Library and Information Center Management

Library and Information Science Text Series

Library and Information Center Management

Sixth Edition

Robert D. Stueart

Barbara B. Moran

2002
LIBRARIES UNLIMITED
A Division of Greenwood Publishing Group, Inc.
Westport, Connecticut • London

To our grandchildren,
Annika, Jacob, Madison, Magnus, and Molly—
the lights of our lives,
and
in memory of a dear friend and colleague
Elfreda A. Chatman.

LIBRARIES UNLIMITED
A Member of The Greenwood Publishing Group, Inc.
88 Post Road West,
Westport, CT 06881
1-800-225-5800
www.lu.com

Library of Congress Cataloging-in-Publication Data

Stueart, Robert D.
  Library and information center management / Robert D. Stueart, Barbara
B. Moran.-- 6th ed.
    p. cm. -- (Library and information science text series)
Includes bibliographical references and index.
  ISBN 1-56308-986-6 -- ISBN 1-56308-990-4 (pbk.)
  1. Library administration--United States. 2. Information
Services--United States--Management. I. Moran, Barbara B. II. Title.
III. Series.
  Z678 .S799 2002
  025.1--dc21
                              2002008905

Contents

Section 1: Evolving

Section 2: Planning

Section 4: Human Resources

Section 5: Leading

Section 6: Coordinating

Section 7: Managing in the 21st Century

Figures and Tables

Figures

Tables

Foreword

Libraries are among the oldest social and cultural institutions in existence. Many great libraries flourished in ancient times, just as they continue to influence modern societies. Although they have been developed by various nations and cultures, these institutions share one overriding feature—all had and still have a body of information recorded on some type of medium: from stone to clay tablets, papyrus and palm leaf to vellum, paper to synthetics and film, scrolls to books, hand-copied to printed books, and most recently print-on-paper to magnetic media to optical and interactive multimedia and to the Internet, the vast web of information sources. The recording media and devices used for that recording remain secondary to the availability and accessibility of the information contained therein.

Today, the issue of how the "library" performs its role is vastly different from what it was in the past, although its primary role of providing access to information, which can be converted by the user into knowledge and ultimately wisdom, remains. Today, knowledge workers in libraries or information centers are most concerned with providing the right amount of information to the right person at the right time for the right reason and in the right format. They also have an ethical commitment to society to see that this is done within accepted standards of behavior. The realization is that a seeker of information does not care whether the needed information is contained in the big red book on the top shelf of the upper floor of a closed-stack physical building called the library or in an online database accessible from the other side of the world. Concern is no longer simply with preservation but also with purveying the information. This paradigm shift requires a commitment and a change in service goals.

In that more leisurely past, it is likely that there was as much concern and consternation among information professionals working in organizations when scrolls were replaced by books as there is today with print-on-paper technology being supplemented and even supplanted by online interactive access mechanisms. The medium remains secondary to the structure of the organization required to offer services that allow retrieval and accessibility of information in a timely, efficient, and effective manner. Such structuring requires creating a management process that facilitates work and a work environment aimed toward achieving those goals. It requires flexibility and adaptability to a constantly changing environment.

Over the centuries, the science—or some would call it an art—of management has changed as dramatically as have the libraries and information services. From the days of slaves managed by a few privileged classes to the age of the free artisans or traders; to the age of cottage industries, in which a whole family worked to produce a living; to the age of the Industrial Revolution, which caused a violent social upheaval; to the Information Age, where knowledge and its management is the single most important source in the political, economic, social, and technological development of society, and information professionals in knowledge-based organizations play a key role as information advocates and intermediaries—standards of management and approaches to viewing management have drastically and dramatically changed.

Libraries and other information-intense enterprises have, over the years, adopted and adapted many management principles from business, industry, religion, and government. In some cases, as part of a government structure, libraries and information centers have been required to do so. In other cases, it makes good sense to adopt and to adapt principles that guide organizational efficiency and instill a climate of success.

Libraries and information centers are businesses that must be operated efficiently and effectively; they are accountable to the larger organization of which they are a part. There is, of course, a major difference between most libraries and a profit-driven enterprise, and different parameters of services are likely to exist for certain information centers. Nevertheless, whatever the nature of the enterprise, it must operate to please the customer or client, to give the employees and employers a sense of well-being and self-esteem, to maintain an attractive and healthy environment, and to provide consistent and efficient services.

The image that a library or information center presents to its constituency is very important. A cluttered, unattractive workplace can only lead to disregard of its importance by customers. A laissez-faire attitude toward organizational structure and service objectives can be both demoralizing and destructive. A high turnover of staff likely indicates a personnel problem affecting service. A budget deficit at the end of a reporting period reflects lack of proper attention to control. If libraries and information centers are to remain viable entities in this new century and be able to compete with the aggressive information industry, they must achieve an efficiency and then maintain an effectiveness that will ensure that success.

Preface

The contemporary title of this edition and the previous one published five years ago reflects a coming of age and a continual development of principles and processes of management in libraries and information center organizations. Twenty-five years ago, when the first edition of this book was published, little had been written about the management of libraries and information centers. Those seeking advice, examples, and information about how organizations function were forced to seek answers in the literature of public administration or business management. Since then, there has been a spate of articles and monographs on various aspects of management as applied to library and information center operation.

The first edition of *Library Management*, published in 1977, was conceived as a basic text for library and information science curriculum, primarily in North America—because the authors were both faculty members in schools on that continent. Many students in programs for which the textbook was intended had work experience in libraries or other types of information centers before entering graduate school, but they had little understanding of the theories or philosophies that direct and control the environments in which they worked or would be working in the future. They simply accepted patterns of library and information center organization, personnel procedures, budgetary controls, and planning processes, with their mission and goals—if they were even stated—as a given, without understanding why processes and procedures were followed. They were subjected to the "what and how" without understanding the "why." Even when examples and forms, such as budgetary and personnel evaluation forms, were available, these were mostly regional or type-of-center specific and did not reflect a broad cross-section of libraries and information centers in the United States, not to mention the rest of the world. The second edition, written by colleagues Robert D. Stueart and John T. Eastlick, was much broader in scope. While maintaining its usefulness as a basic text, it also served as a primary source of information and contemplation for lower- and middle-management personnel. Its geographic scope broadened to be more representative of practices throughout North America. The third edition, published in 1987, addressed new and more complex issues and reflected contemporary developments in addition to the basic core of information. A new co-author with Stueart in this edition—Barbara B. Moran—brought additional insight, expertise, and depth to the discussions. With the fourth edition, published in 1993, the two authors expanded the coverage to include themes for an international audience. In the meantime, previous editions had been translated into several languages—some without prior knowledge of the authors and publisher. The edition also changed its title to *Library and Information Center Management* to reflect more accurately the focus and to incorporate a deeper discussion on each topic, with new materials, features, topics, examples, and insights. Quotes by experts were used to emphasize particular points.

The fifth edition identified trends, updated discussion of research and theories, and was greatly expanded to include many examples of practice in modern libraries and information centers.

The present edition updates and expands the materials contained in the previous five editions and discusses new thoughts and techniques as well as reemphasizes those which have stood the test of time and trial. This edition uses contemporary examples to illustrate discussions on such themes as strategic planning and human resources management.

Since publication of the first edition of *Library Management*, libraries and information services have changed drastically. This change has been precipitated by both the internal and the external environment. This continuous process requires a more systematic approach to reviewing functions and developing strategies in the organization's setting. Technology and the political, economic, and social environments are powerful forces that influence the planning for information services today. New knowledge, skills, and techniques are required by staff at every level of the enterprise's operations. Different organizational structures, communications techniques, and budgeting strategies are required in the information age, when the focus is upon strategic initiatives for services necessary to connect the customer with the information being sought—whether for cultural, education, entertainment, or information purposes. Even while established theories and practices of management have been modified and expanded, new theories, concepts, and practices have been developed. For example, the relatively new contingency management concept is essential for the planned growth and viability of an institution in the current social and technological climate. The virtual library concept, accompanied by changing demographics; ethical issues; social responsibilities; and other economic, social, and technological forces, requires reexamination of how effectively and efficiently resources of a human, material, and technological nature are used.

Teaching colleagues, practicing librarians and other information managers, and students require a text addressing established theories and reflecting contemporary practices. The volume has been rethought, reworked, and reedited to reflect recent changes and new issues in the information services environment. A great deal of thought has been given to restructuring the volume. Citations and examples have been updated, and additional readings are suggested. Examples of library and information service practice are included. They are from U.S. institutions, but their purpose has international appeal. Some provide direct application for those seeking to establish new processes and procedures; others provide useful guidelines for establishing standards throughout the world. A website has been established accommodating those and other relevant sources.

The basic theme of the book remains unchanged. The book focuses upon the complex and interrelated functions common to all organizations and is intended specifically for managers and future managers of services and staffs. Concepts previously covered in seven chapters have been expanded into seven sections in sixteen chapters, covering all of the important functions involved in library management and development. Although these functions are presented and discussed separately, it is important to remember that they are carried out simultaneously and concurrently. The actual operation of a library or information center follows no precise linear pattern. Most managerial functions progress simultaneously; they do not exist in a hierarchical relationship. For instance, budgeting is not likely to be reflective of the enterprise's success without some measure of planning where goals and objectives are established. Therefore, management cannot be viewed as a rigid system, and the concepts discussed in this text must be viewed as a whole. In this volume, each concept discussed is related to or builds upon others, and each relates to all levels of management and supervision in information service organizations. The purpose of separating and individually discussing the functions that comprise the management process is to examine the various threads in the fabric of what managers actually do.

This book was not written in a vacuum, nor is it intended for use in one. In-basket exercises, case studies, action mazes, and other simulation techniques should be used to supplement and magnify the principles discussed. Volumes on case studies may be helpful. Anderson's[1] volume was specifically developed as a companion piece for earlier editions of this text. The most applicable cases from Anderson are available on the website for this volume. In writing this treatise, the authors drew freely from writings and research in cognate fields, including business management, public administration, and the social sciences. The readings and the footnotes represent a classified bibliography on covered topics.

Finally, it is important to point out that anyone who is supervising another person is involved in the management process. Further, anyone involved in an organizational setting that requires interaction among individuals should understand the dynamics that relate to managing situations and organizations. Therefore, the principles discussed in this volume have relevance for each person whose job involves interacting with others to achieve the common goals and objectives of their organization.

Notes

1. A. J. Anderson, *Problems in Library Management* (Littleton, CO: Libraries Unlimited, 1981).

Acknowledgments

As with previous editions, many people have contributed to the final product of this, our sixth edition, spanning twenty-five years of management practice. Faculty and students of programs in North America, Europe, Australia, and Asia have made encouraging comments and useful suggestions to improve the text. Many of those suggestions have been incorporated into this latest edition, and to these people we are indebted. The authors would like to thank others, too numerous to name here, who read and made comments on the content of various chapters. Colleagues throughout the world have offered encouragement in the development of this new edition by indicating their appreciation and continuing use of previous editions of this general text, covering principles important for the practice of good information services. To them we are also grateful.

We would especially like to thank Linda Watkins, the GSLIS librarian at Simmons College, who is one of the best reference librarians we have ever known, and Mari Marsh, Amy Pattee, Pnina Fichman-Shachaf, and Rebecca Vargha from the University of North Carolina at Chapel Hill for their help in this new edition.

Grateful acknowledgment is also due to Martin Dillon, adviser and friend, who provided invaluable advice, assistance, and encouragement as the new edition emerged. We also owe gratitude to those library and information center directors who permitted us to cite documents that are used as examples in the book and on the website—thank you. Their management practices and procedures make our discussions and illustrations of the issues and challenges more relevant and effective.

Finally, to colleagues at Libraries Unlimited—under new direction of Edward Kurdyla Jr. as general manager, and the very capable staff of associates, particularly Carmel Huestis, managing editor—for their efficiency and continuing encouragement to write yet another edition of this successful textbook.

The Website

One noticeable exciting change with the current edition is the initiation of a "living" website. It will be continuously updated, and suggestions are sought from readers and users of the textbook for new items to be added to the site.

The address is http://www.eLearning@lu.com/management.

Instead of including a limited number of specific examples of documents, for instance, strategic plans, organizational charts, job descriptions, or other practical items as appendixes in the textbook, there will be sections of the website that include not only full-text examples, but also indications of links to web pages that give examples or explain processes in greater detail than a printed textbook can accommodate. A core of book "references" is included at the beginning of each section of the text for ready reference, and this is augmented on the web by extensive bibliographies of general and LIS management literature in book, article, and website format. References to other websites are important both for classroom activities and as guides for libraries and information centers' colleagues embarking on or maintaining a "change process" mentality.

Many examples have international appeal and application and are cited as colleagues in Australia, Britain, Canada, and other countries, as well as the United States, continue to explore issues important to international information service. All of the initial websites that are cited have been checked and are valid as of April 1, 2002. Others will be verified as they are added, and some attempt will be made to remove those that are no longer pertinent or functioning. These examples provide basic directions for faculty, students, and practitioners seeking to understand, establish, or redevelop programs, processes, policies, and procedures. They serve as guidelines for establishing standards for information services throughout the world.

The initial categories of materials include:

♦ readings—an extensive bibliography of pertinent materials;

♦ case studies—several cases from Dr. A. J. Anderson's useful *Problems in Library Management* have been included, with his permission;

♦ in-box exercises—including in-basket exercises and other simulated problem-solving activities;

♦ exhibits—including, for instance, full-text strategic plans of both academic and public libraries, organizational charts, performance assessment forms and job descriptions; and

♦ discussion forum—a separate protected web page for ongoing discussions on topics of interest to LIS management faculty and students.

Managing change is the primary characteristic of future-focused, knowledge-based library and information centers as they pursue their mission of creating, organizing, analyzing, and providing access to knowledge for their customers. The globalization of information services, made most evident in the technological applications on a worldwide scale, presents a challenging profile. The only constant in library and information service organizations today is change. Recognizing that change is inevitable, coping with its effects, and embracing its outcome are vital steps for libraries and information centers. Today's turbulent environment requires that a holistic view be taken, identifying techniques, skills, and knowledge to accomplish priorities and initiatives in order to satisfy customer needs. Tolerating ambiguity and risk-taking are factors in organizational change and are reflected in each element of a structured work environment. The practice of managing in such an environment requires awareness of the political, economic, social, and technological factors and strengths, weaknesses, opportunities, and threats, internally and externally, that influence what is done and the way it is done.

Just as organizations change over their lifetime, over a span of years, theories that can be identified and have been applied are reinterpreted, and new ones are developed. What is right at one point in an organization's development may not be appropriate at a different stage when the organization has metamorphosed into a more sophisticated organism or, perhaps, has taken a completely different direction. Likewise, some theories that have developed over the years may no longer have relevance for organizations in this new century. But many of the principles developed over the years continue to provide a framework for development of modern organizations, even if as historical elements. Knowing where one has been helps put into perspective where one wants to be.

Those two components—change and historical perspective—form the basis for this first part of the textbook.

Readings

Axelrod, Richard H. *Terms of Engagement: Changing the Way We Change Organizations*. San Francisco: Bernett-Koehler, 2000.

Bates, Anthony W. *Managing Technological Change*. San Francisco: Jossey-Bass, 2000.

Belasco, James A. *Teaching the Elephant to Dance: Empowering Change in Your Organization*. New York: Crown, 1990.

Brown, John Seely, and Paul Duguid. *The Social Life of Information*. Boston: Harvard Business School Press, 2000.

Burton, Terrence T., and John W. Moran. *The Future Focused Organization*. Englewood Cliffs, NJ: Prentice Hall PTR, 1995.

Cargill, Jennifer, and Gisela M. Webb. *Managing Libraries in Transition*. Phoenix, AZ: Oryx Press, 1988.

Carson, Kerry David, Paula Phillips Carson, and Joyce Schonest Phillips. *The ABCs of Collaborative Change*. Chicago: American Library Association, 1997.

Champy, James. *Reengineering Management: The Mandate for New Leadership*. New York: Harper Business, 1995.

Connor, Patrick E., and Linda K. Lake. *Managing Organizational Change*. 2d ed. Westport, CT: Praeger, 1994.

Crawford, W., and Michael Gorman. *Future Libraries, Dreams, Madness and Reality*. Chicago: American Library Association, 1995.

Davenport, Thomas H., and Laurence Prusak. *Working Knowledge*. Boston: Harvard Business School Press, 1998.

Drucker, Peter F. *Managing in a Time of Great Change*. New York: Truman Talley Books/Dutton, 1995.

Gallecher, Cathryn. *Managing Change in Libraries and Information Services*. London: ASLIB, 1999.

Gibson, Rowan, ed. *Rethinking the Future*. London: Nicholas Brealey, 1997.

Gryskiewicz, Stanley S. *Positive Turbulence*. San Francisco: Jossey-Bass, 1999.

Hammer, Michael. *Beyond Reengineering the Corporation*. New York: Harper Business School Press, 1996.

Handy, Charles. *Beyond Uncertainty: The Changing Worlds of Organizations*. Boston: Harvard Business School Press, 1996.

Imparato, Nicholas, and Oren Harari. *Jumping the Curve: Innovation and Strategic Choice in an Age of Transition*. San Francisco: Jossey-Bass, 1994.

Kanter, Rosabeth Moss. *Evolve—Succeeding in the Digital Culture of Tomorrow*. Boston: Harvard Business School Press, 2001.

Lampikoski, Karl, and Jack B. Emden. *Igniting Innovation: Inspiring Organizations by Managing Creativity*. New York: John Wiley & Sons, 1996.

May, G. H. *The Future Is Ours: Foreseeing, Managing and Creating the Future.* Westport, CT: Praeger, 1996.

Penfold, Susan. *Change Management for Information Services.* London: Bowker-Saur, 1999.

Peters, Thomas J. *The Circle of Innovation.* New York: Alfred Knopf, 1999.

Senge, Peter M. *The Fifth Discipline: The Art & Practice of the Learning Organization.* New York: Doubleday, 1990.

Stacey, Ralph D. *Managing the Unknowable: Strategic Boundaries Between Order and Chaos.* San Francisco: Jossey-Bass, 1993.

Vaill, Peter B. *Learning as a Way of Being: Strategies for Survival in a World of Permanent White Water.* San Francisco: Jossey-Bass, 1996.

Want, Jerome H. *Managing Radical Change.* New York: John Wiley & Sons, 1995.

Weaver, Richard G., and John D. Farrell. *Managers as Facilitators: A Practical Guide to Getting Work Done in a Changing Workplace.* San Francisco: Bernett-Koehler, 1997.

Worley, Christopher G. *Integrated Strategic Change.* Reading, MA: Addison-Wesley, 1996.

Wren, Daniel. *The Evolution of Management Theory.* 3d ed. New York: John Wiley & Sons, 1987.

Chapter 1

Change—The Innovative Process

> *If we are reactive and let change overwhelm us or pass us by, we will perceive change negatively. If we are proactive, seek to understand the future now, and embrace change, the idea of the unexpected can be positive and uplifting.*[1]
>
> —Bill Gates,
> *Business @ the Speed of Thought*

Impetus for Change

The cliché that the future isn't what it used to be holds true today more than ever before in the provision of good knowledge-based services where the focus is no longer on processes but rather on seekers and users of information. Not only is the future not what one could imagine it to be even five years ago, but the speed of change is increasing in all sectors of society. A good example of a traumatic experience with change is that of *Encyclopedia Britannica*, the most comprehensive and authoritative encyclopedia, almost 250 years old with fifteen editions, whose sales reached $650 million in 1990. However, since then sales have plummeted by eighty percent. Why? The introduction of give-away encyclopedias, available on CD-ROM, have practically destroyed the printed encyclopedia business.[2] Was Britannica ready for that, or were they in denial?

For libraries and other knowledge-based organizations, the ongoing knowledge revolution has launched a gigantic wave of change. Uncertainty about the impact of the political, economic, social, and technological climate worldwide renders it almost futile to anticipate the future. Yet, immediate decisions still must be made to commit resources in support of the future of technology, employee development, and other ongoing or new priorities or initiatives. Organizations must be managed, or more appropriately guided, in a way that decisions can be made, or else nothing can get done. And the time frame for identifying and implementing change has continued to shorten. This requires managers and other staff to be accountable for their performance as a result of those decisions. In many instances decisions are likely to be made, not with the aid of a crystal ball, but based upon best-guess assumptions about the future. In such a scenario some management theorists and consultants advocate redesigning organizations through such popular techniques as that of reengineering,[3] a phrase that has become synonymous with redundancy and downsizing. Such a process of radical change requires reinventing the structure, systems, and services of libraries and information centers to achieve improvement and to present a value-added profile. Other theorists and consultants encourage restructuring, whereas a few take it one thought farther, forecasting the need to cope with what has been called an "age of unreason." With few dissenting opinions, it is accepted that the present time of discontinuity and ferment—what some have called chaos[4]—demands reevaluation, renewal, revamping, even redesign of previously stable library and information service organizations. In that process futurists, trying to predict outcomes, are making forecasts concerning the importance of various forces that have been growing for some time. To coin an alliterative phrase, confusion about comprehensive change complicates compliance with contemporary conditions in library and information service.

In this time of great entrepreneurial ferment, old and staid institutions suddenly have to become very limber. Changes that have affected many knowledge-based libraries and information centers are those relating to:

♦ Introduction of new technologies, which creates new industries and renders existing industries obsolete;

♦ Emergence of a world economy that involves a world market and a global shopping center;

♦ Development of a changing political and social matrix, involving much disenchantment with the status-quo; and

♦ Creation of a "knowledge economy" in which about half of the funds available are spent on procuring ideas and information and in which knowledge has become the central factor of production.[5]

The PEST (political, economic, social, and technological) factors place intense pressures on knowledge-based organizations and must be reckoned with if knowledge-based organizations are to survive.

> Transferring knowledge depends on factors such as the nature of knowledge, the organizational environment and technology.[6]
>
> —Michael C. Jensen and William H. Meckling,
> "Specific and General Knowledge and Organizational Structure"

Of course, the one force that has received greatest attention is technology because it is the most obvious force. Historically the introduction of new technology—from electricity to the typewriter and the duplicating machine to the computer has resulted in major change in the organization of work. But it should be remembered that technology is a tool, and it is the people, their attitude, and their acceptance of change that are the primary cause for change or lack thereof; technology simply enables it.

Knowledge-based nonprofit organizations, including most libraries and information centers, have felt dramatic change pressures, precipitated by such internal factors as ethics and social responsibility and the desire for team building and empowerment. Internally a sometimes planned, but too often unplanned, change process occurs in relation to values and attitudes toward work life, organizational structures, and application of different management theories and practices in library and information service organizations. Change in the knowledge-based environment, with focus on the knowledge base within the organization and providing access to customers, has occurred in the way that information is created, organized, accessed, used, and valued as it is refined into knowledge.

As a philosophy for knowledge-based organizations, knowledge management, a relatively recent concept for libraries and information centers, is proving to be a catalyst agent for change—creating an atmosphere where focus is no longer upon processes taking place in buildings called libraries, but upon knowledge workers, those professionals who possess the knowledge, and upon organizing a system to capture that knowledge embedded therein and then transmitting it to those customers who seek answers.

This process is spawning a new set of information-to-knowledge management vocabulary terms—knowledge work, knowledge workers, knowledge management, and the ultimate concept of a knowledge society. Knowledge now is the primary resource, and the dynamics of knowledge impose change in the very structure of knowledge-based organizations.

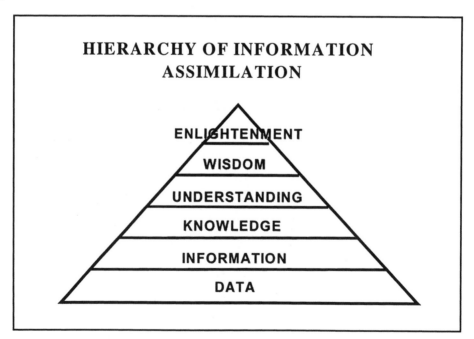

Figure 1.1. Hierarchy of Data to Enlightenment

Links between information, the services and systems to access it, and the application of knowledge, with the conversion to wisdom being the desirable outcome, affect every library and information service organization's development, management, and performance. However, this change phenomenon produces a paradox because an organization's success depends upon its ability to maintain stability while managing change. A delicate balance between the concept of control and the need to inspire on the part of management requires planning, development, and maintenance. Knowing what to change and how to change are imperative for the process, and this requires an understanding of how a knowledge-based organization's direction of change and innovation can shape the level of knowledge transfer because implementing that transfer requires self-direction and teamwork.

Both deliberate planning and directional change are required because without the order that planned change provides, an organization is crippled, and without change, a knowledge-based organization is no longer viable, becomes obsolete, and is quickly superceded by other entities willing and ready to take the risk, unfortunately oftentimes with a profit motive.

Environmental trends point to a future in which organizational vitality and ambiguity will be essential to effectiveness and services.[7]
—James G. Neal and Patricia Steele,
"Empowerment, Organization and Structure"

Factors that are directly driving strategic initiatives for change in library and information services include costs of services, speed of delivery, changing values and expectations of both customers and knowledge workers, entrepreneurial activities, and quality of the value-added service, all enhanced by a technological climate and global communication system that promotes a reconfiguration of knowledge-based organizations and their services. In such an environment the significance of what is done and how it is done is challenged by questioning why it is done or, in some cases, why "it" is not done. Resources—people, materials, and methods; knowledge and skills; techniques and tools; components to which long established management principles traditionally have been applied—remain the core of a changing knowledge-based organization's life, and its success depends upon their knowledge and commitment.

But with each one of those components being affected by this phenomenon of change, each presents its own challenge to an effective process of change. For too long many workers and managers in some knowledge-based organizations have discounted change as a force in the organization's life, while at the same time embracing it in their own personal lives. As an example, almost a third of all American workers are "discounters," who routinely reject the significance of potential future change; another 40 percent are "extrapolators," who believe that the trends of the recent past will continue into the foreseeable future. However, 40 percent of the discounters and extrapolators indicate that they are currently going through a major, self-initiated change in their own lives or careers, and another 40 percent are actively planning to undertake such a change.[8] How can this dichotomy of attitude toward acceptance of change in personal lives but resistance to change in the organizational life be explained? Perhaps the answer lies in an organizational culture and value system that traditionally would present barriers to change. Those barriers can be identified as:

1. failure to create a sense of urgency for change;

2. lack of a clear vision;

3. not removing the obstacles to change;

4. failure to anchor changes into the organization's culture; and

5. a failure to follow through with plans.[9]

When libraries and information centers are confident of their success and believe that they are necessary, complacency easily becomes a trap. Although historic success has been built on innovative ideas, there is a common tendency to rest upon those past laurels. But a continuation of that success requires a reawakening and renewal in today's competitive environment, and this is an active and deliberate process.

> The organization of the future will be networks, clusters, cross-functional teams, temporary systems, ad hoc task forces, lattices, modules, matrices—almost anything but pyramids.[10]
>
> —Warren Bennis,
> *An Invented Life: Reflections on Leadership and Change*

From the human side, barriers to that success are both psychological and institutional, with most being in the minds of knowledge workers rather than on organization charts.[11] Predictably this requires a reorientation and recommitment of all people, managers and nonmanagers, professional and support staff, working in knowledge-based organizations. It also requires a marketing program that informs both customers and potential customers that their information and knowledge needs can be met. It is obvious that without due preparation, change can place any organization on a confrontation course because it is a threatening process and change can easily get out of control. To address that resistance one must look at what is happening in knowledge-based libraries and information centers.

Paradigm Shift

The most important avenues of change have produced paradigm shifts. In library and information service organizations there has been a paradigm shift in the resources, in the services, and in the user orientation within those knowledge- based organizations and in knowledge workers' responsibilities for services and systems in those organizations. This continuing paradigm shift now presents the best yet opportunity for comprehensive organizational change.

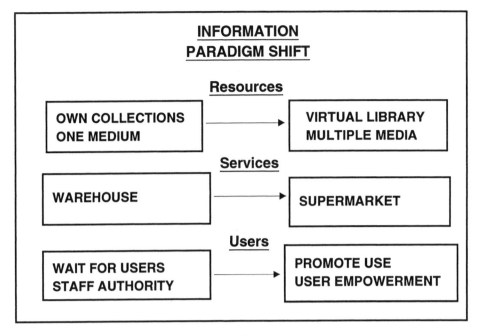

Figure 1.2. Information Paradigm Shift

Change is now more accurately portrayed as unpredictable, unstoppable, and transformational rather than incremental, predictable, and controllable.[12]
—Richard M. Dougherty,
"Being Successful (Nimble and Agile)
in the Current Turbulent Environment"

Change, of course, is just as threatening to managers as to other members of the organization because much decision making of a more mundane nature now can be made by nonmanagers in the organization or even by machines, rather than by managers. In addition, the refinement of responsibilities of teams of knowledge workers also diminishes the image of a finger-snapping manager making all the decisions. In the developing scenario, some managers may feel a loss of authority, being unable to control certain outcomes, and that is exactly what does occur if the management style is not one of openness and collaboration. From the top and through every level of the organization, this reorientation requires acceptance of new ideas, learning new skills, breaking old habits, and adaptation of new behavioral patterns. This threatening process of change requires a calculated approach with much deliberate preparation and gentle persuasion. In such a setting each member of the organization is expected to become a risk-taker and must be prepared to abandon things that are currently being done but no longer work. Tough questions must be asked—What sort of work is left as smart technologies are developed and employed? What do knowledge professionals do better than the technologies? How can knowledge workers be organized for optimum impact? It seem obvious that knowledge-based organizations are moving from individualism, or task orientation, to teamwork and process development. Empowerment is the key factor in today's changing knowledge access marketplace, and accountability is the motto. However, because change remains difficult to quantify and somewhat elusive to manage, there is no one successful model to follow. But change can be accomplished when it is done to improve, innovate, and exploit the knowledge base, and a new organizational profile can emerge. Of course, risk is the primary factor in this equation. But what is the alternative?

Change seems to have a way of sneaking in on a series of irregular waves, each one providing added stimulus to motivate people. Staff participation in the decision-making process; unionization and collective bargaining efforts; decentralization of information services; flattening of organizational hierarchies; and collaborative employer/employee workplace arrangements, including programs like maternity and parental leave, flex-time and flex-place, part-time and job-sharing, and an end of mandatory retirement age—all of which are designed to meet changing needs and interests—are examples of change factors that are having an impact on organizational culture and character and have helped produce a feeling of shared responsibility toward achieving a vision of knowledge-based services. A common mission holds the organization together, and team effort is the vital link to achieving benchmarks toward that mission.

Educating, informing, and involving knowledge workers is a very important step in planning change because information about needed change helps individuals and organizations adjust to the inevitable and helps them view change as an opportunity rather than a threat. Of course, in the process an organization must not abandon recognition of prior achievements of individuals and the organizational whole because that could demoralize people who contributed to those past successes. The "looking around" aspect of the planning process, the performance evaluation and motivational aspects of the human resources function, the motivational aspects of the leading function, and the feedback options and budgeting applications of the controlling endeavor, provide important information about both external and internal forces promoting and facilitating change and offer options for making tough choices, decisions about future directions of the knowledge-based organization.

Change from a warehouse to a supermarket mentality, from a passive role of preservers of print-on-paper technology to one of purveyors of knowledge, brings greater emphasis on specialized value-added services libraries and other information centers offer. The effects of this paradigm shift are not limited to any one country, developed or emerging, or one type of setting, whether it is a public, academic, school, or special library or information center. Libraries and other information centers in every part of the world are experiencing the challenging phenomenon that shifts focus from an ownership mentality with concentration upon in-house activities to a universal information access attitude, creating, collaborating, and sharing resources and services. Just look at the Collaborative Digital Reference Service maintained by the Library of Congress and one sees that.[13]

In addition, change in organizations that provide knowledge-based services, as has been mentioned, comes from a variety of other sources: pressures of the external environment (customers, governing authorities, and other stakeholders), change in directions (goals and objectives of the parent organization), reconfiguration of technology (systems development and access to international communications sources, primarily through the Internet), and modification of the overall physical plant (buildings and branch campuses with libraries and offices, sometimes spread throughout the world). Also e-learning and campus-without-walls concepts present new challenges. All of these have had an effect on libraries and other information centers and are causing evolutionary changes in the structure, the individuals' attitudes, and the individuals' responsibilities, both as managers and as workers.

Change also requires constant awareness of each identified organizational role in the goal-oriented, information-intense, knowledge-based organizations where the previously mentioned teamwork and process is replacing individualism and a task orientation. This involves designing, implementing, and evaluating programs to meet the market's needs and desires and using effective financing or resources, communications of services, and distribution of systems to inform, motivate, and service a market that is also fluid.

> The key to success in a customer-driven organization is caring about people, learning about customer expectations, exceeding customer expectations, and maintaining long term, productive relationships.[14]
> —Miriam Drake,
> "Technological Innovation and Organizational Change"

In the knowledge service sector the needs of customers, or clients, or patrons, or users—whatever term is most acceptable to the individual institution—have become the focus of all services, with every member of the organization recognizing the potential of direct communication with the customer or, at the very least, recognizing their role in performing supporting activities that facilitate access. Future-focused knowledge empowering organizations anticipate and redefine customer needs on a regular basis and expand and shift services in the fluid environment. *Re*examination often times requires:

♦ *Re*ordering priorities;

♦ *Re*training staff;.

♦ *Re*organizing space;

♦ *Re*newing equipment;

♦ *Re*structuring the hierarchy; and

♦ *Re*directing financial resources.

Current worldwide economic constraints coupled with accelerated technological developments encourage greater inter-type and intra-type international cooperative efforts in systems (creating, acquiring, and organizing) and services (accessing, evaluating, and distributing) offered by libraries and other knowledge-based information centers from cooperative acquisitions and cataloging to computerized interlibrary loan; and from resource sharing (networking, online access, CD-ROM purchasing and use, etc.) to other online information services offered in conjunction with publishers, vendors, other information centers and, indeed, other units of the parent organization. International organizations, particularly the International Federation of Library Associations and Institutions (IFLA) and UNESCO have become important partners in addressing issues of international standards, systems, and services. This dynamic environment is one of inter-activity, both online and on paper. Technology is a primary driving force, and for the first time in history, technological developments and innovations are outpacing the human endeavor to cope and to develop services and systems that technology is capable of supporting. This simple fact, combined with the social, political, and economic pressures of the day, necessitates organizations to have a very fluid profile.

Organizing for Change

Only a few short years ago, managers of libraries and other information centers spent little time on external matters. Today a major portion of every manager's time is spent on external matters: with civic organizations, trustees, or corporation members at board meetings and individually; with fund-raising by cultivating relationships with philanthropic-minded individuals and foundations as well as other potential funding authorities; with lobbying government officials and other decision makers at many levels; in collective bargaining sessions, Friends of Libraries group meetings, meetings with higher administration and funding agencies or authorities in defense of the budget or support of strategic planning efforts; and on other public relations matters such as gathering and disseminating information to the press, to decision makers, to customers, and to colleagues. That activity is an important part of the change paradigm.

The need and desire to be constantly in touch with an organization's primary customers and other important stakeholders; to gauge their information/knowledge-seeking patterns; and to assess their information/knowledge needs in order to develop plans, policies, practices, and procedures that satisfy those needs bring new challenges in changing patterns and attitudes. "The whole world is by now a richly interactive system"[15] that requires managers to be proactive in their relations with external bodies and to scan the environment to discern outside pressures and workers to be committed to the priorities of the organizations. This developing interactive system has facilitated tentative organizational moves away from what has been called the authoritarian hierarchy to smaller work groups in which people manage themselves, and the response time to action is shortened in the process.

What is required is a transformation, not a refining of organizational structure, work, and external and internal relationships.[16]

—Carla J. Stoffle,
"Choosing Our Futures"

The library or other information services center is a complex organization, relying upon a trusting relationship among its various units. Workers' roles in adopting a change environment are enhanced as they are allowed, as far as capabilities permit, to grow beyond a traditional hierarchical job to the point of being involved in team problem-solving activities.[17] Work design is becoming more flexible and self-organized, and in many cases human networking is replacing the pyramid as the organizational form. In order for libraries and other information centers to achieve their unique mission of becoming both knowledge-based organizations and organizations that facilitate knowledge acquisition, professional information intermediaries working in those no longer institution-bound organizations are challenged to become educators, coordinators, and facilitators. The trend toward the flattening of the organization means that communication and decisions are more immediate and apparent within groups of workers at appropriate levels, and those changes are not easily portrayed in solid lines, or even dotted lines, on organization charts. This flattening of organizations requires greater collaboration as new approaches are developed in management planning, personnel development, systems analysis, and control activities. Seeking a balance between initiative, delegation, and control is a meaningful challenge for those who are ultimately responsible for action.

The introduction of highly specialized staff affects library and information management, decision making, staff empowerment, and responsibilities, and this challenges organizations to offer new incentives to workers. Employees are more sophisticated, articulate, and unwilling to settle for what management theorists call the lower-level needs. "Managing participation is a balancing act: between management control and team opportunity; between getting the work done quickly and giving people a chance to learn; between seeking volunteers and pushing people into it; between too little team spirit and too much."[18] This requires that managers become teachers and coaches, mentors and developers of human potential, rather than "whip-wielding autocrats trying to force change."[19] The idea of a virtual organization is not unthinkable as the digital library becomes a concept, replacing the idea of the library organization being just a building called "the library." Management's focus becomes one of motivation and trust as managerial style changes, as organizations move from "hierarchical to networked organizations characterized by informality and equality, with lateral, diagonal and bottom-up communications."[20]

The way change is managed is as important as the outcome of the change process itself. Change does not come by edict; it is no longer possible for the traditional top management figure to decree that change will occur and then to expect others to make it happen. Such a dictatorial approach, without proper preparation, only creates an atmosphere of heightened uneasiness and mistrust that is sure to have an adverse effect. To implement new ideas and services requires participation by those most affected by such change. The thought of restructuring requires consensus and a common vision of the organization's future. As mentioned before, managers are learning to acknowledge this transition and to cope with the continuous barrage of new ideas, advanced technologies, sophisticated information access, and the need for interpersonal and intra-organizational relations. Therefore, understanding what the change process means and then becoming committed to it is a continuing process from the time that an organization first officially recognizes, and therefore encounters, the need to change until the point when change is internalized, institutionalized, and valued, as illustrated in figure 1.3.

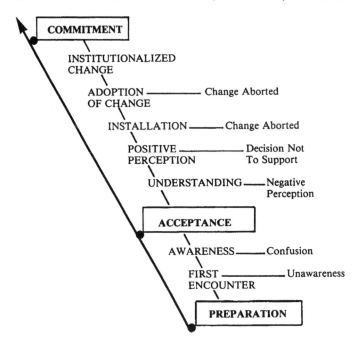

Figure 1.3. The Continuum of Change

At every point along that continuum of change, the process can be, and often is, aborted for a variety of reasons. For instance, with the "understanding" point in that continuum, a person or group can have a "positive perception," in which the process continues, or a "negative perception." If it is negative, steps must be taken to bring that person or group along to the point of understanding and having a positive response. This does not mean coercion, rather education and gentle persuasion.

Diagnosing Change

Two types of change are prevalent in library and information service organizations. One is unplanned change, likely to be disastrous, which presents a situation that forces the organization to react. Unplanned change usually occurs when pressures for change are out of control or the process is being mismanaged; either one can prove destructive to an organization. Negative forces, such as poor management and lack of vision, which can cause organizational decay, have forced change just as much as positive forces, including expansion or organizational redirection, have facilitated change.

Conversely, planned change encourages all to buy in to the process, which then brings about renewal or recommitment on the part of the organization and the people working in it. Although change is sometimes forced upon an organization from outside, causing it to react, successful change efforts most often come from within as calculated effort on the part of people working in organizations who have recognized the need. An informed approach to managing change enables library and information center personnel to join together in strategic thinking and envisioning a strategic vision for the organization while at the same time deciding upon necessary choices about technological and facility investments, staffing, and service needs. This process involves a deliberate progression toward renewing the organization by creating conditions, encouraging participants, and soliciting resources to accomplish that transition. Change is expensive to implement yet inevitable in the current life cycle of libraries and other knowledge-intensive organizations. The question is not how much it costs but rather what its ultimate value is. One is tempted to paraphrase a quote by Oscar Wilde, "Everyone knows the price of everything and the value of nothing."

The difference between planned and unplanned change, then, is that of being proactive rather than reactive when the time is right. Proactive change: recognizes the need for change, easily revealed in a SWOT analysis which considers the Strengths and Weaknesses in the organization as well as the Opportunities and Threats that exist in the external environment. This deliberate approach can guide the identification and establishment of goals for change, can help diagnose relevant variables, and can aid in the selection of a change technique to be employed. It also sets the stage for planning the initiation of change, implementing the process, and then evaluating its impact.

> Deep change differs from incremental change in that it requires new ways of thinking and behaving. It is change that is major in scope, discontinuous with the past and generally irreversible. The deep change effort distorts existing patterns of action and involves risk taking. Deep change means surrendering control.[21]
>
> —Robert E. Quinn,
> *Deep Change*

Theorists, when they describe the change process, talk about either incremental or fundamental change, with incremental being based upon preserving successful aspects of what has been created before and building upon that, whereas fundamental change is based upon abandoning what has gone before, challenging those old concepts, and doing things in a new, completely different way. There are proponents of both approaches, each stating the strengths and logic of a particular approach. In any case, it is apparent that organizations must be flexible and agile.

Two approaches to bring about positive change in libraries and information centers can be identified. One is that the organization conducts the process in-house with staff assuming responsibilities for developing the plan led by individuals within the organization (self-appointed or management-appointed teams to address various aspects necessary in the process). Guidelines for this method are found in the professional literature. A second approach is that of employing change agents, brought in from outside the organization, who are responsible for helping to adapt the organization's structure to a changing environment, directing the speed and focus of organizational change, and controlling conflict. One effective process using that approach is the "Star of Success Model,"[22] which provides consultants for change with an objective way of addressing a series of questions and factors to consider in a process of organizational change.

> The consultant must keep a continual focus on the simultaneous and sometimes conflicting realities that exist in the internal and external environment of the organization.[23]
>
> —Dannemiller Tyson Associates,
> *Whole-Scale Change*

Effective change agents, whether brought in from outside or whether members of the staff, ensure that people are not afraid of what is to come and are able to put the "traditions of the organization" into some perspective because they recognize that "We've always done it that way" is a strong argument on the side of those satisfied with the status quo. Those doubters must be persuaded that yesterday's success may be tomorrow's failure. Gentle but firm persuasion and inclusiveness all along the way is needed in changing not only the way that people act, but also the way they think. This positive process, then, requires trust and participation by all.

The internal environment that fosters change includes the organizational structure itself, the strategic planning process, the decision-making process, strategies for improving communication and staff morale, team building and conflict management, and the accountability factor that controls what is done and the way it is done, all of which must be encouraged by management and gently directed by leaders in the organization. Modification of attitudes and behavior of individuals, a delicate process and one that cannot be management controlled, is just as important as those other factors in the internal environment. The culture of the organization and the set of beliefs and expectations that are shared by members, in other words the ethics and social responsibilities, must be identified and preserved.

Just as with any major process, there must be a plan for change, a road map of getting from where the organization is now to where it wants to be. This process is facilitated by a few simple questions, prevalent in all good planning exercises (who, what, when, where, how, and, most importantly, why). Proper groundwork is necessary because lack of preparation and imaginative follow-through are ingredients for sure failure in a change initiative.

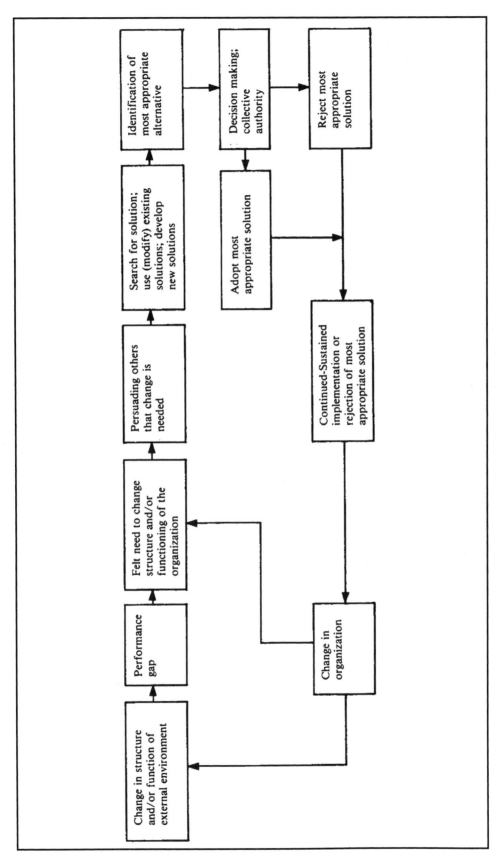

Figure 1.4. Change Is an Evolutionary, Cyclical Process. From *Innovations and Organizations* by G. Zaltman, Duncan, and Holbek, copyright 1973. Used with the permission of John Wiley & Sons, Inc.

> Success requires a more complete makeover, namely rethinking the model for how to organize the work of the whole organization. It requires challenging traditional assumptions about relationships with customers, internal and external communication, decision making, operating style, management behavior, employee motivation and retention—and they define a new way.[24]
>
> —Rosabeth Moss Kanter,
> *Evolve—Succeeding in the Digital Culture of Tomorrow*

The change is evolutionary because tasks, technologies, and even organizational structure are dictated by constantly changing environmental pressures and relationships. Those influence the attitudes, habits, and values of persons working in the organization, in a changing political, economic, social, and technological climate. As an example, change in attitude among elected officials as to the government's role and responsibilities has direct impact on government support for libraries and information centers. This shifting focus can be capitalized upon as elected officials and decision makers begin to recognize the importance of information, converted into knowledge in the social services and economies of countries and local areas. The question of fee-based services versus free services in public libraries, with the concomitant issues of the data-rich but information-poor is a specific example of a social question that influences individuals working in libraries and information centers and their guiding principles and operations. These are but examples of library and information services reacting internally to external opportunities or pressures. Those various components must be considered as a whole because each one affects and interacts with all of the others. Figure 1.5 represents internal and external pressures.

Libraries and Information Centers as Open Systems

The library or information center today is, basically, an open system that receives input from the outside, absorbs it, transforms that information, and then transmits it back into the environment. The organization contains a number of subsystems that respond to this change cycle. Any change in any one component of the organization leads invariably to a change in all components.[25] This means that goals and objectives are determined to a great extent by that larger environment or subsystem, and, if the organization is to be successful, it depends on that outside input to be able to produce usable output measured against which the success of those goals and objectives can be measured. Further, the psychosocial subsystem is formed by individuals and groups interacting both within the system and with groups of individuals outside the system. Additionally, the structure of the organization subsystem determines the way assignments are divided and work is carried out, those being reflected in documents such as organization charts, performance evaluation processes, policies relating to service and structure, and procedures manuals. Finally, the technical subsystem is shaped by the specialized knowledge, skills, and techniques required, and the types of technological equipment and other machinery involved. These subsystems continually interact in informal and formal ways within the overall system. Each points to the challenge of developing a multidimensional knowledge–rich, technologically savvy environment and the need to

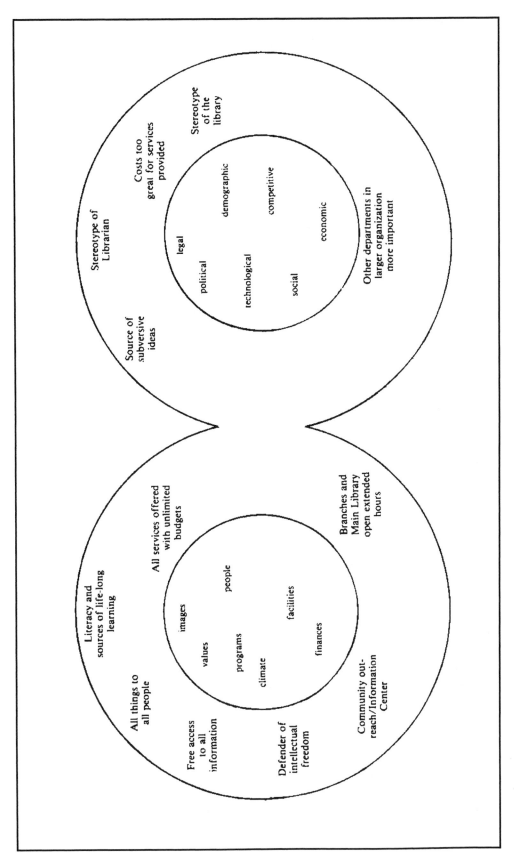

Figure 1.5. The Internal/External Environment of Libraries

plan for that eventuality. This interaction is reflected in the larger managerial subsystem that encompasses components of the entire organization and is subject to the greatest change. Figure 1.6 illustrates the interrelationships of the various subsystems.

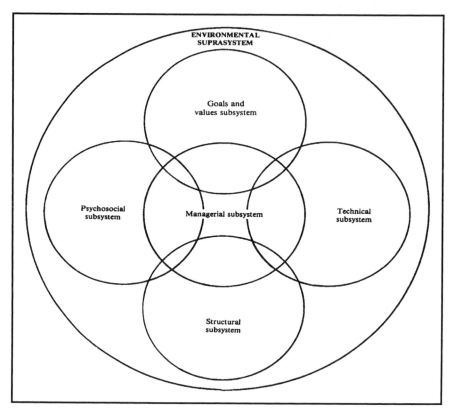

Figure 1.6. Organizational System. From *Organization and Management* by F. E. Kast and J. E. Rosenzweig, 1985. Used with the permission of McGraw-Hill Book Company.

> Literature on organizational change indicates the relative weakness of efforts to change only structure (e.g., job design), only people (e.g., sensitivity training), or only technology (e.g., introducing new equipment or a new computer).[26]
> —Clayton P. Alderfer,
> "Change Processes in Organizations"

Change in both placid and turbulent organizations, whether it is planned or unpredicted, almost always is accompanied by tension, anxiety, resistance, and conflict. Those negative forces can be analyzed and minimized to facilitate the success of the change process. Change, affected unilaterally by the hierarchy where the "definition and solution to the problem at hand tends to be specified by the upper echelons and directed downward through formal and impersonal control mechanisms,"[27] is a recipe for disaster because that attitude and approach is one of the major causes of tensions, anxiety, conflict, and resistance to change. Human nature dictates that change initiatives sometimes fail because the primary factor of people working in organizations is not adequately accounted for. Indeed, research suggests that 90 percent of change initiatives fail because human factors are not taken into account.[28]

Resistance to Change

Resistance to change, oftentimes destructive but sometimes creative, relates primarily to emotional, philosophical, and procedural conflicts among individuals and groups and within the process. It is natural, in human nature, to be tentative about change if they do not understand why it is being initiated. Resistance can provide important feedback and, when identified early and managed properly, can facilitate the change effort with minimum difficulty. Empowerment is the key factor. With that in mind, it is important to remember that 90 percent of change initiatives that fail do so because human factors are not taken into account adequately. Resistance occurs for a variety of reasons:

1. *People do not understand* or do not want to understand the need for change. Some truly do not understand, and too often this reaction is interpreted by change advocates as defiance. Other persons may disagree with the need for change, basically denying that it is necessary. Certain categories of people resist change more than others. It has been pointed out that people who have been in an organization longer are more resistant to change because they have more time and money invested in the status quo. People who have less time invested have no strong commitment to the old way and are more adaptable to new situations.

2. *People have not been fully informed* about the process and are skeptical about the success of the effort. If resistance is viewed as noncompliance with change, it can build the change climate to a higher intensity of resistance. Communication is the key in any change process, and it is management's responsibility to see that everyone is kept fully informed. Unfortunately, information about change is sometimes restricted, thereby causing resistance. Several experts have pointed out that not only will providing opportunities for individuals to have influence over and participate in the change process lessen resistance to change, but also providing continuing involvement after the initial change effort "will produce significant increases in motivation, satisfaction, and performance."[29] Lack of understanding of how and what to change causes confusion.

3. *People's habits and securities are threatened.* Sometimes, people may feel their basic assumptions, personal values, sources of security, or friendships are being threatened. Change introduces new conditions and requires different skills and knowledge. People may become anxious about their

own personal situations and about their future responsibilities or even if they have a future in the organization. Self-preservation becomes paramount in the mind because self-confidence is threatened.

4.   *People may be satisfied with the "status-quo,"* with the way things are now and with current priorities and working relationships, particularly because groups of individuals may be comfortable working together. Group norms and pressure from the group may influence their attitudes toward change, forcing the burden of proof upon those seeking change. They may lack motivation and therefore do little to support its implementation.

5.   *People have vested interests and definite perceptions of what is needed* or wanted, even if they agree that change is necessary. They may want change to occur, but only on their terms. With increasing complexity in organizations comes a greater disparity of backgrounds, attitudes, and values, thereby allowing greater likelihood of individual or group resistance.

6.   *The speed with which change occurs causes greater strain* on the organization. The organization itself may not be able to cope. When overwhelmed by change, people resist. Rapid change makes people nervous, and fear becomes an inhibitor. On the other hand, once the process has begun, some may become impatient with the slowness of progress, which leads directly to the next point.

7.   *Inertia* in an organization requires considerable effort in order to be redirected. Such strain forces pseudoconsensus on groups and places greater reliance on managers as coordinators, negotiators, and arbitrators, as well as motivators.

8.   *The organization may not be ready for change.* Certain preconditions, as previously discussed, are required, but may not yet be in place. Speed in instituting those preconditions cannot be forced. Trust must be established at all levels, and leaders must be ready and capable of implementing the proposed change and must exude that confidence.

9.   *Rapidly changing technology and societal conditions render some individuals obsolete.* It is impossible to remain in the same job for life, and even if a person did remain in one position, the job itself would change. Obsolescence is one of the most serious problems facing individuals in today's society. Obsolescence means the degree to which a person lacks the up-to-date knowledge or skills necessary to maintain effective performance on the job. In addition, many things, including the information explosion and dynamic change stimulated by the knowledge revolution; personal characteristics, particularly psychological; and work environment and climate influence obsolescence. The acceleration of change has resulted in a progressive decline in the useful lifetime of previous formal education and training, thereby requiring continual education on the part of individuals and staff development on the part of organizations.

10. *Change is difficult to implement.* Any type of transformation or transition is difficult. It is difficult to let go of a way of doing things, a way of organizing work and working life, to imagine a different future. Change cannot be forced upon the organization by the dictate of managers; no person wishes to have change in his or her working environment forced upon him or her. Likewise, every effort must be expended to preserve the agreed upon traditions, values, and character that are vital to the organization's life.

In any case, it can be anticipated that there will be some resistance to change, and resistance must be recognized, valued, and managed. The organization as a whole must explore the core of that resistance, validate its existence, and try to minimize its impact through understanding and problem-solving. This kind of negotiation is what experienced change agents are good at, facilitating change in organizations.

Change within an organization is also driven, or at least influenced, by change in the external environment. A status quo attitude in times of universal change can render stagnation, and stagnation condemns organizations to obsolescence.

> In today's environment, nothing is constant or predictable. . . . Three forces, separately and in combination, are driving today's (organizations) . . . Customers, Competition and Change.[30]
>
> —Michael Hammer and James Champy,
> *Reengineering the Corporation*

Conclusion

Change in organizational behavior of libraries and information centers is the result of recognition that today's knowledge-intense climate requires a different structure, attitude, and outcome on the part of those organizations. It requires collaboration and cooperation among all levels of workers, primarily in self-directed teams. Managerial systems and practices in some libraries and information centers were introduced in a more leisurely past without the current rate of change, and some of those systems, created in that more stable, predictable world, may no longer work effectively. For example, bureaucratic control, a holdover from the past, is being replaced by peer control, customer control, and automated control. In many successful library initiatives teamwork, team building, team sharing of core knowledge and new directions, and team incentives now provide flexibility and total organizational learning modes.

Organization charts now depict new organizations of groups with collective responsibility for service to customers, with a focus on customer requirements. The challenge is to convert resistance into commitment and status quo attitudes into new initiatives as the change concept is implemented. The remaining chapters of this textbook discuss components necessary to be considered as that change is instituted in knowledge-based library and information service organizations.

Notes

1.   William H. Gates, *Business @ the Speed of Thought* (New York: Warner Books, Inc., 1999), 414.

2.   Phillip Evans and Thomas S. Wurster, *Blown to Bits: How the New Economics of Information Transfer Strategy* (Boston: Harvard Business School Press, 1999), 2–7.

3.   Charles Handy, *The Age of Unreason* (Boston: Harvard Business School Press, 1990).

4.   Dirk van Gulick, *Encounter with Chaos* (New York: McGraw-Hill, 1992).

5.   Peter F. Drucker, *The Age of Discontinuity: Guidelines to Our Changing Society* (New York: Harper & Row, 1979), 17.

6.   Michael C. Jensen and William H. Meckling, "Specific and General Knowledge and Organizational Structure," in Paul S. Miller, ed., *Knowledge Management and Organizational Design* (Boston: Butterworth-Heinemann, 1996), 19.

7.   James G. Neal and Patricia Steele, "Empowerment, Organization and Structure," *Journal of Library Administration* 19 (1993): 49.

8.   Daniel Yankelovich, *New Rules: Searching for Self-Fulfillment in a World Turned Upside Down* (New York: Random House, 1981), 79.

9.   John Kotter, "Leading Change: Why Transformational Efforts Fail," *Harvard Business Review* 73 (March–April 1995): 59–67.

10.   Warren Bennis, *An Invented Life: Reflections on Leadership and Change* (Reading, MA: Addison-Wesley, 1993), 105.

11.   L. Hirschenhorn and T. Gilmore, "The New Boundaries of a Boundaryless Company," *Harvard Business Review* 70 (1992): 104.

12.   Richard M. Dougherty, "Being Successful (Nimble and Agile) in the Current Turbulent Environment," *Journal of Academic Librarianship* 27 (July 2001): 265.

13.   http://www.loc.gov/rr/digiref/tech-docs.html.

14.   Miriam Drake, "Technological Innovation and Organizational Change," *Journal of Library Administration* 19 (1993): 49.

15.   Stafford Beer, "The World We Manage," *Behavioral Science* 18 (1973): 198.

16.   Carla J. Stoffle, et al., "Choosing Our Futures," *College and Research Libraries* 57 (May 1996): 214–15.

17.   Victor Turner, *The Ritual Process* (Chicago: Aldine, 1996), 47.

18.   Rosabeth Moss Kanter, *The Change Masters: Innovations for Productivity in the American Corporation* (New York: Simon & Schuster, 1983), 275–76.

19.   John Naisbitt and Patricia Aburdene, *Re-inventing the Corporation* (New York: Warner Books, 1985), 54.

20.   David Birchall and Laurence Lyons, *Creating Tomorrow's Organizations* (London: Pitman, 1995), 91.

21.   Robert E. Quinn, *Deep Change: Discovering the Leader Within* (San Francisco: Jossey-Bass, 1996), 3.

22.   *Ibid.*

23. Dannemiller Tyson Associates, *Whole-Scale Change: Unleashing the Magic in Organizations* (San Francisco: Berrett-Koehler, 2000), 9.

24. Rosabeth Moss Kanter, *Evolve—Succeeding in the Digital Culture of Tomorrow* (Boston: Harvard Business School Press, 2001), 72.

25. B. Burnes, *Managing Change: A Strategic Approach to Organizational Development and Renewal* (London: Pitman, 1992), 43.

26. Clayton P. Alderfer, "Change Processes in Organizations," in Marvin D. Dunnett, ed., *Handbook of Industrial and Organizational Psychology* (Skokie, IL: Rand McNally, 1976), 670.

27. L. E. Greiner, "Patterns of Organization Change," *Harvard Business Review* 45 (1967): 120.

28. Steve Morgan, "Change in University Libraries: Don't Forget the People," *Library Management* 22 (2001): 58.

29. Alan C. Filley, R. J. House, and S. Kerr, *Managerial Process and Organizational Behavior* (Glenview, IL: Scott, Foresman, 1976), 491.

30. Michael Hammer and James Champy, *Reengineering the Corporation* (New York: Harper Business, 1993), 17.

Chapter 2

Evolution of Management—Its Impact on Libraries and Information Centers

> *Each body of theory purports to rest on a scientific*
> *foundation. . . . Each theory offers its own version of what*
> *organizations are like and its own version of what they should*
> *be like. . . . A modern manager who wants to improve an*
> *organization thus encounters a cacophony of different*
> *voices and visions. . . . As managers . . . turn to the theory*
> *base for help, they will find a conceptual pluralism:*
> *a jangling discord of multiple voices.*[1]
>
> —Lee G. Bolman and Terrence E. Deal,
> *Reframing Organizations*

Introduction

Anyone studying the history of management who thought, with a glimmer of hope, that past practices might shed some guiding light on future operations is likely to be both enlightened and disappointed. Experiences and experiments add to a body of knowledge. For the field of management this relates to how organizations were created in a more leisurely past and how persons working in those organizations interacted with each other and within organizations. But those experiences and experiments are relative and when placed into a modern context of constant change, therefore often present interesting reading but little insight. Further, unlike principles in other disciplines where there seems to be specific agreement, there is none for management, where focus seems to vary from time to time and from society to society. Only some segments of the management process have developed their own principles and ethics, such as personnel management, marketing, and planning, and some general theories do present a solid foundation upon which to view the present management milieu.

A hundred years ago most organizations were relatively small, and focus was upon techniques, with little recognition of underlying principles that guided development. Since then, organizations have grown in size and multiplied in numbers. Some have disappeared completely, whereas others have been able to build upon their initial strengths to become stronger and more focused over time. Most dynamic organizations have changed; some dissolved and reappeared in different configurations. New ones have emerged with strength and vitality. There also have been mergers, splits, and strategic partnerships that form the nucleus of today's organizational life. Networking and adaptation to change, both technological and personal, now play primary roles in all organizational life. Both profit-making and not-for-profit organizations are now struggling with changes brought on by political, economic, social, and technological (PEST) forces.

Libraries and information centers have not been immune to those dynamic developments discussed in the first chapter. Today most libraries and information centers are market driven, with service performance and customer satisfaction being primary criteria for resource allocation, with measurement against set standards becoming the norm. Entrepreneurship and risk-taking have become a way of life in modern libraries and information centers that have traditionally adopted various management theories and techniques.

Myriad concepts and theories have developed, particularly over the decades of the past century, as historians and management theorists struggled with identifying the experiments and defining the influences and functions that influence organizations in their development. They have tried to envision those which are likely to survive into future generations of organizations through the twenty-first century. Several thoughts, theories, and trends have merged in the current management practice. They have been driven by consideration of the work, the people who perform it, and the environment that influences both.

> A person who knows only the skills and techniques, without understanding the fundamentals of management, is not a manager, he (she) is, at best, a technician.[2]
>
> —Peter F. Drucker,
> *Management: Tasks, Responsibilities, Practices*

Today's management has evolved from earliest practice, principles, and research that provide a body of scientific knowledge about organizations and the way they function. Throughout the development of the art of management, philosophers have tried to capture the concepts of what is happening and why and to condense those notions into theories to be tested and expounded upon. Several attempts have been made to identify and to delineate the "schools of thought" and approaches to management theories, both developed during the twentieth century. Adding to those experiments and theories, one also can learn from many management experiences recorded before modern times. For a variety of reasons, the categorization of the ideas and findings into various schools of thought continues to be met with as much confusion as clarity. Some researchers and instructors place a particular idea, theory, or observation into one "school" while others might place it in a different, though aligned, "school." Sometimes these have been further delineated as "approaches" to management thought.

The topic of management and observations about how it works have been of concern to organized society throughout civilized history, although its systematic study as a separate branch of human knowledge received most attention during the second half of the twentieth century, primarily after World War II. Although formal management inquiry and research are relatively recent phenomena, historical records make it obvious that the forces that affect organizations today are much the same as those of the past: *P*olitical, *E*conomic, *S*ocial, and *T*echnological. PEST is perhaps an appropriate acronym for those forces. It will be discussed in subsequent chapters.

The twentieth century produced a critical mass of larger, profit-driven organizations, as well as a variety of smaller institutions that were limited in size and scope. Some of them were social or other not-for-profit agencies or units, including most libraries and information centers. Organization profiles provide great opportunities for observation and speculation. Through analysis, researchers working in schools of thought have attempted to formulate scientifically underlying principles of management and to postulate various theories based upon the practice of the occasion, as is evidenced in those various types of organizations.

A retrospective glance at the development of management science or art reveals that, in most situations, management actions can be observed to have been guided by underlying theory or theories observable in practice. Thus management can be described either as a science, grounded in theory, or an art, practiced by those who have the inspiration and drive to encourage others in their assigned organizational responsibilities. Theory provides the cornerstone, the *why*, whereas practice provides the laboratory for observation, the *what* and *how*.

Management in Ancient History

As early as 3000 B.C.E., the Sumerians kept records on clay tablets; many of those records applied to the management practices of the priests of Ur. Early Babylonia implemented very strict control of business enterprises with its Codes of Akkadian and Hammurabi. Nebuchadnezzar, for instance, used color codes to control production of the Hanging Gardens of Babylon, considered to be one of the great wonders of the ancient world. Checks were performed every week and cumulated yearly, with rewards being given for piecework, thereby establishing some of the earliest norms for performance. The Hebrews's understanding of hierarchy and the importance of delegation is reflected in the Old Testament, particularly in Exodus, chapter 18:25–26, in which Moses "chose able men out of all Israel and made them heads over the people, rulers of thousands, rulers of hundreds, rulers of fifties, and rulers of tens. And they judged the people at all seasons; the hard cases they brought unto Moses, but every small matter they judged themselves."

Construction of one pyramid in Egypt around 5000 B.C.E. was accomplished by about 100,000 people working for 20 years. It is obvious that such a magnificent feat could not have been accomplished without extensive planning, organizing, and controlling.

Around 2000 B.C.E., the principle of decentralized control was introduced, as is illustrated by the vesting of control in the individual states of Egypt; it was only later that the pharaoh established central control over all.[3] There is also evidence that Egyptians employed long-range planning techniques and staff advisers. Interpretations of early Egyptian papyri, extending as far back as 1300 B.C.E., indicate that the bureaucratic states of antiquity recognized the importance of organization and administration. Similar records exist for activities in ancient China. Claude George points out that one could find, in the China of 3000 years ago, "concepts that have a contemporary managerial ring: organization, functions, cooperation, procedures to bring efficiency, and various control techniques."[4] The staff principle, later perfected by military organizations, was used very effectively by Chinese dynasties as far back as 2250 B.C.E.

Although the records of early Greece offer little insight to the principles of management, the very existence of the Athenian commonwealth, with its councils, popular courts, administrative officials, and board of generals, indicates an appreciation of various managerial functions. Socrates's definition of management as a skill separate from technical knowledge and experience is remarkably close to current understanding. The Greek influence on scientific management is revealed in their writings; for example, Plato wrote about specialization, and Socrates described management issues.[5]

In ancient Rome the complexity of the administrative job evoked considerable development of management techniques. It is thought that the secret of the Roman Empire's success lay in the ability of the Romans to organize work and people for the cause. Confucius, the great Chinese sage, a civil servant and teacher of management around 500 B.C.E., wrote parables that offered practical suggestions for public administration. Some of them are still quoted in and applied to modern organizations.

Many ancient leaders were not only charismatic individuals but skillful organizers as well. Hannibal's crossing of the Alps in 218 B.C.E., with his Carthaginian troops and equipment, was a remarkable organizational feat. About the same time, Qin Shi Huang Di, the first emperor of China, was able to organize hundreds of thousands of slaves and convicts to create his burial complex at Xian and to connect portions of the Great Wall. He also unified warring factions and standardized weights and measures as part of his centralization initiative. It is for that reason he is referred to as the "first" emperor of China.

The earliest documentation of motion studies appeared in the time of Cyrus, the Persian king, about 600 B.C.E. Records of those studies indicate that musical instruments—the flute and the pipe—governed workers' tempo and motions, while songs designated each of the various tasks. The Persians further added to the developing body of management practice by introducing rhythm, standard motion, and other motion-related work aspects. Thus, many of the techniques that are employed today in modern organizations can be traced to ancient times and civilizations.

Modern History of Management Thought

Bringing the management process into modern times, the most efficient formal organization in the history of Western civilization has been the Catholic Church. This is not only because of the sustained appeal of its objectives but also because of the effectiveness of its organization and management techniques. The scalar chain of command, which established a path of communication from the highest level in the organization, the pope, down to the bottom rung of a ladder-like hierarchy, can be traced to its introduction early in the organization of the church, along with the concept of specialization.

The Arsenal of Venice in Italy, probably the sixteenth century's largest industrial plant, is an outstanding example of organizational efficiency. It appeared during the time of Machiavelli, whose writings emphasized the principle that authority develops from the consent of the masses. His ideas, particularly as set forth in his classic work *The Prince*, apply to current study of leadership and communications.

Some of the most important principles and practices of modern business management can be traced to military organizations. The principles of unity of command, staff advisers, and division of work all evolved from early military order, probably as early as Cyrus and certainly refined by Alexander the Great of Russia, who effectively used staff organization to coordinate activities.

The military has been a strong organization in many countries throughout history. Among the most important management practice developed by the military is the staff principle. For example, the general staff, organized under a chief of staff, furnishes specialized advice and information and supplies auxiliary services. The general staff and its services have come to be essential features of not only the military but also of business enterprises. In addition, the line-of-command concept originated in the armies of antiquity and medieval times, and the scalar principle, to be discussed later, is still a very important part of military organizations today.

The development of technology during the Industrial Revolution, at the end of the nineteenth and beginning of the twentieth centuries, produced a factory system that brought workers into a central location and into contact with other workers. It was during the development of effective and efficient management control of these newly founded organizations that many management concepts began to emerge. Adam Smith in his writing, particularly in *The Wealth of Nations*, described division of work and time-and-motion studies as they should be employed in organizations. Other writers of the period, including Robert Owen, Charles Babbage, and Charles Dupin, wrote about the problems of management in factories.[6] Many of the principles that were later reemphasized and further refined in the scientific management approach and the human relations approach were first developed by those writers during the eighteenth and nineteenth centuries. For instance, Babbage, a mathematician, stressed the importance of distinguishing mental activity from physical work and wanted to improve efficiency by encouraging managers to use time-study techniques, to centralize production, to inaugurate research and development, and so forth.[7] He contributed much to the scientific management approach and was a pioneer in developing the principles that are used in computing. Both Owen and Babbage identified human resources as a major contributing force to the success of organizations. Owen was committed to human comforts, including working conditions and wages, whereas Babbage emphasized staff benefits, including profit sharing.

> Those who look for library administrative theory search for it outside of librarianship. Because library administration is so pragmatically oriented, it seems impossible that a theoretical framework for viewing administrative practice already exists within libraries. Yet this is indeed the case. It remains only to ferret it out.[8]
>
> —Charles McClure,
> *Strategies for Library Administration*

Various methods have been used in the study of management in this century. The first systematic approach was legalistic, being devoted to a study of the organization, powers, activities, and limitations of public authorities. Later, a more scientific approach was considered, concerned chiefly with the administrative organization as an instrument of management. An attempt was made to determine, on the basis of empirical evidence, rules for administrative organization and operation. More recently, behavioral scientists have used the methods of psychology, sociology, and anthropology in efforts to secure a better understanding of group behavior, leadership, and decision making. These pioneering contributions to schools, movements, or approaches are referred to by various names, but the major focus or core of each can be recognized, although factors sometimes overlap.

No student of management thought can afford to be unfamiliar with the contributions of the major pioneer thinkers in the field. This is not to say that their ideas must be accepted without question. However, their ideas are the basis for the development of management techniques currently in practice, and their contributions provide insight into the background theories that are the essence of management today.

> There are the behaviorists . . . who see management as a complex of interpersonal relationships and the basis of management theory, the tentative tenets of the new and undeveloped science of psychology. There are also those who see management theory as simply a manifestation of the institutional and cultural aspects of sociology. Still others, observing that the central core of management is decision-making, branch in all directions from this core to encompass everything in organization life. Then, there are mathematicians, who think of management primarily as an exercise in logical relationships expressed in symbols and the omnipresent and ever revered model. But the entanglement of growth reaches its ultimate when the study of management is regarded as one of a number of systems and sub-systems, with an understandable tendency for the researcher to be dissatisfied until he [or she] has encompassed the entire physical and cultural universe as a management system.[9]
>
> —Harold Koontz,
> "The Management Theory Jungle"

It is apparent when one studies the schools of management thought developed in the last century that each reflects the problems of the changing times. There is a progression of concerns detailed in those studies. In management practice, the theory that is most relevant and applicable at one point in its evolution seems not to be the most appropriate one at the next level of the organization's development. Also, the theory that is prominent at one point in time may no longer be in vogue during the next decade. A few theories have survived and continue to influence management thought and practice today. For purposes of discussion, these are grouped into three approaches: scientific, human relations, and systems, with brief discussion of contemporary theories.

For the purposes of this chapter, the major management theories have been placed in categories that are frequently used in the management literature. These categories have been labeled with terms drawn from the literature, although writers disagree about which terms can best be used in a strict classification of management theory. All of the approaches are concerned with the management process, but no one theory can begin to provide a comprehensive view. All have strong points and weak points, and some of the best and some of the worst of each can be observed in library and information center operations today.

Scientific Approach

Scientific Management Movement

The term *scientific management* is said to have been coined in 1910 by Louis Brandeis in his appearance before the Interstate Commerce Commission in the United States. The basic assumption of this school of thought is that workers at the operational level are primarily economically motivated and that they will put forth their best efforts if they are rewarded financially. Further, the emphasis is on maximum output with minimum strain, eliminating waste and inefficiency. Planning and standardization of efforts and techniques are viewed as important factors. In the United States, the pioneering work of Frederick Winslow Taylor dominates the thinking of this school. Although one cannot say that he developed the theory, his concepts, based upon experiments on the shop floor, have contributed to general management theory of the scientific management movement.

> Scientific management requires the establishment of many rules, laws and formulae which replace the judgment of the individual [worker] and which can be effectively used only after having been recorded, indexed, etc.[10]
> —Frederick W. Taylor,
> *Principles of Scientific Management*

During his day, Taylor's views coincided closely with those of proponents of the Protestant work ethic, who had no difficulty with the fusion of religion and worldly success. Taylor's attitude toward work was that the human and the machine are similar. "It is no single element, but rather the whole combination, that constitutes scientific management, which may be summarized as: Science, not rule of thumb; Harmony, not discord; Cooperation, not individualism; Maximum output, in place of restricted output; The Development of [all workers to their] greatest efficiency and prosperity."[11] Taylor expounded several principles:

- ◆ To gather all traditional knowledge and classify, tabulate, and reduce it to rules, laws, and formulas to help workers in their daily work.

- ◆ To develop a science for each element of humanity's work to replace the rule-of-thumb method.

- ◆ To select scientifically and then train, teach, and develop the worker.

- ◆ To cooperate with workers to ensure that work is done according to developed scientific principles.

- ◆ To effect an almost equal division of work and responsibility between workers and managers; that is, managers are to be given work for which they are best fitted, as are employees.[12]

Efficiency was Taylor's central theme. As a steel works manager in Philadelphia, Pennsylvania, in the United States, he was interested in knowing how to get more work out of workers who were "naturally lazy and engage[d] in systematic soldiering." This attitude, he speculated, was fostered by poor management. He observed "when a naturally energetic man works for a few days beside a lazy one, the logic of the situation is unanswerable. 'Why should I work hard when the lazy fellow gets the same pay that I do and does only half as much work?' "[13] Taylor proposed using scientific research methods to discover the one best way to perform a job. He felt that faster work could be assured only through enforced standardization of methods; enforced adaptation of the best instruments to be used for the work; adoption of good, hygienic working conditions; and enforced cooperation. This attitude moved away from a more experiential approach to a more scientific one. Among the several experiments he performed were:

- ◆ Work study. One particular experiment detailed movements of workers in a shop and suggested shortcuts and/or more efficient ways of performing certain operations. Within three years of implementation of the new ways, the output of the shop had doubled.

- ◆ Standardized tools for shops. In another area he found that the coal shovels being used weighed between 16 and 38 pounds. After experimenting, it was found that 21–22 pounds was the best weight. Shovels weighing that amount were employed. Again, after three years, efficiency increased as 140 men were doing what had previously been done by between 400 and 600 men.

- ◆ Selecting and training workers. Taylor insisted that each worker be assigned to do what he or she was best suited for and that those who exceeded the defined work be paid bonuses. With this motivation, production, as might be expected, rose to an all-time high.

As a result of these experiments, Taylor also advocated assigning supervisors by function, that is, one for training, one for discipline, and so on. As can be imagined, this required the principles of planning, organizing, and controlling as input measures to increase output. A related functional approach is still successful as is evident today in many organizations, including some libraries and other types of information centers throughout the world.

However, in the industry of that time, Taylor's efforts were resented by unions and managers alike: managers because their intuition and discretion were challenged, unions because their role was questioned. Taylor was fired from his original job in Philadelphia. He then went to Bethlehem Steel, still in Pennsylvania, where again he was fired after only three years. The unions, indignant by this time, were instrumental in having his methods investigated by a special U.S. congressional committee; they succeeded in forbidding the use of stopwatches and bonuses in U.S. army arsenals until World War II. His concepts, however, spread to Europe and Great Britain and later to the Soviet Union after the Russian Revolution. Many researchers and scholars maintain that this movement represented techniques only and thwarted the development of a true philosophy of management.

An often-repeated criticism of the scientific management approach is that it overemphasizes productivity and underemphasizes human nature. Amitai Etzioni wrote that "although Taylor originally set out to study the interaction between human characteristics and the characteristics of the machine, the relationship between these two elements which make up the industrial work process, he ended up by focusing on a far more limited subject: the physical characteristics of the human body in routine jobs—e.g., shoveling coal or picking up loads. Eventually Taylor came to view human and machine resources not so much as mutually adaptable, but rather man functioning as an appendage to the industrial machine."[14] Similar criticism could be leveled at other movements within the scientific management approach.

Even though Taylor was the most important advocate of the scientific management movement, others worked in the same arena, including Frank and Lillian Gilbreth. Frank, an engineer, and Lillian, who held a doctorate in psychology, were concerned with the human aspects of managing, and they expanded the concepts of motion study and fatigue. Their merit systems eventually evolved into performance analysis and appraisals. They tried to identify the one best way to perform a task in the most comfortable manner. In the process they identified seventeen basic elements in on-the-job motions, such as grasp, hold, position, and search. These motions came to be called THERBLIGS, *Gilbreths* spelled backward, with one transposition.[15] Taylor's experiments and the Gilbreths's work were complementary, Taylor stressing time study, and the Gilbreths emphasizing motion study. From these two merged systems emerged the industrial engineering discipline.

Henry L. Gantt, experimenting at about the same time, developed the task-and-bonus system, which was similar to Taylor's awards incentive. Gantt's system set rates of output; if those rates were exceeded, bonuses were paid. In some cases, production more than doubled; therefore, he developed what might be considered the first set of output measures. The Gantt Chart is still widely used in production schedules and is used in many libraries and information systems to chart and calculate work schedules. Along the horizontal axis of the chart, Gantt placed the time, work schedule, and work-completed aspects; along the vertical axis he placed the individuals and machines assigned to those schedules. In this way, the path to completion could be easily calculated.

In its early development, scientific management had little concern for the external environment of the organization but was almost exclusively concerned with internal operations. Taylor took many of his concepts from the bureaucratic model developed by Max Weber in Germany, particularly in regard to rules and procedures for the conduct of work in organizations. Weber, the first to articulate a theory of authority structure in organizations, distinguished between power and authority, between compelling action and voluntary response. He identified three characteristics that aided authority: charisma (personality), tradition (custom), and bureaucracy (through rules and regulations). This concept of bureaucracy developed on one side of the Atlantic at about the same time as scientific management was developing on the other. Insights on specialization of work, levels of authority, and control all emerged from Weber's writings.

Weber was more concerned with the structure of the organization than with the individual. Most of his writings and research related to the importance of specialization in labor, regulations and procedures, and the advantages of a hierarchical system in making informed decisions. Weber, a German behavioral scientist, characterized a bureaucratic organization as an organization of functions bound by rules in which:

♦ Area of competence or division of labor provides specialization and contributes to standardization;

♦ The principle of hierarchy exists;

♦ Promotion into management ranks is only by demonstrated technical competence; and

♦ Rules are to be recorded in writing.[16]

Weber further stated that "experience tends universally to show that the purely bureaucratic type of administrative organization . . . is, from a pure theoretical point of view, capable of attaining the highest degree of efficiency and is in this sense formally the most rational known means of carrying out imperative control over human beings."[17] But Weber later recognized the dangers of too rigid a bureaucratic control.

> It is horrible to think that the world could one day be filled with nothing but little cogs, little men clinging to little jobs and striving toward bigger ones. This passion for bureaucracy is enough to drive one to despair.[18]
>
> —Max Weber, in J. P. Mayer,
> *Max Weber and German Politics*

Classical Movement

Another movement began to develop in France about the same time as Taylor's experiments in the United States. Using some of the same scientific management methods, it sought to establish a conceptual framework for management, to identify principles, and to build a theory. However, unlike the scientific management movement, which focused on shop operations, this approach, referred to as the classical or traditional or universalist school, took a holistic view of the organization in order to define an ideal structure. Some refer to the body of knowledge that emanated from this process as the "administrative management theory."[19]

The father of the classical or generalist theory movement was a Frenchman, Henri Fayol. Fayol took a scientific approach, but he looked at administration from the top down. As an industrialist, he concentrated on the roles that managers should perform as planners, organizers, and controllers. He believed that managers needed guidelines, basic principles upon which to operate, and he emphasized the need to teach administration at all levels. He identified elements in the administration of organizations as including planning, organization, command, coordination, and control. Briefly, his stated principles are:

♦ Division of work. As the enterprise grows, there should be an early division of duties. The activities concerning management should be separate and distinct. Specialization naturally develops with division of work.

♦ Authority. The authority that individuals possess in an organization should be equal to their responsibility. A person who is responsible for the results of a task should be given the authority to take actions necessary to ensure its success.

♦ Discipline. There should be complete obedience to, total energy devoted to, and behavior in the best interest of the organization.

♦ Unity of command. An employee should receive orders from only one superior. (This unity of command is in direct opposition to Taylor's idea of having workers take instructions from several superiors.)

♦ Unity of direction. A body with two heads is a monster and has difficulty in surviving. There should be one head and one plan to ensure a coordinated effort.

♦ Subordination of individual interest to general interest. Primary concern should be the growth of the organization.

♦ Remuneration of personnel. Wages should be fair.

♦ Centralization. Everything that goes to increase the importance of the subordinate's role is decentralization, everything that goes to reduce it is centralization. Centralization is the desirable arrangement within an organization.

♦ Scalar chain. Gangplanks should be used to prevent the scalar chain from bogging down. The gangplank (illustrated in Figure 2.1) can be used without weakening the chain of command, as long as the gangplank relationship is advisory and not policy-making.

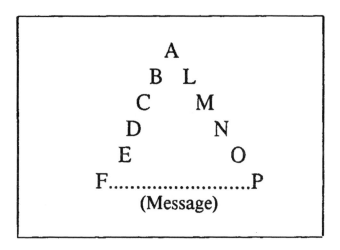

Figure 2.1. A Gangplank Can Be Used to Communicate Across Scalar Boundaries

♦ Order. There is a right place for everything and everyone in the organization. That place or job must be identified.

♦ Equity. Equality of treatment must be taken into account in dealing with employees. Justice should be tempered with kindness.

♦ Stability of tenure of personnel. It is important to keep people on the job.

♦ Initiative. Incentive rewards must be provided to stimulate production.

♦ Esprit de corps. Communication is the key to a satisfied working group.[20]

Like Taylor, Fayol believed workers are naturally lazy, resist work more effectively when working in groups, must be subjected to sharp discipline, can best be motivated by the incentive of higher wages, can do much better when properly instructed, and differ markedly in native ability and capacity. Unlike Taylor in other views of the organization, Fayol was more concerned with human relations and defining the activities of managers. He and Luther Gulick, among others, advised managers to break down complicated jobs into specialized activities. This was achieved through a "pyramid of control." Gulick and Lyndall Urwick followed Fayol's lead by popularizing several principles:

1.   Fit people to the administrative structure.

2. Recognize one top executive as the source of authority.

3. Adhere to unity of command.

4. Use special and general staff.

5. Departmentalize by purpose, process, person, and place.

6. Delegate and use the exception principle.

7. Make responsibility commensurate with authority.

8. Consider appropriate spans of control.[21]

> When management principles can be developed, proved and used, managerial efficiency will inevitably improve. Then the conscientious manager can become more effective by using established guidelines to help solve . . . problems, without engaging in original laborious research or the risky practice of trial and error.[22]
>
> —Harold Koontz and Cyril O'Donnell,
> *Principles of Management*

Taylor and Fayol, then, may be considered the founders of the theory of management. There is little doubt that many organizations, libraries, information centers, and other information agencies still depend heavily on these classic theories for the base of their formal organization. The greatest criticisms of those schools is that they place undue emphasis on the formal aspects of organization and neglect entirely the effects of individual personality, informal groups, intra-organizational conflicts, and the decision-making process on the formal structure.

Organization and System Movement

World War I gave great impetus to the study of efficiency, and by 1930 the idea of applying theory to organization and system was emphasized in the organization and system movement. This theory distinguished between administration, representing the ownership point of view, and scientific management, an approach to work at the operational level, as they related to organization and system. This movement expanded the work of Fayol and at the same time began to explore the behavioral aspects of management. Weber's theory about authority structures in complex organizations is a classic foundation of the system movement.[23] Mooney and Reiley added further substance to the systems movement by focusing on principles of coordination, scalar chaining, functionality, and staffing.[24] Organization charts, job descriptions, and policy manuals for procedures in organizations were developed by them.

Other significant writers about this movement, already mentioned above, were Lyndall Urwick, an Englishman, and Luther Gulick, an American, who edited a landmark work on scientific administration. In a paper presented to U.S. President Franklin Roosevelt in 1937, they summed up an executive's functions in the acronym POSDCORB. The focus was on:

Planning, that is, working out in broad outline the things that need to be done and the methods for doing them in order to accomplish the enterprise's set purpose.

Organizing, that is, the establishment of the formal structure of authority through which work subdivisions are arranged, defined, and coordinated for the defined objectives.

Staffing, that is, the whole personnel function of bringing in and training the staff and maintaining favorable conditions for work.

Directing, that is, the continuous task of making decisions and embodying them in specific and general orders and instructions and serving as the leader of the enterprise.

Coordinating, that is, the all-important duty of interrelating the various parts of the work.

Reporting, that is, keeping those to whom the executive is accountable informed through records, research, and inspection.

Budgeting, that is, all that goes with budgeting in the form of fiscal planning, accounting, and control.[25]

Readers will quickly realize that the early systems approach, originally developed by those two, is a simplified yet comprehensive way of viewing management. It is based upon a combination of experiences and philosophy. The reader will also recognize that the concepts detailed in their work, with modifications and additions, have been used as a framework in developing some of the discussion in this textbook. It is a simplified view of management, recognizing that there are many segments of management, each of which has developed its own principles. For instance, when one talks about organizing and directing, it is obvious that principles of human resources management come into play.

Human Relations Approach

During the 1930s, management studies began to give more attention to the concerns of individuals working in organizations. The primary espoused belief of this approach was that because managing involves getting things done through people, management study should naturally center on interpersonal relations. The main emphasis of observation and study became that of the individual and the informal group in the formal organization; the primary concern was with integrating people into the work environment. The phrase *personnel administration* came into prominence, and increasing efforts toward democratization and staff participation were evident. It became important to study people as human beings rather than as work units, individuals rather than cogs in a wheel.

Of paramount concern in this approach is the recognition of basic human needs, with the idea that once those primary needs are satisfied and a willing ear given to suggestions and complaints made by the individual, morale will increase and production will go up. The maxim "a happy workforce is a productive workforce" well describes this approach. Both sociologists and psychologists have contributed to these developments.

Human Behavior Movement

This movement focuses on behavior of the individual and his or her quality of life in the organization, the individual's needs, aspirations, and motivations, as well as those of the group and the organization. The major assumption is that if management can make employees happy, maximum performance will result. Mary Follett, a political philosopher writing in the early 1900s, was one of the first to be concerned with the human aspect. She emphasized the psychological and sociological aspects of management, viewing it as a social process and the organization as a social system in which coordination was the most important principle: coordination by direct contact with the people concerned, coordination that was a continuous process, coordination found in the initial steps of every endeavor, and coordination as a reciprocal process. Her main concern was with workers and their involvement in deciding their destiny within the organization.

Early efforts in this type of research were conducted in the United States by Elton Mayo and a group of industrial psychologists at the Western Electric Hawthorne Plant in Chicago, Illinois. Mayo promoted internal communications by providing decision makers with insights into the attitudes of workers, by looking at the informal groups, and by focusing on human factors. Researchers, led by Mayo, began to study physical working conditions and their influence on worker productivity.[26] The studies established that each individual is different; that individuals act to protect their own position in a group rather than to help management achieve higher production; and that this self-interest has an impact upon the behavior of others within the group. These studies also revealed the importance of social interaction and psychological factors in determining productivity and satisfaction. Principles that have been demonstrated in their studies are:

1. Workers are more motivated by social rewards and sanctions than by economic incentives.

2. Workers' actions are influenced by the group.

3. Whenever formal organizations exist, both formal and informal norms exist.

The researchers, after hypothesizing that motivation and supervision, as well as basic social relations on the job, were responsible for increased productivity, found that indeed, when the work group felt itself to be in opposition to management, productivity stayed close to the minimum accepted level. For the first time it was recognized that those social factors were important to organizational output. In general, the human behavior movement maintains that if the organization makes employees happy, it will gain their full cooperation and effort and reach optimum efficiency.

‖ A major concern of management must be that of organizing teamwork, that is to say, of developing and sustaining cooperation.[27]

—G. Elton Mayo,
The Social Problems of an Industrialized Civilization

Mayo's conclusions were quite opposite from those of Taylor, who stated that a person at work is an entirely economic person. Mayo maintained that workers are primarily motivated by togetherness and crave individual recognition within the group.

Self-Actualizing Movement

This movement is closely related to the human relations movement and is often confused or intertwined with it. It encourages management to let employees develop social groups on the job, to move toward employee participation in management, and to allow democracy in the organization. The spiritual father of this movement was Chester Barnard, who dwelled on the contribution-satisfaction equilibrium as he examined the organization as a social system. He was the first to introduce the issue of social responsibility of management, including fair wages and security and the creation of an atmosphere conducive to work. He identified four inducements: material inducements, including money and other physical securities; personal, nonmaterial opportunities for distinction, prestige, and personal power; desirable physical conditions of work; and ideal benefactions, such as pride of craft, sense of adequacy, loyalty to the organization, and so on.[28] Barnard emphasized communication as the first function of managers.

‖ Man is a perpetual wanting animal. The average member of society is most often particularly satisfied and particularly unsatisfied in all of his wants.[29]

—Abraham Maslow,
"A Theory of Human Motivation"

Several later theories and concepts regarding the individual have emerged from the works of other authors in this movement. Abraham Maslow's needs theory builds on the concept that humans have a hierarchy of needs, starting with the basic physical necessities of food, shelter, and clothing, and ascending five steps to the intangible needs of self-actualization and fulfillment, with emphasis on self-actualization.[30] The whole concept of organizational behavior has been advanced by this motivational theory espoused by Maslow. Management by objectives, another management concept introduced in the 1950s by Peter Drucker, is supported by Douglas McGregor in his Theory X and Theory Y work, which advocates substituting a more participative approach for that of authoritarianism.[31] Chris Argyris suggests that organizational structure can curtail self-fulfillment.[32] The theories share the idea that information sharing is desirable and that management and workers should share planning and analysis of operations. Other disciples of this approach include Rensis Likert, Warren G. Bennis, and Robert Blake and Jane Mouton. Discussions of these and other theorists are incorporated into the discussions in a later chapter.

The average person learns, under proper conditioning, not only to accept but to seek responsibility. The capacity to exercise a relatively high degree of imagination, ingenuity and creativity in the solution of organizational problems is widely, not narrowly, distributed in the population.[33]

—Douglas McGregor,
The Human Side of Enterprise

Systems Approach

During the last half of the twentieth century, attention began to be paid to the matter of individuals and group behavior in the work situation and the relationship between individuals and groups within a larger social, cultural, and political system. Concepts emerging from the Japanese management approach fall into this category. A topic of current exploration is the behavior of both individuals and groups within organizations and the behavior of organizations as social systems in the environment.

The systems approach, also known as the decision theory approach, regards the organization as a total system. Terms common in this approach include management science and operations research. In many ways, it is similar to the earlier scientific management approach. As Herbert Simon points out, "no meaningful line can be drawn any more to demarcate operations research from scientific management or scientific management from management science."[34] Proponents of this approach gather information by micro-studies of units in the system to discern how individual units interrelate and depend on other units to create a whole.[35] Generally, the systems approach draws on the basic science and theory of several disciplines and relates those principles to the structure and management of organizations.

Decision Theory Movement

Since the 1950s, such disciplines as mathematics, statistics, and economics have contributed to management through the use of mathematical models for decision making and prediction. Control techniques, such as cost-benefit analyses, linear programming, systems analysis, simulation, Monte Carlo techniques, and game theory, have been used in creative planning. However, even though this is a recent phenomenon, an operations research team was used as early as the 1940s in England when the various phases of operations research were developed.[36] The disciplines of psychology and sociology have contributed to theories of leadership and organization, human motivation and behavior, organizational relationships, and the nature of authority. Elements from each of those theories and disciplines have been drawn together in the decision theory movement to focus on the process of making decisions.

The decision theory movement is primarily concerned with the study of rational decision-making procedures and the way managers actually reach decisions. The implication is that mathematical models and quantitative processes can serve as the basis for all management decisions. Many of the researchers have concentrated on describing the decision-making process, drawing on psychology and economics,[37] or on prescribing how decisions should be made.[38] The mathematical branch of the decision theory movement is concerned with both what to measure and why, the goal being to indicate how best to improve a system or solve a problem. Managing information for timely decision making has become a major focus of some research efforts. Management information systems (MIS) developed as a sophisticated technique for systematically gathering relevant information for decision makers. The advent of technology has greatly aided researchers in the development of management information systems and has allowed others to test more quickly theories using simulation models. This approach has now been further facilitated and enhanced, even superceded by the development of decision support systems (DSS) using computer technology to address complex problems requiring human decisions.[39]

Management scientists share common characteristics, namely the application of scientific analysis to managerial problems, the goal of improving the manager's decision-making ability, high regard for economic effectiveness criteria, reliance on mathematical models, and the use of computers.[40] The decision theory movement, primarily through the decision support systems (DSS), uses techniques such as game theory, simulation, and linear programming in presenting alternatives for decision makers to consider.

General Systems Theory Movement

Undoubtedly the most widely accepted theoretical base for modern management is called the general systems theory (GST). This movement integrates knowledge gleaned from the biological, physical, and behavioral sciences. Its disciples, who call themselves revisionists, are working to combine the thoughts of the behavioral scientists with those of systems theorists, mathematicians, statisticians, and computer scientists by merging the theories of the scientific management movement with those of the human relations movement. Some of the previously mentioned researchers are also part of this movement, including Mary Parker Follett, Chester Barnard, Herbert Simon, Chris Argyris, and Rensis Likert. They maintain that workers' attitudes are influenced by external and internal forces. Therefore, it is important to encourage interaction with both environments to benefit the organization. Effective planning systems, organizing systems, and controlling systems, discussed later in this text, are cognizant of this unifying drive. The emphasis is upon communications and developing organizational structures best suited to benefit the organization. Some consider the GST movement not a theory but "a direction in the contemporary philosophy of science."[41]

Ludwig von Bertlanffy is considered the founder of GST because he was the first to talk about the "system theory of the organism."[42] He defines a system as "a set of elements standing in interrelation among themselves and with the environment. The really important aspect is the interaction among the elements to create a whole, dynamic system. This system, if it is an open one, interacts with its environment."[43] The system draws from the environment and feeds back into it. The system is influenced by the environment and in turn influences the environment. If the system is dissected, it becomes evident that it comprises a number of subsystems; likewise, the organization is but one subsystem of a larger environment. Fremont Kast and James Rosenzweig summarize nicely by stating that "an organization is not simply a technical or a social system. Rather, it is the structuring and integrating of human activities around various technologies. The technologies affect the types of inputs into the organization, the nature of the transformation processes, and the outputs from the system. However, the social system determines the effectiveness and efficiency of the utilization of the technology."[44]

Psychological Movement

Brief mention should be made of a fledgling psychological movement that, in many ways, fits into several categories already discussed. Based upon personality theory, the psychological movement views the human as a complex being metamorphosing through physiological and psychological stages to maturity. The ego, as it develops, learns to adjust to factors of the environment, the conscience, and basic sexual and aggression drives. Work is the great equalizer in this development; therefore, the organization becomes an important psychological tool, if you will. The major theorists of this movement are Harry Levinson, Abraham Zaleznik, and Elliott Jaques.

Believing that an individual can fashion his or her own existence, researchers have explored how unconscious motives affect decision making and how irrational behavior relates contemporary pressures to childhood conflicts. The researchers are attempting to create a psychology model that identifies the driving force behind the ego, believing that one's self-esteem is a product of the gap between ego ideal and self-image.

Contemporary Theories

Contingency Approach

Several management theories have gained some attention in recent years; among them is that of contingency management. This concept takes the situational approach. It considers the circumstances of each situation and then decides which response has the greatest chance of success.[45] The contingency or situational approach asserts that:

♦ there is no best management technique;

♦ there is no best way to manage;

♦ no technique or managerial principle is effective all of the time; and

♦ should the question be posed as to what works best, the simple response is, "It all depends on the situation."[46]

Technological impact, size, and outside influences, among others, play a role in determining the structure of the organization. The challenges of the contingency approach are in perceiving organizational situations as they actually exist, choosing the management tactic best suited to those situations, and competently implementing those tactics.[47] The approach requires an analysis and diagnosis of the entire managerial environment, thereby synthesizing all approaches. "It promises to integrate the best of the existing strands of management knowledge."[48]

Recent Management Theory Development

Other modern movements recognize that the bureaucratic approach of the earliest schools, which concentrated decision making and power at the top of the organization, may not be the most appropriate approach to today's organizational development in the world of innovation and change. Most of the current management theorists take the view that individuals and teams in organizations, all workers, are not simply drones in the organizational hive but that, as members of the enterprise, they have an active role to play in identifying the organization's future and have a commitment to its success. Theories in this general range include:

◆ Field Theory—where teams and individuals participate in deciding the structure, participate in decision making, and encourage certain management styles.

◆ Open Systems Theory[49]—where subsystems are identified and related in the total system, and a view maintains that when one subsystem changes the whole system must change.

◆ Organizational Development[50]—which uses many of the factors in the human relations approach and other later ones to place the focus upon individuals and groups as learners ready to contribute to organizational development.

Current Theories Influencing Information Services

In the 1990s two other approaches to organizational management developed to focus on what has been called theories of knowledge and learning organizations, in other words, the knowledge-based theories of information management and learning organizations. Both of them focus efforts on the change process in organizations by concentrating on the total organizations knowledge base[51] as it resides in the minds and attitudes of workers and on the need to develop learning organizations.[52] They complement each other, with learning organizations focusing on self-development of individuals through enrichment of responsibilities and knowledge management emphasizing the creation of systems to capture human knowledge residing in the knowledge base of individuals in the organization.

> The library is the purest form of knowledge manager: its role is to identify, select, collect, organize, store, archive, and distribute knowledge.[53]
>
> —Martin Dillon, *Knowledge Management Opportunities for Libraries and Universities*

The learning organization[54] maintains open communications, decentralized decision making, and a flattened organization. It profiles an organization that can overcome limitations, understands the pressures against it, and yet seizes opportunities. The basic principles are made up of five core areas:

1. Personal mastery, with people identifying what is important in the process;

2.   Mental models, with the organization continuously challenging in order to improve members' mental models;

3.   Shared vision, requiring a visioning of what the organization should be;

4.   Team learning, through cooperation, communication, and compatibility; and

5.   Systems thinking, recognizing the organization as a whole.

Leaders assume various roles—innovator, broker, director, producer, coordinator, monitor, facilitator,[55] teacher, steward, and designer of learning processes—serving the staff rather than controlling it.[56]

We are entering a period of change: the shift from the command-and-control organization, the organization of departments and divisions, to the information-based organization, the organization of knowledge specialists.[57]

Summary

The scientific movement's approach to organization is to study the activities that need to be undertaken to achieve objectives; the human relations approach starts with the study of people's motives and behavior; the decision theory (systems) approach concentrates on the decisions that need to be made to achieve objectives; and the knowledge-based theories approach emphasizes the need for collaboration and identification of the knowledge base in existence in the organization so that systems can be developed to provide excellent service to clients. All of these approaches interrelate to provide a total management picture.

This general overview does not permit detailed discussions of concepts or theories, rather, it only mentions them because the intent is to provide the basic background necessary for a student or other interested professional who can then place into perspective the observed theories as they apply to today's libraries and information centers. Applications of some of those theories mentioned are cited in later chapters of this text. For instance, theories—such as McGregor's Theory X and Theory Y, Herzberg's motivation-hygiene theory, and Maslow's hierarchy of needs theory—are discussed in appropriate chapters.[58] This discussion of the various approaches to management provides a perspective of the foundation upon which contemporary management rests. The various approaches, each with its own techniques and proponents, contribute to an understanding of the nature of management and how it can be practiced more skillfully.

One way to view management is as a set of common processes or functions that, when properly carried out, lead to organizational efficiency and effectiveness. Another way is to think of management as the roles played by managers. Henry Mintzberg observed what managers did over a period of time and from his observations drew conclusions about what managers actually do. Based on that research, managers undertake various roles. These roles can be grouped into three broad categories: interpersonal roles, information roles, and decision roles.[59] This approach offers an interesting and useful alternative to the traditional view of managerial functions. Mintzberg sees managers performing many activities, such as acting as a figurehead and representing the organization to the outside world, that have not been considered strictly managerial functions. This is not surprising because many of those roles are performed only by top managers.

> Most managers spend most of their time on things that are not "managing."
> A sales manager makes a statistical analysis or placates an important customer.
> A foreman repairs a tool or fills out a production report. A manufacturing
> manager designs a new plant layout or tests new material. A company
> president works through the details of a bank loan or negotiates a big
> contract—or spends hours presiding at a dinner in honor of long-service
> employees. All of these things pertain to a particular function. All are
> necessary and have to be done well. But they are apart from the work
> which every manager does whatever his (or her) function or activity, what-
> ever rank and position, work which is common to all managers and
> peculiar to them.[60]
>
> —Peter F. Drucker,
> *Management: Tasks, Responsibilities, Practices*

Although management can and should be viewed as a synthesis of functions and roles, several functions common to all managers at all levels can be identified. The remaining chapters of this text identify and discuss those common functions and roles. If a manager is able to perform all of these functions skillfully, he or she will ensure that the organization is managed well.

Management theory has expanded greatly over recent decades, influenced by new ideas that helped "new cohorts of professional managers climb up the bureaucratic ladder; mathematicians, natural scientists, economists, computer programmers, artificial intelligentsia, and even humanistic psychologists came to influence."[61] The proliferation of management theories has resulted in semantic difficulties and tension among proponents of the various schools as each has tried to establish its approach as the most logical. Perhaps the best way of viewing the maze called management theory is to consider each movement as a subsystem that contributes to the overall system of people working together in organizations that are changing. Each theory brings new means of examining organizations. The current political, economic, social, and technological climate is forcing a reevaluation of systems and structures and reexamination of some of the early theories, with a view of applying new ones.

Library and Information Center Management

The Historical Perspective

From its very inception, library and information center management, as might be expected, showed no identifiable characteristic that set it apart from other types of organizational management. Trends, theories, and techniques introduced into organizations and discussed in the management literature easily found their way into library practice and over the years have been adapted with varying degrees of success. The integration of those theories and techniques into library operations has been extensively reported in the world's library literature during the last 115 years.

In 1887, F. M. Cruden, then librarian of the St. Louis Public Library, stated that "the duties of a chief executive of a library differ in no essential way from those of a manager of a stock company. . . . The librarian may profit by the methods of the businessman."[62] Arthur E. Bostwick, addressing the New Zealand Library Association in 1891, advocated adoption of the methods of business efficiency in the operation of the library.[63] Other early library leaders, including Charles C. Williamson, emphasized the value to libraries of industrial methods, pointing out that "no one has attempted yet to treat comprehensively the principles and philosophy of library service or library management."[64] This was stated at the time of the development of the scientific management school, whose theories had already been applied to a number of industrial situations but not yet to libraries. It was not until the 1930s that particular attention was paid to the application of scientific management to libraries. Donald Coney emphasized the "new" approach by stating that "scientific management furnishes library administrators with a useful instrument for orientating their activities."[65] Twenty years later, in 1954, Laurence J. Kipp published an article that discussed the application of scientific management to library operations for the period of 1920 to 1950.[66] Arthur T. Kittle, in his dissertation, pointed out that scientific management did not receive serious attention in libraries until after World War II.[67]

> Data processing methods stimulated interest in scientific management, as is evident in the first detailed presentation of principles and techniques of scientific management as they apply specifically to library oriented problems.[68]
> —Richard M. Dougherty and Fred J. Heinritz,
> *Scientific Management of Library Operations*

Ralph R. Shaw began his landmark studies of the scientific management of library operations in the late 1940s and early 1950s. In one study he analyzed two trends in library management—specialization and integration of specialties into a functional organization.[69] These two conflicting trends, which he termed micro-management and macro-management, are still evident in library organization today. In 1954, Shaw, writing as editor of an issue of *Library Trends*, noted "a trend toward the application of scientific management to libraries."[70] Some librarians have always been reluctant to use scientific management tools because they do not believe that library work lends itself to systematic analysis. "They overlook, however, the high percentage of library tasks that consist of repetitive, mechanical routines that do lend themselves to such analysis."[71]

The influence of the human relations school on library and information service also became particularly evident in the early 1930s; the issues relating to people working in libraries began to receive attention, and preparation for library administrators emphasized the personnel relations approach. An article by J. Periam Danton emphasized the trend toward analyzing the human side, where personnel administration became paramount to the democratization of the library organization.[72] This was further expounded in Clara W. Herbert's 1939 volume on personnel administration.[73] Among Herbert's recommendations were greater attention to personnel administration, greater consideration of basic organization directed toward the simplification and coordination of activities, greater staff development, and better working conditions.[74]

F. W. McDiarmid and John M. McDiarmid in the late 1930s recognized two paramount problems applicable to libraries: the need to delegate authority to the level of responsibility and the need to define library objectives and their influence on the administration.[75] Amy Winslow, in her 1953 paper, emphasized staff participation in "democratic organization."[76] Ernest J. Reese's 1959 article on library administration noted, among other things, an increase in staff participation in management of libraries.[77]

With respect to the social systems school, several works cited the development of library management in relation to the larger institution and the community the library serves. C. B. Joeckel, a pioneer in the field of library management, suggested that "library administrators will do well to seek models from comparative study in the fields of public administration, in business, in industry, and in education."[78] The Library Institute at which Joeckel's paper was presented was, perhaps, the landmark event in the analysis of library administration. Twenty years later, Paul Wasserman supported Joeckel's contention that "in a very real sense library administration is only an extension of public administration."[79]

Elizabeth W. Stone's analysis of the situation thirty-five years ago showed a tendency toward "emphasis upon theory and principles and basic functions, bringing with it corresponding de-emphasis upon specific technical skills."[80] This observation is substantiated when one examines the literature on organization and administration of specific types of libraries—academic, public, school, and special.

In recent years issues of major research journals, chapters in management collection treatises, and monographs on librarianship and information management make it clear that management topics are receiving increasing attention. The proceedings of several national conferences, including those of the Association of College and Research Libraries, the Public Library Association, the Special Libraries Association, the American Association of School Libraries, as well as those of the Library Association in the United Kingdom, the Australian Library Association, the New Zealand Library Association— and other national and international associations (the International Federation of Library Associations and Institutions [IFLA] in particular)—present the thoughts and concerns of academic and research librarians in several major areas, including administration and management.[81] An issue of *Library Trends* addressed the dilemma of "How we can optimally integrate the technical and human resources that we manage toward achieving the library's service mission and, at the same time, manage working arrangements and role relationships so that people's needs for self-worth, growth, and development are significantly met in our libraries?"[82] On the same topic, Elizabeth W. Stone researched a commissioned study for the National Commission on Libraries and Information Science (NCLIS). In addition, the issue of participative management has been addressed in research studies.[83] An example, drawn from a number of volumes on the subject of personnel in libraries, is a report done for the Illinois State Library, which identifies the kinds of activities that are typical of the training and background of individuals working in libraries.[84] A King Research study attempted to identify competencies needed by professionals working in libraries.[85] Other important and timely views have been presented by Sheila Creth and Frank Duda as well as Barbara Conroy in their examinations of staff training and development.[86] Buckland[87] proposes a redesign of library services, and Dougherty and Hughes[88] look at future steps, whereas Crawford and Gorman[89] identify factors influencing future developments. Drabenstott provides a useful bibliography on the "Library of the Future."[90]

It is also important to look at the quantitative, or mathematical, school and the influence it has had on library operations. From the late 1960s managers of libraries have used applied operations research in decision making.[91] In the 1960s an original group of researchers, led by Philip Morse at MIT, and a later group, headed by Ferdinand Leimkuhler at Purdue, studied library problems using operations research. Two reports from other sources illustrate this trend. In 1972 the Wharton School at the University of Pennsylvania finished a study that had been supported by a federal grant to design and develop a model for management information systems in universities and large public libraries.[92] That report classified library functions into seventeen categories, and it proposed that those categories be used as a basis for program budgeting systems in libraries. Chin-chih Chen, in her dissertation, demonstrated how operations research techniques could be used by library administrators in their everyday decision making.[93]

Special issues of *Library Trends* have focused on "Effective Resource Allocation in Library Management," which examined "evaluative techniques and procedures used by librarians to determine the effectiveness of their programs (e.g., surveys, cost accounting, systems analysis, operations research, PPBS, MBO, PERT)," and "Systems Design and Analysis for Libraries," which viewed systems analysis as a management tool to be used in "seeking out the fundamentals of a situation and applying to this study rigorous scientific methods, with the aim of finding an optimal solution to the problems facing managers."[94] Those topics, and their subtopics, are constantly revisited.[95] In addition, Charles McClure's thorough review and writings on the topic of planning, including issues of the *Journal of Library Administration* and a feature article in the *ALA Yearbook*,[96] as well as Donald Riggs's treatise[97] on a particular aspect of planning, keep that important topic foremost in the minds of leaders in the profession and managers of information services organizations. The importance of measurement and evaluation of library services continues to receive attention, as is evidenced by major works on the topic.[98]

Reports on networking present the state of the art. *Resources and Bibliographic Support for a Nationwide Library Program* was commissioned by NCLIS. A second report, cosponsored by NCLIS, addressed the structure and governance of networks. "Library Networks: Promise and Performance" emphasized the need for developing networks that include all types of libraries. *Networks for Networkers* took what is probably the most comprehensive view on problems and potentials of library networking. Susan K. Martin's periodical state-of-the-art reviews are tools of awareness of the ferment in networking.[99]

One unit that continues to contribute significantly to the study of library management is the Association of Research Libraries, with a sister organization in Australia. Through funding from the Council on Library Resources, the association developed its Office of Management Studies, now the Office of Leadership and Management Studies, which is responsible for a number of projects relating to library management. One primary activity has been the issuing of "SPEC kits" on topics of major interest, including goals and objectives, collective bargaining, performance evaluation, job analysis, and planning. The office developed a self-study guide, "Management Review and Analysis Program" (MRAP), for larger academic libraries and an Academic Library Development Program for smaller academic libraries. Through task forces, both guides, aimed at improving productivity and staff morale, examine planning and control processes, organizational development, and personnel needs and relationships in individual libraries. During the late 1980s, many university libraries in North America implemented the planning process using that technique. Since then, MRAP has been transformed, no longer using a manual but now providing a general framework and using the "assisted self-study" approach to engage a steering committee in "just-in-time" planning. Through its University Library Management Studies Office, the Association of Research Libraries publishes occasional papers on relevant topics. Another analytical study of note is the by-now classic one for Columbia University Libraries.[100]

Most important, the issue of women and minorities as managers has received due consideration. Although in numbers the profession is female-dominated, the majority of top management positions in North America are still held by males, mostly white males. The cause for this has been discussed in the literature, at conferences, and in institutes. Organizations, including the Status of Women in Librarianship Committee of the American Library Association, and the literature, through writings and research studies, have also identified issues and have proactively promoted partners in developing a vital, previously neglected, resource.[101] The outlook has gradually changed as the mentoring system, as opposed to the "old-boy network," has begun to function and as individuals are hired and promoted based on their abilities and qualifications rather than gender or race.

Conclusion

Collections of readings on management topics of interest to knowledge-management team leaders should prove helpful to both the novice and the experienced manager in considering issues of importance to the management process.[102] Before leaving the topic, it is useful to introduce some of the issues to be discussed in other sections of this text as they relate to the future of libraries and information services. Discussions, reported in the literature, at conferences, and elsewhere, confirm activities in relation to revitalizing libraries and information centers at the beginning of this knowledge-development century for the next century. These include individual organization's strategic thinking[103] and group thinking.[104] Most of these reports and discussions identify financial constraints, automation, organizing for efficiency and effectiveness, and vision and change for the next century as major focal points for consideration of organizational restructuring.

It is evident that the various management theories developed—scientific management, human relations, open system, and quantitative—are being applied to library and information center operations today. The continued use, development, and refinement of those thoughts and techniques will result in more efficient and effective library and information service in knowledge-based organizations. The remaining chapters of this textbook discuss components necessary to be considered as change is instituted in knowledge-based library and information services organizations.

Notes

1.   Lee G. Bolman and Terrence E. Deal, *Reframing Organizations* (San Francisco: Jossey-Bass, 1991), 10–11.

2.   Peter F. Drucker, *Management: Tasks, Responsibilities, Practices* (New York: Harper & Row, 1973), 17.

3.   J. H. Breasted, *Ancient Records* (Chicago: University of Chicago Press, 1906), 150–250.

4.   Claude S. George Jr., *The History of Management Thought*, 2d ed. (Englewood Cliffs, NJ: Prentice-Hall, 1972), 12.

5.   Daniel Wren, *The Evolution of Management Theory*, 3d ed. (New York: John Wiley & Sons, 1987).

6.   Larry N. Killough, "Management and the Industrial Revolution," *Advanced Management Journal* 7 (July 1970): 67–70.

7.   Charles Babbage, *On the Economy of Machinery and Manufacturers* (London: Charles Knight, 1831).

8.   Charles McClure, *Strategies for Library Administration* (Littleton, CO: Libraries Unlimited, 1982), 11.

9.   Harold Koontz, "The Management Theory Jungle," *Academy of Management Journal* 4 (December 1961): 174–75.

10.   Frederick W. Taylor, *Principles of Scientific Management* (New York: Harper & Row, 1941), 47.

11.   Frederick W. Taylor, *Scientific Management* (New York: Harper & Row, 1947), 10.

12.   Taylor, *Principles of Scientific Management*, 36–37.

13.   Taylor, *Scientific Management*, 31.

14.   Amitai Etzioni, *Modern Organizations* (Englewood Cliffs, NJ: Prentice-Hall, 1964), 21.

15.   Edna Yost, *Frank and Lillian Gilbreth* (New Brunswick, NJ: Rutgers University Press, 1949), 262.

16.   Max Weber, *The Theory of Social and Economic Organizations*, A.M. Henderson and T. Parsons, trans. and eds. (Oxford: Oxford University Press, 1947).

17.   Weber, *The Theory of Social and Economic Organizations*, qtd. in Gerald D. Bell, ed., *Organizations and Human Behavior* (Englewood Cliffs, NJ: Prentice-Hall, 1967), 88.

18.   J. P. Mayer, *Max Weber and German Politics* (London: Farber, 1956), 127.

19.   James G. Marshall and Herbert A. Simon, *Organizations* (New York: John Wiley & Sons, 1958), 22.

20.   Henri Fayol, *General and Industrial Management*, trans. by Constance Storrs (New York: Pitman, 1949), 22.

21.   Luther Gulick and Lyndall Urwick, eds., *Papers on the Science of Administration* (New York: Institute of Public Administration, Columbia University Press, 1937).

22.   Harold Koontz and Cyril O'Donnell, *Principles of Management*, 5th ed. (New York: McGraw-Hill, 1972), 14–15.

23.   Weber, *The Theory of Social and Economic Organizations*.

24.   James D. Mooney and Alan C. Reiley, *Onward Industry* (New York: Harper & Row, 1931).

25.   Gulick and Urwick, *Papers on the Science of Administration*.

26.   G. Elton Mayo, *The Social Problems of an Industrialized Civilization* (New York: Macmillan, 1933), 30.

27.   G. Elton Mayo, *The Social Problems of an Industrialized Civilization* (London: Routledge, 1949), 76.

28.   Chester I. Barnard, *The Functions of the Executive* (Cambridge: Harvard University Press, 1938).

29.   Abraham Maslow, "A Theory of Human Motivation," *Psychological Review* 50 (July 1943): 394.

30.   Abraham Maslow, *Toward a Psychology of Being* (Princeton: Van Nostrand, 1964).

31.   Douglas McGregor, *The Human Side of Enterprise* (New York: McGraw-Hill, 1960).

32.   Chris Argyris, *Integrating the Individual and the Organization* (New York: John Wiley & Sons, 1964).

33.   *Ibid.*, 78.

34.   Herbert A. Simon, *The Shape of Automation for Men and Management* (New York: Harper & Row, 1965), 69.

35.   D. Katz and D. Kahn, *The Social Psychology of Organization* (New York: John Wiley & Sons, 1966), 18.

36.   C. West Churchman, Russell L. Ackoff, and E. Leonard Arnoff, *Introduction to Operations Research* (New York: John Wiley & Sons, 1957), 12–13.

37.   James G. March and Herbert A. Simon, *Organizations* (New York: John Wiley & Sons, 1958).

38.   Sheen Kassouf, *Normative Decision Making* (Englewood Cliffs, NJ: Prentice-Hall, 1970).

39.   Paul R. Watkins, "Perceived Information Structure: Implications for Decision Support System Design," *Decision Sciences* (January 1982): 38–59.

40.   Richard M. Hodgetts, *Management: Theory, Process and Practice* (Philadelphia: W. B. Saunders, 1975), 113.

41.   Anatol Rapoport, "General Systems Theory," in David Sills, ed., *International Encyclopedia of the Social Sciences*, vol. 15 (New York: Macmillan, 1968), 452.

42.   Ludwig von Bertlanffy, "The History and Status of General Systems Theory," *Academy of Management Journal* 15 (December 1972): 407.

43.   *Ibid.*, 417.

44.   Fremont E. Kast and James E. Rosenzweig, *Organization and Management: A Systems and Contingency Approach*, 4th ed. (New York: McGraw-Hill International Editions, 1985), 113.

45.   Don Helbriegel, J. S. Slocum, and R. W. Woodman, *Organizational Behavior* (St. Paul, MN: West, 1986), 22.

46.   Chimezie A. B. Osigweh, *Professional Management: An Evolutionary Perspective* (Dubuque, IA: Kendall/Hunt, 1985), 160.

47.   Samuel C. Certo, *Modern Management*, 5th ed. (Boston: Allyn & Bacon, 1992), 48.

48. Fred Luthans, "The Contingency Theory of Management: A Path Out of the Jungle," *Business Horizons* 16 (June 1973): 62.

49. B. Burns, *Managing Change: A Strategic Approach to Organizational Development and Renewal* (New York: Pitman, 1992).

50. J. Steward, *Managing Change Through Training and Development.* 2d ed. (New York: Pitman, 1996).

51. T. H. Davenport and L. Prusak, *Working Knowledge: How Organizations Manage What They Know* (Boston: Harvard Business School Press, 1998).

52. M. Pearn and C. Mulrooney, *Learning Organizations in Practice* (New York: McGraw Hill, 1995).

53. Martin Dillon, "Knowledge Management Opportunities for Libraries and Universities," in *American Reference Book Annual* 32 (Englewood, CO: Libraries Unlimited, 2001), 3.

54. Peter M. Senge, *The Fifth Discipline: The Art and Practice of the Learning Organization* (New York: Doubleday/Currency, 1990).

55. Sue R. Faerman, "Organizational Change and Leadership Styles," *Journal of Library Administration* 19 (1993): 62.

56. Diane Worrell, "The Learning Organization: Management Theory for the Information Age or New Age Fad?" *Journal of Academic Librarianship* 21 (September 1995): 356.

57. Peter F. Drucker, *The Coming of the New Organization.* Originally published in January–February 1988, Reprint 88105, p. 19.

58. McGregor, *Human Side of Enterprise.* Frederick Herzberg, *Work and the Nature of Man* (Cleveland, OH: World, 1966). Abraham Maslow, *Motivation and Personality,* 2d ed. (New York: Harper & Row, 1970).

59. Henry Mintzberg, *The Nature of Managerial Work* (New York: Harper & Row, 1980).

60. Peter F. Drucker, *Management: Tasks, Responsibilities, Practices* (New York: Harper & Row, 1974), 399–400.

61. Stephen P. Waring, *Taylorism Transformed: Scientific Management Theory Since 1945* (Chapel Hill, NC: University of North Carolina Press, 1991), 203.

62. Gertrude G. Drury, *The Library and Its Organization* (New York: H. W. Wilson, 1924), 83–84.

63. Arthur E. Bostwick, "Two Tendencies of American Library Work," *Library Journal* 36 (January 1911): 275–78.

64. Charles C. Williamson, "Efficiency in Library Management," *Library Journal* 44 (February 1919): 76.

65. Donald Coney, "Scientific Management in University Libraries," in G. T. Schwennig, ed., *Management Problems* (Chapel Hill, NC: University of North Carolina Press, 1930), 173.

66. Laurence J. Kipp, "Scientific Management in Research Libraries," *Library Trends* 2 (January 1954): 390–400.

67. Arthur T. Kittle, "Management Theories in Public Administration in the United States" (Ph.D. dissertation., Columbia University, 1961).

68. Richard M. Dougherty and Fred J. Heinritz, *Scientific Management of Library Operations,* 2d ed. (Metuchen, NJ: Scarecrow Press, 1966, 1982), 8.

69.   Ralph R. Shaw, "Scientific Management in the Library," *Wilson Library Bulletin* 21 (January 1947): 349–52.

70.   Ralph R. Shaw, "Scientific Management," *Library Trends* 2 (January 1954): 359–483.

71.   *Ibid.*

72.   J. Periam Danton, "Our Libraries—The Trend Toward Democracy," *Library Quarterly* 4 (January 1934): 16–27.

73.   Clara W. Herbert, *Personnel Administration in Public Libraries* (Chicago: American Library Association, 1939).

74.   *Ibid.*, xiii-xiv.

75.   E. W. McDiarmid and John M. McDiarmid, *The Administration of the American Public Library* (Chicago: American Library Association, 1943).

76.   Amy Winslow, "Staff Participation in Management," *Wilson Library Bulletin* 27 (April 1953): 624–28.

77.   Ernest J. Reese, ed., "Current Trends in Library Administration," *Library Trends* 7 (January 1959): 333–36.

78.   C. B. Joeckel, ed., *Current Issues in Library Administration: Papers Presented Before the Library Institute at the University of Chicago, August 1-12, 1938* (Chicago: University of Chicago Press, 1939), vii–ix.

79.   Paul Wasserman, "Development of Administration in Library Service: Current Status and Future Prospects," *College & Research Libraries* 19 (November 1958): 288.

80.   Elizabeth W. Stone, *Training for the Improvement of Library Administration* (Urbana, IL: Graduate School of Library Science, University of Illinois, 1967), 15.

81.   Robert D. Stueart and Richard D. Johnson, eds., *New Horizons for Academic Libraries* (New York: K. G. Saur, 1979). Michael D. Kathman and Virgil F. Massman, eds., *Options for the 80's: Proceedings of the Second National Conference of the Association of College and Research Libraries* (Greenwich, CT: JAI Press, 1983). Suzanne C. Dodson and Gary L. Menges, eds., *Academic Libraries: Myths and Realities: Proceedings of the Third National Conference of the Association of College and Research Libraries* (Chicago: American Library Association, 1984). Danuta A. Nitecki, ed., *Energies for Transition: Proceedings of the Fourth National Conference of the Association of College and Research Libraries* (Chicago: American Library Association, 1986).

82.   Elizabeth W. Stone, ed., "Personnel Development and Continuing Education in Libraries," *Library Trends* 20 (July 1971): 3.

83.   U.S. National Commission on Libraries and Information Science, *Continuing Library and Information Science Education*, submitted by E. Stone et al. (Washington, DC: American Society for Information Science, 1974). Maurice P. Marchant, *Participative Management in Academic Libraries* (Westport, CT: Greenwood Press, 1976).

84.   Myrl Ricking and Robert E. Booth, *Personnel Utilization in Libraries: A Systems Approach* (Chicago: American Library Association, 1974).

85.   Jose-Marie Griffiths and Donald W. King, *New Directions in Library and Information Science Education* (Westport, CT: Greenwood Press/ASIS, 1986).

86.   Sheila Creth and Frederick Duda, eds., *Personnel Administration in Libraries* (New York: Neal-Schuman, 1981). Barbara Conroy, *Library Staff Development and Continuing Education* (Littleton, CO: Libraries Unlimited, 1978).

87.   Michael Buckland, *Redesigning Library Services: A Manifesto* (Chicago, IL: American Library Association, 1992).

88. Richard M. Dougherty and Carol Hughes, *Preferred Futures for Libraries* (Mountain View, CA: Research Libraries Group, 1991).

89. Walt Crawford and Michael Gorman, *Future Libraries: Dreams, Madness & Reality* (Chicago: American Library Association, 1995).

90. Karen M. Drabenstott, *Analytical Review of the Library of the Future* (Washington, DC: Council on Library Resources, 1994).

91. Don R. Swanson and Abraham Bookstein, eds., *Operations Research: Implications for Libraries* (Chicago: University of Chicago Press, 1972).

92. Morris Hamburg et al., *Library Planning and Decision Making Systems* (Cambridge, MA: MIT Press, 1974).

93. Ching-chih Chen, *Applications of Operations Research Models to Libraries* (Cambridge, MA: MIT Press, 1976).

94. William Axford, "Effective Resource Allocation in Library Management," *Library Trends* 25 (April 1975): 547–72. F. Wilfrid Lancaster, "Systems Design and Analysis for Libraries," *Library Trends* 21 (April 1973): 463.

95. Donald H. Kraft and Bert R. Boyce, *Operations Research for Libraries and Information Agencies* (New York: Academic Press, 1991).

96. Charles R. McClure, ed., "Planning for Library Services," *Journal of Library Administration* 2 (1982); and "Library Planning: A Status Report," in *The ALA Yearbook of Library and Information Services, 1986* (Chicago: American Library Association, 1986), 7–16.

97. Donald E. Riggs, *Strategic Planning for Library Managers* (Phoenix, AZ: Oryx Press, 1984).

98. Ernest R. DeProspo, E. Altman, and K. E. Beasley, *Performance Measures for Public Libraries* (Chicago: American Library Association, 1973). Lowell Martin et al., *Library Response to Urban Change: A Study of the Chicago Public Library* (Chicago: American Library Association, 1969). F. Wilfrid Lancaster, *The Measurement and Evaluation of Library Services* (Washington, DC: Information Resources Press, 1977). Douglas Zweizig, *Output Measures for Public Libraries* (Chicago: American Library Association, 1982; 2d ed. forthcoming). *See also* Charles R. McClure et al., *A Planning and Role Setting Manual for Public Libraries* (Chicago: American Library Association, forthcoming).

99. U.S. National Commission on Libraries and Information Science, *Resources and Bibliographic Support for a Nationwide Library Program*, submitted by Vernon E. Palmour et al. (Rockville, MD: Westat, 1974). Allen Kent and Thomas J. Galvin, eds., *The Structure and Governance of Library Networks* (New York: Marcel Dekker, 1979). Leon Carnovsky, ed., "Library Networks: Promise and Performance," *Library Quarterly* 39 (January 1969): 1–108. Barbara E. Markuson and Blanche Woolls, eds., *Networks for Networkers: Critical Issues in Cooperative Library Development* (New York: Neal-Schuman, 1980). Susan K. Martin, *Library Networks, 1986-1987* (White Plains, NY: Knowledge Industry Publications, 1986).

100. Allen Booz and Hamilton, Inc., *Organization and Staffing of the Libraries of Columbia University* (Westport, CT: Redgrave, 1973).

101. Ching-chih Chen, ed., *Library Management Without Bias* (Greenwich, CT: JAI Press, 1980). E. J. Josey and Kenneth E. Peeples, *Opportunities for Minorities in Librarianship* (Metuchen, NJ: Scarecrow Press, 1977). Kathleen M. Heim, *The Status of Women in Librarianship* (New York: Neal-Schuman, 1983). Betty Jo Irvine, *Sex Segregation in Librarianship* (Westport, CT: Greenwood Press, 1985).

102.   Ruth J. Person, ed., *The Management Process: A Selection of Readings for Librarians* (Chicago: American Library Association, 1983). Beverly P. Lynch, ed., *Management Strategies for Librarians: A Basic Reader* (New York: Neal-Schuman, 1985). Margaret S. Jennings et al., *Library Management in Review*, vol. 2 (Washington, DC: Special Libraries Association, 1987).

103.   Joanne Euster et al., "Reorganizing for a Changing World" (personal correspondence April 3, 1997). Mary Elizabeth Clack, "Continued Organizational Transformation: The Harvard College Library's Experience," *Library Administration and Management* 10 (April 1996): 98–104. Beth J. Shapiro and Kevin Brook Long, "Just Say Yes: Reengineering Library User Services for the 21st Century," *Journal of Academic Librarianship* (Nov. 1994): 285–90.

104.   "Strategic Visions for Librarianship: Issues," LIBADMIN Listserv, December 15, 1991. "Strategic Visions Discussion Group: Values and Qualities of Librarianship," Discussion Draft, LIBADMIN Listserv, January 18, 1992. Richard M. Dougherty and Carol Hughes, *Preferred Library Futures II: Charting the Paths* (Mountain View, CA: Research Libraries Group, 1993).

Section 2: Planning

A s the change process, discussed in Section 1, more and more affects information services, what is done, and how it is done, libraries and information centers must strategically rethink and take action to revise and revitalize in order to meet such challenges. With the future no longer being predictable as an extrapolation from the past, a recommitment to core values, a clear vision of the future, and a solid plan for achieving the mission of the library or information center are all vital initial steps toward creating that future. All of these factors must be developed with a keen awareness of outside forces that may facilitate or frustrate the planning efforts. Technology, of course, is such a force, but it is only one and it is only a tool that can positively or negatively affect programs, depending upon how it is perceived and used. The political, economic, social, and technological climates all must be recognized, and libraries must be responsive to that as they focus their plans for developing knowledge-based services.

Strategic planning enables libraries and information centers to make decisions that respond to changes in the greater environment. Involving stakeholders—users and financial supporters—in the process empowers the organization to move forward in a more rapid fashion. In order to garner that kind of support for such plans, those libraries and information centers are required to develop marketing strategies for support.

Several planning techniques are available to facilitate such a process. Those planning trends and techniques are the focus of the next two chapters.

Readings

Allison, M., and J. Kaye. *Strategic Planning for Nonprofit Organizations*. New York: John Wiley & Sons, 1997.

American Association of School Librarians. *A Planning Guide for Information Power: Building Partnerships for Learning*. Chicago: AASL, American Library Association, 1999.

American Library Association. *Guidelines for the Development of Policies and Procedures Regarding User Behavior and Library Usage*. Chicago: American Library Association, 1993.

Anthony, Robert N., J. Deardon, and V. Govindarajan. *Management Control Systems*. 7th ed. Homewood, IL: Irwin, 1992.

Asantewa, Doris. *Strategic Planning Basics for Special Libraries*. Washington, DC: Special Libraries Association, 1992.

Baltimore County Public Library. *Balancing Tradition and Technology, Baltimore County Public Library's Strategic Plan V*. Chicago: American Library Association, 2000.

Baughman, Steven A., and Elizabeth A. Curry, eds. *Strategic Planning for Library Multitype Cooperatives: Samples and Examples*. Chicago: ASCLA, American Library Association, 1997.

Biesecke, Joan. *Scenario Planning for Libraries*. Chicago: American Library Association, 1998.

Bremer, Susanne W. *Long Range Planning: A How-To-Do-It Manual for Public Libraries*. New York: Neal-Schuman, 1994.

Bryson, John M. *Creating and Implementing Your Strategic Plan: A Workbook for Public and Nonprofit Organizations*. San Francisco: Jossey-Bass, 1996.

Cassell, Kay Ann, and Elizabeth Futas. *Developing Public Library Collections, Policies, and Procedures*. New York: Neal-Schuman, 1991.

Corrall, Sheila. *Strategic Management of Information Services: A Planning Handbook*. London: Aslib, 1999.

Georgantzas, N. C., and W. Acar. *Scenario-Driven Planning*. Westport, CT: Quorum Books, 1995.

Goodstein, Leonard David, Timothy M. Nolan, and J. William Pfeiffer. *Applied Strategic Planning: A Comprehensive Guide*. New York: McGraw-Hill, 1993.

Goodwin, B. Terence. *Write on the Wall: A How-To Guide for Effective Planning in Groups*. Alexandria, VA: American Society for Training and Development, 1994.

Hayes, Robert M. *Models for Library Management, Decision-Making, and Planning*. San Diego: Academic Press, 2001.

Himmell, Ethel, and Bill Wilson. *Planning for Results: A Public Library Transformation Process* and *The Guidebook*. Chicago: American Library Association, 1998.

Hitt, William D. *Guide for Building a Learning Organization*. Columbus, OH: Battelle Press, 1998.

Larson, Jeanette, and Herman L. Totten. *Model Policies for Small and Medium Public Libraries*. New York: Neal-Schuman, 1998.

Levesque, Paul. *Breakaway Planning*. New York: AMACOM, 1998.

Loggins, Ann. *Library Policy Manuals: A Guide to Their Creation.* Ft. Worth, TX: North Texas Library System, 1989.

MacLachlan, Liz. *Making Project Management Work for You.* London: Library Association, 1996.

Makridakas, Spyros G. *Forecasting, Planning and Strategy for the 21st Century.* New York: Free Press, 1990.

Mason, Marilyn Gell. *Strategic Management for Today's Libraries.* Chicago: American Library Association, 1999.

Mayo, Diane. *Wired for the Future: Developing Your Library Technology Plan.* Chicago: American Library Association, 1999.

Migiore, Henry, et al., eds. *Strategic Planning for Not-for-Profit Organizations.* New York: Hayworth Press, 1994.

Mintzberg, Henry. *The Rise and Fall of Strategic Planning.* Upper Saddle River, NJ: Prentice-Hall, 1994.

Nelson, Sandra. *New Planning for Results: A Streamlined Approach.* Chicago: American Library Association, 2001.

Oster, Sharon M. *Strategic Management for Non-Profit Organizations.* New York: Oxford University Press, 1995.

Prytherch, Ray, ed. *Handbook of Library and Information Management.* Hants, UK: Gower House, 1998.

Public Library Association, Policy Manual Committee. *PLA Handbook for Writers of Public Library Policies.* Chicago: American Library Association, 1993.

St. Clair, Guy. *Total Quality Management in Information Services.* New Providence, NJ: Bowker-Saur, 1997.

Tjosvold, Dean. *Teamwork for Customers: Building Organizations That Take Pride in Serving.* San Francisco: Jossey-Bass, 1993.

Watstein, S. B., et al., comps. *Formal Planning in College Libraries.* Chicago: American Library Association, 1994.

Chapter 3

Planning Information Services

*Management has no choice but to anticipate the future, to
attempt to mold it, and to balance short-range and
long-range goals. . . . The future will not just happen if one
wishes hard enough. It requires decisions—now. It imposes
risk—now. It requires action—now. It demands allocation
of resources, and above all, of human resources—now. It
requires work—now.[1]*

—Peter F. Drucker,
Management: Tasks, Responsibilities, Practices

Introduction

Planning services and systems in libraries and information centers is all of the
above—and more. In its most structured form, it encompasses activities directed toward
developing a vision and a mission, and then setting goals, motivating individuals,
appraising performance of both personnel and systems, evaluating results, developing
a financial base to accomplish all of that, and then adjusting directions to account for
the outcome of those activities. Planning is at the heart of management activities
because its effectiveness—or in some cases ineffectiveness—is reflected in every segment of an organization's developmental process. As an analytical process it involves
assessing the future, determining a desired direction for the organization in that future,
creating objectives in the context of that future, developing programs of action for
such objectives, selecting an appropriate agenda from among those alternatives that are
priorities, and pursuing a detailed course of action. A variety of approaches have developed
over the years to address this need. Only currently used ones will be discussed in this
and the following chapter. Others, which the professional literature describes, have
been superseded, or the concepts have been incorporated into current processes.

Despite the obvious need to plan, a systematic planning process remains one of the most elusive and easily avoided activities in libraries, information centers, and other for-profit and nonprofit organizations. This phenomenon continues to exist despite the fact that planning is THE most basic function—all other functions must reflect it, and the growth or decline of an organization depends in no small measure upon the soundness of its planning process.

Those recently imposed change factors, discussed in the first chapter of this textbook, now have come together to force planning decisions and focus on more systematic processes than was necessary in a more leisurely past. The multidimensional interrelationship between external and internal forces and among levels of staff in the organization now demands a systematic approach to developing services and marketing their benefits. Changing environments and anticipated future environments—including declining or stabilized budgets, inflation, technological developments, the explosion of information in many formats, staffs' growing sophistication coupled with their needs and expectations, patterns of use, user interests and satisfaction, and nonuser resistance and reasons thereof—all make planning for information services more vital and more alive today than it has ever been. This dynamic environment provides an opportunity to redefine the organization and reinvent information sources and services, for growth and survival, but primarily to meet a growing need in society for access to information. An added benefit, of course, is that it is likely that staff at various levels in library and information center organizations, as they become engaged in the process, are most likely to be committed to an agreed upon vision of the organization and to dedicate themselves to pursuing the goals and objectives that are the outcomes of planning. Once this happens, all members of the organization are more committed to becoming spokespersons and advocates in explaining, enhancing, and enveloping the identified needs and directions to other staff members, governing agencies, and the customer/client/patron/user base.

Although there are numerous reasons given for why libraries and other information centers neglect planning, the main reason seems to be that it is an extremely difficult and time-consuming, and can be a confusing, sometimes threatening, process. That is further complicated by the macro-environment, including economic uncertainty, technological innovations that are necessary, shifting demographics, changing societal priorities, and shrinking financial support from primary sources. Further, changes occur in reporting relationships in organizations of which libraries and information centers are a part—university presidential and corporate officials' tenures are shorter, sometimes another administrative layer is inserted in the chain of command, and boards of trustees change, as do school committees, corporate boards, and mayors or other chief management officers in organizations of which the information services is just one part. Such changes may force libraries and information centers to make decisions now that will affect operations in the foreseeable future and, in some cases, even to project needs beyond that immediate future. Added to the complications and resistance is the fact that many managers and other staff members simply avoid proper planning, whereas others naively do not understand how to plan.

Some library and information center professionals in decision-making positions tend to emphasize current operations at the expense of planning for the future. Resistance to systematic and comprehensive planning is often couched in such phrases as "Planning is just crystal ball gazing in these days of technological change," or "There is no time to devote to planning because we are too busy with our work." Some managers in libraries and information centers continue to look to past success as a guide for projecting future trends, whereas others rely on intuition as a decision-making device. Former successful operations that were the result of an overabundance of funds are sometimes attributed to the manager's own imagination and intuition. Lack of success, on the other hand, is blamed on "circumstances beyond the library's or the information center's control" instead of on a lack of planning.

Planning styles and approaches, where they can be identified, often are more retrospective in nature, drawing upon past experiences with the hope of projecting those past successes into the future. When the organizational climate, internal and external, was more stable than in current turbulent times, such experience was acceptable as a basis for decision making. This is no longer a realistic approach. Although experience still is one legitimate factor in the overall analysis of a plan, it is no longer the only and certainly not the most important factor. Experience, intuition, and snap judgments made by one person are no longer effective methods with so many new variables now likely to determine eventual outcomes. As libraries and other information centers have matured organizationally, and in order to avoid continual crisis, information professionals have taken it upon themselves or, in some cases, have been mandated by parent institutions to think more strategically and to act more strategically by developing future-oriented plans in an attempt to anticipate the processes, programs, and priorities that will be desirable and sustainable in the future. That future isn't what it used to be. The outcome of such strategic thinking and planning then becomes the basis for financial considerations leading to operational plans covering staff utilization, materials acquisition, technological development, and physical plant maintenance, each of those cost factors being a part of the total service matrix. Many libraries and information centers have introduced a self-evaluation planning process in order to identify strengths and weaknesses that support or hinder priorities identified in the process. Some are surprised that those identified priorities may be completely different from what was previously perceived to be the primary focus of activities.

> Institutions are often the product of a formative idea. The extent to which an institution is successful depends on the degree to which it is guided by this idea and its underlying principles and assumptions. . . . The enormous growth in the quantity and kinds of research materials, escalating publication costs, the introduction of new technologies, changing patterns of research and institutions, and finite resources have undermined the assumptions of the past and prompted the library to seek a new vision and a strategy for creating it.[2]
>
> —Harvard College Library,
> *Commitment to Renewal*

Anticipating the Future

Change, as has been discussed in the first chapter of this textbook, is the key factor, the driving force in this equation. Change can be viewed from opposite extremes: It can be unplanned, therefore random, haphazard, unpredictable, and often destructive, or it can be planned and deliberate, anticipated, and reasonably controlled by actions taken to adjust the organizational thinking about the challenges and opportunities of the future. When actions are forward-looking, deliberate, conscious, and consensual, there is greater likelihood of successfully incorporating change as the dynamic force it can be. Various change dimensions and predictive management approaches are used in the planning process and are extensively discussed in the literature. *Crisis management, contingency planning*, and *conditional thinking* are terms found in the literature to describe the art of predicting and planning. Most new techniques capitalize on opportunities to change, not on the threats that unplanned change can bring. They are techniques for minimizing some of the risk and uncertainty from an organization's future, replacing that uncertainty with some measure of control over the direction and outcome of the future, and placing the organization on a deliberate, successful course through the planning jungle. Planning gives direction, redresses impact of change, minimizes waste and redundancy, and sets standards used in controlling.

Because planning is an effort to anticipate future change, it can be accomplished by choosing from among several possible alternatives. Planning in the past was most often accomplished as a *line* function, performed only by managers in a direct supervisory relationship. Now many large libraries and information centers have developed cadres of people whose primary function is planning. Officers in *staff* positions augment and support team-based planning efforts, sometimes acting as information sources, sometimes as catalysts, sometimes as advisers, and sometimes as devil's advocates. Those individuals might, for example, provide factual data and propose new services, but their primary role is to coordinate the entire planning program. Some libraries and information centers have instituted planning committees or groups, whereas others, mainly large public and academic library systems, have created planning offices within the staff structure of the library. Information centers in for-profit organizations are more likely to relate a portion of their activities to a planning division and with knowledge management becoming such an important component of their responsibilities, are likely to be represented at a high level in the organization because knowledge management plays an important role in those initiatives. These groups are responsible for developing or guiding the development of certain plans, particularly those that are long range or more strategic in nature. Such groups, with clearly defined responsibilities, are usually able to perform more intensive investigations and to analyze and to coordinate plans more thoroughly.

One of the earliest examples of such units in libraries was established at Columbia University more than thirty years ago when the library's Planning Office was created and administered by the then newly created position of assistant university librarian for planning. The specific objectives of that office were to:

1. Provide a direction and framework for library and information service operations that will guide decision making and problem-solving.

2. Improve library service, operations, and fiscal control through the application of computer technology and management science to library procedures.

3. Ensure the rational and effective development of information services and resources in the context of university academic planning.

4. Permit the anticipation of future resource needs for information service by establishing plans based on present decisions.

5. Bring the skills and experience of university and library staff members into the planning process.[3]

It is a pattern that has been successfully repeated and refined in information-oriented organizations of all types. Oftentimes one finds a senior staff member in the position of "Director of Strategic Planning and Change." Over the years, to encourage and facilitate the planning process, several libraries have used self-study guides, such as those developed by the Office of Management Studies of the U.S.-based Association of Research Libraries, including its *Library Management Review and Analysis Program* (MRAP), the *Planning Process for Small Academic Libraries*, and the *Academic Library Development Program* (ALDP), which were particularly popular during the 1980s and 1990s, as well as other planning guidelines for public, academic, and school libraries that have been developed by divisions of the American Library Association.[4]

Now, more than ever before, a new, more formalized approach to planning, based upon forecasting and examination of environmental factors, is the key to success in library and information services. However, this simply stated feat is not easily accomplished. Librarians and information specialists new to the planning process should be cautioned that some formal planning methods and models can be quite complicated and may not apply to current library and information service needs of their own organization. Some of these sophisticated models do not lend themselves to smaller information service operations and, therefore, may not be cost-effective; others are so complex that they may be of no use in a particular library or information center setting.

It is also important to recognize that, because of rapid environmental changes, many plans may become dated or obsolete before they can even be implemented. Therefore, it should be a process that never ends, continuously revisited and revised as opportunities and circumstances dictate. A balance between efforts expended and outcome is desirable. However, it should be recognized that there is a down side to an extensive planning process. If, in the larger organization, the library or information center is the only unit, or one of the few, that performs a planning process, it may be held strictly accountable for the priorities in its plan or risk being criticized for not meeting stated expectations. This alone should not divert librarians and information specialists from planning strategically, and such cautions should not be viewed as discouragement but as reminders that planning is an evolving process with political overtones.

The Planning Concept

A plan is not just a document prepared to be brought out and admired on special occasions, but an active program, incorporating certain beliefs; schedules, specifying steps to be taken; a theory or concept to be explored, relationships to be considered; and a precedent, established for existing decisions. A textbook definition of planning is that it is an "analytical process which involves an assessment of the future, the determination of desired objectives in the context of that future, the development of alternative courses of action to achieve such objectives and the selection of a course, or courses, of action from among these alternatives."[5]

Planning is both a behavior and a process; it is the process of moving an organization from where it is to where it wants to be in a given period of time by setting it on a predetermined course of action and committing its human and physical resources to that goal. The analogy of a road map is an appropriate one—if one doesn't know where he or she is, and doesn't know how to get to where he or she wants to be, many roads lead to a dead-end, or at least a retracing of steps. Basic questions of "who, what, when, where, and how" are preceded by the most important philosophical question of "why," and all must be addressed in the process. Perhaps the most important reasons for planning are: to offset uncertainty and to prepare for change, to focus attention on a clear direction for the future, to gain economic control of the operation, and to facilitate control and to demonstrate accountability. It is, of course, not only impractical but also impossible to plan for every single action. Put in perspective, because there are many levels of planning, the extent and sophistication of planning depend upon the situation at hand, whether it is charting the future of the library or information center or negotiating next month's staffing of the reference/information desk. Although both of those examples require some planning effort, the intensity of thought being given to needs, the level, and the required involvement in developing plans is very different.

A successful planning approach must build an understanding of the library's or information center's reason for existence and capabilities as an essential first step to identifying future directions. To create a planning attitude, the concept must involve all levels of the organization, beginning at the top and filtering down throughout the various levels to be accepted and implemented through policies, procedures, projects, and programs that can be developed as a result. The outcome, a planning document, becomes today's design for tomorrow's action, an outline of the steps to be taken starting now and continuing into the future. The process leading to the development of a written document involves all segments concerned with and affected by the process, both inside the immediate library and information center and outside through customers with programmatic interests and individuals and organizations with vested financial interests. This planning process forces action on the part of the "whole" of the institution. Although the idea of involving every single person in the process is an idealistic approach, it is so only because it is not feasible for everyone to participate in every single aspect of the stages of a planning process.

Because planning is a delicate, complicated, time-consuming process, it cannot be forced on an organization that is not prepared for self-analysis and the change that will result from the process. A bifurcation exists, in which scientific evidence and rational thinking must be balanced by a planning attitude and the interpersonal skills that facilitate the process. Discretion must be exercised so that overinvolvement in the planning process, by individuals and by groups, does not interfere with fulfillment of the basic mission of the organization, while at the same time they must be assured that they are an important component in the success of the process. Occasionally, services can suffer if resources are diverted to the planning process and staff become so wrapped up in planning that current basic library and information services tasks are ignored. On the other hand, the success of the effort requires commitment that must be earned. One cautionary note relates to the fact that when large amounts of energy and resources are committed, expectations are likely to be high, foreseeing miraculous results and significant instant change. Such expectations must be quickly brought into a realistic perspective.

The degree of extensive staff involvement in planning depends on cost, time, the importance of the particular plan, and the perceived knowledge and interest of participants. It is imperative that each person involved knows clearly the purpose of the planning, the expected outcomes, and his or her role as well as that of every other individual throughout the process. Keeping the whole organization informed about the plans that are taking shape is also an important component. If this type of communication and involvement takes place, a greater commitment is likely to be achieved. Even previous to the start of the process, the right organizational climate must be established to encourage the success of the planning process. If the staff, the customers, and the funding authorities are in agreement at this initial stage and buy into the process, then it is realistic to expect that members of the library or other information service organizations will consistently use the written plan as a guide.

After the plan is accepted as a document for future directions, progress toward achieving the intent of the plan should proceed in a timely manner, addressing activities and developing procedures to achieve the objectives identified in the plan. The planning process should never be considered as just an activity that management uses occasionally, when they think there is time for it. Without daily planning as follow-up, decisions revert back to becoming ad-hoc choices, activities become random, and confusion and chaos can prevail.

Factors in Planning

The impetus for the type of planning today, which is now a required approach for most complex organizations and a desirable approach for others, came primarily after World War II when postwar planning was necessary in for-profit organizations. This was true because technology was changing, becoming more expensive, and companies had to be sure of the need to expend resources in that arena. Factors in the planning process can be arbitrarily divided into at least five elements: time, collecting and analyzing data, levels of planning, flexibility, and accountability.

Time Frame

There are two categories of plans with respect to time: long-range or strategic plans and short-term, annual, or operational plans. These categories refer to the span of time over which the plan is effective, starting with the time when the plan is initiated and ending with the time when the objectives of the plan are actually measured for achievement.

A variety of terms, including *long-range, normative, strategic,* and *master planning* have been used to describe what is now most popularly conceived, with a few variations, as the strategic planning process. It is a type of planning that has become widely used and accepted over the last couple of decades. There are nuances of differences in each of those approaches but, for purposes of this text, the focus will be on thinking and planning strategically. Strategic planning has become the most central outcome of many organizations' strategic thinking. Exacerbating, or one should say encouraging, this approach are technological developments and applications combined with circumstances and external forces that are mostly beyond the library or information center's immediate environment and control. Those forces dictate an organized, extended view to planning library and information service operations. The strategic planning concept has more or less absorbed what was previously viewed as the intermediate long-range view. Long-range, strategic, and master planning each necessitate looking at library and information center operations in a critical and comprehensive way in order to develop a planning network and time frame that combines the subplans of departments, divisions, project units, or program coordinators of the library or information center into one master plan that charts the course of the whole organization for a foreseeable future. As an example, perhaps the best known long-range plans have been those produced by various national governments in the form of five- or ten-year plans.

On the other hand, short-term, operational, or tactical plans encompass the day-to-day planning that takes place in any organization; a type of planning that is more task-oriented. It involves a shorter time frame and the resolution of specific problems, usually of an internal nature. Such plans often coincide with the accounting or bookkeeping year and are deadline driven. An example of short-term plans is the calculation of one year's budget, which is expressed in operational terms. Short-term plans provide the guidelines for day-to-day operations and the procedures by which they are accomplished. These plans are much more detail-intensive and immediate than strategic plans, and their objectives are much more short-term and specific. They encompass more known factors and, therefore, are more quantitative. Short-term plans bring the general guidelines developed in long-range plans to the operational level. One might view the two approaches as complementing each other—strategic plans providing the overview and operational plans providing the specific budgetary factors for a specified period of time. Because short-term plans are specific and immediate, they do not carry the uncertainty that strategic plans do. However, both types of plans can be considered action-oriented and, therefore, measurable and attainable.

Collecting and Analyzing Data

The more pertinent the information on which a plan is based, the better the planning process will be. Therefore, the second element in planning is collecting and analyzing data. This step includes systematic collection of data concerning the library or information center, its activities, operations, staff, use, and users over a given period of time, as well as the external environment, which affects what the organization wants to do and the way it can do it. In other words, it is an analytical study of the whole organization and its operation. One must fight the urge to allow data collection to dominate or to bog down the planning process, rather viewing this step as a means to an end—the collection of data relating to past activities with the view of making decisions about future ones. Needs assessment and data collection cannot be stressed to the exclusion of translating the needs into goals and objectives, developing programs to address those needs, and evaluating the effectiveness of new and ongoing library operations and programs. Evaluation as an element of the planning process and techniques for collecting data are discussed in later chapters of this textbook.

Levels of Planning

All supervisors, coordinators, or team leaders, whatever their level of responsibility within the organizational structure, should engage in planning on two levels. They should be responsible for planning in their individual units or groups, and they should work with others in the organization to develop the overall plan. In addition, involvement of lower echelon personnel in planning has the advantage of incorporating the practical point of view of those closest to the scene of operations while enticing them to recognize the need for planning and to support the direction the plan takes. Traditionally, long-range planning has been carried out primarily by the upper echelons, whereas short-term planning usually is conducted by supervisors or coordinators at the point-of-impact of services. In libraries and information centers that have planning committees or officers, and in smaller organizations, a hierarchical approach is abandoned in favor of input from all levels and segments of the organization.

It should be easy to recognize the consequences of failing to coordinate long-range and short-term plans because the whole concept of planning is to create a network of mutually dependent components ranging from overall, mission-oriented plans to detailed, technical plans for specific operations.

Flexibility

Flexibility, or adaptability in meeting changing needs, is the essence of good planning. Flexibility applies to both short-term and strategic planning processes. Any planning that is too rigid to accommodate change as it occurs is an exercise in futility. This is why it is important to review plans on a scheduled basis with the intent of revising priorities that might change over the short term, as well as identifying objectives that have been accomplished. In this respect, a planning process is never completed; it is continuously reviewed, revised, and renewed. Having said that, it is important that the library's or the information center's plans remain compatible with those of the larger organization of which the information unit is a part and that they reflect the changing environment in which the library or information center exists.

Accountability

Accountability is key to future success. Accountability requires obligation and initiative to carry out established plans. For managers, this means delegating authority and making individuals or teams responsible for achieving the plan's objectives once they have been established. Ultimately, however, the manager is accountable for the action—or inaction—toward the established goals. This ties control to the planning process. A plan can be no better than the control mechanisms established to monitor, evaluate, and adjust efficiency and effectiveness toward the ultimate success of the endeavor.

Environment for Planning

Planning is committing library or information center resources—physical, personnel, and material—based upon the best possible knowledge of the future. It requires systematically organizing the effort needed to use these resources and requires measuring the results of planning decisions through systematic feedback so that needed changes can be effected. In libraries and other information service organizations, the planning process may be resisted by individuals and groups who fear that change—in goals and objectives as well as in responsibilities and organizational structure—will threaten their positions in the organization. In its extreme, this planning climate can create a competitive relationship with other departments in the larger organization—whether they are academic units of an educational institution, departments of a governmental entity, part of a school district, or divisions of a business or foundation—of which the library is a part. This competition places greater responsibility on the librarian to sell programs and exert pressures for their successful execution.

Environmental Assessment

Political, economic, social, and technological (PEST) trends all significantly influence success in achieving the mission of a library or information center in today's volatile climate. For instance, commerce and technology are globalizing, international resource needs are increasing, and the world political climate is changing daily as governments and organizations react to changes. Also, economic factors, including publisher price increases, foreign exchange rates, varying tax revenues from funding authorities, increasing costs of electronic resources, inflation, and global intellectual property issues affect buying power. In the social arena, an increasingly urban population, disenfranchised from mainstream society and economically disadvantaged, requires the library and information center to aggressively promote itself to its public, stressing its benefits to society. The technological environment, including the Internet, World Wide Web, and electronic bibliographic and full-text resources that are now ubiquitous, requires customer assistance, both informational and technical, for effective use.

Planning Techniques

Many techniques must be considered for use in the planning process. However, they should not be mistaken for the process itself. Some of the most important techniques are developing standards and guidelines and forecasting.

Developing Standards and Guidelines

One concise definition of *standards* is being able to designate any measure by which one judges a thing as authentic, good, or adequate. Standards are measurable, enforceable, and can be directly related to goals. They should provide guidance for actions in the present climate while being flexible enough to allow for future development. General, industry-wide, or profession-wide standards or guidelines established by various professional groups provide a basis for planning. For examples of standards developed by the American Library Association, the Library Association (UK), and the Special Libraries Association, see "Readings" on the website. Those serve as guidelines and are based on actual, or known, demands for library services. But these standards are not plans; they are a means of defining acceptable service. Each individual library must develop its own plans based on the demands of its clientele, using those industry standards as guidelines. Both human and technical factors must be considered in developing sound standards.

Forecasting

> Planning is an effort to anticipate the future and the inevitable change that comes with it. It must be accomplished by choosing from among possible alternatives, and with full knowledge and use of techniques and tools available for such action.[6]
>
> —Robert D. Stueart,
> "Long-Range Planning in U.S. Public Libraries"

The term *forecasting* elicits visions of crystal ball gazing, but more appropriately designates a process of projection or prediction. Predictions are, basically, opinions about facts. Projections, on the other hand, are based on some type of systematic review, whether that review employs quantitative data analysis or qualitative judgment using techniques like the Delphi method (see below). Forecasts are predictions based on assumptions about the future. Forecasting helps reduce uncertainty because it anticipates the results of a decision about a course of action described in the forecast.

Forecasting is the most valuable planning technique. It attempts to find the most probable course of events or range of possibilities. H. G. Wells, more than a century ago, argued that if the long-term course of events is principally determined by society's collective response to economic and technological circumstances, we can, in fact, make meaningful projections of what the future is likely to bring through the continued use of analytical tools, including forecasting.[7] A problem very basic to planning in any library is estimating future trends, influences, developments, and events that will affect the library but are beyond the control of the library manager. Forecasts account for this uncertainty; they are the foundation on which managers plan. Forecasting requires good information on trends and developments in society and the economy as well as in the profession and its system of user interaction. Many techniques, some of which are subjective and qualitative, can be used to prepare forecasts, but effective forecasting involves both qualitative and quantitative approaches. Three strategies for forecasting are:

1. *Deterministic.* This strategy assumes that there is a close causal relationship between the present and the future. This strategy places great reliance upon information about the future.

2. *Symptomatic.* This strategy searches for signs that might be indicators of the future, for example, the leading economic indicators. This approach is based on the concept that the sequence of events in a cycle is a consistent pattern.

3. *Systematic.* This strategy looks for underlying regularities over a period of time. Econometrics is an example of this type of forecasting.[8]

Various new techniques are currently employed to predict the future. From opinion polling to informal gathering of information, qualitative approaches are used. Futurology has become particularly popular among managers of business enterprises. Some forecasting techniques used in industry have been adapted for library and information services. These include the survey approach, which is used in technological forecasting. Probably the most important type of technological forecasting, one that is popular among librarians and information specialists, is the Delphi technique. Delphi is most useful when judgment is required, when several responses to an issue might be viable, or when it is politically expedient to have strong support for the alternative that eventually will be chosen. The steps for this technique are:

1. A panel of experts on a subject, for example, library funding, is identified.

2. Working independently, selected members of the panel predict developments over a specified period of time. There is no group interaction.

3. The list of predictions is used to create a survey that is sent to each panelist for further reaction.

This process is repeated and ideas are refined until the investigator is convinced that no further refinement is necessary. This technique, based on the opinions of experts, is sure to gain popularity as more libraries and information centers become involved in strategic planning.

Other forecasting techniques that have been used quite effectively in libraries and other information centers include trend projection and environmental scanning. In its more formal approach, trend projection graphically plots future trends based on past experience and current hard data. For instance, the number of volumes put on reserve and the number of times they have circulated during a semester, if plotted on a graph, can reveal significant trends for future planning. Environmental scanning is carried out to anticipate and to interpret change and sometimes to provide a competitive edge. Although libraries have not yet gotten completely into the competitive intelligence area of environmental scanning, seeking basic information about competitors and global scanning are examples of techniques necessary to assimilate the knowledge. Another technique that has come out of forecasting efforts is that of benchmarking, a process that searches for the best practice, assuming that an organization can be improved by analyzing and copying other successful organizations. Therefore, data are collected and analyzed to determine the performance gaps between that particular organization and others who are more successful. From that analysis, an action plan is developed.

These are only examples of the forecasting techniques that can be used in libraries and information centers. Other mathematical and statistical models are used by for-profit organizations to provide quantitative data, and econometric models of the economy are also used. Some of these models are appropriate for nonprofit organizations. With the availability of computers for modeling and the development of software for that purpose, it is certain that forecasting techniques will become even more attractive to library and information services planners. However, it would be virtually impossible to mold all the various factors into any one explicit, well-defined model that can be used to quantify and to solve problems via computational techniques. Therefore, the emphasis is likely to remain, at least for the immediate future, on collecting and analyzing the most relevant information and introducing that information into a flexible framework to serve as a guide for library and information service development. Several modeling efforts, using computer programs that provide means for estimating staff, materials, and costs needed to handle library operations and services, have been developed and are discussed in the literature.

Before leaving the topic of techniques, it is useful to briefly discuss two applications that have been used in both for-profit and not-for-profit organizations, including libraries and information centers. Both of these techniques, MBO (Management by Objectives) and TQM (Total Quality Management), are no longer as popular as they were a few years ago, perhaps because many of the components have been absorbed into other techniques, some of them into strategic planning, which will be discussed in the next chapter.

Management by Objectives

One technique that has been used to supplement the planning process relates specifically to merging organizational goals and objectives with the personal ones of individuals working in the organization in order to achieve greater success. MBO has been informally applied in some libraries (though perhaps not consciously) to combine individual and institutional goal setting with the decision-making process. Much has been written on the technique of MBO, a process that has been in and out of favor with industry and commerce for some time. Some now believe that its time has passed, whereas others feel it is now reemerging. It is mentioned here because it is a style of thinking that is still widespread and pervasive in both private and public organizations.

One large organization that is currently going through a merger review, but still uses the essence of MBO in its activities, termed the "Hewlett Packard way," is the Hewlett Packard Company (www.hp.com/ hpinfo/abouthp/corpobj.htm#management/)

Because some of its concepts (relationships among units are closely linked through common technologies, customers, values, goals, and objectives) are so closely aligned with those of strategic management, and its focus for the future is on providing a framework for the management process, some discussion is warranted. For example, in an analysis of seventy studies on the use of management by objectives, it was found that the MBO process has become more widely used in both government and business where they have been supported by top management.[9] However, MBO has seen its greatest success in for-profit organizations,

> MBO is a participative system of managing in which managers look ahead for improvements, think strategically, set performance stretch objectives at a beginning period, develop supporting plans, and give accountability for results at the end of the period.[10]
>
> —Paul Mali,
> *MBO Updated*

Although MBO allows one to direct oneself and one's work, it can also mean domination of one person by another. "Objectives are the basis of 'control' in the first sense; but they must never become the basis of 'control' in the second, for this would defeat their purpose. Indeed, one of the major contributions of Management by Objectives is that it enables us to substitute management by self-control for management by domination."[11]

Description of the technique has been refined to a process whereby the superior and subordinate managers of an organization jointly identify its common goals, define each individual's major areas of responsibility in terms of the results expected, and use these measures as guides for operating the unit and assessing the contribution of each of its members.[12] In essence, MBO means establishing objectives and approaching them as a team over a stated period of time. Objectives must be measurable, with time limits, and they must require specific and realistic action. Perhaps the two most important factors in this process are interactive goal setting and the performance appraisal. The interactive aspect identifies mutually agreed upon objectives for a person to pursue, making that person accountable for results. In true interactive sessions, both the supervisor and the employee give input to the goal setting and the appraisal. This follow-up requires open and free communication without fear of retaliation and without judgment, but with trust and respect. Some feel that these sessions can be "self-defeating over the long run because they are based on a reward-punishment psychology that serves to intensify the pressure on the individual."[13] Indeed, the process is a very delicate one that can improve with experience, but it is not a process based upon threat or intimidation.

Management by Objectives is perhaps one of the most evident examples of participative management because it involves everyone, to an extent, in the management process. It can clarify responsibilities, strengthen planning and control, and establish better relationships between supervisors and other staff members. In this process, at the start of appraisal periods, supervisor and subordinates agree upon specific results to be obtained during this period; they establish what is to be done, how long it will take, and who is to do it. The process rests upon several premises:

1. Clearly stated objectives. If they are not clear, they should be clarified.

2. A succession of specific objectives. Benchmarks must be established to measure progress.

3. Delegation of specific objectives. Certain people should be responsible for accomplishing specific objectives.

4. Freedom to act. Subordinates should be given objectives and authority and then be charged with accomplishment of those objectives.

5. Verifiable objectives. To achieve objectives, it is best to quantify them. If they are nonquantifiable objectives, they may relate to quantifiable ones. For example, if one wants to reduce absenteeism by fifty percent, the reasons for absenteeism must be considered. If the reasons relate to morale, then morale must be improved.

6. Clear communication. This exists only when objectives are specific, are agreed upon by all parties, are budgeted, and are known by all individuals who have a reason for knowing.

7. Shared responsibility. Team effort is the key to management by objectives.

8. Personal accountability. Each person must be accountable for the achievement of his or her assigned objectives.

9. Improving management ability. Management is able to plan more objectively when these premises are accepted.

Management by Objectives occurs in phases: finding the objectives, setting the objectives, validating the objectives, implementing the objectives, and controlling and reporting the status of the objectives. Research studies have confirmed that the process does, indeed, improve communications, increase mutual understanding, improve planning, create positive attitudes toward the evaluation system, employ management abilities, and promote innovation within organizations that have used it.[14] Simply stated by George Odiorne, MBO helps solve management problems by:

1. providing a means of measuring the true contributions of managerial and professional personnel.

2. defining the common goals of people and organizations and measuring individual contributions to them. It enhances the possibility of obtaining coordinated efforts and teamwork without eliminating personal risk taking.

3. providing solutions to the key problem of defining the major areas of responsibility for each person in the organization, including joint or shared responsibilities.

4. gearing processes to achieving the results desired, both for the organization as a whole and for the individual contributors.

5. eliminating the need for people to change their personalities as well as for appraising people on the basis of their personality traits.

6. providing a means of determining each manager's span of control.

7. offering an answer to the key question of salary administration, "How should we allocate pay increases from available funds if we want to pay for results?"

8. aiding in identifying potential for advancement and in finding promotable people.[15]

Some libraries and information centers have explored this technique's potential for their operations. In practicing MBO one must guard against making the individual's objectives too easy, making them too difficult, setting objectives that conflict with policy, or setting objectives that hold an individual accountable for something beyond his or her control. Also, some concern has been expressed as to whether there is a deterioration of motivation over time. Such deterioration is reflected in lack of participation by all members, stacks of paperwork, emphasis on quantitative aspects, and increased administrative concerns.[16]

Total Quality Management (TQM)

TQM no longer has the success it experienced several years ago, particularly in Japan where it originated, and many no longer advocate the approach. Some organizations report success in using TQM; others have tried it and abandoned it. Some, such as Douglas Aircraft, invested a great deal of money in TQM, only to find it unworkable because of business setbacks that required large layoffs. Florida Power and Light, which had won Japan's Deming Prize for quality management, curtailed its program when employees complained about excessive paperwork. The Wallace Company, a Houston oil supply company, implemented TQM but subsequently filed for Chapter 11 bankruptcy protection.[17] Proponents of TQM argue that these setbacks are temporary and that TQM will eventually produce results. They point out that the Japanese began using quality improvement efforts in the 1950s and did not begin to see significant rewards until the 1970s.[18] During the end of enamorment with the technique, it was argued that TQM does not work, not because its focus on quality is misguided, but because the TQM operations often become so cumbersome that they overshadow the mission of the organization.[19]

It is true that TQM can result in the formation of more bureaucracy to implement quality, particularly when it is first being implemented, because it tends to add to the workload of everyone. "If quality does not become 'the religion, organizing logic, and culture of the firm, but instead gets stalled as internal programs run by technocrats, it will fail.' "[20] If TQM is adopted as a quick fix, forgetting that quality is a never-ending journey, or if the managers of an organization only pay lip service to the technique, it will not succeed. However, TQM did find success in corporate America as companies sought ways to excel in the global economy, and in some large library and information services organizations as those organizations sought ways of implementing a planning process, whether by strategic planning, TQM, focus groups or task forces, etc.

> Libraries must build into their organizational structures and their approaches to work, the ability to identify, anticipate, and quickly respond to constantly changing customer needs. They must be capable of leaps forward and breakthrough performance. They must reduce cycle times for implementing new services. They must be able to anticipate those needs rather than wait for customer needs to be articulated fully. And they must be ready to abandon formerly successful approaches to work, strategies, processing systems, services and products that do not continually prove their value to customers.[21]
>
> —Carla J. Stoffle et al.,
> "Choosing Our Futures"

Some libraries and information centers, like other organizations as they sought to pay more attention to quality, turned to TQM as a system that allows them to do so. All libraries and information agencies have certain processes, for example, copy cataloging or overdue billings, which could be greatly improved by TQM methods. In addition, the TQM emphasis on improving quality in service could help libraries and other service organizations maintain the support of their "customer" base in an era of increasing competition. Even though TQM has not been widely accepted by not-for-profit organizations, its emphases on quality and customer service can be examined as a model for managers and staff in these organizations. Because even though TQM is fading as a management tool, it leaves behind its "own important legacy in two key concepts. The first is the need to focus on the customer in the development of products and the delivery of services. The second is the need to be constantly aware of process both in development and delivery, and vigilant for opportunities for improvement."[22]

It is easy to dismiss TQM and other techniques as just management fads, but those fads often have something valuable to teach us. TQM provided a way to make libraries and information centers more interested in quality, customers, teamwork, and getting things done right the first time.

Other recent trends in industry, which will not be discussed here in any depth, include reengineering, which basically calls for complete change—as was discussed in the first chapter. What has happened is that there has been a continuum of planning strategies that has brought libraries from looking first at incremental change to the more dramatic comprehensive change. Some of the best of both techniques has been incorporated in current strategic thinking and planning exercises as libraries and information centers look to the future. Benchmarking, which is a part of the process, is one good example.

Policy Making

It is important to distinguish between objectives and policy. Objectives emphasize aims and are stated as expectations; policies emphasize rules and are stated as instructions intended to facilitate decision making.

In many discourses, policy making and decision making are synonymous terms. In practice, however, policy making is one part of decision making, in that policies emanate from the original decisions and become general statements or understandings that channel thinking in future decision making and serve as guidelines for actions, particularly those of a repetitive nature, in order to create some sense of uniformity in the conduct of an organization. Policies can be viewed as contingency plans because they are based on decisions that set the course of the plan. Policies, even though they are sometimes expressed in positive terms, are essentially limiting because they dictate a specific course of action and are aimed at preventing deviations from a set norm. They attempt to eliminate differences that sometimes result from personality conflicts or irrational forces. Policies become effective tools for transferring decision making through the various levels in the organization because, within the broad policy outline, individuals at all levels can be charged with making operational decisions. A good working definition of policy making might be "a verbal, written, or implied overall guide setting up boundaries that supply the general limits and direction in which managerial action will take place."[23]

Both policies and objectives are guides to thinking and action, but there are differences between them. Objectives, as already discussed, are developed at one point in the planning process, whereas policies channel decisions along the way toward meeting those established objectives. Another difference is that a policy is usually effective or operational the day it is formulated and continues to be in effect until it is revised or deleted. A policy, then, leads to the achievement of objectives and aids in the decision-making process. As mentioned before, policies can give guidance to all levels of the organization. For example, by adopting an equal employment opportunity policy, an institution ensures that all qualified individuals are seriously and equally considered by all hiring units within the organization for any position vacancy. The policy does not dictate the choice of a particular individual but does eliminate one factor—discrimination—as an element in the final decision.

Policy making is not reserved for top management. Policies include, on the one hand, major policies involving all segments of the organization and, on the other hand, minor policies applicable only to a small segment of the organization. Many policies in libraries and information centers provide basic direction toward the achievement of stated goals, including policies relating to materials purchasing, personnel employment, equipment use, and monetary allocation. Examples of library and information center policies might be:

1. All new staff will be rotated through all departments during their first year of employment (a staff-development policy).

2. Library materials should present all sides of controversial issues (a materials selection policy).

Policy manuals usually enumerate an organization's policies in relation to its goals and objectives. A policy manual is an important record and is invaluable as a decision-making guide and as a way of communicating within the organization. It is also a basic tool for indoctrinating new staff members and assuring some degree of uniformity in approaches or responses to issues. Of course, it also serves as a historical record of decisions made.

All libraries have policies, whether they are written or unwritten, sound or unsound, followed or not followed, understood or not understood, complete or incomplete. It is almost impossible to delegate authority and clarify relationships without policies because one has difficulty carrying out decisions without some kind of guideline. It is important to remember that policies can provide freedom as well as restrict it, and that there are as many cases of frustration within organizations about the lack of rules, regulations, procedures, and policies as there are about arbitrarily established ones. In the absence of policy, each case is resolved on its own merit and at one particular time, so consistency is lacking. Lack of policy means that the same question may be considered time after time, by a number of different individuals, in several units of the organization, with the result that energy is wasted, redundancy is established, conflicting decisions are made, and confusion develops. Policies ensure some degree of consistency in the operation. They may be stated in the form of guiding principles (these being broad, comprehensive, and basic) or may be specific or operational and deal with day-to-day activities.

Sources of Policy

Policies can be categorized according to their source as follows:

1. Originated policy. This type of policy is developed to guide the general operations of the library or information center. Originated policies flow mainly from the objectives and are the main source of policy making within the organization. An example of an originated policy is the previously mentioned policy to adhere to the concept of equal employment opportunity.

2. Appealed policy. Certain decisions may be needed by managers in their assigned areas of responsibility, and the staff is required to take it through the chain-of-command, where a common law is established. This type of policy can cause tension because it forces a decision or policy that, consequently, often does not have the thorough consideration that is required.

To draw an extreme example, it may be the appealed policy of the catalog department to make no more than two subject headings for each monograph. That policy, derived from practice, has a great effect on the reference department's ability to work with patrons. Oftentimes, appealed policies are made by snap decisions.

3. Implied policy. This type of policy is developed from actions that people see about them and believe to constitute policy. Usually, this type of policy is unwritten. For instance, repetitive actions, such as promotion from within, may be interpreted as policy. This may or may not be the case. Particularly in areas relating to personnel, staff must be informed so that misunderstandings do not arise. When implied policies are recognized, policies should be developed or other statements used to clarify the issue.

4. Externally imposed policy. These policies, which come through several channels, dictate the working of an institution but may be beyond its control. For example, local, state, and federal laws have a direct bearing on the policies that libraries may formulate. These laws may be general, such as those relating to destruction of public property (Malicious Damage Act of 1861), or specific, such as those relating to copyright (Copyright Act of 1976). When policies are being formulated, they must be checked for compliance with law before they can be finalized.

No matter what policies are set for libraries and information centers, the policies are subject to government regulation. In the case of public libraries, objectives must adhere to government policy on the local, state, provincial, and/or national levels. If, for instance, a local authority decides, for local economic reasons, to reduce drastically the library service hours to the point that the library no longer meets state standards for allocating funds to that library, such an action could be in conflict with its obligation and thus be illegal. Or, if a library replans its service points and closes a branch library, people living nearby may petition their representatives or other local officials, who may decide that such a policy does not secure an improvement and may prevent the library from carrying out its decision on policy.

Laws governing information services often relate to finances. Standards for capital investment, percentage of budget spent on physical and electronic materials, qualifications of staff, and so on, are developed by library officials. Because this is an external control upon all public library spending, it necessarily affects the planning and administration of public libraries.

Effective Policy Development

Policies fall into two groups: those that deal with the managerial functions of planning, organizing, staffing, directing, and controlling, and those that deal with the functions of the enterprise, such as selection and development of technology, resources, finance, personnel, and public relations. Both types of policies relate to the characteristic behavior of the library to achieve its objectives.

Several basic rules should be considered when policies are being formulated. Some of these may seem simplistic, mundane, and even redundant, but it is surprising how many organizations ignore these basics when they are formulating policy. To be most effective, policies should be reflective of the objectives and plans of the organization. These should complement each other and build on that common strength. For this reason, any policy should receive detailed consideration before being proposed and certainly before implementation. Characteristics of good policies would include them being:

1. Consistent. This maintains efficiency. Again, the existence of contradicting policies dissipates desired effects.

2. Flexible. Policies must change as new needs arise. Unfortunately, many organizations adhere to out-of-date policies. On the other hand, a laissez-faire approach to policy formulation and revision may lead to disillusionment on the part of those who are charged with carrying out the policies. Some degree of stability must be maintained. Policies should be regularly revisited and controlled through careful review. Although the application of policies requires judgment, violation of the policy under the guise of flexibility should be avoided.

3. Distinguished from rules and procedures. Rules and procedures are firm, while policies, as guides, allow some discretion and latitude.

4. Written. A clear, well-written policy helps facilitate information dissemination. Because many policies affect individuals who have not been involved in their formulation, the policies should be discussed and widely distributed through letters, memoranda, announcements, and policy manuals.

Stated policies have several advantages.

1. They are available to all in the same form.

2. They can be referred to, so that anyone who wishes can check the policy.

3. They prevent misunderstanding through use of a particular set of words.

4. They indicate a basic honesty and integrity of the organization's intentions.

5. They can be readily disseminated to all who are affected by them.

6. They can be taught to new employees easily.

7. They force managers to think more sharply about the policy as it is being written, thus helping achieve further clarity.

8. They generate confidence of all persons in management and in the fact that everyone will be treated substantially the same under given conditions.[24]

Implementing Policy

Policies are carried out or enforced by procedures, rules, and regulations. Procedures are guides to action and therefore are subordinate to policies. They establish a method of handling repetitive tasks or problems and may be thought of as means by which work is performed. Basically, procedures prescribe standardized methods of performing tasks to ensure uniformity and consistency. Greater efficiency in routine jobs can be achieved through procedures that identify the best way of getting the job done. Procedures tend to be chronological lists of what is to be done. Examples of procedures are: a timetable for budget preparation, a sequence of steps to be followed in searching and ordering library materials, and interlibrary loan procedures. Procedures are helpful in routine decisions because they break down the process into steps.

The relationship between procedures and policies can be best indicated by an example. Library policy may grant employees a month's annual vacation. The procedures specify how vacations are to be scheduled to avoid disruption of service, maintain records to assure each employee is allocated the right length of vacation days, and elucidate procedure for applying for additional entitled time off.

Rules and regulations, constituting the simplest type of a plan, spell out a required course of action or conduct that must be followed. A rule prescribes a specific action for a given situation and creates uniformity of action. Rules may place positive limits (should), negative limits (should not), or value constraints (good or bad) on the behavior of individuals working in the institution or on individuals using the institution as a service. Rules ensure stable, consistent, and uniform behavior by individuals in accomplishing tasks, addressing personnel issues, and relating to both the internal and external environment. Like procedures, rules and regulations guide action, but they specify no time sequence. Similar to decisions, rules are guides, but they allow no discretion or initiative in their application. Examples of rules might be the prohibition of smoking in the library or information center or the fact that materials in the reference collection do not circulate. Regulations also establish a course of action that is authoritative, with failure to adhere to regulations eliciting discipline.

Decision Making

Regardless of formal position in the organization, the librarian is an information processor—not only in the provision of services to the patrons but also as a decision-maker in the operation of the library. It is this second role of information processor to which attention must be drawn, for it is in this role that the librarian affects the decisions being made in the organization.[25]

—Charles R. McClure,
Information for Academic Library Decision Making

Some writers consider decision making synonymous with management,[26] and indeed it is a part of the planning process. There is no doubt that it is an important part of management, one of the basic planning principles. Selection from among alternatives is the core of planning. A decision is a judgment. It is a choice between alternatives but is rarely a choice between right and wrong. "It is at best a choice between 'almost right' and 'probably wrong'—but much more often a choice between two courses of action neither of which is probably more nearly right than the other."[27] Decision making, therefore, complements planning because it involves choosing the best alternative for the future of the enterprise, and those decisions with organization-wide implications are related specifically to the planning process. A decision must be made, with a course of action in mind, by choosing the alternative that one thinks is best. This is not necessarily the alternative that is best because that can be determined only later. Of course, such a choice implies an awareness of alternatives and the important factors that need to be considered.

Decision making is a conscious choosing, and it is a much slower process than some would like to imagine. The stereotype of finger-snapping and button-pushing fades with the realization that decisions, affecting important future outcomes, require systematic research and analysis. The decision-making process involves a blend of thinking, deciding, and acting; information is key to the process. Deliberation, evaluation, and thought must be brought into play. Although many decisions are mundane, others are of unmeasured consequence and could change the information center's course of action. An example of the latter is the decision to open a new branch library or to purchase a totally integrated online system for the library's or the information center's operation. Such decisions can be made only after long, thoughtful review, analysis, discussion, and deliberation. The manager who has the ultimate responsibility must make a decision that will have a great impact on the operation of the library and on many people, staff, customers, and other stake holders. Attention paid to the final act—the decision itself—obscures the fact that a number of steps and minor decisions are made along the way, and the announcement of the decision is only the final step in the process.

Decision making at a formal level involves a series of scientific steps: defining the problem, analyzing it, establishing criteria by which it can be evaluated, identifying alternate solutions, selecting the "best" one, implementing it, and evaluating the results. The decision-making procedure can be divided into four phases:

1. Intelligence gathering. The environment inside and outside the organization is searched for conditions requiring a decision, and information is assembled with respect to those conditions.

2. Design. The available courses of action are determined and analyzed to determine their relative values as solutions to the problems that have been detected.

3. Choice. An available course of action, which is designed to convert the present, less-desirable situation into a future situation judged to be more desirable, is selected.

4. Review. Assessing the past choices and adjusting new directions.[28]

These phases, of course, do not have clear-cut boundaries or strict sequence. Although this discussion is primarily about the steps in the major decision-making process, it is important to remember that everyone makes decisions every day and that most of these decisions are, to some degree, reached by the same process discussed here. Some organizational decision making, which was once reserved for the executive, is now being delegated to and assumed by others in the organization. Decision making can no longer be confined to the very small group at the top. In one way or another almost every knowledge worker in an organization will either have to become a decision maker himself or herself or will at least have to be able to play an active, an intelligent, and an autonomous part in the decision-making process. What in the past was a highly specialized function, discharged by a small and usually clearly defined unit within the organization, is rapidly becoming a normal if not an everyday task of every single unit in the open system of a large-scale knowledge-based organization. The ability to make effective decisions increasingly determines the ability of every knowledge worker to be effective.

One of the characteristics of an effective decision maker appears to be "the ability to distinguish between problems for which existing procedures are appropriate and those for which new ground must be broken. It is ineffective and inefficient to deal with an exceptional problem as though it were routine, or a generic problem as though it were an exceptional case."[29]

Group Decision Making

The approach to decision making by groups is somewhat different from individual decision making, primarily because of group dynamics. However, group decision making should follow the same process if it is to be constructive. Herbert Simon points out that "almost no decision made in an organization is the task of a single individual."[30] Not everyone would agree. When Max Weber formulated the concept of bureaucracy with emphasis on the position rather than the person, he detailed the delegation of responsibility, channels of communication for decision making, and the need for specialization for decision-making purposes. His theory, for all intents, rejects interaction among subordinates for decision-making purposes. Those attitudes may be outdated but certainly have not been abandoned. There are, nevertheless, several advantages to group decision making, including:

1. Group judgment. The old adage "two heads are better than one" applies here. Group deliberation is important in identifying alternative solutions to a problem.

2. Group authority. There is a great fear of allowing one person to have too much authority. Group decisions prevent this problem to an extent. However, it must be remembered that one person must ultimately answer for decisions that have been made. Thus, the role of leadership in the organization is not diminished but altered.

3.   Communication. It is much easier to inform and receive input from all parts of the organization through a group. Also, if various interest groups have been represented during the process of making major decisions, there is less resistance to the decisions. Communication permits a wider participation in decision making and therefore can have some influence on employee motivation.

There are also distinct disadvantages to the group approach. As a cynic once wrote, a committee is a group of "unfits appointed by the incompetent to do the unnecessary." More realistically, disadvantages potentially include:

1.   Cost. Group decision making requires a great deal of time, energy, and, therefore, money.

2.   Compromise. Group decisions can be diluted to the least common denominator. Pressures of uniformity force compliance. There are two ways to view this. The major drawback may be that majority rules. The desirability of a consensus should not take precedence over critical evaluation in such a situation. On the other hand, a group can prevent an individual from going off the track by forcing him or her into line with the thinking of the rest of the group.

3.   Indecision. There are delays in reaching a final decision because of the lengthy deliberations required. Groups are often accused of engaging in too much irrelevant talk and not enough concrete action.

4.   Power. One individual usually emerges as a leader. This person should be in a position of influence in the organization. The authoritarian personality of an administrator can be used as a tactical weapon so that the group process simply becomes one of minimizing opposition to an action that has already been decided on by the administrator. The cohesiveness of the group and the attitudes of one person toward another are important factors in the group process.

5.   Authority. Groups are frequently used to make decisions that are beyond their authority. This can cause great delay and only enhances a feeling of frustration on the part of members, particularly if the group decision is rejected by management. The responsibility and authority of the group should be clearly set out at the beginning.

The democratic approach of group decision making improves morale, stresses the team approach, keeps individuals aware, and provides a forum for free discussion of ideas and thoughts. Traditionally, librarians and information managers have not demanded a greater voice in decision-making affairs because they have had an employee rather than a professional orientation. In the past, the higher a person was on the administrative scale, the less aware he or she was of the inadequate opportunities available for staff participation. This is an area of great discussion and disagreement in all types of organizations and one that is rapidly changing as team-based organizations proliferate.

Steps and Factors in Making Decisions

If the organization's goals are clear, the next important step in decision making is developing alternatives. This step is possible in almost all situations. Effective planning involves a search for these alternatives. If there is only one solution, management is powerless to devise alternatives, and no decision is required, although some adjustments may be necessary. In most cases, however, several alternatives exist. Final selection of a course of action is a matter of weighing expected results against enterprise objectives. What is best for one segment is not necessarily best for the whole. Making only two subject entries in the catalog, for instance, is easier for the cataloging department but harder for the reference department. Choosing a course of action commits the entire enterprise to the chosen position.

The scientific approach to decision making requires that one first identify the problem. Once that has been done, the decision-maker must collect and analyze all data available on the problem. This includes intuition, opinion, and impression, in addition to concrete data. It may involve operations research. After all alternatives have been developed, one must select what appears to be the most appropriate alternative. Often this alternative, if adopted, is then expressed as policy for the functioning of the organization. This selection process involves a great deal of risk-taking as well as uncertainty because it is only after the decision has been implemented that one can determine whether or not it was appropriate. The final step of implementation brings the decision into the control and evaluation aspect of the decision.

> Participative management is not decision making by committee or by staff plebiscite. Good management requires that when all the facts have been gathered and analyzed and all the advice is in, the appropriate administrator has to make the decision and take responsibility for it. Knowing when and how to seek and take advantage of consultative advice and prior approval of decisions where appropriate is one of the most important managerial skills.[31]
>
> —Richard DeGennaro,
> "Library Administration and New Management Systems"

Several factors influence decision making for libraries and other information centers. The PEST analysis, to be detailed later, suggests a community analysis should be conducted before final decisions can be made on services to be offered by the library. Selection from among alternatives is then made on the basis of the following:

1.   Experience. In relying on one's experience, mistakes as well as accomplishments should act as guides. If experience is carefully analyzed and not blindly followed, it can be useful and appropriate.

2. Experimentation. This approach toward deciding among alternatives, although legitimate in many situations, is expensive where capital expenditures and personnel are concerned.

3. Research and analysis. Although this is the most general and effective technique used, it may be somewhat expensive. However, the approach is probably more beneficial and cheaper in the long run, particularly for large academic, public, and special libraries. This topic is discussed in the chapter on controlling.

Another important factor in the decision-making process is the perceived level of importance of a particular decision. There are two basic types of decisions: a major one affecting the total organization and a lesser one, which has less effect on the overall organization but is nonetheless important. The routine decisions comprise as much as ninety percent of decisions made in an organization. Most decisions of lesser importance do not require the thorough analysis described here.

Politics is paramount in decision making, as is consideration of the human factor. Acceptance of change is essential to the success of a decision. It is desirable that those who will be affected also be involved in the decision from the beginning. The following suggestions may facilitate involvement in the decision-making process:

1. Distinguish big from little problems to avoid getting caught in a situation that is rapid-fire and not effective.

2. Rely on policy to settle routine problems, and subject the big problems to thorough analysis.

3. Delegate as many decisions as possible to the level of authority most qualified and most interested in handling the problem.

4. Avoid crisis decisions by planning ahead.

5. Don't expect to be right all the time; no one ever is.

Decision making is at the heart of any organization. The approach that the librarian and the information specialist take to decision making and to the involvement of others will determine the direction the library or information center will take in the future.

Conclusion

Preparing for the planning process is an important aspect of sustaining an organization's viability. It requires examining the factors in the process, setting a proper environment within the organization, and making decisions based upon sound guidelines. Once the process is in place, an organization can view the big picture and begin to address the questions of "Why are we here?" and "Where do we want to be?" organizationally.

There are several techniques being used in libraries and information centers today to help an organization do that. Perhaps the most widely used one is strategic planning, which is discussed in the next chapter.

Notes

1.   Peter F. Drucker, *Management: Tasks, Responsibilities, Practices* (New York: Harper & Row, 1974), 121–22.

2.   Harvard College Library, *Commitment to Renewal* (Cambridge, MA: Harvard College Library, 1992), 1.

3.   Columbia University, "Detailed Organization Description of the Columbia University Libraries" (effective June 1973), 11.3.1. (Mimeo, 12 April 1973).

4.   Joan Giesecke, ed., *Strategic Planning for Libraries* (Chicago: American Library Association, 1998). Ethel Himmell and Bill Wilson, *Planning for Results: A Public Library Transformation Process and the Guidebook* (Chicago: American Library Association, 1998). Richard W. Clement, *Strategic Planning in ARL Libraries* (OMS EC Kit 210, Washington, DC: Association of Research Libraries, 1995). Nancy Van House et al., *Measuring Academic Library Performance: A Practical Approach* (Chicago: American Library Association, 1990). S. Easun, "Beginner's Guide to Efficiency Measurement: An Application of Data Envelopment Analysis to Selected School Libraries," *School Library Media Quarterly* 22 (1994): 103–6. C. Guyonneau, "Performance Measures for ILL: An Evaluation," *Journal of Interlibrary Loan and Information Supply* 3 (1993): 101–26. K. Hendrickson, "Standards for University Libraries: Evaluation of Performance," *College and Research Libraries News* 50 (1989): 680–81. S. B. Watstein et al., comps., *Formal Planning in College Libraries* (Chicago: American Library Association, 1994). Nancy van House, B. Weil, and Charles McClure, *Measuring Library Performance* (Chicago: American Library Association, 1990). Ethel Himmel and William James Wilson, cons., *Planning for Results: A Public Library Transformation Process* (Chicago: American Library Association, 1998). American Library Association, *Standards for College Libraries, 2000* (www.ala.org/guides/college .html). Sandra Nelson, *The New Planning for Results: A Standard Approach* (Chicago: American Library Association, 2001).

5.   Bernard Taylor and John R. Sparkes, *Corporate Strategy and Planning* (New York: John Wiley & Sons, 1977), 3.

6.   Robert D. Stueart, "Long-Range Planning in U.S. Public Libraries," in H. Ernestus and H. D. Weger, eds., *Public Libraries Today and Tomorrow: Approaches to Their Goals and Management* (Boston Spa, England: British Library Research and Development Department, 1986), 40.

7.   Quoted in David P. Snyder and Gregg Edwards, *Future Forces* (Washington, DC: Foundation of the American Society of Association Executives, 1984), 1.

8.   Leonard S. Silk and M. Louise Curley, *A Primer on Business Forecasting* (New York: Random House, 1970), 3–4.

9.   Robert Rodgers and John E. Hunter, "A Foundation of Good Management Practices in Government: Management by Objectives," *Public Administration Review* 52 (January–February 1992): 27–39.

10.   Paul Mali, *MBO Updated* (New York: John Wiley & Sons, 1986), 47.

11.   Stephen J. Carroll Jr., and Henry L. Tosi, *Management by Objectives* (New York: Macmillan, 1973), 3.

12.   George S. Odiorne, *Management by Objectives* (New York: Fearon-Pitman, 1965), 55–56.

13.   Harry Levinson, "Management by Whose Objectives," *Harvard Business Review* 48 (July–August 1970): 134.

14.   Stephen J. Carroll Jr., and Henry L. Tosi, "Goal Characteristics and Personality Factors in a Management-by-Objectives Program," *Administrative Science Quarterly* 15 (1970): 295–301.

15.   Odiorne, *Management by Objectives*, 55.

16.   John M. Ivancevich, "A Longitudinal Assessment of Management by Objectives," *Administrative Science Quarterly* 17 (March 1972): 127.

17.   Jay Mathews with Peter Katel, "The Cost of Quality," *Newsweek* 120 (September 7, 1992): 48–49.

18.   *Ibid.*

19.   Oren Harari, "Ten Reasons TQM Doesn't Work," *Management Review* 38 (January 1997): 38–44.

20.   Tom Peters, "Strategic Planning," *Total Quality* 5 (October 10, 1994): 1.

21.   Carla J. Stoffle, et al., "Choosing Our Futures," *College and Research Libraries* 57 (May 1996): 213–33.

22.   Susan Jurow, "Tools for Measuring and Improving Performance," in Susan Jurow and Susan B. Barnard, eds., *Integrating Total Quality Management in a Library Setting* (Binghamton, NY: Haworth Press, 1993), 125.

23.   M. Valliant Higginson, "Putting Policies in Context," in Alfred Gross and Walter Gross, eds., *Business Policy* (New York: Ronald Press, 1967), 230.

24.   Dalton E. McFarland, "Policy Administration," in Alfred Gross and Walter Gross, eds., *Business Policy* (New York: Ronald Press, 1967), 230.

25.   Charles R. McClure, *Information for Academic Library Decision Making* (Westport, CT: Greenwood Press, 1980), 5.

26.   Herbert A. Simon, *The New Science of Management Decision,* 2d ed. (New York: Macmillan, 1966), 143.

27.   Peter F. Drucker, *The Effective Executive* (New York: Harper & Row, 1967), 143.

28.   Simon, *New Science of Management Decision*, 39.

29.   Jerry W. Koehler et al., *Organizational Communication* (New York: Holt, Rinehart & Winston, 1976), 218.

30.   Herbert A. Simon, *Administrative Behavior* (New York: Macmillan, 1957), 133.

31.   Richard DeGennaro, "Library Administration and New Management Systems," *Library Journal* 103 (December 15, 1978): 2480.

Chapter 4

Strategy — Thinking and Doing

Organizations engage in formal planning, not to create strategies but to program the strategies they already have, that is, to elaborate and operationalize their consequence formally.[1]

—Henry Mintzberg,
The Rise and Fall of Strategic Planning

Strategic Thinking

Demands of a changing environment require the use of systems, methods, models, and options that are responsive to a rapid and sometimes unpredictable future. This requires strategic thinking as a basis for development. To be truly strategic in actions, ambiguity must be tolerated, and uncertainty is evident. Before one can plan strategically, one must think strategically. With an unknown future, knowledge-based organizations must put into place the process, discussed in the first chapter, of converting information to knowledge through staff endeavors and for the benefit of customers in order to steer a successful course for the organization into the future. Such strategic thinking is a continuous process of making entrepreneurial, even risk-taking, decisions systematically and with the greatest possible knowledge of their future consequences.

In a way, it is a rethinking of the organization, its vision for the future and a mission that is required to achieve that vision. It requires reexamining the organization's strengths and weaknesses and identifying threats as well as opportunities that exist to hinder or encourage future directions. Managers and other staff, working together, are required to explore future options or directions in a systematic way. Three primary questions guide this future strategic thinking exercise:

1. What seems to be happening? This requires addressing how one builds the relevant knowledge base (perceiving).

2.   What possibilities are presented? This requires addressing how one determines the significance or use of the knowledge base (understanding).

3.   What is the organization going to do about it? This requires addressing how to determine the significance or use of the knowledge base (reasoning).[2]

This involves identification and recognition of the political, economic, sociological, and technological forces external to the organization (PEST analysis, relating to this topic, will be discussed later), which have a bearing on what can eventually be accomplished. A knowledge base of those forces, including input from customers and competitors, also allows the organization to develop scenarios of what information services could be. If those are compared to the organization's own strengths and weaknesses, possibilities for the future begin to emerge. Intangible inputs in this strategic thinking process, including the culture, values, vision, and mission can be converted into the outputs of trust identified through honesty, openness, and reliability; satisfaction; team spirit; and commitment of pride, loyalty, and ownership of the process. Strategic planning assists libraries and information centers by developing a thinking mode that facilitates projecting the organization into a desired future.

Strategic Planning

Strategic planning is the systematic outcome of that thinking process that enables libraries and information centers to organize efforts necessary to carry out these decisions and to measure the results of these decisions against the expectations through organized, systematic feedback and adjustments. Libraries and information centers as customer-focused organizations develop services to meet their needs and also market to nonusers who are potential customers. Therefore, strategic planning must start with the customer. That focus is primary in all types of libraries and information centers today.

Strategic planning is a major tool for effective identification and development of organizational priorities in that milieu. Although it was introduced in the business world more than thirty years ago to address market shifts, it now has much wider, almost universal, application in not-for-profit organizations as well. The concept is relatively new to libraries and information centers, whether one considers university planning, affecting academic libraries; city planning, affecting public libraries; school systems planning, affecting media centers; or corporate planning, affecting special libraries. Most large library and information centers and many smaller ones are now involved in some form of strategic planning. Figure 4.1 illustrates the strategic planning process common to libraries and other information centers.

Although strategic planning is automatically associated with growth and new resources management, today it is equally important for successful retrenchment and maintenance of efforts. Strategic planning requires describing a vision for the organization, identifying a mission within that context, setting realistic goals, establishing attainable objectives, and developing activities that can be carried out as policies and procedures that accomplish those goals and objectives. In its simplest definition, it is a process of

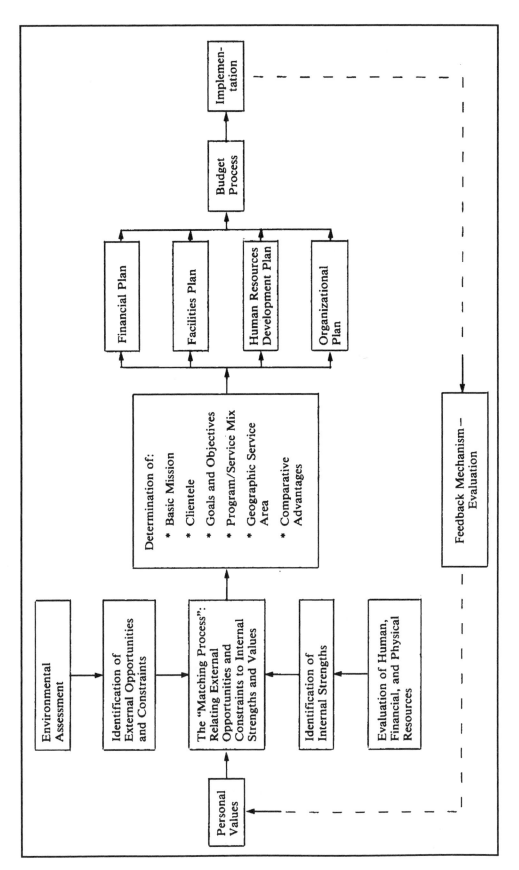

Figure 4.1. Strategic Planning Is a Continuous Process

translating decisions into policies and policies into actions. The approach is being used more and more by both for-profit and nonprofit organizations that have recognized the need for change and are determined to make a successful transition, not only from where they are to where they want to be, but also from the current scenario to that of one envisioned for the future.

Systematic, planned change is the most effective way to implement new services and preserve important existing ones, and it eliminates those whose usefulness has passed. This requires an organizational arrangement that makes orderly change possible and attainable within a realistic time frame. Flexibility in development, implementation, and time constraints presents the greatest challenges to a "strategic" planning effort. "Change at the Speed of Thought" is the metaphor of the day, and this requires a flexible process, perhaps even "preferred futuring."[3]

To establish a climate for strategic planning within the library or information center, at least two things are desirable: The entire organization should be informed of the process, be committed to its success, and be kept updated as it progresses, and the larger institutional administration should know decisions, commitments, and efforts as a result of the planning activities. Within this climate, the library or information center can proceed with a systematic planning process that has a chance of maximum success with a minimum amount of resistance.

Most experts agree that strategic plans should attempt to project at least five years and that those efforts should be part of an ongoing, periodic planning process, not a one-time affair resulting in a document that is never again consulted. In fact, with today's changing climate, many libraries and information centers are revisiting their strategic planning efforts on a more abbreviated basis. The ongoing process addresses one of the most difficult aspects of strategic planning, which is that of projecting and making assumptions about external forces. A good example is that of monitoring population trends for higher education or urban settings. The further ahead one projects, the greater the uncertainty and therefore the greater the challenge. Uncertainty makes it even more imperative that strategic long-range plans receive periodic review and assessment so that certain aspects can be updated, deleted, or rethought as the library's goals are achieved and as priorities shift. One weakness is that strategic planners seldom, if ever, plan for failures. But strategic planning is attempting to address that eventuality with shortened timelines and more effective monitoring.

> To be effective planners librarians and information services managers need a great deal more information about their own organizations and their environment than most have tried or been able to gather. Effective goal-setting and decision making for the future are dependent upon extensive, up-to-date, and accurate information about the current state of the organization.[4]
> —Edward R. Johnson,
> *Academic Library Planning, Self-Study, and Management Review*

Self-Analysis—A Part of the Plan

An added benefit of strategic planning is that it also can be thought of as a self-analysis or self-study that identifies the organization's strengths and weaknesses and develops priorities within the framework of the organization's physical and financial capabilities. The library or information center is an open, social system with specific goals of service. It interacts with the larger environment through the underlying values that it exists to support—sources and services for the social/informational/educational good upon which an open environment depends. To state an overused example, "the right amount of information, to the right person, at the right time, in the right format, at the right cost, and for the right reason" is a plan of service. The self-examination begins with identifying the beliefs, values, and ethos that guide the library's or information center's service goals. Commitment of individuals, working in the organization, to organizational strategies is most evident through those common values and shared beliefs or ideologies that are deemed good and desirable and that should act as guidelines that influence actions and the implementation of decisions.

Self-examination allows the library or information center to coordinate what it would like to be, envisioned in the mission statement, with what it can afford to be, regulated by the organization's physical and financial capabilities. If great disparity exists, a resolution must be sought by reducing expectations and/or increasing resources. Both for-profit and nonprofit organizations often focus their planning strategies on similar concerns: new directions, marketing, growth, finances, organizational concerns, personnel, and public relations.

Strategic planning supplies a forum for announcing, selling, negotiating, rationalizing and legitimizing strategic decisions, and it also offers means for controlling their implementation.[5]

—Arthur Langley,
The Role of Formal Strategic Planning

Strategic thinking about those factors includes serious discussion of who the organization is and what is its set of core values or philosophy. As an example, the concept of "right to know" encompassed in the Library Bill of Rights[6] might be one aspect of the value system discussion. Focus on the organizational values most commonly agreed upon by members of the workforce helps create a vision and sets the stage for both decision making and daily work. Those shared values and understanding of a vision help build commitment to the organization's reason for being, not just to provide jobs for those working there.

The existence of a vision gives . . . a context for planning activities, choosing courses of action, and making informed decisions.[7]

—Nancy Bolt,
"Critical Issues in Library Management"

From that analysis emerges a concise understanding of what the organization is, who it serves, and how it intends to achieve its plan by identifying priorities of service and directing decision making.

Strategic planning, components of which can be found in some other planning activities, analyzes capabilities, assesses environmental pressures and opportunities, sets objectives, examines alternate courses of action, and implements a preferred course. However, strategic planning differs from other forms of planning in that it deliberately attempts to concentrate resources in those areas that can make a substantial difference in future performance and capability. Thus, strategic planning is more a frame of reference and a way of thinking than a set of procedures. It does not concentrate, as long-range planning often does, upon projecting past experiences into future practices. Rather, it concentrates upon understanding the environment into which the library or information center is moving. It encourages creativity, has the potential of improving communications within the organization, markets the initiative to its users, and allows libraries and other information organizations and their staffs to identify and adopt options that may be unique to their individual settings and at a particular time in the organization's life. The plan itself encourages managers to experiment with various alternatives before committing resources by promoting a systems approach in:

♦ providing a mechanism to avoid overemphasizing organizational parts at the expense of the whole;

♦ guiding managers to make decisions that are in line with the aims and strategies of the whole organization;

♦ providing a basis for measuring the performance of the organization as a whole, of an operating unit, and of an individual;

♦ forwarding to higher levels of management those issues of strategic importance with which they should be concerned;

♦ serving as a training device by requiring participants to ask and answer the very questions that managers must address; and

♦ improving managerial motivation and morale through a sense of creative participation in the development of known expectations.[8]

Models for Strategic Planning

Several models have been developed for strategic planning, including some sophisticated ones developed with the aid of appropriate computer software. Each model has its strengths and weaknesses. To identify those systems would not be appropriate for this discussion. Descriptions of them can be found in the literature of library and information science, as well as in the more extensive literature of business and management. Those sources should be consulted by those who are seriously debating the subject of strategic planning and those who wish more detail than is possible to present in this brief overview.

It is important to note that, although somewhat mechanical planning models can be helpful in many situations, a desirable approach relies upon creativity and innovation. "The key to uniqueness is creativity."[9] Figure 4.2 shows the steps taken by the Board of Library Commissioners in Massachusetts as they developed a first strategic plan for public library service in the Commonwealth In addition to the steps in the planning process, the figure indicates which segments a strategic planning committee might be expected to complete and which are the responsibility of the organization staff. Strategic thinking is the key component in that creativity.

Scenario Planning

One preliminary planning technique that is receiving some attention in the for-profit sector is that of scenario planning, which is also a group process that promotes creative thinking. It encourages workers to discover new ways to solve problems, to develop services, and to institute plans by sharing knowledge and sharing a vision for becoming a learning organization. Scenario planning is being developed using Peter Senge's five disciplines approach.[10] It maintains that multiple possible futures exist and discusses the process necessary for an organization to create its own future by exploring all possible alternatives to the present.

> A learning organization is an organization skilled at creating, acquiring and transferring knowledge and insights.[11]
>
> —David Garvin,
> "Building a Learning Organization"

Since the intent is not to develop only one vision, it is flexible in creating views of the future as part of the planning process. David Garvin[12] categorizes the strategies into three possible scenarios:

1. Probable: Key trends and constraints of current situations are explored. Develop implications for continuation, increase or decline of what is current.

2. Possible: What might change? What would one envision if the organization had better and more? Imagination and speculation are tools for deciding.

3. Preferable: Develop a vision of what is a preferred, idealized condition.

By choosing the most likely to succeed, actions can be converted into an agenda through the planning process. The technique could be useful for libraries and information centers as they try to envision the unknown future and to plan strategically.

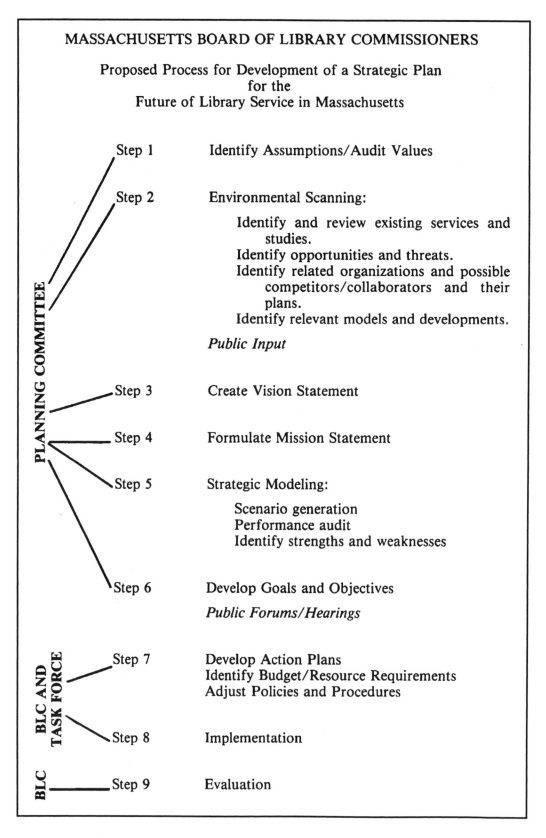

MASSACHUSETTS BOARD OF LIBRARY COMMISSIONERS

Proposed Process for Development of a Strategic Plan
for the
Future of Library Service in Massachusetts

PLANNING COMMITTEE

Step 1 — Identify Assumptions/Audit Values

Step 2 — Environmental Scanning:

    Identify and review existing services and studies.
    Identify opportunities and threats.
    Identify related organizations and possible competitors/collaborators and their plans.
    Identify relevant models and developments.

Public Input

Step 3 — Create Vision Statement

Step 4 — Formulate Mission Statement

Step 5 — Strategic Modeling:

    Scenario generation
    Performance audit
    Identify strengths and weaknesses

Step 6 — Develop Goals and Objectives

Public Forums/Hearings

BLC AND TASK FORCE

Step 7 — Develop Action Plans
Identify Budget/Resource Requirements
Adjust Policies and Procedures

Step 8 — Implementation

BLC

Step 9 — Evaluation

Figure 4.2. Before Strategic Planning Can Begin, Its Strategy Must Be Mapped

Getting Started

> The mission, vision and values statements are the principal products of the ... strategic planning process. They, and the process itself which, either directly or indirectly, involve nearly every member of the library staff, are the glue that binds and connects the various parts of the community to the whole.[13]
> —Richard DeGennaro,
> *Shared Understanding*

One initial step in undertaking strategic planning is to identify a planning team that will be responsible for carrying out the major planning phase and will involve other work teams and task forces at appropriate times in the process. Many organizational planning teams work with a strategic planning consultant, who facilitates the process. The primary role of a consultant is to help the team decide what data are to be collected, how they will be collected and by whom, and how they will be analyzed and used. The consultant acts as a catalyst and facilitator in identifying organizational goals and objectives. He or she does not force opinions on the group because experience shows that no two organizations are alike, even if they have similar missions and goals. A realistic time frame, realistically not less than six months but probably not more than a year for the initial plan, should be set for an initial strategic planning process. During that time, the team will need a number of concentrated periods of work to complete its charge.

Before the team or task force begins the strategic planning process, several basic questions need to have been adequately answered: Why plan strategically and, particularly, why at this point in the organization's life? Who should be involved, and how involved should they be? What does strategic thinking and planning entail, and what needs to be known beforehand? Is there understanding, among all the primary players, of the factors to be considered and how they relate to each other? What additional resources are needed, will they be available, and how long will it take? How will the process be implemented, and how will it be evaluated? What kind of support is likely to be forthcoming from the parent organization to facilitate success of the process? What factors are in place or likely to develop in the larger context, including the global environment, that will affect the end result?

The latter question can be answered using a formal process, such as environmental scanning or "looking around," the SWOT analysis (*S*trengths and *W*eaknesses within the organization, and *O*pportunities and *T*hreats from outside the organization) in order to develop strategies to deal with that external PEST (*P*olitical issues, including governmental institutions' attitude toward information services and information policies; *E*conomic force, looking at systems and general economic conditions and trends within and outside the country; *S*ocial forces, including the norms and values that characterize the local culture; and *T*echnological forces, developing software and hardware systems that are likely to have impact) change that is occurring or may occur in the near future. The review process views the environment in at least two ways:

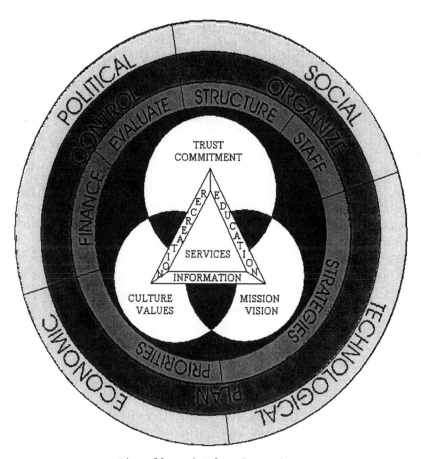

Rings of factors in Information Services

Figure 4.3. Political, Economic, Social, and Technological (PEST) Factors Impact Planning

♦ looking at the overlapping layers in the macro-environment—economic trends, inflation, demographics, and technological factors; the customer environment—who they are and what their needs are; and the internal environment—facilities, personnel resources, and structure of the organization. Positive and negative events inside and outside of the library or information services organization can influence changes in any or all of these categories; and

♦ looking at the micro-environment as a simple dichotomy: the external opportunities and constraints, factors identifiable in the opportunities and threats categories of PEST and internal analysis with strengths and weaknesses being identified—personnel, tasks to be done, finances available, and organizational structure, which is the second part of the SWOT analysis process. Both views help focus planning on the mission of the organization.

LOOKING AROUND

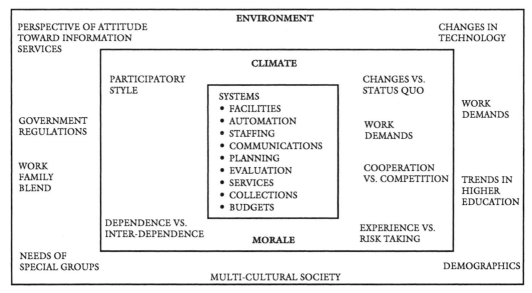

Figure 4.4. Looking Around Aspect of the Planning Process

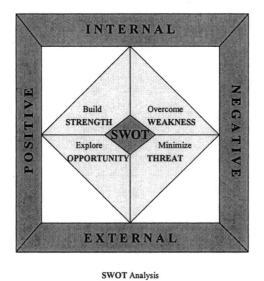

SWOT Analysis

Figure 4.5. Strengths, Weaknesses,
Opportunities, and Threats (SWOT)

Internal forces, identifiable in the strengths and weaknesses portion of a SWOT exercise, include facilities, technology, staffing, communications, and financial resources, all of which are tangible input factors, as well as intangible ones of morale, values, and style of management. All must be factored into the strategic thinking and planning process.

The external environmental scan and the internal self-analysis come together in the process to provide the focus for developing strategies and converting them into plans, policies, processes, and procedures.

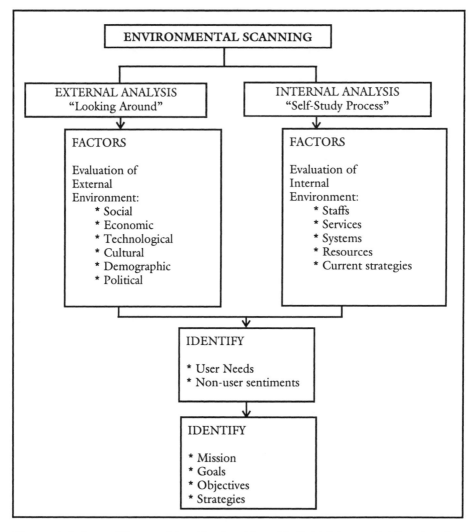

Figure 4.6. Several Factors Must Be Considered in Initial Strategic Planning Steps

The steps in the strategic planning process, after the planning team has been identified and the environmental scan and strengths/weaknesses exercise have been carried out, are to:

1. Identify the organizational culture and the values or assumptions that are the organization's guiding principles; this leads to creation of a vision statement that focuses on a better future by communicating enthusiasm and excitement.

2. Formulate the vision and mission statements that identify a distinctiveness.

3. Develop the goals and objectives.

4. Develop strategies and action plans. This requires identifying resource funds and developing policies and procedures to accomplish the objectives.

5. Implement the strategic plan.

6. Monitor, evaluate, and adjust the plan as objectives are accomplished and as priorities shift.

An initial strategic planning exercise, just as with planning of any magnitude, should be viewed as only the initial step in a continuous process. No plan, no matter how well formulated, can or will implement itself. It requires direction and commitment to succeed. Therefore, the final step in the cycle is one of monitoring, the evaluating and adjusting that is essential to the process. Following through with clearly developed implementation steps, measuring progress toward the goals, and incorporating feedback are a continuation of the process of planning. The greatest cause for failure of the process lies in poor execution of the plan, a lack of follow-through accompanied by a lack of commitment to see that it is accomplished or that adjustments are made so that it can be accomplished.

Planning Information Services

Values

In order for the process to proceed smoothly at the operational level, there should be a common understanding of the meanings of terms used in the strategic planning process. The vision, acceptable as an act of foresight, and values, accepted as principles intrinsically desirable, are inextricably tied together. They are set within a context of the future, envisioning changes that will affect systems and services. Values are usually stated in terms of respect for other people, their honesty and integrity, social responsibilities to society, and commitment to innovation and excellence in services. As examples: Miami University of Ohio Libraries' staff is "dedicated to providing quality library and information services. . . . In providing those services we value: the diversity of our clients and our own staff; equal and open access to information for all members of the Miami

University community; the intellectual freedom to pursue information and knowledge without censorship or reprisal; a current and balanced array of diverse information sources in a variety of formats; creating a welcoming environment for our clients and colleagues; respectful communication with our clients, regardless of their location, background or experience, through individual attention, active listening and unbiased, efficient assistance; sharing of our expertise through formal and informal instruction, with both individuals and groups; offering state-of-the-art equipment and services; exceeding the expectations of our clients. As colleagues we value: mutual courtesy and respect regardless of position or assignment; the contribution each individual can make to the organization; an environment characterized by cooperation, a strong work ethic, mutual recognition, meaningful rewards, collaboration and teamwork; innovation and continual improvement; honest, open, accurate and timely communication, internal and external; a flexible, well-managed organization; well-designed, ergonomic workspaces and facilities; a healthy sense of humor."[14]

Vision

Developing a vision statement requires drawing upon the imagination of a perfect world. A formal technique of "visioning" is used by some organizations to help develop vision statements as part of their strategic planning by examining and understanding all of the possibilities available for them to envision a scenario for the future. Vision focuses on the ultimate end result of an effort, not how to get there. As a guiding statement, it should answer the question "What is the preferred future for this organization?" For example, the vision statement of the California State University, Northridge, "is inspired by the belief that our commitment to educational opportunity, inclusion and excellence will extend the promise of America to succeeding generations. Our graduates will be the vanguard of leaders for the next century—committed to sustaining a democracy in which diverse people share in the rights and responsibilities of citizenship, proficient in applying technology to wise purposes, and dedicated to securing a humane world community and sustaining the bounty of the Earth. As an institution of higher learning, we will: be a high performing, model university in which student achievement levels are among the highest of peer universities; create a community of shared values in which faculty, students, staff, administrators, and alumni will experience personal satisfaction and pride in our collective achievements; be the first choice for university applicants who seek a rigorous, collaborative teaching/learning experience in a technologically rich environment; be the leader in enhancing the educational, cultural, and economic resources of our region; and receive local and national recognition for our distinctive achievement in teaching, learning, scholarship, and service,"[15]

> It is difficult enough for an individual to identify and describe accurately a personal vision for the future; it is even more difficult to create one for an organization. . . . However the journey or the process is as important as the goal.[16]
>
> —Peter Senge,
> *The Fifth Dimension*

The procedure of "visioning" seeks to create a compelling picture of a desirable future that represents quantum changes from the past. It has many critics who maintain that it can generate impractical and ungrounded concepts. When visioning focuses on generating a thoughtful vision statement, a process engaging people in the exploration of possibilities, it can be energizing and enlightening for an organization. It can help distance a library from a constrained view of the future and is a particularly powerful way of tying values to action.

The vision is the result of imagining a preferred future for the organization. It draws upon the beliefs and the environment of the organization that make the path toward satisfying the vision a realistic one. Simply stated, it should be an inspiring statement of the future, which can become the guide for actions and behaviors toward the accomplishment of the mission.

Following from the identified values and a vision for the future, the organization's mission, and other components necessary to accomplish it, can be more accurately stated. One of the difficulties in stating components in the strategic thinking and planning process is the confusion that exists in the terminology used. In the literature, objective is often used as a generic term variously referring to philosophy, vision, mission, purposes, goals, guiding principles, strategies, targets, quotas, policies, activities, and even deadlines. Because of the lack of consistency in the use of the terms, confusion arises. The hierarchy of activities in the strategic thinking and process include: preliminary SWOT analysis, with a PEST considerations component; value audit; vision statement; mission identification; goals development; objectives formulation; activities assignment; and the final performance audit.

To help clarify the terminology, at least for the purposes of this discussion, a chart of planning terminology (see Figure 4.7) has been devised to help in the strategic planning process.

A hierarchical process, yet integral relationship, exists among components after the vision has been articulated: the mission preceding goals, which precede objectives, which precede activities and strategies from which policies and procedures emanate. Each of these components builds on the lower one.

With those understandings, activities and policies can be developed and directed toward the achievement of the goals and objectives based upon mission, vision, and value formulation, through strategic thinking, and through strategy analysis. Clear formulation of all of those levels encourages consistent planning and decision making over the long term and at various levels of the knowledge-based organization. Unfortunately, sometimes parts of that whole exist in the thinking of management but are not made explicit by verbalizing and sharing them. Such a casual approach can lead to confusion, discouragement, and resistance. A great deal of energy can be expended on such faulty and secretive assumptions. It is difficult, if not impossible, to be accountable for achieving portions of a plan if they have not been clearly articulated and communicated.

Activity	a predetermined act toward achieving an objective
Action plan	a plan to achieve an initiative through actions and strategies
Aim	a determinant to a course of action
Aspiration	a strong desire for high achievement
Deadline	a time before which something must be done
Ethos	a guiding belief
Goal	a broad statement of purpose toward which effort is directed
Indicator	a measurement for success of an initiative
Initiative	a project that contributes to the achievement of a goal
Mission	a bold statement that takes the organization forward
Objective	a measurable action to be achieved
Outcome	an indicator of the success of an initiative
Performance	measure a benchmark for success
PEST factors	an environmental consideration of the political, economic, social, and technological factors influencing a plan
Philosophy	a viewpoint, a system of values
Plan	a method of achieving an end, implying mental formulation
Planning theme	a broad area within which action must be taken
Policy	a written guideline for action
Principle	an assumption
Priority	a ranking assigned to goals based on impact
Procedure	a particular way of accomplishing something
Purpose	an intention that derives from core values—reason for being
Quota	a production assignment
Strategic direction	an identified process for achieving stated goal
Strategy	a guide for making decisions
SWOT analysis	a process of examining strengths, weaknesses, opportunities and threats for the organization
Target	a desired goal to be achieved
Task	an assigned undertaking
Value audit	a process of identifying the vital organizational values
Values	a set of intrinsically desirable principles that govern
Vision	an overarching view of the future that is realistic

Figure 4.7. Planning Terminology

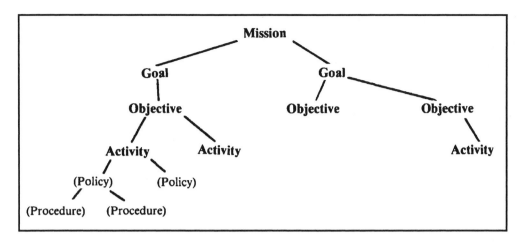

Figure 4.8. Strategic Planning Identifies Hierarchy of Interactive Goals, Objectives, and Activities

Mission

Identification of this broad service aspiration is the first step in the planning process. The mission statement is a short, succinct statement focusing on the purpose of the organization, its reason for existence, and what it hopes to accomplish. This overarching concept or principle guides the organization in establishing goals and developing strategies to achieve those goals. Defining its mission is the most important strategic step an organization can take. The effort is based upon the values and beliefs previously identified in the organization's vision. The mission statement should answer three primary questions: "Who (customers)?, What (services)? and How (activities)?" all focused by the previously answered question of "Why (the vision)?" A concise mission statement, for example, from Baltimore County, Maryland states that its "residents will have access to innovative library services, delivered in an efficient and effective manner, which will: Provide the information services needed to answer their questions; Support their ability to find and use information in a variety of formats; Provide the materials, programs and services needed to meet their recreational needs; Help prepare children to enter school ready to learn and then succeed in their studies; Assist everyone to continue to grow and learn throughout their lives."[17] In some expansive statements questions answering When? and Where? are added to guide future management decisions.[18]

Only by closely examining external forces and perceived constraints (political, economic, social, and technological) and by analyzing internal strengths and weaknesses can an effective mission statement be formulated. A clearly formulated, broadly discussed, and mutually accepted statement enables all parts of an organization to work toward common goals. Taken together, these can provide a focus for policy making and for management decisions of all types and all levels. After this has been answered, and the mission has been put into place in the strategic thinking of the organization, then quantitative and qualitative goals and objectives can be developed. This concise mission statement should be shared with all members of the organization, funding authorities, and supporters so that everyone understands and is committed to its principles. This reduces the possibilities of fragmentation and dissension, and the statement itself is an important marketing tool.

Of course, libraries and information centers are typically created with a mission of service. For public libraries, this mission has traditionally included education, information, and recreation or entertainment; and the library's services have emerged as a vehicle to accomplish a broader mission. In formulating goals, planners must go one step further by defining the overlap between the needs of the users and the physical and financial capabilities of the library or information center. This intersection is the foundation of the library's goals. Failure to identify concisely and correctly this common ground leads to the selection of goals—and later objectives and activities—that are unrelated and unrealistic, subject to false starts and ultimate failure. Likewise, it must be recognized that goals and objectives are likely to change over time and, therefore, must be viewed as flexible and changeable.

Some form of an organization's mission statement is often set forth in a charter, constitution and bylaws, annual report, or other authoritative pronouncements of the organization. Although one might assume that the mission will not change, it does, sometimes subtly, sometimes dramatically. Consider the Baltimore County (Maryland) system. Twenty-five years ago its mission was "to make readily available to the greatest possible number of county residents the most wanted library materials of all kinds, and to serve as a point of access for any needed information." Five years later, the mission statement had been changed to: "To make readily available to Baltimore County residents library materials and information services proportionate to levels of demand and use, and to provide access to materials and information outside the library system." The next system's mission statement was "to make readily available to Baltimore County residents library materials and information services in a cost-effective manner, proportionate to levels of demand and use, and to provide access to resources outside the library system," and in the current statement it is: "Baltimore County residents will have access to innovative library services, delivered in an efficient and effective manner, which will: Provide the information services needed to answer their questions; Support their ability to find and use information in a variety of formats; Provide the materials, programs and services needed to meet their recreational needs; Help prepare children to enter school ready to learn and then succeed in their studies; Assist everyone to continue to grow and learn throughout their lives."[19] To insure that a library or information center continues to respond appropriately to the changing environment, it should be obvious from this example that its mission should be reviewed periodically.

Goals

Goals are the organization's broad aspirations defined in operational terms, leading to measurable objectives with strategies and activities emanating from them. Goals provide direction and are intended to produce effectiveness. They also provide a framework for future planning and help motivate individuals. Goals must be flexible and are also subject to constant modification to reflect change. However, goals are not specific enough to be considered operational; therefore objectives and activities quantify goals. They are the basis for development and measures against which the success or failure of the plan can be determined. Goals are action-oriented in that they cannot be merely stated; action must follow in the form of objectives, which specify means of achieving the goals. Often, two types of goals function in an organization—stated goals and real goals. Although stated goals and real goals may be identical, sometimes they are different. If they are real goals, they will have an impact on the organization's policies, structure, operations, and, in general, on the behavior of people. The differences between stated goals and real goals are subtle and often financially driven. For instance, a library may want to offer bookmobile service (stated goal), but, if it does not adequately finance the operation, it cannot offer high-quality bookmobile service (real goal). As an example: The University of Iowa Libraries state one of several goals within the context of distinction for the library's services as: "Distinction: Providing leadership in the application of information technology in assuring access to resources, provision of services and creating greater efficiencies in all operations and activities throughout the library system; Goal 3: Maintain state of the art technology; Strategic Direction: Provide leadership in adopting new information technologies in support of information resources and services."[20]

Objectives and Strategies

Objectives can and should set the pattern for the structure of the organization and, therefore, must be action-oriented. The objectives cannot be viewed as passive but rather should provide direction as well as incentive toward achievement. Objectives can be conservative or expansive, but always should be stated in terms and conditions that stretch the enterprise. They are specific objectives to achieve goals that specify activities to be accomplished in order to achieve the vision. There is a real danger of setting objectives that are really hopes and not attainable ends or, on the other hand, so easily attainable that they are not challenging. In setting objectives, many things must be taken into account: the strengths of the library, the limitations of the library and how much can be accomplished with the financial and material resources available, and the objectives of the larger institution of which the library or information center is a part. Questions that must be addressed in the objective-setting exercise are:

- ◆ Is the objective suitable for this library/information center at this time?
- ◆ Does the objective help achieve the goal to which it is related?
- ◆ Does it take the organization in the direction it wants to go?
- ◆ Does it support the overall mission of the library/information center?
- ◆ Is it compatible and complementary with other objectives?
- ◆ Is it acceptable and understandable to the majority who will be charged with implementing it?
- ◆ Is it affordable for the organization?

♦ Is it measurable and achievable?

♦ Is it ambitious enough to be challenging?

The library or information center must be able to prove to both its staff and to the funding authority that the objectives are suitable, sustainable, and measurable. For example, one objective, in a previous plan of the Montgomery County (Maryland) Library System, was that within three years "85 percent of the residents of nursing homes, senior residential facilities, senior nutrition sites and facilities for the handicapped will be provided access to library materials and services through outreach to the facilities on a regularly scheduled basis." The concomitant reasoning they noted at that time was that there were "approximately 102 facilities . . . housing and serving those in the elder community who may find it difficult or impossible to utilize regular library services and programs. . . . Approximately 78 percent of the more than 3,800 households in continuing care/sheltered housing facilities for seniors presently have access to library services and materials. . . . Residents of all nursing homes . . . presently have access to library materials. . . . Ninety percent of the clients of nutrition sites and adult day care centers have access to programs and materials and 56 percent of the . . . clients of senior centers have access to outreach services at these centers."[21]

Elements involved in objectives formulation include:

♦ Clients—who they are and who they are not (with the potential of converting those who are not);

♦ Services—what new services are needed, which existing ones should be retained, and which should be deleted;

♦ Personnel resources—what professional and support skills are needed to provide identified services;

♦ Technological resources—what can be accessed when and where (many organizations are now instituting a separate strategic plan for technological development);

♦ Financial resources—what and where they are and how to maintain them; and

♦ Community responsibilities—the library's obligations as a social institution.

There should be a maximum degree of compatibility among goals and objectives if the organization is to achieve its mission. If an individual working in the organization does not see a relationship between his or her well-being and success, in regard to his/her own personal goals, and the well-being and success of the organization, then he or she is likely to have little motive to serve the objectives of the organization. It is also important to remember that many forces influence the process of planning and achieving goals; therefore, the process must be viewed from a number of perspectives. The three primary perspectives are:

1. Environmental, that is, considering constraints imposed on the organization by society in general;

2. Organizational, that is, considering the organization as an open system; and

3. Individual, that is, considering the personal goals of the individuals working in the organization.

A balance must be achieved between what is realistic and obtainable and what is challenging and idealistic but not necessarily completely attainable. As was mentioned under the goals discussion, the greatest problem in planning is bridging the gap between what is desirable (stated objectives) and what is possible (real objectives).

Unlike for-profit organizations, where the first objective is often to create the greatest profit base, most libraries and other information centers have among their primary objectives "the public good," that is, to pay adequate wages, to make the organization a good place in which to work, to provide a useful and needed service, and to attract a competent staff. Libraries and information centers, however, are responsible to higher authorities that may restrict those social objectives. Objectives can be forced upon libraries and information centers by the community, through social obligations, or by the employees, through collective bargaining or other means. Therefore, just as profit objectives in business organizations and their sometimes conflicting social objectives can dictate opposing courses that force compromise, so in information services organizations an individual's personal objectives and those of the organization as a whole can create conflict and sometimes force compromise.

Specific objectives can be departmental, unit, or team-based objectives or even short-range objectives of the whole organization. Most objectives are tangible or measurable, but others are not. For example, one objective may be to improve morale, but how can a person measure morale? Nonetheless, objectives should be stated in terms of activities that are in some way quantifiable and measurable.

Another challenge results from multiple service goals and related objectives with attempts to avoid any conflict in those activities. For example, when one examines the primary service goal of a university library, is it to provide needed curricular materials for students at the undergraduate level, or is it to provide materials that will allow faculty and graduate students to conduct research and advance the state of knowledge? Are they mutually exclusive? Can one be chosen over another? How does this relate to the mission of the organization?

Activities, Tasks, and Initiatives

These elemental tasks are directly related to the objectives and are a way of achieving the objectives. They are usually short-term, repetitive, measurable, and numerous at the operational level. They require effective policies and procedures to facilitate their achievement. Activities guide the everyday functioning of the organization, and in that sense are pragmatic and narrow. At the end of established time periods, reports are made to appropriate individuals and groups as to the progress and success. A fuller discussion of this aspect is covered in the later chapter on coordination.

Implementation of the Plan

Evaluation is vital to the strategic effort. Performance measures must be in place to measure the success of the effort and to indicate adjustments that may need to be incorporated in the plan. Once a strategic plan to achieve goals has been developed and objectives have been stated and approved, guidelines can be established for monitoring progress in terms of daily decision-making operations as well as guidelines for overarching decisions for policy making. Someone has to be responsible for monitoring progress toward each objective that has been established. A person or team is identified in relation to the success of each goal, and that person or team is responsible for developing a timeline for accomplishing the objective, identifying measures to evaluate progress, and establishing processes and procedures at the functional level. Individual strategies are assigned to one or more units or teams within the organization for execution, and these units in turn assign activities to individuals or specific sections of the unit. If this process is followed, the strategic plan can automatically be used at the functional level for decision making. This, of course, entails designating responsibilities for implementing the various steps in the planning process.

Ideally, each unit executes several plans simultaneously, making consistent progress toward several objectives in keeping with the established priorities. In practice, this may not always work effectively. By nature, some people tend to invest more time in fulfilling objectives related to their own particular interests, thus losing sight of the priorities established for the unit. For example, the priority objective of a catalog department may be to catalog all current, incoming materials as quickly as possible. Other objectives (such as getting rid of a backlog or reclassifying portions of the already classified collection) may take priority with some staff members, so the department falls behind in achieving its primary objective. In addition, unforeseen circumstances, such as the loss of a key person, can jeopardize the achievement of objectives or can, at least, force major revisions or delays.

Unfortunately, many people carry out tasks; they do not achieve objectives. Some employees do not even know the objectives of an organization. Ask that person what justifies their position, and they will nearly always answer by listing the work they do, the tasks they perform, or the machines they control or supervise. These individuals are concerned with means and methods and may be unable to describe the goals and objectives. Perhaps the main benefit of setting goals and objectives is to provide a new way to look at those jobs; it concentrates thought and gives a sense of purpose and commitment. Organizations with clear goals and objectives tend to have higher staff morale. Understanding those goals and objectives and their environment and actively participating in understanding them and carrying them out is the best assurance of loyalty to the plan of service. By developing a plan and establishing written goals and objectives and communicating them to the staff and the organization's customers, the organization encourages individuals to think through logical courses of action and provides a yardstick for decision making and ongoing activities. Such a planning exercise is the most effective way of measuring output for the organization.

Example of the Hierarchy of a Plan

An example of the hierarchy of mission to goals to objectives to activities is illustrated below from the strategic plan of Syracuse University Libraries. Only one example is selected from each of the elements in each component of the strategic plan—therefore they are selective examples (i.e., one of several planning themes; one of several goals). (See website for references to examples of full strategic plans.)

Purpose: To build and organize enduring accessible collections and to provide expert services which promote scholarship, learning, and discovery.

Vision: Our Vision of Syracuse University Library—its people, services, collections, and facilities—is of a nationally significant research library that understands the needs of its users and has actively developed the resources and methods to meet those needs now and in the future.

Mission: By 2005, we will transform the Library into the University's primary gateway for scholarly information. To accomplish this mission we must:

- ◆ develop and sustain a highly user-centered culture
- ◆ secure staff, facilities, technology, and funding that support and promote this new culture
- ◆ deliver information literacy programs that enable effective use of our services, collections and resources

Planning Theme 2: User services provide and promote expert user services that are available at the time and place of need. The following goals and initiatives focus on this critical area:

Goal 2.1: Information literacy provides every SU student with the opportunity to acquire information literacy skills.

Rationale: Information literacy contributes to lifelong learning, which is increasingly necessary for success in today's world. Library staff have unique expertise in information access and evaluation and in providing information literacy instruction. We must enhance collaborative efforts with faculty to this end.

Success indicator 2.1: Increase in the number of integrated instruction sessions courses.

Initiatives 2.1.2: Focus the Information Literacy Program on efforts to increase librarian/ faculty member collaboration and conducting a broader range of course-integrated instruction campus-wide.

Figure 4.9. Syracuse University Library Strategic Plan 2000–2005 (modified November 2001)[22]

Technology—An Important Factor

As libraries and information centers plan strategies for the future, one of the most important components is developing a strategy that anticipates technological needs and integrates that into the planning process. Technology is the major force in changing library and information services today, and it is recognized that it continues to outpace humankind's ability to envision how it can be most effectively used. Additionally, the lifetime of a technological innovation is reduced by the constant upgrade of both hardware and software.

Technology planning, as an important component in the strategic planning process, helps translate the library's vision and mission into options and actions. A reasoned approach to technology planning would require establishing standards, norms, and methods for evaluating, purchasing, implementing, and using technology, including hardware, other equipment, software, and staff training. Assuming that such a plan is already in place or is progressing simultaneously, a technology component should be articulated and integrated into the strategic plan.

> Successful technology application for information services is based on its fit to actual needs, as well as realistic expectations of what can be accomplished using technology. The way to achieve this is through proper strategic planning.[23]
>
> —Richard P. Hulser,
> "Integrating Technology into Strategic Planning"

The challenge is to develop scenarios based upon realistic assessments of technology's potential and how it can be integrated into good information services. The best way to do this is through the strategic planning process, involving both staff and stakeholders in the process. Experience has shown that such a team-based approach ensures greater success in technology's integration into the vision of information services. In the "looking-around" aspect of the environmental scan and the SWOT analysis, clients, customers, patrons, users, or other stakeholders and their needs will already have been identified. Identifying how technology applies in satisfying their needs is therefore paramount to successful mission accomplishment. Because technology plays such an important role in information services, planning its integration is embedded in almost every aspect of strategic planning processes (see examples of strategic plans on the websites listed). If one examines the "objectives" statements in many strategic plans, one clearly sees how technology is integrated into the overall strategic planning process. Technological consideration in the strategic plan is also a good point to reexamine policies and procedures, particularly relating to access of information.

As an example of this integration, West Virginia University sets forth the following five strategic directions for its "Framework for an Information Technology Superstructure": "1) Engage the Student; 2) Empower the Faculty; 3) Infuse the Curriculum; 4) Enhance Research Capabilities; and 5) Fulfill Our Duty to Serve."

Marketing—A Necessary Strategic Component

Once the strategic plan has been developed, the plan itself can serve as an important tool for communication and marketing within the community. This thought will have been built into the plan at the very beginning by involving the whole community in the planning process and, thereby, encouraging everyone to buy into the outcome. The strategic planning process has not only identified goals and objectives but also the means by which the library will accomplish them. Perhaps the most important component is that of assuring or reassuring customers that their needs, identified in the process, will be met. That fact is translated into terms that everyone can understand in a marketing process. This requires special focus on a communication plan to promote those priorities of information services. A comprehensive marketing program, of course, encompasses not just the strategic plan, but because the major components of "what we are here for" have been identified in the plan, it makes sense to extensively market the goals and objectives of the plan, as the showpiece of the wide range of activities that are involved in meeting the needs of customers and giving value to those efforts. In that sense, marketing components must be obvious in every aspect of the plan; otherwise, once a service is identified, how do customers know it exists? Viewing strategic planning and marketing in the same context adds strength to both components and recognizes marketing as an important management tool.

Marketing the strategic plan presents the opportunity to move from the "push" mentality of persuasion to a "pull" mentality of identifying what is needed, a process that has been carried out in the strategic planning process. It involves all of the elements already discussed under strategic thinking and planning. For instance, when thinking about an environmental scan (SWOT, with its PEST component), a marketing audit would have been included in the community analysis component. Therefore the marketing audit and planning process must be bundled together in a single process in order to reach a successful comprehensive planning outcome.[24]

Conclusion

Strategic planning is the most popular approach, in today's knowledge-based organizations, to define the organization's reason for being and mission. Because the planning process can be a costly proposition, improper selection or faulty specification of objectives wastes planning time and money, results in frustration, and renders the entire planning activity futile. Every library needs to spell out its own goals and objectives, instead of relying on those of other organizations, because those components determine the policy, procedures, and organizational structure of the library or information center. Planning represents the beginning of a process upon which other principles are based.

Notes

1.   Henry Mintzberg, *The Rise and Fall of Strategic Planning* (Upper Saddle River, NJ: Prentice-Hall, 1994), 333.

2.   Stuart Wells, "To Plan, Perchance, To Think; Aye, There's the Rub," *Information Outlook* 5 (September 2001): 10–11.

3.   Ronald Lippitt, "Futuring Before You Plan," in R.A. Ritvo and A. G. Sargent, *The NTL Managers' Handbook* (Arlington, VA: NTL Institute, 1983).

4.   Edward R. Johnson, "Academic Library Planning, Self-Study, and Management Review," in Charles R. McClure, ed., *Planning for Library Services* (New York: Haworth Press, 1982), 72.

5.   Arthur Langley, "The Role of Formal Strategic Planning," *Long Range Planning* 21 (1988): 48.

6.   American Library Association, *Library Bill of Rights* (adopted June 18, 1948) *with Amendments* (Chicago: American Library Association).

7.   Nancy Bolt, "Critical Issues in Library Management" in *Organizing for Leadership and Decision Making* (Urbana, IL: GSKIS, University of Illinois [35th Allerton Institute], 1995), 64.

8.   Benjamin B. Tregue and John W. Zimmerman, "Strategic Thinking," *Management Review* 68 (February 1979): 10–11.

9.   Richard Cyert, "Designing a Creative Organization," in *Handbook for Creative Managers* (New York: McGraw-Hill, 1988), 186.

10.   Peter M. Senge, *The Fifth Discipline: The Art & Practice of the Learning Organization* (New York: Doubleday, 1990).

11.   David Garvin, "Building a Learning Organization," *Harvard Business Review* 78 (July/August 1993): 80.

12.   *Ibid.*

13.   Richard DeGennaro, "Shared Understanding," in *Harvard College Library 1995* (Cambridge, MA: The Harvard College Library, 1995).

14.   Miami University Library. *Preserving the Past, Embracing the Future.* 2000–2004 Strategic Plan. www.lib.muohio.edu/libinfo/strategic/Intro.html.

15.   California State University Northridge–Strategic Plan www.library.csun.edu/susan.curzon /stratpln.html.

16.   Peter Senge, *The Fifth Dimension* (New York: Doubleday, 1990), 89.

17.   Baltimore County Public Library Strategic Plan, www.bcplonline.org/libpg/lib_facts.html.

18.   Benjamin B. Tregue and John W. Zimmerman, *Top Management Strategy: What It Is and How to Make It Work* (New York: Simon & Schuster, 1980).

19.   Baltimore County website, www.bcplonline.org/libpg/lib_facts.html.

20.   University of Iowa Libraries–Strategic Plan 2000–2004 (rev. March 2001), www.lib.uiowa .edu/admin/strategic-plan.html.

21.   "Public Services Plan for Public Libraries in Montgomery County, MD," FY93-88 (Montgomery County Government, Rockville, MD, May 1982), 4, 6.

22.   Syracuse University Libraries–Targets for Transformation: Strategic Plan for Syracuse University Library 2000–2005, www.syr.edu/information/strategicplan.

23.   Richard P. Hulser, "Integrating Technology into Strategic Planning," *Information Outlook* 2 (February 1998): 24.

24.   Darlene E, Weingand, *Marketing/Planning Library and Information Services,* 2d ed. (Englewood, CO: Libraries Unlimited, 1999).

Section 3: Organizing

The planning and organizing functions are closely linked. The planning process described in the previous section helps an organization define its goals and objectives. After these are established, the next function of management is to design an organizational structure that will facilitate the achievement of those goals and objectives. Organizing involves determining what tasks are to be done, who is to do them, how the tasks are to be grouped, and how all the tasks are to be coordinated. So organizing divides an organization into smaller, more manageable units and makes the work done in each unit compatible with that done in the others. As a result of organizing, the structure of the organization is formed.

In this section, the component pieces of the organizing process are examined. Ways in which the organization is broken apart (specialization) as well as the ways in which the organization is brought back together (coordination) will be discussed. Various aspects of organizing, covering the *why*, *how*, and *when*—why organizing is important, how to choose the most appropriate structure, and when reorganization should be considered—are examined. The classic theories of organization are covered in addition to more contemporary views on the topic. Finally, the different types of organizational structures that libraries and other information agencies have adopted are examined.

Readings

Ashkenas, Ronald. *The Boundaryless Organization: Breaking the Chains of Organizational Structure*. San Francisco: Jossey-Bass, 1995.

Belbin, Meredith. *The Coming Shape of Organization*. Oxford: Butterworth-Heinemann, 1996.

Burns, Tom, and G. M. Stalker. *The Management of Innovation*. London: Tavistock, 1966.

Chilton, Kenneth, Murray Weidenbaum, and Robert Batterson. *The Dynamic American Firm*. Boston: Kluwer Academic Publishers, 1996.

Collins, Jim. *Good to Great: Why Some Companies Make the Leap . . . And Others Don't*. New York: Harper Business, 2001.

Davenport, Thomas H. *Process Innovation: Re-engineering: Work Through Information Technology* Boston: Harvard Business School Press, 1993.

Davenport, Thomas H., and Laurence Prusak. *Working Knowledge: How Organizations Manage What They Know*. Boston: Harvard Business School Press, 1998.

Deevy, Edward. *Creating the Resilient Organization*. Englewood Cliffs, NJ: Prentice-Hall, 1995.

Drucker, Peter F. *Managing the Non-Profit Organization*. New York: HarperCollins, 1990.

Eustis, Joanne D., and Donald J. Kenney. *Library Reorganization and Restructuring* (SPEC Kit 215). Washington, DC: Association of Research Libraries, 1996.

Evans, Philip, and Thomas S. Wurster. *Blown to Bits: How the New Economics of Information Transforms Strategy*. Boston: Harvard Business School Press, 2000.

Fritz, Robert. *Corporate Tides: The Inescapable Laws of Organizational Structure*. San Francisco: Berrett-Koehler, 1996.

Galbraith, Jay R. *Designing Organizations: An Executive Guide to Strategy, Structure, and Process Revised*. San Francisco: Jossey-Bass, 2001.

Gates, Bill, with Collins Hemingway. *Business @ the Speed of Thought: Using a Digital Nervous System*. New York: Warner Books, 1999.

Gomez-Meija, Luis R., and Michael W. Lawless, eds. *Organizational Issues in High Technology Management*. Greenwich, CT: JAI Press, 1990.

Hackman, J. Richard, and Greg R. Oldham. *Work Redesign*. Reading, MA: Addison-Wesley, 1980.

Hammer, Michael, and James Champy. *Reengineering the Corporation: A Manifesto for Business Revolution*. New York: HarperBusiness, 1993.

Howard, Jennifer, and Laurence Miller. *Team Management: Creating Systems and Skills for a Team-Based Organization*. Atlanta, GA: Miller Howard, 1994.

Kanter, Rosabeth Moss, Barry A. Stein, and Todd D. Jick. *The Challenge of Organizational Change: How Companies Experience It and Leaders Guide It*. New York: Free Press, 1992.

Kotter, John P., and James L. Heskett. *Corporate Culture and Performance*. New York: Free Press, 1992.

Lawler, Edward E., III. *From the Ground Up: Six Principles for Building the New Logic Corporation.* San Francisco: Jossey-Bass, 1996.

Martin, Lowell A. *Organizational Structure of Libraries.* rev. ed. Lanham, MD: Scarecrow Press, 1996.

Mintzberg, Henry. *The Structuring of Organizations: A Synthesis of the Research.* Englewood Cliffs, NJ: Prentice-Hall, 1979.

Morhman, Susan A., Jay R. Galbraith, and Edward E. Lawler III. *Tomorrow's Organization: Crafting Winning Capabilities in a Dynamic World.* San Francisco: Jossey-Bass, 1998.

Nadler, David A., and Michael Tushman. *Competing by Design: The Power of Organizational Architecture.* New York: Oxford University Press, 1997.

Osborne, David, and Ted Gaebler. *Reinventing Government: How the Entrepreneurial Spirit Is Transforming the Public Sector.* Reading: MA: Addison-Wesley, 1993.

Palmer, Ian, and Cynthia Hardy. *Thinking About Management: Implications of Organizational Debates for Practice.* London: Sage Publications, 2000.

Pasternack, Bruce A., and Albert J. Viscio. *The Centerless Corporation: A New Model for Transforming Your Organization for Growth and Prosperity.* New York: Simon & Schuster, 1998.

Pearson, Gordon. *The Competitive Organization: Management for Organizational Excellence.* New York: McGraw-Hill, 1992.

Schein, Edgar H. *The Corporate Culture Survival Guide.* San Francisco: Jossey-Bass, 1999.

———. *Organizational Culture and Leadership.* 2d ed. San Francisco: Jossey-Bass, 1992.

Tushman, Michael L., and Charles A. O'Reilly III. *Winning Through Innovation: A Practical Guide to Leading Organizational Change and Renewal.* Boston: Harvard Business School Press, 1997.

Chapter 5

Organizations and Organizational Culture

By now, however, it should have become clear that there is no such thing as the one right organization. There are only organizations, each of which has distinct strengths, distinct limitations and specific applications. It has become clear that organization is not an absolute. It is a tool for making people productive in working together. As such, a given organizational structure fits certain tasks in certain conditions and at certain times.[1]

—Peter F. Drucker,
"Management's New Paradigms"

There is a close link between the planning and the organizing functions of management. First, managers plan in order to establish the organization's goals and objectives. Then managers organize to provide a structure that will allow the organization to achieve its strategic objectives. Today, managers in both for-profit and not-for-profit organizations are very attentive to the organizing function because the structure of the organization is seen as a key element in making an organization successful. It is essential for both managers and nonmanagers to understand the function of organizing. Although most of the decisions about organizing are made by upper-level managers (often with the input of mid-level managers), all employees work within an organizational structure, and it is important to know why the organization is shaped as it is. In addition, most organizations today face rapidly changing environments, and it is often necessary for organizations to change their structures. An understanding of organizing as a managerial function will help employees to understand both the organization they are working in now and the structure of the one they may be employed in tomorrow.

As the name implies, *organizing* provides shape and structure to the organization. Organizing involves looking at all the tasks that have to be done and deciding how they will be done and by whom. Organizing has long been central to the study of management. The classical management writers such as Henri Fayol provided more guidelines and principles about organizing than to any other managerial function. These classical writers viewed an organizational structure as a lasting entity. Their overall perception was that organizations were stable structures, almost always arranged in hierarchical fashion, with the power flowing in an orderly fashion from the individuals at the top of the hierarchy to those below.

As Henry Mintzberg has written:

> It probably would not be an exaggeration to claim that the vast majority of everything that has been written about management and organization over the course of this century . . . has had as its model, usually implicitly, [this] form of organization. With its dominant vertical hierarchy, sharp divisions of labor, concentration on standardization, obsession with control, and of course, appreciation of staff functions in general and planning in particular [this] type has always constituted the "one best way" of management literature.[2]

One of the most striking changes in management in the past decades has been a rethinking of organizational structure. Much of this rethinking has been forced on managers by rapid changes in the environment, especially increasing competition and the growing importance of computerized information in all types of organizations. The old conventions about organizational stability have been challenged and discarded in many types of organizations, including libraries and information centers.

> Recent interest in various new organizational forms has meant that managers today are bombarded with a plethora of design solutions that purportedly solve a host of organizational problems. They are told to de-layer and downsize; to re-engineer, restructure and rightsize; to be fast and flexible; to empower and collaborate; and to dismantle hierarchy, bureaucracy, and boundaries. . . . Organizational structure is acknowledged to be a key strategic variable and problem-solving device in meeting contemporary management challenges.[3]
>
> —Ian Palmer and Cynthia Hardy,
> *Thinking About Management*

In an attempt to become more efficient and effective, organizations have begun to change their structures. Hierarchies have been flattened by the removal of layers of middle managers. The new model of organization being touted by management experts is flexible and adaptable to change, has relatively few levels of formal hierarchy, and has loose boundaries among functions and units.[4] Many of these new organizations employ teams of workers who work together on a specific task on a semipermanent or permanent basis.

Libraries, like other organizations, are restructuring in response to changes in their external environments. But, unlike many other organizations, libraries have an additional compelling reason to reorganize. Over the past few decades, libraries have evolved from organizations where traditional print resources predominate into ones where the traditional resources co-exist with digital electronic resources. Today's libraries are hybrids containing both print-based and electronic materials with the proportion of electronic resources in most libraries increasing year by year.[5] Users who once expected to have to come to the libraries to gain access to resources now expect access to much material to be available through electronic gateways both inside and outside the library. Libraries now are as much about access to materials as the materials themselves. It is not surprising then that libraries, which have always been structured to provide onsite access to print resources, need to change their organizational patterns.

What organizational structure is best suited for the new hybrid library? As will be seen in this section, there is no one answer to that question. At the present time there is a growing interest in organizational structure, and many librarians are actively engaged in looking for a way to restructure their organizations to answer the challenge presented by the change from print-based to digital materials. What is required for this transformation? What organization best suits the new reality of libraries? In this section, various approaches that libraries have taken and are taking to organizing will be discussed.

Before discussing organizing, it is important to understand what organizations are. We live in a world that is full of organizations of many types. All of these organizations share certain characteristics.

What an Organization Is

What are organizations? One definition is that organizations are goal-directed, boundary-maintaining, and socially constructed systems of human activity.[6] Let us examine that definition a bit more closely. Organizations are socially constructed, that is, they are deliberately formed by humans. They are goal directed, which means that they are purposive systems in which members attempt to achieve a certain set of goals. They are boundary maintaining, that is, there is distinction between members of that organization and nonmembers, which sets organizations off from their environments. Those boundaries are almost always permeable because organizations are affected by their environments.

Organizations are the basic building blocks of modern society. The development of organizations is inevitable in any complex culture because of the limitations of individuals. When a single person cannot do all the work that needs to be done, there is no choice but to organize and to use more people to accomplish the task. There are many types of organizations, and they vary greatly in size and in purpose. Although they differ in many ways, the local Rotary Club, the Little League baseball team, and Microsoft are all organizations.

> An organization is a human group, composed of specialists, working together on a common task. Unlike society, community, or family—the traditional social aggregates—an organization is purposefully designed and grounded neither in the psychological nature of human beings nor in biological necessity. Yet, while a human creation, it is meant to endure—not perhaps forever, but for a considerable period of time.[7]

Throughout most of human history, organizations have played a less important role in people's lives than they do now. For instance, over the past 200 years, the United States has changed from a country where almost all workers were self-employed, either as farmers or independent craftspeople, into one in which almost all workers are employed by organizations. Even as recently as the beginning of the twentieth century, farmers constituted more than one-third of the total U.S. workforce.[8] Today, most people spend their work life as one employee among many others working in an organization.

Organizations are, therefore, groups of individuals joined together to accomplish some objective. But organizations are more than an aggregation of individuals. Organizations have characteristics of their own, over and above the characteristics of the people who make them up. For example, organizations have a distinct structure; they have rules and norms that have developed over time; they have a life cycle that goes beyond the lives of individuals; and they usually have goals, policies, procedures, and practices. They exist in an environment that affects many of these characteristics. They are likely engaged in processing some kind of input and turning it into an output. They interact with other organizations, and they have to change internally to keep up with external pressures.[9]

Although there are many organizations in existence in the modern world, most are quite small. In the United States, the Small Business Administration has estimated that about ninety percent of the approximately five million businesses employed fewer than twenty workers. A similar size distribution is seen in the European Union.[10] Libraries display the same type of size distributions: There are many small libraries and a few very large ones. According to the latest American Library Association statistics, there are approximately 122,000 libraries in the United States, and almost 100,000 of these are school libraries. These libraries employ approximately 385,000 people, about one-third of whom are classified as librarians.[11]

Organizations, like people, have life cycles: They come into existence, they grow and become mature. They may flourish for a while but then usually begin to decline and often die. Although some organizations such as the Roman Catholic Church, the Icelandic Parliament, and some universities have been in existence for a long time, most organizations are short-lived, coming and going in a much shorter time period than the humans who formed them.[12] If they wish to continue to exist, organizations have to adapt to meet changing conditions.

The environment in which organizations function has become more competitive and complex, so, as mentioned earlier, many of these entities have begun to experiment with changing their organizational structure. Not surprisingly, most of this restructuring of organizations has occurred in the corporate world, the sector that usually leads the way in organizational transformation. Publicly supported organizations, including libraries, have been slower to change and move away from the traditional organizational structures. But although libraries and other information centers as a whole have not been as radically altered as organizations in the private sector, they have begun to reshape and restructure. Although a few libraries have completely revamped their organizational structure, so far, however, the reorganization in most libraries has been "incremental rather than dramatic."[13]

The need to examine and perhaps reshape the organizational structure is as imperative in libraries as in other organizations. As was discussed in chapter 1, fast-paced change is certainly a part of the environment of all types of libraries. Libraries have undergone vast changes in the past few decades. The changes have led managers in all types of libraries, like managers in other types of organizations, to consider possible restructuring. Many of the same forces that have resulted in the reshaping of other types of organizations have also affected libraries and information centers: increased automation, reduction in budgets, changing information needs and expectations of users, and the need for staff to have more autonomy and control over their work.[14] The boundaries of many libraries, like other organizations, have become more permeable or "fuzzy" as they have collaborated with other libraries in joint ventures, such as statewide licensing consortia, and as they have used outsourcing as a means to attain from outside sources goods and services that they once produced in-house. The traditional structure of the library is being affected by all these changes as libraries make the transition from a paper-based book world to a world of digital materials. As librarians have had to reconsider their systems and the roles their libraries play, they have also had to reexamine the organizational structure of the library itself.

The critical task for management in each revolutionary period is to find a new set of organizing practices that will become the basis for managing the next period of evolutionary growth. Interestingly enough, these new practices eventually sow the seeds of their own decay and lead to another period of revolution. Managers therefore experience the irony of seeing a major solution in one period becoming a major problem in a later period.[15]

There are no pat answers about the way libraries or any other organization should be structured. But wise managers are exploring the options. Clinging to the organizational structure that worked well yesterday may mean that an organization cannot meet the challenges of either today or tomorrow.

Organizational Structure

The terms *organization* and *organizational structure* are often used interchangeably, but more precise definitions are available. The *organization* is the group of individuals joined together to achieve an objective. An organizational structure (sometimes called an organizational design) results from the organizing process and is the system of relations, formally prescribed and informally developed, that governs the activities of people who are dependent on each other for accomplishment of common objectives.

Organizational structure is one of the interrelated components that define any organization. *Structure* refers to the definition of individual jobs and their relationship to each other as depicted on organization charts and job descriptions. An organization's structure is the source of how responsibility is distributed, how individual positions are coordinated, and how information is officially disseminated. When an organization's structure is changed, the process is referred to as *restructuring* or *reorganization.*

Because the structure of organizations is created by people, it should in no way be considered permanent, fixed, or sacred. Traditionally, many managers have been reluctant to alter an organizational structure once it has been established. This may be due to fear of change or failure to recognize that new activities necessitate new or modified organizational structures. It has been said that most of the organizations existing today were created to meet goals and objectives that no longer exist for those organizations. For managers to continue to use an old organizational structure to achieve new goals and objectives results in inefficiency, duplication of endeavor, and confusion. In a period when there is little competition or when changes in the outside environment are occurring slowly, it is possible to get by with an outdated organizational structure, but when competition becomes more intense and the environment more turbulent, an outdated structure will lead to problems.

It is not easy to develop an organizational structure that provides for the efficient achievement of planned goals and objectives. And, as organizational structures get larger and involve more people, more complex problems are encountered. The organizational structure must provide for the identification and grouping of similar or related activities necessary for achieving the organization's goals and objectives; it must permit the assignment of these activities to appropriate units of the emerging organization. It must provide for the coordination of activities under a manager and the delegation of authority and responsibility necessary for the manager to carry out the assigned activities.

Even in the corporate world there is much indecision about reorganization and the best type of structure. As Robert Johansen and Rob Swigart write: "We have outlived the usefulness of models from the industrial era but don't yet have robust organizational models for the information era."[16]

> Business organizations are changing, whether they want to or not. The changes are chaotic—the experience from inside or close to a large corporation, as well as the feeling inside your stomach. The pyramids of corporate strength have flattened into a web of organizational ambiguity. Individual employees no longer have a sturdy structure to climb. Instead, planning a career is more like crawling out on a webbing of rope, grasping for stability that comes and goes quickly.[17]
>
> —Robert Johansen and Rob Swigart,
> *Upsizing the Individual in the Downsized Organization*

In the 1990s many organizations tried to restructure following the principles of business process reengineering (BPR). BPR was the latest of a long line of managerial reforms adopted by businesses in an effort to make organizations more effective and efficient. Two books published in the early 1990s, *Process Innovation Re-engineering:*

Work Through Information Technology[18] and *Reengineering the Corporation: A Manifesto for Business,*[19] triggered the explosive interest in BPR, and organizations all over the world started to "reengineer."

As the name implies, business process reengineering consists of rethinking and transforming organizational processes through the use of information technologies to achieve major improvements in quality, performance, and productivity. BPR is not for the timid; it is radical and difficult to implement. It does not involve gradual change; instead it calls for the total overhaul of an organization. According to Michael Hammer and James Champy, BPR is "the fundamental rethinking and radical redesign of business processes to achieve dramatic improvements in critical, contemporary measures of performance such as quality, service, and speed."[20] One of the results of reengineering was a change in organizational structure as a result of the rethinking of processes.

Although BPR was heavily used in the 1990s, in the past few years even some of the strongest early advocates of BPR have backed away and begun to point out some of its problems. Many of these difficulties resulted from a misunderstanding of the purpose of BPR. Undoubtedly, one of the reasons BPR was so popular when introduced was because of the generally adverse economic conditions of the early 1990s. Management literature was full of dire predictions of what would happen to companies that did not become more cost-efficient in the face of global competition. Many of the organizations that adopted BPR did so primarily as a cost-saving measure, and in numerous cases BPR was used as an excuse to reduce the number of employees. Managers thus were able to avoid taking direct responsibility for making staff redundant—they could argue that these cuts were required by the reengineering effort.[21] Many organizations claimed to be reengineering when their primary purpose was reducing headcount, so in the eyes of many BPR became inextricably linked with downsizing and layoffs.

BPR also fell from favor because it seemed to devalue people. Reengineering often resulted in a demoralization of the organization's staff, especially when the employees did not understand or had little input into the organizational changes. From the employee's point of view, it seemed that the organization's structure was far more important than the people who worked there. Even Thomas Davenport, one of the creators of BPR, called it a failed process: "The rock that re-engineering foundered on is simple: people. Re-engineering treated the people inside companies as though they were just so many bits and bytes, interchangeable parts to be re-engineered."[22] As more and more business organizations reported problems with the process, BPR began to fade from use, at least in the U.S. corporate sector.

However, it would be foolish to ignore the real benefits associated with BPR. BPR as originally designed and sold to organizations had flaws, but many of its underlying concepts were sound. Properly designed processes (e.g., how work is carried out) are vitally important to the success of any organization. Periodically, all organizations do need to examine both the need for and the design of their processes. Any organization that ignores the need to change and improve its processes is risking its future. The pace of change in all organizations, including libraries, is accelerating, and most are experiencing increased competition. Information technology has been widely adopted and should be permitting people to do their jobs in different and better ways. Organizations cannot continue to use yesterday's processes or organizational structures if they want to be in business tomorrow.

Although a number of libraries used some of the principles of BPR in redesigning their internal processes,[23] none followed all of its principles. Instead, most libraries that have reorganized have done so by keeping at least some of the previous structure while making incremental changes in departments and subunits. Libraries and information centers currently are organized in a variety of ways, ranging from very flat to traditional hierarchical organizations. Although libraries and information centers may have many different structures, each may be appropriate; having different structures does not necessarily mean that some are right and some are not. As this section will show, there is no optimum way to organize and no consistent prescription for the best type of organizational structure. Although the trend now is toward flatter structures, it is not true that they are always superior to more hierarchical ones. Traditional hierarchies do work best in some situations, whereas flatter structures are more suitable in others. As in so many other areas of management, the best organizational structure depends on the circumstances in a specific case.

Organizational theorists have moved away from a prescriptive approach and now agree that there is no one best answer. They urge the organization to think about what it hopes to accomplish and to adopt the type of organizational structure that allows it to best achieve its goals. The question then becomes, "which organization design performs better in a particular market and location, and which design best enhances the company's core competencies. . . . The executive's operating focus becomes how to create congruency—the fit among all organizational components consistent to the chosen organization design—so that the organization is the most efficient."[24]

> I have long believed that there is no ideal library organization, and that a finite number of possible permutations exists, each with the potential to be effective in a given situation.[25]
>
> —Joanne R. Euster et al.,
> "Reorganizing for a Changing Information World"

But restructuring is a difficult task. Often organizations have restructured to solve one problem, but the new structure inadvertently created many more. There are no easy answers to how organizations should be designed, but managers of all types should be addressing the question of the most appropriate structure for their organization.

Getting Started with Organizing

One of the most important aspects of organization is choosing the design of the enterprise, both its structure and the allocation of the jobs. As long as the work to be accomplished in an enterprise can be done by one person, there is little need to organize. But as soon as an enterprise grows so that more than one worker is necessary, decisions must be made about its organization.

> As managers move up the hierarchy, and/or as the size of their organization grows, they become more concerned with the issues of organizational design. . . . Managers are concerned with three related goals when they make design decisions: 1) To create an organization design that provides a permanent setting in which managers can influence individuals to do their particular jobs. 2) To achieve a pattern of collaborative effort among individual employees, which is necessary for successful operations. 3) To create an organization that is cost effective.[26]

Most organizations need little structure when they are first started because they are small. There are advantages in small organizations: they are flexible, fairly inexpensive to maintain, and have clear accountability. When OCLC (then the Ohio College Library Center) was founded in 1967, the organization consisted of Frederick G. Kilgour and one secretary. The people at OCLC in its earliest days probably gave little thought to formal organizational structure. When organizations are small, there is less need for organizational structure because decisions can be made by just a few people, and communication can be very informal. But, if an organization is successful and grows larger, the need for a formal structure becomes more critical. There is a need to have written policies and guidelines and to divide the responsibilities and the authority for decision-making. OCLC now employs a large number of people and has operations worldwide. As OCLC expanded and grew into a global organization, its managers needed to think about how to organize the corporation so it could achieve its goals and objectives. Today, OCLC's organizational structure reflects the larger, more complex corporation it has become.

Some organizations remain small and never get to the point where they have to think seriously about organizational structure. For instance, a small public library with a handful of employees will be able to remain relatively informal in its organizational structure. But, every organization that grows reaches the point where a formal organizational structure becomes essential, and those that don't implement a structure will not be able to make a successful transition from a small to a large organization.

> Few successful start-ups become great companies in large part because they respond to growth and success in the wrong way. Entrepreneurial success is fueled by creativity, imagination, bold moves into uncharted waters and visionary zeal. As a company grows and becomes more complex, it begins to trip over its own success—too many new people, too many new customers, too many new orders, too many new products. What was once great fun becomes an unwieldy ball of disorganized stuff.[27]

Library and information agencies reflect the same increasing complexity of organization as they grow larger. For example, consider the case of a small, special library in a fast-growing corporation. When the library is first established, one librarian may be sufficient to perform all the tasks associated with operating the library, including acquisitions, cataloging, reference, interlibrary loan, and online searching. But as the parent corporation grows larger and the demand for information supplied by the library increases, more employees are needed. Now decisions must be made about the organization of that library. The expanded library and its new employees could be structured in many ways. The task of the manager is to try to establish the most effective and efficient structure. It is possible that each employee could do a portion of all the tasks that need to be done, with each one spending some time doing acquisition, reference, cataloging, and so forth. More likely, however, the work will be divided in such a way that each employee will specialize, at least to some extent, in one or more of the tasks that have to be performed.

Since the publication of Adam Smith's *The Wealth of Nations* more than 200 years ago, it has been recognized that division of labor leads to greater efficiency. Smith believed that a nation's wealth could be increased if organizations used a high degree of worker specialization. Instead of having one individual complete an entire job, the job is broken up into its component parts, and each discrete part of the job is completed by a different individual. Smith described one factory in which pins were produced. In this factory, 10 workers produced as many as 48,000 pins a day. The task of making a pin was subdivided into a series of smaller tasks, such as straightening the wire and cutting it. If each worker had been working alone to make the whole pin alone, he or she could produce only about twenty pins a day.[28] Division of labor leads to role differentiation and specialization of function, and thus is an efficient way to structure tasks.

So, specialization usually leads to more efficiency in jobs, but as will be discussed in sections 4 and 5 of this book, too much specialization often results in jobs that are too narrow in scope and thus are boring and dissatisfying to the employee. Specialization is more often found in larger organizations; in smaller ones, employees often have to perform many types of functions, and there is much less differentiation of roles. Contrast the difference between a school library media specialist working as the only librarian in a media center and a librarian working in a large academic research library that employs 300 professionals. Obviously, the school library media specialist will, of necessity, perform a wider range of tasks than the librarian in a specialized position in the large academic library. Persons working in what have been termed "one person libraries"[29] have to be generalists who are able to perform many functions well.

In the case of the corporate library described above, it is likely that the library organizer would decide that each employee should specialize to some extent. In that case, the manager would divide the tasks to be performed, and the tasks would be allocated so that one employee would be in charge of acquisitions, two would focus on cataloging, two would work in reference services, one would perform online searches, and so on. Probably, there would also be one employee accountable for the operation of the entire library. One of that person's responsibilities would be to coordinate all the tasks that have to be done to be sure that all processes work together and all objectives are accomplished. That person would be the library director, the manager who makes the ultimate decisions about the structuring of the organization.

The restructuring of this library illustrates two key concepts in organization: specialization and coordination. When more than one person is working toward an objective, each worker must know what part to do to avoid confusion and duplication of effort. No matter how precisely the work is divided, the workers' efforts will not mesh exactly unless some means of coordination is provided.

Every organization must decide how it wants to divide its tasks or specialize; this specialization involves breaking the whole organization into parts. Then the organization must decide how to integrate all the specialized parts to create a whole product or service. The latter goal is achieved by coordinating. All large organizations must specialize and coordinate. The methods that libraries use to specialize and coordinate will be discussed in chapter 6.

Formal and Informal Organizations

Organizations may be classified as formal or informal. A formal organization is legally constituted or decreed by those in authority. This is the organization as it is supposed to function, based on the deliberate assignment of tasks, functions, and authority relationships. The formal organization is the set of official, standardized work relationships. An informal organization, on the other hand, is more loosely organized and flexible. It is often created spontaneously. Informal organizations can exist independent of formal organizations; for instance, four people who gather to play bridge constitute an informal organization.

However, many informal organizations are found within the confines of a formal organization. After the formal organization has been established, informal organizations arise naturally within its framework. The unofficial relationships within a work group constitute the informal organization. These informal groups often have leaders whose position never shows up on the organizational chart. Unlike the formally appointed leader who has a defined position from which to influence others, the informal leader does not have officially sanctioned authority. Instead, the leader of informal groups is typically the one that the other members feel is critical to the satisfaction of their specific needs at a specific time. Leadership in informal groups often changes rapidly, and different individuals revolve in and out of leadership.

Informal organizations are never found on the organization chart, but they often have a profound impact on the formal organization. Their influence can either contribute to or subvert the organization's effectiveness. Classical management principles usually ignored the existence of informal organizations, and many managers still underestimate the importance of these informal ties. For the individual who is employed by an organization, both the formal and informal relationships affect his or her organizational role.

Libraries as Organizations

This chapter focuses on formal organizations. Libraries are one type of formal organization; most libraries are not-for-profit, service organizations, with special organizational characteristics. As Lowell Martin has pointed out, libraries

♦ are service agencies, not profit-making firms;

♦ purvey information, not more tangible services or products;

♦ perform functions both of supply and guidance, a combination that in the medical field is shared among the doctor's office, the hospital, and the pharmacy;

♦ provide professional service without, in most cases, having a personal and continuous client relationship;

♦ for all their general acceptance, are currently marked by ambiguous goals rather than clear-cut objectives;

♦ during their long history have accumulated set conceptions of function and method that make for rigid structure and resistance to change;

♦ respond both to resources and to clientele in a dual and sometimes conflicting orientation, with some staff characterized as resource-minded and others as people-minded;

♦ function as auxiliaries to larger enterprises, such as universities, schools, and municipalities, and not as independent entities;

♦ because of their auxiliary role, are subject to external pressures from political bodies, faculties, and users;

♦ are staffed in the higher echelons by personnel with graduate training, making for a highly educated core staff;

♦ are administered by professionals who are promoted from the service ranks, not by career managers; and

♦ seek identity and domain within a host of communication and information sources in the community at large and in their parent organization.[30]

Although libraries and information centers are distinct types of organizations, they share many characteristics with other types of organizations. Throughout this section, libraries and information centers will be the focus of attention, but the theories and principles of organizing discussed are the same used in all other types of organizations.

Organization Charts

"When they hear the word *structure,* most organizational people think of boxes on charts. The term has been used for years to describe simple reporting relationships. But the term has been used inaccurately. Who reports to whom does not tell us anything about the structural dynamics that drive an organization to perform and behave as it does. If the real structure is not pondered, explored, and penetrated when designing the organization, it may never be understood."[31]

—Robert Fritz, *Corporate Tides: The Inescapable Laws of Organizational Structure*

A useful aid for visualizing the horizontal and vertical differentiation within an organization is the organization chart. An organization chart is a graphic representation of the organizational structure. Although it includes staff units, its primary function is to show how lines of authority link departments. An organization chart provides valuable information about the organizational structure of the organization, but it must be remembered that the "orderly little boxes stacked atop one another . . . show you the names and titles of managers but little else about the company—not its products, processes, or customers—perhaps not even its line of business."[32]

Lines of authority are usually represented on organization charts by solid lines. Lines that show staff organizational units are often represented by broken lines. Formal communication follows the lines of organizational units and authority. Informal lines of communication are not shown on the traditional organization chart.

On an organization chart, authority flows down and out; it does not return to the point of origin. For example, in Figure 5.1, the main line of authority flows from the director down to the assistant director and from that position down and out to the three functional departments. The business office is supervised by the director only. Authority flows from the director down to the assistant director and continues down and out to the business office, where it stops. In other words, in this library the assistant director "reports" to the director, as does the head of the business department. The heads of the circulation, reference, and technical services departments "report" to the assistant director. Understanding that authority flows out and stops is very important in interpreting organization charts. The business office has no authority over the assistant director or the other organizational units shown in the figure.

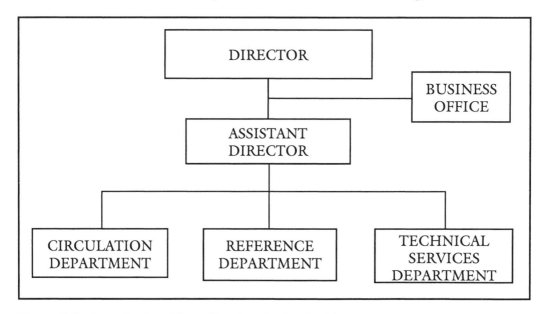

Figure 5.1. Organization Chart Showing Authority Lines

In the library represented in Figure 5.2, the director has authority over the human resources office. Because the human resources office performs a staff function, this authority is depicted with a broken line. The human resources office serves in an advisory capacity to the director and to all other units of the organization, without authority over any unit. However, the human resources office, in its internal operation, has line authority in that it supervises the payroll functions.

Some of the blocks in Figures 5.1 and 5.2 seem to represent individuals (e.g., director and assistant director), whereas others represent functions (e.g., circulation, reference, and technical services). The blocks that represent functions include all assigned activities and a manager. The blocks that seem to represent individuals actually represent all the activities assigned to that position. For the director, activities include the direct supervision of the business office in Figure 5.1 and the human resources office in Figure 5.2. In addition, both charts assume that the director will perform activities such as planning; working with outside groups, organizations, and individuals (such as the public library board or, in a university library, the vice-president for academic affairs); and evaluating library services. In both charts, the assistant director is responsible for day-to-day supervision of the three operating units, but other activities are also assigned to this position. Although it may appear that a unit of the organization structure is designated by an individual's title, one must recognize that the organizational block includes all the activities of that position.

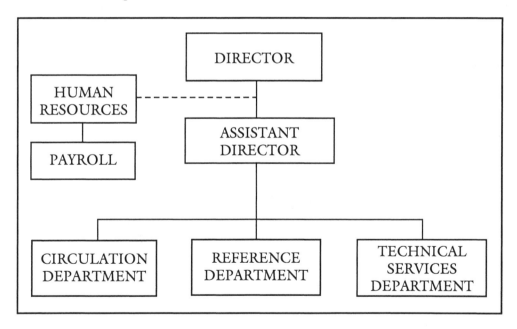

Figure 5.2. Line and Staff Organizational Units

Not many organizations are as simple as those represented by Figures 5.1 or 5.2. Some are very complex. Various means have been developed to show the authority relationship of one unit to another. Some organizational charts are very complex, and because of their size, sometimes confusing. It is commonly believed that the higher on the chart the unit appears, the greater is its status and authority, and, occasionally, the organizational status of a unit is misunderstood because of its location on the organization chart. The importance of an organizational unit is not determined by its position on the organizational chart but by the line of authority and the number of managers that authority passes through before reaching the final authority. Following the line of authority in Figure 6.5 in the next chapter reveals that the assistant director provides immediate supervision to circulation, reference, and technical services. It is apparent that these organizational units are important because they are placed rather high on the organization chart. But what of extension—the unit that provides service outside the central building? It is shown low on the chart. Analyzing the authority line reveals that extension is equal in status, rank, and importance to the other three units. Extension reports to the same position—the assistant director—as do circulation, reference, and technical services.

The organizational charts in Figures 5.1 and 5.2 are traditional. They are based on the hierarchical concept and are designed to show the relationship of one organizational unit to another through lines of authority. A few organizations, although structured traditionally, depict their structure in a nontraditional organization chart. Figure 5.3 is an example of this type of chart. This chart model consists of a series of concentric circles, each of which shows a different level of operation. Top administrators are shown in the center, and successive circles represent the various levels of the organization. Other organization charts have even different configurations. Figure 5.4, on page 138, shows the organization as spokes around a wheel. Neither of these is a different organizational structure, but both are different ways of illustrating a traditional hierarchical structure.

Organization charts can be used to define and describe channels of authority, communication, and information flow. They can be used to show the status or rank of members of the organization, and the span of control of each supervisor can be readily detected. Developing an organization chart helps the manager identify problems or inconsistencies in the organization, such as the assignment of unrelated or dissimilar activities to a unit.

> Organizations don't have tops and bottoms. These are just misguided metaphors. What organizations really have are the outer people, connected to the world, and the inner ones, disconnected from it as well as so many so-called middle managers, who are desperately trying to connect the inner and outer people to each other.[33]
>
> —Henry Mintzberg,
> "Musings on Management"

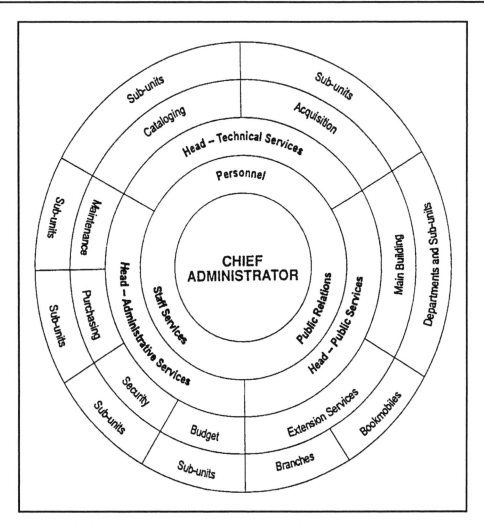

Figure 5.3. Organization Chart Presented as a Circle

Every library, regardless of size, should have an up-to-date organization chart. It should be available to all staff to help them understand relationships within the library. But it must be understood that an organization chart, a static model of a dynamic process, is limited in what it can do. It shows division of work into components; who is (supposed to be) whose boss; the nature of the work performed by each component; and the grouping of components on the levels of management in terms of successive layers of superiors and subordinates. It does not show the importance or status of the organizational units, the degree of responsibility and authority exercised by positions on the same management level, clear distinctions between line and staff, all channels of communication and contact (only the formal ones are shown), all key links or relationships in the total organizational network, and the informal organization that is a logical and necessary extension of the formal structure.[34]

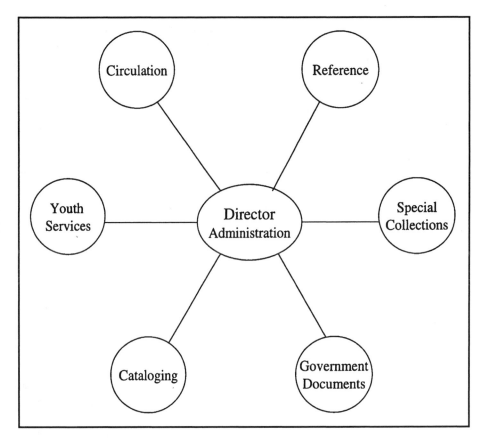

Figure 5.4. Organization Chart Presented as Spokes Around a Wheel

This book's website (www.eLearning@lu.com/management) contains a number of organization charts from libraries and links to the charts of others. Analysis of the charts indicates that the principles of organizing are sometimes violated. On some of the charts, some positions have two or three supervisors. The span of control of some supervisors is larger on some of the charts than is usually recommended. An organization chart often reflects local situations that may be historical or may represent the intent of the top administrator, regardless of the general principles of organizational design.

Organizational Culture

Each organization tends to develop its own organizational, or corporate, culture, as norms of the organization arise and become manifest in employee behavior. In the corporate world, many organizations have very strong cultures. Wal-Mart, for example, has developed a culture based on the belief that its founder Sam Walton's thriftiness, hard work, and dedication to customers is the source of the company's success. IBM has a strong corporate culture that is very different from that at Dell Computer. Organizations with a strong culture are viewed by outsiders as having a certain style or way of doing things.[35]

Most libraries have their own culture. For instance, in some, the employees dress in a businesslike manner; the men wear coats and ties, and the women wear tailored suits and dresses. In others, the employees dress in a much more casual manner. In some libraries, the workers tend to socialize a great deal off the job, whereas in others there is little interaction outside of work hours. In some libraries, the director is always addressed formally using a title, such as Dr. Brown or Ms. Smith. In other libraries, everyone is on a first-name basis. The ways in which workers dress, socialize, and interact with one another are just a few examples of organizational culture.

> The organization itself has an invisible quality—a certain style, a character, a way of doing things—that may be more powerful than the dictates of any one person or any formal system. To understand the soul of the organization requires that we travel below the charts, rule books, machines, and buildings into the underground world of corporate cultures.[36]
>
> —R. H. Kilmann,
> "Corporate Culture"

Organizational culture is defined as the "assumptions that a group discovers it has as it learns to cope with problems of external adaption and internal integration." *External adaption* refers to how the organization finds a niche in and copes with the external environment. *Internal integration* is concerned with establishing and maintaining effective working relations among members of the organization. In both of these categories, the assumptions that have worked well are taught to new members of the group as the correct way to perceive, think, and feel in relation to those issues.[37] In other words, the culture reflects the values of the organization. Organizational culture comes from three main sources: 1) the beliefs, assumptions, and values of the organization's founder; 2) the learning experiences of group members as the organization evolves; and 3) new beliefs, values, and assumptions brought in by new members and leaders.[38] The major influence on an organization's culture is usually the organization's top management, which "not only creates the rational and tangible aspects of organizations, such as structure and technology, but also is the creator of symbols, ideologies, language, beliefs, rituals and myths."[39]

Organizational culture is composed of many elements. Among the most common are:

♦ Symbols are objects or acts that convey meaning to others. Some symbols that are found in libraries are whether employees work in traditional offices or in cubicles, the type of decorations on the wall, and whether or not supervisors keep their office doors open or closed.

♦ Language is the shared terminology that helps cement an organization's identity. In libraries, there is great use of various acronyms such as LC or AACR2 that are understood by most librarians but by few outsiders.

♦ Group norms are the implicit standards or ways of acting that evolve within an organization. In some libraries, all staff meetings start exactly on time; in others, they tend to start five to ten minutes late.

♦ Slogans are phrases or sentences that express an organization's values. Sometimes these slogans are found in the organization's mission statement.

♦ Heroes are the men and women who exemplify the attributes of the culture. The experienced reference librarian who always finds the right answer or the library director who is able to defend the library against proposed budget cuts might be held up as heroes within their organization.

♦ Myths or stories are the retellings of real (or sometimes imagined) things that happened to figures associated with the organization, typically in the past. These stories are retold to new employees because they reinforce the organization's values. Stories about the founder or the early leader of an organization are common.

♦ Ceremonies are the rituals that mark a special event. Many libraries have ceremonies each year, for example, an employee appreciation dinner or a reading of banned books during National Library Week.

All of these elements and often many more go into defining an organization's culture.

Organizational culture has various levels. Some of it is visible, and some of it is less easy to see. Edgar Schein describes three levels of culture: artifacts, espoused values, and shared basic assumptions:

♦ *Artifacts* are visible manifestations of underlying cultural assumptions, such as behavior patterns, rituals, physical environment, stories, and myths. Artifacts are easily discerned and relatively easy to understand. For example, the dress codes that some organizations have are artifacts. Schein warns that it is dangerous to try to infer the deeper levels of organization culture from the artifacts alone because individuals inevitably project their own feelings and reactions. For example, if an individual sees a very informal organization, he or she may interpret that as inefficient if that individual's own perceptions have been colored by the assumption that informality means playing around and not working.

♦ *Espoused values* are the shared values of the organization. For example, many libraries have mission statements that inform both employees and patrons about what the library strives to accomplish. Adoption of codes such as the American Library Association's Code of Ethics could be considered as part of the espoused values of a particular library. These values are statements of why things should be as they are. The set of values that become embodied in an organization serves as a guide to dealing with uncertain or difficult events.

♦ *Basic assumptions* are the invisible but identifiable reasons why group members perceive, think, and feel the way they do about certain issues. These basic assumptions can be so deeply held in a group that members will find behavior based on any other premise inconceivable. Basic assumptions are so deeply imbedded that they are likely to be neither confronted nor debated, and thus they are extremely difficult to change. Basic assumptions often deal with "fundamental aspects of life—the nature of time and space; human nature and human activities; the nature of truth and how one discovers it; the correct way for the individual and the group to relate to each other; the relative importance of work, family, and self-development; the proper role of men and women; and the nature of the family."[40]

Schein argues that the pattern of basic underlying assumptions can function as a cognitive defense mechanism for individuals and the group; as a result culture change is difficult, time-consuming, and anxiety provoking. "The bottom line for leaders is that if they do not become conscious of the cultures in which they are embedded, those cultures will manage them. Cultural understanding is desirable for all of us, but it is essential to leaders if they are to lead."[41] Schein stresses the need for senior management to focus upon the third level of culture. Artifacts can be changed and new values can be articulated. But unless the basic assumptions are addressed, the organization's culture is likely to stay the same.

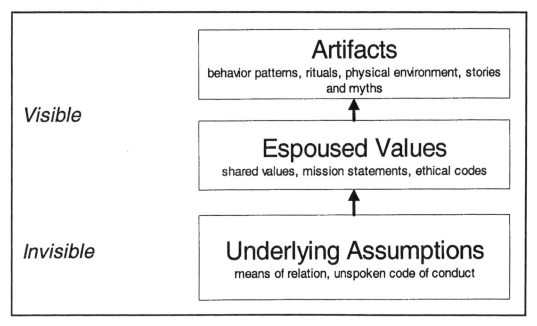

Figure 5.5. The Three Levels of Corporate Culture

Getting to Know the Culture

One of the first things that newly hired employees learn is "the way things are done here," including information about the organization's history, its cast of characters, and expectations about employee behavior. Often when employees are unhappy in a job, it is because there is not a good fit between the organization's culture and what the employee had expected. In many cases when this mismatch occurs, employees resign from their jobs or are asked to leave because they cannot conform to the culture. So it is important for prospective employees to find out as much about the organizational culture as possible before they accept a job.

Just as employees are always happier when they can accept the culture of the organization in which they work, organizations look for this fit when filling positions. They do this because an organization's culture is largely maintained through recruiting employees who fit into the culture. In addition to hiring individuals they think will fit into the culture, managers reinforce the organizational culture by 1) what they pay attention to; 2) the way they react to critical incidents and crises; 3) how they allocate rewards; 4) the way they carry out role modeling and coaching; 5) what methods they use for selection, promotion, and removal; and 6) their various organizational rites, ceremonies, and stories.[42] If an organization wishes to change its organizational culture, it has to restructure all of the factors listed above.

As can be seen, each organization has its own individual culture. Although the culture of two organizations of the same type may be similar, each one will have its own distinctive culture. In the corporate world where there have been so many mergers in the past few years, one of the most difficult things to accomplish in these mergers has been the bringing together of the corporate cultures of the two firms. Although mergers are less common in the not-for-profit sector, libraries, too, sometimes face the need to merge. In the academic libraries that have merged with university computing centers, the clash of cultures between those two types of institutions has often been a challenge. Public libraries that have merged with academic libraries, as in San Jose, California, or Cologne, Germany,[43] likely face a similar challenge in making the two institutions one.

Obviously, it is not easy to change the culture in an organization because it is usually deeply ingrained in the employees and managers. Organizational culture is often the cause of inflexibility in organizations. Employees are resistant to change because they have "always done it that way." However, some organizations, such as Toyota, have consciously shaped a corporate culture that welcomes change.[44] Research has shown that the most successful organizations not only have strong cultures but they have adaptive ones.[45] The so-called learning organization described in chapter 9 is distinguished by its adaptive culture. Employees in learning organizations are rewarded for questioning the status quo and the current way of doing things. This type of organization values risk-taking and change. Most experts feel that an adaptable organizational culture will be critical for the success of tomorrow's organizations.

Organizational culture needs to be able to change because cultural values that have worked in the past may become outdated, and an organization needs to adapt its culture to new conditions Ironically, it is sometimes the most successful organizations that are the most resistant to change; their past success has convinced them that their ways are the right ones. They think that they have the answers so they are not as responsive to their constituencies. They are not willing to take risks. They become resistant to change, which allows new organizations to gain ground on them and to begin to take away market share.

Libraries have an organization and a structure that have worked well in the past, but now these organizations are faced with increasing competition as they make the transition from paper-based to digitally based collections. It is easier to cling to the "tried and true" than to make changes, especially when there is no new model that has been shown to be a reliable replacement. But if libraries wish to continue to exist in the future, they have to continue to experiment with changes in their organization and their culture. As Philip Evans and Thomas Wurster state: "The paralysis of the leading incumbent is the greatest competitive advantage enjoyed by new competitors. It is an advantage they often do not deserve, since if the incumbent would only fight all-out by the new rules, the incumbent would often win."[46] But, it is hard to make radical changes in the way things are done, and it is very difficult to walk away from the things that organizations have done well over the years—from those "core competencies that were built over decades, the object of personal and collective pride and identity."[47]

What will happen if libraries refuse to change? One view of the consequences comes from the planning team of an academic library in the midst of organizational restructuring.

> Unlike commercial enterprises that fail to keep up with changing customer expectations or that make a product that no longer sells, the Library probably will not go out of business, at least not in our lifetimes. There is a very strong possibility, however, that we WILL be bypassed by competing information providers. Faculty and students who can go elsewhere for what they need, and who can get it more quickly and with less "hassle," are unlikely to keep coming to us for help. As the information-seeking behavior of our clients changes, services that depend on old models—for example, providing assistance only at desks physically located within library buildings—will see a decline in use, and it will become harder and harder to justify the resources that support them. For many people in our community, the Library will become a place one visits infrequently and for an ever-narrowing number of purposes. . . . We must also remember that the Library has something very valuable to contribute to the information environment of the 21st century, namely a long tradition that values free access to information, and the organization and preservation of knowledge for use across the centuries. If the Library does not carry those values forward into this new age—and it can't do that unless it continues to adapt—then we will be replaced by something harder, more commercial, less altruistic, and less able to support the University's academic mission.[48]

Libraries of all sorts have a rich tradition of access to information and preservation of knowledge. But, if libraries are to continue to flourish, they must do more than rest on their laurels. They must make changes. Library managers face an enormous challenge in trying the "organize" libraries to meet the demands of tomorrow. They must develop a different mindset, one that welcomes change, and welcoming change is far easier to accept intellectually than actually to do. But librarians will need to persist in experimenting with different types of organizational structures and with modifications in the organizational culture. If librarians are not willing to make these changes, not willing to "deconstruct" their own organizations, someone else will do it to them.[49]

Conclusion

This chapter has provided an overview of organizations and their cultures. Chapter 6 will cover the methods that organizations use to specialize and coordinate. Chapter 7 will look at the prevailing organizational designs of libraries and ways that some libraries are beginning to redesign their organizational structures.

Notes

1.   Peter F. Drucker, "Management's New Paradigms," *Forbes* 62 (October 5, 1998): 152.

2.   Henry Mintzberg, *The Rise and Fall of Strategic Planning: Reconceiving Roles for Planning, Plans and Planners* (New York: Free Press, 1994), 399.

3.   Ian Palmer and Cynthia Hardy, *Thinking About Management: Implications of Organizational Debates for Practice* (London: Sage Publications, 2000), 11.

4.   Rosabeth Moss Kanter, Barry A. Stein, and Todd D. Jick, *The Challenge of Organizational Change: How Companies Experience It and Leaders Guide It* (New York: Free Press, 1992), 3.

5.   For more about hybrid libraries, see http://hylife.unn.ac.uk/toolkit/.

6.   Howard E. Aldrich, *Organizations Evolving* (London: Sage Publications, 1999), 2–3.

7.   Peter Drucker, *Post-Capitalist Society* (New York: HarperBusiness, 1993), 48.

8.   John Naisbitt, *Megatrends: Ten New Directions Transforming Our Lives* (New York: Warner Books, 1982), 14.

9.   John H. Jackson and Cyril P. Morgan, *Organization Theory: A Macro Perspective for Management* (Englewood Cliffs, NJ: Prentice-Hall, 1978), 3.

10.   *Ibid.*, 10.

11.   See http://www.ala.org/library/fact1.html and http://www.ala.org/library/fact2.html.

12.   Aldrich, *Organizations Evolving*, 8.

13.   Joanne D. Eustis and Donald J. Kenney, *Library Reorganization and Restructuring* (SPEC Kit 215) (Washington, DC: Association of Research Libraries, 1996).

14. Joe A. Hewitt, "What's Wrong with Library Organization? Factors Leading to Restructuring in Research Libraries," *North Carolina Libraries* 55 (Spring 1997): 3.

15. Larry E. Greiner, "Revolution as Organizations Grow." *Harvard Business Review* 76 (May–June 1998): 58.

16. Robert Johansen and Rob Swigart, *Upsizing the Individual in the Downsized Organization: Managing in the Wake of Reengineering, Globalization, and Overwhelming Technological Change* (Reading, MA: Addison-Wesley, 1994), 13.

17. *Ibid.*, x.

18. Thomas N. Davenport, *Process Innovation : Re-engineering Work Through Information Technology* (Boston: Harvard Business School Press, 1993).

19. Michael Hammer and James Champy, *Reengineering the Corporation: A Manifesto for Business Revolution* (New York: Harper Business, 1993).

20. *Ibid.*, 46.

21. E. Munford and R. Hendricks, "Business Re-engineering RIP" *People Management* 2 (1996): 22–26.

22. Thomas Davenport, "The Fad That Forgot People," *Fast Company* (1995), http://www .fastcompany.com/online/01/reengin.html.

23. For example, see B. J. Shapiro and K. L. Long, "Just Say Yes: Reengineering Library User Services for the 21st Century," *Journal of Academic Librarianship* 20 (1994): 285–90; T. W. Shaughnessy, "Lessons from Restructuring the Library," *Journal of Academic Librarianship* 22 (1996): 251–56; N. R. Smith, "Turning the Library Inside Out: Radical Restructuring to Meet the Challenge of Sudden Change," in *Computers in Libraries International 96* (Oxford: Learned Information Europe, 1996), 71–82; N. Roitberg, "Library Leadership and Re-Engineering— An Israeli Experience," *IATUL Proceedings, New Series. Vol. 8* (1999); Sandra Yee, Rita Bullard, and Morell Boone, "We Built It and They Came: Client Centered Services in a New Building," *Proceedings of the ACRL Tenth National Conference* (Chicago: American Library Association, 2001), 261–64.

24. Miles H. Overholt, "Flexible Organizations: Using Organizational Design as a Competitive Advantage," *Human Resources Planning* 20 (1997): 23.

25. Joanne R. Euster et al., "Reorganizing for a Changing Information World," *Library Administration and Management* 11 (Spring 1997): 103.

26. Jay Lorsch, "Organizational Design," in John J. Gabarro, ed., *Managing People and Organizations* (Boston: Harvard Business School Publications, 1992), 313–14.

27. Jim Collins, *Good to Great: Why Some Companies Make the Leap and Others Don't* (New York: Harper Business, 2001), 121.

28. Jay R. Galbraith, *Organization Design* (Reading, MA: Addison-Wesley, 1977), 13.

29. See Guy St. Clair, *Managing the New One-Person Library* (New York: Bowker Saur, 1992), for more information about one-person libraries.

30. Lowell A. Martin, *Organizational Structure of Libraries* (Lanham, MD: Scarecrow Press, 1996), 12–13.

31. Robert Fritz, *Corporate Tides: The Inescapable Laws of Organizational Structure* (San Francisco: Berrett-Koehler, 1996), 14.

32. Henry Mintzberg and Ludo Van der Heyden, "Organigraphs: Drawing How Companies Really Work," *Harvard Business Review* 77 (September–October 1999): 87.

33.   Henry Mintzberg, "Musings on Management," *Harvard Business Review* 74 (July–August 1996): 61.

34.   Harold Steiglitz, "What's Not on the Organization Chart," *The Conference Board RECORD* 1 (November 1964): 7–10.

35.   John P. Kotter and James L. Heskett, *Corporate Culture and Performance* (New York: Free Press, 1992), 15–18.

36.   R. H. Kilmann, "Corporate Culture," *Psychology Today* 28 (April 1995): 63.

37.   Edgar H. Schein, "Organizational Culture," *American Psychologist* 45 (February 1990): 111.

38.   Edgar Shein, *Organizational Culture and Leadership* (San Francisco: Jossey-Bass, 1992), 211.

39.   Andrew Pettigrew, "The Creation of Organizational Cultures" (Paper presented to the Joint EIASM-Dansk Management Center Research Seminar, Copenhagen, 18 May 1976), 11. Quoted in Thomas J. Peters and Robert H. Waterman Jr., *In Search of Excellence: Lessons from America's Best-Run Companies* (New York: Harper & Row, 1982), 104.

40.   Shein, *Organizational Culture and Leadership*, 25–26.

41.   *Ibid.*, 377.

42.   *Ibid.*, 228–53.

43.   Ilene Rockman, "Joint Use Facilities: The View from San Jose," *Library Administration and Management* 13 (1999): 64–67.

44.   A. Taylor, "Why Toyota Keeps Getting Better and Better and Better," *Fortune* 122 (November 19, 1990): 66–79.

45.   John P. Kotter and James L. Heskett. *Corporate Culture and Performance* (New York: Free Press, 1992).

46.   Philip Evans and Thomas S. Wurster, *Blown to Bits: How the New Economics of Information Transforms Strategy* (Boston: Harvard Business School Press, 2000), 65.

47.   *Ibid.*, 66.

48.   Brown University Library, Library Transition Management Group, "FAQ. The Library in Transition" (April 2001). See http://www.brown.edu/Facilities/University_Library/MODEL /LTMG/faq.html#q2.

49.   Evan and Wurster, *Blown to Bits*, 66.

Chapter 6

Structuring the Organization— Specialization and Coordination

Every human activity—from the making of pots to the placing of a man on the moon—gives rise to two fundamental and opposing requirements: the division of labor into various tasks to be performed and the coordination of these tasks to accomplish the activity. The structure of an organization can be defined simply as the sum total of the ways in which it divides its labor into distinct tasks and then achieves coordination among them.[1]

—Henry Mintzberg,
Structure in Fives: Designing Effective Organizations

The larger the organization, the more complex its structure. As was discussed in chapter 5, small organizations have very simple organizational structures. When there are only one or two or three people working in a library or any other type of organization, there is not a great need for either *specialization*—that is, breaking the tasks to be done down into discrete parts for various individuals to accomplish—or *coordination*—that is, being sure that all the tasks are being accomplished in the appropriate sequence. But as organizations grow larger, attention has to be paid to both specialization and coordination if the goals of the organizations are to be accomplished. Structuring involves these two fundamental requirements: the division of labor into distinct tasks, and the achievement of coordination among these tasks. In this chapter, the ways in which the organization is broken apart (specialization) as well as the ways in which the organization is brought back together (coordination) will be discussed.

Specialization

An organization divides the total tasks to be done (or specializes) in two ways. The first is by establishing horizontal specializations, which results in the creation of various departments, each performing specific tasks. The second is by establishing vertical differentiation, or a hierarchy of positions. Vertical differentiation involves structuring authority, power, accountability, and responsibility in an organization.

An organization is structured horizontally by identifying and grouping similar or related activities or tasks into subunits or departments. To identify similar or related tasks sounds simple, but it becomes complex when the tasks are examined to determine how they contribute to the organization's goals and objectives. Grouping tasks creates blocks of activity-oriented tasks and people-oriented tasks. How the blocks are placed in relation to one another will indicate the true goals and objectives of the organization.

Blocks of activity tasks, such as cataloging a book or acquiring materials, put primary emphasis on process, procedure, or technique. These tasks can vary from the most routine, requiring little skill, to very complex tasks, requiring extensive ability and knowledge as well as conformity with a process, procedure, or technique. People-oriented tasks, which place primary emphasis on human relationships, require the ability to communicate, to guide or direct, and to motivate other individuals.

Most of the older forms of organizations put primary emphasis on activity-oriented tasks. Since World War II, however, it has been recognized that people-oriented tasks fulfill very important roles in any organization. Examples of routine activity-oriented tasks in a library are shelving books or copy cataloging; complex activity-oriented tasks might include the selection of books in accordance with a book-selection policy or the development of World Wide Web-based user instruction modules. People-oriented tasks include the relationship of the reference librarian to the library user, the attitude of the supervisor to subordinates, or the ability of the library director to work with officials in government or academic institutions.

Having identified blocks of tasks, the managers designing an organization must place them in a logical order. The manager must answer the questions, "What blocks should be put together or kept apart?" and "What is the proper relationship of the blocks?" Some of the blocks will be of primary importance; others will be secondary.

According to Peter Drucker, it is not as important to identify all tasks that are required in an organization as it is to identify the key tasks. He proposes that an organization design start with the following questions: In what area is excellence required to obtain the organization's objectives? In what areas would lack of performance endanger the results, if not the survival, of the enterprise? He recommends, in short, that organizers ask why the organization exists and build on that basis.[2] These are questions that all library managers need to ask and have answered before organizing.

Organizations are like elephants—They both learn through conditioning. Trainers shackle young elephants with heavy chains to deeply embedded stakes. In that way the elephant learns to stay in its place. Older elephants never try to leave even though they have the strength to pull the stake and move beyond. . . . Like powerful elephants, many companies are bound by earlier conditioned constraints. "We've always done it this way" is as limiting to any organization progress as the unattached chain around the elephant's foot. Success ties you to the past. The very factors that produced today's success often create tomorrow's failures.[3]

—James A. Belasco,
Teaching the Elephant to Dance

In a similar vein, other management experts urge organizations to ask, "What business are you in?" They point to the plight of the American railroad companies, which almost became extinct because they thought they were in the business of trains, not realizing that they were actually in the transportation business. Another example is provided by Pitney Bowes. After that company lost its monopoly on postage meters, Pitney Bowes went through a troubled financial period until it was able to move beyond viewing itself as a "postage meter" company and realized that it could be highly successful if it looked broader and concentrated on providing "messaging" to organizations.[4] In a similar fashion, libraries and information centers have had to reexamine their purpose during the past few decades. Most now consider themselves in the "information business" (and not just in the book or printed material business) and realize that they have competitors in the private sector that did not exist before. Libraries and information centers have had to redefine themselves, and this redefinition will likely require a change in the structure. As a result, some libraries have modified their organizational structure to reflect their new mission.

Parts of an Organization

Organizational design can be seen as the putting together of a fairly standardized set of building blocks; it is a process similar to building a house. Although houses may have many types of design, ranging from traditional colonial to modern contemporary, and although their sizes may range from small cottages to large mansions, almost all houses share common characteristics. They will all have a foundation, a roof, certain essential rooms, and ways to provide such services as electricity and water. Organizations are designed in a similar fashion. Although the variety and number of blocks will vary with the size and the type of institution, with pieces that can be put together in different ways, all organizational structures have a great deal in common. Managers who are attempting to organize (or reorganize) are, metaphorically speaking, the architects of the structure—they are shaping the space to meet the needs and aspirations of the organization.[5]

So, most organizations contain the same basic parts. Mintzberg has categorized the five basic elements of organizations as:

♦ A *strategic apex,* which consists of the organization's top management and is responsible for the overall functioning of the organization.

♦ The *middle line,* which is composed of the mid-level managers who coordinate the activities of the various units. They serve to link the operating core to the strategic apex. One of the major activities of the mid-level managers is to transmit information about the operating core to the top level managers.

♦ The *operating core,* which is made up of the workers who carry out the mission of the organization.

♦ The *technostructure,* which consists of those units that provide the organization with technical expertise.

♦ The *support staff,* which is composed of the workers who provide the organization with expertise in areas such as labor relations or personnel.[6]

These components are illustrated in Figure 6.1.

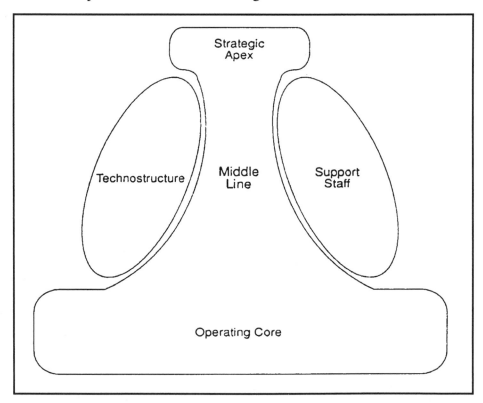

Figure 6.1. Mintzberg's Model of the Organization Is Made Up of Five Components. From *Structure in Fives: Designing Effective Organizations* by Mintzberg, ©1983. Reprinted by permission of Prentice-Hall, Inc., Englewood Cliffs, NJ.

In a large library, the director and the assistant and associate directors form the strategic apex. The heads of the various departments make up the middle line. Employees in units such as library systems and original cataloging comprise the technostructure, whereas employees in units such as personnel and public relations constitute the support staff. The largest group, the operating core, consists of the employees who work in areas such as circulation and reference. They are the ones carrying out the organization's mission of linking people to information. Although some small organizations do not contain all of Mintzberg's categories, most larger ones do, although the size of each component in relation to the others varies according to factors such as type and complexity of endeavor, age of the organization, and its size.

Methods of Departmentalization

In the past business and industry have traditionally used five methods to establish departments: function, territory, product, customer, and process. Libraries and other information agencies have used many of the same methods. In addition, libraries have developed two other methods to establish departments: subject and form of resources. In both businesses and libraries, these methods are used in varying combinations to produce a hybrid structure. Although these methods of departmentalization are being affected in many organizations by new approaches to organizational structure, they still serve as the primary approach for establishing subdivisions within an organization. Each method of departmentalization is discussed below.

Function

In business, the most common organizational design is the functional structure. For instance, a company that makes shoes would have departments dealing with production, marketing, sales, accounting, and so on. In libraries, too, this method of departmentalization is extensively used. The functions of circulation, reference, acquisition, cataloging, and management, to name but a few, historically have been the basis of library organization. The grouping of necessary library activities has resulted in these functional categories.

In some of the organizational patterns that have emerged in the past fifty years, a number of these functions have been combined in one department with subdepartments performing related functions. A good example is the emergence of the major functional department of technical services, which includes many units that once were autonomous functional departments. Order or acquisitions departments, catalog departments, serials departments, binding departments, and book processing departments, previously autonomous, are now combined because their activities are related to the organization's end goal of acquiring and organizing library resources.

Functional design has a number of advantages. It groups specialists with similar backgrounds and interests, and it allows specialization within that function. For instance, a library might have both a Slavic and an East Asian cataloger. Functional design also ensures that higher organizational levels will be aware of the contributions and the needs of the various subunits of the organization. There are, however, three major disadvantages of functional division. First, it may lead to competition among various departments, for example, competition for resources or disagreements over the most appropriate procedures. In some libraries, the reference and cataloging departments may disagree about the best classification or subject headings for a particular book. Second, workers in functional settings may lose sight of the end product of the whole organization, especially when workers are distanced from the ultimate users of the product. Finally, this organizational design is not so effective if the organization has units in different locations. The functional design appears to work best in organizations that do not need close collaboration among the functional departments.

Territory

In industries that operate over a wide geographic area, all activities in a designated geographic territory are commonly grouped together and placed under the direction of a manager. For instance, multinational organizations have divisions to deal with specific parts of the world, such as North America, South America, or Europe. This structure permits the organization to adapt to local situations as far as the local labor market, local needs and problems, and local production problems are concerned. Libraries also use this principle of territory or area in their organizational structure. For instance, public libraries have always been very concerned about the location of their central facility and the areas to be served by their branch libraries, bookmobiles, and storefront libraries. Academic libraries that have branches, such as a science library, an architecture library, or an education library, are concerned that these facilities be in the area where the appropriate clientele will be located. School systems usually have individual schools and their media centers located throughout their service area, and students will typically go to the school geographically nearest to their homes.

The primary advantage of this type of organization for libraries is that the individual units can be located close to their users, can get to know their needs better, and, it is hoped, can serve them better. Territorial organization also provides a training ground for managers because it gives a manager a chance to work relatively autonomously as the manager of a smaller unit that is geographically separated from the central organization. It is not uncommon for a librarian who has been the head of a branch library to be promoted to the head of the library system.

The biggest disadvantage of territorial organization is that it increases the difficulty of coordination and communication within the organization. In addition, rivalries often crop up between the different locations. Many large public libraries hard hit by funding cuts have had to make difficult decisions about whether it is better to maintain the quality of the central collection or to maintain service to various neighborhoods through the branches. Finally, territorial organization often leads to duplication, for example, in resources like standard reference books.

In librarianship there has always been disagreement about the degree of geographic centralization that should prevail. Typically, library administrators have favored a more centralized organization because of the tight control and budgetary advantages associated with that design. On the other hand, users typically prefer a more decentralized system because of its convenience and more personalized service (in spite of the special problems of users working in interdisciplinary areas).

The degree of decentralization varies according to country and type of library. For example, academic libraries in the United States have traditionally been more centralized than those in Europe, especially those within the older European universities where individual units such as institutes or colleges often provided library service before it was provided centrally. Some of the arguments against decentralization have been weakened by the increasing importance of information technology and the advent of new methods of document storage and retrieval that lessen some of the costs involved in duplication of material in decentralized locations.[7] The advent of online catalogs and online access to reference and bibliographic material and full-text journals and books has made decentralization less expensive.

Product

Large industries use this method of organization because it allows for specialization. Organization by product is particularly useful in diversified industries in which production of one product is sufficiently large to employ fully specialized facilities. In such cases, departmentalization by product allows a product manager complete control over all functions related to that product, including profit responsibility. For instance, AOL Time Warner is organized into divisions that are based on product lines: America Online; Time, Inc.; Turner Broadcasting; Warner Brothers; etc.[8]

Product organization is used infrequently in libraries. Although the product of a print shop (a bibliography or a brochure) or a product of the systems office (such as the library's website) might be considered a product, in almost every case, this product is a minor part of the total operation of the library.

Customer

Businesses, especially retail stores, use this structure to appeal to the needs and desires of clearly defined customer groups. Department stores have children's, preteen, men's, misses, and petite departments to cater to specific customer groups. Libraries also use the same structure. Since the late 1800s, special children's sections have been one of the most used sections in public libraries. Public libraries also have aimed their services at other customer groups, such as young adults or business users. Academic libraries have used this structure in establishing undergraduate libraries.

The advantage of this type of departmentalization is that it allows libraries and information centers to meet the special and widely varying needs of users. The disadvantages are similar to those involved in territorial departmentalization. Coordination among departments is difficult, and competition among various departments, especially for resources, may arise. In addition, when budgets get tight, services to special groups may be eliminated.

Some organizations have decided that service to some customers may best be handled in a more general manner. For example, many public libraries have eliminated their young adult departments. In some large universities, previously existing undergraduate libraries have been eliminated because it was felt that undergraduates could be better served by the main library.

Process

In the process method of departmentalization, workers are grouped based on process or activity. A process is "a set or collection of activities that take more than one kind of input and that, taken together, produce a result of value to the customer."[9] So a process approach to departmentalization focuses upon how work is done within an organization. Processes usually have two characteristics. The first is that the process has customers, either internal or external. Second, processes usually cross organizational boundaries; they occur across organizational subdivisions. Consider the common library process of getting a specific book on the shelf. That process could involve several departments, including collection development, acquisitions, cataloging, etc.

So a process is not a function or a department but a series of activities that result in an output that is a value to a customer. An organizational output that is of value only to the organization itself is one that should likely either be improved or eliminated.[10] Looking at functions instead of process often leads to fragmentation and low customer satisfaction because no single department owns the entire process. Because customers are not interested in the steps in the process but in the output, designing libraries around process should lead to greater customer satisfaction.[11]

Focusing on improving processes usually provides a competitive advantage for an organization. Michael Porter and Victor Millar suggest the use of the "value chain" as a means of analyzing processes.[12] The value chain is a representation of the activities carried out in an organization. An organization may gain competitive advantage by managing its value chain more efficiently or effectively than its competitors. Each step in the value chain has both a physical and an information processing element. Competitive advantage is often gained by increasing the information content of parts of the value chain.

> Initially, companies used information technology mainly for accounting and record-keeping functions. In these applications, the computers automated repetitive clerical functions such as order processing. Today information technology is spreading throughout the value chain and is performing optimization and control functions as well as more judgmental executive functions. General Electric for instance, uses a data base that includes the accumulated experience and (often intuitive) knowledge of its appliance service engineers to provide support to customers by phone.[13]
>
> —Michael Porter and Victor Millar,
> "How Information Gives You Competitive Advantage"

Maxine Brodie and Neil McLean describe the components involved in restructuring the provision of information resources within a library and provide an outline of the organizational impact of adopting a process framework.

♦ Steps in the process will be performed in natural order.

♦ Work will be done where it makes most sense.

♦ Work units will change from functional departments to process teams.

♦ Jobs will change from simple to multidimensional.

♦ Processes will not be standardized but will have different versions for different clients.

♦ Staff will become empowered to make decisions.

♦ Performance appraisal measures will shift from activities to results.

♦ Values will cease to be protective and become productive.

♦ Managers will become coaches, not supervisors.

♦ Organizational structure will become flatter.

♦ Top managers will become leaders, not scorekeepers.

♦ A hybrid centralized/decentralized structure may be used based on shared information systems.

♦ A "one-stop shopping" case manager with easy access to all information systems will serve as a single point of contact for users.

♦ Checks and controls will be introduced.[14]

Business process reengineering discussed in chapter 5 is built around the restructuring of process. Total quality management also focuses upon processes. For organizations that have departmentalized using functional or other traditional approaches, changing and focusing upon process is difficult. Although a few libraries have reorganized using the process approach,[15] to date process is not a widely used method of departmentalization in libraries. However, team and matrix organization, discussed later in this section, usually do provide more attention to process than more traditional structures.

In addition to the five conventional ways of establishing departments described above, libraries have used two additional methods: subject and form of resources departments.

Subject

Large public and academic libraries use this method extensively. It provides for more in-depth reference service and reader guidance, and it requires a high degree of subject knowledge on the part of the staff. There is no pattern of subjects included in a subject department and no set number of subject departments. In academic libraries, subject departments are usually broad in scope and include all related subjects in areas like humanities, social sciences, or science. In large public libraries, subject departments such as business, fine arts, and local history are common.

There are definite advantages of subject departments. All materials dealing with one topic are gathered together, which is convenient for users. The librarians working with this material usually have special training in the subject matter. The disadvantages include the increased cost of the necessary duplication of material and the hiring of specialized personnel. Each department must be staffed, even when usage is low. One reference librarian might be sufficient to handle all reference inquiries at a central desk when demand is low; but if there are four subject-area reference desks, four reference librarians are required, even if there are few inquiries. In addition, as has been frequently pointed out, although subject divisions are convenient for users working strictly within a subject field, users who are pursuing interdisciplinary topics spread across subject lines must go to many subject departments to find the materials they need.

Form of Resources

Many libraries have used format, or the form in which resources are issued, as a basis for organization, especially as the quantity of nonbook and nonprint material has increased. It is not unusual to find separate map, microform, audiovisual, periodicals, online services, electronic resources, and documents departments in a library. Many of these specialized forms present special problems in acquisition, storage, handling, or organization. Often, librarians working in format-based departments handle all functions relating to the department's resources, including functions that are normally performed centrally. For instance, a government documents department may order, process, provide reference service for, and circulate all government documents. Format-based departments are most useful for patrons seeking one type of resource, for instance, audiovisual materials. More commonly, however, users seek information on specific topics, and they may easily miss relevant materials that are housed in various format-based departments. As digital material replaces printed material in libraries, departments based on form of resources will need to be restructured.

Summary

Only in the most specialized library would a single organizational method be used. A large public library, for example, generally has a circulation department (function), subject department (combining several functions), branch libraries (territory), children's services (customer), business services (customer), government documents collections (form), and several others.

There is no one right way to establish departments in an organization. There are advantages and disadvantages associated with each method; a manager interested in organization should be aware of both the strengths and the disadvantages. Also, as stated previously, no organizational structure, no matter how good, is intended to last forever. Institutions change, and organizational structures must change to reflect new situations. Managers need to look first at the tasks that need to be accomplished, the people involved in accomplishing them, the users being served, and the pertinent external and environmental factors, and then design a suitable departmental organization. Often, employees feel threatened by any change in organizational structure; managers should communicate the reasons for changes and provide reassurance to employees who need it.

For years the basic questions about how best to organize people and tasks remained the same:

> Do we centralize or decentralize? Do we organize by product or by function? Where do we stick the international operation? The answers were seldom satisfactory. Typically, companies were organized by product, by customer, or by territory, and then switched when those structures stopped working. Whereas senior managers felt the impact of such reshuffling, it rarely affected the rank and file who continued to operate in the same functional, vertical organization where all that changed was the boss's name. Today's management challenge is to design more flexible organizations that affect all members.[16]

The Hierarchy

Within the structure of an organization, specialization exists in two dimensions. We have just discussed the specialization found on the horizontal axis—the grouping of tasks into departments and subunits. The vertical axis contains a different type of specialization—the structuring of authority (see Figure 6.2). In organizations, authority is the degree of discretion conferred on subordinates that makes it possible for them to use their judgment in making decisions and issuing instructions. A manager is assigned to each department or subunit within an organization. Each manager has a measure of responsibility and authority, delegated by his or her superior. The need for such delegation is obvious; if managers are responsible for the accomplishment of designated tasks and the supervision of employees, they must have the authority to guarantee efficient performance. The vertical hierarchy provides a channel through which authority flows from top management down to the managers of subunits. It also provides a means to coordinate the efforts of many individuals performing a variety of tasks. The concept of a vertical hierarchy is central to the classic theories of organizing. Now that so many organizations are using teams, encouraging horizontal communication, and instituting multiple reporting patterns, the vertical hierarchy may be less critical than it used to be. Nonetheless, it is important to understand this concept even if many organizations are deemphasizing its importance.

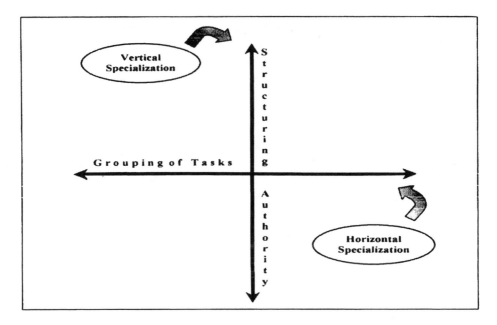

Figure 6.2. Vertical and Horizontal Specialization Within Libraries

The Scalar Principle

As departments and subdepartments are assigned various tasks, primary and secondary units of the organization emerge. Primary organizational departments have numerous tasks and broad responsibilities; secondary or subdepartments have specific tasks and limited responsibility. For example, a copy catalog unit would be a subdepartment of a cataloging department. A subdepartment's tasks contribute to the fulfillment of the responsibilities of the primary department. The manager of the primary department supervises the manager of the subdepartment to assure compliance with the needs of the primary department. Authority flows from the primary to the secondary manager.

The scalar principle requires that there be final, ultimate authority and that lines of authority descend to every subordinate position. The clearer the line of authority, the more effective the organizational performance and communication. Henri Fayol described the scalar principle as:

> the chain of supervisors ranging from the ultimate authority to the lowest ranks. The line of authority is the route followed—via every link in the chain—by all communications which start from or go to the ultimate authority. This path is dictated both by the need for some transmission and by the principle of unity of command, but it is not always the swiftest. It is even at times disastrously lengthy in large concerns, notably in governmental ones.[17]

A clear understanding of the scalar principle by each subordinate is necessary for an organization to function effectively. Subordinates must know to whom and for what they are responsible, and the parameters of each manager's authority are clear.

The vertical hierarchy develops as a result of the ranking of organizational units. A scalar hierarchy may be illustrated as a pyramid, with the ultimate authority at the apex and authority fanning out as it flows down. The positions at the top of the pyramid deal with broader tasks and responsibilities, those at the bottom with more specific tasks and responsibilities (see Figure 6.3). Even though the vertical hierarchy may remain stable over a period of time, tasks and responsibilities may shift as managers and supervisors delegate.

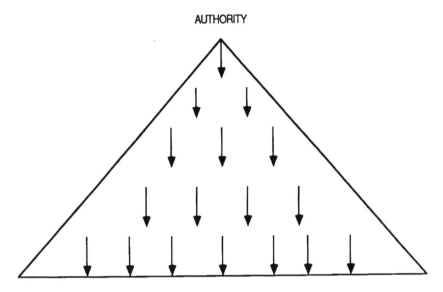

Figure 6.3. The Flow of Authority Within a Traditional Organization

Power and Authority

The words *power* and *authority* are sometimes used interchangeably, but these terms are not synonymous. A person may possess power but not necessarily authority. *Authority* is the legitimate right of a supervisor to direct subordinates to take action within the scope of the supervisor's position. Authority flows down the vertical chain of command within the organization. The authority is vested in the organizational position, not in the person holding that position, and it is accepted by subordinates. *Power* is the potential ability to influence the behavior of others. John French and Bertram Raven have identified five types of power:

1. Legitimate power is the power that comes from a formal management position and is based upon authority recognized in accordance with position in an organizational structure.

2. Reward power stems from the power to provide rewards for people.

3. Coercive power is power that derives from the potential to inflict punishment.

4. Expert power is the power derived from expertise or knowledge. Often people whose positions are not high in the chain of command have a great deal of power because of their knowledge.

5. Referent power refers to power that derives from the respect and esteem accorded to an individual by virtue of personal attributes that command respect and admiration.[18]

Authority is the ability to influence that is associated with a person's position within the organization. Power can be derived from sources other than a formal position. In many organizations there are people who have more power than might be expected as a result of their position.

Delegation

A supervisor with authority may delegate some of that authority downward. *Delegation* is the transfer of authority within closely prescribed limits. In an effective organization, the person in the position holding ultimate authority delegates authority to subordinate managers. The delegation of authority to subordinates does not relieve the ultimate authority of responsibility; a manager is responsible for the actions of subordinates, even if authority has been delegated. A manager can delegate to subordinates almost anything for which that manager has responsibility. Of course, managers cannot delegate all authority without abdicating the managerial role. This is rarely a problem, however. Most managers delegate too little; some clutch tenaciously at authority and dislike delegating anything.

The process of delegation involves determining the expected results, assigning tasks, delegating authority for accomplishing the tasks, and holding people responsible for the accomplishment of tasks. The delegation process should never be practiced only in part, but it often is. Too often managers give subordinates the responsibility to perform designated activities, but withhold the authority to accomplish them. This defeats the purpose of delegating. As Allen Veaner has written:

> Delegation without authority is empty. Before delegating think carefully whether you are willing to permit work to be done without your direct oversight or review. Too much review, especially of professionals, breeds apathy, dependency, and passive resistance, and destroys motivation.[19]

Many managers find it difficult to delegate adequate authority because they fear that a subordinate might make a mistake or perform poorly. In addition, some managers feel that they are not doing their jobs unless they make all of the decisions, even the smaller ones that subordinates could easily make. These managers spend a disproportionate amount of time on minor decisions, not realizing that, by doing so, they are taking time and attention away from the more important decisions that only they can make.

Effective managers have learned to delegate. They are willing to let go of some of their authority and to trust their subordinates. They know that subordinates sometimes make mistakes, and they are willing to take the risk because they realize that delegation is necessary in any organization. In addition, effective managers always remember that responsibility cannot be delegated without authority. A subordinate given responsibility without authority probably will be unable to function efficiently.

Centralization and Decentralization

In describing the departmentalization process in organizations, the issues of centralization and decentralization were discussed. These same issues, although in a different form, are also relevant to a discussion of hierarchy. In the context of the vertical hierarchy of an organization, centralization and decentralization do not refer to geographic dispersal but to the dispersal of authority for decision making. In highly centralized organizations, authority is concentrated in the highest echelons of the hierarchy; almost all decisions are made by those at the top. In the traditional organization, the authority was highly centralized in the hands of top managers. These types of organizations have been termed *command and control* organizations because they were structured to centralize both the command and control of the organization in the ranks of top management. It was assumed that whoever was in command would also tightly control the organization.

In contrast, in decentralized organizations the authority to make decisions is pushed down in the organizational structure. As institutions become larger and more complex, there is a tendency toward decentralization. Centralization and decentralization can best be envisioned as two ends of a continuum. Organizations marked by a high degree of retention of power, duties, and authority by top management are centralized; those marked by a high degree of delegation of duties, power, and authority at lower levels of the organization are decentralized.

Decentralized organizations are often described as "participative" because they allow for greater employee participation in decision making. Organizations run the gamut from being highly centralized to highly decentralized, with most lying between the two extremes of the continuum.

As mentioned earlier, many of today's organizations are moving away from a command and control configuration toward a more decentralized structure. The advantages of decentralization are several. First, the decisions to be made in many organizations are so numerous that if they are centralized, the manager may be overwhelmed by the amount of decision making that needs to be done.

Mintzberg warns against centralization of decision making. He has written that:

> Perhaps the most common error committed in organizational design has been the centralization of decision making in the face of cognitive limitation. The top managers, empowered to design the structure, see errors committed below and believe that they can do better, either because they believe themselves smarter or

because they believe they can more easily coordinate decisions. Unfortunately, in complex conditions, this inevitably leads to a state known as "information overload": the more information the brain tries to receive, the less the total amount that actually gets through.[20]

These managers become overwhelmed by too much information and too many decisions to be made, and the organization becomes paralyzed by their inaction.

Today, more libraries allow decisions to be made at the levels in the organization where the most information about the decisions exists.

> We need to respect those who have the knowledge and experience to make decisions in the areas under discussion and we need to share information so that anyone who might be affected by a decision— or simply has a good idea—can add to the conversation. . . . It's also important that no one has a decision made that affects them without having a chance to be part of that conversation.[21]

This greater access to inclusion in the decision-making process is contrary to practice in the typical bureaucracy, where decisions and the information needed to make them are pushed up the hierarchy to a top manager. Most modern organizations attempt to bring together people who have the necessary information and let them make the decisions that will affect them. The effect is to create groups that can focus on problems, projects, or products better than the traditional hierarchy can. These overlays allow the organization to cut across departmental lines and to decentralize decision making. They make the organization more flexible.

Both centralization and decentralization offer advantages.[22] The major advantage of centralization is that it offers the tightest means of coordinating decision making in the organization. Managers have a great deal of control over the decisions that are made because only a small number of managers are permitted to make them.

> Almost everyone agrees that the command-and-control corporate model will not carry us into the twenty-first century. In a world of increasing interdependence and rapid change, it is no longer possible to figure it out from the top. Nor, as today's CEOs keep discovering, is it possible to *command* people to make the profound systemic changes needed. . . . Increasingly, successful organizations are building competitive advantage through less controlling and more learning—that is, continually creating and sharing new knowledge.[23]
>
> —Peter M. Senge,
> "Communities of Leaders and Learners"

A second advantage of decentralization is that it permits organizations to be more responsive to local conditions. Because the transmission of information for decision making takes time, a decentralized organization is able to make more timely decisions.

A final advantage of decentralization is that it serves as a stimulus to motivation. An organization that wishes to attract and retain creative and intelligent people is better able to do so when it permits them considerable power to make decisions. The idea of decentralization is contrary to the classical concept of hierarchy, which centralizes all authority in the primary administrator. However, some degree of decentralization is practiced by almost all modern organizations.

As mentioned previously, most large organizations have cut back the number of middle managers, resulting in a flatter, more decentralized structure. Much of the flattening of structures has been permitted by the introduction of information technology. Technology has the potential to increase top-down control and to demotivate and deskill jobs, but if it is used to provide employees with information needed for decisions, it can empower employees. Information technology, telecommunications combined with databases and computational programs, makes more reliable information available much more quickly than it ever was before to both top managers and those who work at lower layers in an organization.[24] Mid-level managers have been replaced with information technology.

Now top managers can receive up-to-the-minute information on operations via their computers—information that was once collected and interpreted by middle managers. Information technology also permits the easy sharing of information both up and down the organizational ladder. In organizations such as libraries and information centers, where there are a number of highly educated and skilled workers, it is likely that technology will play a key role in permitting further decentralization of decision making.

Unity of Command

A classical management principle that provides clarity in the vertical hierarchy is that of unity of command. The organizational structure should guarantee that each employee has one supervisor who makes assignments and assesses the success of the employee in completing those assignments. However, in many organizations employees have several supervisors. In libraries, this is often true of the clerical staff and shelvers; in many large libraries, subject bibliographers are responsible to both the head of collection development and the head of technical services. An employee with more than one supervisor is placed in the awkward position of determining whose work to do first, how to do the work, and which instructions to follow. Unity of command protects the employee from such undesirable situations. As modern organizations have become more complex, theorists have realized that employees are often subject to multiple influences. When faced with conflicting pressures, the employee should have a single supervisor who can resolve the conflict. In addition, job descriptions should clearly spell out the worker's duties and the amount of time to be spent on each.

Span of Control

Just as employees should not be accountable to too many supervisors, managers should not be responsible for too many employees. Span of control (sometimes called span of management) refers to the number of people or activities a manager can effectively manage. When a manager supervises a large number of employees, that manager is said to have a wide span of control, whereas one who supervises a small number is said to have a narrow span of control. When the number of subordinates exceeds the span of control of a single manager, something must be done to reduce their number. Managers usually solve the problem by grouping some of the jobs together and by placing an individual in charge of each of the groups. The manager then deals primarily with the individuals in charge of the groups rather than with all of the subordinates. Obviously, span of control is closely related to how many levels exist in an organization's hierarchy. When there is a broad span of control, there are fewer managers, and the organization tends to be flatter.

There is no set number of subordinates that constitutes the ideal span of control. Recent research shows that the size of an effective span of control varies widely, depending on the type of organization and the type of activity being supervised. Managers have moved away from trying to specify the "ideal" span of control to considering which is most appropriate to a specific situation.

> By now you may be asking, what is the right number of levels of management for an organization? How many individuals should report to a single manager? Unfortunately, there are no simple answers to these questions. . . . The correct number has a great deal to do with a manager's skills, the complexity of the work, and the organization's ability to develop self-managing teams.[25]

One of the criteria used to determine the number of people a manager can adequately manage is the number and variety of tasks being managed. If the activities of the units assigned to one manager are similar, the span of control can be increased. If the activities vary extensively and require thorough knowledge, the span of control should be decreased. One must consider what knowledge the manager must have to do an adequate job; the broader and more detailed the required knowledge, the fewer units should be assigned.

Another criterion used to determine span of control is the amount of time available to be spent in communication. Time is a critical element in many enterprises. A manager who has many subordinates must reduce the time spent supervising each. Thus, it will be necessary for the manager with a large number of subordinates to spend more time in the initial training of a new supervisor, to give assignments in broad terms of goals or objectives to be achieved, and to delegate authority so that the supervisors may manage their personnel. If the span of control is wide and the manager fails to function as described, time will be consumed by frequent conferences, daily meetings, and repetitive instruction.

When many organizational units report to one manager, a flat or horizontal organization is created, and a wide span of control prevails. There are few levels of operation in a flat organization. Figure 6.4 shows only two levels of operation—the director and the manager of each unit to which specific activities have been assigned. But the scope of knowledge required of the director is extensive indeed. When a manager has many subordinates, supervision of each unit is likely to be minimal. In organizations with narrow spans of management, a tall, vertical organization is created. Figure 6.5, on page 166, shows a vertical organization with four levels of operation. Each supervisor's span of control is narrow—in this organization the director has direct supervision only over two people—a great reduction from the twelve positions shown in Figure 6.4.

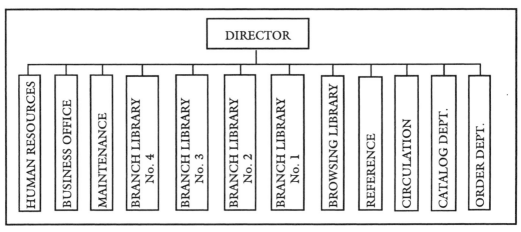

Figure 6.4. A Flat Organization Chart

As would be expected, both narrow and wide spans of control have advantages and disadvantages. A narrow span of control offers tight control and close supervision, frees managers to think of future matters because they are not burdened with an excessive number of present problems, and provides managers of lower quality the chance to perform effectively because they manage fewer and more highly specialized people and activities. If one contrasts the amount of time the director with the narrow span of control spends in supervising with the director with the wide span of control, one can see how there should be more time available for planning and thinking about the "big picture." However, a narrow span of control requires a larger number of managers, which can be costly, and adds complexity to the organization's communication and coordination processes. On the other hand, a wide span of control, in which the manager is unable to exercise close supervision, may promote maturity of subordinates by allowing them to make more decisions on their own. In addition, a wide span of control requires fewer managers; this reduces costs and simplifies communication and coordination. The disadvantages of a wide span of control are that managers are unable to exercise tight control and supervision, and, in general, higher-quality and more costly employees are needed because they have large jobs and must act independently.

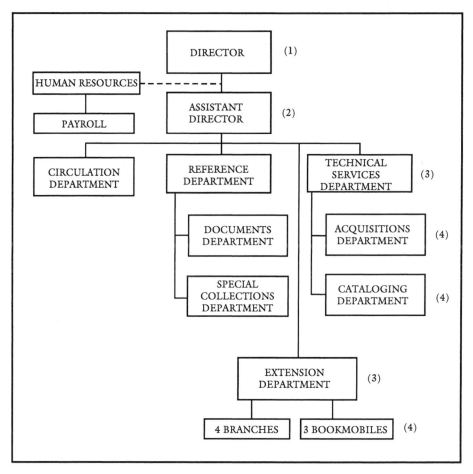

Figure 6.5. A Vertical Organization Chart (figures in parentheses indicate level according to authority lines)

Libraries, like other organizations, are now attempting to flatten structures; this move reverses the pattern of the recent past when organizations have tended to add layers of management to provide tighter control. In the past, many libraries in response to an increase in their size introduced a new layer of administration to avoid a too-wide span of control. As recently as the 1940s, almost all libraries, regardless of size, were organized along departmental lines. Work was apportioned among various departments—circulation, reference, and cataloging, for example—and all department heads reported to the library director. As libraries grew, the number of departments grew also, until the span of control was so wide that either the administration began to break down or the library director became so involved in operational duties that no time was left for broader responsibilities, such as planning or cultivating institutional relationships. Large libraries tried various ways of reorganizing, but by the early 1950s, most adopted a bifurcated organizational structure based on a division of library functions into technical services and readers' services. An assistant or associate library director in charge of each area reported to the director. In that way, the director's span of control was decreased. Although this bifurcated pattern of organizations remains in place in many large libraries, it is being replaced in some by more decentralized structures where the director's span of control is wider. For instance, at the University of Arizona, which has a team-based structure, the dean has a large number of people reporting to her (see Figure 7.4).

The concept of span of control is important. It demonstrates that there is a limit to the number of persons an individual can effectively manage. The optimal width of the span of control depends on a number of circumstances, including the variety of activities assigned, the rate of change, and the amount of time a manager must give each subordinate.

Line and Staff Positions

An important but sometimes confusing authority relationship in any organization is that of line and staff positions. The concept of line and staff has been used for a good many years, but it still causes friction and difficulty. Line positions are responsible and accountable for the organization's primary objectives. Staff positions provide advice, support, and service to the line positions. Line and staff are also distinguished by their decision-making authority. Because line positions are responsible for accomplishing the organization's primary objectives, they have final authority to make decisions. Staff positions, on the other hand, provide suggestions and advice for the line positions but cannot, theoretically, make decisions for the line positions. As the old saying goes, "Line tells; staff sells." The staff must convince the line managers to adopt their suggestions. By maintaining final decision-making authority in the line positions, an organization seeks to keep authority for decision making in the positions accountable for results and to preserve a clear chain-of-command from the top to the bottom of the organization.

As libraries have grown in size and complexity, they have relied more heavily on staff positions to provide support, advice, and information. Many libraries now have a number of staff positions dealing with public relations, systems, personnel, planning, fund-raising, and budgeting. These staff positions are held by individuals skilled in specific functions who provide the facts and information needed by the decision makers. A library human resources office, for example, may be responsible for receiving applications, interviewing applicants, maintaining personnel files, and recommending promotion or transfer. But, generally, the human resources director does not have the authority to make human resources decisions. For instance, the human resources department facilitates the search for a new department head, but the actual decision about whom to hire is made by someone else—most likely by the library director, often with input from a search committee. Only individuals in the line position—the authority position—make these kinds of decisions. Although the head of the human resources department serves in a staff position for the entire library, he or she would at the same time have a line position within the human resources department and make decisions relating to its operation.

> Finally, the best GMs [general managers] use staff people well and expect them to make positive contributions, not to nitpick or "*gotcha*." They appoint strong functional leaders (not line-manager rejects, politicians, or tired old pros) who can provide innovative, idea-driven leadership (not just ask good questions) and can transfer ideas across the organization. As a result, line managers respect and use the staff instead of writing unfriendly memos or playing unproductive political games.[26]
>
> —Andrall E. Pearson,
> "Six Basics for General Managers"

Conflicts often develop between line and staff personnel, usually where there are unclear notions of duties and authority. If staff employees do not understand their role in the organization, they will be frustrated and confused. On the other hand, if line managers continually disregard the advice of the staff, fearing that staff members may undermine the line manager's position and authority, the staff will be underutilized and its expertise wasted. Managers to whom staff employees report should be sure that authority relationships are understood and should encourage line personnel to listen to staff and keep them fully informed so that staff positions can play their intended role of offering support and advice.

Coordination

Division of work, or specialization, is one important task in setting up an organization, but it is equally important to make provisions for coordination. As mentioned earlier, every organization must specialize by dividing the tasks to be done. It must also coordinate or integrate these activities, bringing together all the individual job efforts to achieve a particular objective.

It is sometimes hard for a manager to strike the right balance between too much and too little coordination between departments. If there is too little, each department will focus inward on its own responsibilities. There will be too little attention given to the organization's overall objectives, and likely there will be both duplications and omissions in what is done because of the lack of the overall "big picture" view. At the same time, too much coordinating can lead to departments getting in each other's way and little getting accomplished. Sometimes in libraries one hears the complaint that librarians spend all their time in committee meetings and hence do not have time to do their "real" work. Although this is almost always an exaggeration, it is true that in all types of organizations a great deal of time is consumed by committees and meetings. These are good methods of achieving coordination and integration among units, but if allowed to proliferate uncontrolled, they can take far too much time away from the real work of the organization. Therefore, managers need to strive to maintain a balance between specialization and coordination.

Coordinating Mechanisms

There are a number of ways that coordination can be achieved. The vertical hierarchy is the primary means of providing coordination and integration because the power and accountability associated with the hierarchy help ensure that all parts of the organization work compatibly with one another. The planning techniques discussed in chapters 3 and 4 provide another means of coordinating. Policies, procedures, and rules provide guidance for members of the organization. When organizational members follow agreed-upon guidelines, they are more likely to perform in a manner that is consistent with overall goals. In similar fashion, the organizational manual serves as a coordinating mechanism by specifying the activities that are to be conducted in each unit. The functional statements in the manual are designed to ensure that all work is covered and that the separation of the overall duties and functions provides the mix necessary to achieve organizational objectives. Committees provide another means of coordination among specialized units because they often draw members from various parts of the organization and because they encourage communication and participation in decision making. Staff positions, because they provide assistance and advice to managers throughout an organization, also promote coordination.

Michael McCaskey points out that the more highly differentiated or specialized an organization, the more difficult it is to coordinate.

> The manager/designer must resist differentiating the organization radically—the greater the differences between the units, the harder it is for them to coordinate activities with each other. . . . [W]hen an organization is highly differentiated people have to spend more effort translating and appreciating the framework of people in different units. Most people think in their own terms and it takes an increased effort to move into another's frame of reference. The chances for misunderstandings increase in a highly differentiated organization.[27]

Many management experts recommend that organizations maintain a basic simplicity of form. Thomas Peters and Robert Waterman, in their study of successful organizations, found that the most successful organizations had a simple form that was easily understood by their employees. In their words, "making an organization work has everything to do with keeping things understandable for the tens or hundreds of thousands who must make things happen. And that means keeping things simple."[28] Any good organization structure has to have clarity with a clear delineation of boundaries and accountabilities. Thus, simplicity in form aids in coordination.

Henry Mintzberg provides another viewpoint on coordination. He identifies five mechanisms that explain the fundamental ways organizations coordinate their work. These five mechanisms—mutual adjustment; direct supervision; and standardization of work processes, outputs, and skills—provide the means to hold the organization together.

◆ *Mutual adjustment* means informal communication. Because it is such a simple mechanism, mutual adjustment is the coordinating mechanism used in the simplest of organizations, for example, in a small library with a limited number of employees. Where there are just a few workers, there is no need for elaborate hierarchy, and direct communication among all workers is unimpeded. Hence, informal communication permits the coordination of activities without use of a more elaborate mechanism. And as will be discussed later, mutual adjustment is also used by the most complex of organizations, where sophisticated problem-solvers facing extremely complicated situations must communicate informally to accomplish their work.

◆ In *direct supervision* one individual takes responsibility for the work of others, issuing instructions to them and monitoring their actions. In a library that has individual departments, mutual adjustment does not suffice to coordinate work. A hierarchy in which, as Mintzberg says, "one brain coordinates several hands,"[29] needs to be established.

Mintzberg's remaining methods of coordination involve standardization. With standardization, coordination is achieved before the work is undertaken. In a sense, standardization incorporates coordination into the design of the work; this reduces the need for external coordinating mechanisms.

◆ *Standardization of work processes* occurs when the content of specific jobs is specified and programmed, that is, the processes are standardized to a high degree. Supervisors overseeing such workers have little need to coordinate because a high degree of specificity is built into the jobs that are to be performed. The classic case of this type of standardization is found on assembly lines where workers perform highly specified tasks.

◆ *Standardization of outputs* occurs when the results of the work, for example, the dimensions of the product or the performance, are specified. Certain outputs are standardized in libraries and information centers; for instance, the order of records in a catalog is usually standardized by means of a tool like the ALA filing rules.

Where neither the work nor its outputs can be standardized, some coordination is attained by "standardizing" the worker.

◆ *Standardization of skills* occurs when the training required to perform the work is specified. In most libraries and information centers, an ALA-accredited master's degree is required for entry-level professional positions. Although curricula differ among schools of library and information science, it is assumed that a person who has earned an accredited MLS has acquired the initial skills and knowledge needed to be a professional librarian.

Mintzberg sees the five coordinating mechanisms as a continuum; as organizational work becomes more complicated, the means of coordination shifts from mutual adjustment to direct supervision, to standardization of work processes, to standardization of outputs, and, finally, to standardization of skills. As mentioned previously, the most complex organizations revert to the beginning of the continuum and use the coordinating device of mutual adjustment.

Consider the organization charged with putting a human being on the moon for the first time. The project requires an incredibly elaborate division of labor, with thousands of specialists doing specific jobs. At the outset, no one can be sure exactly what needs to be done; that knowledge develops as the work unfolds. In the final analysis, despite the use of other coordinating mechanisms, the success of the undertaking depends primarily on the ability of the specialists to adapt to each other along the uncharted route.[30]

Although organizations may favor one coordinating mechanism, no organization relies on a single one, and most mix all five. At the least, a certain amount of mutual adjustment and direct supervision is always required, no matter what the reliance on standards. Libraries and information centers use all five of the coordinating mechanisms.

Managers should remember the importance of coordination. It serves as the glue that permits the various units of the organization to move together toward the achievement of organizational objectives. The larger and more complex an organization becomes, the more those coordinating mechanisms are needed.

Conclusion

This chapter has covered the methods that organizations use to decide how to subdivide into smaller subunits to permit specializations and the approaches they use to integrate the organization to permit coordination among the functions. The next chapter will look at the various overall organizational structures that are found in libraries and other organizations today and will discuss how those structures may be different in the organizations of tomorrow.

Notes

1. Henry Mintzberg, *Structure in Fives: Designing Effective Organizations* (Englewood Cliffs, NJ: Prentice-Hall, 1983), 2.

2. Peter Drucker, *Management: Tasks, Responsibilities, Practices* (New York: Harper & Row, 1974), 530.

3. James A. Belasco, *Teaching the Elephant to Dance: Empowering Change in Your Organization* (New York: Crown, 1990), 2.

4. Jim Collins, *Good to Great: Why Some Companies Make the Leap and Others Don't* (New York: Harper Business, 2001), 133–34.

5. Robert Howard, "The CEO as Organizational Architect: An Interview with Xerox's Paul Allaire," *Harvard Business Review* 70 (September/October 1992): 120–21.

6.   Henry Mintzberg, "Organization Design: Fashion or Fit?" *Harvard Business Review* 59 (January–February 1981): 103.

7.   Vesa Kautto and Joma Niemitalo, "Organization and Efficiency of Finnish Academic Libraries," *Libri* 9 (December 1996): 201–8.

8.   See http://www.aoltimewarner.com/about/index.html.

9.   Michael J. Hammer and James Champy, *Reengineering the Corporation: A Manifesto for Business Revolution* (New York: Harper Business, 1993), 3.

10.   Maxine Brodie and Neil McLean, "Process Reengineering in Academic Libraries: Shifting to Client-centered Resource Provision," *CAUSE/EFFECT* 18 (Summer 1995): 42.

11.   *Ibid.*

12.   Michael E. Porter and Victor E. Millar, "How Information Gives You Competitive Advantage," *Harvard Business Review* 63 (July–August 1985): 149–74.

13.   *Ibid.*, 152.

14.   Brodie and McLean, "Process Reengineering in Academic Libraries."

15.   See, for example Sandra Yee, Rita Bullard, and Morell Boone, "We Built It and They Came: Client Centered Services in a New Building," *Proceedings of the ACRL 10th National Conference* (Chicago: American Library Association, 2001), 261–64.

16.   Gregory G. Dess et al., "The New Corporate Architecture," *Academy of Management Executive* 9 (1995): 16.

17.   Henri Fayol, *General and Industrial Administration* (New York: Pitman, 1949), 14.

18.   John R. P. French, Jr. and Bertram Raven, "The Bases of Social Power," in Dorwin Cartwright and Alvin Zander, eds. *Group Dynamics: Research and Theory* (Evanston, IL: Row, Peterson, 1960), 607–23.

19.   Allen B. Veaner, *Academic Librarianship in a Transformational Age* (Boston: G. K. Hall, 1990), 129.

20.   *Ibid.*, 183.

21.   David Lesniaki et al., "Collegial Leadership in Academic Libraries," *Proceedings of the ACRL 10th National Conference* (Chicago: American Library Association, 2001), 236.

22.   Henry Mintzberg, *The Structuring of Organizations* (Englewood Cliffs, NJ: Prentice-Hall, 1979), 181–213.

23.   Peter M. Senge, "Communities of Leaders and Learners," *Harvard Business Review* 75 (September–October, 1997): 30–31.

24.   Kenneth Chilton, "American Manufacturers Respond to the Global Marketplace," in Kenneth Chilton et al., eds., *The Dynamic American Firm* (Boston: Kluwer Academic Publishers, 1996), 166.

25.   Edward E. Lawler III, *From the Ground Up: Six Principles for Building the New Logic Corporation* (San Francisco: Jossey-Bass, 1996), 90.

26.   Andrall E. Pearson, "Six Basics for General Managers," in Joseph L. Bower, ed., *The Craft of General Management* (Boston: Harvard Business School Press, 1991), 17.

27.   Michael B. McCaskey, "An Introduction to Organizational Design," *California Management Review* 17 (Winter 1974): 13–20.

28.   Thomas J. Peters and Robert H. Waterman Jr., *In Search of Excellence: Lessons from America's Best Run Companies* (New York: Harper & Row, 1982), 306.

29.   Mintzberg, *The Structuring of Organizations*, 4.

30.   *Ibid.*, 3.

Chapter 7

Types of Formal Organizations— Today and in the Future

Organizational structure has traditionally been viewed as layers of boxes neatly stacked atop one another, connected by solid and dashed lines. This view focused our attention on hierarchy, reporting relationships, division of labor, and accountability. The new corporate architecture requires a different mindset: the emphasis is on results rather than maintaining internal relationships.[1]

—Gregory Dess et al.,
"The New Corporate Architecture"

Organizations can be of many types and structures. It is widely recognized that no one structure is suitable to all organizations, and factors such as growth, competition, technology, and environmental uncertainty have to be considered in choosing a structure.

> This is a world in which there are now many more choices about organizational alternatives (forms) than there have been in the recent past. It is also a world in which technological alternatives are many and the variations are proliferating. We have gone from a world in which there were only a few "tried and true" organizational designs to one in which there are many. It requires a great deal of "organization design skill" to achieve a good fit between the organizational and technical alternatives available.[2]

Nonetheless, some types of organizations are very common. Today, throughout the world, most large organizations, including libraries, are structured as bureaucracies. In this chapter, the traits and characteristics of bureaucracies are described, and some of the criticisms of bureaucracies as a structure are discussed. Next, some alternatives to the bureaucratic structure are introduced. The chapter concludes with some speculations about how future organizations will be structured.

Bureaucracies

" 'Bureaucracy' is a dirty word. . . . It suggests rigid rules and regulations . . . impersonality, resistance to change. Yet every organization of any significant size is bureaucraticized to some degree."[3] The term *bureaucracy* is used often in a derogatory fashion, with a connotation of cumbersome structure, red tape, and over-organization, but the term has a different origin.

Bureaucracies were first described in the early part of the twentieth century by Max Weber, a German sociologist trained in law, economics, history, and philosophy. His perceptive and incisive theoretical analysis of the principles of bureaucracies is undoubtedly one of the most important statements on formal organizations; it has had a profound influence on almost all subsequent thinking and research in the field.[4]

> The hierarchical kind of organization we call bureaucracy did not emerge accidentally. It is the only form of organization that can enable a company to employ a large number of people and yet preserve unambiguous accountability for the work they do. And that is why, despite all its problems, it has so doggedly persisted.[5]
>
> —Elliot Jaques,
> "In Praise of Hierarchy"

Weber created the concept of bureaucracy as a model for use in his analysis of organized industrial society. He attempted to construct a model of a perfectly rational organization, one that would perform its job with maximum efficiency. Basing his model on reasoning rather than on empirical evidence, Weber described the characteristics of this ideal administrative framework as follows:

♦ Impersonal and formal conduct. Because personality and emotional-based relationships interfere with rationality, nepotism and favoritism not related to performance should be eliminated.

♦ Employment and promotion on the basis of technical competence and performance. Using these criteria ensures that the best-qualified people will pursue a career in the organization and remain loyal to it.

♦ Systematic specialization of labor and specification of responsibilities. All of the work necessary to accomplish the tasks of the organization should be divided into specific areas of competence, with each employee and supervisor having authority over his or her functions and not interfering with the conduct of others' jobs.

♦ A well-ordered system of rules and procedures that regulates the conduct of work. These rules serve (a) to standardize operations and decisions, (b) as receptacles of past learning, and (c) to protect incumbents and ensure equality of treatment. The learning of rules represents much of the technical competence of incumbents because the rules tell them what decisions to make and when to make them.

♦ Hierarchy of positions such that each position is controlled by a higher one. The hierarchy of authority is impersonal, based on rules, and the superior position is held by the individual having greater expertise. In this way, compliance with rules and coordination is systematically ensured.

♦ Complete separation of the property and affairs of the organization from the personal property and affairs of the incumbents. This serves to prevent the demands and interests of personal affairs from interfering with the rational, impersonal conduct of the business of the organization.[6]

Weber's concept of bureaucracy is the basis for much influential thought and investigation into organizations. His work brings together a large number of the concepts already discussed in this section—division of labor, horizontal specialization, hierarchy of authority, and standardization of work processes. The organization of a typical library includes many characteristics of bureaucracy. Almost all libraries are marked by the hierarchical structure, a large number of rules (ranging from cataloging and filing rules to circulation rules), the demands of technical competence, and the systematic specialization of labor.

Since Weber formulated his ideas concerning bureaucracies, many critics have written about the dysfunctional aspects of bureaucracies. A great deal of this criticism of bureaucracy focuses on the internal workings of the organization, especially the unintended consequences of control through rules.[7] Other criticism centers on the relationship of the bureaucratic organization to its environment and the tendency of the traditional bureaucracy to largely ignore the outside world. This criticism considers the bureaucratic organizational model flawed because it treats the organization as if it were a closed system unaffected by the uncertainties of environment.[8] Other criticism faults the bureaucratic model for being overly mechanical and ignoring individual and group behaviors in organizations.[9]

> [Functional bureaucracies] breed dependence and passivity. In a functional organization, there is a natural tendency for conflicts to get kicked upstairs. People get too accustomed to sitting on their hands and waiting for a decision to come down from above. Well, sometimes the decision does come down. But sometimes it doesn't, and even when it does, often it comes too late, because market conditions have already changed or a more nimble competitor has gotten there first. Or maybe the decision is simply wrong—because the person making it is too far from the customer.[10]
>
> —Robert Howard,
> "The CEO as Organizational Architect"

In stable environments, changes occur slowly. For organizations, stable environments mean that customer needs change slowly, and thus, organizations are under little pressure to change their established methods. In a stable environment, organizations handle information that is largely predictable. Carefully developed plans can be made in advance, and exceptions are so few that there is time for upper-level decision-makers to decide what to do. The rules and procedures that are a characteristic of bureaucracies function best in an environment that is stable. Indeed, in most large organizations in stable environments, bureaucracies are likely to be the most efficient types of organizational structure.

Today, however, the environment is not stable but turbulent. The rapid changes taking place in the external environment of today's organizations cause many to question the suitability of the bureaucratic method of organization. Organizations that exist in unstable environments encounter change frequently. They must be adaptable and flexible. Long lists of policies and rules cannot be relied upon; circumstances change too quickly for decisions to be adequately covered by rules. As technology evolves rapidly, frequent product and service changes result from both the changing needs of customers and the pressure of competitors. Bureaucracies are less efficient in a turbulent environment than in a stable environment because they lack the ability to adapt easily to change. Bureaucracies lack this ability because they "are geared to stable environments; they are performance structures designed to perfect programs for contingencies that can be predicted, not problem solving ones designed to create new programs for needs that have never been encountered."[11]

> Hierarchy is an approach to organization that is beginning to lose its once unquestioned authority where it exists in its most extreme form: in multilevel hierarchy, which gives rise to multilevel bureaucracy, and absolute hierarchy, where all work is determined by downward assignment and where peers play no part in distributing work among themselves. History has imposed these forms of organization upon us. They will be displaced only if we find something better.[12]
>
> —Meredith Belbin,
> *The Coming Shape of Organizations*

Although the bureaucracy is the most common form of organizational structure, there are other forms. Tom Burns and G. M. Stalker were among the first to distinguish between two types of organizations: One they called the mechanistic, and the other the organic.[13]

Mechanistic organizational structures are shaped in the traditional, pyramidal pattern of organization. Bureaucracies are an example of the mechanistic organizational structure. This type of organization is designed to be like a machine, hence the name. "People are conceived of as parts performing specific tasks. As employees leave, other parts can be slipped into their places. Someone at the top is the designer, defining what the parts will be and how they will fit together."[14]

Burns and Stalker found that the mechanistic, or bureaucratic, structure worked best for organizations that perform many routine tasks and operate in a stable environment; mechanistic structures were not successful in organizations that were required to adjust to environmental changes. Instead, another form, the organic, functioned best in these environments.

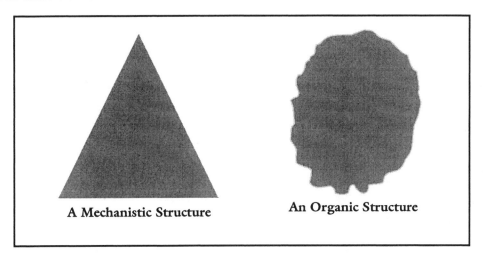

Figure 7.1. The Mechanistic and Organic Organizational Structure

Organic Systems

The organic organization's structure is completely different from the mechanistic organization. This structure is based on a biological metaphor, and the objective in designing such a system is to leave it open to the environment so it can respond to new opportunities. The organic form is appropriate to changing conditions that constantly give rise to fresh problems and unforeseen requirements for action. Organic structures are often more appropriate than bureaucracies for today's better-educated workers who seek greater freedom in their work. An organic structure is characterized by:

♦ an emphasis on lateral and horizontal flows of communication within the organization;

♦ organizational influence based largely on the authority of knowledge rather than an individual's position in the structure;

♦ members of the organization tending to have a system-wide orientation rather than narrow, departmental views;

♦ job definitions that are less precise and more flexible and duties that change as new problems and challenges are confronted; and

♦ a commitment by many members to professional standards developed by groups outside the formal organization. For instance, engineers may identify as strongly with their professional societies as they do with the firms for which they work.[15] In a similar fashion, many librarians identify as much with their profession as with the institutions that employ them.

In almost every respect, the organic institution is the opposite of the classical bureaucracy. Bureaucracies emphasize standardization and formal relations; organic structures are marked by loose, informal working relations, and problems are worked out as needs arise.

> Organizations used to be perceived as gigantic pieces of engineering with largely interchangeable human parts. We talked of their structures and their systems, of inputs and outputs, of control devices and managing them, as if the whole was one large factory. Today the language is not that of engineering but of politics with talk of cultures and networks, of teams and coalitions, of influence or power rather than control, of leadership not management.[16]
>
> —Charles Handy,
> *The Age of Unreason*

Burns and Stalker are careful to emphasize that whereas organic systems are "not hierarchic in the same sense as are mechanistic systems, they remain stratified." Positions are differentiated according to seniority, that is, greater expertise. The lead in joint decisions is frequently taken by seniors, but it is an essential presumption of the organic system that the lead, or the authority, is taken by those who show themselves most informed and capable. The location of authority is settled by consensus.[17]

Organic structures are further marked by workers' commitment to the organization, a blurring of the distinction between the formal and informal organization, and the development of shared beliefs about the values and goals of the organization. However, because of the departure from the familiar clear and fixed hierarchical structure, many managers feel uncomfortable in organic organizations. In many ways, it is harder to be a manager in an organic system than in a bureaucracy because most of the certainties associated with a stable hierarchy do not exist in the organic system. Much more ambiguity is associated with the organic pattern of organizing, and managers must be able to tolerate that ambiguity.

It takes a different style of management to succeed in organic structures. And, as we will see, it is not easy for a manager to switch from managing one type of structure to the other.

> Executives who have good interpersonal skills, are comfortable with delegating, and enjoy the intellectual challenge of a healthy debate, favor flatter more participative designs. Executives who have a high need for control, a genius for detail, and a strong ability to organize prefer hierarchical, closely managed configurations. Debates among the differing styles are often endless and pointless, for the argument regresses into one of personal preference.[18]

Mechanistic and organic systems are on the extreme ends of a continuum. A small group of scientists working in a laboratory represents an organic structure; a highly structured factory producing a standard product for a stable market represents a mechanistic one. Most institutions fall somewhere between these two extremes. And, an organization can contain both organic and mechanistic units. Burns and Stalker characterized whole organizations as mechanistic or organic, but others have found these terms often describe units within an organization.[19]

Few libraries are structured as pure organic systems. Some small, special libraries come close to this model, as do small academic libraries that have adopted a collegial system of organization similar to that used in academic departments.[20] Some small public and school libraries are also organic in structure. This type of organizational structure is possible only when the number of people working in an organization is relatively small. There it often makes much more sense than a mechanistic organization structure. The librarians in one small library who decided to change from a hierarchical to a collegial structure explained their reasoning as follows:

> [W]e previously had a vestigial hierarchy, laid out in a pyramid shaped chart, that mimicked standard library organizations: we had a director, heads of technical and public services, and the remaining librarians in a third tier. But having three layers of hierarchy among six librarians makes about as much sense as having a captain and a first mate in a rowboat. . . . In fast-changing times, we couldn't work within a system, however vestigial, in which some of us stood around waiting for orders—or in which people best positioned to make informed decisions felt compelled to go through layers of command for approval. And in practice, we usually ignored those vestiges of traditional hierarchy. It made sense to us that the best decisions are made by a group of people

working together with a shared knowledge base and a shared sense of responsibility for the entire operation.[21]

In the collegial system, instead of a single final authority position, a group of individuals participates in making decisions that affect the whole organization. The collegial organization has been successful in some small libraries, but the large number of professional and nonprofessional employees in most libraries make this form of organization impossible. But even in large libraries, you see subunits of the library becoming more organic in structure. The use of self-managing teams, which will be discussed later, is an example of how a mechanistic organization can become more organic.

> Traditionally, libraries have been organized along hierarchical lines, internally structured according to function. In this structure responsibility for decision making is placed with the head of the library, and authority diminishes with descending levels of the organizational pyramid. While this organization has its advantages, it is prone to becoming an uncompromising bureaucracy. Too often it results in poor communication, organizational stratification, stifled initiative, and bureaucratic overstaffing.... Lack of coordination within and between departments and competition among units over priorities, resources, and means to attain library objectives increase the likelihood of conflict and misunderstanding between organizational units. Divided by factional interests, staff members focus on their own narrow domains.... In a stable environment, this structure has managed to function effectively. However, it is clearly ill equipped to face the challenges of the electronic information age.[22]
>
> —Susan Jacobson, "Reorganization"

Modifying Library Bureaucracy

Although many organizations are attempting to move away from the bureaucratic model, most libraries and information centers, because of their size, the technology they use, and the services they perform, are still organized in this fashion. But as libraries "have been criticized for their inability to keep up with social and individual expectations and their failure to change quickly enough to meet competitive challenges,"[23] they have begun to search for new forms of organizational structure. There is a growing acceptance of the fact that the traditional hierarchical system needs to be modified. As Michael Gorman writes:

> Hierarchies are not hospitable to creativity and self-fulfillment. Such structures are inimical to the open and flexible nature of library work . . . other negative characteristics of hierarchical library organizations are their innate internal rigidity and uniformity within substructures. . . . Beyond such examples, there is the

enormous difficulty of carrying out change within the hierarchical structure. The hierarchy is inherently resistant to internal chance and *must* be replaced by an open structure of clusters of staff interacting with each other in a multidimensional and innovative manner.[24]

There has been a widespread belief that the adoption of new technologies will inevitably lead to radical changes in the organizational structures of libraries. To date those radical changes have not occurred. Since 1973, the Association of Research Libraries (ARL) has published a series of volumes containing the organizational charts of the large research libraries that are members of ARL. The latest of these ARL volumes was published in 1996.[25] A comparison of the four collections provides a quick overview of some of the structural changes that have occurred in North American university libraries over the past three decades. Although changes have been made in organizational structures, the hierarchical structure still prevails in large academic libraries as it does in other large libraries.

But it is also obvious that these large libraries are involved in organizational change. For the latest ARL compilation, in addition to contributing organizational charts, libraries were also asked to respond to a survey about restructuring. Fifty-three libraries responded, and of these seventeen were in the process of or had recently completed a library-wide reorganization. An additional thirty-four libraries were engaged in or had recently reorganized specific units, most often reference, cataloging, acquisitions, interlibrary loan, circulation, or reserves. Declining resources and the need for greater productivity precipitated much of this reorganization. Many university libraries reported losing staff positions. Twenty-three libraries had lost support staff (an average of 10.5 individuals), and twenty libraries had lost professional positions (an average of 5.5). The survey results showed that the most common outcomes of the reorganizations had been "combining of units within the libraries, new partnerships with other university units, greater emphasis on networked information, new and expanded user services, elimination of some services, and a decreased emphasis on catalog maintenance and on the collection of print materials."[26] Although the bifurcated pattern of organization remained in place in some libraries, it was being replaced in others by more decentralized structures where the director's span of control was wider. The charts and the survey results demonstrate that although many of these large university libraries were feeling the need to restructure, most had merely reorganized around the edges instead of completely discarding their old structure and beginning anew.

Instead of radically restructuring, the structure of libraries has changed in a way that is not reflected on the organizational chart. Libraries and information centers are becoming more hybrid in structure by organizing some departments more organically than others or by employing "overlays," or modifications imposed on the basic bureaucratic organizational structure. The pyramid remains largely intact, but modifications are in place in many libraries that are flattening the pyramid and allowing more employee input into decision making.

Some Commonly Used Modifications

Libraries rely heavily on various types of coordinating positions and temporary groups to deal with increasing complexity, but, in most cases, these modifications are superimposed upon the traditional bureaucratic structure. Modifications may be traditional, such as committees, or innovative, such as quality circles; they may be permanent, such as matrix organizations, or more transitory, such as temporary task forces. But in libraries and information centers of all types, the hierarchical structures are being modified by a number of means. A discussion of some of these modifications follows.

Committees

One of the most common modifications to libraries' hierarchical structure is a committee. Committees are especially useful when a process does not fall within the domain of any one chain of command, so a committee consisting of representatives from all the units involved is established. Standing committees often deal with ongoing issues, such as staff development, automation, and personnel. Ad hoc, or temporary, committees are formed as required. For instance, many libraries use search committees in the hiring process. The power held by committees varies from library to library. In some libraries and information centers, committees have the authority to establish policy; in others, they play an advisory role.

Committees provide a means to bring a wide variety of knowledge and experience to bear on a topic. They also are useful in obtaining commitment to policies and decisions. However, committees are often slow to act, and they are costly because of the time required of participants. All of the advantages and disadvantages of group decision making discussed in chapter 3 pertain to decision making by committees.

Task Force

Task forces are similar to committees, except that their assignment is generally full-time rather than part-time: That is, employees leave their primary jobs to devote all their time to the task force. A task force has a specific, temporary task to perform, and when the task is completed, the members of the group return to their primary jobs. Task forces are particularly valuable when the undertaking is a one-time task that has a broad scope and specific, definable results; is unfamiliar or lacks precedent; calls for a high degree of interdependence among the tasks; and involves a high stake for the task force in the successful completion of the project. In libraries and information centers, task forces are often called upon to deal with new, unfamiliar, or involved projects, such as the installation of a new online catalog or the building of a new facility.

Matrix Organizational Structure

One of the significant innovations in organizational design is the matrix organizational structure. In task forces or project management, group members are withdrawn from their departments and temporarily assigned to the project manager. For the duration of the project, group members have a reporting responsibility to both the project manager and their department supervisor. In matrix management, dual assignments become part of the permanent organizational pattern. Matrix management represents an attempt to retain the advantages of functional specialization while adding the project management's advantage of improved coordination. Aerospace firms were the first to use the matrix structure by experimenting with organizational structures that combined project management with departments organized by function. Functional departments continued to exist in the traditional vertical hierarchy, but project management was superimposed over those departments as a horizontal overlay, hence the name matrix.

The matrix is a fairly complex structure that violates many management principles, especially the principle of unity of command. Although many businesses, including banks and insurance and chemical companies, use a matrix organizational pattern, it is still not common. One reason that this type of structure has not been more widely adopted is that it is often confusing: The simple chain of command is replaced by multiple authority relationships, and managers need to function as team leaders rather than as traditional managers.[27] People working in such an environment need to be able to tolerate a great deal of ambiguity. As two library managers wrote, matrix management is "difficult to implement. It runs against our cultural bias, and it is sufficiently complex and ambiguous that it requires virtually constant monitoring to keep it running well. Most of us have lived in hierarchical organizations all of our lives, and it is difficult for us to even visualize, much less adapt to, another form of organization."[28]

> Any discussion of matrix management must recognize the role played by conflict. Decision makers who introduce matrix management into organizations expect interpersonal, intergroup and interorganizational conflict as a consequence. The organizational objective that makes a matrix structure desirable creates, by its very nature, a situation prone to conflict.[29]
>
> —Peggy Johnson,
> "Matrix Management:
> An Organizational Alternative for Libraries"

One of the first published accounts of matrix management in libraries describes the experience of San Francisco State University. This library was looking for a way to increase organizational effectiveness, particularly in reference services and collection development. After considering the options, the library decided to adopt a matrix management organization. Program coordinators were chosen for the various services provided by the readers services division: user education, online, reference, and collection development. Librarians working in the readers services division had a dual reporting responsibility to the assistant director for public services and to the program coordinator of their specific service unit.[30]

The organizational structure of that library is illustrated in Figure 7.2.

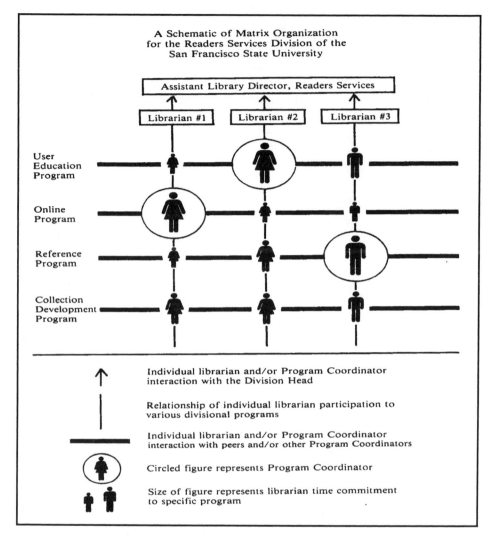

Figure 7.2. A Matrix Organizational Structure. From Joanne Euster and Peter Haikalis, "A Matrix Model of Organization," in *Academic Libraries: Myths and Realities, Proceedings of the Third Annual ACRL Conference* (Chicago: American Library Association, 1984). Reprinted with permission of American Library Association.

Even in the for-profit sector, a number of corporations experimented with and then eliminated the matrix management organizational pattern because of its complexity and lack of clear-cut authority lines. Although few libraries have adopted the pure form of matrix organization, matrix-like structures exist in many libraries today, either as part of their overall organizational structure or in specific units of the library. Libraries that are using teams or task forces as organizing devices are good examples of the incorporation of matrix-like structures into the organization.[31]

Quality Circles

Quality circles are not committees or task forces but small groups of employees that meet regularly and voluntarily to recommend solutions to quality and productivity problems. Quality circles make recommendations only; it is up to management to implement them. Quality circles allow employees greater control over their working conditions and, because they permit line employees greater opportunities for decision making, they increase decentralization. Without a commitment from management, however, quality circles cannot succeed.

Generally, six to twelve volunteers from the same work area make up the circle. The members receive appropriate training, usually from a facilitator who is a specially trained member of management. The facilitator helps ensure that the circles run smoothly. Typically, the circles meet for four hours a month during the work day. Members of the group choose the work-related problems they wish to solve.[32] The quality circle concept was imported from Japan and for a while received widespread acceptance in the United States. At one time in the 1980s it was estimated that more than 90 percent of the Fortune 500 companies had such programs.[33] But after an initial period of enthusiasm, the popularity of quality circles in the United States began to fade. Although quality circles seemed to have some positive impact shortly after their formation, sustaining successes over a longer period of time demanded considerable effort.[34] The quality circles that are still in existence today in the United States are generally part of a larger TQM program.

Self-Managing Teams

If interest in the use of quality circles has waned, there has been an increased interest in the use of teams in the workplace. The team approach provides a basic redesign of how work is accomplished: Instead of groups being managed, there is a shift to groups that manage themselves. When a number of employees work as a group to perform related tasks, it is possible to redesign the overall work, not as a set of individual jobs but as a shared group task. Self-managing or autonomous teams take over many of the functions traditionally reserved for managers, including determining their own work schedules and job assignments.

> The major difference between self-directed work teams and their predecessors, such as quality circles, is that team direction isn't a program but a profound change in how companies do business. It involves using the collective brain-power of all employees as a competitive strategy, empowering them with the responsibility for all functions of the business.[35]
>
> —Jana Schilder,
> "Work Teams Boost Productivity"

Self-managing teams sometimes have other names depending on the organization but their duties are similar.

> Self-managed work teams are known by many different names: self-directed, self-maintaining, self-leading, and self-regulating work teams to name a few. No matter which name is used, by definition they are groups of employees who are responsible for a complete, self-contained package of responsibilities that relate either to a final product or an ongoing process. Team members possess a variety of technical skills and are encouraged to develop new ones to increase their versatility, flexibility, and value to the work team. The team is responsible for monitoring and reviewing the overall process or product (through performance scheduling and by inspecting the team's own work), as well as assigning problem-solving tasks to group members. The teams create a climate that fosters creativity and risk taking, in which members listen to each other and feel free to put forth ideas without being criticized.[36]

Some people have questioned how the use of teams differs from the use of committees, which have been used by libraries of all types for many years. There are, in fact, distinct differences between teams and committees. Committees are marked by the following characteristics:

1.   Members are appointed by administration.

2.   Leadership is usually appointed.

3.   They have a specific charge and are result-oriented.

4.   Agendas are set with the charge.

5.   Broad participation is not required.

On the other hand, teams are marked by these characteristics:

1.   Members are those "who do the work."

2.   Leadership is chosen by the team.

3.   They are process-oriented.

4.   Agendas are set by the team.

5.   Everyone participates.[37]

Self-managed teams began to be used in libraries in the late 1980s, and their use grew in the 1990s. Today, self-managing work teams are the most common overlay to the bureaucratic structure of large libraries. Whereas some of these libraries, such as the ones at California State University at San Marcos or the University of Arizona, have used the team approach for the entire library, others use teams only in a few departments.[38] Figures 7.3 and 7.4 show how the organizational chart of the University of Arizona's libraries changed with the implementation of a team approach to organization.

The role of a manager changes when teams or work groups are used. In an organization that uses teams, the core behaviors of a manager are developing the talents and skills of the team members, getting them excited about the mission of the team, and fostering effective working relations. A team leader needs skills in the following:

1. developing self-motivated staff capable of setting its own goals and evaluating its own efforts;

2. helping diverse members of the team learn to generate and implement their own ideas;

3. developing teams that manage their own daily work;

4. championing cross-functional efforts to improve quality, productivity, and service; and

5. anticipating, initiating, and responding to changes caused by forces outside the organization.[39]

Work teams are gaining increasing popularity in library settings, and they provide yet another way to provide greater decentralization within the hierarchical structure. As all of the accounts of organizations that have switched to the team approach note, it is not an easy or a fast process. The hierarchical approach, with all of its deficiencies, is one that both managers and employees are most familiar with, and sometimes the old certainties look very alluring. It is important for any library considering teams to understand that a team-based organization means undergoing a radical change in organizational culture, and that the process is neither fast nor easy. Chapter 12 contains more information on managing teams and team building.

Reshaping the Library's Organizational Structure

Library conferences and library journals are abuzz with talk of paradigm shifts . . . the non-library . . . the library without walls . . . the library as electronic switching center . . . and on and on. Meanwhile, most librarians get on with the essential daily tasks, involved in incorporating new technologies into existing services; maintaining and improving existing collections; and generally making real if unspectacular progress in the face of financial adversity.[40]

—Walt Crawford and Michael Gorman,
Future Libraries: Dreams, Madness, and Reality

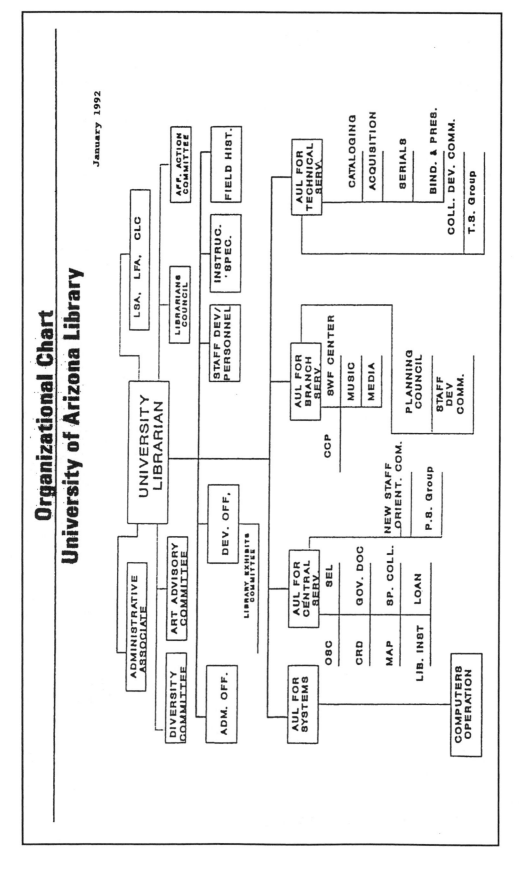

Figure 7.3. The University of Arizona Library Organization Prior to Reorganization

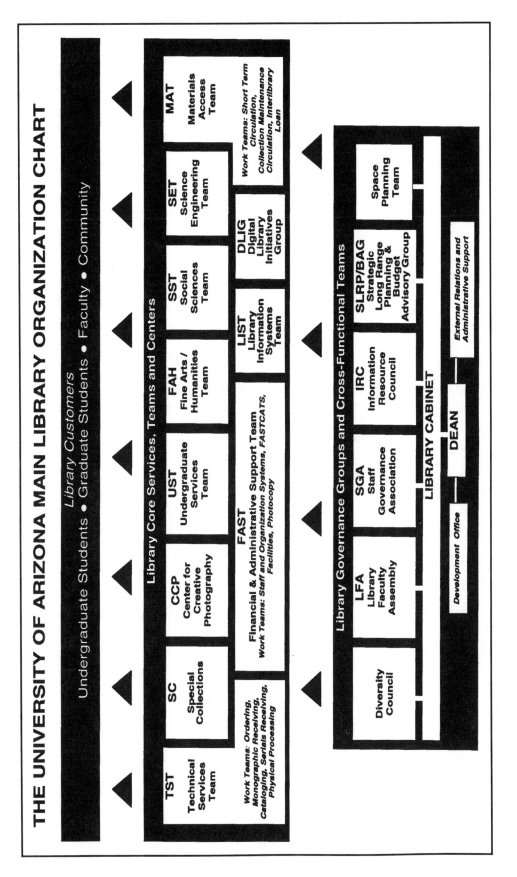

Figure 7.4. The University of Arizona Library Organization After Reorganization

Although there are as yet few signs of radical reorganization of libraries, librarians in all types of libraries and information centers are thinking about the future and trying to devise organizational structures that will allow them to reach their goals most successfully. Most libraries are considering ways to flatten the structure and make the organization more flexible and responsive. These changes are being considered while the library is "getting on with essential daily tasks." Any reorganization is of course complicated because "current services must be maintained while the infrastructure is being built to support the information needs of the 21st century."[41]

Librarians are restructuring to meet the challenges of tomorrow. Rosabeth Moss Kanter has said that tomorrow's organization must possess the following characteristics:

♦ focused—organizations must choose areas in which they can excel and meet high standards;

♦ fast—because no centralized organization with top-down managers can respond to change as rapidly as smaller divisions and departments can, organizations must rely on action taken by individuals. The primary job of the management is to transmit values and priorities;

♦ flexible—job definitions need to be broader; team skills are necessary, and employees need to be able to bridge functions and departments; and

♦ friendly—people need to find work pleasurable and satisfying.[42]

If a library wants to reorganize, what will be involved in making the change? Before even beginning the process, it is important to realize that a significant change in structure will most likely be difficult and time-consuming. It is easy to discuss organizational change in the abstract, but when it comes to implementation, change is usually more difficult than expected.

> In my opinion, organization structure is so important to the future of our libraries that it is often worth undertaking the complicated three- to five-year process of changing a library's basic character if its existing structure is at odds with contemporary needs for change.[43]
>
> —Jerry D. Campbell,
> "Building an Effectiveness Pyramid for
> Leading Successful Organizational Transformation"

In a recent study of large research libraries that had undergone reorganization or restructuring, Joe Hewitt found that there were four major factors precipitating this action. These reasons are similar to those found in other types of organizations. They are:

♦ a need for organizational flexibility;

♦ a need for a stronger external and client-centered orientation;

♦ a need to provide for more staff empowerment and work satisfaction; and

♦ a need to improve management processes, such as communication, coordination, and planning.[44]

A number of accounts of library organizational restructuring have appeared in the recent literature. These reorganization attempts vary in the way they were carried out, and most resulted in different types of restructuring. But there are some common elements found in most successful efforts to change. Miles Overholt has summarized these as follows:

1. determine and select the organizational design that best matches the organization's strategy;

2. assess whether the organization's employees can work well in the preferred design; and

3. then develop a plan for how to move the organization from the current configuration to the new one.[45]

If a library decides to proceed with reorganization, the *first step* is to decide what type of structure is needed. Peter Drucker, who has written so much about organizational structure, provides three ways to determine the type of structure necessary for a specific organization: 1) activities analysis; 2) decision analysis; and 3) relations analysis.[46]
The activities analysis requires the manager to perform a detailed and thorough analysis of activities so that it can be determined what work has to be performed, what activities belong together, and where the activities should be placed in the organizational structure. The decision analysis identifies the kinds of decisions that are needed, where in the structure of the organization they should be made, and the degree of involvement of each manager in the decision-making process. The relations analysis emphasizes the relationships among the units of the organizational structure and the responsibilities of each manager to the various units as well as the responsibilities of the various units to each manager. After performing these three analyses, a manager would have information to be used in determining the structure needed for the organization.
Therefore, planning for the type of structure chosen is important. Analyses such as the ones Drucker proposes would be helpful in gathering information about the type of structure to be implemented. Often other data, especially on library use and satisfaction, are gathered. Techniques such as those used in Business Processing Reengineering that focus upon reexamining the critical processes within an organization can also be useful.
Managers interested in implementing change in an organization's structure should learn as much as possible from reading on the topic and talking to others who have implemented change, but the structure chosen for a particular organization should be based on that organization's specific needs and not chosen because a certain type of organizational structure is being implemented elsewhere. Some libraries and information centers have used consultants in this planning process, others have done it with planning committees drawn from library employees, whereas others have used both of these approaches.

The *second step* in any structural change is a consideration of whether the employees will be able to work well in the proposed new structure. One part of this consideration concerns the personal style of the organization's managers. Not all present-day managers adjust well to a flatter, less bureaucratic style of organization. They learned to manage in the command and control mode, and they feel more comfortable using that style. If a library is considering drastic changes to its structure, it needs to consider whether this new structure will be congruent with the present managers' styles. If not, it will likely fail unless the structural changes are adopted in tandem with other changes, such as changes in management personnel or providing in-depth training to managers in how to manage in the new environment.

> One of the reasons that the traditional command-and-control approach has been so effective in the past and is so hard to change in the present is precisely that its elements reinforce each other. Leaders for example are trained and selected to behave in a hierarchical manner. Status symbols reinforce their authority, pay plans reward them for moving up hierarchies and staff support and information flows allow them to coordinate and make decisions more effectively than anyone else. Movement away from this model requires not just a change in their behavior, but a change in how the organization is designed, managed and structured.[47]

It is not just top-level managers, however, who will likely need help in adjusting to a new structure. Many lower-level staff and middle managers may also find the adjustment difficult. Staff development needs to be provided to all employees to ready them for the new organizational structure. Much attention has to be paid to the human side of the organization.

> Perhaps the library personnel who have to make the greatest changes and who will face the most difficulties in the transformation of the library are library administrators. The roles of the director, assistant directors, and department heads must change from managers, controllers, directors of activities, deciders and evaluators to leaders, coaches and facilitators. All these administrators must be willing to give up a great deal of decision-making authority and become much more comfortable with being challenged, having to explain, not having the last say, and living with ambiguity and uncertainty.[48]
>
> —Carla J. Stoffle et al.,
> "Choosing Our Futures"

It cannot be stressed too much that different types of structures will demand different types of management expertise and different types of employee skills. Inevitably there will be both managers and employees who will not be effective or comfortable in a newly restructured organization. These individuals will either have to be retrained and made comfortable or be replaced; any planning for change must take these needs into account. As the director of one library that has reorganized wrote:

> The key to making the reorganization work is staff education and training. This point cannot be overemphasized. Moreover, educational efforts must target all staff, including management. The staff needs to learn how to participate in the new organization. . . . Not only do staff members need to acquire new knowledge and skills, but, also their attitudes and philosophies must be reexamined and refined.[49]

The staff development and training required to bring about organizational transformation successfully, both in the planning and implementation phases, requires a large amount of monetary and time investment.

The *third step* is to develop the strategy for moving from the current configuration of the organization to the new configuration. This is the implementation stage of the process. Recently published accounts of how certain libraries and information centers have approached restructuring can provide some insights into strategies being employed.

The accounts of successful restructuring have all included a great deal of employee input. Unless employees understand the reasons for the change and "buy into" the change proposed, it is unlikely to be effective. Staff members must understand the concepts underlying the new structure to ensure their full participation.

There is a critical need throughout the entire process, beginning from inception, for effective communication. This communication needs to be both external—for the library is usually a part of a larger organization that needs to be informed about the proposed changes—and internal. Organizational communication will be discussed in chapter 13, but it should be noted here that if employees are not kept well informed of proposed changes, rumors will be rampant. Changes in organizational structures can be very threatening; good communication keeps everyone informed about proposed changes and helps to alleviate employee anxiety.

Almost all the descriptions of organization transformation in libraries and other settings have stressed the time and effort involved in the process, with most commenting that it took longer than they had anticipated to implement. It is also not an inexpensive undertaking. As the librarians at one institution described:

> The process has been expensive. It has taken an enormous amount of time, in total length and in staff weeks. It has required consistency and constancy of vision over a span of several years. Sometimes it also has required, uncomfortably, that we remain flexible and adaptable and that we recognize that ambiguity is an ongoing part of our organization life, not an occasional problem to be eradicated. Would we do it again? Most emphatically *yes*.[50]

The *last step* is to realize that once the reorganization is accomplished, the process is likely not finished. A method of assessment needs to be built into the process so it can be determined whether the new structure is successfully carrying out the organization's goals and objectives. This assessment should attempt to pinpoint the things that are working well and the things that still need to be changed. In most settings, the reorganization is viewed as an iterative process. Typically, everything does not work well with the first reorganization attempt; some things need to be fine-tuned, and mistakes need to be corrected. Once greater flexibility is built into the system, it will be easier to face future changes and to view any restructuring process as an evolutionary one.

In summary, any structural reorganization requires effort and cannot be implemented quickly. Mistakes will be made in the process, and there will be many times in the course of the process when almost everyone will wonder why they ever wanted to consider reorganization. It is important to reward small successes along the way and to keep employees focused on the expected results of the reorganization. It should be encouraging to any organization that feels itself mired in structural change to look to the published reports of libraries that have finished the initial stages of reorganization. Almost all report greater productivity, increased flexibility, better communication, and improved decision making.

The Library Organization of the Future

Libraries and information centers, like all other institutions, are moving toward new organizational structures. They are changing, slowly, away from rigid hierarchies to more organic forms of organization. The move is appropriate because there has often been tension in libraries between the professional status of many of their employees and the bureaucratic organizational form.

Libraries have been struggling to identify the most appropriate new organizational structure for many decades now. During that time, writers have speculated about the type of libraries and information centers that will exist in the future. Most of these writers have expected increased decentralization. In 1984, Hugh Atkinson predicted that the academic library of the future would be decentralized. He felt the "ideal library is one with one or two librarians, one or two library clerks, a handful of student assistants, a homogeneous identifiable clientele, and a collection large enough to suit that clientele."[51] About the same time, Charles Martell proposed restructuring the library into small, client-centered work groups, with librarians operating at all points where the library interacts with its user groups. Each member of the work groups would perform a number of library functions: advanced reference, development of the collection, client instruction, original cataloging, and other forms of information service.[52] Client-centered organizations are decentralized organizations that provide an opportunity for teamwork, greater work variety, and the promise of an improvement in the quality of service.

These early advocates of decentralization were thinking in terms of the decentralization of the library as a physical entity. Today, we have moved away from thinking of libraries just as places. Libraries contain elements of "bricks, books, and bytes,"[53] and the electronic information component of the library is making place less important.

Although a great deal has been written about the "virtual library" and the "library without walls," that type of structure does not exist at the present time and likely will not come into existence in the near future. In the strictest sense, this type of library would not be a physical entity at all, and the storage function traditionally performed by libraries would be eliminated because all information would be available via computer technology. The libraries in some corporations have gone the furthest in assuming this type of structure. In some large multinational corporations, much of the information provision is done by professionals in widely separated locations using electronic resources. Typically these types of libraries have very small collections. The professionals employed in these libraries function as parts of virtual teams and work together although they rarely see one another face to face.

It is in these types of libraries that we see the closest approximation to a new model of organization structure being implemented in some for-profit organizations. These new organizations, often called boundaryless, virtual, or networked organizations, give us a preview of what the organizational structure of a completely new type of library might be. The terms "virtual," "boundaryless," and "networked" are used slightly differently by different people, but in general they all describe a new type of organizational structure that is geographically dispersed and supported by information and communication technology. These types of organizations are not defined or limited by horizontal, vertical, or external boundaries imposed by a predetermined structure. Rather than being housed under one roof, these organizations are widely dispersed and they grow and they shrink as needed. Usually, they have a small hub that coordinates the functions, but most of the rest of the organization is subcontracted.[54] Firms such as Dell Computer, which buy all of their products ready-made or handle only the final assembly, are examples of networked organizations.

These types of organizations provide a high level of flexibility. They can grow or contract as circumstances demand. They are able to change directions swiftly. There is little administrative overhead. At the same time, these organizations have disadvantages. They are hard to coordinate because the parts are so scattered. There is very low employee loyalty because there is a very weak link between employees and the organization.[55] A networked organization is shown in Figure 7.5.

As libraries become less dependent on place, more of them may begin to assume the networked or virtual structure. Perhaps the first true virtual library might be part of one of the universities that has been established to serve only distance students. These universities are not places but are "knowledge servers" linked into a vast network that provides classes to students situated in geographically diverse locations across the country and the world.[56]

These emerging universities provide one model of higher education in the future, and it is possible to imagine a library with a network-type of organizational structure associated with them. In the networked organization, there is a central core or hub that coordinates the organization, and all of the other functions are subcontracted or outsourced to other groups that are linked electronically to that core. Rather than being housed under one roof, the functions of the library would be geographically dispersed. The individuals in the core of the library might still be housed near the central offices of the university, but the other units could be almost anywhere in the world, with all of them

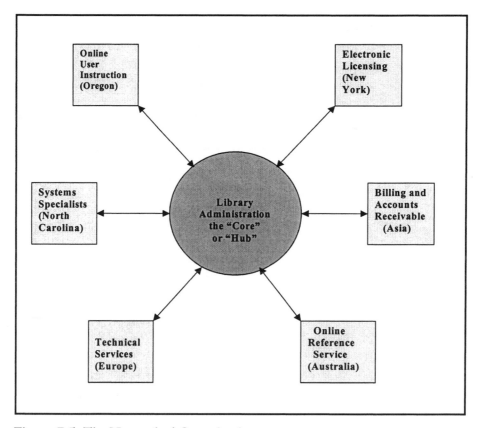

Figure 7.5. The Networked Organization

being electronically linked to the core. The individuals in the core would outsource the acquisition and licensing of electronic materials, including both books and journals (assuming those types of formats still exist). The core would outsource user assistance and perhaps user instruction to help students wherever they might be. If users were billed for the use of material, the accounting department could be located offsite. Systems specialists could be located at a distance also. The people in the center would be the nexus. They would administer and coordinate this networked library, but all of its functions would be supplied from elsewhere. The only interaction between librarians and users would be electronic. This type of library would be truly virtual.

But at least in the foreseeable future, few libraries will take this route. Instead, libraries will be hybrids—combining both paper and electronic resources. But many of these hybrid libraries are displaying at least some components of virtual organizations. For instance, the libraries that are member of the Library of Congress's Collaborative Digital Reference Service project provide professional reference service to their users wherever they are located through an international, digital network of libraries.[57] Most libraries now have access to collections of electronic resources that are not owned or managed by the library itself but by some sort of a library aggregator.

Despite these moves toward the virtual organization, libraries as physical places will continue to exist in the near future, but they will likely become more and more "boundaryless" each year. For instance, academic libraries could have small satellite libraries scattered throughout the campus containing just a few books and journals; these branch libraries would provide most access to information electronically. Students and faculty would also have access to electronic resources from their dormitory rooms, offices, or homes. Public libraries could be much more decentralized, with small branches or kiosks in government offices, businesses, shopping malls, or other locations. With computer technology, the branches would not have to own a large number of materials, but the librarian could have needed material available via a computer workstation and could respond to users' needs upon request. Public library patrons who own computers would have access to materials from their homes. Most special libraries will continue to have small collections, and more and more of their information will be provided electronically.

New technologies will doubtless have a major impact on the departmental patterns of all types of libraries and information centers, but at this point, one can only speculate about what the ultimate effects will be. It seems likely, however, that automation will permit libraries and information centers of the future to be more decentralized and thus provide their users with the geographically dispersed, individualized service they have always preferred. It also seems likely that efforts to introduce more flexibility into libraries and information centers, including the use of cross-functional teams, will lead to libraries and information centers where the barriers between departments are much less fixed. There will likely be more frequent changes in library structure, and workers will become accustomed to working in organizations that are periodically reshaped to fit new needs. In the libraries and information centers of the future, it will be even more important for managers to observe closely the organizational structure of the library to see whether it is still adequate to achieve its goals and objectives.

But we are still moving toward those new organizational structures. Today's libraries are not like the libraries of twenty years ago, but we must also realize that the libraries of 2020 will be different from those of today. To date the biggest changes in the organizational structure of libraries is the flattening of the hierarchy, the use of teams, and the greater inclusion of employees in decision making that has resulted from the decentralization of the library.

> Although the organizational charts may still appear fairly hierarchical, these organizations have begun the metamorphosis into a new type of organization. Whatever the risks or advantages of alternatives to hierarchy, the fact is that few models are in existence in libraries at present.[58]
>
> —Joanne Euster,
> "The New Hierarchy"

When libraries cease to "warehouse" printed materials, their organization structures will change drastically. But until then, it is doubtful that many large libraries will ever adapt a strictly organic organizational form although some small libraries and some subunits within larger libraries may. Large libraries are somewhat limited in the organizational changes they can make because of their size, the large number of routine tasks performed, and the type of product they produce. But some large libraries have changed their structure, and even those that have not will continue to experiment with modifications and expansions or overlays that will permit some decentralization of decision making with some measure of hierarchical control. But the perfect organizational design for today's libraries has not been found, and many failures can be expected as part of the process. There will not be just one successful model but a number of different models. The design of an organization should be contingent upon the environment in which it operates, the tasks the employees must perform in this environment to achieve the organization's objectives, and the characteristics of the employees.[59] Each library will need to discover what works best for it, which organizational structure is most effective and efficient in allowing the organization to achieve its purposes and reach its objectives. And, as Clifford Haka wrote, there is no need for just one type of structure for an entire organization.

> Even within the same organization, there is no one or best way to design operations. For example, would anyone seriously contend that you want the management of your accounts receivable "organized" in the same way with the same amount of control as a team working on developing software for an artificial intelligence (AI) system? I certainly hope not. In one case, there is a clear need for tight control and adherence to procedures, whereas the other situation begs for unbridled creativity.[60]

Regardless of the structure chosen, it must be one that will facilitate flexibility and change. The age of the rigid, unchanging organizational structure is over, and organizations must be ready to change their forms to meet changing conditions and needs. At the same time, there must be a core of stability built into the structure because no organization or its employees can function effectively if there is frequent complete restructuring. As Thomas Peters and Robert Waterman observed in describing excellent companies, "[They] appear to be reorganizing all of the time. They are; but most of the reorganization takes place around the edges. The fundamental form rarely changes that much."[61] In their view, the best organizations have found a way to build stability into the structure but at the same time have incorporated organizational features that allow innovation and responsiveness to the external environment. Libraries and information centers that have maintained the traditional hierarchical structure modified with various overlays are attempting to achieve the same objectives.

Like everything else, management trends change over time. Right now the flat organizational structure is in fashion. Some experts confidently predict that the age of bureaucracies is finished and that hierarchical structures are doomed,[62] but others take a different viewpoint. David Fagiano, president of the American Management Association, recently wrote, "As we have with most management concepts . . . we have driven the dismantling of traditional corporate structure to Luddite proportions. Each time we reach this point, momentum shifts, and the pendulum of change begins to swing back toward a more centrist position."[63] Fagiano predicts that the recent trend toward flatter structures will inevitably reverse and that hierarchical business structures will return to favor soon.[64]

> For example, one hears a great deal today about "the end of hierarchy." This is blatant nonsense. In any institution there has to be a final authority, that is, a "boss"—someone who can make the final decision and who can then expect to be obeyed in a situation of common peril—and every institution is likely to encounter it sooner or later. If the ship founders, the captain does not call a meeting; the captain gives an order. And if the ship is to be saved, everyone must obey the order, must know exactly where to go and what to do and do it without "participation" or argument. Hierarchy, and the unquestioning acceptance of it by everyone in the organization, is the only hope in a crisis.[65]
>
> —Peter F. Drucker,
> "Management's New Paradigms"

Despite the praise of flattened, flexible library organizations, they too have their critics:

> A traditional pyramid organization disperses power throughout itself, with gradations evenly spread over the different strata. However, in the flattened library with no middle managers, the director emerges as the sole political player with sanctioned executive authority, a potentially very powerful person. The team-based library has lost not only its career ladder, but also in sociological terms, its middle classes. It possesses one powerful "have" and numerous "have-not." Without the check and balances of a properly stratified organization, the flattened library may slip from authority into autocracy rapidly.[66]

What we should learn from the pendulum swing of management trends of all types is that there is not just one answer to any problem and that it is a mistake to adopt any prevailing model, dealing with organizing or anything else, without seeing whether that answer suits the circumstances of a particular organization. The rush to flatten structures has taught us a great deal, and in certain types of organizations, flatter structures will provide more efficiency and effectiveness. However, flattening is not the only or necessarily the best approach to use in fashioning every organization's structure. Library managers need to try to avoid the pendulum swings by systematically addressing the entire range of organizational issues, including organizational structure and culture. Each organization must consider its own needs and design a structure to allow it to achieve its objectives. And, as much as possible, managers should involve the library's employees in the design of the new organization. Broad employee participation will create a better structure because the employees' detailed knowledge of the way that specific parts of the organization work will ensure that the rationale behind the new structure is understood and will make implementing the new structure easier because participation builds people's commitment to change.

Conclusion

Each organization must be structured to achieve its goals and objectives. The organizational structure must allow workers to specialize, while coordinating and integrating the activities of those workers at the same time. Although organizing is one of the most important managerial functions, it must be remembered that it is not an end in itself but merely a means to allow the organization to reach its objectives. The design principles discussed in this section are tools, which are neither good nor bad in themselves. They can be used properly or improperly; and that is all. To obtain the greatest possible simplicity and the greatest "fit," organization design has to start out with a clear focus on *key activities* needed to produce *key results*. They have to be structured and positioned in the simplest possible design. Above all, the architect of the organization needs to keep in mind the purpose of the organization he [or she] is designing.

As Peter Drucker writes: "Organization is a means to an end rather than an end itself. Sound structure is a prerequisite to organizational health but it is not health itself. The test of healthy business is not the beauty, clarity, or perfection of its organization structure. *It is the performance of people.*"[67]

Organizational structures fail if they do not encourage workers to perform at their highest levels. As many experts have noted, too much reengineering and reorganization can result in a demoralized workforce, especially when the employees do not understand or have little input into the organizational changes. From the employees' point of view, it can appear that the organizational structure is far more important than the people who work there. In many of the reengineered structures, reorganization and downsizing have resulted in many workers losing their jobs and in feelings of instability and overwork among those who remain. At the same time, the managers in these restructured organizations are stressing the importance of their employees and touting the importance of "the performance of people."

An organization's structure is important, but it is never more important than its employees. So, while libraries and other types of organizations search for better, more efficient structures, they must keep in mind that the effectiveness of the structure depends primarily on the performance of the people working there.

Today, the most successful organizations are those where top executives recognize the need to manage the new environmental and competitive demands by focusing less on the quest for an ideal structure and more on developing the abilities, behavior, and performance of individual managers.[68]

The next two sections of this book will focus on the organization's employees and will discuss the managerial functions dealing with human resources and leading. They will discuss how to handle the important and challenging issues associated with the people who work within an organization.

Notes

1. Gregory G. Dess et al., "The New Corporate Architecture," *Academy of Management Executive* 9 (August 1995): 16.

2. Harvey F. Kolodny, "Some Characteristics of Organizational Designs in New/High Technology Firms," in Luis R. Gomez-Mejia and Michael W. Lawless, eds., *Organizational Issues in High Technology Management* (Greenwich, CT: JAI Press, 1990), 174.

3. Charles Perrow, *Organizational Analysis: A Sociological Review* (Belmont, CA: Wadsworth, 1970), 50.

4. Peter M. Blau and W. Richard Scott, *Formal Organizations* (San Francisco: Chandler, 1962), 27.

5. Elliot Jaques, "In Praise of Hierarchy," *Harvard Business Review* 68 (January–February 1990): 127.

6. John H. Jackson and Cyril P. Morgan, *Organization Theory: A Macro Perspective for Management* (Englewood Cliffs, NJ: Prentice-Hall, 1978), 77.

7. See, for example, Robert K. Merton, "Bureaucratic Structure and Personality," *Social Forces* 18 (May 1940): 560–68; Philip Selznick, *TVA and the Grass Roots* (Berkeley, CA: University of California Press, 1969); Alvin W. Gouldner, *Patterns of Industrial Bureaucracy* (New York: Free Press, 1954).

8. See, for instance, James D. Thompson, *Organizations in Action: Social Science Bases of Administrative Theory* (New York: McGraw-Hill, 1967).

9. Warren G. Bennis, *Changing Organizations: Essays on the Development of Human Organization* (New York: McGraw-Hill, 1966); Rensis Likert, *The Human Organization: Its Management and Value* (New York: McGraw-Hill, 1967).

10. Robert Howard, "The CEO as Organizational Architect: An Interview with Xerox's Paul Allaire," *Harvard Business Review* 70 (September–October 1992): 110.

11. Henry Mintzberg, *The Structuring of Organizations: A Synthesis of the Research* (Englewood Cliffs, NJ: Prentice-Hall, 1979), 375.

12. Meredith Belbin, *The Coming Shape of Organizations* (Oxford: Butterworth-Heinemann, 1996), vi.

13. Tom Burns and G. M. Stalker, *The Management of Innovation* (London: Tavistock, 1966), 119–20.

14. Michael B. McCaskey, "An Introduction to Organizational Design," *California Management Review* 17 (Winter 1974): 14.

15. Burns and Stalker, *Management of Innovation*, 122.

16. Charles Handy, *The Age of Unreason* (Boston: Harvard Business School Press, 1989), 89.

17. Burns and Stalker, *Management of Innovation*, 122.

18. Miles H. Overholt, "Flexible Organizations: Using Organizational Design as a Competitive Advantage," *Human Resources Planning* 20 (1997): 23.

19. Paul R. Lawrence and Jay W. Lorsch, *Organization and Environment: Managing Differentiation and Integration* (Boston: Graduate School of Business Administration, Harvard University, 1967).

20. David Lesniaki, Kris (Huber) MacPherson, Barbara Fister, and Steve McKinzie, "Collegial Leadership in Academic Libraries," *Proceedings of the ACRL Tenth National Conference* (Chicago: American Library Association, 2001), 233–39.

21. *Ibid.*, 234.

22. Susan Jacobson, "Reorganization: Premises, Processes and Pitfalls," *Bulletin of the Medical Library Association* 82 (October 1994): 370.

23. R. Euster and Peter D. Haikalis, "A Matrix Model of Organization for a University Public Services Division," in *Academic Libraries: Myths and Realities* (Chicago: American Library Association, 1984), 357.

24. Michael Gorman, "The Organization of Libraries in the Light Of Automation," *Advances in Library Automation and Networking, Vol. 1* (Greenwich, CT: JAI Press, 1987), 160–61.

25. Association of Research Libraries, *Library Reorganization and Restructuring* (SPEC Kit 215) (Washington, DC: Association of Research Libraries, May 1996).

26. *Ibid.*, 4.

27. Alex Bloss and Don Lanier, "The Library Department Head in the Context of Matrix Management and Reengineering," *College and Research Libraries* 58 (November 1997): 499–508.

28. Euster and Haikalis, "Matrix Model of Organization," 359–60.

29. Peggy Johnson, "Matrix Management: An Organizational Alternative for Libraries," *Journal of Academic Librarianship* 16 (September 1990): 226.

30. Euster and Haikalis, "Matrix Model of Organization."

31. For example, see Alex Bloss and Don Lanier, "The Library Department Head in the Context of Matrix Management and Reengineering," 499–508.

32. Edward E. Lawler and Susan A. Mohrman, "Quality Circles After the Fad," *Harvard Business Review* 63 (January–February 1985): 64–85.

33. *Ibid.*, 64–71.

34. E. E. Adam, "Quality Circle Performance," *Journal of Management* 17 (1991): 25–39.

35. Jana Schilder, "Work Teams Boost Productivity," *Personnel Journal* 71 (February 1992): 69.

36. Moshen Attaran and Tai T. Nguyen, "Self-Managed Work Team," *Industrial Management* 41 (July/August 1999): 24.

37. Rush G. Miller and Beverly Stearns, "Quality Management for Today's Academic Library," *College and Research Libraries News* 55 (July/August, 1994): 408.

38. See, for example, Joseph F. Boykin Jr. and Deborah Babel, "Reorganizing the Clemson University Library," *The Journal of Academic Librarianship* 19 (May 1993): 94–96; Joanne R. Euster et al., "Reorganizing for a Changing Information World," *Library Administration and Management* 11 (Spring 1997): 103–14; Joan Giesecke, "Reorganizations: An Interview with the Staff from the University of Arizona Libraries," *Library Administration and Management* 8 (Fall 1994): 196–99; Susan Jacobson, "Reorganization: Premises, Processes and Pitfalls," *Bulletin of the Medical Library Association* 82 (October 1994): 369–74; John Lubans, "I Ain't No Cowboy, I Just Found This Hat: Confessions of an Administrator in an Organization of Self-Managing Teams," *Library Administration & Management* 10 (Winter 1996): 28–40; Nancy Markle Stanley and Lynne Branche-Brown, "Reorganizing Acquisitions at the Pennsylvania State University Libraries: From Work Units to Teams," *Library Acquisitions: Practice and Theory,* 19 (1995): 417–25.

39. Maureen Sullivan, "The Changing Role of the Middle Manager in Research Libraries," *Library Trends* 41 (Fall 1992): 275–76.

40. Walt Crawford and Michael Gorman, *Future Libraries: Dreams, Madness, and Reality* (Chicago: American Library Association, 1995), 123.

41. Joanne D. Eustis and Donald J. Kenney, *Library Reorganization and Restructuring* (SPEC Kit 215) (Washington, DC: Association of Research Libraries, 1996), 2.

42. Rosabeth Moss Kanter, "Mastering Change," in S. Chawla and J. Renesch, eds., *Learning Organizations: Developing Cultures for Tomorrow's Workplace* (Portland, OR: Productivity Press, 1995), 70–83.

43. Jerry D. Campbell, "Building an Effectiveness Pyramid for Leading Successful Organizational Transformation," *Library Administration and Management* 10 (Spring 1996): 86.

44. Joe A. Hewitt, "What's Wrong with Library Organization? Factors Leading to Restructuring in Research Libraries," *North Carolina Libraries* 55 (Spring 1997): 6.

45. Overholt, "Flexible Organizations," 24.

46. Peter F. Drucker, *The Practice of Management* (New York: Harper & Row, 1954), 195–201.

47. Edward E. Lawler III, *From the Ground Up: Six Principles for Building the New Logic Corporation* (San Francisco: Jossey-Bass, 1996), 17.

48. Carla J. Stoffle, Robert Renaud, and Jerilyn R. Veldof, "Choosing Our Futures," *College and Research Libraries* 57 (May 1996): 223.

49. Jacobson, "Reorganization," 373.

50. Euster et al., "Reorganizing for a Changing Information World," 105.

51. Hugh C. Atkinson, "The Impact of New Technology on Library Organization," in *The Bowker Annual of Library & Book Trade Information*, 29th ed. (New Providence, NJ: R. R. Bowker, 1984), 113, 114.

52. Charles R. Martell Jr., *The Client-Centered Academic Library: An Organizational Model* (Westport, CT: Greenwood Press, 1983), 67.

53. "Books, Bricks, and Bytes," *Daedalus* 125 (Fall 1996).

54. Sirkka L Jarvenpaa and Blake Ives, "The Global Network Organization of the Future: Information Management, Opportunities, and Challenges," *Journal of Management Information Systems* 10 (Spring 1994): 25–57.

55. Janet Fulk and Gerardine DeSanctis, "Electronic Communication and Changing Organizational Form," *Organization Science: A Journal of the Institute of Management Sciences* 95 (July/August 1995): 337–39.

56. J. J. Duderstat, "A Choice of Transformations for the 21st Century University," *The Chronicle of Higher Education* (4 February 2000): B6.

57. See http://www.loc.gov/rr/digiref/ for more information.

58. Joanne R. Euster, "The New Hierarchy: Where's the Boss," *Library Journal* 115 (May 1, 1990): 43.

59. Jay Lorsch, "Organizational Design," in John J. Gabarro, ed., *Managing People and Organizations* (Boston: Harvard Business School Publications, 1992), 315.

60. Clifford Haka, "Organizational Design: Is There An Answer?" *Library Administration and Management* 10 (Spring 1996): 75.

61.   Thomas J. Peters and Robert H. Waterman Jr., *In Search of Excellence: Lessons from America's Best-Run Companies* (New York: Harper & Row, 1982), 311.

62.   See, for example, Tom Peters, *Liberation Management: Necessary Disorganization for the Nanosecond Nineties* (New York: Knopf, 1992).

63.   David Fagiano, "Pendulum Swings Back," *Management Review* 86 (September 1997): 5.

64.   *Ibid.*

65.   Peter F. Drucker. "Management's New Paradigms." *Forbes* 162 (October 5, 1998): 155.

66.   Phillip J. Johnson, "Individual Accountability and Individual Authority," *Library Administration & Management* 14 (Summer 2000): 143.

67.   Peter F. Drucker, *Management: Tasks, Responsibilities, Practices* (New York: Harper & Row, 1974), 602.

68.   Christopher A. Bartlett and Sumantra Ghoshal, "Matrix Management: Not a Structure, A Frame of Mind," *Harvard Business Review* 68 (July–August 1990): 138.

First, a library plans and establishes its goals and objectives. As a result, an organizational structure is put into place to allow the organization to reach its goals. Establishing the structure would be meaningless unless there were qualified people to fill the positions in the structure. The human resources function encompasses all the tasks associated with obtaining and retaining the human resources of an organization. These tasks include recruitment, selection, training, evaluation, compensation, and development of employees.

Until recently, all of these functions dealing with human resources were termed "personnel management," but in recent years that term has been displaced by another—"human resources management." Although the two phrases are still sometimes used synonymously, human resources management has been the favored term since 1989, when the American Society for Personnel Administration (ASPA) voted to change its name to the Society for Human Resources Management (SHRM). The name change was symbolic of the expanding role that human resources, another term for the organization's employees, play in the modern workplace. Employees are no longer looked upon just as "costs" to the organization; instead, they are "resources," just as the budget and the physical plant are resources. All resources are important, but good human resources are the greatest asset an organization can have.

This section of the textbook provides an overview of the major activities associated with the employees who work in libraries and information centers. Chapter 8 describes the different types of staff found in a typical library, discusses the organizational framework of various types of positions that must be established before an organization can hire a staff, and provides an overview of the process of recruiting and hiring staff to fill those positions. Chapter 9 focuses on the functions that relate directly to individuals holding jobs within an organization. These employee functions include training, developing, evaluating, compensating, and disciplining. Finally, chapter 10 looks at some of the general issues that have had a major impact on human resources in libraries. The chapter will cover such topics as personnel procedures and policies, career development, mentoring, health and safety, external regulations, and unionization.

Readings

Allen, David. *Getting Things Done: The Art of Stress-Free Productivity.* New York: Viking Press, 2001.

Argyris, Chris. *Integrating the Individual and the Organization.* New Brunswick, NJ: Transaction Publishers, 1990.

Baldwin, David A. *The Academic Librarian's Human Resources Handbook.* Englewood, CO: Libraries Unlimited, 1996.

Becker, Brian E. *The HR Scorecard: Linking People, Strategy, and Performance.* Boston: Harvard Business School Press, 2001.

Benaud, Claire-Lise, and Sever Bordeianu. *Outsourcing Library Operations in Academic Libraries: An Overview of Issues and Outcomes.* Englewood, CO: Libraries Unlimited, 1998.

Casteleyn, Mary, and Sylvia P. Webb. *Promoting Excellence: Personnel Management and Staff Development in Libraries.* London: Bowker Saur, 1993.

Crawford, Walt, and Michael Gorman. *Future Libraries: Dreams, Madness, and Reality.* Chicago: American Library Association, 1995.

Creth, Sheila, and Frederick Duda, eds. *Personnel Administration in Libraries.* 2d ed. New York: Neal-Schuman, 1989.

Davis, Keith, and John W. Newstrom. *Human Behavior at Work: Organizational Behavior.* 11th ed. New York: McGraw-Hill, 2001.

Davenport, Thomas O. *Human Capital: What It Is and Why People Invest It.* San Francisco: Jossey-Bass, 1999.

Garvin, David A. *Learning in Action: A Guide to Putting the Learning Organization to Work.* Boston: Harvard Business School Press, 2000.

Goodson, Carol F. *The Complete Guide to Performance Standards for Library Personnel.* New York: Neal-Schuman, 1977.

Kanter, Rosabeth Moss. *Evolve!: Succeeding in the Digital Culture of Tomorrow.* Boston: Harvard Business School Press, 2001.

Kratz, Charles E., and Valerie A. Platz. *The Personnel Manual: An Outline for Libraries.* 2d ed. Chicago: American Library Association, 1993.

Lawler, Edward E., III. *Rewarding Excellence: Pay Strategies for the New Economy.* San Francisco: Jossey-Bass, 2000.

Limerick, David, and Bert Cunnington. *Managing the New Organization.* San Francisco: Jossey-Bass, 1993.

Metz, Ruth. *Coaching in the Library.* Chicago: American Library Association, 2001.

Orlov, Darlene, and Michael T. Roumell. *What Every Manager Needs to Know About Sexual Harassment.* New York: AMACOM Books, 1999.

O'Neil, Sharon Lund, and Elwood N. Chapman. *Your Attitude Is Showing: A Primer of Human Relations.* Upper Saddle River, NJ: Prentice Hall, 2002.

Rubin, Richard E. *Human Resource Management in Libraries.* New York: Neal-Schuman, 1991.

Senge, Peter M. *The Fifth Discipline: The Art & Practice of the Learning Organization.* New York: Doubleday, 1990.

Ulrich, David. *Human Resource Champions.* Boston: Harvard Business School Press, 1997.

Urgo, Marisa. *Developing Information Leaders: Harnessing the Talents of Generation X.* London: Bowker Saur, 2000.

Wexley, Kenneth N., and Gary P. Latham. *Developing and Training Human Resources in Organizations.* 3d ed. Upper Saddle River, NJ: Prentice Hall, 2002.

Woodsworth, Anne, and Theresa Maylone. "Reinvesting in the Information Job Family: Context, Changes, New Jobs, and Models for Evaluation and Compensation." CAUSE Professional Paper Series, # 11. Boulder, CO: CAUSE, 1993.

Zingheim, Patricia K., and Dr. Jay R. Schuster. *Pay People Right!: Breakthrough Reward Strategies to Create Great Companies.* San Francisco: Jossey-Bass, 2000.

Zey, Michael G. *The Mentor Connection: Strategic Alliances in Corporate Life.* New Brunswick, NJ: Transaction Publishers, 1990.

Chapter 8

Staffing the Library

*Librarianship is a people-based profession. Its core
values revolve around managing and serving people.
To take people out of the future of the profession is to
empty it of its substance.*[1]

—Marisa Urgo,
*Developing Information Leaders:
Harnessing the Talents of Generation X*

Libraries could not exist without people. To a large extent, any organization's employees are the key to its success or failure. Even in highly automated settings, people are required to coordinate and to control the automated functions. Libraries are becoming more and more reliant on technology, but they are still highly labor-intensive organizations. Most of them still devote between fifty and sixty percent of their budgets to employee costs. In such labor-intensive organizations, the human resources are especially critical to success because almost everything else in the organization depends on them. A library can have an outstanding collection of print and electronic materials, access to a wealth of online resources, cutting-edge automated systems, and an award-winning building, but if it does not have a well-trained, competent staff, the patrons using the library will not be served effectively. So, in libraries as in most other organizations, one of the manager's most critical functions is to provide the human resources needed to carry out the functions of the organization. Not surprisingly, like so much else in libraries, there are changes occurring in the types of people needed to work in today's library. Digital information libraries have human resource requirements that are different from those in more traditional libraries.[2]

In the past, employees have sometimes been considered as interchangeable, easily replaced components of the organization. Modern organizations no longer view employees this way. They are no longer looked upon just as "costs" to the organization but as resources, just as the funding to run the organization and the building in which the organization is housed are resources. All resources are important, but good human resources are the greatest assets an organization can have.

> The organization which treats people as assets, requiring mainte-
> nance, love and investment can behave quite differently from the
> organization which looks upon them as costs, to be reduced
> whenever and wherever possible.[3]

The human resources function of management has been transformed by this new attitude toward employees. Now that human resources (usually abbreviated as HR) are recognized as one of the most valuable assets of organizations, the role of HR specialists has also been redefined. HR specialists are now considered a strategic part of management instead of paper-pushing, clerical workers. Today's HR specialists spend a large part of their time matching organizational problems with human resource solutions, demonstrating the impact that HR have on the "bottom line" of the organization.[4] Because there is a realization that the organization is the people who work there, those specialists who work with employees are recognized as essential parts of the organization.

> Human-resources issues must move up near the top of the agenda in discus-
> sions of the company's strategic priorities. That means that a first-class human-
> resources executive must be at the CEO's right hand. Eventually, traditional
> strategic-planning processes will need to be overhauled and the financially
> calibrated measurement and reward systems will have to be redesigned
> to recognize the strategic importance of human as well as financial
> resources.... Recognizing that the company's scarce resource is knowl-
> edgeable people means a shift in the whole concept of value management
> within the corporation.[5]
>
> —Christopher A. Bartlett and Sumantra Ghoshal,
> "Building Competitive Advantage Through People"

Large libraries have specially trained individuals who work exclusively on the HR aspects of management. These individuals, usually called human resources or personnel directors, are responsible for directing the human resource functions. Other information centers or special libraries located in larger organizations use the HR services of the parent organization. In a large organization, the HR department consists of a director (and possibly other professional level workers) and support staff members who perform the clerical functions. In libraries, the human resources/personnel directors are usually individuals who have MLS degrees with additional coursework and experience in HR management, but sometimes the human resources/personnel director is not a librarian.

Most libraries and information agencies, however, are too small to have one person who is a full-time HR or personnel specialist. Instead, the director usually performs the top-level HR functions that relate to the entire organization, or many of the HR functions are done by the library's parent organization (for instance, the appropriate county or city government office for a public library). But in every library, even in those large enough to have an HR department, all managers, from directors down to first-line supervisors, are involved in HR functions. For instance, many librarians have supervisory responsibility over others, and HR management comes with that responsibility because the training and evaluation of library employees are usually performed within a specific department by an employee's immediate supervisor. Although the degree of responsibility for HR increases as a manager moves up the hierarchy, it is a basic task for every manager. For that reason, the principles of good HR management should be widely understood throughout the organization. Because the largest allocation of the budget goes toward personnel costs, library managers must be able to handle people if they want their organization to be effective and efficient.

> Because of the differences among people, no single way of dealing with individuals is ever likely to be the best way. Further, the whole approach of treating people in a standardized manner runs counter to the desire of many people to be treated and recognized as individuals.[6]
>
> —Edward E. Lawler and David Finegold,
> "Individualizing the Organization"

The need for HR skills usually appears early in a manager's career, and some librarians never have an opportunity to learn effective HR management before they must practice it. Many new librarians in their first positions are called upon to supervise other workers, oftentimes workers with a great deal more seniority than themselves. Usually, one of the most challenging and sometimes frustrating aspects of every manager's job is dealing with people-related problems. Because no organization is static, the people in it and the problems associated with them change. Often, no sooner is one personnel problem solved than another develops. It is much more difficult to deal with people than with inanimate objects because each person is different. Some managers proceed on the mistaken notion that everyone can be treated identically, but every employee is unique, and often techniques that have worked well with one employee will not be effective in dealing with another. So, although it is relatively easy to learn the basic principles of HR management, dealing with employees is a never-ending challenge.

The Increasing Complexity of Human Resources Management

Managing HR has become more complex in the last few decades for a number of reasons. One of the reasons is the increasing diversity of the workforce. As the workforce becomes less homogenous, a manager has to learn to deal with people from many different backgrounds. The American workforce is being transformed from a group composed largely of white males into one in which the majority of workers will be women, African Americans, Hispanics, and employees who have recently immigrated from another country. Diversity is a broad term encompassing not only race, ethnicity, and gender but also characteristics such as age and physical ability. So today's workforce is varied in many different aspects. This diversity provides organizations with great opportunities but can also present problems unless managers understand the needs of these new workers and accept the challenge of managing a heterogeneous workforce.

> In the next century, nearly one out of two Americans will be a member of what today is considered a minority group. America will be many faces and many races with no one majority group in the workforce. The question is not whether there will be change but how we manage that change so that all may benefit. It is not so much a choice as a challenge.[7]
>
> —U.S. Department of Labor, *Futurework— Trends and Challenges for Work in the 21st Century*

Another reason for the increasing complexity of HR management centers around the expectations of most contemporary workers, especially well-educated employees. These employees expect to have jobs that are meaningful and that provide opportunities for promotion and career advancement. No longer are most employees content to remain in dead-end jobs where they have no input in the decisions that affect them and their jobs. Most managers realize that autocratic management is not an effective way of dealing with most of today's employees. Instead, managers who wish to have productive employees must empower workers. The library profession is seeking ways to empower library employees by decentralizing decision making and increasing employees' control over their work environment.

Still another factor changing the nature of managing people in libraries and information centers is technology. In the past two decades, technology has restructured many library jobs, created others, and eliminated still others. Technology brings many benefits for library employees and users; at the same time, it complicates the jobs of managers and employees. Some employees find it difficult to adapt to an environment where there is constantly changing technology. In some organizations, technology is used to monitor the amount of work that employees perform, which many employees view as an invasion of their privacy. In addition to psychic stress, technology can also produce physical problems, often caused by the repetitive motions involved in using keyboards for long periods of time. Some employees develop technology-related ailments, such as carpal tunnel syndrome or back and neck injuries. Managers have had to become more knowledgeable about the potential and pitfalls of technology and its impact on employees.[8]

Jobs are not only being restructured because of technology, but, as discussed in the last section, many of the hierarchical organizational patterns are also being modified. Instead of a group of workers reporting to one supervisor, in many types of organizations the workforce is now structured into teams, which manage themselves to a large extent. Team organization brings benefits to workers, but it also presents new challenges to managers.

In addition, many organizations have downsized and become smaller. In many cases, fewer employees are employed doing more work than previously. Other organizations are relying more heavily on part-time or temporary workers. Others have outsourced processes that used to be performed internally. Organizations that are in the process of downsizing or those that are handling the same amount of work with a "leaner and meaner" employee pool or those that have a large number of temporary employees provide additional complexities to HR managers.

> Organizations clearly comprise more than their organizational charts. In particular they are made up of people. Managing people is a key challenge to contemporary organizational life. We are repeatedly told that "people are our most important asset." Such words ring hollow in the ears of many since such statements are often made at the same time that organizations undertake massive corporate restructuring with traumatic consequences for victims and "survivors" alike.
>
> —Ian Palmer and Cynthia Hardy,
> *Thinking About Management*

Finally, the job of the manager has become more complicated because of the growing number of external regulations, especially those from state and federal governments. The purpose of these regulations is to make organizations safer and more equitable. External regulations are not new; laws relating to pay, safety, and labor relations have been in place for decades. However, the number of regulations with which organizations must comply has increased, and managers dealing with people need to be knowledgeable about the various, often complex, regulations that pertain to their employees.

All of these factors will be discussed in greater depth in the three chapters in this section, which provide an overview of the HR functions in libraries and information centers. Chapter 8 describes the different types of staff found in a typical library, provides information about the organizational framework of various types of jobs that must be established before an organization can hire a staff, and then discusses recruiting and hiring. Chapter 9 focuses on the HR functions that relate directly to individuals holding jobs within an organization. These functions include training, evaluating, compensating, and disciplining employees. Finally, chapter 10 examines some of the external issues, especially legal issues and unionization, which have had a major impact on HR in libraries.

Types of Staff

Like other types of organizations, libraries employ a diverse group of employees with various levels of education and responsibility. As libraries have incorporated more technology in their processes, the staff employed by libraries has necessarily become more varied. Professional librarians almost always constitute the smallest group of library employees. Usually, to be considered a "professional" librarian, an individual has earned a master's degree in library or information science (LIS), but sometimes these professionals also hold a second master's degree in a subject field or a doctorate. The professional staff works at the predominantly intellectual and nonroutine tasks, those requiring "a special background and education on the basis of which library needs are identified, problems are analyzed, goals are set, and original and creative solutions are formulated for them, integrating theory into practice, and planning, organizing, communicating, and administering successful programs of service to users of the library's materials and services."[9] Professional librarians serve in leadership roles, directing the total organization and the various departments and subunits. They also provide the expertise needed to fulfill the information needs of the library's patrons.

The support staff consists of workers with a wide range of skills, from paraprofessional to clerical. The support staff is usually the largest group of full-time employees in a library, and the activities of these employees cover a wide range of essential duties, including the tasks of entering, coding, and verifying bibliographic data; maintaining book funds; ordering; circulating materials; claiming serials; filing; and copy cataloging. The support staff handles the routine operations in most departments. The educational background of these workers varies widely. Some may have only a high school diploma, but many have a bachelor's degree, and some have graduate degrees of various kinds. And in the past few decades especially, libraries have needed both librarians and support staff with a strong technology background. Many libraries and information centers now employ specialists to work specifically with technology, for instance, to manage the library's local area network or to maintain web pages. These technology specialists have a variety of types of degrees and training.

Libraries usually employ a large number of part-time employees. Part-time employees, such as pages in public libraries and student assistants in academic libraries, work at easily learned, repetitive tasks such as retrieving items from the stacks or shelving returned books. Because these workers typically work for only a limited period of time, they require a great deal of training and supervision in proportion to the number of hours they work.

As mentioned earlier, libraries are labor-intensive organizations, and traditionally, the largest part of their budgets has been devoted to staff. In the past the traditional rule of thumb for dividing library budgets was sixty percent for personnel, thirty percent for materials, and ten percent for other expenses. This budget ratio is rapidly being discarded. Many libraries are now confronted with no-growth or shrinking budgets whereas costs for library technology and library materials are climbing rapidly. A number of libraries have tried to reduce the size of their staffs to cut the cost of their HR component. Like private corporations, libraries have become "leaner and meaner" organizations. Some feel that for libraries to remain viable, still larger changes must be made.

For instance, one library director has advocated that research libraries "reverse the current standard in budget ratios. The new look should be 33 percent for staff, 50 percent for materials/access, and 17 percent for 'other.' "[10] A change of this magnitude will be difficult to implement without an accompanying reduction in service and a loss of employee morale.

Nonetheless, libraries and information centers, like other organizations, must strive to improve their productivity. Many libraries and information centers are turning to part-time and contract workers in an attempt to achieve more flexibility and to save money. A recent survey showed that almost ten percent of MLS graduates in the year 2000 are working in temporary professional positions.[11] Other libraries and information centers are employing part-time workers and using contract workers to perform such services as janitorial and groundskeeping functions.

A number of libraries have decided to outsource certain functions, including such core functions as cataloging, to outside agencies. The term outsourcing refers to purchasing from an outside source certain services or goods that an organization previously provided or produced for itself. Although a recent study found no evidence that outsourcing has a negative impact on library services and management,[12] it is obvious that a library that begins to outsource probably will need fewer employees as a result.

All of these new methods of getting work done with different types of workers have the possibility of presenting problems to a manager. There is often a potential clash of attitudes about values and service between the permanent staff and these more temporary workers.[13] Long-term contract workers, hired as a cost-cutting measure to do basically the same job as regular employees but without being paid benefits, often resent the dual standard of compensation.[14] A library has less control over employees who are doing "outsourced" work than it does over employees who work within the organization itself. Libraries, like other organizations, must become more productive, but managers must realize that these economizing measures can make both the manager's work and the employees' lives more difficult.

Despite all of these attempts to downsize the number of employees,[15] the results have not produced significantly lower percentages of the library budget being devoted to staff. According to the National Center for Education Statistics, in 1998 public libraries still devoted almost 65 percent of their budgets to staff.[16] Academic libraries reported a lower percentage of their budget, 50.4 percent, was spent on salaries and wages.[17] When technology was first introduced into libraries, it was predicted that the number of employees would decline as a result. This has not proven to be true. Like other types of organizations, libraries have invested large amounts of funding in computers and information technology but have not seen an increase in productivity.[18] To date, library technology has done more to change the nature of jobs in the library than to cut the number of people needed to provide effective library service. In many cases, the introduction of technology has increased the demands for the services provided by libraries and information centers and has resulted in a need to add additional staff to meet the needs of users.

Librarians of electronic information find their job now a radically restructured one—they must consciously construct human attention structures rather than assemble a collection of books according to commonly accepted rules. They have, perhaps unwillingly, found themselves transported from the ancillary margin of the human sciences to their center. If this is so—and can it be doubted?—how should we train librarians, much less plan the buildings where they will work?[19]

—Richard A. Lanham,
The Electronic Word: Democracy, Technology, and the Arts

One of the most difficult issues that library administrators continue to face is matching the appropriate level of work to the appropriate type of employee. For many years, professional librarians spent at least part of their working day engaged in tasks that did not require a professional background. This was especially true in small libraries because in many small libraries, the only employee was a professional librarian. During the 1930s and early 1940s, it was not uncommon to find libraries in which fifty percent or more of the total staff was classified as professional librarians. In the past few decades, the tasks that professional librarians perform have become more clearly demarcated from those done by other staff members, and, in many cases, tasks that previously had been done by professionals have been transferred to members of the support staff. These transfers have been made possible by the increase in the number of staff members in most libraries and by the introduction of new technologies. As Allen Veaner writes:

> The movement of task oriented work from the professional staff to the support staff has been under way for at least a generation and has been well documented. The shift illustrates an important social aspect of the "technological imperative" in that once a technology is applied to carry out very complex, routine mental work, that work is driven downward in the work hierarchy, away from professionals whose work then expands to comprehend new and more challenging responsibilities, such as those librarians now carry out. Thus in losing a "job," the librarians acquired a much more clearly definable professional responsibility. The change has provided magnificent professional enrichment opportunities for librarians and has similarly enriched the jobs of support staff.[20]

Although some small libraries still have only one professional librarian and perhaps a clerical worker, in most larger libraries today, the ratio is usually one professional librarian to three support staff members, and in some libraries the proportion of professional to support staff is even smaller. As library technology advances, it may be feasible to turn over still more functions to support staff, and the ratio of professional to nonprofessional may decrease even further.

The "LIS Education and Human Resource Utilization" Policy

The most comprehensive attempt to clarify desirable staffing patterns in libraries is the American Library Association's recently revised "Library and Information Studies Education and Human Resource Utilization" policy.[21] This document demonstrates 1) that skills other than those of librarianship are needed in libraries; and 2) that nonlibrarians must have equal recognition in both the professional and the support ranks.

Skills other than those of librarianship also have an important contribution to make to the achievement of superior library service. There should be equal recognition in both the professional and supportive ranks for those individuals whose expertise contributes to the effective performance of the library. To accomplish this goal, the document recommends that libraries establish a dual career lattice that allows both librarians and nonlibrary specialists to advance in their chosen careers.

In addition to recognizing the importance of specialists, the "LIS Education and HR Utilization" policy recommends that librarians be permitted to advance within an organization without becoming administrators. In many libraries, promotion and advancement are possible only when the employee assumes greater supervisory responsibility. However, there is a great need for administrators to recognize and to reward financially the important role that nonadministrative librarians play. The "LIS Education and HR Utilization" policy advocates that there "are many areas of special knowledge within librarianship which are equally important [as administration] and to which equal recognition in prestige and salary should be given. Highly qualified persons with specialist responsibilities in some aspects of librarianship—archives, bibliography, reference, for example—should be eligible for advanced status and financial rewards without being forced to abandon for administrative responsibilities their areas of major competence."[22]

Although the original version of the "LIS Education and HR Utilization" policy was produced more than thirty years ago, most libraries and information centers have yet to deal successfully with some of its recommendations. Many libraries, despite the influx of nonlibrarian specialists, have not yet adopted dual career lattices to allow nonlibrarians to advance. Most libraries also still need to develop organizational patterns that will allow employees to advance in salary and in professional rank without becoming administrators.

Staffing patterns in libraries have been changed and complicated by the changes that technology has brought to the work environment. Most large libraries now employ a number of technology specialists—some of these specialists have library degrees, others do not. Largely as a result of technology, tasks that were once assigned solely to professional librarians have drifted downward, and almost all tasks performed in libraries are more complex and intellectually demanding than before. The strict demarcation that was once observed in most libraries between support staff and professional librarians has eroded as virtually all employees of libraries have become knowledge workers.[23] Support staff members are being used increasingly in "new and reconfigured roles, in many cases performing tasks previously considered to be the exclusive province of librarians."[24]

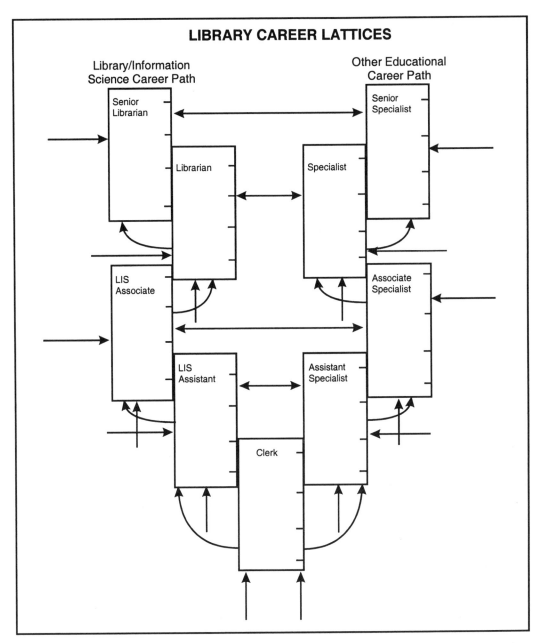

LIBRARY CAREER LATTICES

Library/Information Science Career Path

Other Educational Career Path

Senior Librarian

Senior Specialist

Librarian

Specialist

LIS Associate

Associate Specialist

LIS Assistant

Assistant Specialist

Clerk

If one thinks of Career Lattices rather than Career Ladders, the flexibility intended by the Policy Statement may be better visualized. The movement among staff responsibilities, for example, is not necessarily directly up, but often may be lateral to increased responsibilities of equal importance. Each category embodies a number of promotional steps within it, as indicated by the gradation markings on each bar. The top of any category overlaps in responsibility and salary with the higher category.

Figure 8.1. Dual Career Lattices. From "Library and Information Studies Education and Human Resource Utilization" (Chicago: American Library Association, 2002), p. 5. Reprinted by permission of the American Library Association.

This overlap sometimes causes tension, and even resentment, among support staff as paraprofessionals "see themselves performing the tasks they have watched librarians perform for years, as well as the challenging new tasks created by automation, but for less money and lower status."[25]

Both professional librarians and support staff have new names that reflect this increasing diversity. For instance:

> librarians are not just called librarians anymore. Increasingly their job responsibilities and titles provide a framework for the technological role that they play within the library. Professional journals and electronic mailing lists reflect these new roles. They are filled with openings for Technology Consultant, Technology Training Coordinator, Head of the Digital Information Literacy Office, Information Systems Librarian, Head of Computer Services, Webmaster, Cybrarian, and Internet Services Librarian.[26]

In a similar way, the old "clerical" functions of library support staff have been transformed. Some of the many job classifications of support personnel can be seen in Table 8.1.

Table 8.1. Types of Support Staff

The types of support workers employed in libraries and information agencies have increased, reflecting the changing and varied responsibilities of the support staff in today's libraries. The titles listed below were collected in a recent survey of support staff classifications.[27]		
Delivery Worker	Applications Systems Analyst	Human Resources Specialist
Development Associate	Systems Specialist	LA Specialist/Coordinator
TV Repair Supervisor	Public Information Officer	Photographer
Curatorial Assistant	Business Coordinator	Fiscal Officer
Learning Disabilities Specialist	Graphic Design Specialist	Adult Literacy Specialist
Bookmobile Driver	Marketing Specialist	Volunteer Resources
Gallery Manager	Electronic Technician	Network Specialist

The library profession has not come up with a uniform model addressing the types of staffing patterns. Libraries and librarians need to look at the necessary qualifications for all levels of library work and hire a workforce that has qualifications matching those needed. One approach to attempting to match qualifications to positions is through the use of competencies in professional education. In contrast to traditional education that centers on inputs—students are exposed to a segment of a curriculum and expected to learn it—competency-based learning specifies the outcomes that students should be able to demonstrate upon leaving the system. These outputs are clearly specified and education is focused upon, ensuring that students master these outcomes. Recently, there has been a great deal of interest in competency-based education, and many library-related groups have issued guidelines on the competencies needed by practitioners in a particular type of setting.[28]

It seems inevitable that the staffing patterns of libraries will continue to shift in the twenty-first century and that the realities of budgeting will force libraries to look for economical ways to provide the staffing needed to carry out the needed functions. Charles Handy has suggested that the organizations of the future will be "shamrock" organizations, made up of three different groups of workers, "groups with different expectations, managed differently, paid differently, organized differently."[29] The first leaf of the shamrock is composed of the core workers, the permanent employees, which are essential to the organization. This core group is becoming smaller in all types of organizations. Work is increasingly being done by workers in the two other leaves: the contract workers and the part-time and temporary workers. Although these other groups of workers have always existed, what is different today is the relative size of the three groups. The core workers are decreasing in number and the other two groups are being used more because their use allows greater flexibility if budget cuts need to be made.[30]

Like other types of organizations, libraries and information centers are increasingly relying on a smaller core group with a greater use of part time workers and of outsourcing. They are employing increasing numbers of support staff to perform diverse duties. The old patterns of staffing are disappearing, but the patterns of the future are not yet clear.

The Organizational Framework for Staffing

As described in the previous section, organizations are formed and jobs are created when the overall task of the organization is too large for any one individual. Libraries, like all organizations, are networks of interacting components. Jobs are the individual building blocks upon which the organization is built.

Although the terms job, position, and occupation are often used interchangeably, each has a distinct definition in human resources terminology. A position is a collection of tasks and responsibilities that constitute the total work assignment of one person. Thus, there are as many different positions in an organization as there are people employed there. The Slavic language cataloger in a large academic library holds a position as does the bookmobile driver in a public library. A job, on the other hand, is a group of positions that generally involve the same responsibilities, knowledge, duties, and skills. Many employees, all performing slightly different work, may be classified under the same job title. A library may employ many catalogers, all of whom have different responsibilities but whose duties are similar enough to be classified in the same job group. An occupation is defined as a general class of job found in a number of different organizations; for example, librarianship is considered to be an occupation.

A job should always be a planned entity consisting of assigned tasks that require similar or related skills, knowledge, or ability. Ideally, jobs should never be created haphazardly at the whim of an employee or to suit the special knowledge or ability of a particular individual. Instead, jobs should be carefully designed to ensure maximum organizational effectiveness. It is the responsibility of the library administration to identify the tasks that are to be included in a job. The tasks should be similar or related. All the tasks to be accomplished by a specific job should require approximately the same level of education. One task should not be so excessively complex that extensive education is required, whereas another is so simple that it could be performed by an individual with much less education. Further, the tasks assigned to any one job should require comparable experience. Some tasks can be performed only after extensive experience, whereas others can be executed by novices. And last, tasks assigned to a job should require comparable responsibility. Some tasks have end responsibility, which means that there is no review of what is done. The action of the individual in a job having end responsibility is final. Such end responsibility is frequently found in reference services, book selection, and top administration. Other jobs require little or no end responsibility. Work is reviewed. Revisers in a catalog department may have end responsibility, whereas the catalogers whose work is revised have no end responsibility. To summarize, a well-defined job has assigned to it tasks that are 1) comparable in the amount of education required; 2) comparable in the amount of experience required; and 3) comparable in the degree of responsibility required.

It was long a principle of job design that all the tasks that comprised a job should, if possible, be related to the accomplishment of a single function, process, or program or should be related to the same subject field or type of material. In large institutions, this was easily accomplished; in small institutions, however, workers often had to work at multiple tasks. Although in terms of specialization, the assignment of a single function, process, or program to a job makes sense in terms of efficiency, it can be carried too far. There is now a much greater interest in jobs that allow workers to practice multiple skills. This new interest reflects a growing belief that to make a job too narrow may, in many cases, be detrimental to workers and managers. To increase flexibility within organizations, jobs are now being designed to take advantage of multiple skills. More organizations are encouraging cross-training, that is, having employees learn the techniques associated with jobs that are not their own so that if the need arose, there would be additional employees who would know how to get a specific job done. Workers are being encouraged to work both with and across other functions and units.

This flexibility and broadening of job responsibilities is a change in the way that jobs have traditionally been structured. The allotment of narrow, specialized portions of a large task to specific workers is known as division of labor. Adam Smith, in The Wealth of Nations (1776), first wrote about the benefits of division of labor.[31] When each job consists primarily of a few simple, repetitive tasks, the skill level and training required for performing that job are low.

In the United States during most of the last century, the scientific management principles popularized by Frederick W. Taylor and the Detroit style of mass production introduced by Henry Ford heavily influenced the thinking of individuals who designed jobs. There was widespread acceptance of the principle of dividing tasks into small component units and having each worker responsible for just a small portion of the overall task. This type of job design promoted efficiency and ease of training. More recently, there has been a realization that this approach to job design neglects the psychological nature of the worker and often leads to worker dissatisfaction and alienation. Often workers who perform one small task over and over begin to feel like cogs in a machine. Now, many industries are trying to provide job enrichment by redesigning jobs so they comprise a wider variety of tasks and more responsibility. In addition, in the spirit of continuous improvement, all organizations, including libraries and information centers, are rethinking the design of jobs in an attempt to find better ways of accomplishing the objectives of the organization.

> Job enrichment will not be a one-time proposition, but a continuous management function. . . . The argument for job enrichment can be summed up quite simply: if you have employees on the job, use them. If you can't use them on the job, get rid of them, via automation or selecting someone with lesser ability. If you can't use them and you can't get rid of them, you will have a motivation problem.[32]
>
> —Frederick Hertzberg,
> "One More Time: How Do You Motivate Employees?"

Although few library jobs were ever as narrow and confining as those on an assembly line, the principle of job enrichment is especially important in organizations like libraries and information centers. The educational level of most of the employees in a library is typically quite high, and well-educated workers are usually seeking jobs that are intellectually challenging. A job should not be so restrictive that assigned tasks are quickly mastered and soon become dull, monotonous, and boring. Instead, the scope of a job should be large enough to challenge and encourage employees to grow in skills, knowledge, and abilities. Some jobs in libraries must be performed according to prescribed procedures to maintain uniformity or because of standardized methodologies. These jobs are generally low in the hierarchy. Nevertheless, even at this level, the employee should be given every opportunity to be creative, to exercise initiative, and to vary the routines, as long as the established standards are maintained. The "judicious expansion" of certain jobs leads to higher productivity, lower absenteeism, and increased job satisfaction, whereas routine and repetitive tasks discourage initiative and tend to produce apathetic and uncommitted workers.[33]

Technology has had the greatest impact on lower-level jobs, where work is routine, and less on higher-level jobs where decision-making is concentrated. Just adding technology to a job function does not in itself make the job more interesting. Instead, sometimes information technology leads to deskilling when the computer takes decision making away from an employee. A recent study of paraprofessional technical services positions found that the introduction of technology had changed the positions over time primarily by changing the tools by which the work is done. It had done little to add autonomy, authority, and decision making to the positions.[34]

It is not easy to redesign jobs to make them more fulfilling to workers, and some workers resist job enrichment. Although the buzzword now in all types of organizations is "empowerment," it must be remembered that there are some workers who do not want to be empowered.

> People work in organizations for many reasons: to earn a paycheck, to get away from home, to contribute to society, to make friends, to master particular skills, to get recognition and the like. Some people even come to work because they enjoy being told what to do, or they feel most secure in a structured, well-ordered environment, or they get satisfaction out of doing one thing well, over and over. In other words, not all people want to be empowered to make their own decisions, and assuming that they do can create dysfunction.[35]

A basic rule to HR management is to match the individual to the job. Following that principle, workers who do not want autonomy and empowerment should not be placed in positions where they will need to work without supervision and direction.

Nonetheless, the talents of great numbers of workers are underutilized at the present time, and it benefits both the worker and the organization to create jobs that allow employees to work up to their full potential. If libraries want their employees to be innovative and responsible, they must provide jobs that give employees an opportunity to develop these attributes.

Hackman and Oldham have proposed a model of job enrichment that identifies five core job dimensions that are essential to job enrichment. These dimensions are:

- ◆ Skill variety—the extent to which a job requires a number of different activities using a number of skills and talents.

- ◆ Task identity—the extent to which a job requires completing a whole piece of work from beginning to end.

- ◆ Task significance—the worker's view of the importance of the job.

- ◆ Autonomy—the extent to which employees have the freedom to plan, schedule, and carry out their jobs as desired.

- ◆ Feedback—the extent to which a job allows the employee to have information about the effectiveness of their performance.

As Figure 8.2 illustrates, these core job characteristics lead to critical psychological states that allow the worker to experience the meaningfulness of the work, the responsibility for the outcome of the work, and the knowledge of the actual results of the work. These psychological states affect an employee's feeling of motivation, quality of work performed, satisfaction with work, and lead to low absenteeism and turnover.[36]

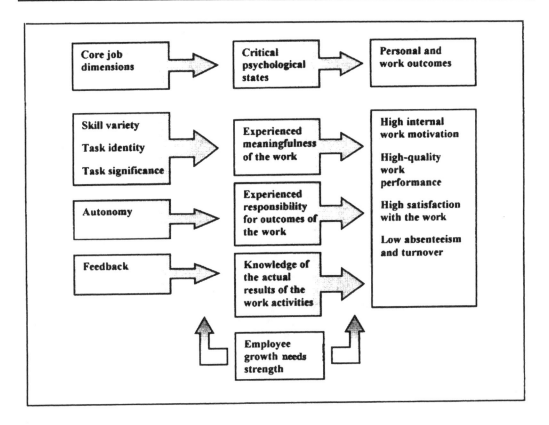

Figure 8.2. Hackman and Oldham's Core Job Characteristics

Despite a great deal of interest in the area of job design, no new model has arisen to replace the Hackman and Oldham job characteristics model.[37]

> Job design continues to be a dominant area of interest for theorists and researchers. . . . Jobs are the window through which individuals perceive, experience, and contribute to organizations. Similarly, jobs are also the window through which organizations direct the work of individuals in productive ways, assess their value to the organization and undertake efforts to motivate their behavior.[38]

Just as organizations are changing, so are the jobs within organizations. Managers need to look at the jobs in the organization and see if they are designed in a way that balances the need for efficiency with the need for a more enriched job to ensure employee motivation. Since the Hackman and Oldham model has been found to be an effective way of understanding job design, jobs should be designed as much as possible to provide the core elements of job variety, autonomy, task significance and identity, and feedback.

Job Descriptions

After a job has been established, the next step is to write a job description that specifies the duties associated with that job; the relationship of the job to other units of the institution; and the personal characteristics, such as education, skill, and experience, required to perform the job. Today, most government agencies and private industries require job descriptions for all employees. Job descriptions vary from organization to organization, but generally contain the following elements:

1. Job identification. This section of the description typically includes the job title, line number, and department.

2. Job summary. This section of the job description provides a description of the major responsibilities and provides a justification for the existence of the job.

3. Job activities and procedures. This section includes a description of the tasks performed by the incumbent in the job, sometimes including the percentage of the job that is devoted to each of the tasks. There should be clear delineation of what the duties and responsibilities of the job are, although some flexibility often is inserted by the use of a phrase such as "and other duties on occasion as assigned." The enumeration of the job's activities and procedures is the most important part of the job description. This enumeration identifies for the employee the exact tasks for which he or she will be responsible. It also indicates to the supervisor those tasks that require training, supervision, or task evaluation. Without this section of the job description, neither the employee nor the supervisor knows what the employee is expected to do. The tasks assigned should be, of course, comparable in the amount of education, experience, and responsibility required and should demand similar or related skills, knowledge, and abilities.

4. Relationship of the job to the total institution. This section states the title of the person to whom the incumbent reports, the number of employees or the organizational unit supervised by this job, and the internal and external relationships required by the job.

5. Job requirements. Job requirements are established by each organization and identify the minimum acceptable qualifications required for an employee to perform the job. Requirements often include amount of education; amount of experience; and special skills, knowledge, or abilities demanded. All job requirements should be necessary for the successful performance of the job. For some jobs, requirements are set unrealistically high, which artificially restricts the pool of possible applicants. Sometimes, job specifications reflect what the organization would like to have and not what is necessary to perform the job effectively. Job specifications (for example, an educational requirement such as a college degree) that are not essential

for successful job performance are invalid and may violate Title VII of the 1964 Civil Rights Act.

Job descriptions fulfill several important administrative and HR needs. A job description may be used in recruiting new employees. Not only does the recruiter know exactly the capabilities for which to search, but the candidate also knows exactly what would be expected if the job were accepted. For this reason, the job description always should be made available to applicants for their study and review. After an individual has been hired, the job description becomes the basis for determining training needs and identifying tasks that require special effort before the employee can perform them well. Later, the job description becomes the basis for formal performance appraisal. Job descriptions are also used to evaluate job worth to aid in developing a compensation structure. Figure 8.3 shows a job description from an academic library. Other job descriptions can be seen on this book's website.

Job Analysis

In principle, a job should be stable over time. Once the job has been defined and the characteristics necessary to perform it have been specified, the job should not be appreciably changed by the incumbents holding the job or by different situations. In reality, though, jobs are dynamic and often change considerably over time. New machinery or equipment may be introduced. Departments or even entire libraries may be reorganized. Changing technology may alter the skill requirements necessary for a job. In libraries, for instance, the job of cataloger has changed greatly since the introduction of the bibliographic utilities. Thus, it is important to remember that job descriptions and specifications must be kept up-to-date to ensure that they still describe the activities and characteristics of that job.

> Job categories change constantly in an evolving economy. Once all telephone calls were made through an operator. . . . Today there are comparatively few telephone operators, even though the volume of calls is greater than ever. Automation has taken over.[39]
>
> —Bill Gates,
> *The Road Ahead*

Because all jobs change over time and because employees, by emphasizing or deemphasizing certain portions of their jobs, can produce drastic changes in the job, all organizations should occasionally perform a job analysis. The job analysis allows the institution to gather information about what is actually being done by employees holding specific jobs. A variety of methods may be employed for a job analysis. Some of the most common include direct observation of the job, interviews, written questionnaires, or requesting employees to record what they do on a job by means of a daily log or diary. Each of these methods has its advantages and disadvantages. It is beneficial to acquire data using more than one method to make sure that sufficient information is

Acquisitions Librarian and Associate Head, Technical Services Department

Manages, plans, and supervises all acquisitions operations to provide users with rapid access to library materials in all formats. Establishes and maintains effective business relationships with book vendors and subscription agents and oversees expenditures for a book and serials budget of over $7 million. Assists with overall leadership of Technical Services to sustain and shape its role in the rapidly changing environment of information resources. Reports to the Head of Technical Services.

Responsibilities

- Manages, plans, and supervises all phases of development, implementation, and evaluation of Acquisitions operations. Staff consists of 22.75 FTE organized into two service units: Order Processing Unit and Receipts Processing and Accounting Unit. Activities include annually placing orders for over 22,000 monographs and serials; receiving over 80,000 monographs and serials, including more than 16,000 standing order titles and titles received through 22 approval plans; providing full-level copy cataloging for nearly 18,000 monographs upon receipt; and processing payments totaling over $7 million.

- Formulates policies, sets goals and priorities. Exercises leadership in developing cost-effective procedures and workflow for ordering, receiving, and paying for library materials.

- Establishes and maintains effective business relationships with publishers and vendors of both print and electronic information; monitors and evaluates vendor performance and makes adjustments, as necessary; advocates for the most effective delivery of library resources for the Duke community.

- Defines and clarifies roles and responsibilities of staff, setting forth clear expectations and performance standards. Works to create an environment that fosters respect, trust, and accountability. Analyzes and reports on the work of the Acquisitions operation, documenting progress, identifying trends, and making recommendations regarding staffing, equipment, training, etc.

- Works with other areas of Technical Services, Resource Specialists, and the Head, Collection Development Department to coordinate policies, procedures, and standards and to facilitate cooperation and communication at all levels.

- Works closely with the Electronic Resources Librarian to ensure that the acquisitions process for these materials is efficient.

- Participates in local and national meetings, conferences, and workshops on acquisitions-related topics; stays abreast of developments and trends in all areas of relevance to acquisitions; and contributes to discussions of library issues, including formal service on committees and task forces.

- Carries out special projects and performs other related duties as assigned by the Head of Technical Services.

Qualifications

Required: master's degree from an ALA-accredited program or an equivalent combination of education, experience, and training that demonstrates the conceptual, analytical, interpersonal, and problem-solving skills required to manage and lead a complex operation; at least three years of relevant professional experience in acquisitions and serials management; demonstrated success in supervising staff and administering acquisitions and serials work in an academic or research library; demonstrated knowledge of the domestic and foreign book and serial trade, including electronic information products; proven expertise in fiscal management and bibliographic control; excellent oral and written communications skills; and extensive experience with at least one bibliographic utility and an automated acquisitions system (OCLC and INNOVACQ preferred). Highly desirable: reading knowledge of one or more European languages; knowledge of trends in e-book publishing, and familiarity with licensing of electronic resources.

04/17/01

Figure 8.3. A Job Description for an Acquisitions Librarian

gathered. The results of the job analysis can be useful in writing new job descriptions, in specifying the skills and abilities needed by workers holding the job, and in determining the appropriate compensation for that job. A job analysis can also indicate when a job needs to be redesigned. Although sometimes employees feel threatened by a job analysis, in most cases the data provided by the analysis allow an organization to manage its HR effectively and to provide better training, performance evaluation, and promotion and compensation opportunities.

Because a complete job analysis of all positions is not only time-consuming but demands extensive expertise, complete analyses are not performed regularly in libraries. When they are, library administrators often call in special HR or management consultants to help accomplish the analysis. Another approach found in some libraries is to use the HR department of the parent institution to perform the analysis. For example, the HR department of a municipal or county government or of a college or university might assist in designing and carrying out the job analysis program.

To keep jobs up-to-date between complete analyses, supervisors should report any significant changes in the makeup of tasks in their units. Some institutions conduct periodic audits of the jobs in every department. The audit involves checking the tasks that are actually being performed against the ones specified on the job description. When discrepancies are found, either changes are made in the work habits of the employee, if certain essential tasks are not being carried out, or changes are made in the job description so that it will reflect the changes that have occurred in the job for legitimate reasons (for example, the introduction of new equipment or technology).

Job Evaluation

After jobs have been designed and accurate job descriptions written, all the jobs within the organization are arranged in hierarchical order. An attempt is made to enumerate the requirements of each job and its contribution to the organization and then to classify it according to importance. Skill, education, experience, and the amount of end responsibility are common criteria used in making this evaluation. A number of methods can be used to assign jobs to ranked categories.

Some organizations use the point method. These organizations develop a quantitative point scale that identifies the factors involved in a job and assign weights to the factors. The higher the number of points, the higher the job is in the hierarchy. Other organizations use a factor system, which is calculated by comparing jobs one with another and also by subdividing jobs into factors that have dollar values attached to them. The factor method is similar to the point method but with a monetary scale in place of a point scale.

Two nonquantitative systems are widely used for evaluating jobs. Simple ranking systems compare actual positions to one another to create a ranked hierarchy. The job classification system defines classes of jobs on the basis of duties, skills, abilities, responsibilities, and other job-related qualities. The jobs are grouped into classes arranged in a hierarchy. Regardless of the system used, it is always the job that is classified, not the employee holding the job.

The hierarchically arranged jobs are divided into groups, which vary from library to library. Usually, all professional librarian positions fall into one group; library associates or paraprofessionals into another; and library technicians, clerks, and custodians into still others. Within each group, there will be hierarchical levels based upon the experience, education, and responsibility associated with each job. A job title is assigned to each level, usually modified by the use of a numeral. Jobs requiring the same level of education, experience, and responsibility are given the same title, although the tasks associated with each may be different. Both an experienced reference librarian and an experienced cataloger could be classified as Librarian III. Figure 8.4 shows a hierarchy of professional library positions.

Job Title	Education	Experience	End Responsibility
Librarian IV	MLIS from an accredited LIS school plus an Advanced Certificate	10 years with 3 years in supervisory positions	Final responsibility for the operation of the institution
Librarian III	MLIS from an accredited LIS school plus subject specialization	5 years of professional experience	Under general supervision and according to policies, end responsibility for a department
Librarian II	MLIS from an accredited LIS school	2 years of professional experience	Under general supervision and according to policies, responsible for a unit of a department
Librarian I	MLIS from an accredited LIS school	0 years of experience	Under general supervision and according to policies, performs assigned task

Figure 8.4. A Hierarchy of Professional Positions

The same procedure is used for all other job groups. A hierarchy for clerical level jobs is shown in Figure 8.5. There is no standard for the number of levels in each group. In larger institutions there may be many, in smaller ones only a few.

Job Title	Education	Experience	End Responsibility
Clerk III	High school plus business school graduate	3 years of experience	Under general supervision, end responsibility for payroll
Clerk II	High school plus some business school	2 years of experience	Under general supervision, end responsibility for verifying invoices
Clerk I	High school diploma	0 years of experience	Under close supervision, perform assigned tasks

Figure 8.5. A Hierarchy of Support-Level Positions

Recruitment and Hiring

Recruiting and Attracting a Qualified Work Force

Once a library has its positions established, they need to be filled. Filling these jobs is a multistep process, which is illustrated in Figure 8.6. The first step is recruiting applicants to apply for the jobs.

Recruitment involves seeking and attracting a pool of applicants from which qualified candidates for a vacant position can be chosen. Recruiting has become an important consideration in filling library jobs because many libraries are finding it difficult to attract enough qualified applicants to fill vacant librarian positions. More and more libraries are experiencing extremely small applicant pools and/or failed searches. This is quite a change from the situation a few years ago when there were sometimes hundreds of applicants for an opening in a library. It can certainly be argued that having hundreds of applicants for each opening is just as troubling as having only a few—particularly to those applying for positions. But, without a doubt, libraries are going through another period where there is an imbalance between the number of positions open and the number of qualified candidates ready to fill those positions. Librarianship, like most other professions, has gone through these imbalances before. In the last forty years, there have been three periods when there were not enough librarians and two when there was an overabundance.[40] At the present time there are too few people applying for positions in libraries always to ensure quality applicant pools and the successful filling of positions on the first attempt. Most experts attribute this shortage to low salaries, competition from the private sector, and the beginning of the retirement of the Baby Boom Generation.[41] Some LIS graduates have sought nonlibrary jobs after graduation because of the lower salaries in librarianship compared to similar jobs in the private sector. Although it is thought that competition from the private sector will inevitably drive up the salaries of librarians, there have been no dramatic increases in pay to date.[42]

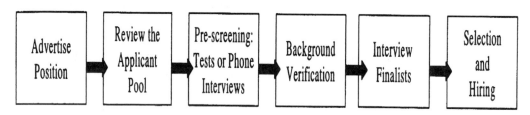

Figure 8.6. The Stages in Recruiting and Hiring

Recruitment has become a critical issue for the profession as a whole. How do we attract talented people to the profession? How do we get them in the pipeline so that when a library has a need for a specific type of librarian, there will be someone there to fill the position? The need for attracting new professionals is especially critical for libraries because of the demographics of the library workforce. Research has shown that overall librarians are significantly older than most other professionals. For instance, a study that examined the age of librarians in the large Association of Research Libraries (ARL) institutions showed that relative to comparable professions, librarianship contains one-third the number of individuals aged thirty-five and under and almost seventy-five percent more individuals aged forty-five and older.[43] Another recent study that looked at age distribution of librarians showed that a very large percentage of librarians will reach the age of 65, the traditional age of retirement, between 2005 and 2014.[44] The percentages can be seen in Figure 8.7 As the report states, "The data presented here indicates that the shortage reported from coast to coast in 2001 is likely to become more troublesome in the immediate future."[45]

Librarians of all types need to begin to think about more active recruitment. What is needed at the most basic level is to begin with creating greater interest in entering librarianship as a career. Because people choose to enter librarianship at so many stages of their lives, there is no one tried and true method of recruiting. Instead, librarians need to think about a variety of types and times of recruiting, remembering that librarians themselves are the most effective recruiters. Most people who choose to become librarians do so because at some time in their lives, a librarian made an impression on them and made them think that they would like to follow that career.

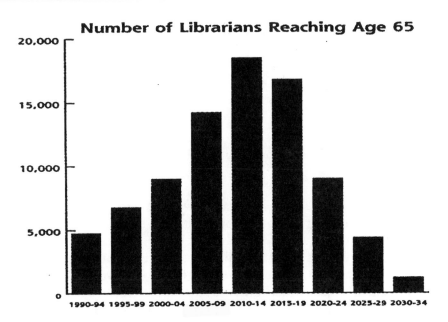

Figure 8.7. The Percentage of U.S. Librarians Reaching Age 65, 1990–2034. Reprinted by permission of the American Library Association.

Filling Vacant Positions

Whenever librarians begin to design a search to fill a vacant position, they need to consider the labor market from which candidates will be drawn. In most libraries, support staff positions are filled from the local labor market. Openings are advertised only in local publications, and almost all support staff positions are filled by individuals already living in the area. On the other hand, in many libraries candidates for professional vacancies are filled from the national labor market. Almost all libraries and information centers recruit top administrators nationally. In these cases, libraries and information centers advertise in national periodicals, such as *American Libraries*, *Library Journal*, or *The Chronicle of Higher Education*, in the hope of attracting a large number of well-qualified applicants.

The Internet is changing the way that open positions are being advertised. The classified sections of many newspapers and specialized publications are available on a website, for instance *The Chronicle of Higher Education*'s position openings can be seen at http://chronicle.com/jobs/, and ALA's *American Libraries* position openings can be seen online at http://www.ala.org/alonline/index.html. There are also sites specifically devoted to employment advertisements (such as http://monster.com/) where job seekers can search job openings by category and find useful tips to aid in a job search. Many individual libraries publicize open positions on their own websites. Others post positions to be filled on specific listservs that are apt to be read by people with the appropriate background and interest for the job vacancy. Advertising using the Internet is advantageous to both the organization with the open position and the job seeker because it usually permits access to information about positions to be distributed to individuals who might not see the printed ad, especially if it were in a regional newspaper that the job seeker did not usually read.[46] The cost is generally lower also.

Attracting a Diverse Work Force

Diversity among staff is becoming increasingly more valued in all types of institutions.

> Women, Hispanics, Asian Americans, African Americans, Native Americans—these groups and others outside the mainstream of corporate America don't bring with them just their "insider information." They bring different, important, and competitively relevant knowledge and perspectives about how to do work—how to design processes, reach goals, frame tasks, create effective teams, communicate ideas and lead. When allowed to do so . . . [a diverse work force] can help companies grow and improve by challenging basic assumptions about an organization's functions, strategies, operations, practices and procedures.[47]

Because libraries serve a multicultural clientele, most libraries try to hire a culturally diverse staff. These efforts sometimes are unsuccessful, especially at the professional level. Despite attempts to increase the number of minorities in the profession, minorities are still underrepresented. Recent statistics show that in academic and public libraries fewer than fifteen percent of the librarians belong to racial or ethnic minorities, and the percentages are far below the representations of these groups in society.[48]

In an attempt to increase the number of minorities in libraries, both libraries and LIS schools have tried a number of approaches. Some libraries have introduced undergraduate internship programs designed to bring more minorities into the profession. Others have established minority residency programs to attract new MLS graduates. Many libraries have instituted diversity plans to coordinate their efforts to produce a more diverse work force. LIS schools have attempted to diversify their enrollment by more active recruitment efforts and by offering special scholarships. The American Library Association has instituted a new Spectrum Initiative to provide scholarships to African American, Latino/Hispanic, Asian/Pacific Islander, and Native American/Alaskan Native students for graduate programs in library and information studies.

> One of the most visible means to demonstrate the library's commitment to diversity is through the establishment of internship/apprentice/residency and/or visiting librarians programs. These programs require a commitment of human and fiscal resources and they represent one of the highest forms of sharing in the profession.[49]

—James F. Williams,
"Managing Library Diversity"

Despite these efforts, the profession has been relatively unsuccessful in attracting minorities to the field. Librarianship must compete with more lucrative professions and, not surprisingly, often comes in second in terms of attracting minority entrants. Despite the difficulties, at each hiring opportunity managers should make an effort to attract qualified minority applications to diversify their workforce.

Internal and External Applicants

Applicants for a job often include both internal candidates—individuals already employed by the organization who are seeking job transfers or promotions, and external candidates—individuals from outside the organization. There are advantages and disadvantages associated with both the external and internal recruiting of personnel. The first advantage of recruiting external candidates is the larger pool of talent that can be tapped. The second advantage is that new employees bring fresh insights and perspectives to the organization. The major disadvantage to external recruiting is that filling a position with an external candidate generally takes a longer time and is more expensive than filling it with an internal candidate. It also takes a longer time for an employee hired from the outside to become oriented to the organization because the new employee must acquire familiarity with the people, procedures, and special characteristics of a new organization.

The biggest advantage of filling positions with internal candidates is that it usually fosters high morale. Employees in organizations that have a policy of promotion from within have an additional incentive for good performance because they know they will be considered for a promotion when openings occur. Another advantage of recruiting from within is that management can more accurately appraise the suitability of the candidate. The internal candidate is a known factor, whereas the external candidate is less well known; therefore, there is less risk in the selection and placement of an internal candidate. However, if the position is an attractive one and there are many internal candidates, the ones not chosen may react very negatively. For that reason, it is extremely important to build procedural fairness into this as well as every other search so that the unsuccessful candidates will feel that the process was a fair and objective one.[50]

There are, however, inherent problems and limitations of always relying on internal promotion. Probably the most dangerous is organizational inbreeding. When all subordinates have been employed by the same organization, they all may know just one way of doing things. When these subordinates are promoted, they tend to perpetuate what they have seen done in the past, and the organization may not be exposed to new ideas and innovation. In general, the best policy is probably filling the majority of vacancies from within when there are fully qualified individuals to assume these positions. But, it is also wise to fill at least some high-level positions by outsiders to inject new ideas into the organization.

Matching the Applicant to the Position

Selection refers to the process of actually choosing the individual who will most likely perform the job successfully. The fundamental goal of selection is to achieve a good fit between the qualifications of the applicant and the requirements of the position.

Successful matching of an applicant to a position is very important because failures are not only costly to the persons hired but also to the organization. If the match is bad, corrective measures, such as training, transfer, demotion, or termination of employment, are often required.

The time spent in selecting the right person for a position is time well spent. Oftentimes, organizations do not realize the large investment of scarce organizational resources that may be committed to each new employee. One study that looked at the investment a library would make in a new entry-level librarian who would stay in the job for twenty-five years estimated that the investment would be in excess of one million dollars, not including the costs of office furnishings, training, travel expenses, moving costs, or even the cost of recruitment itself.[51] Offering the position to the wrong applicant can be an expensive mistake, both in time and in money. An interesting calculator on the Internet allows an employer to calculate the cost of a bad hire (see http://www.advantagehiring.com/calculators/fs_hfcalcs.htm). Because each new person hired represents a large sum of resources, it is wise to ensure that the best applicant is selected for each position. This has always been important, but is even more so now when there is often little staff turnover in many libraries. If the right candidate cannot be found the first time, it is better to readvertise the position and try again than to hire someone who may not be able to do the job.

One selection tool used more frequently in private corporations than in libraries is the assessment center. Assessment centers use comprehensive standardized procedures to make HR decisions, primarily about hiring and promotion. Multiple assessment procedures, such as job simulations and situational exercises, are used to evaluate individuals. Trained management evaluators assess each individual's performance in exercises like discussion groups, in-basket exercises, and presentations, and then make recommendations about the candidate's strengths and potential. Assessment centers have been shown to have a high degree of accuracy in predicting success in the job, and the techniques have been accepted by the Equal Employment Opportunities Commission (EEOC) as a valid, racially blind method of selecting personnel.[52] Assessment centers are becoming more prevalent in the public sector, and some libraries are beginning to make use of this technique.[53]

The Selection Process

Each organization should have a well-designed selection system. Typically, the selection process includes application forms, applicant testing, personal interviews, verification of past performance and background, and hiring.

Application Forms. Libraries often use standard application forms for vacant positions. In some cases, a cover letter and a résumé are substituted for the application form. The application form is used by the employer to gain written information about the candidate. The typical application form contains questions that identify the applicant, such as name, address, and telephone number; questions about an individual's education and work experience; and questions related to the specific requirements of the job or the organization. The employer receiving an application form must ensure that the applicant has the experience and the education needed for the job. The employer looks for steady progress in experience and asks questions about unexplained gaps in the work history. Information on the application form allows tentative judgments to be made about an applicant's suitability for a position; it also screens out obviously unqualified candidates.

Applicant Testing. Some libraries use tests to see if an applicant possesses the skills needed for a specific job. These tests are most useful when the job requires certain skills that can be easily tested. For instance, a typist might be given a typing test to ensure that the applicant's speed and accuracy are satisfactory. The most useful tests are a sample of the work itself or a task that closely resembles the work and requires the same skills and aptitudes. If a test is used for selection, the EEOC requires that the employer establish the validity and reliability of the test.

Interviewing the Candidate

When the pool of candidates has been narrowed down, the most promising applicants are invited for an interview. Sometimes, libraries initially interview candidates by telephone, but, in most cases, telephone interviews are used to narrow a pool of candidates and to choose those who will be invited for a personal interview. The job interview is the single most important tool in the selection process. Although few libraries use tests in selecting employees, almost all interview the candidate. In many libraries, multiple interviews are held, thus allowing a wider participation in the selection process.

The purpose of the interview is to supplement information obtained through other sources. The interviewer uses this opportunity to find out more about the applicant's technical and professional knowledge, experience, and personal characteristics. The applicant finds the interview useful to learn more about the job itself, to clear up any uncertainties about the position or the organization, and to be introduced to the staff that he or she would work with if hired.

The sole focus of the interview should be job requirements, and questions should be designed to provide information about an individual's suitability for the job that is being filled. It is important to remember that all questions asked during an interview should be job-related. The EEOC has forbidden the use of interview questions that are not related to job requirements. Candidates may not be asked questions about race, religion, gender, national origin, age, or handicaps. Specific questions that are prohibited are listed in Table 8.2.

Interviewing is a skill that can be improved with practice. To start, interviewers should prepare for the interview. They should be familiar with the information provided by the candidate on the application form. An interviewer should plan an outline of questions to be asked and specify the information needed to be obtained. The same basic questions should be asked of all individuals being interviewed for a specific position. The interviewer should also arrange a place for the interview that will be private and free of interruptions.

Table 8.2. Permitted and Prohibited Questions in Employment Interviews

Topic	Permitted	Prohibited
Marital status	None	Are you married? Are you planning to get married? What does your spouse do? Do you have children?
Sexual Orientation	None	Do you live alone?
National origin	None	Where were you born?
Citizenship	Are you a citizen of the United States? If hired, are you able to prove eligibility to work in the U.S.?	What country are you a citizen of? Are you a naturalized American citizen?
Religion	None. If you wish to know if an applicant is available to work on Saturday or Sunday, ask about working on those days and ask the questions to each applicant.	Do you go to church? Synagogue?
Race	None	What is your race?
Criminal History	Have you ever been convicted of a crime?	Have you ever been arrested?
Age	If hired, will you be able to provide proof that you are at least 18 years old?	How old are you?
Disability	Are you capable of performing the essential functions of this position with or without reasonable accommodation?	Are you disabled? Do you have any health problems?

Since the establishment of Affirmative Action, it has been universal practice to compile a uniform list of key questions for all candidates. Even if there were no legal requirement, a consistent instrument applied to all candidates would be the most sensible, rational course in recruiting, and a definite aid to minimizing bias.[54]

—Allen B. Veaner,
Academic Librarianship in a Transformational Age

One of the first rules of interviewing is to put the applicant at ease. A relaxed applicant will display a more normal behavior pattern than a tense applicant. The candidate should be encouraged to talk, but the interviewer must maintain control of the interview and remember that the objective is to gather information that will aid in the selection process. Too often, interviewers spend an excessive amount of time discussing the organization and the position and never obtain from the applicant the information needed to make a good hiring decision. The best interview is one in which the applicant does most of the talking.

The interviewer must listen carefully and note pertinent facts. He or she should refrain from excessive note-taking, however, because it will inhibit the applicant. Questions should be phrased correctly. Open-ended questions elicit the best answers because they force a candidate to think through a situation. The interviewer should avoid leading questions, that is, questions that signal the desired answer. Instead of asking, "You wouldn't object to weekend work, would you?" say, "Tell me how you feel about working weekends." The interviewer should never be judgmental. By refraining from expressing disbelief or shock at a candidate's response, the interviewer encourages the person to reveal failures as well as successes. As soon as the interview is over, the interviewer should record his or her impressions about the applicant. If this is delayed, valuable information and impressions about the applicant will be forgotten.

Background Verification

At some point, either before or after the interview, an employer will want to verify information provided by the candidate by contacting references and previous employers. Most jobs require that the applicant list references: personal, school, or past employers. Personal references are unreliable because few applicants would list a person who would not give a highly favorable reference. If the applicant has a work history, previous employers are the most valuable source of information. An applicant should give written permission to have references checked before the individuals listed as references are contacted.

Reference checking is frequently conducted by telephone. It is felt that individuals provide more frank and specific information on the telephone than in writing. Some organizations, however, divulge information about past employees only in writing, and the amount and type of information provided varies from organization to organization. Fear of lawsuits makes reference checking harder than ever these days as former employers have become hesitant about giving references for fear of possible lawsuits from their ex-employees. A few organizations are now willing to confirm only that an individual had been employed there. Usually, however, a prospective employer is able to verify the accuracy of the information the applicant provides, such as position held, last salary, supervisory responsibilities, and reasons for leaving. The prospective employer may also ask whether the previous employer would be willing to rehire the employee and why. Although previous or present supervisors usually provide accurate assessments, sometimes they may give a better recommendation than the applicant deserves—either because they would like to see that applicant leave his or her present place of employment or because they do not feel comfortable giving negative information about individuals. The reference checkers should probe and follow up if they feel that the person giving the reference is hesitant or not responding to the questions being asked.

The same set of basic questions should be asked of all references about all candidates. Only questions relating to an applicant's job performance should be asked. Even if references are checked on the telephone, the prospective employer should also ask to have a written reference so that there will be written documentation if an employment decision is challenged.

If an applicant does not list supervisors from recent jobs as references, a prospective employer might want to contact them anyway. Very few applicants falsify their credentials, but it is always wise to verify the information given. If a particular educational background is required, the applicant's school record should be confirmed. A person's job history might be verified by calling the organizations listed to ensure that the person has indeed worked there. The investigation into an applicant's background is sometimes overlooked by prospective employers. It costs little in either time or money and is worth the effort because it cuts the risks that an organization will make an unwise hire.

Making the Hiring Decision

The last step in the selection process is choosing the individual who will be hired to fill the vacant position. In some libraries, many people contribute to the final decision, especially for professional positions. Search committees, which are commonly used in academic and other types of libraries, are one way of allowing peer involvement in the selection process. The search committee usually recommends a ranked list of finalists for the position, then an administrator usually makes the final choice. In some libraries and information centers, the director always makes the final decision; in others, the immediate supervisor is allowed to choose, subject to the approval of higher management. If the appropriate information has been gathered and if the steps in the selection process have been performed effectively, the likelihood of making a good decision is quite good; the applicant's qualifications will match the job requirements, and the fit should be successful.

If good hiring practices are not followed, an organization may be plagued by a high level of turnover in its staff. Although turnover can have many causes, one of the most common is job dissatisfaction. Even though a certain amount of turnover is healthy, and allows an organization to bring in employees with new ideas and experiences, excessive turnover can be detrimental. It is costly because an employee has to be replaced, and a new one has to be retrained. A great deal of turnover also can threaten morale in an organization because the remaining employees feel that there is a lack of continuity and that the organization is in a constant state of change. An excessive amount of turnover should be a warning to a library to examine carefully its hiring and recruitment practices.

Conclusion

After the steps that are delineated in this chapter are finished, the library's positions will be established, and there will be individuals hired for each of those spots. Hiring the staff is just the first step in working with HR in the library. Chapter 9 will look at some of the processes involved in training, evaluating, and compensating those employees.

Notes

1.   Marisa Urgo, *Developing Information Leaders: Harnessing the Talents of Generation X* (New Providence, NJ: Bowker-Saur, 2000), 2.

2.   Peter R. Young, "Librarianship: A Changing Profession," in *Books, Bricks and Bytes. Daedalus* (Fall 1996): 124.

3.   Charles Handy, *The Age of Unreason* (Boston: Harvard Business School Press, 1989), 24.

4.   Sharon Lobel, "In Praise of the 'Soft' Stuff: A Vision for Human Resource Leadership," *Human Resources Management* 36 (Spring 1997): 135–39.

5.   Christopher A. Bartlett and Sumantra Ghoshal, "Building Competitive Advantage Through People," *MIT Sloan Management Review* 43 (Winter 2002): 36.

6.   Edward E. Lawler III and David Finegold. "Individualizing the Organization: Past, Present, and Future," *Organizational Dynamics* 29 (Summer 2000): 1.

7.   U.S. Department of Labor, *Futurework—Trends and Challenges for Work in the 21st Century* (Washington, DC: Department of Labor, 1999), 10. (Available online at http://www.dol.gov /asp/futurework/execsum.pdf.)

8.   See Shoshana Zuboff's *In the Age of the Smart Machine* (New York: Basic Books, 1988) for a thoughtful discussion of the impact of technology on work.

9.   American Library Association, *Library and Information Studies and Human Resource Utilization* (Chicago: American Library Association, 2002), 4.

10.   Jerry D. Campbell, "Academic Library Budgets: Changing 'The Sixty-Forty' Split," *Library Administration and Management* 3 (Spring 1989): 78.

11.   Tom Terrell and Vicki L. Gregory, "Plenty of Jobs, Salaries Flat," *Library Journal* 126 (October 15, 2001): 34.

12.   Robert S. Martin, *The Impact of Outsourcing and Privatization on Library Services and Management* (Chicago: American Library Association, 2000). Available online at http://www.ala .org/alaorg/ors/outsourcing/index.html.

13.   Ann Lawes, "Managing People for Whom One Is Not Directly Responsible," *The Law Librarian* 26 (September 1995): 421–23.

14. A recent federal appeals court ruled that Microsoft must provide long-term contractors with benefits. See Beverly Ma, "Independent Contractor Pitfalls: Lessons from Microsoft," *Human Resources Forum* (June 1997): 1.

15. See "Changing the Way We Downsize," *Library and Personnel News* 8 (January–February 1994): 3, for a description of how to downsize in a more humane fashion.

16. U.S. Department of Education, National Center for Educational Statistics, *Public Libraries in the United States: Fiscal Year 1998* (July 2001): 83. (Available online at http://nces.ed.gov /pubs2001/2001307.pdf).

17. U.S. Department of Education, National Center for Educational Statistics, *Academic Libraries: 1998* (July 2001): 38. (Available online at http://nces.ed.gov/pubs2001/2001341.PDF).

18. Chris Hare and Gary Geer, "The Productivity Paradox: Implications for Libraries." Contributed paper presented at the ACRL 9th National Conference, 1997. (Available online at http://www.ala.org/acrl/paperhtm/c22.html.)

19. Richard A. Lanham, *The Electronic Word: Democracy, Technology, and the Arts* (Chicago: University of Chicago Press, 1993), 134.

20. Allen B. Veaner, "Librarians: The Next Generation," *Library Journal* 109 (April 1984): 623–24.

21. American Library Association, *Library and Information Studies and Human Resource Utilization.*

22. *Ibid.*, 2.

23. Allen B. Veaner, "Paradigm Lost, Paradigm Regained? A Persistent Personnel Issue in Academic Librarianship, II," *College and Research Libraries* 55 (September 1994): 390.

24. Larry R. Oberg, "Library Support Staff in an Age of Change: Utilization Role Definition, and Status," *ERIC Digest*, EDO-IR-95-4, May 1995. (Available online at http://www.ed .gov/databases/ERIC_Digests/ed382197.html.)

25. *Ibid.*

26. Linda W. Braun, "New Roles: A Librarian by Any Name," *Library Journal* 127 (February 1, 2002): 46.

27. Ed Martinez and Raymond Roney, "1996 Library Support Staff Salary Survey," *LibraryMosaics* (March/April 1997): 6–10.

28. See, for example, Special Libraries Association, "Competencies for Special Librarians of the 21st Century," (can be seen at http://www.sla.org/content/SLA/professional/meaning /comp.cfm); American Library Association, Young Adult Library Services Association, "Young Adults Deserve the Best: Competencies for Librarians Serving Young Adults" (http://www .ala.org/yalsa/yalsainfo/competencies.html); or the Association of Southeastern Research Libraries, "Shaping the Future: ASERL's Competencies for Research Librarians" (http://www .aserl.org/statements/competencies/competencies.htm).

29. Handy, *Age of Unreason*, 90.

30. *Ibid.*, 94.

31. Adam Smith, *An Inquiry into the Nature and Causes of the Wealth of Nations* (New York: Modern Library, 1937).

32. Frederick Hertzberg, "One More Time: How Do You Motivate Employees?" *Harvard Business Review* 46 (January–February 1968): 53.

33. Chris Argyris, *Integrating the Individual and the Organization* (New Brunswick, NJ: Transaction Publishers, 1990).

34. Carol P. Johnson, "The Changing Nature of Jobs: A Paraprofessional Time Series," *College and Research Libraries* 57 (January 1996): 59–67.

35. Ron Ashkenas et al., *The Boundaryless Organization: Breaking the Chains of Organizational Structure* (San Francisco: Jossey-Bass, 1995), 55.

36. J. R. Hackman and G. R. Oldman, *Work Redesign* (Reading, MA: Addison-Wesley, 1980).

37. Ricky W. Griffin and Gary C. McMahan, "Motivation Through Job Design," in Jerald Greenberg, ed., *Organizational Behavior: The State of the Science* (Hillsdale, NJ: Lawrence Erlbaum Associates, 1994), 33–34.

38. *Ibid.*, 40.

39. Bill Gates, with Nathan Myhrvold and Peter Rinearson, *The Road Ahead* (New York: Viking, 1995), 253.

40. James M. Matarazzo, "Library Human Resource: The Y2K Plus 10 Challenge," *Journal of Academic Librarianship* 26 (July 2000): 223–24.

41. Mary Jo Lynch, "Reaching 65: Lots of Librarians Will Be There Soon," *American Libraries* 33 (March 2002): 55–56.

42. Mary Jo Lynch, "Librarian Salaries: Annual Increase Drops Below Average," *American Libraries* 29 (November 1998). (Available online at http://www.ala.org/hrdr/salaries.html.)

43. Stanley J. Wilder, *The Age Demographics of Academic Librarians: A Profession Apart* (Binghamton, NY: Haworth Information Press, 1999).

44. Lynch, "Reaching 65," 55.

45. *Ibid.*, 56.

46. Marydee Ojala, "Recruiting on the Internet," *Online* 21 (March/April 1997): 78–81.

47. David A. Thomas and Robin J. Ely, "Making Differences Matter: A New Paradigm for Managing Diversity," *Harvard Business Review* 74 (September/October 1996): 80.

48. Lynch, "Librarians' Salaries," 68. (Also available as "Racial and Ethnic Diversity Among Librarians: A Status Report," at http://www.ala.org/alaorg/ors/racethnc.html.)

49. James F. Williams II, "Managing Library Diversity: Library Management in Light of the Dismantling of Affirmative Action," *Journal of Library Administration* 27 (1999): 45.

50. Ken Jordan, "Play Fair and Square When Hiring from Within," *HR Magazine* 42 (January 1997): 49–52.

51. Constance H. Corey, "Those Precious Human Resources: Investments That Show You Care Enough to Keep the Very Best," *Library Administration and Management* 2 (June 1988): 128.

52. Peter Hiatt, "Identifying and Encouraging Leadership Potential: Assessment Technology and the Library Profession," *Library Trends* 40 (Winter 1992): 514.

53. *Ibid.*, 515.

54. Allen B. Veaner, *Academic Librarianship in a Transformational Age* (Boston: G. K. Hall, 1990), 279.

Chapter 9

The Human Resources Functions in the Library

Although there are many facets to a management job, most involve considerable interaction with people. A management job involves counseling, leadership development, and building a competent staff. Some corporate presidents devote over 80 percent of their time to people problems. It is true that an executive manages resources and capital, but the first priority is working with people.

—Sharon Lund O'Neil and Elwood N. Chapman,
Your Attitude Is Showing

Hiring an employee is just the first step. The new employee arrives at the library for that first day of work. Immediately there is a need for orientation and training this new worker. There has to be a compensation and benefits package in place for him or her. And for as long as the employee stays in the position, there are HR functions that must be performed. In this era of rapid change, there are always demands for training and staff development. Each year an employee needs to have a performance appraisal and consideration for a salary adjustment. Sometimes an employee has to be disciplined or wishes to file a grievance. Occasionally an employee needs to be terminated because of poor job performance. All of these activities and many more are an integral part of the HR responsibilities of managers. This chapter will provide an overview of the major HR functions from the initial day on the job until the employee leaves the organization.

Training and Staff Development

Training is a never-ending process. It seems that there are always new employees that need training or new systems that involve training. Almost all practicing librarians have some assigned responsibilities that involve training other employees. The trainee may be a shelver, a beginning clerical employee, or another professional. As a professional librarian assumes a greater role as manager, training will become a major responsibility.

In a library, as in any institution, there are many levels of training. Some training is received by everyone; other parts of the training program are more individualized. Although training is expensive in terms of the time it takes, it is false economy to try to minimize it. Over a period of time, the cost to the institution is returned in quality performance.

Orientation

The first type of training typically received is an *orientation*. After an employee has been hired, he or she needs a general orientation to the organization. Usually, if a number of new employees come in at about the same time, a general orientation meeting is held. This general orientation for all employees provides information that all employees need, regardless of level or place of employment within the institution. Perhaps some of the information was transmitted during the selection process, but it is wise to reinforce that knowledge. A general orientation usually includes two basic areas: general information and the goals, objectives, and philosophies of the organization.

The general information part of the orientation covers rules and policies applicable to all employees, including information concerning pay periods, how vacation and sick leave are accumulated and how they can be used, requirements for reporting illness, and the use of time sheets. Many libraries have specific ways of answering telephone calls, such as requiring that the name of the library or department and the individual's name be given. The reason for this requirement is explained. Some libraries require employees to wear name tags. Again, the reason for this is given. The overall policies that affect all employees are interpreted in a way that makes the new employee a part of the organization and sympathetic with general requirements.

> [M]ore often than not, after the new employee is chosen, the contract is signed, and the beginning work date is set, the people involved in the hiring process wipe their brows (with a muttered "Thank goodness that slot is filled!"), and move back into the flow of business as usual without making adequate preparations for their newly appointed librarian.[2]
>
> —Dorothy E. Jones,
> "I'd Like You to Meet Our New Librarian"

Each employee, regardless of level or place of employment in the library, needs to know its overall goals, objectives, and basic service philosophies. The director should make the presentation on these topics, not only because he or she best knows the philosophies, goals, and objectives of the institution, but also because the new employee is impressed and more readily accepts such information when it comes from the chief administrator. New employees who receive a careful introduction to policies and procedures will more easily assume a productive role in the organization.

Although some libraries still treat orientation sessions in a casual manner, others have given careful thought to what should be included. For instance, Figure 9.1 illustrates the checklist used by Kent State University in its orientation for new employees. The form asks for signatures of all the individuals involved to ensure accountability.[3] More orientation forms and links can be found on this book's web page.

New employees need more orientation to the institution than that provided by the general orientation; they also need an understanding of the responsibilities of the various organizational units of the library. Units, such as the HR office, the public information office, and various subject or functional departments, are described so that employees see their role in the total organization. The managers of the individual units usually conduct these training sessions. Using visual presentations and permitting extensive discussion and questions make such sessions productive.

Initial Job Training

As soon as a new employee reports for work, the immediate supervisor begins training in the specific tasks of the job. Occasionally, this training is given by the person leaving the job. The practice of having the incumbent train the new employee is risky, particularly if the departing employee has been a problem. The practice perpetuates the departing employee's work habits and patterns, and it frequently establishes attitudes and opinions toward the supervisor, the department, and the organization. For these reasons, it is recommended that the immediate supervisor be in charge of training new employees.

There are many ways of training. The worst way is to describe verbally in a few minutes the tasks to be performed. The new employee, already uneasy by being in a new environment with new responsibilities, probably will hear little of the supervisor's remarks. Some employees are able to observe other employees, figure out the job from the job description, or learn the job on their own, in spite of the supervisor. Others fail, and their failure is the fault of the supervisor.

Training must be carefully planned. The following principles guide a good trainer:

1. Teach the simple tasks first.

2. Break down the task into its basic components.

3. Teach only the correct procedures.

4. Keep teaching cycles short, and reinforce them with practice.

What Every New Libraries/Media Services Employee Should Know
CHECKLIST

√ **DIRECTOR OF STAFF SERVICES discusses:**

I. Introduction to Kent State University and Libraries/Media Services

	DATE		DATE
• University ID card		• Community information: what does Kent offer ... Portage and Summit Counties ... greater Akron/ Cleveland metropolitan areas ... Ohio	
• Parking permit			
• Map of campus; tour of especially relevant offices, such as Personnel		• Library circulation policies	
		• When the library operates	
• Tours: department, main library, branch libraries, regional libraries as appropriate		• List of University paid holidays	
• Introductions to staff		• Keys and getting into the building outside of normal work schedule	
• Promotional materials about University services and organizations (e.g., Wellness Center, physical fitness facilities, Audio Visual Services, Professional Women of Kent State University)		• Completion of *Confidential Vital Information Record*	
		• Safety manual	
• Copies of undergraduate and/or graduate catalogs		• University/corporate perks (e.g., Sea World, Sam's Club, American Express card)	

II. Personnel Policies and Procedures

	DATE		DATE
• Breaks: length, frequency, where allowed physically, coordination with co-workers, etc.		• Changing one's regular schedule	
• Lunch/dinner, including bringing food into the library		• Attendance at University and library functions and meetings, such as May 4 Remembrance, Women's Day events, etc.	
• Flextime availability		• Timecards	
• Calling supervisor, forms to fill out for sick leave, vacation, leave of absence		• Professional development: meetings, conferences, seminars; travel reimbursement	
• Court leave		• Pay raises	
• Use of radios and radio/headphones on the job		• Promotions	
• Making/receiving personal telephone calls		• Exiting the University	
• Dress codes		• Faculty issues: reappointment, tenure, sabbatical, faculty committees, mentors, library liaison program, use of research leave, exit interviews	
• Attending classes, completing class assignments			

III. Information About the Job and the Organization

	DATE		DATE
• Information about the relationship with the supervisor, including: chain of command; administering discipline/ rewards; performance evaluations; communicating with supervisor, including what supervisor needs to know and what is confidential		• L/MS personnel structure: organizational charts, personnel rosters, descriptions of committees, how to become involved	
• Information about relationships with co-workers: when and how to discuss mutual interests and concerns; what to tell the supervisor		• L/MS communication methods: memo writing protocol, telephone protocol, availability of committee reports, *Local Data Record, Inside, Matrix, Connect,* other publications and reports, communicating with others	
• Information about relationships with supervisees: policies as for supervisors above		• List of L/MS telephone numbers	
		• List of radio stations to tune in if snow might close down University operations	

Director of Staff Services sign-off: _____

New Employee sign-off: _____

continued

√ SUPERVISOR discusses:

DATE

- Training information: how long is training period, when reviewed, who reviews performance, when is a decision about employment binding, implications with respect to layoffs _____

- Job description/outline of job responsibilities _____

- Procedures manuals: personal copy or knowledge of ready availability _____

- When the department operates _____

- Work schedules of co-workers and supervisor _____

- Personal schedule: regular working hours, timeliness _____

DATE

- Getting into the department outside of regular working hours _____

- Relationship with supervisor: the chain of command, expectations of the supervisor, departmental meetings, how to request other meetings, when and how to discuss issues and concerns _____

- If new employee supervises others, the supervisor may make recommendations on how the new employee should relate with supervisees _____

- Word processing: availability of computers and software for on and off the job _____

- Supplies and equipment: when and how to request _____

Supervisor sign-off:

_____

New Employee sign-off:

_____

√ PERSONNEL – STAFF BENEFITS OFFICE discusses:

DATE

- Benefits: tuition waiver, insurance (life, medical, dental), retirement, travel reimbursement _____

DATE

- Explanation of Benefits Fest _____

Personnel Office sign-off:

_____

New Employee sign-off:

_____

Figure 9.1. Checklist for New Employees. From Shelley L. Rogers, "Orientation for New Library Employees: A Checklist," *Library Administration and Management* 8 (Fall 1994): 213–17. Used by permission of the American Library Association.

5. Develop skills through repetition.

6. Do not train too far in advance of the need for it to avoid forgetting what was learned.

7. Motivate the trainee.

A library's responsibility for training and education does not end when a new employee is properly trained for his or her position. Periodically, following the initial orientation, the institution provides continuing training programs for new employees and for selected groups of employees.

Training for new employees goes on for a long time as these new hires become socialized into the organization's culture, with its norms for acceptable and unacceptable behavior. These new employees will look to more senior staff members to serve as role models. When they are faced with a gap in knowledge, they will usually turn to more senior employees to act as their teachers or coaches. Experienced staff plays a vital role in helping new employees make an effective transition to a new setting.[4]

Training and Staff Development for Established Employees

Any organization develops people; it has no choice. It either helps them grow or it stunts them. It either forms them or it deforms them.[5]

—Peter F. Drucker,
Managing the Non-Profit Organization

It is not only new employees who need training. Any staff member who works in a library needs continuous updating to stay current. The rapid changes taking place in all types of libraries compel library managers to attach new importance to training and staff development. Although the terms "training" and "staff development" are often used synonymously, a distinction is sometimes made. Often *training* refers to learning skills or knowledge that are to be used on the present job, whereas *staff development* involves learning of a larger scope that goes beyond the present job and looks toward the future. But because it is often difficult to make a distinction between the two types of continuing learning, this book will treat them together. Another related function, career development, will be covered in chapter 10.

Training and staff development can be offered in various ways. On a recurring basis as specific training needs are identified, selected groups of employees might receive training in specific topics, such as how to conduct good performance evaluation interviews, how to prepare performance evaluation reports, how to prepare departmental budget recommendations, or how to do task analysis for job description revisions. These training sessions, which concern all units of the organization, may be conducted by a specialist within the institution or by an authority brought into the institution for this purpose.

The training programs described so far are developed and presented by the institution. In addition, many training and educational programs exist outside the institution; these should be available to employees. Attendance at local, regional, and national conferences and workshops provides opportunities for employee development and growth. Some librarians may need extensive continuing education to prepare them to work with a new computer system or to prepare them for new positions in other parts of the library. More and more training is being offered by means of online courses or teleconferences. Many institutions provide tuition funds for employees who take formal courses that are job related. The need to take courses beyond the first professional degree increases as library operations become more complex. There must be continued emphasis on training and staff development in all types of libraries.

Some organizations, including many libraries, are attempting to transform themselves into "learning organizations." These are organizations where "people continually expand their capacity to create the results they truly desire, where new and expansive patterns of things are nurtured, where collective aspiration is set free and where people are continually learning how to learn together."[6] Peter Senge contends that most modern organizations have learning disabilities—fundamental problems in the way jobs and organizations are structured, which result in organizations learning poorly. He recommends that organizations adopt specific tools or disciplines that will help them learn better. These disciplines are:

- ♦ Systems thinking—understanding the whole system and not just individual parts;

- ♦ Personal mastery—individuals continually clarifying and deepening their personal vision, focusing their energies, developing patience, and seeing reality objectively;

- ♦ Mental models—the deeply held visions of how the world works;

- ♦ Building shared vision—the leader's vision is transmitted and shared by all employees; and

- ♦ Team learning—the process of developing the capacity of a team to create the results its members desire.[7]

The learning organization is marked by a team-based culture, open flows of information, empowered employees, and decentralized decision making. As a result, the learning organization is able to grow and change in response to environmental changes. These learning organizations attempt to formalize exchanges of information. Managers in learning organizations must be open to suggestions, be able to admit mistakes without fear of reprisal, and be willing to make changes. Learning organizations have become adept at translating new knowledge into new ways of behaving.[8] Many of the recent changes in libraries of all types are allowing them to become more like learning organizations.

Another change in training comes from the newly adopted attitude in many organizations to view managers and supervisors as "coaches" for the employees they supervise. Like a good coach, a supervisor should act as a role model, help the employee set realistic goals, give feedback on performance, provide suggestions on how to improve, and provide reinforcement and encouragement. The supervisor and the employee should not view themselves as adversaries. Instead, they are on the same team, each trying to improve the overall performance of the organization. A commitment to coaching "sends the message that continuous learning is the accepted practice. By coaching, we model how we must interact with each other if we are to achieve our best individual and organizational performance."[9]

> Technology has created a dynamic workplace "learning curve" for every employee of the organization. We are mud-caked dirt bikers, scrambling up slippery slopes to meager plateaus with no place to rest and more slopes ahead. The need to learn is ceaseless.[10]
>
> —Ruth F. Metz,
> *Coaching in the Library*

In the section of chapter 13 dealing with team-building, there will be more about coaching as a specific means of staff development.

No library is exempt from change, and at times it seems the pace of change becomes more rapid each year. If librarians are to remain up-to-date, there is no choice but to continue to learn. Every library, regardless of size or type, needs a planned staff development program. Such activities are not haphazardly scheduled but are organized on a structured continuum. Such programs provide the means by which employees can grow on the job and prepare to advance as opportunities become available. Good staff development programs contribute to employees' career development; through such programs, employers can identify potential supervisors and prepare them for that responsibility. Human resources are too valuable for any institution to fail to invest in the training programs that the times require.[11]

Performance Appraisals

> Giving employees honest feedback on their performance can be one of the toughest jobs a manager can do. Leaders often shy away from delivering the honest feedback their employees need because it is uncomfortable and can seem overwhelming to deal with. Yet without good feedback, our operation cannot improve productivity and your employees cannot grow and learn.[12]
>
> —Paula Peters,
> *"Seven Tips for Delivering Performance Feedback"*

Performance appraisal is the systematic evaluation of an individual employee's job-related strengths and weaknesses. In all types of organizations, employees have to be evaluated. Some workers are better than others at specific jobs. Some workers take the initiative and carry through an assignment with little supervision. Others may be unreliable or must always be closely supervised to ensure the successful completion of a project. When decisions have to be made about pay increases or promotions, the supervisor must have a way to distinguish the excellent performers from the mediocre. Before systematic performance appraisals were developed, those decisions were often made on the basis of supervisors' subjective, spur-of-the-moment impressions. A systematic, written performance appraisal system provides a sounder method of distinguishing among the performances of employees.

Not every management expert advocates performance appraisal. For instance, W. Edwards Deming claimed that performance appraisal is one of the seven deadly diseases afflicting Western management.[13] He states that

> what is wrong is that the performance appraisal or merit rating focuses on the end product . . . not on leadership to help people. . . . Merit rating rewards people that do well in the system. It does not reward attempts to improve the system. . . . Moreover a merit system is meaningless as a predictor of performance. . . . Traditional appraisal systems increase the variability of performance. The trouble lies in the implied preciseness of rating systems. . . . One of the main effects of evaluation of performance is nourishment of short-term thinking and short-term performance.[14]

However, Deming is in the minority in his view. Most managers, although they realize that performance appraisals are not perfect tools, are advocates of their value.[15]

There has been a shift in some organizations in the focus of evaluations as a result of other changes in the organization. Especially in team-based organizations, there has been a move to see the supervisor as more of a coach than a boss. If the supervisor is functioning as a coach, the feedback to the employee is continuous throughout the year. Even in these types of organizations, formal performance assessments may still only be done once a year, but there should be no surprises. Learning theory suggests that immediate feedback helps learners increase their performance. All employees need feedback more than once a year, and good supervisors provide it. Usually, the frequent feedback is done on a more informal, spontaneous fashion, whereas the annual evaluation is done in a more formal, structured manner.

Personnel Appraisal (pers'-n-el a-pra'zel) noun: given by someone who does not want to give it to someone who does not want to get it.[16]

—Anonymous

Judging another's performance is usually difficult, and often both supervisors and subordinates feel ambivalent about performance appraisal. Some writers have likened appraisals to paying taxes. They are something that managers are obligated to do but would like to avoid. Although most employees want feedback on how they are doing, they would prefer feedback that is consistent with their image of themselves as good performers.[17]

Why Appraisals Are Done

Formal performance assessments have two main objectives. The first objective of a performance appraisal is to determine how well an employee performs on the job. Performance appraisals have a second objective, that is, to help an employee know how well he or she is doing so that if improvement needs to be made, the employee knows in what area performance is falling short. Thus, performance appraisal can be used to encourage the growth and development of an individual worker. To achieve the second objective, the evaluation of an employee's performance must be communicated to the individual. Without this transfer of information and the development of a remedial process or plan, the employee cannot be expected to achieve improvement or redirection in performance.

Most managers regard performance appraisals as useful tools with several important functions. A good performance appraisal system can serve as a basis for HR decisions relating to promotion, demotion, and termination of employees. It facilitates the promotion of outstanding workers and the weeding out or transfer of poor performers. Systematic, written assessment of a worker by a number of raters over a period of time helps make these decisions reasonable and sound. Performance appraisal also can serve as the basis for wage and salary treatment. Many organizations relate at least some decisions about the size and frequency of pay increases to an employee's performance appraisal rating. If properly conducted, the performance appraisal will give every level of management a better understanding of the individual worker's capabilities and potential. The entire appraisal process can facilitate understanding between supervisors and employees. Performance appraisal provides concrete feedback to employees that allows them to improve their performance by making them aware of weaknesses and how to correct them.

> A formal review is more than once-a-year paperwork and more even than a "people program." It is a way to link performance with corporate strategy. Because a review provides the occasion to open the books and share information, it can be a powerful idea generator and a rich source of improvement. Take the time to do it right.[18]

So, appraisals aid in creating and maintaining a satisfactory level of performance by employees. The performance appraisal process should help employees establish personal goals that will enable them to grow and develop and that, in turn, will further the goals of the institution. In addition, performance appraisals can serve as information-gathering tools that provide data to be used in determining both organizational and individual training needs.

Good performance appraisal systems are careful to make a distinction between the variations of performance of employees caused by shortcomings on the part of the employee and those caused by inadequacies of the organization. For instance, the best employee cannot be productive if there is a problem with getting materials—a cataloger cannot catalog if there is a backlog in acquisitions that prevents the books getting to the cataloging department. An appraiser must be careful never to blame the deficiencies of the organization on the individual employee because these improperly done appraisals "can jeopardize morale, adversely affect teamwork, and leave an individual feeling unfairly criticized."[19]

When to Do Appraisals

Each organization determines when performance appraisals will be administered. There should be a definite schedule, and the schedule should be public knowledge. Performance appraisals are most commonly done on a yearly basis. Ideally, though, performance appraisals would be done frequently enough to let employees know if their performance is satisfactory and, if not, the steps that need to be taken for improvement. For some employees, this cannot be accomplished solely through an annual performance appraisal. It is recommended that informal performance appraisals be done several times a year to supplement the formal annual appraisal.

New employees need more frequent appraisals than do long-established workers. In most organizations, new staff members serve a probationary period before permanent appointment is made. That probationary period may vary from a few months for clerical positions to up to one year for professional positions. A performance rating should be administered at the end of the probationary period, but a good supervisor will review the job description and the quality of job performance with the new employee several times during the probationary period.

After the probationary period, performance appraisals are administered on a recurring basis. Some institutions schedule all employee evaluations at the same time. This practice permits the supervisor to compare most easily the performance of all subordinates. But grouping all the appraisals presents drawbacks. Supervisors with a large number of appraisals to complete can be overwhelmed, resulting in poorly prepared performance evaluations. Not enough time is allowed for thoughtful, careful evaluation. To avoid overload, some institutions do performance evaluations on each anniversary of the employee's appointment to permanent status. This timetable distributes the work load over the entire year and permits careful judgments to be made.

Who Does Appraisals

Who should do the performance evaluations? By far, the most common practice in libraries, as in other institutions, is to have the immediate supervisor evaluate the performance of his or her subordinates because that individual has the greatest opportunity to observe the subordinate and, thus, is most familiar with that employee's performance. Because the supervisor is accountable for the successful operation of his or her unit, it is appropriate that the supervisor have authority over HR administration affecting that unit.

Although the custom of having the immediate supervisor evaluate subordinates is most common, other types of evaluations replace or supplement this practice in some institutions. Peer ratings are used to evaluate some professional librarians, primarily academic ones. Because many academic librarians have faculty status, the librarians have adopted the same type of peer review of performance that is used for most faculty members in institutions of higher education. Professional librarians interact with one another and are usually familiar with each other's work. In addition many elements of the librarian's work, particularly at the departmental level, require cooperative work. Thus, they should be good judges of each other's performance.[20]

> Peer appraisal begins with the simple premise: the people best suited to judge the performance of others are those who work most closely with them. In flatter organizations with looser hierarchies, bosses may no longer have all the information they need to appraise subordinates. But it doesn't necessarily follow that peers will eagerly step into the breach. They may tend to give fairly conservative feedback rather than risk straining relationships with colleagues by saying things that could be perceived negatively. Consequently, the feedback gathered from peers may be distorted, overly positive, and in the end, unhelpful to managers and recipients.[21]
>
> —Maury A Peiperl,
> "Getting 360° Feedback Right"

In some organizations, subordinates are allowed to appraise the performance of their immediate supervisor. Considerable trust and openness are necessary to make this type of appraisal successful, and, in most cases, subordinates do not assess their bosses without guaranteed anonymity. When subordinates do evaluate their superiors, the appraisals are not used to determine pay raises; often, employee appraisals are not seen by anyone but the managers. Instead, these evaluations serve primarily as a tool for the guided self-development of the manager and as a means of giving employees a way to express their opinions. Several studies of upward evaluations have shown that usually staff feels supervisors have used the upward evaluations and improved as a result.[22] One study showed that upward feedback was most helpful to those managers who received low rankings and that managers who met with subordinates to discuss the results of the evaluation improved more than those managers who did not.[23]

Upward evaluations provide supervisors with information that can be used to improve performance and thus can be very useful. But, because inaccurate and inadequate information gathered about a supervisor could lead to a distorted view of the supervisor's performance and thus potentially could lead to legal challenges, it is important that a formal process be developed and a valid and reliable instrument used.[24]

A growing number of organizations are using what is termed "360-degree" or "multirater" feedback, a process where an employee's performance is assessed through confidential feedback from a variety of sources, including direct reports, managers, peers, internal and external customers, and the individual employee. Oftentimes the questionnaires used in 360-degree evaluations are computerized and the feedback sheets computer generated. The reviews from each of these sources are anonymous, and usually the HR department collects and compiles the reviews into a report to be given to the employee. This 360-degree feedback allows an employee to get feedback on facets of performance that are often overlooked in a traditional top-down performance assessment. Another reason for its growing use is the number of organizations that have eliminated layers of middle managers. With the span of control for managers becoming wider, it becomes more difficult for a manager to provide assessments for the large number of employees being supervised. The increase in the number of organizations using self-directed teams is another impetus for the adoption of 360-degree feedback. The members of the team are in the best position to know the performance of other team members.

This type of evaluation yields valuable data, but it can be very threatening to individual managers.[25] It can also be very time consuming. If a library had thirty employees and decided to institute this type of performance appraisal, and on average each employee was to be evaluated by six other employees using an appraisal instrument that took forty-five minutes to complete, it is easy to see how this appraisal becomes expensive in terms of time.

If a library decides to institute 360-degree appraisals, the process should be planned carefully. It will take time to implement a well-designed system. As with all other appraisal systems, there needs to be support from the top management. Because employees know their jobs best, they should be involved in the development of the appraisal criteria. Training in both giving and receiving 360-degree feedback should be given to everyone participating in the process. If employees are given feedback without being told what to do with the results, they do not know what actions to take. As one expert states, "there is often too much focus on getting the feedback and mining the data and too little focus on using the feedback for job-related or behavior change."[26] As with any new system, the procedure should probably be pilot tested in one area before being adopted library–wide, and managers should monitor the system to be sure it is performing as designed and be ready to modify it if it isn't.

Some organizations permit employee self-evaluation. Employees can usually give an accurate picture of their own strengths and weaknesses. If an employee is accurate in identifying strengths and weaknesses, the supervisor only has to confirm and help the employees set goals to improve the weaknesses. Individuals are much less defensive if they themselves have pointed out their shortcomings instead of having those shortcomings pointed out by their manager. But, unfortunately, not all employees are able to evaluate themselves accurately, and there is often low agreement between the employee's evaluation and that of the supervisor.[27] Employee self-appraisal is most useful in employee development and identifying training needs. If self-appraisal is used as part of employee evaluation, it is almost always used in conjunction with another type of appraisal.

Whatever type of performance appraisal program is instituted, it must be strongly supported by senior management. Senior management must orient and train supervisors in systematic evaluation and convince them of its value. Management must also give supervisors sufficient time to carry out the appraisals. Most supervisors dislike the process of evaluating their employees and, in particular, try to avoid discussing deficiencies with the employee. Unless the upper echelons of management indicate their support, the program likely will be ineffective.

One of the major challenges of performance appraisal is establishing the standards of performance against which an employee's work is judged. Standards that need to be established usually fall clearly into three categories:

1. *Quality-quantity standards.* How well does the employee perform the various tasks in the job description, and how much of each task is actually accomplished?

2. *Desired-effect standards.* Is work complete, accurate, and performed on time, benefiting the goals and objectives of the institution and users? Are sound data gathered as a basis for judgment and decisions?

3. *Manner of performance standards.* Is the work accomplished in cooperation with others, without friction? Can the employee adapt to new programs or processes?

Because no two supervisors interpret these standards in exactly the same way, top management must define the standards. This is sometimes done by issuing a performance evaluation manual to be used by supervisors in evaluation. If supervisors interpret standards differently or give greater weight to one standard over another, inequity in evaluation from department to department will result.

Problems in Rating

Because appraisals are carried out by humans, they are subject to a number of weaknesses and errors. The most common errors found in performance appraisal are:

1. The *halo effect.* Supervisors often let the rating they assign to one characteristic unduly influence their rating on all factors. For example, if a supervisor thinks an employee is outstanding in one area, the supervisor gives that employee excellent ratings on all the factors being evaluated. One way to minimize the halo effect is to have the supervisor evaluate all subordinates on the same factor before going on to the next.

2. *Prejudice and partiality.* Sometimes a supervisor allows personal feelings about a subordinate to affect the rating given to that subordinate. It is a serious error for a supervisor to let personal likes and dislikes interfere with evaluating an employee's work performance. In addition, it is not only an error of judgment but a constitutional violation to consider race, creed, color, religion, politics, nationality, or gender in evaluating work performance.

3. *Leniency or strictness.* When some raters are extremely lenient and some are extremely strict, employees working at the same level of performance receive vastly different ratings depending on their supervisor. Some supervisors give all their subordinates relatively high ratings because they do not want to face any resentment or disappointment that might result from lower

ratings. This leniency causes all the ratings to be so close to the top of the scale that they are worthless to management and unfair to the really good employees. The error also creates an unrealistic feeling of success when improvement in performance may be badly needed and often possible. Less common but equally damaging is the practice of giving low ratings to all employees. Sometimes these overly strict raters have artificially high standards that few subordinates can ever achieve. Both of these errors are caused by the subjectivity of the ranking process, and both can be alleviated, to some extent, by careful training of the evaluators.

4. *Central tendency.* Some appraisers are reluctant to use either the high or low extremes of the rating scale and cluster all their ratings about the center. On a normal distribution curve, more people will be rated closer to the mean than to any other point on the scale. However, when all ratings are clustered at the center, most of the value of the systematic performance appraisal is lost.

5. *Contrast.* This error occurs when the supervisor does not measure the work the employee has actually done but measures what he or she thinks the employee has the potential to achieve.

6. *Association.* Sometimes raters with a number of evaluations to complete rate factors at the same level merely because they follow each other on the page. This may also happen when the supervisor is tired or bored and tries to make hurried judgments without all the facts.

7. *Recency.* This is the error of a rater who appraises only the work the employee has done in the recent past, rather than the work done over the entire period of time covered by the appraisal.

A number of techniques can reduce errors in performance appraisal. As mentioned earlier, training can reduce errors. Some errors can be lessened by keeping good records of employee performance. Errors can also be reduced if supervisors have input into the type of appraisal system that is used. If raters have participated in developing the system, they will use it more effectively. Finally, errors can be minimized if the organization's top management makes it clearly understood that all supervisors are to take performance appraisal very seriously. Not only should good appraisals be expected, they should be rewarded. When the organization not only expects good appraisals but systematically rewards supervisors who carefully and conscientiously perform those appraisals, it lays the foundation for an effective system of performance evaluation.

Methods of Performance Appraisal

There are no standard methods of performance appraisal and no method that works best in all settings. Instead, there are a number of effective methods that can be used. Institutions do not have to select a single method, but generally one method or combination of methods is agreed upon for the entire institution. The method used may be that used by the parent institution, as in the case of a library that is part of a larger municipal or academic system. Some examples of performance appraisals forms are available on this book's website.

If the library is free to select its own method, staff committees may have input into selecting the method. In larger libraries and information centers, the HR office often plays a key role in the selection and development of the method used. The performance appraisal methods most commonly used are essays, ranking, forced distribution, graphic ratings scales, and the behaviorally anchored rating scale. Management by objectives also provides a means of performance appraisal (see chapter 3 for more information). Regardless of the type of instrument used, all factors being assessed should be job-related.

In the essay method, the rater describes an individual's performance in a written narrative. The essay can be unstructured, but usually the rater is asked to respond to general questions relating to the employee's job knowledge, strengths and weaknesses, and promotion potential. The major drawback of essays is that their length and content may vary, and consistency is hard to achieve. The rater's writing ability may also affect the appraisal. An employee might receive a comparatively poor rating because the rater does not write well. Essays are most effective when they are combined with some other appraisal technique.

Several ranking systems are used in employee appraisal. Using the simple ranking method, the supervisor ranks the employees from highest to lowest—from best employee to worst. In alternative ranking, the supervisor first chooses the best and the poorest performers. Then the next-best and the next-poorest performers are chosen, alternating from top to bottom, until all employees have been ranked. The paired comparison method is an organized way of comparing each employee with every other employee, one at a time. The advantage of the ranking system is its simplicity. The major disadvantages are that it does not reveal the degree of difference between persons in adjacent ranks, and individuals with the same performance rating must be given separate ranks. In addition, it is difficult to compare various groups of employees because the ones ranked highest in one unit may not be as good as those ranked highest in another unit.

A common problem with rating scales is that too many people are rated on the high end of the scale. The forced distribution rating system is designed to prevent this clustering. Forced distribution requires the rater to compare the performance of employees and to place a certain percentage of employees at various performance intervals. Usually, a supervisor must allocate ten percent to the highest category and ten percent to the lowest, with the other employees proportionately assigned as follows. As can be seen in Figure 9.2, this process results in a distribution identical to that found in the normal bell shaped curve.

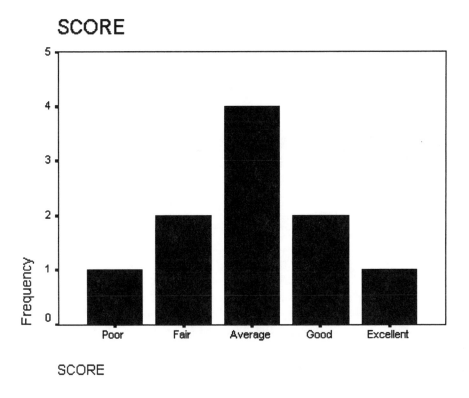

Figure 9.2. The Distribution of a Forced Distribution Rating System

The forced distribution method assumes that the performance in a group of employees is distributed according to a normal curve. In many units, this assumption may be untrue. The method of performance appraisal is most difficult to use when evaluating a small number of people.

The graphic rating scale is the most commonly used method of performance appraisal in libraries and information centers. The rater evaluates the employee on such factors as quantity of work, dependability, initiative, job knowledge, and accuracy. Some organizations use a very simple form, with the factor being evaluated, listed, and defined, followed by a multiple-choice format for the rating. The supervisor indicates the rating of the employee for each factor by placing a mark on the horizontal line.

Accuracy is the correctness of work performed.				
Poor	Fair	Average	Good	Excellent

It is very difficult for supervisors to agree on the meaning of *average*, *fair*, or *excellent*. No matter how much training supervisors receive, different individuals will interpret these terms differently.

In recent years, most institutions have improved the graphic rating scale by eliminating such terms as poor, fair, and excellent. In their place, a short phrase is used to describe the different levels of performance. The most difficult part of developing these new scales is to provide a short phrase that cannot be misinterpreted, thus assuring comparable interpretations by various supervisors. Using this type of form, accuracy might be evaluated as follows:

Accuracy is the correctness of work performed.				
Makes frequent errors	Careless, often makes errors	Usually accurate. Only makes average number of errors	Requires little supervision. Is exact and precise most of the time	Requires absolute minimum of supervision. Is almost always accurate

It does not make any difference how many levels of an element are defined; generally four or five are given, as in the example above. The fact that graphic rating scales require relatively little time to construct and administer doubtlessly contributes to their popularity. Graphic rating scales also force an evaluator to consider several dimensions of performance, and they are standardized and comparable across individuals. Their biggest drawback is that they are susceptible to errors such as halo, central tendency, or leniency. In addition, all rating scales tend to look backward, judging an employee's performance over the period of time being assessed instead of helping the employee set goals for improvement. An example of a graphic rating scale may be seen in Figure 9.3.

Behaviorally anchored rating scales (BARS) were developed to correct some of the deficiencies in the graphic rating scale. In developing BARS, the active participation of job holders and supervisors helps to identify key job dimensions and areas of responsibility. Each job is likely to have several job dimensions and separate scales for each. The anchors are specific, written descriptions of actual job behaviors that supervisors agree represent specific levels of performance. To carry out a performance appraisal using BARS requires the rater to read through the list of anchors on each scale (i.e., for each job behavior) until the anchor that best describe the employees' job behavior are identified. The scale value opposite the anchor is checked. The evaluation is obtained by combining the scale values chosen for each job dimension. BARS take more time to develop than graphic rating scales, and a separate form must be developed for each job. The use of BARS can help reduce errors if good behavioral statements are provided as anchors. Also, because BARS are developed with the participation of managers and job holders, the likelihood is higher that this appraisal method will be accepted. Figure 9.4 shows a BARS that was designed to evaluate the job dimension of project planning, which is a function of many managerial positions. BARS are often impractical because each job requires its own scale, and often in smaller organizations there are not enough employees in each specific job to use them.[28] To date BARS are not widely used in libraries.[29]

Parkville Public Library
Employee Performance Evaluation

Employee's Name _____   Classification _____

Evaluation Period: From _____ To _____   Department _____

> PLACE CHECK MARK IN BOX THAT MOST APPROPRIATELY INDICATES YOUR JUDGMENT ON EACH FACTOR BEING APPRAISED. COMPLETE ALL ITEMS FOR ALL EMPLOYEES.

Job Knowledge

1	2	3	4	5
Serious gaps in knowledge of essentials of job	Satisfactory knowledge of essentials of job	Adequately informed on most phases of job	Good knowledge of all phases of job	Excellent understanding of job

Attitude

1	2	3	4	5
Uncooperative, resents suggestions, no enthusiasm	Often cooperates and accepts suggestions	Satisfactory cooperation; accepts new ideas	Responsive, cooperates well; helpful to others	Excellent in cooperation and enthusiasm; welcomes new ideas; very helpful

Judgment

1	2	3	4	5
Decisions often wrong or ineffective	Judgment usually sound but makes some errors	Good decision resulting from sound analysis of factors	Sound, logical thinker	Consistently makes sound judgments

Quantity of Work

1	2	3	4	5
Falls below minimum requirements	Usually meets minimum requirements	Satisfactory quantity	Usually well exceeds minimum	Consistently produces high quantity

Quality of Work

1	2	3	4	5
Poor quality, many errors	Quality usually all right, some errors	Satisfactory quality	Quality exceeds standards	Consistently high quality

Figure 9.3. A Graphic Rating Scale

Scale values	Anchors
7 [ ] Excellent	Develops a comprehensive project plan, documents it well, obtains required approval, and distributes the plan to all concerned.
6 [ ] Very good	Plans, communicates, and observes milestones; states week by week where the project stands relative to plans. Maintains up-to-date charts of project accomplishments and backlogs and uses these to optimize any schedule modifications required.
	Experiences occasional minor operational problems, but communicates effectively.
5 [ ] Good	Lays out all the parts of a job and schedules each part; seeks to beat schedule and will allow for slack.
	Satisfies customers' time constraints; time and cost overruns occur infrequently.
4 [ ] Average	Makes a list of due dates and revises them as the project progresses, usually adding unforeseen events; instigates frequent customer complaints.
	May have a sound plan, but does not keep track of milestones; does not report slippages in schedule or other problems as they occur.
3 [ ] Below average	Plans are poorly defined, unrealistic time schedules are common.
	Cannot plan more than a day or two ahead, has no concept of a realistic project due date.
2 [ ] Very poor	Has no plan or schedule of work segments to be performed.
	Does little or no planning for project assignments.
1 [ ] Unacceptable	Seldom, if ever, completes project because of lack of planning and does not seem to care.
	Fails consistently due to lack of planning and does not inquire about how to improve.

Figure 9.4. A Behaviorally Anchored Rating Scale. From "Developing Behaviorally Anchored Rating Scales (BARS)," by C. E. Schneier and R. W. Beatty, August 1979. Reprinted from the August 1979 issue of *Personnel Administrator*. Reprinted with the permission of *HR Magazine*, published by the Society for Human Resource Management, (www.shrm.org) Alexandria, VA.

The Performance Appraisal Review Process

Institutions structure the performance appraisal review process in various ways, but some elements are common to almost all reviews. First, the office that is responsible for distributing evaluation forms to supervisors distributes the appropriate forms. The office that has this responsibility varies according to the size of the organization. An HR office, the library director's office, or an administrative assistant's office might be responsible. That office identifies the individual whose performance is to be evaluated, the department in which the job is located, the name of the person responsible for completing the form, and the date the form is due back in the initiating office. In an increasing number of organizations, computer software is used in performance appraisals as a means of making the process more efficient and standardized.

The person who received the form then needs to evaluate the employee's performance. As mentioned earlier, the rater is most commonly the employee's immediate supervisor, who is supposed to know the most about the job and the employee being evaluated. It is the rater's responsibility to complete the form thoughtfully and carefully. Usually, it is wise for the rater to base judgments on notes or a diary kept over a period of time. The rater must have proof of evaluations given, particularly negative evaluations. The rater must consider the employee's work from the last period of rating to the current time; evaluation should not be based solely on what happened recently.

The rater must not be afraid to give a negative rating. With today's emphasis on accountability, it is the rater's responsibility to be accurate and truthful in the evaluation of an employee's performance. Not infrequently, a rater rates an employee as adequate or good, but requests the employee's discharge or transfer a few months later. If the employee's performance is bad, say so, but have proof.

Sometimes, a rater is consciously or unconsciously prejudiced against an employee. Prejudice arises not only from race or creed, but also from color of hair, personality, sexual preference, physical characteristics, or other factors. In order to make sure that no prejudice or bias influences an evaluation, the rating should be reviewed by the supervisor's supervisor—the next person in the hierarchy. Together the rater and his or her supervisor should review the proposed performance evaluation and come to a consensus on the accuracy of the evaluation.

After the evaluation form is complete, the rater must share the results with the employee. This information is usually provided in a performance appraisal interview. Conducting the performance appraisal interview is probably the most difficult part of the process—at least, it is the part most dreaded by employees and supervisors. Some well-defined steps should be taken to prepare for the interview. To prepare the employee, the supervisor should make an appointment with the employee and make the purpose of the appointment clear. Before the meeting is held, the supervisor should give the employee the completed performance appraisal form. The employee should have at least twenty-four hours to review the evaluation of his or her work and to consider its fairness and appropriateness. In addition, the supervisor must prepare for the meeting. The supervisor might examine previous performance appraisals to review the employee's progress. Certainly, the supervisor will plan the meeting's structure. Accomplishing these two steps eliminates two of the most prevalent errors in performance appraisal interviews. First, the employee has time to study the appraisal instead of being suddenly handed an appraisal without time to think about it. Second, the supervisor plans the meeting instead of calling it on impulse in an attempt to get it out of the way.

> Thou shalt treat employees as adults and with respect, and not lose sight of the fact that they are people, not just human resources. . . . The surest way for a business to fail is to suggest, through its actions or statements, that people are nothing more than useful commodities. As managers, we must never forget that we are dealing with people— real human beings who deserve to be treated with fairness, honesty, and respect.[30]
>
> —Kent E. Romanoff,
> "The Ten Commandments of Performance Management"

Most employees are apprehensive about these performance appraisal interviews. Once an interview time has been established, the supervisor should make every effort to hold to the schedule because postponements or other schedule changes increase the employee's worry and concern. Because of the sensitivity of this interview, the supervisor must establish as informal an atmosphere as possible. Frequently, supervisors move away from their desks to an area with more informal furniture because the supervisor's desk, a symbol of authority, functions as a barrier and a psychological obstacle to many workers. Supervisors should allow for uninterrupted time with provisions made so there will be no telephone calls or other people interrupting the interview. The supervisor should employ techniques of good interviewing. He or she should ask questions or make comments that encourage the employee to talk. The supervisor should not lecture the employee. If the employee is encouraged to talk, the discussion will naturally center on the performance appraisal. The employee has the opportunity to express concern or approval of the appraisal, and the supervisor can explain why certain elements were rated as they were.

In this interview, the supervisor's objectives are to identify problems the employee has in performing any assigned tasks; to plan methods or procedures by which these problems might be resolved; to determine the employee's general level of satisfaction with the job, the institution, and the working environment; and to help the employee plan personal programs and activities that will make him or her more effective in the job or that will help him or her prepare for advancement. The last objective is particularly important. Together, the employee and the supervisor are establishing current and long-range goals for the employee. After mutual agreement, the goals are recorded on the performance evaluation form; at the next evaluation interview, progress toward the goals is measured. By signing a performance evaluation form, the employee indicates acceptance of the evaluation and proposed goals.

Of course, not all interviews go smoothly. In some cases, the supervisor may have to demote or to terminate an employee. The supervisor should be able to anticipate when such action might be necessary and be prepared. Previous and current performance appraisals, as well as the known attitude and behavior of the employee, provide indications that difficulty might be encountered. The wise supervisor is seldom caught unprepared for any direction the interview takes.

Performance appraisal is a necessary though difficult part of HR administration. The rationale is that if employees are told where their performance is deficient, they will take steps to improve it. But, as Saul Gellerman points out, this is an oversimplification. "It would be more accurate to say that most [people] would want to correct the deficiencies in their performance if they agreed that they were deficient and if there appeared to be enough advantage in correcting them to justify the effort."[31] Difficulties in communication and lack of trust are the reasons performance appraisal frequently results in resentment and tension between the supervisor and the employee.

Granted, performance appraisal may be an imperfect tool of HR administration. If it is viewed as a tool of second- or third-level supervisors, it loses its clout and encourages strife. But if it is given strong support from top-level management and if it uses objective standards for evaluation, it helps employees understand where they stand—and that is something all employees want to know.

Discipline and Grievances

At one time or another, almost every manager has to deal with an employee who fails to comply with the requirements of the job or the organization. That employee's supervisor may need to invoke some sort of disciplinary procedure to resolve the problem. Conversely, sometimes an employee has a complaint about the organization or its management. In that case, the employee may need to use the grievance procedure to resolve the problem.

Discipline is the action taken by an organization against an employee when that employee's performance has deteriorated to the point where action is necessary or when that employee has violated an institutional rule. Discipline is a method of communication to employees that they need to change their behavior to come up to established standards. Discipline may need to be administered for reasons ranging from excessive absenteeism to theft. Discipline is one of the most challenging areas in dealing with employees. The supervisor must be aware of the dual objectives of discipline: preserving the interests of the organization and protecting the rights of the individual.

Most organizations have formal policies and procedures for handling discipline. It has been estimated that only about five percent of employees ever need discipline—the vast majority are good workers who want to do the right thing.[32] But the policy and procedures must be in place to deal with the few who need them. Before establishing disciplinary procedures, each institution must develop rules and regulations governing employee performance and must take measures to ensure that these rules and regulations are clearly understood by each employee. If an employee violates a rule or work standard, disciplinary action is taken. Before this is done, however, it should be established that the cause of the poor performance is not caused by external factors, such as poor training, insufficient supervision, or inadequate equipment.

Disciplinary actions take various forms, depending on the nature and frequency of the offending behavior. Most organizations employ what is known as progressive discipline, which provides for a series of steps before dismissal so that an employee will have the opportunity to correct the undesirable behavior. The mildest disciplinary action is the simple oral warning. The penalties escalate to an oral warning noted in the employee's personnel record, then to a written warning, then to suspension without pay for varying lengths of time, and finally, to the harshest penalty, discharge from the job. In the case of gross misconduct, such as assault on a supervisor or theft, however, an employee can be dismissed without going through all the steps. To prevent possible litigation, documentation should be kept at each step of the process.

> Management has the responsibility for building an organizational climate of preventive discipline. In doing so, it makes its standards known and understood. If employees do not know what standards they are expected to uphold, their conduct is likely to be erratic or misdirected. Employees are more likely to support standards that they have helped create.... They usually want to know the reasons behind a standard so that it will make sense to them.[33]
>
> —Keith Davis and John W. Newstrom,
> *Human Behavior at Work*

To administer discipline effectively, the penalties must be imposed consistently and fairly and with advance warning. Many HR experts refer to the "red-hot stove" method of administering discipline. When someone touches a red-hot stove, the punishment is immediate, given with warning, consistent, and impersonal. The best disciplinary systems have these characteristics. Discipline should be carried out impersonally, without a feeling of animosity on the part of the supervisor. A supervisor should never hesitate to use discipline when necessary but should always remember that discipline is not intended to humiliate an employee but to correct a problem or to modify job behavior. Discipline should be administered privately and in a calm manner. The supervisor should encourage two-way communication and allow the employee to speak. A follow-up plan for improving behavior should be agreed upon. If possible, the interview should end on a positive note so that the employee can believe that the supervisor and organization want him or her to succeed.[34]

No one likes to administer discipline, but if handled properly, a disciplinary system can be an effective tool in handling job-related employee problems. In addition to the individual being disciplined, discipline may prevent others from acting in a similar fashion, assure others that inappropriate behavior will not be tolerated, and communicate the manager's commitment to a high standard of conduct.[35]

Firing or Termination

When none of the discipline procedures are effective, a manager may have to discharge an employee. *Firing* is the term that is usually used for a for-cause dismissal. An employee who has committed a major transgression, such as stealing, gross insubordination, or the like, would be fired. *Termination* results from an employee's failure to meet job expectations after a reasonable amount of time.[36] Discharging an employee is never easy, but the process must be handled correctly because the mishandling of terminations is a major cause of employee lawsuits. Documentation is important in all HR decisions but especially important in the case of terminations. All evidence supporting the need for termination should be available in case of litigation.[37] Managers should treat the employee with respect and understand how traumatic it is to lose a job for whatever reason. At the same time, however, it is the duty of a manager to remove poorly performing employees before they affect the morale of other workers and impede the work being done in the unit.

Grievance Systems

Discipline is concerned with the problems organizations have with employees. A grievance system, on the other hand, provides a method for employees to deal with problems they have with supervisors or with the organization. A *grievance* is any dissatisfaction relating to one's employment that is brought to the attention of an organization's management. Grievance procedures are found in both unionized and nonunionized organizations, but the procedure is apt to be more formal and well-defined in unionized situations.

Often, in nonunionized institutions, the open-door policy is used to solve employee grievances. This policy is based on the assumption that when supervisors encourage employees to come to their office voluntarily at any time to discuss problems and complaints, they will feel free to do so. But this assumption is not completely sound. The open-door policy works only when the supervisor has been able to instill in employees a feeling of trust. Employees must feel that any problem or complaint will be objectively heard and fairly resolved and that the supervisor will not hold it against them or consider them troublemakers. The open-door policy works when the supervisor is skilled in human relations and is sensitive to employee needs and feelings. The open-door policy gives the supervisor an opportunity to explain why certain action was taken and to resolve the complaint or grievance through direct communication.

The open-door policy, though it can operate in a unionized organization, is more likely to function in a nonunionized organization. In the absence of a union contract, the supervisor has more freedom and more options to resolve problems. Factual problems are probably the easiest to resolve because they involve working conditions, hours of work, or changes in the procedures of a job. Problems involving feelings or emotions are much more difficult to handle. Here, the supervisor must constantly ask, "Why does the employee feel this way?" The answer will depend on the supervisor's understanding of people.

In a unionized institution, the collective bargaining agreement establishes the procedures to be used for handling employee complaints. The grievance procedure goes through certain steps outlined in the union contract. In general, the first step is for the aggrieved employee to meet with his or her union steward, who is the union representative for that employee's unit. The employee and the union steward discuss the grievance and together bring the grievance to the grievant's supervisor. If a mutually satisfactory solution cannot be reached at this stage, the grievance is put in writing, and the process is continued with the next level of management. If the problem still is not resolved, higher management and the HR department usually become involved. If a solution to the grievance cannot be arrived at in the organization, the grievant can request arbitration, a process by which both the employer and the union representing the employee agree to settle the dispute through an outside, neutral third party. The decision made by the arbitrator is binding for all parties involved.

It is essential that organizations have a written, public grievance procedure. In a unionized organization, this procedure is part of the union contract. In a nonunionized organization, management must see that such procedures are established. A grievance procedure defines: the manner in which grievances are filed (written or oral), to whom the grievance is submitted, how the grievance proceeds through the organization's hierarchy, where decisions about the grievance can be made, and the final point of decision. Usually, the procedures identify actions that aggrieved employees can take if they are not satisfied with the final decision.

Grievance procedures are ways of removing the employee from the direct and complete control of the immediate supervisor. Grievance procedures may discipline supervisors and act as guarantees to employees. They exist to assure employees that justice is available when they have a legitimate complaint against the organization.

Employee Compensation

The ultimate aim of salary administration is to arrive at an equitable system of compensating employees for the work they perform. Unlike many corporations, which operate for profit and often provide annual bonuses, stock options, or other special incentives to reward employees, most libraries and information centers offer only salaries and benefits.

Most libraries differentiate between wages and salaries. *Wages* refers to compensation of employees whose pay is calculated according to the number of hours worked each week, and *salary* refers to compensation that is uniform from one pay period to the next. Wages are usually reported as being so much per hour, whereas salaries are reported in terms of so much per year.

Two other terms are used to describe the two kinds of workers. Wage-earning employees are often referred to as nonexempt personnel. Generally, nonexempt employees work in nonsupervisory positions and are covered by the Fair Labor Standards Act. Nonexempt employees must be paid "time-and-one-half" (the hourly wage multiplied by 1.5) for overtime work. Salaried workers are often referred to as exempt personnel. Exempt employees are usually managerial or professional employees who are exempt from the Fair Labor Standards Act. Employers are not required to pay such employees overtime regardless of the number of hours worked.

Both wages and salaries come from the same general pool. Most libraries receive the bulk of their salary funding from the institution to which they are attached. For public libraries, this funding comes from the municipality, the county, or other political structure. Academic libraries receive their funds from the parent educational institution, as do school media centers. Special libraries draw their funding from their parent institution. In addition, a few libraries receive a smaller amount of personnel funds from endowments, federal or foundation grants, or, very occasionally, from earned income. Funds received from federal or foundation grants are allocated to specific projects or programs on a temporary basis; such funding is often called *soft* money.

Private businesses and institutions are not required to make public the wages or salaries of any individual or group of employees. Indeed, in many industries, salary information is a closely kept secret. The justification for salary secrecy is to prevent discontent among employees. Most public institutions, on the other hand, are required to make salary information available to anyone. In many states the salaries of state employees are considered a public record and are available in personnel offices and libraries and/or are printed in a newspaper.

Some employees dislike having salaries disclosed because they may feel strongly that the disclosure violates their privacy. Sometimes public disclosure of salaries may lead to envy and a loss of morale. On the other hand, open disclosure of salaries is thought to curb favoritism and to lessen pay discrimination among employees. Many HR specialists feel that, if possible, a compromise between the two positions is best. An organization should disclose the pay ranges for various jobs within the organization but not reveal what any particular individual is earning.

In libraries as in other organizations, a salary administration program consists of three parts: the determination of what salary to pay, the development of a salary scale, and the process of awarding salary increases.

Determination of Salary

All institutions that pay personnel for services rendered must determine what is a fair and equitable compensation for the education, experience, and responsibility required in the job. A job that requires more of each of these three criteria should receive more pay than a job that requires less. The determination of the salary associated with any job should be directly related to the job evaluation. In general, the higher the job is evaluated, the higher the salary.

Institutions that wish to recruit and retain highly qualified personnel must offer salaries that are competitive in the job market. Individuals who have specialized education, who have demonstrated capability resulting from successful work experience, and who are willing to accept responsibility are always in demand. Thus, the compensation must be adequate to attract them. Although money may not be the most important motivator for some people, it is still very important to most. Institutions that strive to obtain and retain the best people will usually offer salaries higher than institutions that will accept lower performance and anticipate turnover.

> When it comes to salaries and benefits there are several forces pushing at each other and none wants to budge. On the one hand, there is the continued pressure to increase salaries or at least keep them competitive. . . . On the other hand, budgets are being slashed and compensation and benefits are tempting chunks to take a whack at. The result of this tug-of-war is that HR sits in the middle. It is expected to maintain a delicate balance recruiting and retaining the best employees while keeping payroll manageable.[38]
>
> —Todd Raphael,
> "Hold the Line on Salaries and Benefits"

In the private sector more and more companies are paying employees on the basis of some sort of performance measure.[39] This "pay-for-performance" can range from the piece-rate method of paying factory workers to the lump-sum bonuses given to employees who are considered to have contributed to a company's productivity or profits. These programs differ from the usual compensation systems because they link pay directly to productivity or performance, not just to spending time in a job. This type of compensation system is found rarely in publicly funded libraries.

The question of fair pay generally involves two general issues: 1) internal equity, or what the employee is paid compared to what other employees in the same organization are paid; and 2) external equity, or what the employee is paid compared to what employees in other organizations are paid for performing similar jobs. If organizations are to avoid dissatisfaction about pay, employees must be convinced that both internal and external equity exist. Pay dissatisfaction can have a negative influence on the employee's work. Lawler illustrates the results of pay dissatisfaction among employees (see Figure 9.5). Employees who are dissatisfied about pay not only desire more compensation but find their jobs less attractive as well. The consequences of these two conditions are detrimental to the organization as well as the employee.[40]

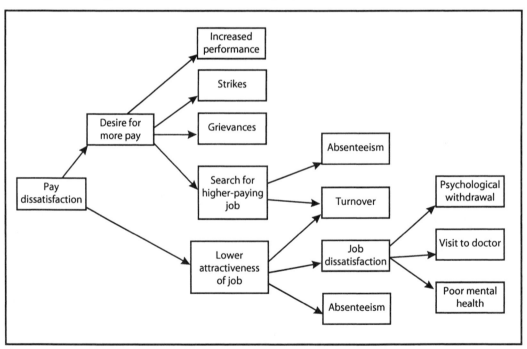

Figure 9.5. Model of Consequences of Pay Dissatisfaction. From E. E. Lawler, III, *Pay and Organizational Effectiveness* (New York: McGraw-Hill, 1971). Reprinted with permission of Edward E. Lawler, III.

In general, the salaries of professional librarians are competitive nationally, although there are sometimes regional and local conditions that affect salaries. In large metropolitan centers, such as New York City or San Francisco, the cost of living is greater than in smaller communities. Factors of this nature affect the level of salary offered. The annual report of professional salaries received by current graduates of accredited schools of library and information science, usually published in an October issue of *Library Journal,*[41] shows the regional variation of beginning salaries as well as the national average and median salaries. It must be remembered that this information is provided for only beginning or entry-level positions.

The entry-level position is the only position for which the job requirements can be accurately described. Although there are some exceptions, the entry-level position generally requires five or six years of education beyond the secondary school, with the years of education culminating in graduation from an accredited LIS school; no professional experience; and minimal or moderate end responsibility in job performance. The requirements of other levels of professional positions vary from institution to institution. Thus, many institutions use the entry-level salary as the basis of their salary scale and build upon it to compensate more experienced employees.

In addition to the *Library Journal* survey, there are several ways to gather information on entry-level salaries as well as on the salaries of other professional levels. Periodically, the Special Library Association conducts an in-depth survey of its members.[42] The American Library Association periodically reports information about salaries in *American Libraries.*[43] The Association of Research Libraries publishes an annual salary survey.[44] Some state libraries issue salary data for all libraries in that state. An institution may wish to gather these data by conducting a salary survey or by simply evaluating salaries offered in advertisements in professional periodicals. Regardless of the method used, great care must be taken to assure that all the data gathered apply to positions that have the same job requirements.

Salaries for library positions other than those held by professional librarians usually are determined by the going rate of pay in the community in which the library is located. A national overview of salaries for library support staff is published on an irregular basis by *Library Mosaics.*[45] Information concerning local salaries can be obtained from agencies and institutions, such as the school system, local government, employment agencies, or Chamber of Commerce. There are Internet sites, such as www.salary.com, which provide information about salaries for specific jobs in various geographic locations. If desired, a library can conduct a salary survey within a community. Of course, careful attention must be paid to the requirements of each job to be sure that the employee receives adequate compensation for the required education, experience, and responsibility.

Information technology has altered the jobs of most librarians, and often the job classifications and the pay scales have lagged in recognizing these changes. In many organizations the tasks that librarians perform are similar to those performed by computer or systems workers, but because they are classified differently, they are paid less.

> Despite growing confluence in the use of information technologies, performance of seemingly comparable work, and sometimes strong administrative connections in such organizations, institution policies (as reflected in classification and compensation systems) appear not to be keeping pace with changes in actual job content. The job streams or "families" with their differing evaluation structures, pay scales and benefit status that have been in existence for decades have not been adjusted to take into account the significant alterations occurring at the working levels on campus.[46]

If libraries and information centers wish to attract the most talented employees, efforts must be made to be sure that the salary offered to their employees is as attractive as that offered to employees performing similar functions working elsewhere. The disparity in salaries between technologically proficient workers in libraries and in the corporate world is one of the reason that libraries today are having such problems in recruiting new employees.

Development of a Salary Scale

A salary scale establishes the amount of money that will be paid for the accomplishment of duties designated in the job description. The scale has a minimum and a maximum amount that will be paid for that job. The minimum represents the beginning or entry-level salary, and the maximum amount should indicate the value of the job to the institution when it is performed with maximum efficiency and thoroughness. The difference between the minimum and the maximum are steps on the salary scale that designate salary increases awarded the employee as proficiency increases or as experience is gained. After an employee has reached the top step of a grade, the only way he or she can receive a pay increase is by moving to a higher range.

Each library has to develop its own salary scale, but such scales are influenced by many external factors. For instance, there are numerous constraints on how these scales can be developed. Federal and state laws concerning minimum wage put a floor under the compensation of the lowest paid employees. In 2002, the federal minimum wage remained at $5.15 per hour. The existence of a union contract may affect how employees are paid. The salaries paid in competing institutions influence the salary scale. Finally, the law of supply and demand plays a part; employees in high-demand specialties may have to be paid more than employees with more common expertise.

The establishment of the salary scale is closely linked to the process of job evaluation. Regardless of which method of job evaluation has been used (for instance, the factor method or the classification method), the ultimate objective is to ascertain the correct rate of pay for all jobs and the relationship in terms of salary between all jobs in the organization.

Although some institutions have salary scales that do not overlap, it is much more common for the ranges of adjacent pay grades to overlap. The use of an overlapping pay scale allows an outstanding performer in a lower grade to make a higher salary than a below-average worker in a higher grade. In a like fashion, an experienced worker in a lower grade would make a higher salary than a beginning worker in a higher grade.

In administering a salary scale, some commonsense principles should be kept in mind. First, there should be equal pay for equal work. If two jobs have equal requirements in terms of education, experience, and responsibility, the pay should be the same. Of course, this does not prevent having a salary range with individuals at different steps within the range. Second, employees are not required to enter a salary scale at the first step. Most institutions recognize previous related work experience and allow a new employee to enter higher on the scale. Third, if an employee is promoted from one rank to another, for instance, from Librarian I to Librarian II, the employee should not be forced to take a pay cut if the beginning salary of Librarian II is lower than the salary the employee earned as Librarian I. Instead, the employee should be given a somewhat higher salary to compensate him or her for assuming more responsibility.

Salary Increases

Three common methods of determining salary increases in libraries and information centers are length of service, merit, or some combination of length of service and merit. Length of service equates increased pay with seniority. The underlying assumption is that an organization should recognize the fact that an experienced worker is more valuable than an inexperienced one. Librarians working in public schools usually have pay schedules with predetermined steps; with each year of experience, the librarians advance a step on the salary scale. Often, public employees receive a uniform salary increase, for example, a five percent increase, and all employees receive the same percentage increase. This is a way of rewarding seniority. Every employee who completes another year of employment receives the same percentage increase.

The merit system is based on the concept that salary increases should be awarded only for quality performance. In any organization, it is obvious that some workers contribute more than others. Merit pay allows the organization to reward the employees who work the hardest and who are the most valuable. It is presumed that merit pay will encourage all employees to perform more efficiently in the hopes of receiving a larger pay increase.

There are drawbacks to each of these methods. The automatic increase, though easy to administer, does not allow the organization to reward exceptional performers. The merit system is much more difficult to administer, and it is almost impossible to construct a plan of merit increases that will please all employees. Supervisors are often accused of using merit systems to reward their favorite employees. Because all merit systems are at least partially based on subjective judgment, it is difficult to construct a merit system. The merit system also presents problems when many employees receive no pay increase at all. During periods of high inflation, employees who are given no salary increase are seriously affected by a loss of spending power. Automatic Cost of Living Adjustments (COLAS), which are found in some industrial union contracts, are provided by very few libraries. So if employers do not give some kind of across-the-board raise to all employees, workers will not be able to maintain the same standard of living from year to year.

Most libraries use some combination of merit and seniority to award pay increases. All employees may be awarded a certain amount of money for a pay raise, with that amount increased if their job performance is meritorious. If a merit system is used, it should be carefully designed, well publicized, and closely related to the employees' performance appraisals.

> Today's organizations may have visionary strategies, networks, team-based designs, and the latest advanced information technologies in place, but unless organizational participants are reinforced for their performance-related behaviors, these strategies, designs, and technologies may have little impact.[47]
>
> —Fred Luthans and Alexander D. Stajkovic,
> "Reinforcing for Performance:
> The Need to Go Beyond Pay and Even Rewards"

The increased use of teams has complicated the awarding of salary increases. Traditionally, employees have been compensated based on their individual performance, but with the increasing number of organizations moving toward teams, many employees are being evaluated and paid according to the performance of their teams. Team-based pay is a growing phenomenon in the corporate sector. Obviously, if an organization wants to reinforce the value and importance of teams, it is important to reinforce team behavior. Rewarding team performance, not individual performance, achieves that goal. But the team-based reward only works well when all team members contribute equitably. Team-based pay has the potential of giving "free riders" as great a pay increase as those who have worked much harder. Determining equitable pay for team members is difficult, but libraries need to continue to find a way to provide equitable ways of administering team-based rewards. Whatever the shape of the final compensation plan, it must be one that can be communicated easily and one that is felt to be fair by the employees.

Recognition and Rewards

Individuals working in libraries rarely receive the monetary nonsalary rewards, such as stock options, that are available to employees in the private sector. Nonetheless, many libraries have tried to structure some no-cost or low-cost way to reward employees and to show that they are appreciated. For instance, the Duke University Library has had an employee recognition program in place for many years to recognize outstanding employees. Other organizations have tried to devise much broader recognition systems. At the library of the University of Wisconsin—Eau Claire, each employee is given a blank award certificate to give to any university employee for either an especially meritorious action or for excellence sustained over time. This type of award fits well with the total quality management principle that states to each employee, "If you see a problem, you own it" because these awards clearly tell an employee, "If you see great performance, recognize it."[48]

Employee recognition programs usually are successful because employees are motivated by recognition. People who feel appreciated identify with the organization and are more productive than those who do not feel appreciated. Managers of successful reward systems must be sure that rewards are tied to the organization's needs, the reward system is flexible and fair, rewards are publicized and if appropriate presented in a public forum, and the timing is right. It is best to schedule frequent reward presentations so employees receive the reward soon after the achievement being recognized.[49]

> Good leaders need to make sure that each member of a unit realizes that his or her work is respected and appreciated by the administrator, by the parent body, and by his or her coworkers. This does not mean that administrators should spend their days going around patting everyone on the back. It does mean, however, that administrators are responsible for communicating appreciation for work done well.[50]
>
> —Joan M. Bechtel,
> "Leadership Lessons Learned from
> Managing and Being Managed"

Although some reward programs are expensive to implement, others cost very little. Celebrations and awards can be effective morale boosters and can increase productivity and quality. They also contribute to building a strong organizational culture.

Employee Benefits

A major portion of employees' compensation packages consists of benefits. The number and variety of benefits provided by libraries and information centers for their employees has grown over the years to the point where items of this nature represent a major factor in total compensation. Because of the importance of benefits as a part of compensation, many employers have stopped using the term "fringe" when referring to benefits.

The package of benefits offered to employees is determined by the individual library or by the library's parent institution. Some benefits are required by federal or state law, and, in unionized institutions, some are mandated as part of a collective bargaining agreement. Federal and state regulations apply to almost all workers in the United States. Among the benefits required by these laws are Social Security, unemployment insurance, and workers' compensation. Unemployment insurance and workers' compensation are financed solely by employer contributions. Social Security is financed by equal contributions from employer and employee. The amount of Social Security tax has increased rapidly over the years. In 1937, the combined employer-employee tax rate was 2 percent on a maximum of $3,000 in earnings. In 2002, the combined rate was 15.3 percent on a maximum of $84,900. For many low-paid employees, contributions to Social Security are larger than their federal income tax.

In addition to benefits mandated by federal or state law, organizations provide many types of employee benefits. For some of the benefits, the employer pays the full cost, and for others, the employee pays a portion of the cost. In private industry, a recent trend is the use of flexible, or cafeteria, plans, which allow employees some discretion in choosing the specific elements of their benefit program from a range of options. This approach allows employees to tailor a program to their needs. For example, an employee who is covered by a spouse's health insurance plan might forgo the health insurance option and instead select a larger amount of life insurance. To date, however, few public institutions provide such cafeteria plans.[51] The benefits most commonly found in libraries include group insurance policies, paid time off, retirement plans, employee assistance programs, and miscellaneous benefits, such as job sharing.

Most libraries provide several types of group insurance plans. Medical insurance, often including major medical coverage of catastrophic illness, is a benefit provided by most organizations. The cost of medical insurance has escalated in the past few years, and organizations in some cases are looking at double-digit percentage cost increases.[52] As a result, many organizations have shifted more of the cost of this insurance onto the employee and have increased the deductibles. More organizations are now mandating the use of health maintenance organizations (HMOs) by their employees in an attempt to control the cost of medical insurance. In addition to health insurance, many organizations provide both group life insurance and disability insurance; the latter tides employees over during periods of disability caused by sickness or accident. Dental insurance is provided by some libraries. The payment for these types of insurance varies; in some libraries, the institution pays the full cost, but, more commonly, the employee pays a portion of the cost, especially for coverage of dependents.

Paid time off includes holidays, vacations, and various types of leave. It is also standard practice in many organizations to pay employees for rest periods and lunch breaks.

Employee retirement plans are pension or retirement plans offered by most libraries and information centers in addition to Social Security. Commonly, both the employer and employee make contributions to the plan.

Many employees are offered access to Employees Assistance Programs (EAPs). These programs provide assessment and referral for employees who have problems with depression, family dissension, substance abuse, and financial or legal problems. At one time, employees with personal problems were fired if these problems got in the way of work performance. Many organizations now provide EAPs to help employees work through these problems and to improve work performance.

Librarians may be offered a wide variety of other benefits, depending on where they work. Some of these monetary benefits include travel and moving expenses, tuition refunds, and access to subsidized daycare.

Some of the benefits offered by libraries are related to the rise in the number of two-career families. Especially when couples in a two-career marriage have children, benefits that allow them flexibility in order to meet family responsibilities are among the most valuable.

> For the vast majority of working families, Ozzie and Harriet are demographic dinosaurs. For others, they were always a myth. Today, Harriet usually does not stay home. Nearly three out of four women with children are in the workforce. Often, neither Ozzie nor Harriet gets home by 5:00 p.m. The time that married women with children spend working outside the home nearly doubled in 30 years—translating into 22 fewer hours per week families can spend with their children.[53]
>
> —U.S. Department of Labor,
> *Futurework—Trends and Challenges for Work in the 21st Century*

A nonmonetary benefit found more and more in libraries and information centers is the alternative work schedule. Instead of requiring all employees to work the same hours, alternative work schedules, such as flextime or the compressed work week, allow employees some freedom in choosing the hours and days they work. This flexibility, of course, can be granted only if appropriate provision is made to cover service to users and supervisory and training responsibilities. Before instituting any type of alternative work schedule, administrators should develop clear plans of action, with targeted jobs tested in advance to determine the likely effects of the new schedule.

Telecommuting refers to working away from the office, on a full-time or part-time basis, often at home, usually using a computer and the Internet, telephone, and/or fax machines as a way to keep in touch with the office. Telecommuting has advantages for both employer and employee. The employer does not have to provide a place for the employee to work. The employee gains benefits from a more flexible job schedule, no interruptions, no commuting, and the maximum amount of freedom in terms of structuring the work environment. Although telecommuting is becoming increasingly popular in the for-profit sector, it is not used as frequently in libraries. Where it is used, it is usually on a temporary or part-time basis. However, some librarians are allowed to work out of their homes at least part-time for such tasks as website design, online reference, and writing projects. To be a successful telecommuter it is important "to be self-motivated, focused, and organized, and to have a family life that won't create frequent work interruptions."[54] Telecommuting does provide ultimate flexibility for people holding the type of job that lends itself to being done offsite.

A few libraries have instituted the practice of job sharing. Job sharing splits one job between two individuals. Usually, the salary is shared; benefits, such as medical insurance, are sometimes prorated, but, in the best cases, both employees receive benefits. Flextime, telecommuting, and job sharing are attractive to employees with small children because these alternative approaches to work enable the parents to spend more time with their children. Other employees also find these options beneficial; their existence sometimes allows organizations to keep valuable employees they would otherwise lose.

Many employees take their benefits for granted, not realizing that benefits are a sizable part of the total labor cost of any organization. Benefits add significantly to the salary of an employee because of the contributions made by the employer. On a percentage basis, the cost of benefits has increased substantially in recent years. The Bureau of Labor Statistics reports that, for all domestic industries in 1999, the total cost of all benefits was almost thirty percent of total annual wages.[55]

Both employers and employees gain from a well-designed and well-administered benefits program, despite its cost. In considering a benefits program, a manager must carefully study each element of the program to determine its future financial impact on the institution. After determining that the program is needed and desired by the employees, the manager must carefully define the program and establish the policies and procedures necessary to assure its fair and equitable implementation. Finally, the manager should communicate information about the benefits package to all employees to inform them what is available, when they are eligible, and what procedures are involved in obtaining benefits. Supervisors should be able to speak knowledgeably about the entire benefits package because many employees turn to their immediate supervisors for information of this type.

Conclusion

This chapter has covered the primary functions related to maintaining the HR in the library. The next chapter looks at some of the general issues affecting HR management. That chapter will cover topics such as personnel procedures and policies, career development, mentoring, external regulations, and unionization.

Notes

1.   Sharon Lund O'Neil and Elwood N. Chapman, *Your Attitude Is Showing: A Primer of Human Relations*, 10th ed. (Upper Saddle River, NJ: Prentice-Hall, 2002), 220.

2.   Dorothy E. Jones, "I'd Like You to Meet Our New Librarian," *Journal of Academic Librarianship* 14 (September 1988): 221.

3.   Shelley L. Rogers, "Orientation for New Library Employees: A Checklist," *Library Administration and Management* 8 (Fall 1994): 213–17.

4.   Mary M. Nofsinger and Angela S. W. Lee, "Beyond Orientation: The Roles of Senior Librarians in Training Entry-Level Reference Colleagues," *College and Research Libraries* 55 (March 1994): 161–70.

5.   Peter F. Drucker, *Managing the Non-Profit Organization* (New York: Harper Business, 1990), 145.

6.   Peter M. Senge, *The Fifth Discipline: The Art & Practice of the Learning Organization* (New York: Doubleday, 1990).

7.   *Ibid.*

8.   David A. Garvey, *Learning in Action: A Guide to Putting the Learning Organization to Work* (Boston: Harvard Business School Press, 2000).

9.   Ruth F. Metz, *Coaching in the Library: A Management Strategy for Achieving Excellence* (Chicago: American Library Association, 2001), 2.

10.   *Ibid.*, 4.

11.   For a more in-depth look at staff development, see Sheila D. Creth, *Effective On-the-Job Training: Developing Library Human Resources* (Chicago: American Library Association, 1986).

12. Paula Peters, "Seven Tips for Delivering Performance Feedback." *Supervision* (May 2000): 12.

13. W. Edwards Deming, *Out of the Crisis* (Cambridge, MA: Massachusetts Institute of Technology Center for Advanced Engineering Study, 1982), 101–2.

14. *Ibid.*

15. However, see Rao Aluri and Mary Reichel, "Performance Evaluation as a Deadly Disease," *Journal of Academic Librarianship* 19 (July 1994): 145–55, for an application of Deming's viewpoint applied to library performance evaluations.

16. Taken from James S. Bowman, "Performance Appraisal: Verisimilitude Trumps Veracity," *Public Personnel Management* 28 (Winter 1999): 557.

17. Michael Beer, "Making Performance Appraisal Work," in John J. Gabarro, ed., *Managing People and Organizations* (Boston: Harvard Business School Publications, 1992), 196.

18. Nancy K. Austin, "Updating the Performance Review," *Working Woman* (November 1992): 35.

19. Brendan McDonagh, "Appraising Appraisals," *The Law Librarian* 26 (September 1995): 425.

20. Necia Parker-Gibson and Lutishoor Salisbury, "The Process of Peer Review," *Arkansas Libraries* 53 (February 1996): 3–7.

21. Maury A Peiperl, "Getting 360° Feedback Right," *Harvard Business Review* 79 (January 2001): 143.

22. Gay Helen Perkins, "The Value of Upward Evaluation in Libraries—Part II," *Library Administration and Management* 9 (Summer 1995): 166–75.

23. Alan G. Walker and James W. Smither, "A Five-Year Study of Upward Feedback: What Managers Do with Their Results Matters," *Personnel Psychology* 52 (Summer 1999): 393–423.

24. Richard Rubin, "The Development of a Performance Evaluation Instrument for Upward Evaluation of Supervisors by Subordinates," *Library and Information Science Research* 16 (Fall 1994): 315–28. This article provides considerable detail about the development of a valid and reliable instrument used in one public library.

25. Bodil Jones, "How'm I Doin'?" *Management Review* 86 (May 1997): 9–18.

26. Susan J. Wells. "A New Road—Traveling Beyond 360-Degree Evaluation," *HR Magazine* 44 (September 1999): 84.

27. George C. Thornton, "The Relationship Between Supervisory and Self-Appraisals of Executive Performance," *Personnel Psychology* (Winter 1968): 441–55.

28. Bowman, "Performance Appraisal," 561.

29. Joyce P. Vincelette and Fred C. Pfister, "Improving Performance Appraisal in Libraries," *Library and Information Science Research* 6 (April–June 1984): 191–203.

30. Kent E. Romanoff, "The Ten Commandments of Performance Management," *Personnel* 66 (January 1989): 24.

31. Saul W. Gellerman, *Management by Motivation* (Chicago: American Management Association, 1968), 141.

32. "Breaking with Tradition: Changing Employee Relations Through a Positive Employee Philosophy," *Library Personnel News* 8 (January–February 1994): 4.

33. Keith Davis and John W. Newstrom, *Human Behavior at Work: Organizational Behavior*, 8th ed. (New York: McGraw-Hill, 1989), 424.

34. D. Day, "Training 101: Help for Discipline Dodgers," *Training and Development* 47 (May 1993): 19–22.

35. Richard E. Rubin, *Human Resource Management in Libraries: Theory and Practice* (New York: Neal-Schuman, 1991), 157–58.

36. Steven A. Jesseph, "Employee Termination, 2: Some Dos and Don'ts," *Personnel* 66 (February 1989): 36.

37. Karen L. Vinton, "Documentation That Gets Results," *Personnel* 67 (February 1990): 43.

38. Todd Raphael, "Hold the Line on Salaries and Benefits," *Workforce* 80 (September 2001): 38.

39. Fred Luthans and Alexander Stajkovic, "Reinforcing for Performance: The Need to Go Beyond Pay and Even Rewards." *Academy of Management Executive* 13 (May 1999): 49–56.

40. Edward E. Lawler III, *Pay and Organizational Effectiveness: A Psychological View* (New York: McGraw-Hill, 1971), 233.

41. The last survey available, published in 2001, reported the 2000 results. The average beginning salary for a 2000 MLS graduate was $34,871, up 2.63 percent from the previous year's average. Tom Terrell and Vicki L. Gregory, "Plenty of Jobs, Salaries Flat." *Library Journal* 126 (October 15, 2001): 34–40.

42. Information about the latest survey can be seen at http://www.sla.org/content /memberservice/researchforum/salarysurveys/salsur2001/index.cfm.

43. For the latest, see Mary Jo Lynch, "Librarian Salaries: Annual Increase Drops Below U.S. Average," *American Libraries* 32 (September 2001): 64.

44. For the latest ARL salary survey, see http://www.arl.org/stats/salary/2000-01/ss00.pdf.

45. For the latest survey, see Charlie Fox and Raymond G. Roney, "Library Support Staff Salary Survey, 2000," *Library Mosaics* 11 (July/August 2000): 8–12.

46. Anne Woodsworth and Theresa Maylone, *Reinvesting in the Information Job Family: Context, Changes, New Jobs, and Models for Evaluation and Compensation*, CAUSE Professional Paper Series #11. (Boulder, CO: CAUSE, 1993), 1–2.

47. Luthans and Stajkovic, "Reinforcing for Performance," 53.

48. Steve Marquardt and Leslie Foster, "The Groo Award: Participative Recognition of Peer Performance," *Library and Administration & Management* 8 (Fall 1994): 209–11.

49. Philip C. Grant, "How to Make a Program Work," *Personnel Journal* 71 (January 1992): 103.

50. Joan M. Bechtel, "Leadership Lessons Learned from Managing and Being Managed," *The Journal of Academic Librarianship* 18 (January 1993): 355–56.

51. Marjorie Watson, "Employee Benefits: Emerging Trends for Librarians," *Bottom Line*, charter issue (June 1986): 29–33.

52. Raphael, "Hold the Line on Salaries and Benefits," 40.

53. U.S. Department of Labor, *Futurework—Trends and Challenges for Work in the 21st Century* (Washington, DC: Department of Labor, 1999): 10. (Available online at http://www.dol .gov/asp/futurework/execsum.pdf.)

54. Karen Schneider, "The Untethered Librarian," *American Libraries* 31 (August 2000): 72.

55. Bureau of Labor Statistics, *Employer Costs for Employee Compensation 1986–1999*, Bulletin 2526 (March 2000), 2. (Available online at http://stats.bls.gov/ncs/ect/sp/ecbl0013.pdf.)

Chapter 10

Other Issues in Human Resource Management

The term knowledge worker flows easily off the tongues of managers these days. It borders on cliché status, still it is too important to dismiss because people use it loosely. Economy wide employment trends illustrate the growing importance of work whose value comes from what people know, instead of what they produce with their physical powers.[1]

—Thomas O. Davenport,
Human Capital

Many HR functions are related to day-to-day activities such as the ones discussed in the last chapter. There are, however, some things that lie at the periphery of the HR functions that nonetheless are very important to the management of the human resources in any organization. This chapter will look at some of those topics, ranging from policies and procedures to health and safety issues in the workplace. In addition there are a number of external forces that affect HR management. Two of the most important of these, legal protections for workers and unionization, will be discussed.

Human Resources Policies and Procedures

The first of these topics is a very basic one. Throughout this section of the book, much has been written about HR policies and procedures. The importance of both types of documents cannot be overemphasized. The development of policies and procedures is an integral part of the HR function of libraries and information centers.

Every library should have a set of human resources policies. A policy is a statement of action that commits management to a definite plan or course of action. Policies, for example, concerning hiring and promotion, play an important role in every organization. They are used as guidelines for decision making. By reducing ad hoc decision making, human resources policies lead to greater consistency and continuity in an organization.

Clearly defined policies are essential to an effective HR program. All employees need to understand, through written policy statements, topics such as what the HR program is, how it operates, why salaries are administered in a particular way, how and when performance appraisals will take place, and what benefits are available.

> If your company policies are scattered throughout a series of memos, e-mails and other documents and there's no one place to find the answers to policy questions (except to knock on your door), then it's time to create an employee manual. And, if your manual has not been revised in a while—and major legislation has been passed or practices have changed since then it is time to compile a new or updated handbook.[2]
>
> —Betty Sosnin,
> "Packaging Your Products"

Even in larger libraries and information centers with specialized human resources departments, the formulation of policy usually is the responsibility of the library director. In all types of libraries, the director should establish policy with input from others. The preparation of policy statements should be an opportunity for involvement of other groups. A group of supervisors or staff members might recommend the establishment or modification of a policy. Discussing, evaluating, and writing the policy statement can encourage the participation of the groups that will be affected by it.

An effective set of human resources policies serves a number of functions. First, the formulation of such policies requires library management to think through the needs of both employees and the organization. Second, such policies provide consistent treatment for all employees. Because each supervisor follows the same policies, the equal treatment of each employee is assured. Clearly stated policies minimize both favoritism and discrimination. Third, such policies assure continuity of action, even during periods when managers or supervisors change. New managers have a written standard to follow, and policy remains stable. Employees need not endure vacillations in policies when supervisors resign or retire.

A human resources policy may be broad. For instance, "The X Library does not discriminate against any employee on the basis of age, gender, race, religion, or national origin." Policies may also be narrow. For instance, "All employees are entitled to four weeks of paid vacation each year." It must be remembered that a policy is a general statement of intent and does not spell out the exact methods by which it will be implemented. That function is accomplished by the procedure. A procedure provides the methods for carrying out a policy. It sets forth the steps that are essential to accomplish a particular result. A library will have procedures as to how vacation times will be allotted or how equal opportunity will be assured.

In addition to policies and procedures, organizations also have rules. A rule is defined as a law, regulation, or prescribed guide for conduct or behavior. Rules can be considered minimum standards of conduct that apply to a group of people. Rules apply uniformly to the group concerned. Libraries, like all other institutions, must have rules. Examples of rules are the number of hours to be worked each day or how many absences an employee can have. Rules serve to insure predictability of behavior so that the organization can achieve its goals and function without undue disruption.

Obviously, the policies, procedures, and rules of an organization should be written down. If they exist only in the mind of the director, they fail to serve the purposes for which they are developed. But, they must be more than written; they must be communicated to and understood by all employees. Policies locked in the director's desk are just as ineffective as those that are unwritten.

How are policies, procedures, and rules communicated through an organization? First, special care must be taken to communicate these documents to supervisors so that they can administer them equitably and uniformly. Often, organizations have special training sessions to acquaint supervisors with policies or to review them periodically. Nonsupervisory employees commonly learn about the policies, procedures, and rules through the employee's handbook, which is usually given to each new employee during orientation. The information contained in the handbook should be followed up with oral explanation, and any changes in policies, procedures, or rules should be communicated and explained by the employee's immediate supervisor.

Career Development

In the knowledge economy, a company's most important asset is the energy and loyalty of its people—the intellectual capital that, unlike machines and factories, can quit and go to work for your competition. And yet, many managers regularly undermine that commitment by allowing talented people to stay in jobs they're doing well at but aren't fundamentally interested in. That just doesn't make sense. To turbocharge retention, you must first know the hearts and minds of your employees and then undertake the tough and rewarding task of sculpting careers that bring joy to both.[3]

—Timothy Butler and James Waldroop,
"Job Sculpting: The Art of Retaining Your Best People"

The topics of training and staff development were covered in chapter 9. Career development differs from both training and staff development. It is a long-term attempt to help employees shape careers that are satisfying to them. A career is usually defined as a series of positions occupied by an individual during the course of a lifetime. Ultimately, of course, career development is the responsibility of the individual employee. Although career development is not the duty of the employing organization, the best organizations pay some attention to this topic. Helping employees, especially high-performing employees, achieve the type of career that they aspire to cuts down on turnover and enables an organization to keep valuable human resources. At the very least an organization should recognize the complex issues that employees face as they attempt to manage careers in the changing environment of the twenty-first century workplace.

Typically careers are thought to go through certain stages. These stages are illustrated in Figure 10.1.

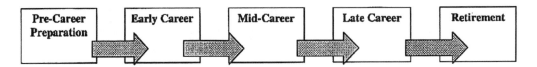

Figure 10.1. The Stages of a Career

Each of the stages is marked by different needs and perceptions. The first stage is organizational entry where an individual enters the job market and begins to establish a career. A newly minted MLS graduate taking a first professional job in a library would be at the entry stage. The challenges of this stage are getting a first position and becoming established in the organization. After a few years in a career, the individual enters the mid-career stage. He or she is familiar with the field now and perhaps has been promoted into some sort of managerial position. Plateauing, discussed below, is one of the common problems associated with the mid-career stage. The late career stage is when individuals are firmly established in an organization and typically of great value because of their expertise and organizational knowledge. These are the people who likely will serve as mentors to younger professionals. Individuals toward the end of that stage are likely to be looking ahead to retirement.

The last stage in a career is retirement. Once most people retired at age 65, but with the end of mandatory retirement, employees are retiring at different ages. Even some of those who have retired return to the workplace as part-time or temporary workers, either at their previous organization or at another one. These career stages are not always as clear-cut as Figure 10.1 might imply. People move through them at varying rates of speed, and in an era when many people switch careers, some may not go through all the steps outlined, whereas others might go through them several times.

In the past, at least in the for-profit sector, employees often expected to go to work for one company and stay there until they retired. That old pattern has been upended by the increased number of companies that have downsized, merged, or turned to temporary or contract workers. No longer can an employee in the for-profit sector expect a career working in a single company. Instead, the new pattern is one where individuals are active agents in their own career development. In the not-for-profit sector, the organizational upheavals have been fewer, but still employees are affected by the new "organizational" rules that are in effect. The career ladders in most libraries are flatter than they used to be. An entry-level librarian who wants to move up the ladder to eventually become a library director encounters many obstacles. The flattened organizations discussed in chapter 7 do not have as many levels of hierarchy as the ones they replaced, and new team-based organizations found in many libraries have also eliminated the need for many mid-level managers. The career progression pattern that used to exist in most large libraries of becoming a department head, and then an assistant or associate director, and finally a director is not as commonly available as before.

> Equally important is managing your own career. The stepladder is gone, and there's not even the implied structure of an industry's rope ladder. It's more like vines, and you bring your own machete. You don't know what you'll be doing next, or whether you'll work in a private office or one big amphitheater or even out of your home. You have to take responsibility for knowing yourself, so you can find the right jobs as you develop and as your family becomes a factor in your values and choices.[4]
>
> —T. George Harris,
> "The Post-Capitalist Executive:
> An Interview with Peter F. Drucker"

In fact, careers are being viewed differently. There is a realization that not everyone wants to be library director or a manager of any type. Different people have different aspirations. That is why the dual career ladders found in the "LIS Education and Human Resources Utilization" policy statement discussed in chapter 8 are helpful in allowing individuals who do not aspire to management to progress within a library. Also, there is some evidence that there are differences between age cohorts and that the wants of Generations X and Y may be different from those of the Baby Boom Generation.[5]

But assuming an individual does want to progress up the administrative ladder, there are roadblocks in the way for many. Most libraries have been in a nongrowth stage for a number of years. Well-qualified employees may find their career advancement blocked because there are no openings in the positions directly above them, and, even worse, many of these positions are held by individuals who are only slightly older than the employee who is seeking advancement. Until the large number of Baby Boomers employed in libraries begins retiring, this situation will likely prevail.

Plateauing

When employees wish to progress but are unable to do so, they are said to be "plateaued." Plateauing should be of great interest to managers because many plateaued workers are frustrated, depressed, and nonproductive. Plateauing can occur in two ways. Structural plateauing occurs when an individual is no longer promoted within the organization; content plateauing means that a job has become routine, and no challenging tasks are added to it.[6] Both types of plateauing result in employees who are stuck and no longer stimulated by promise of promotions or new job content.

A special type of plateauing is sometimes referred to as the glass ceiling. The glass ceiling is an invisible barrier that prevents women and minorities from ascending the institutional hierarchy. Although in the past two decades, women and minorities have made significant progress into lower and middle-management levels, neither is represented in upper management in proportion to their numbers in the general population.

> It is not the ceiling that's holding women back; it's the whole structure of the organizations in which we work: the foundation, the beams, the walls, the very air. The barriers to advancement are not just above women, they are all around them. But dismantling our organizations isn't the solution. We must ferret out the hidden barriers to equity and effectiveness one by one [and replace them] with practices that are stronger and more equitable, not just for women but for all people.[7]
>
> —Debra E. Meyerson and Joyce K. Fletcher,
> "A Modest Manifesto for Shattering the Glass Ceiling"

Although some employees accept plateauing as an inevitable part of a career, others do not. Supervisors often find that personnel problems such as irritation with fellow employees and intolerance of bureaucracy develop more frequently with plateaued employees than with others. In addition, organizations can lose valuable workers who seek employment elsewhere when they feel that they are "stuck" in a no-promotion situation.[8]

Managers can use a number of strategies, including those listed in Table 10.1, to help employees overcome the stress of plateauing. These strategies include job enrichment, lateral transfers, cross training, restructuring organizations to make them more horizontal so that decision-making power increases in the lower ranks, and educating employees about plateauing so that they will be prepared for periods of stagnation in their career development.[10] Employees can be encouraged to take advantage of mentoring and networking opportunities to offer career support and possibilities for change. Managers of libraries, as well as other organizations, should attempt to find ways to make jobs interesting and keep workers' enthusiasm alive if they want to maintain the effectiveness of employees whose careers have become plateaued. To crack the glass ceiling, managers should encourage women and minorities to apply for promotions as openings occur.

Mentoring

Mentoring is a specialized form of career development. Although mentoring has always existed in organizations of all types, only in the last few decades has the importance of this process been recognized. There has been a growing interest in mentoring in all fields. The reason for this interest is the clear link between career success and having a mentor. Many studies provide evidence of this link; their findings are fairly consistent in stating that very few individuals advance to the top administrative ranks in an organization without the help of a mentor.[11]

Today, the term *mentor* is used to describe an influential person who significantly helps another, usually a younger person, reach his or her major goals. A mentor is a person who oversees the career and development of another person. Michael Zey, in *The Mentoring Connection*, identifies four functions of mentoring: teaching, psychological counseling and emotional support, organizational intervention, and sponsoring. The context and meaning of the term is adjusted slightly by each mentor and protégé. No two mentoring experiences are exactly alike because no two people or set of organizational circumstances are exactly alike.[12]

Table 10.1. Human Resource Practices That Help Overcome the Problems of Plateauing

---

Performance Management

1) Fight negative stereotyping with accurate appraisals

2) Ask around to appreciate fully how employees contribute

Training

1) Train for the future, not for advancement

2) Train everyone to contribute, not just the fast trackers

Career Development and Staffing

1) Broaden opportunities to grow on the job

2) Remove roadblocks to lateral and downward moves

3) Help employees identify new challenges

Compensation

1) Pay employees for performance, knowledge, or teamwork

2) Look beyond financial compensation

3) Check to see if your perks send the right messages

Human Resources Planning

1) Determine how many employees are plateaued

2) Determine what proportion of plateaued employees are successful[9]

    The need for the mentor varies at different points in the protégé's career, and the things a mentor does for a protégé also differ. New employees need a mentor to help them learn more about the details of the job and the organization. As they become more technically competent and begin to ascend the organizational ladder, the need for teaching might be less important than the need for emotional support. When the appropriate times for promotion and advancement occur, the mentor can be most helpful by providing organizational intervention and sponsoring the protégé.

    The advantages to the protégé are clear. But, since mentoring involves a considerable investment on the part of the mentor, it may be harder to understand what causes individuals to serve in such a capacity. Most mentors do not enter into such a relationship from altruism alone. The benefits are almost always mutual, and the mentoring role is almost always professionally rewarding. Sometimes, the mentor receives job assistance from the protégé and secures a valuable ally within the organization. In addition, the mentoring procedure causes the mentor to reexamine the day-to-day workings of the organization, which usually causes the mentor to learn more about the organization. Often, the protégé can serve as a sounding board for the mentor's ideas.

> Mentoring is a complex subject. There are advantages and disadvantages to the practice. Obviously, those in the organization who don't have mentors may resent those who do. . . . [I]f one wishes to continue to advance, developing a network that includes a mentor greatly enhances the probability of success.[13]
>
> —Joseph Berk and Susan Berk,
> *Managing Effectively*

A protégé who succeeds can make a mentor look very good. One of the responsibilities of present-day management is developing talent. The protégé validates the mentor's worth to the organization. Having protégés who can help perform the mentor's job shows the mentor to be a highly productive manager who knows how to delegate well. The mentor also gains a reputation as an individual who is able to spot and develop new talent. And, as a protégé advances, the mentor not only shares in the glory but builds up a strong network of past and present protégés. Finally, many mentors derive great personal pleasure out of the process. They enjoy teaching and feel a sense of personal gratification as the protégé's career advances. They are pleased to see the continuity of their own work carried on by the protégé.

The benefits of mentoring spill over to the organization. These benefits include properly socialized employees, integrated workers, and a smoothly functioning managerial team. Mentoring is almost always a three-way beneficial process. The benefits of mentoring are illustrated in Figure 10.2.

There are more individuals who would like to have mentors than those who actually have them. Some organizations have established formal mentoring programs where new employees are provided a mentor. These programs sometimes succeed, but mentoring relationships that arise spontaneously usually are more successful because both the mentor and the protégé see the value of each other without being forced into a relationship. With most library employees now having access to electronic mail, some mentors are now off-site and advise through email.[14]

Mentoring relationships, both formal and informal, should be encouraged by organizations as a means of career development and growth. But it must be remembered that mentoring can sometimes have a darker side. Harris has pointed out that because mentoring is by definition designed just for a few individuals, it may pose barriers that impede the progress of many librarians who are interested in career advancement but are not chosen as protégés.[15] Another problem with mentoring is that mentors are usually drawn toward mentoring those that are like themselves, and this unconscious bias often leads to an uneven availability of mentoring opportunities. And because mentoring requires the development of a personal relationship between the mentor and the protégé, it occasionally results in claims of sexual harassment or discrimination.[16] There may be a need for formal guidelines to accompany a mentoring program. Overall, however, the benefits of a well-designed program to provide mentoring seem to outweigh the disadvantages.

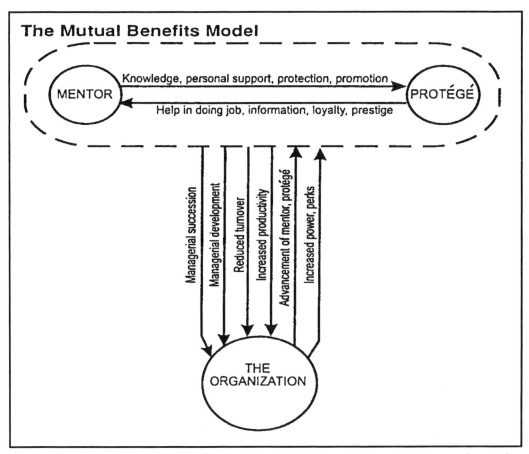

Figure 10.2. Benefits Provided by Mentoring. From Michael G. Zey. *The Mentor Connection: Strategic Alliances in Corporate Life.* New Brunswick, NJ: Transaction, 1990. Reprinted with permission.

Health and Safety Issues in the Library

Employers have a responsibility to ensure the health and safety of their employees. Today's workers are demanding a more healthful environment in which to work, and most managers are trying to provide such a workplace. Most libraries today are smoke-free so that non-smokers are not exposed to second-hand smoke. Many libraries have security and disaster procedures in place to attempt to meet unexpected emergencies.

Physical Stress

Overall, libraries provide fairly safe workplaces. One type of physical problem being found more commonly in libraries today is injury caused as a result of the use of computers. Now that computers are used as a tool by almost every category of worker in a library, more and more employees are suffering from a condition known as repetitive stress injury (RSI)—most frequently carpal tunnel syndrome. RSI has been common for a long time in employees working in factories who perform the same motion repetitively throughout the day. Now the same condition is appearing in libraries and information centers where staff spends a large part of the day working on computer keyboards. Repetitive keyboarding can lead to carpal tunnel syndrome.

The number of employees in organizations reporting repetitive stress injuries climbs each year. According to the U.S. Occupational Health and Safety Administration (OSHA):

> Over the past 20 years ergonomic injuries have gained recognition as a major factor in work place health. About one-third of all occupational injuries and illnesses stem from over exertion and/or repetitive motion. Cost to the nation in direct work's comp costs range as high as or exceed $20 billion.[17]

One survey found that 3.1 percent of staff members in ARL libraries are affected by carpal tunnel syndrome.[18] As more employees spend more time in front of computers, the number of these repetitive stress injuries is likely to increase.

Libraries and information centers have begun to take steps to prevent RSI and to provide relief to those already exhibiting symptoms. Many libraries have invested in ergonomic chairs, workstations, and keyboards. Other libraries have instituted more frequent breaks, increased the types of activities within a job, started exercise sessions, and provided training in attempts to alleviate and prevent RSI. Many libraries have established ergonomic standards to govern the use of computers.[19] Because the use of computers will continue to be an essential function in the work life of most library employees, managers of all types need to be mindful of this physical stress to prevent the development of more cases of carpal tunnel syndrome among employees.

RSI appears to be the most harmful result of using computers. Although a few years ago there was concern about radiation resulting from video display terminals (VDTs), studies have shown that the radiation produced by computer terminals of all types is slight. More common complaints are of eyestrain, back and neck aches, and body fatigue, which probably result from sitting in one position for too long. Again, good ergonomic practices, such as proper positioning of monitors, supportive chairs, good lighting, adequate ventilation, and more frequent breaks from working on the computer can alleviate many of these complaints.

Before President Clinton left office, OSHA had proposed a rigorous set of ergonomic standards to attempt to reduce the number of repetitive stress injuries, with the final standards set to go into effect January 16, 2001, with a compliance date of October 2001. When the new Bush administration came into office, those standards were scuttled. Critics said the standards would be far too costly. The Department of Labor has said it will pursue a "comprehensive approach to ergonomics, which may include new rule making, that addresses the concerns levied against the current standard." To date, however, no new standards have been issued.[20]

Workers Compensation

Before the enactment of workers' compensation laws, employees injured on the job had to pay for their own medical care and went without pay until they were able to return to the job again. Things began to change in the early 1900s when some states enacted legislation to cover the medical costs of employees injured on the job. Job-related injuries became viewed as a responsibility of the employer and not the employee. Workers' compensation is now found in all states and is a state-administered and employee-funded program. These programs provide medical and financial assistance to workers injured in the course of their job, including total disability for those who are not able to work again and survivors' assistance to the families of workers killed on the job.

Job-Related Mental Stress

Employees in all types of organizations are susceptible to stress. Although libraries are sometimes considered to be stress-free environments, they are not, and library employees can be subjected to various sources of stress. Stress is the body's response to any demand placed upon it.

> Stress is not something "out there" or inherent in "stressful" things or situations. Rather stress is within a person—i.e., a response. The source of the demand or challenge is referred to as a "stressor." A stressor for one person may cause a completely different response in another.[21]

Today, more employees in all types of organizations, including libraries, are reporting feeling stress or tension as a result of their jobs. Without a doubt, among librarians part of the cause of this stress is the increasing rate of change within the profession. Librarians, now more than ever, are being asked to master new methods and technologies for doing their jobs. Technology has speeded up the way things are run; email and faxes have cut the time needed in communication but have added pressure to get things done faster. Organizational change of all types, if too rapid and frequent, may result in stress. In addition, because of budget cutbacks in many libraries, librarians are being asked to assume more responsibilities.

Stress arises from many sources. Role ambiguity arises when positions are poorly defined and employees do not know what is expected of them. Some librarians feel the stress of what is known as role conflict when different groups of people hold different views about how that employee should behave. Oftentimes in libraries and information centers, there is tension between the professional and support staff when roles are blurred and changing.[22] In some organizations interpersonal demands cause stress when an employee must constantly deal with unpleasant or abrasive coworkers or supervisors. In addition, in many libraries the effect of downsizing has resulted in a smaller number of employees doing the same amount of work.

Of course, not all stress-related disorders are caused by workplace stress; many employees have stresses caused by off-the-job reasons, such as family or financial problems. Sometimes stress can be produced by the conflict between job and home responsibilities, especially in two-career families with children. Table 10.2 shows some of the common causes of stress.

Table 10.2. Common Causes of Stress

Common Causes of Stress	
Personal causes	Financial problems
	Family problems
	Illness
Organizational causes	Interpersonal demands
	Role conflict or ambiguity
	Technology
	Downsizing
	Constant change

Stress is not always bad, and different employees are able to tolerate different levels of stress. Without some stress in organizations, there would likely be much less energy and productivity. Many people work more effectively under conditions of mild stress. When there are deadlines looming, many people work faster and better. The same deadline can often cause other employees to experience extreme stress. It is when stress is severe and unending that it becomes destructive.

Although it has been commonly thought that managers feel more stress than lower-level employees, recent research has shown that that is not true. For example, a study of 270,000 male employees at a large corporation found that the rate of coronary disease increased at successively lower levels of the organizations. It is thought that top-level executives feel less stress because they have greater control and predictability over their work than employees at lower levels.[23] The more control employees have over their own work and the more information they have about possible changes that will occur, the less likely they are to feel job-related stress.

> Fast-paced, turbulent work contexts, fueled with ambiguity through organization downsizing, restructuring and redesign, technological change, and mergers and acquisitions suggest that stressful work environments are becoming even more noxious, causing physical and mental health-related illness to be at an all time high.[24]
>
> —Pamela L. Perrewé et al.,
> "Political Skill: An Antidote for Workplace Stressors"

Stress may be evidenced in a number of ways, including absenteeism, irritability, tardiness, and inability to perform well. One of the jobs of the manager is to help identify the cause of the stress and try to help eliminate it if possible. All managers need to be aware of the individual differences in their employees and help them to cope with the stresses in their lives. If the effects of the stress are more than can be handled by the manager, the employee should be referred to a health professional for diagnosis and treatment.

Burnout

Burnout is a specific type of stress-induced condition that affects individuals engaged in "people" work. Burnout results from emotional strain and the stress of interpersonal contact, especially from dealing with people who are having problems. Individuals suffering from burnout typically experience exhaustion, both physical and emotional; a negative shift in the way they respond to other people; and a loss of self-esteem.[25]

Remedies for burnout can be found at two levels. At the personal level, employees should structure their lives outside of work to give them a sense of comfort and control. Employees should pursue an active life outside of the work environment. The managerial responsibilities for aiding workers with burnout include knowing the symptoms of burnout and making workers familiar with them, holding staff meetings that can be used for staff support, and fostering a sense of teamwork among the staff. If staffing patterns permit, managers may also restructure jobs so that librarians do not spend as much time with patrons or revise schedules to shorten periods of time spent at public services desks. Workshops in stress management or time management can also be useful.[26]

It is important to try to prevent burnout because it is rarely confined to one worker. "If one worker complains of the work environment and/or questions the worth, rewards, or necessity of his or her work, it is sure to have some effect on co-workers."[27] To keep burnout from spreading, managers need to recognize the symptoms and prevent it whenever possible.

Violence and Crime in the Workplace

[W]orkplace violence is a fact of modern life. And libraries, unfortunately, are as susceptible to the problem as any other workplace. Although often seen as something of a refuge for many people, libraries are a part of modern society and are not immune to current societal trends and ills. It is necessary for us to recognize these problems and to be familiar with countermeasures and remedies.[28]

—Daniel P. Keller,
"Special Problems in the Library Setting"

Violence is an increasingly serious problem in almost all workplaces. Libraries are not workplaces where violence often occurs, but violence is not unknown in libraries. There have been several recent cases of librarians being murdered while on the job, and assault and robbery in libraries (both of staff and patrons) is unfortunately relatively common. Libraries have tried hard to make themselves seen as accessible places, and this accessibility has sometimes left them vulnerable.

Library managers are now more aware of the possibility of workplace violence, and many are taking measures to attempt to lessen it. Robert Willits has suggested a three-tier approach to dealing with violence in libraries:

1. Preventive measures with such steps as thorough background checking of all applicants, including checking for criminal records, training of supervisors in techniques such as conflict resolution and stress management, and having a grievance system that is perceived as fair.

2. Threat management such as having a plan to deal with workplace violence, including a threat management team.

3. Crisis/Post-Trauma management dealing with a tragedy that has taken place in the library. In addition to a well-rehearsed and ready-to-go plan, there should be an individual designated to deal with the public and the press. People who were witness to the violence must be dealt with in a compassionate manner, families of victims must be notified, and cleanup and repairs must be tended to as soon as permitted by law enforcement.[29]

Most libraries have preparedness programs for natural disasters such as floods or hurricanes, but fewer have instituted such programs for violence in the workplace. All libraries need manuals relating to emergencies, and librarians should be trained in what to do in the event an emergency arises. It is the responsibility of library managers to provide a safe environment for both personnel and patrons so that they do not have to fear for their personal safety.[30]

Overall, most libraries are focusing more than ever before on the health of their employees. Many encourage employees to participate in exercise programs or other wellness programs. Employee assistance programs have been instituted at a number of organizations to provide help for employees with various types of personal problems, such as alcoholism or drug use. Many library managers are becoming better at helping to prevent both physical and mental stress. Managers realize that it is cost-effective to invest in the health of employees because healthier employees are more productive than those who are suffering from physical or mental conditions. Making the workplace environment a safe and healthy one is a win-win situation for employees and employers.

External Impacts on HR—Legal Protections

All of the subjects discussed so far relate to specific internal HR functions found in libraries and information centers of all types. There are, however, two broader external forces that have had a profound impact on human resources work in many libraries These issues are 1) legal protections for employees; and 2) unionization.

The number of federal and state regulations relating to the HR function of management has increased over past decades, and today, virtually every human resource function from hiring to firing is affected by these regulations. These regulations have provided workers with more legal protection—especially in the area of equal employment. Nonetheless, there are still some areas where employees have very few rights. Almost every employee not covered by a collective bargaining contract or civil or state service rules is at risk for dismissal because of the "employment-at-will" principle that permits either party to an employment contract to cancel it at-will. Although legislation protects workers from firing for such reasons as age, gender, national origin, or disability, workers not covered by either collective bargaining or civil service regulations have few legal remedies to combat being fired or discharged.

There are other areas where workers have limited protection. Although the right to free speech is guaranteed by the First Amendment to the U.S. Constitution, managers in the private sector can legally discipline workers who say something damaging about the corporation or its practices. The right to privacy is another area where employees, especially those in the private sector, do not have clear protections.

Privacy issues have become a growing concern for workers with the growth of electronic technologies of all types. For instance, although the Electronic Communications Privacy Act of 1986 prohibits outside interception of electronic mail by a third party, the act does not affect inside interception, and unless an individual organization has a policy prohibiting it, employers can read their staff's email, listen in on telephone conversations, install small video cameras anywhere, and search employees' lockers and desks. The use of electronic surveillance is growing as more and more organizations monitor people using personal computers by counting keystrokes and mistakes.[31] On the whole, these new monitoring technologies are considered to be extensions of managerial prerogatives, and employees currently have few legal tools to combat them.[32]

Obviously, this electronic monitoring can be beneficial if it can prevent or disclose misconduct or if supervisors use it in training to give constructive feedback to help individual workers improve. But studies have shown that employees who know that they are monitored are more likely to be highly dissatisfied and to suffer from such conditions as fatigue and hostility.

Suggestions for reform on electronic monitoring have come from many sources, and the proposed reforms almost all agree in advocating that employers do the following: monitor in the open, monitor only relevant activities, monitor only periodically, and encourage employee participation in setting up the monitoring standards and practices.[33] Employers have the right to monitor employees' communications and activities but should take care that such activities are only used when necessary. Employees should be familiar with and understand the policies relating to surveillance and monitoring.

Another challenging legal issue in the workplace is that of random testing for the use of drugs. Many employees feel that drug testing is a violation of privacy, but in most states employers of all types have the right to screen employees for drug and alcohol use. These types of tests are often mandatory for certain positions, such as airline pilot.

Although the rights of employees are better protected now than in the past, there are still areas where few protections exist. Because the employment at will rule allows employers the right to discharge workers for any cause, employees who wish to maintain a job sometimes are subjected to practices in the workplace that they feel violate their privacy. Many of these privacy issues are particularly resented by workers and cause mistrust and ill feelings on the job. The rights of both employers and employees need to be balanced. Supervisors should strive, as much as possible, to show respect for employees' privacy and dignity even when they are not legally obliged to do so.

Equal Employment Opportunities

Many of the legal protections enjoyed by workers are found in the area of equal employment opportunity (EEO). Equal employment opportunity refers to the right of all people to be hired and to advance in a job on the basis of merit or ability. Discrimination against protected classes of people in any aspect of employment is now prohibited by law in the United States.

Before the passage of equal employment opportunity laws, employers were able to hire, promote, or fire whomever they wished. Today, women, racial minorities, older workers, and people with disabilities have acquired substantial employment rights under law. The equal employment opportunity laws have exerted a profound influence on the American labor scene. HR functions, such as hiring, interviewing, testing, training, promoting, appraising, disciplining, and compensating, have been affected by equal employment opportunity law.

In almost every situation, there will be more candidates for a job opening or a promotion than there are openings and promotions available—it is almost always necessary to select some candidates instead of others. The preference of one candidate over another is permitted as long as the preference is based upon what can be shown to be job-related criteria.

▌ Ignoring *any* source of talent and motivation will unduly restrict a company.[34]
—Rosabeth Moss Kanter,
"Men and Women of the Corporation Revisited"

The laws that influence human resources activities are too numerous to discuss comprehensively in this section. Instead, only the highlights of the legal framework and the impact of the laws will be presented. Readers who are interested in this area should turn to a more complete treatment for additional information.

The Civil Rights Act of 1964

Although federal laws prohibiting discrimination against certain groups of employees go back more than one hundred years to the Civil Rights Acts of 1866 and 1871, the biggest impetus to equal employment opportunity came with the passage of the Civil Rights Act of 1964, which President Lyndon Johnson signed into law. Title VII of that act prohibits discrimination based on race, color, religion, sex, or national origin in all employment practices, including hiring, firing, promotion, compensation, and other conditions or privileges of employment. The primary aim of the legislation is to make overt discrimination actionable in all phases of employment. The act does not guarantee that women and minorities must be hired for vacant positions or promoted within a library; rather, it requires that they be fairly considered and neither excluded nor hindered because of race, sex, religion, or national origin.

Title VII has been interpreted in the courts many times since passage of the act. Court decisions have established that an employer's practices are discriminatory if they affect any one of the groups protected by Title VII in an adverse manner, even if the employer had no intention to discriminate.

It is against the law for any organization to have policies and practices that have an adverse impact on any protected groups, unless that organization can demonstrate that those policies and practices are justified by business necessity. Business necessity has been narrowly interpreted to mean that the employer must show overriding evidence that a discriminatory practice is essential to the safe and efficient operation of the firm. Once a plaintiff shows a *prima facie* case of discrimination by demonstrating adverse impact upon any protected group, the burden of proof falls on the organization to justify its employment policy or practice.

Title VII as amended by the Equal Opportunity Employment Act of 1972 covers all private employers of fifteen or more people, all private and public educational institutions, state and local government, employment agencies, labor unions, and apprenticeship and training programs. Thus, most libraries in the United States are covered by Title VII. It is enforced by the Equal Employment Opportunity Commission (EEOC), a five-member independent agency appointed for a five-year term by the president, with the advice and consent of the Congress. The EEOC investigates discrimination complaints and develops guidelines to enforce Title VII.

It is sometimes forgotten how much the civil rights rulings have changed the entire field of human resource management. For just one example of the change, see the job advertisements listed in Table 10.3. These advertisements were printed in *Library Journal* in 1959 before the advent of civil rights protection for job applicants. Advertisers were free to look for applicants of a specific gender or age.

The Civil Rights Act of 1991

The Civil Rights Act of 1991 was enacted in response to a number of Supreme Court decisions that limited the enforcement of Title VII and created a heavier burden for plaintiffs. The Civil Rights Act of 1991 reverses seven Supreme Court decisions; it creates rights to compensatory and punitive damages, including the right to jury trial, for individuals who are the victims of intentional discrimination as defined by Title VII of the Civil Rights Act of 1964 and the Americans with Disabilities Act. There are caps on both the compensatory and punitive damages, except for racial discrimination; these caps are based not on the seriousness of the discrimination but on the size of the employer's work force.

Table 10.3. Job Advertisements Before Civil Rights Legislation

Stymied in your present job? Want to broaden your experience? Like to work in a brand-new building under ideal conditions? Insist on liberal fringe benefits? Want faculty status? If so, and you are a male, you may be interested in the position of Assistant Cataloger. . . .

Circulation-Reference Librarian needed immediately for active modern library in progressive community with 20,000 residents. Real opportunity for young woman with initiative. . . .

Assistant Director. Male. Newly enlarged public library in historic. . . .

Position in small college for young woman interested in cataloging and general reference.

Cataloger (Assistant Librarian) needed for small, midwestern liberal arts college. MA, MS, in librarianship. or M.Lbn. desired. Either young female or male (preferred). . . .

Cataloger (half time or less) Reference, rank of assistant librarian, faculty status, needed by small midwestern university. Woman under 40. . . .

Director, Male, Challenging opportunity in fast-growing Long Island Suburb of 40,000. New air-conditioned building. . . .

Assistant librarian, Responsibility for main library service in a city-county. Man or woman under forty.

Taken from the classified advertising sections in the
January 15th and July 1959 issues of *Library Journal.*

Executive Order 11246 and Affirmative Action

Executive Order 11246 was issued by President Lyndon Johnson in 1965 and was amended by Executive Order 11375 in 1967. The most significant action of this order is the section that requires government contractors to have a written plan of affirmative action to remedy the effects of past discrimination. Any organization that holds a government contract of a certain size is required to have a written affirmative action plan. Many other institutions have voluntarily produced such plans.[35] The Office of Federal Contract Compliance Programs (OFCCP) of the Department of Labor administers the order.

Affirmative action refers to a set of specific procedures designed to ensure an equitable distribution of women and minorities within an institution. Despite the belief of some, affirmative action does not require fixed quotas, preferential hiring, or the employment of unqualified people. Affirmative action does require an organization to determine whether there are fewer minorities and women working in particular jobs in the organization than would reasonably be expected by their availability in the workforce and to establish goals and timetables for remedying any underutilization that might be identified.[36]

The EEOC leaves little room for doubt about what it expects of employers. The most important measure of an affirmative action program is its results. Extensive efforts to develop procedures, analyses, data collection systems, and report forms and to file written policy statements are meaningless unless they result in measurable, yearly improvements in hiring, training, and promotion of minorities and females in all parts of the organization.[37]

> Affirmative action should be consistent with and include merit—it is our responsibility within our individual libraries to define what qualities, charac- teristics, perspective and experience are truly needed to strengthen services to our specific academic community. From such a review, we may determine that diversity is an important and vital need that exists in our particular library. Therefore, as we search for and interview candidates diversity (as defined by the individual library context) should be part of the criterion for assessing candidates—thus merit has not been diminished at all but enhanced.[38]
>
> —Sheila Creth,
> "Securing Full Opportunity in American Society"

Despite the impact of affirmative action legislation over the past three decades, both the federal and state commitment to affirmative action seems to be weakening, and the future of affirmative action is unclear. Opponents of affirmative action have two major objections to it. They either argue that it has worked so well that it is no longer needed or that it is a means of reverse discrimination against individuals who are not in the preferred classes, and thus it favors women and minorities at the expense of more qualified white males.[39] Opponents to affirmative action have scored a number of recent successes. For instance, in 1996 California's voters passed a referendum banning gender or race preferences in state hiring. Some recent Supreme Court rulings such as *Adarand Constructors v. Pena* have narrowed the scope of affirmative action. In that case the court did not reject affirmative action programs but said that they must be subject to a rigorous standard of judicial review, known as strict scrutiny, that puts the burden on the government to show that a program being challenged is constitutional.[40] At this point all affirmative action programs are under increasing scrutiny, and their future is uncertain.

The Equal Pay Act of 1963

The Equal Pay Act of 1963 requires all employees to provide equal pay to men and women who perform work that is similar in skill, effort, and responsibility and that is performed under similar working conditions. The only disparity permitted in pay- ment of wages is when such disparity is the result of a seniority system, a merit system, a system that measures earning by quantity or quality of production, and a differential based on any factor other than sex. The law is administered by the EEOC.

Comparable worth, an issue that is closely related to equal pay, began to be discussed in the 1980s. At the heart of this issue is the fact that many occupations in our society are segregated by gender; men are heavily concentrated in certain types of occupations, and women are concentrated in others. At the same time, women who work are, on the average, paid less than men who work. In 2000, the median earnings of women who worked full time were seventy-six percent of the earnings of men who worked full time.[41] Part of this disparity can be attributed to the fact that the occupations in which women are concentrated pay less than occupations in which men are concentrated. Because librarianship is a profession that is approximately 80 percent female, salaries of both male and female librarians are adversely affected. The Equal Pay Act, passed in 1963, made it illegal to pay one gender less than the other for doing substantially the same work on jobs under similar working conditions requiring equivalent skills, effort, and responsibilities. It is clearly illegal to pay different wages to men and women in substantially equal jobs who have equivalent skills and experience.

Advocates of comparable worth say the concept of equal pay for equal work should be broadened to include equal pay for comparable work. For example, a job in a profession dominated by women, such as librarianship, which requires a certain level of education and experience, should pay the same salary as a job in a profession dominated by men, such as engineering, if that job requires comparable (but not identical) education and work experience. Comparable worth is based not on jobs being the same but being comparable, based on a comparison of the intrinsic worth or difficulty of that job in comparison to other jobs in that organization or community. Proponents of comparable worth base their claims on Title VII of the Civil Rights Act, which, in a broader fashion than the Equal Rights Act, forbids discrimination in compensation.

There are two main problems with instituting comparable worth: the difficulty of establishing the mechanism to measure the worth of jobs, and the sizable increase in labor cost to employers. There is still a great deal of controversy concerning comparable worth, and perspectives on the topic differ widely, even among librarians. Recent court decisions indicate the courts will not require employers to implement comparable worth policies nor find them liable of discrimination for using market values in setting salaries. But nothing prohibits an employer from adopting comparable worth standards. There is no doubt that employees in many fields, especially those employed by state or local governments, will continue to press to have comparable worth issues addressed.

The Age Discrimination in Employment Act

This act prohibits age discrimination against persons who have reached the age of forty in hiring, discharge, retirement, pay, and conditions and privileges of employment decisions. This act is also administered by the EEOC. Until recently, individuals over the age of seventy were excluded from protection; Congress has removed that restriction. The major effect of the amendment has been the removal of a mandatory retirement age in almost all occupational fields except for individuals such as police officers, firefighters, and airline pilots.

Americans with Disabilities Act

One of the most sweeping pieces of civil rights legislation, the Americans with Disabilities Act (ADA), was passed in 1990. The legislation bars discrimination against individuals who have disabilities. A person is considered disabled if he or she has a physical or mental impairment that substantially limits one or more of life's major activities, has a record of such an impairment, or is regarded as having such an impairment.[42] The definition of disability is very inclusive; it is estimated that as many as 43 million people may be covered by the act. The provisions of the act dealing with employment became effective in July 1992 for both public and private employers with twenty-five employees or more and in July 1994 for employers with fifteen or more employees. The provisions of the ADA are more extensive than those of the earlier Vocational Rehabilitation Act of 1973, which applied to government contractors, agencies of the federal government, and other programs and activities that receive federal funds. Almost all human resources practices are covered by the ADA, including application, testing, hiring, assignment, evaluation, disciplinary actions, training, promotion, medical examinations, compensation, leave, benefits, layoff, recall, and termination.

> The ADA was not written to provide unlimited opportunities for those labeled "disabled." Instead it was written as a means to provide the disabled with equal access to all those parts of life that others have had the opportunity to enjoy for centuries.[43]
>
> —Teri R. Switzer,
> "The ADA: Creating Positive Awareness and Attitudes"

Employers have the following legal obligations under the ADA:

1. An employer must not deny a job to a disabled person if the person is qualified and able to perform the essential functions of the job, with or without reasonable accommodation.

2. If a disabled person is otherwise qualified but unable to perform an essential function without accommodation, the employer must make the accommodation, unless that would cause the employer undue hardship.

3. An employer does not have to lower existing performance standards if the standards are job related and applied uniformly to all employees and applicants for the job.

4. Qualification standards that screen out or tend to screen out individuals on the basis of disability must be job related and consistent with business necessity.

5. Any test or other procedure used to evaluate the qualifications of applicants must reflect the skills and abilities of an individual rather than the impaired sensory, manual, or speaking skills, unless those are the job-related abilities the test is attempting to measure.

To prevent litigation, all employers should examine their practices to be sure they are in compliance with the ADA. In addition, supervisors and nondisabled workers should be informed about the act and its implications. All employees will have to become better educated and more sensitive about people with disabilities. Policies should be in place and managers should provide education about disabilities such as AIDS that produce concern on the part of other employees.[44] Employers and coworkers will be seeing types of workers in the workplace they are not used to seeing. Staff needs to be trained and made to feel comfortable about working with disabled individuals of all types—both as co-workers and as library patrons.

The Family and Medical Leave Act

This legislation became effective in August 1993 and was established so that workers could take time off from jobs to attend to sick children, parents, or their own illnesses. The Family and Medical Leave Act (FMLA) requires covered employers to provide up to twelve weeks unpaid, job-protected leave to employees for causes including childbirth, adoption, their own serious health problems, or those health problems of a close family member. This legislation recognizes that employees have responsibilities outside of work and that sometimes the family needs of the employee must take precedence over those of the employer. With the passage of FMLA, workers no longer have to choose between their jobs or taking time off to care for an ailing family member or themselves. As with any other benefit, the organization should have a clear policy on FMLA covering the rights of employees to take leave, the steps necessary in requesting leave, and the medical certification required when leave is taken. Supervisors need to be familiar with the organization's FMLA policy, and employees should be informed of their rights.[45]

Sexual Harassment

A relatively new area of federal regulation is that of sexual harassment. The Supreme Court has only recently recognized sexual harassment as a form of sexual discrimination, but according to the Equal Employment Opportunity Commission, it is now the fastest growing employee complaint. The number of sexual harassment charges filed between 1990 and 2001 grew by 150 percent, increasing from 6,127 cases in 1990 to 15,476 in 2001.[46] This increase is attributed to an increased willingness on the part of women to file formal complaints and a Supreme Court ruling, *Harris v. Forklift Systems, Inc.*, that made it easier for plaintiffs to win their cases.[47]

Sexual harassment violates Title VII of the Civil Rights Act of 1964. According to EEOC, sexual harassment includes but is not limited to:

♦ The victim as well as the harasser may be a woman or a man.

♦ The victim does not have to be of the opposite sex.

♦ The harasser can be the victim's supervisor, an agent of the employer, a supervisor in another area, a co-worker, or a nonemployee.

♦ The victim does not have to be the person harassed but could be anyone affected by the offensive conduct.

♦ Unlawful sexual harassment may occur without economic injury to or discharge of the victim.

♦ The harasser's conduct must be unwelcome.[48]

There are two types of sexual harassment. One, the *quid pro quo* type, occurs when a supervisor or someone in authority demands a sexual favor in exchange for some type of employee benefit, such as a pay raise or promotion. The other type of sexual harassment, the hostile work environment, occurs when an employee is forced to work in an environment where behaviors considered offensive to an employee, such as sexual jokes or teasing, occur. The *Harris v. Forklift Systems, Inc.* case expanded the concept of the hostile workplace ruling by determining that an employee does not have to suffer psychological injury to have suffered sexual harassment. The plaintiff must demonstrate only that the environment created by the offensive conduct was hostile and abusive.

> Recognizing sexual harassment is often no easy task because the workplace consists of many complicated interpersonal relationships and corporate structures or mentalities that may dictate how employees are expected to react toward one another. . . . You may treat some subordinates favorably, while others get the cold shoulder, for a variety of reasons. You also may have a social relationship outside the office with some of your subordinates or co-managers, which will obviously affect how you treat these individuals on the job. Relationships between coworkers also cover a wide spectrum, from the best of friends to archenemies. As a manager, you need to be perceptive about these relationships in order to assess any workplace misconduct, including sexual harassment. Sexual harassment is perhaps the most difficult type of employment discrimination to decipher and deal with because it is rooted in behaviors that strike at the most intimate, and perhaps confusing, aspect of human existence: a person's sexuality.[49]
>
> —Darlene Orlov and Michael T. Roumell,
> *What Every Manager Needs to Know About Sexual Harassment*

Sexual harassment is a violation of federal law, and, in most cases, employers are considered liable for the actions of supervisors. In addition, employers can be held liable for the harassment of employees by nonemployees or third parties, defined as customers and/or clients. If, for example, a public services librarian were continually harassed by a library patron, and the employer knew of the harassment but took no corrective measures, the employer could be held liable.[50] Although most victims of sexual harassment are female, the regulations also apply to female-on-male harassment and homosexual harassment.[51]

The field of equal employment opportunity is rapidly changing. The interpretations of the laws pertaining to EEO are changing as new regulatory agency rulings and court decisions are issued. Library managers dealing with any of the HR functions should attempt to remain abreast of changes in these regulations and apply them to their organizations. Although federal and state EEO laws have constrained employers in their human resources actions, the laws have worked to make workplaces in the United States more diversified and equitable. The ultimate aim of all EEO regulation is to ensure that every individual, regardless of age, race, gender, religion, or national origin, has an equal right to any job for which he or she is qualified.

Unionization

From the 1970s onward, there was an accelerated movement toward unionization in various white-collar and professional jobs. A substantial number of public school teachers are unionized, as are a large number of nurses and college professors. Like their colleagues in other professions, a large number of librarians belong to labor unions. Although there are no exact figures available, the most recent estimate is that approximately thirty-three percent of librarians work in unionized situations.[52]

The history of American workers' attempts to get fair and equitable treatment and to have a voice in the decisions that affect their lives goes back to the earliest days of the colonies. In 1636, a group of Maine fishermen protested the withholding of their wages. The first local craft union was formed in Philadelphia in 1792 by shoemakers. The first national organization of workers that has continued to the present day is the Typographical Union, founded in 1752.[53] Labor continued to strive for better working conditions, shorter hours, and better pay through the 1800s and early 1900s. Some of the conflicts between labor and management were violent, and many people were hurt or killed.

The real foundation of the American labor movement was laid in 1935, when the National Labor Relations Act, popularly known as the Wagner Act, was passed. The act gave employees the right to organize unions and to bargain collectively with employers. The purpose of the act was to encourage the growth of unions and to restrain management from interfering with this growth. To investigate violations and unfair labor practices, the act established the National Labor Relations Board (NLRB). This board has the authority to establish the rules, regulations, and procedures necessary to carry out the provisions of the Wagner Act.

After passage of the Wagner Act, unions began to grow rapidly and continued to grow until the mid-1950s. Although the number of individuals who are members of unions has increased, the proportion of the total labor force that is unionized has shown a decline since then. This decline is attributed primarily to the decreasing number of jobs in manufacturing industries, where the greatest number of unionized workers traditionally were found. But the downsizing and cost-cutting efforts of many organizations has also led to a new interest in unionization in many organizations where the workers who remain feel overworked and underpaid. In inflation-adjusted dollars, the average weekly wage of most hourly workers has declined, while the gap between the pay of top-level management and workers has increased.

To compensate for this loss of membership in the blue-collar industries, many unions initiated extensive organizing campaigns in the white-collar sector, particularly of public sector employees, such as government workers and public school teachers. Although there is no clear definition of the white-collar worker, the Bureau of Labor Statistics includes professional, technical, managerial, sales, and clerical workers in this category. Until the mid-1950s, white-collar workers constituted a minority of the nation's work force. Since that time, they have come to outnumber blue-collar workers, and the gap continues to widen as automation and foreign competition reduce the demand for factory workers.

In 2001 union members totaled 13.5 percent of all workers.[54] This is a decline in the percentage of unionized workers even from 1983, when slightly more than twenty percent of all workers were unionized. The decline in unionization has been concentrated in the private sector. While 37.4 percent of workers in the public sector are members of unions, the percentage in the private sector has dropped from 16.5 percent in 1983 to 9 percent in 2001.[55] The percent of workers in labor unions varies from state to state. In 2001, New York, Hawaii, Alaska, and Michigan had union membership rates over 20 percent, whereas North Carolina and South Carolina had memberships rates below 5 percent.[56]

Some white-collar workers, particularly professionals, have been ambivalent about joining unions. Many professionals have felt that membership in a professional organization is the best way to advance their interests and the profession. Some professionals have believed themselves to be more allied with management than with production workers. Other professionals felt that, although unions might be desirable for hourly workers, professionals, with their higher status, did not need them. Nonetheless, as unionization has become more common in the public sector, increasing numbers of librarians, like other professionals, have joined unions. Often librarians are given little choice when the library is part of a larger bargaining unit, such as municipal or university employees. One of the major attractions of unions for most workers is the hope that collective bargaining will improve their salaries and benefits.

> Unionization invariably takes place in a negative working environment. It does not take place by accident or by conspiracy. There are, however, many positive outcomes of unionization both for the employer and the employees. There is a natural synergy, I believe, between librarians and the activities of collective bargaining, particularly when librarians share the bargaining unit with other professionals.[57]
>
> —Deanna D. Wood,
> "Librarians and Unions: Defining
> and Protecting Professional Values"

Many studies have demonstrated that the primary reason employees turn to unions is because they do not feel that management is responsive to their demands. The two factors influencing employees' interest in unions are a dissatisfaction with their working conditions, and a perception that they cannot change these conditions.[58] Employees usually seek out unions when they think that they cannot get management to address working conditions, such as pay, benefits, job security, or chances for promotion. Because many librarians are joining unions or wondering whether such a move might be in their best interest, an understanding of the unionization process is very important to human resources managers regardless of whether or not their own library is presently unionized.

Forming a Union

The impetus for a union organizing campaign may come from several sources. Union organizers may start talking to employees while they are off the job about the benefits of unionization. If a union represents part of the labor force of a specific organization, members of the unionized group or union organizers may talk to employees of nonunionized units. Employees of a nonunionized organization who are dissatisfied with the policies and practices of the organization may solicit the help of an organizer or may submit a petition signed by at least thirty percent of the employees of the unit to the National Labor Relations Board.

If the employees initiating the unionization action are successful in obtaining signatures of the required thirty percent of all employees, an election is usually held to determine the desire of all the employees to unionize and to determine the agency that will be designated as the bargaining agent. If the union receives a majority of the votes cast, the union becomes certified as the exclusive bargaining unit of the employees within the organization. The election is carefully supervised by representatives of the National Labor Relations Board, and procedures are carefully observed by management and union representatives to be sure that no unfair labor practices occur. (Conversely, unions can be decertified if a majority of employees within the organization vote to rescind the union in another election conducted by the NLRB.)

After the local union is established, officers are elected by the dues-paying members. The elected officials usually consist of a president, a vice president, and a secretary-treasurer. Several committees are formed, such as the bargaining or negotiating committee, which is appointed to negotiate the contract for the union, and the grievance committee, which is appointed to handle the grievances of members. A number of departmental or shop stewards—one from each department—are elected. Their primary responsibility is to listen to worker complaints, to handle grievances, and to observe that the supervisors live up to the terms of the contract. In all but the largest local unions, union officials work at their regular jobs but are allowed some working time to attend to union business.

Collective Bargaining

After a union has been certified as the exclusive bargaining agent for a group of employees or for a total company, management and the union must bargain. Matters that will be discussed in the bargaining sessions include wages, hours, work rules, and conditions of employment. When agreement on these matters is reached, a contract that both sides are willing to sign and abide by for a stipulated time is prepared.

Although the form such bargaining actually takes varies from situation to situation, it most commonly proceeds as follows: Generally, the organization designates one person as its representative to carry out the bargaining process and to represent management. In a library, that person may be the library human resources officer, an industrial relations specialist, or any other individual delegated to represent management. The union also appoints an individual to act as its chief spokesperson. Its demands almost always involve increased costs and conditions that restrict management's freedom, for instance, requiring a firm to provide job security for employees. The union's initial demands are more than it expects to receive. The spokesperson for management resists the first demands and offers less than the union desires. (It must be remembered, however, that although bargaining is usually thought to involve union demands only, in the recent past, many companies have demanded union concessions or "give-backs," such as reductions in pension plans or medical insurance, and, in many cases, have gotten them.) Many bargaining sessions may be required before both parties agree and a new contract is produced. Although the negotiating process is complex and frequently frustrating, the vast majority of contracts are negotiated without a strike.

Managers of libraries and information centers must recognize that unionization will affect their organizations and their methods of management. As a result of the bargaining process and the signing of a labor contract, the power and authority of management are diminished. Policies and practices affecting employees, which were previously decided by management alone, become subject to joint determination. Wages, hours, conditions of employment, the handling of grievances, and other items relating to employees are determined by the negotiating process.

To date, unionization in libraries has brought mixed results. On the plus side, unions have contributed to the formalization of human resources policies and procedures, improved communications, increased fringe benefits, and improved working conditions. According to one study, university librarians in California who are represented by unions feel great loyalty to them. They feel greater loyalty to their membership in the union than to their membership in professional organizations.[59]

On the negative side, unions have caused substantially more paperwork, have contributed to the establishment of more rigid work rules, and have created an adversarial relationship between librarians and library managers. A recent study showed that unionized professional librarians in academic research libraries were less satisfied with their jobs than nonunionized librarians although the relationship between job satisfaction and unionization was also affected by the variables of salary and part-time status of the respondents.[60]

Not enough research has been done yet about the effects of unionization on libraries. Unionization is a complex issue, and because of its importance and possible impact on the library profession, more facts are needed to document and implement future planning.[61] In libraries, as in all other types of organizations, harmonious working relations are necessary between management and workers. The adversarial relationship that has often resulted from unionization needs to be overcome so that organizations can function more effectively—both for the good of the managers and the workers.

Conclusion

The human resources function is becoming increasingly important in all types of libraries and information agencies. As these organizations become larger and more complex, HR becomes an even more vital part of library management. In the present era of downsizing and tight budgets, managers need to pay even more attention to HR processes than ever before. As this section has shown, the tasks involved in HR are many and diverse. For an organization to function efficiently, the HR function must have a high priority for every manager. All of the component parts of this function must be integrated into a smoothly functioning system that enables employees to fill their work roles in such a way that the organization can operate effectively.

Providing for the best human resources to meet the HR needs of today presents problems and challenges, but these problems and challenges must be met. Effective organizations are those that are constantly trying to provide the best HR so that the organization can fulfill its mission, both now and in the future.

Notes

1.   Thomas O. Davenport, *Human Capital: What It Is and Why People Invest in It* (San Francisco: Jossey-Bass: 1999), 9.

2.   Betty Sosnin, "Packaging Your Products," *HR Magazine* 47 (July 2001).

3.   Timothy Butler and James Waldroop, "Job Sculpting: The Art of Retaining Your Best People," *Harvard Business Review* 77 (September–October 1999): 152.

4.   T. George Harris, "The Post-Capitalist Executive: An Interview with Peter F. Drucker," in Joan Margretta, ed., *Managing in the New Economy* (Boston: Harvard Business School Press, 1999), 162.

5.   Marisa Urgo, *Developing Information Leaders: Harnessing the Talents of Generation X* (New Providence, NJ: Bowker-Saur, 2000).

6.   Judith M. Bardwick, "Plateauing and Productivity," *Sloan Management Review* 24 (Spring 1983): 67.

7.   Debra E. Meyerson and Joyce K. Fletcher, "A Modest Manifesto for Shattering the Glass Ceiling," *Harvard Business Review* 78 (January–February 2000): 136.

8.   Barbara Conway, "The Plateaued Career," *Library Administration and Management* 9 (Winter 1995): 14.

9.   Adapted from Deborah E. Ettington, "How Human Resource Managers Can Help Plateaued Managers Succeed," *Human Resource Management* 36 (Summer 1997): 228.

10.   Bardwick, "Plateauing and Productivity," 69–72.

11.   David Marshall Hunt and Carol Mitchell, "Mentorship: A Career Training and Development Tool," *The Academy of Management Review* 8 (July 1983): 475–85.

12.   Michael Zey. *The Mentor Connection: Strategic Alliances in Corporate Life* (New Brunswick, NJ: Transaction Publishers, 1990).

13.   Joseph Berk and Susan Berk, *Managing Effectively: A Handbook for First-Time Managers* (New York: Sterling, 1991), 93–94.

14.   Tinker Massey, "Mentoring: A Means to Learning," *Journal of Education for Library and Information Science* 36 (Winter 1995): 52–54.

15.   Roma Harris, "The Mentoring Trap," *Library Journal* (October 15, 1993).

16.   Jonathan A. Segal, "Mirror-Image Mentoring," *HR Magazine* 45 (March 2000): 157–66.

17. Occupational Health and Safety Administration, Technical Links, "Ergonomics" (http://www.osha-slc.gov/SLTC/ergonomics/).

18. Joyce K. Thornton, "Carpal Tunnel Syndrome in ARL Libraries," *College and Research Libraries* 58 (January 1997): 9–18.

19. For instance, see the University of Florida's plan at http://web.uflib.ufl.edu/pers/develop/Ergo_Guidelines.pdf.

20. Rebecca Adams, "GOP-Business Alliance Yields Swift Reversal of Ergonomics Rule," *CQ Weekly* 59 (March 10, 2001): 535–39.

21. Charles A. Bunge, "Stress in the Library Workplace," *Library Trends* 38 (Summer 1989): 93.

22. Julita Nawe, "Work-Related Stress Among the Library and Information Workforce," *Library Review* 44 (1995): 30–37.

23. Stanley J. Modic, "Surviving Burnout: The Malady of Our Age," *Industry Week* 238 (February 20, 1989): 28–34.

24. Pamela Perrewé et al., "Political Skill: An Antidote for Workplace Stressors," *Academy of Management Executives* 14 (August 2000): 115.

25. Marcia Nauratil, "Librarian Burnout and Alienation," *Canadian Library Journal* 44 (December 1987): 385.

26. Mary Haack, John W. Jones, and Tina Roose, "Occupational Stress Among Librarians," *Drexel Library Quarterly* 20 (Spring 1984): 67.

27. Beth Blevins, "Burnout in Special Libraries," *Library Management Quarterly* 11 (Fall 1988): 20.

28. Daniel P. Keller, "Special Problems in the Library Setting," *Library Administration and Management* 11 (Summer 1997): 165.

29. Robert L. Willits, "When Violence Threatens the Workplace: Personnel Issues," *Library Administration and Management* 11 (Summer 1997): 166–71.

30. *Ibid.*

31. Janine Kostecki, "Privacy Issues in the Workplace Increasing," *Library Personnel News* 8 (March–April 1994): 1–2.

32. Michael Levy, "The Electronic Monitoring of Workers: Privacy in the Age of the Electronic Sweatshop," *Legal References Quarterly* 14 (1995): 12–14.

33. Edward D. Bewayo, "Electronic Management and Equity Issues," *Journal of Information Ethics* 4 (Spring 1995): 70.

34. Rosabeth Moss Kanter, "Men and Women of the Corporation Revisited," *Management Review* 76 (March 1987): 16.

35. See, for example, the Association of Research Libraries, Systems and Procedures Exchange Center, *Affirmative Action in ARL Libraries* (Washington, DC: Association of Research Libraries, 1998).

36. Margaret Myers and Beverly P. Lynch, "Affirmative Action and Academic Libraries," *Directions* 1 (September 1975): 13.

37. Equal Opportunity Employment Commission, *Affirmative Action and Equal Employment for Employers*, Vol. 1 (Washington, DC: Government Printing Office, 1974), 3.

38. Sheila Creth, "Securing Full Opportunity in American Society: If Affirmative Action Is Not Our Best Strategy, Then What?" *Invited Paper, ACRL 1997 National Conference.* (Available online at http://www.ala.org/acrl/invited/creth.html.)

39. *Congressional Quarterly Almanac, 104th Congress, 2nd Session, 1996,* Vol. 52 (Washington, DC: Congressional Quarterly, Inc., 1996), 5–37.

40. Dan Carney, "Effort to Ban Racial Preference at Federal Level Restarted," *Congressional Quarterly Weekly Report* 55 (June 21, 1997): 1454.

41. U.S. Department of Labor, Bureau of Labor Statistics, *Highlights of Women's Earnings in 2001.* (Washington, DC: August 2001), 1. (Available online at http://stats.bls.gov/cps/cpswom2000.pdf.)

42. Wayne E. Barlow and Edward Z. Hane, "A Practical Guide to the Americans with Disabilities Act," *Personnel Journal* 71 (June 1992): 53.

43. Teri R. Switzer, "The ADA: Creating Positive Awareness and Attitudes," *Library Administration & Management* 8 (Fall 1994): 207.

44. Willie Mae O'Neal, "AIDS: A Perspective on Management Issues," *Emergency Librarian* 21 (January/February 1994): 26–27.

45. Teresa Brady, "The FMLA: No Free Vacation," *Management Review* (June 1997): 43–45.

46. The U.S. Equal Employment Opportunity Commission, "Sexual Harassment Charges: EEOC & FEPAs Combined: FY 1992–FY 2001" (see at http://www.eeoc.gov/stats/harass.html).

47. Larry Reynolds, "Sex Harassment Claims Surge," *Human Resources Forum* (May 1997): 1.

48. The U.S. Equal Employment Opportunity Commission, "Facts About Sexual Harassment" (see at http://www.eeoc.gov/facts/fs-sex.html).

49. Darlene Orlov and Michael T. Roumell, *What Every Manager Needs to Know About Sexual Harassment* (New York: AMACOM Books, 1999), 1.

50. Teresa Brady, "Added Liability: Third-Party Sexual Harassment," *Management Review* 86 (April 1997): 45–47.

51. Laura N. Gasaway, "Sexual Harassment in the Library: The Law," *North Carolina Libraries* 49 (Spring 1991): 14–17.

52. Barry T. Hirsh and David A. Macpherson, *Union Membership and Earning Data Book: Compilations from the Current Population Survey* (Washington, DC: Bureau of National Affairs, 1997).

53. Wendell French, *The Personnel Management Process: Human Resources Administration,* 3d ed. (Boston: Houghton Mifflin, 1974), 725.

54. U.S. Department of Labor, Bureau of Labor Statistics. "Union Membership" (see at http://stats.bls.gov/news.release/union2.nr0.htm).

55. *Ibid.*

56. *Ibid.*

57. Deanna D. Wood, "Librarians and Unions: Defining and Protecting Professional Values," *Education Libraries* 23 (1999): 13.

58. J. M. Brett, "Why Employees Want Unions?" *Organizational Dynamics* 8 (1980): 47–57.

59.   Renee N. Anderson, John D'Amicantonio, and Henry DuBois, "Labor Unions or Professional Organizations: Which Have Our First Loyalty?" *College & Research Libraries* 53 (July 1992): 331–40.

60.   Tina Maragou Hovekamp, "Unionization and Job Satisfaction Among Professional Library Employees in Academic Research Institutions," *College & Research Libraries* 56 (July 1995): 341–50.

61.   An overview of the advantages and disadvantages of unions in libraries is contained in John Berry's "Directors' Take on Unions," *Library Journal* 122 (November 1, 1997): 47–49.

Section 5: Leading

One common definition of management is "getting things done through people." Leading (sometimes also referred to as directing or commanding) is the managerial function that enables managers to get things done through people—individually and in groups. Leading is related to the human resources function because both of these are concerned with the organization's employees, but the two functions are quite different. They each focus on distinct aspects of working with people. Human resources is concerned with providing and maintaining the individuals working in an organization. The function of leading, as the name implies, involves directing and motivating these human resources. Leading builds upon the human resources functions; it takes the human resources of an organization and guides and coordinates them toward achieving the organization's goals. So, although both functions are concerned with the human side of the organization, they are distinct and different.

Leading is complex because it requires that managers understand the human element in the organization. Thus, it draws heavily on the behavioral sciences such as psychology and sociology for the insights they provide in understanding individuals and their behaviors in the workplace. To be effective at leading, managers must be familiar with what type of rewards are most effective in motivating individuals, and they must know what styles of leadership are most likely to work best in any given situation. They also must understand the importance of communication within the organization. Because each individual is different, leading can be a complicated and time-consuming part of a manager's work. Indeed, if a manager is not careful, the interpersonal aspects of leading can consume inordinate energy and time.

This section presents an overview of the leading function. First, the major research relating to human behavior in the work environment is examined. The three major aspects of leading—motivation, leadership, and communication—are considered in turn. This section also contains information on leading in a team-based environment, on ethics, and on conflict within an organization. The section concludes with a discussion of the contingency approach to management that integrates the many theories of leading into a method that managers can use to match their styles to the needs of specific groups of employees in specific work settings.

Readings

Bennis, Warren, and Nanus Burt. *Leaders: Strategies for Taking Charge*. New York: Harper & Row, 1985.

Berk, Joseph, and Susan Berk. *Managing Effectively: A Handbook for First-Time Managers*. New York: Sterling, 1991.

Brophy, Peter, and Kate Coulling. *Quality Management for Information and Library Managers*. Aldershot, Hampshire, UK: Aslib/Gower, 1996.

Buckingham, Marcus, and Curt Coffman. *First, Break all the Rules: What the World's Greatest Managers Do Differently*. New York: Simon & Schuster, 1999.

Conner, Daryl R. *Managing at the Speed of Change: How Resilient Managers Succeed and Prosper Where Others Fail*. New York: Villard Books, 1993.

Daley, Dennis M. *Strategic Human Resource Management: People and Performance Management in the Public Sector*. Upper Saddle River, NJ: Prentice Hall: 2002.

Edward Deevy. *Recreating the Resilient Organization: A Rapid Response Management Program*. New York: Prentice Hall, 1995.

Dewey, Barbara I., and Sheila D. Creth. *Team Power: Making Library Meetings Work*. Chicago: American Library Association, 1993.

Dobyns, Lloyd, and Clare Crawford-Mason. *Quality or Else: The Revolution in World Business*. Boston: Houghton Mifflin, 1991.

Drucker, Peter F. *Managing the Non-Profit Organization*. New York: Harper-Business, 1990.

Fisher, Roger, William Ury, and Bruce Patton. *Getting to Yes: Negotiating Agreement Without Giving In*. 2d ed. New York: Houghton Mifflin, 1992.

Fulk, Janet, and Charles Steinfield, eds. *Organizations and Communication Technology*. Newbury Park, CA: Sage Publications, 1990.

Galbraith, Jay R., Edward E. Lawler III and Associates. *Organizing for the Future: The New Logic for Managing Complex Organizations*. San Francisco: Jossey-Bass, 1993.

Gardner, Howard. *Leading Minds: An Anatomy of Leadership*. New York: Basic Books, 1995.

Giesecke, Joan. *Practical Strategies for Library Managers*. Chicago: American Library Association, 2001.

Goldsmith, Marshall, et al. *Coaching for Leadership: How the World's Greatest Coaches Help Leaders Learn*. San Francisco: Jossey-Bass, 2000.

Hackman, J. Richard, ed. *Groups that Work (and Those That Don't)*. San Francisco: Jossey-Bass, 1990.

Helgesen, Sally. *The Female Advantage: Women's Ways of Leadership*. New York: Doubleday, 1990.

Hersey, Paul, Kenneth H. Blanchard, and Dewey E. Johnson. *Management of Organizational Behavior: Utilizing Human Resources*. 7th ed. Upper Saddle River, NJ: Prentice Hall, 1996.

Huddleston, Kathleen. *Back on the Quality Track: How Organizations Derailed and Recovered.* New York: American Management Association, 1995.

Kanter, Rosabeth Moss. *Evolve!: Succeeding in the Digital Culture of Tomorrow.* Boston: Harvard Business School Press, 2001.

Lawler, Edward E. *High Involvement Management: Participative Strategies for Improving Organizational Performance.* San Francisco: Jossey-Bass, 1986.

Metz, Ruth F. *Coaching in the Library; A Management Strategy for Achieving Excellence.* Chicago: American Library Association, 2001.

Nicholson, Nigel. *Managing the Human Animal.* London: Texere, 2000.

Quinn, Robert E. *Beyond Rational Management.* San Francisco: Jossey-Bass, 1988.

Tannen, Deborah. *The Argument Culture: Stopping America's War of Words.* New York: Ballentine, 1999.

Vroom, Victor H., and Arthur G. Jago. *The New Leadership: Managing Participation in Organizations.* Englewood Cliffs, NJ: Prentice-Hall, 1988.

Weick, Karl E. *Sensemaking in Organizations.* Thousand Oaks, CA: Sage, 1995.

Wilson, Lucile. *People Skills for Library Managers: A Common Sense Guide for Beginners.* Englewood, CO: Libraries Unlimited, 1996.

Wenger, Etienne. *Communities of Practice: Learning, Meaning and Identity.* New York: Cambridge University Press, 1999.

Chapter 11

The Human Element of the Organization

Managing professionals can present a true dilemma for today's managers. How do you manage, in the traditional sense, professionals or other managers who expect to have the authority and freedom to do their jobs? They are trained as experts in their fields. Why would they want you to manage them? Why would you think you could or should manage them?[1]

—Joan Giesecke,
Practical Strategies for Library Managers

The managerial function called "leading" focuses upon the human elements in the organization. Many of these human elements are invisible at first glance, but they play an important role in any organization. Employees' attitudes, personality attributes, and perceptions affect the way they work within organizations. As Abraham Zaleszik has written, each employee brings to his or her job "all the frailties and imperfections associated with the human condition" and the "complexity in human nature . . . leads managers to spend their time, smoothing over conflict, greasing the wheels of human interactions and unconsciously avoiding aggression."[2] Zaleszik warns that managers often spend too much time trying to maintain the human element of the organization. He urges that managers maintain a balance between what are often two competing organizational functions: functions he terms the "interpersonal" and the "real work," such as marketing and production. Obviously, managers do a disservice to the organization if they spend a disproportionate amount of time on the interpersonal aspects of management. Balance must be maintained. But the interpersonal functions of management cannot be neglected because the human element is essential to the performance of the "real work" of organizations.

320

The managerial function of leading (also sometimes called directing or commanding) draws heavily upon the field of study known as organizational behavior (OB). As the name implies, organizational behavior is the study of how people individually and within groups behave in organizational settings. For the last century, managers have looked to the behavioral sciences, such as psychology, sociology, anthropology, and political science, for useful insights to help in dealing with the people working in an organization, and they have applied many of these findings to the workplace. This borrowing has been useful because it has provided managers with many theories to explain human behavior. However, because there has been so much research and because the results of this research have often seemed contradictory, a manager seeking information on the best way to lead often becomes confused and frustrated. It must be remembered that the research was never intended to provide a single, simple prescription for all managers. Indeed, it has become clear that there is no one best way, and no universal theory that is appropriate in all cases.[3] What behavioral science research does provide, however, is a framework for managers to use in assessing their methods for dealing with the human element and a mechanism to suggest possible avenues of improvement. The more managers know about the research relating to motivation, leadership, and communication, the more able they are to draw from this research the elements that will be most useful to them.

Like other managerial functions, leading is done by managers at different levels throughout the organization. In most typical organizations, including libraries, management can be divided into three levels. Top management, which in libraries usually means the director and the assistant and associate directors, is responsible for the overall functioning of the entire organization. Middle management is in charge of specific subunits or functions of the organization. In libraries and information centers, department heads are middle managers. Their management functions are concentrated on the successful functioning of individual areas of the library. The managers in the lowest position of the management hierarchy are supervisors, sometimes called first-line managers. Supervisors lead the activities of individual workers to accomplish the desired organizational objectives. Because supervisors lead the work of all nonmanagement employees, they play a major role in influencing the performance of a work unit and are an important factor in determining the job satisfaction and the morale of the individuals supervised. Although this tripartite division of management is being affected by the organizational changes discussed in section 3, and the layers of management may be much less distinct in organizations that have adopted team management, even the flattest organizations still have managers who are concerned with leading.

> Every supervisor and team leader in an organization leads by example, even when it is a bad example. Every one of them has influence on the organization, even if it is a bad influence. We just naturally imitate those in charge. What senior leaders do, what they believe and value, what and whom they reward, are watched, seen, interpreted, and imitated throughout the whole organization.[4]
>
> —Kathryn Huddleston,
> *Back on the Quality Track*

In most organizations, managers on the highest levels have the power to establish organization-wide policy and are influential in setting the style of leading throughout the organization. Middle managers, in addition to leading their specific subunits or functions, also serve as liaisons between top management and supervisors. Finally, because supervisors are the managers in direct contact with most employees, much of the leading function in an organization is done by these lower-level managers; they, like upper-level managers, must be skilled in leadership and human relations functions.

Managers at all levels should be familiar with the techniques of good leading so they can create a climate in which people can work together to fulfill the organization's goals. Leading is a difficult undertaking because its focus is on human behavior. Human behavior is always unpredictable because it arises from people's deep-seated needs and values systems. As Keith Davis and John Newstrom state, "There are no simple formulas for working with people. There is no perfect solution to organizational problems. All that can be done is to increase our understanding and skills so that human relations at work can be upgraded."[5]

Although the function of leading has many aspects, the three major ones are motivation, leadership, and communication. This chapter will begin with a brief overview of some of the most important research relating to human behavior in the work environment. Then the first major aspect of leading, motivation, will be discussed. Leadership and communication will be discussed in the following two chapters.

The Human Element of the Organization

Before managers can lead, they must understand as much as possible about the human element of the organization. For instance, what causes workers to act the way they do? What needs do workers have? How should workers be treated to make them most productive? It was not until the early part of the twentieth century that managers began to realize the importance of the employees and their behavior in organizations. If the ultimate goal of all managers is a more effective organization, it is obvious that the people who work in those organizations are key factors in achieving success.

As was discussed in chapter 2, the first management studies were prompted by a desire to improve the productivity of workers. Most of the early management theorists, including Frederick Taylor and Frank and Lillian Gilbreth, were interested primarily in the efficient performance of employees. These early theorists thought that workers were motivated by economic rewards, and they concentrated on applying the principles of scientific management to design jobs for optimal productivity. Taylor and other early theorists thought that the individual workers could meet all of their needs by monetary rewards, which could be used to buy what the workers wanted or needed.[6] In their opinion there was a simple solution to motivation: Money motivates, and that is all a manager needed to know. Today, we realize that individual workers have a variety of needs, many of which would not be answered by money. The desire to understand individuals and what motivates them has resulted in a large number of studies dealing with the human element in the organization.

The Hawthorne Studies

The Hawthorne studies in the late 1920s were among the first studies that demonstrated the importance of the human side of organizations. Elton Mayo's research at the Western Electric Company in Hawthorne, Illinois, has become a landmark in the modern concept of effective human relations.[7] Interestingly, the studies were begun as an attempt to find a way of increasing efficiency and effectiveness by varying the level of illumination for workers in the organization.

As efficiency engineers at the Hawthorne plant were experimenting with various forms of illumination, they noted an unexpected reaction from employees. When illumination was increased, productivity increased. That was not so surprising as the fact that when illumination was decreased, production continued to increase. This same increase in production occurred when the illumination was not changed at all. Mayo was asked to examine this paradox, and the Hawthorne studies resulted.

The studies consisted of two parts. One part involved special six-woman teams of workers. Working conditions for these teams were constantly changed to determine worker fatigue and production. Not only was the illumination changed, but other factors were manipulated, such as rest periods, length of the work day, and coffee breaks. Every change that was made caused production to go up. Baffled by these results, the experimenters decided to return to the original conditions. This change was expected to cause production to decrease. Instead, production jumped to a new all-time high. Why? The answer lay not in the changes in the working conditions but in the changes in the way the workers felt about themselves. By lavishing attention on the workers, the experimenters had made these women feel as though they were an important part of the company. These previously indifferent employees coalesced into congenial, cohesive groups with a great deal of group pride. Employees' needs for affiliation, competency, and achievement were fulfilled, and their productivity increased.

> Each [woman] knew that she was producing more in the test room than she ever had in the regular department, and each said that the increase had come about without any conscious effort on her part. It seemed easier to produce at the faster rate in the test room than at the slower rate in the regular department. When questioned further, each [woman] stated her reasons in slightly different words, but there was uniformity in the answers in two respects. First the [women] liked to work in the test room: "it was fun." Secondly the new supervisory relation, or as they put it, the absence of the old supervisory control, made it possible for them to work freely without anxiety.[8]

The second part of the Hawthorne studies involved interviewing approximately 20,000 workers. Two things became apparent from the interviews. First, work in the factory was dull at best, and most employees accepted it passively and with a feeling of futility. Second, it was found that there were informal groups of workers through which an individual employee acquired a feeling of belonging and being welcome.

Management considered these groups to be threats, which was not entirely in error, because one of the primary functions of the groups was to provide a safe retaliation for poor managerial techniques. Slowdowns in production, poor or careless work, and the forcing of all workers to comply with the group's behavior were within the power of the group. But Mayo believed that the group could become a positive force for increasing productivity if management changed its attitude toward the group and used it for positive action.

> People need to be involved in a meaningful way if they are to be motivated. They need to feel they are part of something bigger than themselves and to understand how their efforts contribute to the big picture. The assumption that workers are content to be treated as outsiders, without access to business information, is one of the major fallacies of the bureaucratic organization.[9]
>
> —Edward Deevy,
> *Recreating the Resilient Organization*

The Hawthorne studies are important because they show that:

♦ employees respond to managerial efforts to improve the working environment;

♦ employees respond to being allowed to make decisions that affect their work patterns and job behavior;

♦ the informal group can be a positive force helping management achieve its goals;

♦ the informal group needs to develop a sense of dignity and responsibility and needs to be recognized as a constructive force in the organization; and

♦ the worker must feel needed and welcomed by management.

In short, the Hawthorne studies are a landmark in management research because they were the first to recognize that organizations are social systems and that the productivity of workers is a result not of just physical factors but of interpersonal ones also.

McGregor's Theory X and Theory Y

Two influential groups of assumptions about workers were developed by Douglas McGregor in the 1950s.[10] McGregor called these sets of assumptions Theory X and Theory Y. The first set of assumptions, Theory X, reflects what McGregor saw as the traditional, autocratic, managerial perception of workers. McGregor's Theory X assumes:

♦ Average human beings have an inherent dislike of work and will avoid it if they can.

♦ Because of this human characteristic of dislike of work, most people must be coerced, controlled, directed, and threatened with punishment to get them to put forth necessary effort toward the achievement of organizational objectives.

♦ The average human being prefers to be directed, wishes to avoid responsibility, has relatively little ambition, and, above all, wants security.

Theory X is a very pessimistic assessment of human nature. Managers who hold Theory X assumptions about their employees feel the need to tightly structure jobs and supervise workers. This theory assumes that the goals of the employee and the organization are incompatible and places major reliance upon the use of authority to control workers.

After describing Theory X, McGregor questioned whether this perception of workers is adequate in a democratic society in which the work force enjoys a rising standard of living and has an increasing level of education. McGregor put forth an alternative set of generalizations about human nature and the management of human resources, which he called Theory Y. Theory Y assumes:

♦ The expenditure of physical and mental effort in work is as natural as play or rest.

♦ External control and the threat of punishment are not the only means for bringing about effort toward organizational objectives. Individuals will exercise self-direction and self-control in the service of objectives to which they are committed.

♦ Commitment to objectives is a function of the rewards associated with their achievement. Positive rewards, such as ego satisfaction and self-realization, are the most significant and can be direct products of efforts directed toward organizational objectives.

♦ The average human learns, under proper conditions, not only to accept but to seek responsibility.

♦ The capacity to exercise a relatively high degree of imagination, ingenuity, and creativity in the solution of organizational problems is widely, not narrowly, distributed in the population.

♦ Under the conditions of modern industrial life, the intellectual potential of the average human being is only partly utilized.

Theory Y presents a much more positive picture of people, but the assumptions that constitute this theory are more challenging to managers. These assumptions imply that human nature is dynamic, not static. They indicate that human beings have the capacity to grow and develop. Most important, Theory Y makes management responsible for creating an environment that permits the positive development of individual employees. Managers who accept Theory Y do not try to impose external control and direction over employees but allow them self-direction and control.

> The conditions imposed by conventional organization theory and by the approach of scientific management for the past half century have tied [workers] to limited jobs which do not utilize their capabilities, have discouraged the acceptance of responsibility, have encouraged passivity, have eliminated meaning from work. . . . People today are accustomed to being directed, manipulated, controlled in industrial organizations and to finding satisfactions for their social, egoistic, and self-fulfillment needs away from the job.[11]
>
> —Douglas M. McGregor,
> "The Human Side of Enterprise"

McGregor's assumptions had a powerful influence in making many managers aware that they had overlooked the potential of individual workers. But, despite their impact on management practice, these assumptions do not represent a panacea for a manager. In the first place, it must be remembered that these are assumptions only, and assumptions as such have no proof. Theory X and Theory Y were not based upon research but upon intuitive deduction, although later researchers have looked at these variables in many settings and cultures.[12]

It was never McGregor's intention that Theory X be viewed as always bad and Theory Y as always good. As he states, most people have the potential to be self-motivated and mature. Some may not realize that potential, however, and the manager may have to create a structured and controlled work environment for those employees. Even though McGregor was aware of the difficulties of what he proposed, nonetheless he urged managers to examine their assumptions about workers to see if the managers themselves are responsible for creating the very behaviors they dislike. He presented a convincing argument that most management actions flow directly from whatever theory of human behavior managers hold.

Argyris Immaturity-Maturity Theory

Chris Argyris developed a conceptual framework that addresses the incompatibility between the values of many organizations and those of mature individuals.[13] According to Argyris, as people mature, their personalities change in several ways. First, people move from the passive state of infancy to the increasingly active state of adulthood. Second, an individual moves from a state of total dependency as an infant to a state of relative independence as an adult. Third, individuals mature from infants who have only limited modes of behavior to adults who are capable of behaving in many ways. Fourth, individuals have only shadowy, erratic interests as infants, but as adults they are capable of deeper and stronger interests. Fifth, infants and children have only a short time perspective, but adults have a time perspective that includes not only the present but the past and the future. Sixth, individuals as infants are subordinate to everyone, but as they mature, they move to equal or superior positions in relation to others. Finally, as infants or young children, individuals lack an awareness of self, but, as adults, they have an awareness of self and are able to control this self. According to Argyris's theory, maturation is a continuum. The healthy personality develops along the continuum from immaturity to maturity, although, sometimes an individual's culture or personality limit maturation. Thus, impediments of various types keep some people from reaching full maturation.

Argyris argued that, not only do most organizations ignore these maturation patterns, but in fact many individuals are kept from maturing because of the management practices of the organizations where they work. Many organizations expect workers to behave in an immature way; thus, the work environment is tightly structured, and the individual employee is closely controlled. Employees are encouraged to be dependent and passive—to remain immature. Because workers are treated as immature, they experience frustration, tension, and aggression and often behave immaturely. For instance, workers may display excessive absenteeism, apathy, or lack of effort.

> An analysis of the basic properties of relatively mature human beings and formal organization leads to the conclusion that there is an inherent incongruency between the self-actualization of the two. This basic incongruity creates a situation of conflict, frustration and failure for the participants.[14]
>
> —Chris Argyris,
> *Personality and Organization*

Argyris encouraged organizations to take steps to alleviate this situation and give employees a chance to grow and mature as individuals on their jobs. Like McGregor's Theory Y, Argyris's theory contended that people can be self-directed and creative at work if they are given the opportunity. He recommended that managers make fundamental changes that would allow employees to increase their individual responsibility and encourage employee participation in decision making. If organizations were more participative, flexible, and responsive to the contributions that employees can make, and if conditions in these organizations were compatible with the needs of mature individuals, it would be beneficial to both the workers and to the organization. Many modern methods of management, such as TQM, have adopted these perspectives on workers. Advocates of this type of management view workers as motivated, mature participants who will work to ensure the success of the organization.

Structuring the Human Element in Organizations

Research concerning people in organizations provides managers with some insight into how to structure the human relations aspect of any organization. As Keith Davis and John Newstrom point out, there are four basic assumptions about people that every manager should keep in mind:

1. Individual differences. People have much in common, but each person is an individual. From the day of birth, each person is unique, and individual experiences make people even more different. Because of these individual differences, no single, standard, across-the-board way of dealing with employees can be adopted.

2. A whole person. Although some organizations wish they could employ only a person's skill or brain, they must employ the whole person. Various human traits may be separately studied, but, in the final analysis, they are part of one system making up a whole person. People function as total beings. Good management practice dictates trying to develop a better employee, but it also should be concerned with developing a better person overall in terms of growth and fulfillment.

3. Motivated behavior. Psychology has shown that normal behavior has certain causes. These may relate to an individual's needs or the consequences that result from acts. In the case of needs, people are motivated not by what we think they ought to have but by what they want themselves. To an outside observer, an individual's needs may be illusory or unrealistic, but still they are controlling.

4. Value of the person. This is more an ethical philosophy than a scientific conclusion. It confirms that people are to be treated differently from other factors of production because they are of a higher order in the universe. It recognizes that because people are of a higher order, they want and deserve to be treated with respect and dignity. Any job, regardless of how simple, entitles the people who do it to proper respect and recognition of their unique aspirations and abilities. This concept of human dignity rejects the old idea of using employees as economic tools.[15]

To a large extent, the human factor in any organization is shaped by managerial actions. Managers have a tremendous impact on the growth and development of individual employees. J. Sterling Livingston used the George Bernard Shaw play *Pygmalion* (the basis of the later musical *My Fair Lady*) as an analogy for the role he thinks managers play in developing able subordinates and stimulating their success.[16] Just as in *Pygmalion* Henry Higgins transformed the flower girl into the society lady by treating her as if she were a lady, managers have the potential to transform their employees. According to Livingston, a manager's expectations are the key to the subordinate's performance and development. If a manager thinks the employee is going to succeed, that employee usually will succeed because that employee will want to live up to the manager's high expectations.

> Some managers always treat their subordinates in a way that leads to superior performance. But most managers ... unintentionally treat their subordinates in a way that leads to lower performance than they are capable of achieving. The way managers treat their subordinates is subtly influenced by what they expect of them. If managers' expectations are high, productivity is likely to be excellent. If their expectations are low, productivity is likely to be poor. It is as though there were a law that caused a subordinate's performance to rise or fall to meet his manager's expectations.[17]
>
> —J. Sterling Livingston,
> "Pygmalion in Management"

When a new worker comes into an organization, he or she may be treated in one of two ways. Typically if the manager has high expectations of that new worker, the manager is friendly toward the worker and gives the worker opportunities to assume responsibility, and if that new worker fails at some task, the manager may view the failure as lack of proper training and may try to see that the worker receives the training necessary to succeed. On the other hand, if a manager has low expectations of a worker, the manager likely will oversee the worker closely; will not trust the worker to do much independent work; and if mistakes are made, will blame the worker. The manager with the low expectations is setting the worker up to fail.[18]

First impressions are very important. The first information received about a person may evoke reactions that lead to a self-fulfilling prophecy. For instance, a poorly dressed new worker may evoke a reaction in the manager's mind that ultimately leads to that new worker failing in the job. Whatever assumption is adopted may serve as a self-fulfilling prophecy because if managers believe that something is true, they will behave in a way that helps that belief to come true. If a manager believes that employees are irresponsible, immature, and lazy, he or she will treat them as if they were. Employees will respond by being frustrated, aggressive, and apathetic, and thus the manager's beliefs will be fulfilled. On the other hand, if employees are treated as responsible, capable, and interested in the organization's goals, they usually will respond in like fashion and thus fulfill that prophecy.

Motivation

Managers are interested in motivation because it affects both employee performance and organizational effectiveness. Managers motivate by providing an environment that induces workers to contribute to the goals of the organization. Many questions about employees' behavior can best be understood by understanding motivation. In every organization, there are some employees who work very hard, and others who do as little as possible; some employees who show up on time for work every day and work after hours when necessary, and others who are frequently late and sometimes fail to come to work at all. It is often said that the first group of employees is motivated and the second is not. But what causes some workers and not others to be motivated? This is a question that has puzzled managers for a long time.

> Most people in this world, psychologically, can be divided into two broad groups. There is that minority which is challenged by opportunity and willing to work hard to achieve something, and the majority, which really does not care all that much. . . . Psychologists have tried to penetrate the mystery of this curious dichotomy. Is the need to achieve (or the absence of it) an accident, is it hereditary, or is it the result of environment? Is it a single, isolatable human motive or a combination of motives—the desire to accumulate wealth, power, fame? Most important of all, is there some technique that could give this will to achieve to people, even whole societies, who do not now have it?[19]
>
> —David C. McClelland,
> "That Urge to Achieve"

Motivation is the willingness to expend energy to achieve a goal or a reward. Thus, motivation is a process governing choices made by individuals among alternate voluntary activities. Motivation at work has been defined as the sum of processes that influence the arousal, direction, and maintenance of behaviors relevant to work settings.[20]

Evidence has shown that most people do not work to the fullest extent of their capabilities and that most jobs do not require that they do so. In some of the earliest research on motivation, William James of Harvard University discovered that hourly workers working at twenty to thirty percent of their ability were performing well enough not to lose their jobs.[21] He also found that highly motivated workers performed at eighty to ninety percent of their ability. That gap between twenty to thirty percent and eighty to ninety percent is the area that can be affected by motivation. Many, if not most, people do not work up to their full potential. Because the success of any organization depends on how well its employees perform, it is not surprising that motivating workers is a concern of managers. The motivation process can be seen as a sequence with the efforts of an employee resulting in the achievement of the goals of the organization, which then leads to the employee's needs being satisfied.

What motivates individuals varies from individual to individual, and even in the same person over time. Motivation is influenced by a number of internal and external forces. Because each human being has a complex psychological makeup, motivation is a complicated, multifaceted characteristic related to various desires, drives, needs, and wishes. A human need is a "personal unfilled vacancy that determines and organizes mental processes and physical behavior so that fulfillment can occur."[22] Individuals may recognize some of their needs and take care of them, but other needs are not as well recognized and may be fulfilled subconsciously.

Many theories and models have been developed to explain human motivation. These theories and models fall into two major groups: the content model and the process theory. The content models try to explain what workers want and need. They attempt to explain the nature of individual needs because according to these theories, workers' needs are tools that managers can use to motivate. The second group of theories is categorized as the process theories, which focus on how managers can use their knowledge of workers' needs and desires to motivate behavior.

The Content Models

Because workers are so individualistic in what appears to motivate them to work, a number of the motivational theories and models attempt to specify the exact needs and desires that motivate a worker. All of these theories assume that individuals possess preexisting needs and that these needs are complex but that organizations can motivate employees by addressing these needs. The relationship between the individual and the organization is a synergistic one; the individual has his or her needs fulfilled, and the organization obtains productivity. Psychologist Abraham Maslow proposed one of the earliest and best known of these theories of motivation in the 1940s.

Maslow's Hierarchy of Needs

Maslow postulated that all individuals have needs and that these needs can be ranked in one predetermined hierarchy. One level of need must be satisfied before an individual pursues the satisfaction of a higher level need. As needs are satisfied, they lose their motivational properties until they are again aroused. Only unsatisfied needs serve as motivators. Maslow identified five levels of needs:

1. Physiological. The basic needs of a human are food, water, shelter, sleep, and other bodily needs. All are essential to human survival, and until they are satisfied to the degree necessary to sustain life, the other needs will provide little motivation.

2. Safety and security. These are the needs to be free of the fear of physical danger and the deprivation of the basic physiological needs.

3. Social or affiliation. After the first two needs are met, an individual develops a need to belong, to love and be loved, and to participate in activities that create a feeling of togetherness.

4. Esteem. After the social needs have been fulfilled, people need to be more than just a member of a group. Individuals want to be held in esteem, both by themselves and by others. The satisfaction of these needs produces feelings of power, self-confidence, and prestige.

5. Self-actualization. At the highest level, the individual achieves self-actualization, which means maximizing one's potential to become everything that one is capable of becoming.[23]

Figure 11.1 is a graphic presentation of Maslow's hierarchy of needs.

Thus [the human] is a perpetually wanting animal. Ordinarily the satisfaction of these wants is not altogether mutually exclusive, but only tends to be. The average member of our society is most often partially satisfied and partially unsatisfied in all of his [or her] wants. The hierarchy principle is usually empirically observed in terms of increasing percentages of non-satisfaction as we go up the hierarchy.[24]

—Abraham H. Maslow,
"A Theory of Human Motivation"

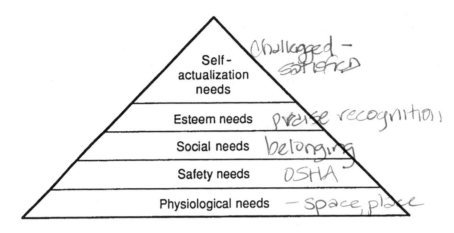

Figure 11.1. Maslow's Pyramid of Human Needs

The implications of the hierarchy of needs can be useful in understanding what motivates workers. If a person's basic physiological needs are not met—if he or she does not have sufficient food, water, clothing, and shelter—none of the higher-level needs will be of sufficient strength to be a motivator. In most cases, physiological needs can be satisfied as long as an individual has enough money. Thus, money, not in itself but because of what it will purchase, is a powerful motivator. In an affluent society like ours, the physiological needs of most individuals are filled and, thus, do not serve as effective motivators.[25]

After a worker's physiological needs are met, filling the security or safety needs becomes paramount. Some security needs are clear: for example, the need to avoid physical harm, accidents, or attacks. Most organizations provide physically safe places to work. But the need for security extends beyond the present into the future. Organizations are able to allay some concerns about the future by providing benefits, such as life and accident insurance and pensions. Job security is very important to most workers; the desire for job security is often a strong motivator, especially when jobs are scarce and unemployment is high.

After the physiological and safety needs have been fulfilled, the worker's social needs become predominant. Humans are social animals; they want to interact with others and be affiliated with a group. The informal organization described by Mayo in the Hawthorne studies arises to fulfill workers' needs to socialize and belong to a group.

The esteem needs include both self-esteem and the esteem of others. Workers desire not only to have their work valued by their superiors and their peers but by themselves; they need to derive self-satisfaction from their work. Some employees stay on a job that does not pay well because of the self-satisfaction they get from it. The desire for prestige and power is also a part of esteem needs, as is the competitive desire to outdo other workers. These esteem needs are rarely completely filled. The desire for recognition is never-ending for most workers, and esteem needs can be a potent and reliable source of motivation.

> Our society during good times almost has a built-in guarantee of physiological and safety needs for large segments of the population. Since many physiological and safety needs are provided for during those times, it is understandable why people would become more concerned with social, recognition, and self-actualization motives. Managers must become aware of this fact and strive to create organizations that can provide the kind of environment to motivate and satisfy people at all need levels.[26]
>
> —Paul Hersey and Ken Blanchard,
> *Management of Organizational Behavior*

The final level of need described by Maslow is self-actualization, or the need to maximize one's potential. This is the most complex of Maslow's levels. Self-actualization goes beyond the boundaries of everyday life and requires individuals to have an almost religious fervor to fulfill their human potential.[27] This need is rarely completely satisfied, although some individuals, such as Mahatma Gandhi, are credited with having reached full self-actualization.

Maslow's hierarchy has been criticized for being simplistic and artificial. Because every individual is different, many individuals do not pursue needs in the order postulated by Maslow, especially at the higher levels. In addition, it appears that the needs frequently overlap and combine to some extent.

Because Maslow's theory was based upon American culture, it is also limited in its applicability to other cultures. Although other Western countries might have cultures that are similar, countries with different value systems might have different hierarchies. For example, E. C. Nevis studied individuals in China and found that the hierarchy of needs there was very different from those that Maslow had proposed. Nevis found that there were only four need categories relevant in Chinese culture. Maslow's hierarchy was based upon workers fulfilling their own individual needs, whereas Chinese culture stressed the importance of needs related to society. According to Nevis, the order of needs in the proposed Chinese hierarchy are:

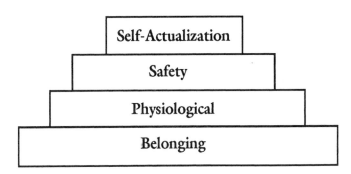

The need for belonging is the most basic need in Chinese culture, and there is no category for self-esteem included. Even self-actualization is defined by the contributions made to society.[28] Most of the models of motivation being discussed in this chapter are, like Maslow's, based upon American culture, and although they may have applicability in other cultures, they are not meant to be universal.

Although Maslow's theory does have flaws and limitations, it has been popular with managers because it provides a conceptual means of understanding the motivation of employees. By identifying an employee's current position in the hierarchy, the manager has an indication of what motivator would be most effective to use in guiding, counseling, and advising the employee to achieve better performance. The hierarchy tells managers that unfilled needs are more motivating than fulfilled needs, and it points out that all needs can never be satisfied because an individual who satisfies one need immediately begins to try to satisfy another. Managers must realize that need satisfaction is a continuous problem for organizations. Employees will never have all their needs fulfilled, regardless of how hard an organization tries.

Herzberg's Two-Factor Theory of Motivation

Frederick Herzberg and his research associates developed another content model of motivation in the late 1950s. Herzberg built upon and modified Maslow's hierarchy of needs. Herzberg formulated a theory of motivation that focused specifically upon the motivation of employees in a work environment.[29] Figure 11.2 compares the two theories.

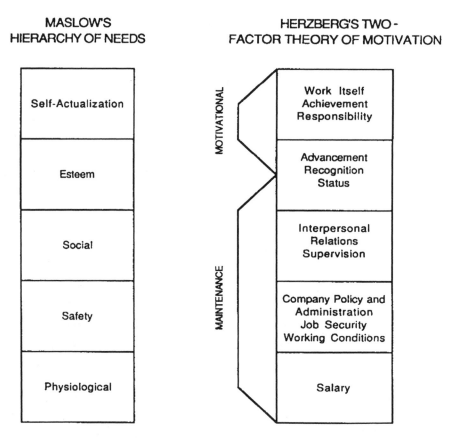

Figure 11.2. Comparison of Maslow's and Herzberg's Motivation Theories

To gather information about what leads to high morale in employees, Herzberg and his associates interviewed approximately 200 engineers and accountants in middle-management positions in the Pittsburgh area. The individuals interviewed were asked to tell what kinds of things about their jobs made them feel happy and satisfied and what kinds of things made them feel dissatisfied.

After the data were analyzed, the researchers discovered that one group of factors contributed to employees feeling good about their jobs. Herzberg called these factors motivators. The motivators, which are closely related to the actual content of the job itself, include achievement; recognition by supervisors, peers, customers, or subordinates of the work accomplished; the work itself—the aspects of the job that give the worker personal satisfaction; responsibility—being able to work without supervision and being responsible for one's own efforts; and advancement. These factors lead to job satisfaction and are effective in motivating individuals to superior performance.

> If I kick my dog (from the front or the back), he will move. And when I want him to move again, what must I do? I must kick him again. Similarly, I can charge a person's battery, and then recharge it, and recharge it again. But it is only when one has a generator of one's own that we can talk about motivation. One then needs no outside stimulation. One wants to do it.[30]
>
> —Frederick Herzberg,
> "One More Time: How Do You Motivate Employees?"

Another group of factors, which Herzberg labeled hygiene or maintenance factors, pertain not to the content of the job itself but primarily to the conditions under which a job is performed. These hygiene or maintenance factors include salary, job security, status, working conditions, quality of supervision, company policy and administration, and interpersonal relationships. These factors did not lead to satisfaction on the job, nor did they serve as motivators. If these factors were inadequate, however, they led to dissatisfaction.

The two sets of factors are relatively independent of each other, and each set affects behavior in different ways. When people are satisfied with their jobs, the satisfaction is connected to the work itself. When they are dissatisfied with their jobs, they are usually unhappy with the environment in which they work. The factors that motivate are intrinsic to the job itself; the factors that cause dissatisfaction are extrinsic.

Later research both supported and rejected Herzberg's model. It appears that his model may be most appropriate for managerial and professional workers. Nevertheless, the two-factor motivational theory has relevance to managers. It implies that the hygiene or maintenance factors must be satisfactory because they provide a base on which to build. If employees are unhappy about their salary, status, or working conditions, they will be discontent in their jobs. But merely providing these maintenance factors is not enough. If managers want employees to be motivated, they must provide what Herzberg called the motivators; that is, managers must ensure that jobs are interesting and challenging to employees. They must emphasize achievement, recognition, the work itself, and growth, all of which are factors that workers find intrinsically motivating.

Herzberg argued that job enrichment is one of the most effective methods of motivating employees.[31] However, he cautioned against horizontal job loading—merely adding more meaningless tasks to be performed by the worker. In a library, allowing a shelver to shelve both books and periodicals is not likely to improve motivation. True job enrichment involves vertical job loading, which consists of making jobs more responsible and challenging. An enriched job uses more of the employee's talents and provides more freedom in decision making. Herzberg's research shows that job enrichment leads to better-motivated and more productive employees.

> If libraries want to recruit people who value stimulating and challenging jobs they need to emphasize the rewards of working in the library. Fortunately, many self-motivated, committed workers place a high value on psychological reward and are not primarily motivated by money. This is not an excuse to underpay library staff; it simply means that even a library that can't pay top dollar should be able to attract workers who seek responsibility and growth.[32]
>
> —Kathlin L. Ray,
> "Toppling Hire-archies"

As a result of interest in job enrichment and its motivational force for workers, many organizations have established quality of working life (QWL) programs. QWL is a broad approach to job enrichment that attempts to satisfy the personal needs of employees through their work experience. The QWL focus on individual needs contrasts sharply with traditional personnel programs with their emphasis on the productive capability of the worker. Proponents of QWL claim that work can be redesigned to meet workers' psychological needs, such as feelings of competency and self-esteem, while at the same time improving productivity. The six major characteristics usually included in QWL programs are: autonomy, challenge, expression of creativity, opportunity for learning, participation in decision making, and use of a variety of valued skills and abilities.[33] There is evidence that links exist not only between QWL programs and employee satisfaction but also between QWL programs and an institution's financial success.[34] Even in libraries that don't have formal QWL programs, attempts are being made to improve working conditions and make jobs more satisfying, both for professional librarians and the support staff.

Herzberg's theory, like Maslow's, was based upon a study of American workers, although in later research Herzberg found similar patterns of satisfiers and dissatisfiers in other countries throughout Europe and in Japan, Israel, India, and South Africa.[35] Although today Herzberg's theory does not have the wide popularity it once had, it has had a strong influence on how jobs are designed and on how managers view the relationship between a worker's job and his or her job satisfaction.

McClelland's Need Theory

David McClelland's work offers a different perspective on what motivates workers. McClelland proposed that there are three major categories of needs among workers:

1. The need for achievement (nAch), which is the drive to excel in relation to a set of standards. It is the drive to succeed.

2. The need for power (nPow) is the desire to have an impact on an organization and to be influential.

3. The need for affiliation (nAff) is the desire for close interpersonal relationships.

Workers with a high need for achievement wish to succeed and advance. They seek situations where they can assume responsibility. Accomplishment is important for its own sake. Those workers with a high need for power want to influence people and make an impact on their organizations. They want to be in charge. If workers have a high need for affiliation, they have a drive to relate to people on a social basis and to have close interpersonal relationships. They prefer cooperative rather than competitive situations.

McClelland's theory also differed from earlier ones in that he thought that the three needs were learned.[36] "Motivation is inculcated in children through the stories and role models presented to them as things admired in their society. As adults, they seek to emulate the heroes and values of their childhood lessons."[37] But McClelland also believed that adults are changeable, and some of his later work deals with the idea of developing greater nAch, especially in workers of other societies. He attempted to train managers in organizations in less developed countries to increase their nAch, thereby increasing the success of their organizations. He claimed to be successful in making these managers increase in nAch. For instance, fifty businesspeople he trained in India invested more money in local ventures, participated in more community development activities, and created more jobs than a control group that was not trained.[38]

McClelland used a projective test, the Thematic Apperception Test (TAT), in this research. The subject was shown a picture and asked to write a story about it. For instance, a picture might depict a boy at a desk with a book. A subject identified as low in nAch might write a story about the boy daydreaming, whereas someone high in nAch would write that the boy was studying hard to do well and was worried about a test that he had to take. In addition to the TAT, McClelland and his associates also used questionnaires asking about such things as career preferences, the role of luck in outcomes, and similar subjects.[39]

McClelland and researchers who have followed him have studied the need to achieve more than either of the other two needs. People with a high nAch strive for personal accomplishment and like jobs that allow them to have personal responsibility and to solve problems. They are not risk-takers but set goals that are moderately high, and they accept personal responsibility for failure or success. Neither the need for power nor the need for affiliation has been studied as extensively as the need for achievement.

Managers using McClelland's theory of motivation would try to match various aspects of the work with the employee's need. Like many of the other theories, McClelland's suggests that the worker has to be matched with a job that fulfills his or her needs if that worker is to be as successful as possible. For instance, a worker with a high nAch should be given a job that challenges him or her and that allows personal responsibility.

The Process Models

In contrast to the content models of motivation, which try to identify the specific needs or values that contribute to motivation, the process models focus on the psychological and behavioral processes involved in motivation. The basic assumption underlying the process models is that "internal cognitive states and situational variables interact in the motivational process. The individual is an active factor, selecting behaviors based on his or her needs and based on expectations about what kind of behavior will lead to a desired reward."[40] Three of the best-known process models of motivation are the expectancy, the behavioral modification, and the goal setting theories.

Vroom's Expectancy Theory

A number of individuals have developed expectancy theories of motivation.[41] The expectancy theory is based upon the belief that individuals act in a way to maximize desirable results and minimize undesirable ones. Among the best known of these expectancy theories is one put forth by Victor Vroom.[42] This theory is more complex than the content theories. It emphasizes how motivation takes place given an individual's needs and objectives. The theory focuses on individual decision making and on the process that an individual goes through in deciding whether or not to exert the effort to attempt to achieve a particular goal.

Vroom's theory states that people will be motivated to perform to reach a goal if they believe in the worth of the goal and if they perceive that what they do will contribute to the achievement of that goal. The expectancy model is composed of four elements. Force is the motivational drive to achieve a goal. Valence is the extent to which an individual desires a certain outcome or goal. Expectancy is the perceived probability that a particular outcome will lead to a desired result, a result that is called the first-level outcome. Instrumentality is the degree to which an individual believes that a first-level outcome is related to a second-level outcome, which is defined as some human need, such as companionship, esteem, or accomplishment. Vroom's model can be stated in the following formula:

Force = Valence x Expectancy x Instrumentality (Motivation)

To illustrate the theory, consider a worker who wants to be promoted. This individual thinks that the best way to achieve the promotion would be to increase job performance. The motivation (force) to improve job performance would be a product of the intensity of the desire for promotion multiplied by the worker's perception of how likely it is that working harder can improve job performance (expectancy) multiplied by the worker's perception of how likely it is that improved job performance will lead to a promotion. In this example, improved job performance is the first-level outcome and promotion is the second-level outcome.

Vroom's formula is a multiplicative one—as soon as the value of any element drops to zero, so does the motivational force. In the example, if the worker felt that despite improved job performance there was no chance for promotion, the motivation to improve job performance would be zero. Likewise, if the worker felt that, despite any effort, there was no way to improve job performance, again the motivation would be nonexistent.

Vroom's theory is important because it highlights how people's goals influence their efforts; the behavior of an individual is a function of 1) his or her belief in the efficacy of that behavior in achieving a goal, and 2) his or her desire to achieve a goal. Because the theory recognizes the importance of various individual needs and motivations, it demonstrates to managers that motivation is highly individualized. A manager must try to learn the special concerns of each employee and what each individual values. The manager must also make clear to employees the connections between performance and reward. It also points out some situations that should be avoided in organizations. If an organization says it has a merit system for awarding pay raises, and if more employees get high evaluations than there is money available for pay raises, there will obviously be less motivation in the future to try to work well enough to get a high evaluation because the reward that was promised was not forthcoming.

Vroom's theory, because it emphasizes the individual, is more difficult to apply than those of Maslow and Herzberg, which are general theories of motivation. But Vroom's theory avoids some of the simplistic features of the content theories and also seems more adequately to account for the diversity in motivational needs seen in employees. There has been extensive research done on this model, and the research bears out the premise that people tend to work hard when they think that working hard will lead to desirable outcomes or avoid undesirable ones.

Behavior Modification

B. F. Skinner, one of the leading proponents of the behavioristic school of psychology, provides managers with still another process model of motivation. Behavior modification, unlike the other motivational theories discussed, is based on observed behavior, not on individual attitudes, desires, and emotions. Skinner's emphasis is on operant behavior, behavior that has been shaped and modified—that is, controlled— by its consequences. Individuals act as they do because of reinforcements received in the past for similar behavior. Reinforcement is defined as a consequence that follows a response and makes a similar response more likely in the future. Reinforcements can be tangible, for instance, money or food, or intangible, for instance, praise or attention.

According to Skinner, there are four methods for modifying behavior: positive reinforcement, negative reinforcement, no reinforcement, and punishment.[43]

> Many things in the environment, such as food and water, sexual contact, and escape from harm, are crucial for the survival of the individual and the species, and any behavior which produces them therefore has survival value. Through the process of operant conditioning, behavior having this kind of consequence becomes more likely to occur. The behavior is said to be strengthened by its consequences, and for that reason the consequences themselves are called "reinforcers."[44]

—B. F. Skinner,
About Behaviorism

Positive reinforcement, according to Skinner, is the most effective long-range strategy for motivating individual behavior. Positive reinforcement is a reward given after a behavior that the motivator wishes to see continued. Positive reinforcement tends to strengthen the act that it follows and makes that behavior more likely to occur again. Managers can offer a wide range of positive reinforcements, including pay increases, promotions, praise, and approval. When a behavior or act is followed by the termination or withdrawal of something unpleasant, it is called negative reinforcement. For instance, if a supervisor criticizes a worker for coming to work late, the worker's desire to eliminate this criticism may cause the worker to come to work on time. No reinforcement leads to the extinction of a behavior. Because the behavior is not reinforced in one way or another, it decreases in frequency and then stops. If the manager neither praises or criticizes the worker who talks loudly to attract the manager's attention, the unwanted behavior is not being reinforced, and it should stop. Punishment is an unpleasant event that follows unwanted behavior; punishment is intended to decrease the frequency of that behavior. Punishments that managers can inflict include demotion and firing.

Skinner's work has been criticized by those who say it treats humans as passive objects and denies the existence of individual free will. In terms of practicality, it is more difficult to apply behavior modification principles in the workplace than in the controlled setting of a laboratory. Scientists working with rats are able to deprive the animals of food so that they are hungry, then provide food immediately after the desired behavior occurs and be certain that no uncontrolled variable influenced the rats' behavior. Although the work environment provides managers many opportunities to practice behavior modification, managers who try to modify the behavior of employees must do it in an environment where uncontrolled variables are always intruding. Nevertheless, some organizations have used Skinner's principles of behavior modification to motivate employees. One of the most frequently cited success stories of the use of behavior modification in business occurred at Emery AirFreight, where, over a three-year period, two million dollars were saved by identifying performance-related behaviors and strengthening them with behavior modification.[45]

Behavior modification, although difficult to institute systematically and thoroughly, provides managers with several principles that can be applied in any type of organization: Be sure that employees who are performing as desired receive positive reinforcement, and remember that positive reinforcement is more effective in modifying behavior than either negative reinforcement or punishment. Although traditionally negative reinforcement and punishment have been popular means of control among managers, they have serious drawbacks and side effects. Among the drawbacks are temporary suspension of behavior rather than permanent change, dysfunctional emotional behavior, behavioral inflexibility, permanent damage to desirable behavior, and conditioned fear of the punishing agent.[46] For example, employees who are punished for talking on the job learn not to talk when supervisors are around but likely still talk in their absence. Also, they are likely to feel resentful about being punished and will find unproductive ways of acting out such feelings by thwarting the supervisors' goals.

Behavior modification works best when a job has specific variables that can be identified and reinforced. Some of the clerical jobs performed by library support staff fall into this category. For instance, error rate is subject to behavior modification techniques. Employees who complete tasks error free could be rewarded in some fashion. When jobs are more complex, it is more difficult to use behavior modification. Much of the work done by librarians is largely intellectual, and it would be difficult to identify, measure, and reinforce many of the behaviors that constitute such work.

Goal-Setting Theory

The last of the process theories to be discussed is the goal-setting theory. This theory, first propounded by Edwin Locke, states that specific goals increase performance and that difficult goals, when accepted by employees, lead to higher performance than do easier goals.[47] There have been more than 500 studies on goal setting in organizational settings in at least eight countries; about 90 percent of the studies have shown positive results.[48]

This theory has a number of propositions:

♦ The more difficult the goal, the higher the performance achievement.

♦ The more specific the goal, the more explicitly performance is regulated.

♦ The best way to get high performance is to make goals both specific and difficult.

♦ Goal setting is most effective when there is feedback.

♦ In order to maximize performance, one must have both goals and feedback.

♦ To get people committed to a goal, they must be convinced that the goal is important and that the goal is reachable or partially reachable.

♦ The higher an individual's self-efficacy,* the higher the goals the person will be willing to set, the more committed the person will be to difficult goals, the more resilient and persistent the person will be in the face of failure, the better task strategies the individual will be likely to develop, and the better the person will perform.

♦ Participation is more valuable as an information exchange device for developing task strategies than as a method of gaining commitment to goals.

♦ The more successful the performance in relation to the goals, the greater the degree of satisfaction experienced.[49]

Goal setting helps point employees toward what is important in the organization. Setting difficult yet achievable goals (sometimes called stretch goals) helps employees know what they should be attempting to achieve. Imagine that you are an original cataloger in a large library. Would it be more motivating to be told that you should do the best you could or to be told that you are to expected to do original cataloging for twelve English-language books a day? Having a goal to meet allows an employee to know the expectations of the employer and gives that employee an objective to try to meet. Finally, achieving a goal that has been set is very satisfying and fulfills both a need for self-esteem and a need for achievement. It often stimulates an employee to try to do even more the next time.

> Unlike needs and values, goals are readily (though not infinitely) change-able. Goals are like values only more specific; people set goals in order to attain values and pursue values in order to fulfill needs. For example, an employee, based on the need for income and self-esteem may choose ambition (getting ahead in life) as a value, and then set goals to do well in a number of specific tasks (both in school and in jobs). The goals help achieve the value that helps satisfy the need. The full sequence is as follows: goals ⇒ values ⇒ needs. Since there are many paths to a given value, many different goals can be set in relation to it.[50]
>
> —Edwin A. Locke,
> "Motivation by Goal Setting"

Goal setting that incorporates only a few of the elements listed above will not be successful. To implement goal setting successfully, the elements illustrated in Figure 11.3 must be included.

---

*Self-efficacy, a concept developed by psychologist Albert Bandura refers to task-specific confidence, in other words, how confident an individual is that he or she is capable of performing a task.

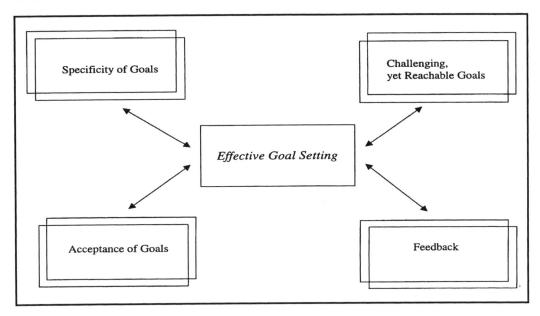

Figure 11.3. Elements of Effective Goal Setting (adapted from Locke, 2001)

How Should Managers Motivate?

> The subject of employee motivation is extremely complex. Furthermore, despite all the research that has been conducted and the thousands of articles that have been written, the various theories fail to complement one another. Rather, they seem to confound one another. This makes it very difficult to synthesize findings from the literature and from practice so as to have something of solid, pragmatic value.[51]
>
> —Charles Martell,
> "Achieving High Performance in Library Work"

Motivation is a complex factor, and the manager faces a wide array of approaches for promoting commitment to jobs within an organization. As one expert states,

> The issue of how to understand and influence human motivation has proven to be one of the most recalcitrant problems in human psychology. The fundamental reasons for this are that motivation at root comes from within the individual and is most directly controlled by the individual. Since motivation is "inside" the person, it cannot be observed directly, and since individuals possess freedom of choice . . . people cannot be controlled directly from the outside.[52]

Raymond Katzell and Donna Thompson have endeavored to summarize the vast body of research on motivation into a series of seven imperatives:

1. ensure that workers' motives and values are appropriate for the jobs in which they are placed;

2. make jobs attractive to and consistent with workers' motives and values;

3. define work goals that are clear, challenging, attractive, and attainable;

4. provide workers with the personal and material resources that facilitate their effectiveness;

5. create supportive social environments;

6. reinforce performance; and

7. harmonize all of these elements into a consistent sociotechnical system.[53]

To carry out all of the seven imperatives is a daunting task, but one that managers need to attempt. There is no one simple formula that can tell managers how to motivate employees. A manager must adopt a managerial style that motivates workers to perform tasks efficiently, but, unfortunately, no one prescribed style assures success. Rather, managers must develop individual approaches based on their personality, managerial philosophy, and knowledge of their workers. The effective manager takes advantage of the worker's reasons for working and offers inducements related to those reasons. Thus, a system of inducements, rather than a single inducement for all workers, emerges. Some inducements may have to be negative, but the majority should be positive. A system of inducements is not designed for across-the-board application but is designed to provide workers with those inducements that best motivate them.

A sound motivational system is based on principles derived from motivation research, on the policies of the organization, and on the manager's philosophy of human needs. Essential to any motivational system is the organization's ability to satisfy employee needs. This is difficult to accomplish because the needs of humans vary greatly and are subject to change. Maslow's hierarchy of needs gives the manager a guide to the range of needs, from basic life requirements to the social, ego, and creative needs. Herzberg's studies provide information about the need for recognition, achievement, advancement, and responsibility. McClelland's work shows that different individuals have different learned needs that affect the way they approach a work situation. Vroom's research demonstrates the importance of considering each individual's aspirations and in coupling performance to reward. Skinner's work makes evident the importance of positive reinforcement to ensure continued desirable behavior. Locke's goal-setting theory shows the significance of goals as a means of helping employees achieve a higher level of performance.

The policies of the organization should be structured so that the capacity to do good work is encouraged. Good productivity reflects the quality of employee motivation. Ideally, an organization's goals and objectives motivate an employee who wants to be part of and contribute to their achievement. Certainly that is so in the library profession. A high degree of success in achieving the goals and objectives creates a positive image of the organization; the worker is proud to be part of the organization and is motivated to promote its success through efficient work.

Conclusion

Any system of motivation depends on managers. The manner in which they apply their knowledge of employee needs and desires, the organizational environment that releases the capacity for work, the quality of training received by capable employees, and the pride the employee has in the organization establish the basic climate of the motivational system. It is the manager's responsibility to exercise sound judgment to make the system work.

Notes

1. Joan Giesecke, *Practical Strategies for Library Managers* (Chicago: American Library Association, 2001), 41.

2. Abraham Zaleznik, "Real Work," *Harvard Business Review* 75 (November–December 1997): 56.

3. John J. Morse and Jay W. Lorsch, "Beyond Theory Y," *Harvard Business Review* 48 (May–June 1970): 61–68.

4. Kathleen Huddleston, *Back on the Quality Track: How Organizations Derailed and Recovered* (New York: American Management Association, 1995), 57.

5. Keith Davis and John W. Newstrom, *Human Behavior at Work: Organizational Behavior*, 8th ed. (New York: McGraw-Hill, 1989), 4.

6. Dennis M. Daley, *Strategic Human Resource Management: People and Performance Management in the Public Sector* (Upper Saddle River, NJ: Prentice-Hall, 2002), 54.

7. Saul W. Gellerman, *The Management of Human Relations* (New York: Holt, Rinehart & Winston, 1966), 27.

8. George C. Homans, "The Western Electric Researches" (1941; reprinted in Management Classics, 3d ed., Michael T. Matteson and John M. Ivancevich, eds. [Plano, TX: Business Publications, 1986], 41).

9. Edward Deevy, *Recreating the Resilient Organization: A Rapid Response Management Program* (Upper Saddle River, NJ: Prentice-Hall, 1995), 48.

10. Douglas McGregor, *The Human Side of Enterprise* (New York: McGraw-Hill, 1960), chaps. 3, 4.

11. McGregor, *The Human Side of Enterprise*, 322.

12. For a description of an application of McGregor's principles in an information center in another culture, see C. S. Champawat, "Douglas McGregor Visits Jaipur Information Centre," *Herald of Library Science* 20 (January–April 1981): 28–37.

13. Chris Argyris, *Integrating the Individual and the Organization* (New York: John Wiley & Sons, 1964).

14. Chris Argyris, *Personality and Organization: The Conflict Between the System and the Individual* (New York: Harper & Row, 1957), 175.

15. Davis and Newstrom, *Human Behavior at Work*, 9–12.

16. J. Sterling Livingston, "Pygmalion in Management," *Harvard Business Review* 47(4) (July–August 1969): 81–89.

17. Livingston, "Pygmalion in Management," 81.

18. Jean-Francois Manzoni and Jean-Louis Barsoux, "The Set-Up-To-Fail Syndrome," *Harvard Business Review* 76 (March–April 1998): 101–13.

19. David C. McClelland, "That Urge to Achieve," *THINK Magazine* 32 (November–December 1966): 19.

20. Meshack M. Sagini, *Organizational Behavior: The Challenges of the New Millennium* (Lanham, MD: University Press of America, 2001), 449.

21. Cited in Paul Hersey and Kenneth H. Blanchard, *Management of Organizational Behavior: Utilizing Human Resources* (Englewood Cliffs, NJ: Prentice-Hall, 1982), 4.

22. O. Jeff Harris and Sandra J. Hartman, *Organizational Behavior* (Binghamton, NY: Haworth Press, 2002), 200.

23. Abraham H. Maslow, *Motivation and Personality*, 2d ed. (New York: Harper & Row, 1970), 35f.

24. Abraham H. Maslow, "A Theory of Human Motivation," *Psychological Review* 50 (July 1943): 395.

25. It is important to remember that workers' basic needs are not fulfilled in all cultures. See, for example, Kalu U. Harrison and P. Havard-Williams, "Motivation in a Third World Library System," *International Library Review* 19 (July 1987): 249–60.

26. Hersey and Blanchard, *Management of Organizational Behavior*, 43.

27. Daley, *Strategic Human Resource Management*, 56.

28. E. C. Nevis, "Using an American Perspective in Understanding Another Culture," *The Journal of Applied Social Behavior* 19 (1983): 249–64.

29. Frederick Herzberg, Bernard Mausner, and Barbara Bloch Snyderman, *The Motivation to Work*, 2d ed. (New York: John Wiley & Sons, 1959).

30. Frederick Herzberg, "One More Time: How Do You Motivate Employees?" *Harvard Business Review* 46 (January–February 1968): 55.

31. *Ibid.*, 53–62.

32. Kathlin L. Ray, "Toppling Hire-archies: Support Staff and the Restructured Library," *Continuity and Transformation: Proceedings of the ACRL 7th National Conference* (Chicago: ACRL, 1995), 85.

33. Charles Martell, "Achieving High Performance in Library Work," *Library Trends* 38 (Summer 1989): 82.

34. R. S. M. Lau and B. E. May, "A Win-Win Paradigm for Quality of Work Life and Business Performance," *Human Resource Development Quarterly* (October 1998): 211.

35. Frederick Herzberg, "Workers' Needs: The Same Around the World," *Industry Week* 234 (1987): 29–31.

36. David C. McClelland, *The Achieving Society* (New York: Free Press, 1961); David C. McClelland, *Power, The Inner Experience* (New York: Irvington, 1975).

37. Daley, *Strategic Human Resource Management*, 58.

38. David McClelland and D. G. Winter, *Motivating Economic Achievement* (New York: Free Press, 1969).

39. Hal G. Rainey, "Work Motivation," in Robert T. Golembiewski, ed., *Handbook of Organizational Behavior*, 2d ed. (New York: Marcel Dekker, 2001), 27.

40. Sagini, *Organizational Behavior*, 462.

41. See, for example, Edward E. Lawler, *Motivation in Work Organizations* (Pacific Grove, CA: Brooks/Cole, 1994), and Victor H. Vroom, *Work and Motivation* (New York: John Wiley & Sons, 1964).

42. Victor H. Vroom, *Work and Motivation*.

43. B. F. Skinner, *Science and Human Behavior* (New York: Macmillan, 1953).

44. B. F. Skinner, *About Behaviorism* (New York: Vintage Books, 1976), 44.

45. E. J. Feeney, "At Emery Air Freight: Positive Reinforcement Boosts Performance," *Organizational Dynamics* 1 (Winter 1973): 41–50.

46. F. Luthans and R. Kreitner, *Organization Behavior Modification* (New York: Scott, Foresman, 1975), 118.

47. Edwin A. Locke, "The Ubiquity of the Technique of Goal Setting in Theories and Approaches to Employee Motivation," *Academy of Management Review* 3 (1978): 594–601.

48. Edwin A. Locke, "Motivation by Goal Setting," in Robert T. Golembiewski, ed., *Handbook of Organizational Behavior*, 2d ed. (New York: Marcel Dekker, 2001), 48.

49. Locke, "Motivation by Goal Setting," 44–48.

50. *Ibid.*, 44.

51. Martell, "Achieving High Performance in Library Work," 78.

52. Locke, "Motivation by Goal Setting," 43.

53. Raymond A. Katzell and Donna E. Thompson, "Work Motivation: Theory and Practice," *American Psychologist* 45 (February 1990): 151.

Chapter 12

Leadership

People have been talking about leadership since the time of Plato. But in organizations all over the world—in dinosaur conglomerates and new-economy startups alike—the same complaint emerges: we don't have enough leadership.[1]

—Robert Goffee and Gareth Jones,
"Why Should Anyone Be Led by You?"

Leadership

Leadership has been a topic of interest for thousands of years. But as was recently written:

> There is far more interest in leadership, however, than there is agreement on it. No topic in business is more hotly debated. Can leadership be taught? Are its skills portable? What makes a leader anyway? More to the point, what are the most important tasks of a good leader? How do the most effective leaders invest their time?[2]

Our failure to understand leadership is not the result of any lack of literature on the topic. Writers in a number of fields have churned out hundreds of books and thousands of articles. A recent review listed more than 7,000 books, articles, or presentations on the topic of leadership.[3] According to Robert Goffee and Gareth Jones, in 1999 alone there were more than 2,000 books on leadership published, exhibiting many varying viewpoints on the topic with "some of them repacking Moses and Shakespeare as leadership gurus."[4] There is so much advice available about how to be a leader that it is almost overwhelming.

The definitions of the term "leadership" are not much clearer. One overview of the literature of leadership found 331 different definitions of leadership in works written since the turn of the twentieth century.[5] But regardless of how leadership is defined, there are certain elements that are usually present in the definition. The words "influence," "vision," "mission," and "goals" are usually found in the definitions. It is commonly accepted that an effective leader has the ability to influence others in a desired direction and thus is able to determine the extent to which both individual employees and the organization as a whole reach their goals. Leadership transforms organizational potential into reality.

Because leaders often function in an organizational or institutional setting, the terms *manager* and *leader* are closely related, but they are not the same. One recent account summarized the differences as:

> In general, leaders are viewed to take control of situations, while managers learn to live with them. Other distinctions include: leaders create vision and strategy while managers implement the outcome; leaders cope with change while managers cope with complexity, and leaders focus upon interpersonal aspects of the jobs, whereas managers deal with administrative duties.[6]

Or, as Warren Bennis and Burt Nanus, two of the most respected scholars of leadership, wrote: "Managers are people who do things right and leaders are people who do the right thing."[7] Although some authors still fail to differentiate between the terms "manager" and "leader," more commonly a distinction is made. Leaders are needed to "light the way to the future and to inspire people to achieve excellence."[8] Managers are needed to ensure that the organization operates well on a day-to-day basis.

Individuals can be good managers without being leaders. Our organizations need good managers. Effective managers are highly valued by those who work for them because good managers facilitate employees getting their jobs done. Of course, some managers may also be leaders, but it is a mistake to denigrate what managers do by assuming that they are failures if they are not also leaders.[9] Leadership may not be as important to an organization that is enjoying a favorable, nonturbulent environment. But, when an organization needs innovation more than standardization, it needs a leader rather than a manager as the top administrator. An organization may be managed well but led poorly.[10]

> Leadership has to take place every day. It cannot be the responsibility of the few, a rare event, or a once-in-a-lifetime opportunity.[11]
>
> —Ronald A. Heifetz and Donald L. Laurie,
> "The Work of Leadership"

If managers and leaders are not synonymous, are there qualities that every leader possesses? It must always be remembered that there is no one model of a successful leader, and leaders differ in different cultures and historical periods. But despite this variability, according to most experts, each leader must fulfill two major roles. First, a leader must exercise power wisely and efficiently, and second, each leader must through actions, appearance, and articulated values present a vision that others will want to emulate.[12] Let us look at these two roles a little more closely.

The first role, that of exercising power wisely and efficiently, obviously has close connections to what a good manager does. A leader must be temperate and fair, must set objectives and see that they are carried out, and must make good decisions. The characteristics that we usually associate with a good manager are also found in a good leader.

The second role, that of presenting an image that others will want to emulate, is the aspect of leadership that is often called "vision." A leader must provide a vision, a difficult undertaking in itself, and a lack of vision is one of the major problems of leaders today. As Henry Steele Commanger wrote a few years ago:

> One of the most obvious explanations of the failure of leadership in our time is that so few of our leaders—and our potential leaders— seem to have any road map. It is hard to lead when you yourself are in a labyrinth.[13]

Although a leader must present a vision so that an organization will not drift aimlessly, presenting a vision is not enough. A leader must have his or her vision accepted by the followers; the followers must buy into the vision and adopt that vision as their own. They must be energized so that the vision can be accomplished.[14] With an effective leader at the helm, the goals of the leader and the followers are meshed and congruent.

When leaders fail, it is often because they have not been able to create a vision that is shared. Sometimes people are hired in an organization, and they bring with them a predetermined vision that they want to see fulfilled. They begin to move too quickly, before their vision is accepted by the individuals who are going to have to carry it out. These individuals inevitably fail because they did not sell the vision to those who had to implement it.

In discussing leadership, sometimes the importance of followers is forgotten. A leader is not a leader without followers. Garry Wills has stated that leaders, followers, and goals make up three equally necessary supports for leadership. He defines a leader as "one who mobilizes others towards a goal shared by leaders and followers," and goes on to state that all three elements are an indispensable part of leadership.[15] As Robert Hogan et al. stated: "Leadership is persuasion, not domination; persons who can require others to do their bidding because of their power are not leaders. Leadership only occurs when others willingly adopt, for a period of time, the goals of the group as their own."[16]

Executives have good reason to be scared. You can't do anything in business without followers, and followers in these "empowered" times are hard to find.[17]

—Robert Goffee and Gareth Jones,
"Why Should Anyone Be Led by You?"

One of the things we do know about leadership is that the successful organization is almost always set apart from less successful ones by the fact that it is headed by a dynamic and effective leader. This leader has the ability to influence others in a desired direction and thus is able to determine the extent to which both individual employees and the organization reach their goals. Leadership is an important attribute that, too often, has seemed to be in short supply. For these reasons, both managers and organization theorists have long been interested in how leadership can be encouraged and developed. There have been a number of approaches to studying leadership. Because managers and leaders share many responsibilities and attributes, a number of the studies cited actually studied high-level managers as a method of investigating leadership. Some of the most important studies are discussed below.

Trait Approach to the Study of Leadership

Early studies on the subject of leadership were concerned with identifying the traits or personal characteristics associated with leadership. The studies were based on the premise that leaders were born, not made, and only those who were born with these traits could be leaders. The assumption was that once the traits were identified, leadership selection could be reduced to finding people with the appropriate physical, intellectual, and personality traits. Leadership training would then consist of developing those traits in potential leaders.

> To argue over whether leaders are born or made is an indulgent diversion from the urgent matter of how best to develop the leadership ability that so many have and that we so desperately need. A Nobel Prize awaits the person who resolves the question of whether leaders are born or made. But until some unanticipated break-through occurs or compelling new data emerge, the argument leads nowhere. The need for leadership in every area of public life has become so acute that we don't have the luxury of dwelling on the unresolvable.[18]
>
> —Warren Bennis,
> "The Leader as Storyteller"

Many trait studies were conducted, and traits that were said to be associated with leadership, such as energy, aggressiveness, persistence, initiative, appearance, and height, were identified.[19] However, summaries of this research demonstrate its shortcomings: Each study tended to identify a different set of traits. In one summary of more than 100 studies, only 5 percent of the traits were found in four or more studies.[20] Eugene Jennings concluded, "Fifty years of study have failed to produce one personality trait or set of qualities that can be used to discriminate between leaders and non-leaders."[21] Although some traits have been found to be weakly associated with leadership, these studies show that there is no such thing as a single leader type. Instead, there is much variation in the skills, abilities, and personalities of successful leaders.

Behavioral Approach to the Study of Leadership

After the trait studies fell out of favor, interest grew in the actual behavior of leaders. Researchers turned from looking for a single configuration of leadership characteristics to investigating leadership style. This research examined the behavior of leaders: what they did, what they emphasized, and how they related to subordinates. Three of the most important of these studies are discussed below. All of these studies looked at managers as leaders within organizations.

The University of Iowa Studies

One of the first of these studies was done at the University of Iowa by Kurt Lewin and his associates. These researchers primarily used controlled experiments with groups of children to examine three types of leadership styles: autocratic (a leader who centralizes decisions and makes decisions autonomously), democratic (a leader who allows subordinates to participate in decision making and delegates authority), and laissez-faire (a leader who gives the group complete freedom in decision making).[22] The results of this experiment demonstrated that there was more originality, friendliness, and group cohesion in democratic groups and more hostility, aggression, and discontent in laissez-faire and autocratic groups.[23]

Ohio State Studies

Other early studies were conducted at Ohio State University in the late 1940s and early 1950s. These studies identified two relatively independent dimensions on which leaders differ. One of these dimensions, consideration, refers to the extent to which a leader establishes mutual trust, friendship, respect, and warmth in his or her relationship with subordinates. Initiating structure refers to the leader's behavior in organizing, defining goals, emphasizing deadlines, and setting direction. Consideration and initiating structure are independent of each other; they are not separate ends of a continuum. A high score on one does not necessitate a low score on the other. A leader could be high in both consideration and initiating structure.[24]

University of Michigan Studies

A group of researchers at the University of Michigan's Institute for Social Research conducted similar studies at about the same time as the researchers at Ohio State.[25] The studies, which involved several large clerical departments, tried to identify managers' supervisory styles and their effects on employee productivity. Based on analysis of interview data, the researchers identified three types of managers: predominantly production-centered managers, predominantly employee-centered managers, and those with mixed patterns. Because no person is always the same, the word *predominantly* is important. A production-centered manager was one who felt full responsibility for getting the work done; departmental employees were to do only what the manager told them to do. An employee-centered manager recognized that the subordinates did the work and therefore should have a major voice in determining how it was done. Employee-centered managers thought that coordinating and maintaining a harmonious environment was the supervisor's main responsibility.

> To be an effective leader, you don't have to be hero with all of the answers, and you don't have to be a cop overseeing clones. Instead, imagine that your job is to create an environment where your people take on the responsibility to work productively in self-managed, self-starting teams that identify and solve complex problems on their own. If you concentrate on doing this, you'll find your people will need you only for periodic guidance and inspiration, which frees you to spend your time confronting big-picture, common-fate sorts of strategic and organizational issues.[26]
>
> —Oren Harari,
> "Stop Empowering Your People"

The research results were surprising. Contrary to traditional management thinking, which emphasized that permissive management led to employee laxity and carelessness, the departments that had employee-centered managers produced more than those with production-centered managers. The Michigan researchers had to make an assumption that was radical at the time; that assumption was that many workers like their jobs, want to be productive, and would be productive if given a share of control over their jobs.

Styles of Leadership

The next trend in the study of leadership was the development of ways to assess the style of a leader. The proponents of these typologies used the findings of the leadership behavioral studies to categorize the ways in which leaders lead. The style theorists thought that although many different leadership behaviors were possible, some styles were better than others. Three of the best known of these style theories were Likert's Systems of Management, the Leadership Grid developed by Robert Blake and Jane Mouton, and the Transactional/Transformational model of leadership.

Likert's Systems of Management

Rensis Likert, in *New Patterns of Management*, built on the research done at the University of Michigan Institute for Social Research.[27] Likert describes four prevailing ways that managers lead within organizations. These styles can be depicted on a continuum ranging from System 1, exploitative-authoritative, to System 4, participative.

- ♦ System 1 management is exploitative-authoritative. In this system, management has no trust or confidence in subordinates. Managers are autocratic, and almost all decisions are made at the top of the organization. Subordinates are motivated by fear and punishment and are subservient to management. Almost all communication in the organization comes from the top of the hierarchy.

♦ System 2 management is benevolent-authoritative. Management is condescending to employees, who are expected to be loyal, compliant, and subservient. In return, management treats the employees in a paternalistic manner. This system permits more upward communication than System 1, but top management still tightly maintains control.

♦ System 3 is consultative. In this system, management has substantial but not total trust in subordinates. Top management still makes most of the major decisions but often solicits ideas from subordinates. Control is still primarily retained by top management, but aspects of the control process are delegated downward. Communication flows both up and down in the hierarchy.

♦ System 4 is participative. Managers have complete trust in subordinates, and much of the decision making is accomplished by group participation. Decision making is found on all levels of the organization. Communication flows up, down, and horizontally among peers. Because of their participation in decision making, employees are strongly motivated to achieve the organization's goals and objectives.[28]

In short, System 1 is a highly structured and authoritarian system of management. The assumptions made about employees under this system closely approximate McGregor's Theory X. System 4 is a participative system based on trust and teamwork. Here, the assumptions made about employees are similar to McGregor's Theory Y. Systems 2 and 3 fall between the two extremes.

Likert concludes that the most effective organizations use the System 4 style of management. Although System 1 may yield favorable results in terms of productivity in the short run, over a period of time, production in System 1 organizations will taper off. In addition, the negative effects of System 1 upon people more than offset any short-term gains in productivity. In Likert's opinion, the closer the leadership in an organization is to System 4, the more effective the performance of the organization.

Today's organizations can be found at all points on the continuum. Those that have adopted innovations such as self-directed work teams are moving toward System 4. Undoubtedly, there are more organizations using System 4 now than in the past, but the true System 4 organization is still rare. Most libraries and information centers are still at the System 2 or System 3 level.

The Leadership Grid

The Leadership Grid (first termed the Management Grid) was developed by Robert R. Blake and Jane S. Mouton.[29] The Leadership Grid involves two primary concerns of the organization: concern for production and concern for people. The term "production" as used here, "covers whatever it is that organizations engage people to accomplish."[30] Managers who are most concerned about productivity focus almost exclusively on the tasks that have to be accomplished; managers who are concerned about people are more interested in the human relations part of the organization.

These two concerns and the range of interactions between them are illustrated in Figure 12.1. Concern for production is represented on the horizontal axis, and concern for people is represented on the vertical axis. Each rating is expressed in terms of a nine-point scale of concern, with one in each case indicating minimum concern and nine, maximum concern. A manager with a rating of nine on the horizontal axis has maximum concern for production; a manager with a rating of nine on the vertical axis has a maximum concern for people.

Based on the grid, Blake and Mouton describe five leadership styles. A rating of 1,1 is considered impoverished leadership. Minimum effort is exerted to get the required work done, and minimum concern is paid to employees. A leader with this rating is essentially doing nothing at all for either people or production; he or she has abdicated leadership responsibility. A rating of 1,9 is called "country club leadership." Thoughtful attention to people's need for satisfying relationships leads to a comfortable, friendly atmosphere and work tempo. There is no concern for production. A rating of 9,1 is considered task leadership. Here, operational efficiency results from arranging work conditions in such a way that human elements interfere to a minimum degree. Leaders with this rating are autocratic taskmasters. A rating of 5,5 is middle-of-the-road leadership. Adequate organization performance is achieved by balancing production with maintaining a satisfactory level of morale. Leaders with this rating are adequate in dealing with both people and production but are not outstanding in either capacity. Finally, a rating of 9,9 is team leadership. Work is accomplished by committed people; interdependence, resulting from a common stake in the organization's purpose, leads to relationships of trust and respect. According to this theory, leaders with a 9,9 rating are outstanding in their concern for both people and production.[31]

> Some think that learning how to lead effectively is next to impossible; some believe leadership is a natural ability and either you have it or you don't; and still others think that you can learn it but you can't teach an old dog new tricks. Accepting any of these propositions precludes the possibility of becoming more effective. Though they are value-based beliefs, they rest on false assumptions about human learning. It is as practical to learn to lead effectively as it is to learn arithmetic or to referee a game or to perfect any other applied skill.[32]
>
> —Robert R. Blake and Jane S. Mouton,
> *The Managerial Grid*

The Leadership Grid is most helpful for identifying and classifying leadership styles. It is useful as a theoretical framework for understanding human behavior in organizations. Using this grid, managers at any level should be able to identify their level of concern for people and for productivity.

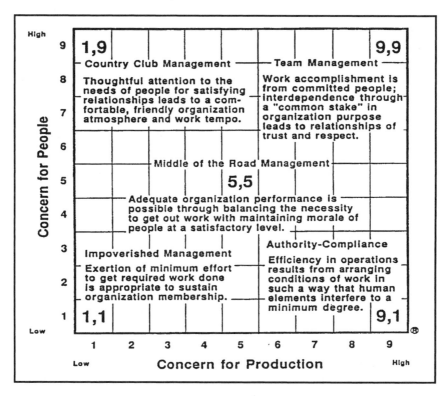

Figure 12.1. The Leadership Grid. From *Leadership Dilemmas—Grid Solutions*, by Robert R. Blake and Anne Adams McCanse. Formerly the Managerial Grid figure by Robert R. Blake and Jane S. Mouton (Houston: Gulf Publishing Company, 1991), 29. Reproduced by permission of the owners.

Transformational/Transactional Leadership

James McGregor Burns first described two types of leadership styles: the transactional and the transformational.[33] Transactional leaders see job performance as a series of transactions with subordinates. The transactions consist of exchanging rewards for services rendered or punishments for inadequate performance. On the other hand, transformational leaders are skilled at getting subordinates to transform their own self-interest into the interest of the larger group. Transformational leaders bring out the best in their subordinates. The described differences between these two types of leaders are reminiscent of the differences that are often said to exist between managers and leaders. The transactional leaders are more like managers, being sure that the job is done, whereas the transformational leader is more like the typical definition of what constitutes a leader because he or she inspires subordinates.

Transformational leaders usually allow more participation on the part of subordinates. Another researcher described transformational leaders as working "to make their interactions with subordinates positive for everyone involved. More specifically, [they] encourage participation, share power and information, enhance other people's self-worth, and get others excited about their work."[34]

> People jockey for position in a transactional group, whereas they share common goals in a transformation group. Rules and regulations dominate the transactional organization; adaptability is a characteristic of the transformation organization.[35]
>
> —Bernard M. Bass,
> "Does the Transactional-Transformational Leadership
> Paradigm Transcend Organizational and National Boundaries?"

Later research has shown that these two types of leadership are not in opposition to each other.[36] Instead, transformational leadership often builds upon transactional leadership. But of the two types of leadership, transformational leadership usually has a greater positive effect on an organization than transactional leadership.[37] But transformational leadership, like so many other models of leadership, is not the answer in every situation. It has been found that transformational leadership alone does not always produce better results. Other factors such as organizational culture, structure, and employee receptiveness influence the effectiveness of transformational leadership.[38]

Situational or Contingency Models of Leadership

Likert's Systems, the Leadership Grid, and the Transformation/Transactional model imply that there is a preferred leadership style. More recent theorists have turned away from the idea that there is one best way to provide leadership. They assert that earlier theorists had little success in identifying consistent relationships between patterns of leadership behavior and group performance. Instead, these contingency, or situational, theorists argue that there is no single ideal type of leader but, instead, a number of leadership styles that may be appropriate, depending on the situation. Employee-centered leadership may be best under some circumstances, and production-centered leadership may be best under others. According to advocates of contingency theories, the task of a leader is to use the style that is most appropriate in any given situation.

Fiedler's Leadership Contingency Model

Fred Fiedler developed one of the best-known contingency theories. According to Fiedler's model, three situational variables determine how favorable any particular situation is for the leader. These three situational variables are:

1. leader-member relations: the degree to which group members like and trust a leader and are willing to follow him or her;

2. task structure: the clarity and structure of the elements of the tasks to be accomplished; and

3. power position: the power and authority that are associated with the leader's position.

Fiedler produced and studied eight combinations of these three variables. The combinations range from the situation that is most favorable to a leader (good relations with followers, highly structured task, and strong power position) to the situation that is most unfavorable to a leader (poor relations with followers, unstructured tasks, and weak power position). Figure 12.2 lists each of the combinations. Fiedler then attempted to assess what would be the most effective leadership style in any of these situations. His theory predicts that the task-oriented leader is most effective in situations at either end of the continuum. When situations are most favorable or least favorable for a leader, the production-oriented style is most effective. The human relations, or employee-oriented, style works best when conditions are either moderately favorable or moderately unfavorable for the leader.

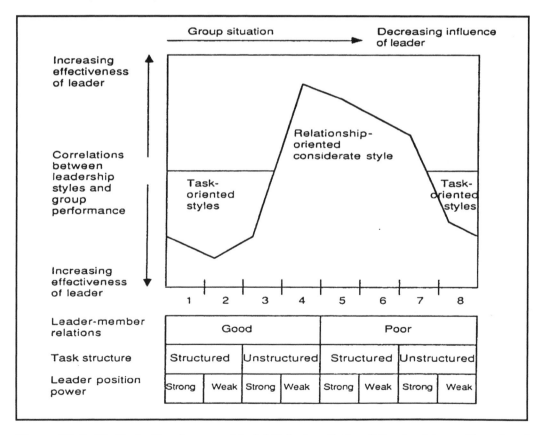

Figure 12.2. Fiedler's Contingency Model Relating Style of Leadership to Situational Variables. From Fred Fiedler, "Correlations Between Leadership Styles and Group Performance," reprinted from *Psychology Today Magazine* (March 1969): 42. Copyright American Psychological Association.

Fiedler concludes, "In very favorable conditions, where the leader has power, informal backing, and a relatively well-structured task, the group is ready to be directed on how to go about its task. Under a very unfavorable condition, however, the group will fall apart unless the leader's active intervention and control can keep the members on the job. In moderately favorable conditions . . . a relationship-oriented, nondirective, permissive attitude may reduce member anxiety or intra-group conflict, and this enables the group to operate more effectively."[39]

Fiedler's research is helpful to managers because it improves their understanding of the relationship of the various situational variables involved in leadership. Leadership effectiveness depends on the variables found in each situation. In Fiedler's view, leadership depends as much on the organizational variables as it does on the leader's own attributes.

Path-Goal Theory of Leadership

Another contingency theory of leadership is called the path-goal theory. This theory, first developed by Robert House, differs from Fiedler's Contingency Theory because its central focus is on the situation and leader's behavior instead of the personality traits of the leader.[40] Unlike Fiedler's view that leaders could not change their behavior, the path-goal model assumes that leaders can adopt different leadership goals depending on the situation.

The path-goal theory arises from a belief that effective leaders clarify the path to help followers achieve work goals, and they make the journey along the path easier by reducing any pitfalls or roadblocks. House thought that the role of a leader is to increase "personal pay-offs to subordinates for work-goal attainment and make the path to these pay-offs easier to travel by clarifying it, reducing road blocks and pitfalls, and increasing the opportunities for personal satisfaction en route."[41] This theory suggests that managers have three ways to motivate: first, by offering rewards for reaching performance goals; second, by making the paths toward these goals clear; and third, by removing obstacles to performance.

House identified four types of leadership behaviors:

1. *Directive leadership* occurs when specific advice is given to the group and clear rules and structure are established.

2. *Supportive leadership* occurs when the needs and well-being of subordinates is considered.

3. *Participative leadership* occurs when information, power, and influence are shared. Subordinates are allowed to share in the decision making.

4. *Achievement-oriented leadership* occurs when challenging goals are set and high performance is encouraged. Achievement-oriented leaders show high confidence in subordinates and help them in learning how to achieve high goals.

A leader may use any of the four types of leadership behaviors depending on the situation. The two most important situational contingencies in the path-goal theory are:

1. The personal characteristics of the workers, such as their experience, ability, motivation, needs, and locus of control;*

2. The environmental factors, including the nature of the work to be done, the formal authority system, and the work group itself.

So, the leader has to take into account both the environment and the characteristics of the followers. For instance, a new employee in an uncertain environment might need directive leadership, whereas an established employee performing a familiar task would be better off with supportive leadership. As is seen in Figure 12.3, different situations require different types of leadership behavior.

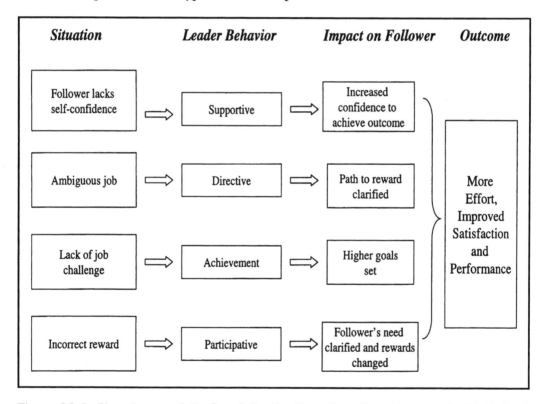

Figure 12.3. Situations and Preferred Leader Behaviors According to the Path-Goal Theory. Adapted from Gary A. Yuki, *Leadership in Organizations* (Englewood Cliffs, NJ: Prentice-Hall, 1981), 146–52.

---

*Locus of control is a personality attribute that measures the degree to which individuals think they control their own fate. Individuals with an external locus of control believe that what happens to them is due to luck or outside forces, whereas those with an internal locus of control think they control their own destinies by their actions.

Some findings that have been drawn from the path-goal theory are:

♦ Directive leadership leads to higher satisfaction when the task is ambiguous, policies are unclear or conflicting, or when there is substantive conflict within the group.

♦ Supportive leadership leads to higher satisfaction when work is stressful or dissatisfying or the subordinate lacks self-confidence.

♦ Participative leadership leads to higher satisfaction when tasks are ego involving or where subordinates are independent.

♦ Subordinates with an internal locus of control will be more satisfied with a participative style, whereas those with an external locus of control will be more satisfied with a directive style.

♦ Achievement-oriented leadership leads to higher satisfaction when individuals are working on ambiguous, nonrepetitive tasks.[42]

The path-goal theory is complex, but it is one of the most respected theories of leadership today. Research to validate its conclusions has generally been encouraging, with most studies supporting the logic underlying path-goal theory.[43] It makes sense that both an employee's performance and satisfaction are likely to be positively influenced when a leader is able to adapt different leadership behaviors to compensate for differences in either the employee or the work setting.

The Leadership Challenge

So, as can be seen, there are many theories to suggest what makes a leader successful. None of the theories completely explains leadership; however, they do help explain many of the variables that contribute to being a successful leader. But as was discussed at the beginning of the chapter, leadership is a complex topic and one that has no easy answers.

> Leaders come to power through both internal and external selection. The internal is self-selection, the force that induces some to seek and others to avoid leadership. Even when one is handed a leadership position on a plate, one's inner self has to acquiesce, especially around three attributes. Are you ready to take on the risks and responsibility (drive)? Do you believe you have the skills to take on the challenge and succeed (ability)? Can you withstand the demands on your energies (constitution)? Many people have succumbed to the lure of the rewards or the encouragement of others and have become bad leaders, when they would have done better to heed their inner doubts.[44]
>
> —Nigel Nicholson,
> *Managing the Human Animal*

It is commonly believed that we are suffering from a leadership crisis in our society. We are dissatisfied with our leaders and confused about the type of leadership we want. In sectors as diverse as the federal government, higher education, and librarianship, the questions are the same. Where are the leaders we need, and why do so many promising individuals fail to live up to our expectations once they assume leadership positions?

As Warren Bennis, one of the foremost authorities on leadership, writes: "It is both an irony and a paradox that precisely at the time when trust in and credibility of leaders are lowest, when people are both angry and cynical, the nation most needs leaders, people who can transcend the vacuum."[45]

Although many of the laments about the lack of leadership are focused on national leaders, the same type of gap between expectations and reality is found in many other arenas, including libraries and information centers. The challenges facing these types of organizations over the next decades will be immense, but the leaders for the transition, those individuals who will guide the organizations through the uncharted waters of tomorrow, have not yet emerged. There are many competent managers, but few that seem to possess a clear vision of the future and the knowledge of how to get from here to there. And, in librarianship as in other areas, the same troubling pattern exists. Too often, after individuals have been chosen for leadership positions, they quickly lose their luster.

It is more difficult for individuals to succeed in leadership roles now for a number of reasons. In the past, people were far less likely to question the authority of a leader. Today's leader must try to inspire confidence and trust in followers who are likely to be at least partially distrustful of authority of all types. Many individuals hold the paradoxical view of leadership described by Bennis. They constantly lament the lack of leadership in our society. They call for better, more effective leadership and purport to believe that strong leadership is the cure for much of what ails our society's institutions and organizations. But at the same time these same people deeply mistrust leaders. As Herb White has stated, "We believe in leaders and in leadership, but . . . on a personal basis few of us want to be led."[46]

Because the present is basically an antiauthoritarian age, it is not surprising that it is easier to diagnose the need for more effective leadership than to effect the cure. It is no wonder that so many contemporary leaders fail when the often turbulent, complex, and crisis-ridden environment in which leadership must now be provided is combined with the modern dislike of accepting authority of any type. Whatever type of leader we have chosen, whether authoritarian or laissez-faire, whether outsider or insider, whether older or younger, too often he or she is less than perfect and fails to live up to our expectations. It is then a common pattern to discard that leader and to begin to look for another.

> In the knowledge era, we will finally have to surrender the myth of leaders as isolated heroes commanding their organizations from on high. Top-down directives, even when they are implemented, reinforce an environment of fear, distrust, and internal competitiveness that reduces collaboration and cooperation. They foster compliance instead of commitment. . . . For those reasons, leadership in the future will be distributed among diverse individuals and teams who share responsibility for creating the organization's future.[47]
>
> —Peter Senge,
> "Communities of Leaders and Learners"

Managers who are concerned with leadership should keep in mind that, despite all the theories about leadership style, research still has not shown whether one style of leadership is superior to the others. The analysis of leadership style is a complex topic, and much of the research that has been done to date has been short-term and scattered. The situational theories, such as Fiedler's Contingency Model and the House's path-goal theory, seem to be the most helpful in dealing with real-life situations. However, such theories, with their emphasis on matching a leadership style to a particular environment or work situation, complicate the manager's task. Many managers would like to be told how to lead; the situational theories say there is no one right way. Instead, effective leaders adapt their style of leadership behavior to the needs of the followers and the situation. Because these factors are not constant, discerning the appropriate style is always a challenge.

Managers should also remember that in most modern organizations, leaders may be found at all levels. To envision the person at the top of the organizational hierarchy as the only leader is to accept an artificially constrained view of leadership. More and more employees at all levels are participating in management and thus are also providing leadership within the organization.

Participative Management

One decision every manager must make is how much employee participation to allow in management. In chapter 13, team-building will be discussed. The use of teams is one example of participative management. Over the past few decades, there has been a change in the outlook of both managers and employees in libraries, as in other types of organizations. As has been discussed previously, traditionally most libraries and information centers were organized in a traditional hierarchical structure, and the normal management style was authoritarian, with the director making all decisions. Today's directors find authoritarian leadership styles to be less effective as librarians demand an increased input into decision making. *Participative management* has been defined as

> both a philosophy and a method for managing human resources in an environment in which employees are respected and their contributions valued and utilized. From a philosophical standpoint, participative management centers on the belief that people at all

levels of an organization can develop a genuine interest in its success and can do more than merely perform their assigned duties.[48]

Many writers have explored the issue of participative management in libraries and information centers. Participative management involves employees in sharing information, making decisions, solving problems, planning projects, and evaluating results.[49] Those who favor greater participation base their opinions on their beliefs that the rank-and-file library staff benefit from having a chance to participate in the governance of the library, that better decisions are made with staff involvement, and that librarians' increased job satisfaction leads to better library service. Writers who take the other view usually support their stand by concentrating on the inexperience of most librarians in management, the amount of time that is consumed by participation, and the inappropriateness of the participative model as a means of operating a complex service organization.

> A strong trend towards more participative management in libraries would be expected since involvement and participation are said to be crucial to meeting the needs of organizations for changed structures and styles in response to the IT revolution, to developing flexibility, to encouraging staff to generate ideas and to tapping their creative talents, to satisfying the increased expectation of individuals for self-realization, and to increasing productivity. There has undoubtedly been such a trend, but it is very difficult to quantify how widespread it is and how far it has gone. As in industry, much of what library directors say about their participative management may be self-deception or lip-service.[50]
>
> —Maurice B. Line, and Margaret Kinnell,
> "Human Resource Management in Library
> and Information Services"

Participative management has the virtue of forcing decision making down to the level where the most relevant information can be found and where the effect of the decision will have the greatest impact. Although few libraries could be considered to operate on Likert's System 4 level, most libraries permit some employee input into decision making, and there is almost always some consultation before decisions are made.

Participative management does not mean that the management relinquishes its responsibility for the final decisions that are made—participative management should not be confused with management by consensus. As Nicholas Burckel has written, "librarians will have to accept that participatory management is no substitute for individual responsibility and leadership. There will likely always be library directors and just as likely they will be paid considerably more than the rest of the non-administrative staff . . . because they are accountable for the operation of the library."[51] Neither does participative management mean that managers involve all their employees in every decision every time, nor do all employees have the same amount of involvement in decision making. The involvement is usually based on familiarity with the decision that needs to be made.[52]

Although management theory advocates the use of participation by employees, it is sometimes difficult to implement with employees who have not had experience with it before. And, on the other hand, it is not easy for some managers to give up control and to let others contribute to decision making and problem-solving. Switching to a more participative system of management requires changes on the part of both managers and employees.

> Not only are many lower-level employees comfortable being told what to do, but many managers are accustomed to treating subordinates like machinery requiring control. Letting people take the initiative in defining and solving problems means that management needs to learn to support rather than control. Workers, for their part, need to learn to take responsibility.[53]
>
> —Ronald A. Heifetz and Donald L. Laurie,
> "The Work of Leadership"

Managers who use participative management are able to use the perspective and knowledge of others in their decision making, and thus the decisions made should be better. The amount of participation permitted varies from library to library, but the issues facing libraries and information centers are so complex and the need for specialized expertise so great that the trend toward shared decision making will likely continue.

Ethics

> Leadership requires courage, good communication skills and the ability to resolve ethical dilemmas. Determining what is right or ethical is one of the most difficult skills an individual must develop. But make no mistake, doing what is "right" is a requirement of effective leadership.[54]
>
> —Robert L. Morehouse,
> "Three Keys to Becoming a Leader"

An overview of ethics has been put in the chapter on leadership because research has shown that the leaders in any type of organization set the ethical tone of that organization. Ethics is part of the organizational climate that was discussed in chapter 5. According to Edgar Schein, organizational cultures "begin with leaders who impose their values and assumptions on the group," and in his view the attribute uniquely associated with leadership is the creation and management of culture.[55] An important dimension of any culture is its approach to ethics. The term *ethical climate* has been coined to describe "the shared perceptions of the *ethical* aspects of an organization's culture."[56]

Top managers serve as leaders within their organizations, and thus they are one of the prime influences in the ethical climate of the organization.[57] One study of more than 100 corporate managers found that 90 percent of them agreed that employee attitudes toward ethical issues directly mirrored executive beliefs.[58] Other researchers have found that the best single predictor of how employees handle ethical dilemmas is the perceived values of top management.[59] There have been numerous other studies that showed that top managers serve as ethical models. If the top managers in an organization routinely engage in questionable ethical principles, such as inflating expense accounts, taking supplies home for personal use, or revealing material that should be kept confidential, then others in the organization will consider those acceptable ways of behaving. It is important for any organization to be clear about its ethical expectations, and the individuals who most commonly act as role models in establishing those expectations are the organization's leaders. They provide guidance for the rest of the organization's employees in what is expected ethically.

Ethics can be defined as the set of principles and values that govern the behaviors of an individual or a group with respect to what is right and what is wrong. Individuals make decisions and act according to their beliefs about what they consider to be right or wrong. These actions and decisions take place both in and outside of the workplace. In this book, the discussion of ethics will be confined to business or managerial ethics, that is, the ethics that are found in the workplace. All though some individuals consider ethics in the workplace to be a frill or an add-on, ethics is an integral part of good business. Organizations that exploit the labor force, take advantage of customers, or deny product defects incur huge costs that ultimately hurt the organization. Consider the difference in ethical approach between the tobacco companies that attempted to cover up and deny the ill effects of nicotine and Johnson & Johnson, which voluntarily recalled all of its Tylenol products in an early product-tampering case. The tobacco companies have been devastated by the effects of the penalty costs imposed by the courts while Johnson & Johnson won widespread praise and customer loyalty by its ethical stand. Organizations that are well respected and profitable are almost always marked by good ethical practices.

> Another characteristic of great managers is integrity. All managers believe they behave with integrity, but in practice, many have trouble with the concept. Some think integrity is the same thing as secretiveness or blind loyalty. Others seem to believe it means consistency, even in a bad cause. Some confuse it with discretion and some with the opposite quality—bluntness— or with simply not telling lies. What integrity means in management is more ambitious and difficult than any of these. It means being responsible, of course, but it also means communicating clearly and consistently, being an honest broker, keeping promises, knowing oneself, and avoiding hidden agendas that hang other people out to dry. It comes very close to what we used to call honor, which in part means not telling lies to yourself.[60]
>
> —Thomas Teal,
> "The Human Side of Management"

Of course, individual employees sometimes act in opposition to the organizational norms. Each employee brings his or her individual ethical values to an organization. These values have been shaped in an individual's early years by parents, teachers, culture, and society, and they represent an individual's basic convictions about what is right and what is wrong. Because these individual values usually differ from person to person, any one organization can have individuals working in it with widely varying ethical values. Each employee, with his or her own values, is then exposed to the norms of the organization. Ideally, these norms would conform to the individual's values, but sometimes that is not the case. However, research has shown that an organization's ethical norms do have an impact on how employees act and their ideas of right and wrong within that organization. So employees' organizational values are influenced by the organization's ethical climate. Unethical actions within an organization "involve the tacit, if not explicit, cooperation of others and reflect the values, attitudes, beliefs, language and behavioral patterns that define an organization's operating culture. Ethics, then, is as much an organizational as a personal issue."[61] Thus it is the responsibility of managers to provide leadership in ethics because those "who fail to provide proper leadership and to institute systems that facilitate ethical conduct share responsibility with those who conceive, execute, and knowingly benefit from corporate misdeeds."[62]

In the past few years, ethics has become an increasingly important concern to all organizations. Many large organizations have been shown to have behaved in ways that were unethical. Not only did these unethical processes bring adverse publicity to the organization, but they caused great damage both to the organization and to people associated with that organization. The latest example of an organization whose unethical practices have caused immense harm is Enron; its corporate misdoings have caused a number of organizations to reexamine their own accounting practices. It has been said that one could teach an entire ethics course by using Enron as an example of what not to do. Although Enron was considered to be a "company of the future," it "sought to circumvent or avoid systems that were designed to protect the company and its shareholders and to bolster the credibility of its dealings."[63] Although no library has had an ethical scandal as immense as that at Enron, given the frequent occurrence of unethical and illegal behavior in highly respected organizations, it is critical to understand and to promote ethical conduct in all types of organizations, including libraries.

Problematic ethical situations often consist of a conflict between the needs of a part and the needs of the whole. These may be the conflicts between the needs of an individual employee and the organization as a whole or between the needs of an organization and society as a whole.

Another type of ethical dilemma often found in a professional situation is that of conflict of interest. A conflict of interest exists when an individual who has to make a job-related decision has an outside interest in the outcome that may influence the objective exercise of his or her duties. Usually these interests are financial, but sometimes they may be personal, for instance, when an individual hires as a summer intern the daughter of a friend instead of doing an objective job search to fill that position. Kenneth Kernaghan and John Langford list seven types of conflicts of interest. All of them might be confronted by librarians in the course of their official duties.

1. *Self-dealing*, which means using your position to your personal advantage. For instance, an example of self-dealing would be a librarian who uses his or her position to secure a contract for a private consulting firm that is partially owned by that librarian's spouse.

2. *Accepting benefits.* These are any benefits that might be thought to affect independent judgment. For instance, some libraries have policies against allowing collection development librarians to be entertained by vendors to avoid having any suggestion that a vendor selection decision might be influenced by accepting a certain vendor's hospitality.

3. *Influence peddling.* This consists of an individual soliciting benefits in exchange for unfairly advancing the interests of another party. For example, a librarian who is instrumental in the selection of a new automated system might be accused of influence peddling if he or she agreed to advocate for a particular system if that organization would offer him or her a part-time position.

4. *Using an employer's property for private advantage.* This could involve taking office supplies for home use or using software licensed to an employer for personal use.

5. *Using confidential information* involves using information that you become privy to as part of your position to your own advantage. Perhaps a reference librarian becomes aware of confidential information about a person by means of a reference interview and reveals that information in a way that advantages the librarian.

6. *Outside employment or moonlighting.* For example, a conflict of interest would arise if an employee spent so much time on his or her outside consulting job that the regular job was neglected.

7. *Post-employment* conflict of interest occurs when an employee uses knowledge or information gained in a position to benefit after leaving that position. Perhaps an employee in the library of a private corporation resigns and uses knowledge from the previous employment to compete directly with his or her former employer.[64]

Ethical Decision Making

When managers or employees are confronted with an ethical dilemma, what should they do? How should they think through the issue, and what factors should they consider?

Obviously, an important first step in analyzing any ethical issue is to get all the facts that are available. Sometimes individuals make wrong decisions because they are not aware of all of the facts concerning the case. But getting the facts is not enough. Facts give us information about a decision, but they do not tell us what should be done. There are a number of different approaches that people can use to deal with ethical issues.

Normative Ethical Frameworks

Philosophers have developed a number of different approaches to dealing with ethical issues, including the development of a variety of normative ethical frameworks that can be used for evaluating behavior. In brief, the most common frameworks are:

♦ Utilitarianism. Using this framework, an individual would behave in a way that produces the greatest good for the greatest number of people. For instance, a manager might decide to ban all smoking in the workplace because more employees benefited from this policy than were hurt by it.

♦ Individual rights. This is the framework that states that all individuals have inalienable rights, such as rights to privacy, freedom of speech, and due process, and that these rights should not be abridged. An employer might make the decision not to look at email logs because he or she considers that a violation of employees' privacy rights.

♦ Social justice. This approach holds that decisions must be based on standards that involve the fair treatment of all, fair application of rules, and fair compensation. For instance, the equal pay legislation discussed in chapter 10 ensures that both males and females doing the same job are compensated equally.[65]

These ethical frameworks give a manager a context to use in considering ethical problems and a means of identifying the most important ethical considerations, but they often do not provide clear-cut solutions. Instead, sometimes they provide different, often contradictory, answers to the problem. For instance, recently the North Carolina Museum of Art had to make a difficult choice about a painting that it had bought to be part of its permanent collection. After its purchase by the museum, this painting was found to have been stolen from its owner during World War II by the Nazis. The descendents of its previous owner asked the museum for restitution of the painting.[66] It could be argued using the utilitarian framework that the greatest good would be produced by leaving it in the museum where many visitors could see it on display. However, other arguments could be mounted using the other two frameworks, which would support the rights of the descendents of the owner from whom the painting was stolen. In this particular instance, a compromise was reached. The museum paid compensation to the owner's descendents for the painting, and it remained in the museum. Unfortunately, sometimes there are no real right and wrong answers in ethical situations, and compromises have to be made. The frameworks give managers a way of viewing ethical dilemmas and putting them in a broader perspective.

Codes of Ethics

Many organizations have codes of ethics designed to guide individuals within the organization in acting ethically. In addition to individual codes in specific organizations, many professional organizations have developed codes of ethics designed to guide individual conduct within a profession. Most large corporations in the United

States and many in other countries around the world have developed their own codes of ethics.[67] Many of these companies' codes of ethics are available on their websites. For instance, Boeing (see http://www.boeing.com/companyoffices/aboutus/ethics /integst.htm) and Johnson & Johnson (see http://www.jj.com/who_is_jnj/cr_usa.html) have their codes of ethics posted on their websites.

Fewer libraries have developed their own individual codes of ethics. Instead, most libraries have subscribed to a professional code of ethics. For example, the American Library Association has a code of ethics that can be seen in Figure 12.4. The Medical Library Association has also developed its own code of ethics (see http://www.mlahq.org /about/ethics.html). National libraries or librarians' associations around the world have developed professional codes of ethics. A large number of such professional codes can be seen at http://www.faife.dk/ethics/codes.htm. Links to other codes of ethics are available on this book's website.

The value of both institutional and professional codes of ethics depends on how they are used. If the importance of a particular code is taught to all employees, if top managers affirm such codes, and if individuals who go against the code are punished, codes can be important in shaping behavior. If such a code is used only as window dressing, it will be ineffective in providing a guide to ethical behavior.

> A code of ethics should enable a health sciences librarian to say, "This is what my profession says I should do. This code gives me the ethical standards I need to enable me to determine the right thing to do in my practice." A code will not tell you the specifics of practice, however. It cannot give you a specific answer in a specific situation. But, it will give you an ethical standard to which you can hold your question, your ethical dilemma, and your ethical difficulty, to help you decide how to act. Your conscience and your code should go hand in hand to help you determine how to practice your profession ethically.[68]
>
> —Richard A. Lyers,
> "Task Force Drafts Codes of Ethics"

Other Frameworks

Experts provide other frameworks, including a list of questions that individuals can use to assess whether they are confronting any problematic situation in an ethical way. For instance, questions such as the ones in Table 12.1 provide guidance to an individual trying to reach an ethical decision. Other managers use such guidelines as asking such questions as: Would you be proud to tell your parents or grandparents about the decision you have made? Are you able to sleep well at night? How would you feel if interviewers from your local television station showed up with cameras to ask about your actions? Questions like these may help to focus an individual's response to a perplexing problem. But ethical dilemmas are not easy; sometimes there are no readily apparent "correct" answers, or there is more than one approach that might be taken.

AMERICAN LIBRARY ASSOCIATION
CODE OF ETHICS

As members of the American Library Association, we recognize the importance of codifying and making known to the profession and to the general public the ethical principles that guide the work of librarians, other professionals providing information services, library trustees and library staffs.

Ethical dilemmas occur when values are in conflict. The American Library Association Code of Ethics states the values to which we are committed, and embodies the ethical responsibilities of the profession in this changing information environment.

We significantly influence or control the selection, organization, preservation, and dissemination of information. In a political system grounded in an informed citizenry we are members of a profession explicitly committed to intellectual freedom and the freedom of access to information. We have a special obligation to ensure the free flow of information and ideas to present and future generations.

The principles of this Code are expressed in broad statements to guide ethical decision making. These statements provide a framework; they cannot and do not dictate conduct to cover particular situations.

I. We provide the highest level of service to all library users through appropriate and usefully organized resources; equitable service policies; equitable access; and accurate, unbiased, and courteous responses to all requests.

II. We uphold the principles of intellectual freedom and resist all efforts to censor library resources.

III. We protect each library user's right to privacy and confidentiality with respect to information sought or received and resources consulted, borrowed, acquired or transmitted.

IV. We recognize and respect intellectual property rights.

V. We treat co-workers and other colleagues with respect, fairness and good faith, and advocate conditions of employment that safeguard the rights and welfare of all employees of our institutions.

VI. We do not advance private interests at the expense of library users, colleagues, or our employing institutions.

VII. We distinguish between our personal convictions and professional duties and do not allow our personal beliefs to interfere with fair representation of the aims of our institutions or the provision of access to their information resources.

VIII. We strive for excellence in the profession by maintaining and enhancing our own knowledge and skills, by encouraging the professional development of co-workers, and by fostering the aspirations of potential members of the profession.

Adopted by the ALA Council
June 28, 1995

Figure 12.4. The Code of Ethics of the American Library Association. Reprinted with permission.

Table 12.1. Questions for Examining the Ethics of a Business Decision

1. Has the problem been defined accurately?

2. Would you define the problem differently if you stood on the other side of the issue?

3. How did the situation occur in the first place?

4. To whom and to what do you give your loyalty as a person and as a member of the organization?

5. What is your intention in making this decision?

6. How does this intention compare with the likely results?

7. Whom might your decision or action injure?

8. Can you discuss the problem with the person or persons likely to be affected before you make the decision?

9. Are you confident that your decision will be just as valid over time as it seems now?

10. Could you disclose without qualms this decision to your boss, your CEO, your board of directors, your family, or to society as a whole?

11. What is the symbolic potential of your action if understood? If misunderstood?

12. Under what conditions would you allow exceptions to this decision?[69]

Ethics Training

Managers must realize that all of the ethical frameworks, codes, and question-asking approaches described previously are useless unless they are communicated to employees and employees are taught to use them. As was mentioned earlier, individuals have their own set of ethical guidelines, and these guidelines can differ a great deal even among employees who are largely homogeneous. As organizations employ a greater diversity of employees, it is important to remember that different cultures often have different beliefs about what is expected ethical behavior, and it can never be assumed that someone understands the ethical expectations of an organization without training. A number of institutions in the private sector have instituted ethics training programs to train employees about the ethical standards expected within the organization on topics varying from sexual harassment to insider stock trading. In addition, some have set up hotlines to allow employees to seek guidance or to report wrongdoings.[70] Although trying to teach people to behave ethically is not an easy thing to do, ethics training can be useful because it reinforces the organization's standards, and it reminds the employee that these standards are important to the organization.

Ethics is an important area, and it is often very complex because there are so many gray areas. Obviously, there are some topics, such as not physically harming another person, which would be agreed upon by almost everyone. But there are many other areas where ambiguity exists, and even people with the best of intentions will come up with two different approaches. A manager should demonstrate the importance of ethics by his or her own behavior, should be certain that appropriate codes of behavior are in place and that employees are informed of them, and should monitor the behavior of employees to be sure that they are complying. Managing ethically is not easy, but it is a responsibility of all managers to uphold high ethical standards within their organizations.

Conclusion

This chapter has looked at the broad topic of leadership, including a discussion of ethics within organizations. The next chapter will examine the topics of communication and some closely related topics, such as conflict resolution and team-building.

Notes

1.   Robert Goffee and Gareth Jones, "Why Should Anyone Be Led by You?" *Harvard Business Review* 78 (September–October, 2000): 64.

2.   "All in a Day's Work," *Harvard Business Review* 79 (December 2001): 55.

3.   Bernard M. Bass, *Bass and Stogdill's Handbook of Leadership*, 3d ed. (New York: Free Press, 1990).

4.   Goffee and Jones, "Why Should Anyone Be Led by You?" 63.

5.   Joseph C. Rost, *Leadership for the Twenty-First Century* (Westport, CT: Praeger, 1991), 44, 70.

6.   Robert G. Isaac, Wilfred J. Zerbe, and Douglas C. Pitt, "Leadership and Motivation: The Effective Application of Expectancy Theory," *Journal of Managerial Issues* 13 (Summer 2001): 213.

7.   Warren G. Bennis and Burt Nanus, *Leaders: The Strategies for Taking Charge* (New York: Harper & Row, 1985), 21.

8.   Fred A. Manske Jr., *Secrets of Effective Leadership*, 2d ed. (Columbia, TN: Leadership Education and Development, 1990), 7.

9.   For an illuminating discussion of the differences between management and leadership, see Joseph C. Rost, *Leadership for the Twenty-First Century* (Westport, CT: Praeger, 1991), 140–52.

10.   Warren Bennis, *Why Leaders Can't Lead* (San Francisco: Jossey-Bass, 1989), 17.

11. Ronald A. Heifetz and Donald L. Laurie, "The Work of Leadership," *Harvard Business Review* 75 (January–February 1997): 124–34.

12. Michael Maccoby, *The Leader* (New York: Simon & Schuster, 1981), 14.

13. Henry Steele Commanger, "Our Leadership Crisis: America's Real Malaise," *Los Angeles Times* (November 11, 1979): 1.

14. Manske, *Secrets of Effective Leadership*, 5.

15. Garry Wills, "What Makes a Good Leader?" *The Atlantic Monthly* 273 (April 1994): 70.

16. Robert Hogan, Gordon J. Curphy, and Joyce Hogan, "What We Know About Leadership: Effectiveness and Personality," *American Psychologist* 49 (June 1994): 493.

17. Goffee and Jones, "Why Should Anyone Be Led by You?" 63.

18. Warren Bennis, "The Leader as a Storyteller," *Harvard Business Review* 74 (January–February 1996): 156.

19. Ralph M. Stodgill, *Handbook of Leadership* (New York: Free Press, 1974).

20. Howard M. Carlisle, *Situational Management: A Contingency Approach to Leadership* (New York: AMACOM, 1973), 124.

21. Eugene E. Jennings, "The Anatomy of Leadership," *Management of Personnel Quarterly* 1 (Autumn 1961): 2.

22. Kurt Lewin and Ronald Lippitt, "An Experimental Approach to the Study of Autocracy and Democracy: A Preliminary Note," *Sociometry* 1 (1938): 292–300.

23. Kenneth E. Reid, *From Character Building to Social Treatment: The History of the Use of Groups in Social Work* (Westport, CT: Greenwood Press, 1981), 115.

24. Ralph M. Stodgill and Alvin E. Coons, eds., *Leader Behavior: Its Description and Measurement*, Research Monograph no. 887 (Columbus, OH: Bureau of Business Research, 1957).

25. Saul W. Gellerman, *The Management of Human Relations* (New York: Holt, Rinehart & Winston, 1966), 32.

26. Oren Harari, "Stop Empowering Your People," *Management Review* 86 (February 1997): 49.

27. Rensis Likert, *New Patterns of Management* (New York: McGraw-Hill, 1961).

28. Rensis Likert, *The Human Organization* (New York: McGraw-Hill, 1967), 4–10.

29. Robert R. Blake and Jane S. Mouton, *The Managerial Grid* (Houston, TX: Gulf, 1964).

30. *Ibid.*, 9.

31. *Ibid.*, 9–11.

32. Robert R. Blake and Jane S. Mouton, *The Managerial Grid III* (Houston, TX: Gulf, 1985), 18.

33. James McGregor Burns, *Leadership* (New York: Harper & Row, 1978).

34. J. B. Rosener, "Ways Women Lead," *Harvard Business Review* 68 (1990): 120.

35. Bernard M. Bass, "Does the Transactional-Transformational Leadership Paradigm Transcend Organizational and National Boundaries?" *American Psychologist* 52 (February 1997): 130–39.

36.   Joseph Seltzer and Bernard M. Bass, "Transformational Leadership: Beyond Initiation and Consideration," *Journal of Management* 16 (December 1990): 693–703.

37.   See, for instance, A. L. Geyer and J. M. Steyrer. "Transformational Leadership and Objective Performance in Banks," *Applied Psychology: An International Review* 47 (July 1998): 397–420.

38.   Badrinarayan S. Pawar and Kenneth K. Eastman, "The Nature and Implication of Contextual Influences on Transformational Leadership: A Conceptual Examination," *The Academy of Management Review* 22 (January 1997): 80–109.

39.   Fred E. Fiedler, "A Contingency Model of Leadership Effectiveness," in L. Berkowitz, ed., *Advances in Experimental Social Psychology*, vol. 1 (New York: Academic Press, 1964), 165.

40.   Robert J. House, "A Path-Goal Theory of Leader Effectiveness," *Administrative Science Quarterly* 16 (September 1971): 321–38.

41.   *Ibid.*, 324.

42.   Alan C. Filley, Robert J. House, and Steven Kerr, *Managerial Process and Organizational Behavior* (Glenview, IL: Scott, Foresman, 1976).

43.   See, for example, J. C. Wofford and L. Z. Liska, "Path-Goal Theories of Leadership: A Meta-analysis," *Journal of Management* (Winter 1993): 857–76; and A. Sagie and M. Koslowsky, "Organizational Attitudes and Behaviors as a Function of Participation in Strategic and Tactical Change Decisions: An Application of Path-Goal Theory," *Journal of Organizational Behavior* (January 1994): 37–47.

44.   Nigel Nicholson, *Managing the Human Animal* (London: Texere, 2000), 115–16.

45.   Bennis, *Why Leaders Can't Lead*, 144.

46.   Herbert S. White, "Oh, Where Have All the Leaders Gone?" *Library Journal* 112 (October 1987): 68–69.

47.   Peter M. Senge, "Communities of Leaders and Learners," *Harvard Business Review* 75 (September–October 1997): 32.

48.   Daryl R. Conner, *Managing at the Speed of Change: How Resilient Managers Succeed and Prosper Where Others Fail* (New York: Villard Books, 1993), 198.

49.   *Ibid.*

50.   Maurice B. Line and Margaret Kinnell, "Human Resource Management in Library and Information Services," in Martha E. Williams, ed., *Annual Review of Information Science and Technology*, vol. 28 (Medford, NJ: Learned Information, 1993), 333.

51.   Nicholas C. Burckel, "Participatory Management in Academic Libraries: A Review," *College & Research Libraries* 45 (January 1984): 32.

52.   Conner, *Managing at the Speed of Change*.

53.   Ronald A. Heifetz and Donald L. Laurie, "The Work of Leadership," *Harvard Business Review* 75 (January–February 1997): 129.

54.   Robert L. Morehouse, "Three Keys to Becoming a Leader," *HR Magazine* 42 (November 1997): 53.

55.   Edgar H. Schein, *Organizational Culture and Leadership*, 2d ed. (San Francisco: Jossey-Bass, 1992), 1.

56.   Dennis Wittmer and David Coursey. "Ethical Work Climates: Comparing Top Managers in Public and Private Organizations," *Journal of Public Administration Research and Theory* 6 (October 1996): 560.

57. See, for instance, Robert Jackyll, "Moral Mazes: Bureaucracy and Managerial Work," *Harvard Business Review* 61 (September–October 1983): 118–30.

58. Marshall B. Clinard, *Corporate Ethics and Crime* (London: Sage, 1983).

59. Shelby D. Hunt, Lawrence B. Chonko, and James B. Wilcox, "Ethical Problems of Marketing Researchers," *Journal of Marketing Research* 21 (1984): 304–24.

60. Thomas Teal, "The Human Side of Management," *Harvard Business Review* 74 (November–December 1996): 37.

61. Lynn Sharp Paine, "Managing for Organizational Integrity," *Harvard Business Review* 72 (March–April 1994): 106.

62. *Ibid.*

63. Ronald Berenbeim, "Enron's Syllabus of Errors: A Primer on Ethics," *Directorship* (March 2002): 8.

64. Kenneth Kernaghan and John W. Langford, *The Responsible Public Servant* (Halifax, NS: Institute for Research in Public Policy, 1990).

65. Gerald Cavanaugh, Dennis J. Moberg, and Manuel Velaquez, "The Ethics of Organizational Politics," *Academy of Management Review* 6 (1981): 363–74.

66. Emily Yellen, "North Carolina Art Museum Says It Will Return Painting Tied to Nazi Theft," *New York Times* 6 (February 2000): 22.

67. Gary R. Weaver, Linda K. Trevino, and P. L.Cochran, "Corporate Ethics Practices in the Mid-1990s," *Journal of Business Ethics* 18 (1999): 283–94.

68. Richard A. Lyers, "Task Force Drafts Codes of Ethics" (March 1994). The code and the explanation can be seen at the MLA website (http://www.mlanet.org/about/ethics2.html).

69. L. L. Nash, "Ethics Without the Sermon," *Harvard Business Review* 58 (November–December 1981): 81.

70. M. J. McCarthy, "How One Firm Tracks Ethics Electronically," *The Wall Street Journal* (October 21, 1999): 81.

Chapter 13

Communication and Related Topics

*The genius of humans is most striking in speech and under-
standing. More than anything else, our gift of language is
what sets us apart from all other known life-forms. It is what
enables us to plan, achieve, reflect, and share our experience.
So if we are born communicators, then how come we do it so
badly in business? Of all the failings of organizations, poor
communication is the most common.*[1]

—Nigel Nicholson,
Managing the Human Animal

Communication is a key ingredient in effective leadership. Since 1938, when
Chester Barnard identified the main task of an executive as that of communication, it
has been commonly accepted that communication is a critical skill for any manager.
Barnard viewed communication as the means by which people are linked together in
an organization in order to achieve a central purpose.[2] Most managers spend a large
part of their time communicating with other people; some estimates of the percentage
of time a manager spends in communication range as high as 95 percent. In his study
of managerial behavior, Henry Mintzberg found that most managerial time was spent
in verbal communication, on the telephone, and in meetings.[3]

Communication in organizations is more varied today than ever before because
so many new communication options are available. Electronic mail, voice mail, instant
messaging, and teleconferencing provide new channels of communication for organizations to use both internally and externally. These methods have helped to minimize
the effects of time and distance, which slow down the communication process. In
knowledge organizations, such as libraries and information centers, communication is the

lifeblood of the organization. Employees in such organizations are constantly involved in the absorption and dissemination of information and ideas. In fact, sometimes people working in information agencies feel that there is so much communication available through so many channels that it leads to information overload and confusion. Many employees receive more information than they can assimilate.

In some ways it seems that communication should be simple. We all communicate every day, and we have all been doing it since we learned to talk (actually before we learned to talk). But what at first glance seems simple is actually quite complex. It is a process composed of many factors. A number of models of the communication process have been developed to help explicate it. Although these models vary, they typically include the following components:

- A *source*. This is the sender of the message. The source has some thought, need, or information to communicate.

- A *message*. The source has to encode the message in some form that can be understood by both sender and receiver.

- The *channel*. The channel is the link between the source and the receiver. The message is transmitted over the channel. A channel can take many forms. For instance, a telephone is an example of a channel that can be used to link the source and the receiver.

- The *receiver*. The receiver is the recipient of the message. The receiver has to decode the message for it to be understood.

- *Noise*. Noise is anything that hinders communication. Noise may occur in the source, the message, the channel, or the receiver. For instance, if the receiver cannot understand the message, noise has occurred. This could be because the message contained ambiguous phrases, because there was static on the channel, or because the message was in a language not understood by the receiver. Even the simplest communication is filled with opportunities for noise to occur.

- *Feedback*. After the receiver receives and decodes the message, the receiver can become a source and provide feedback by encoding and sending a message through some channel back to the original source. Feedback is a response to the original message. Feedback is always useful because it allows the original source to know if the message was properly encoded, transmitted, decoded, and understood. It is this feedback loop that is the difference between one-way and two-way communication. One-way communication is almost never as effective as two-way communication because the sender has no way of knowing if the message was received and understood.

To illustrate this model, imagine a library director wanting to let a department head know about an important meeting. The library director would be the source of the communication. When the library director provided information about the meeting in the form of a written memo, the written memo would be the message. The channel employed for the communication would be the interorganizational mail system. The receiver is the department head who receives the message and reads it. If the interorganizational mail carrier lost the memo, or if the memo had been mutilated in transit that would have been noise. The feedback would be the response the department head sends the library director about the meeting. The elements in this simple communication model are illustrated in Figure 13.1.

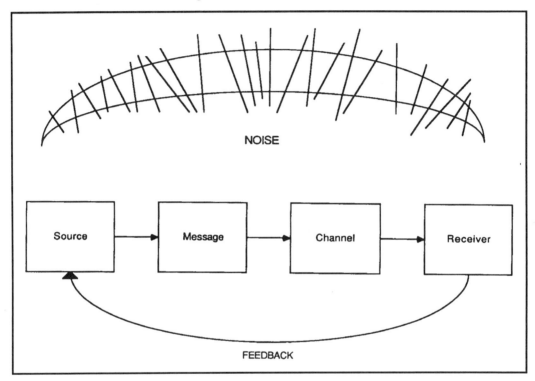

Figure 13.1. A Model of the Communication Process

Communication exists in many forms and in many settings. Often, we think of communication primarily in terms of personal communication. However, every organization must have some way to bind its disparate parts together if it is to achieve its goals and purposes. Communication provides cohesiveness and direction. As Alex Bavels and Dermot Barrett state, "It is entirely possible to view an organization as an elaborate system for gathering, evaluating, recombining, and disseminating information. . . . Communication is not a secondary or derived aspect of an organization—a 'helper' of the other and presumably more basic functions. Rather, it is the essence of organized activity and the basic process out of which all other functions derive."[4] Communication is so important that Peter Drucker has argued that organizations should not be built around hierarchies but around communication.[5] Communication is the process that makes it possible to unify organizational activity.

This chapter will provide an overview of organizational communication, look-ing first at communication as a function within an organization and then discussing two topics closely related to communication: conflict and team-building. The chapter will close with a discussion of the contingency approach to management.

Organizational Communication

Organizational communication has been defined by Gerald Goldhaber as "the process of creating and exchanging messages within a network of interdependent rela-tionships to cope with environmental uncertainty."[6] All organizational communication shares certain characteristics. It occurs within a complex, open system that is influenced by and influences its environment; it involves messages and their flow, purpose, direction, and media; and it involves people and their attitudes, feelings, relationships, and skills.[7]

> Some days it seems that no matter what the problem or issue may be, someone will inevitably say, "It's just a communication problem." It would seem that if we could only communicate better, all problems would disappear.[8]
>
> —Joan Giesecke,
> *Practical Strategies for Library Managers*

Managers should never assume that all workers will understand the messages they communicate. This is especially important to remember as the workforce becomes more diversified. Studies have shown that various ethnic groups and that men and women have different styles of communication. Deborah Tannen has studied gender differences in communication and finds that men's and women's styles vary greatly. She attributes this to different values assimilated by young girls and boys. Males are taught to prize status, independence, and individual power, but females are taught to value connection, interdependence, and the power of community. These differing values lead men and women to communicate in different ways. The resulting differences in the communication styles of men and women can cause misunderstanding in the workplace.[9]

Different ethnic groups also have different styles of communication. For example, in some cultures, it is considered rude to maintain eye contact with someone while they are speaking. Some cultures encourage interruption. Every communication practice is based on certain cultural rules, and as our workplaces become more diversified, managers need to understand the cultural differences that may affect communication flows. Just because two people share a common language does not mean that they can easily com-municate. These differences are often more than linguistic and instead are frequently socio-political-attitudinal in nature. Everyone should try to be aware of the cultural biases that may impede his or her communication and interactions with others.[10]

The difficulty of getting heard can be experienced by any individuals who are not as tenacious as others about standing their ground, do not speak as forcefully at meetings, or do not begin with a high level of credibility, as a result of rank, regional or ethnic style differences, or just personality, regardless of whether they are female or male. Whoever is more committed to compromise and achieving consensus, and less comfortable with contention, is more likely to give way.[11]

—Deborah Tannen,
Talking from 9 to 5

Another barrier that sometimes gets in the way of communication is the use of jargon. Jargon is the specialized language that is developed by individuals in groups, and each profession tends to have its own jargon. That is certainly true of librarianship. Think of all the acronyms and technical terms that are associated with the LIS profession. AACR2, ACRL, ARL, ALA, AASL, ASIS&T, ASCII, ALCS, abstracts, acquisitions, accessions, and authority control are just a few of the ones that begin with the letter "a." Even within the profession, not every individual understands all of these terms, and when librarians begin to communicate with nonlibrarians, it is not surprising that the nonlibrarians are often completely befuddled. Using the language of the communication model presented earlier, it is easy for anyone who understands the jargon to encode it in a message, but it is much more difficult for receivers to decode if they are not familiar with the jargon. Because jargon has the potential of creating "noise," it should be avoided unless it is absolutely certain that the receiver will understand it.

Types of Communication

Communication can be classified in three general categories: written, oral, and nonverbal. Each of these types of communication plays a specific role in organizational communication, and each has certain associated advantages and disadvantages.

Written Communication

Formal channels of command often require written communication. Managers write memos, letters, reports, directives, and policies. Written communication provides a lasting record and ensures uniformity in matters like policy. But written communications often have many problems. Some of these communications may be poorly written and may not fully explain the action desired or completely define the scope of the problem. Employees may be left with ambiguous instructions. Words used in written communications are frequently unclear and ill defined, and written communication allows no opportunity for immediate feedback and clarification. Hence, it may take a long time to know if the message has been received and understood.

Many organizations have tried to improve their written communication, especially their communication with customers. Organizations are urged to scrutinize their written communication to "see if they have value-added components and eliminated fillers and gobbledygook that dilute our purpose and waste the recipient's time."[12]

Electronic mail is a new type of written communication that has become "as common as the sticky note in organizations around the world."[13] It is estimated that 1.3 trillion email messages are being sent annually.[14] Organizations of every sort are connecting people to networks that permit the sending of email both internally and externally. Email in organizations presents a special set of opportunities and problems. Although email is considered "written" communication, it is generally not viewed as being as formal as a paper copy of a letter or a memorandum. It is very convenient for the sender, it speeds the delivery of information, and it can be relatively inexpensive in providing wide distribution of messages for little cost.

Email presents its own set of communication difficulties, however. It has grown as a method of communication faster than rules governing its use. There are established codes of manners concerning face-to-face or telephone communication. No such niceties exist in the email world where it is "frighteningly easy to get into conflicts and misunderstandings with people" because of the "generally hasty, ill-considered and uncrafted nature of electronic communication."[15]

Users are often surprised to learn that email is not necessarily private or completely destroyed when they press the delete key. Just as organizations usually have policies relating to the use of telephones, fax machines, and mail, there should be policies in place concerning the appropriate use of email and corporate practices toward its retention and preservation.[16] And with all such policies, these should be shared with employees.

> As e-mail-communication continues to dominate the business world, it is more important than ever for employers to keep tabs on employee e-mail messages. Not doing so could leave the organization in the midst of legal troubles. In today's electronic age, smart companies will enact and enforce an e-mail usage policy and educate employees and managers as to its purpose and use. It's one measure that could keep your employees safe from inappropriate communications and could save your company millions of dollars in potential lawsuits.[17]
>
> —Patricia S. Eyres,
> "Avoiding Costly E-Mail Disasters"

Oral Communication

Oral communication, conducted through individuals or groups, is usually considered to be the richest communication medium, but it also has problems. Not all oral messages are clearly stated. There remains the problem of the ambiguous or misunderstood word. But in oral communication there is opportunity for feedback through which clarification can be accomplished. Face-to-face oral communication also provides an opportunity for nonverbal communication to help amplify a message. Oral communication often is the best way to resolve conflict situations. On the other hand, oral communication can be time-consuming, especially when many people need to be individually told about something. And unlike written communication, oral statements are not preserved.

Nonverbal Communication

Nonverbal communication is any type of communication that is not spoken or written. Nonverbal communication often consists of various types of body language—for instance, facial cues, hand or arm gestures, or posture. Nonverbal cues are also provided by things such as dress and the positioning of furniture in an office. Nonverbal communication can provide many clues to an observer; as the old saying goes, actions speak louder than words. Some examples of nonverbal communication include:

♦ avoiding eye contact;

♦ a steady stare;

♦ crossing your arms in front of your chest;

♦ perspiring;

♦ sighing;

♦ biting your lips; and

♦ rubbing the back of your head or neck.[18]

Nonverbal communication can contradict, supplement, substitute for, or complement verbal communication. A manager must be especially careful that nonverbal signals do not contradict verbal ones. For instance, consider a supervisor who claims to have an open-door policy and who encourages employees to come to him to discuss any problems that they may encounter. Imagine the nonverbal message that is sent if when an employee enters the supervisor's office to discuss a problem, he or she finds that the supervisor continues to work, does not look up, and fails to establish any type of eye contact with that employee. The supervisor's verbal invitation to feel free to come in to discuss problems is contradicted by the powerful nonverbal message encountered when the employee accepts the invitation. Nonverbal behavior, although sometimes overlooked, is vital to the process of communication. Anytime people communicate using non-face-to-face methods such as fax or email, they do not have the benefit of nonverbal communication, and hence misunderstandings sometime occur.

Different types of communication have different advantages and disadvantages. The truly good communicator knows to pick the right communication channel or medium with which to communicate. Different media vary in degree of richness; information richness is defined as the information-carrying capacity of an item of data. A rich medium is one that conveys a great deal of information, whereas a lean medium is one that conveys the bare minimum.[19] Figure 13.2 shows a classification of different types of communication media according to their richness. Face-to-face communication is the richest in terms of information conveyed because it relies on multiple channels (for instance, words, body language, facial gestures) to reinforce the message. In addition, face-to-face communication provides an opportunity for immediate feedback.

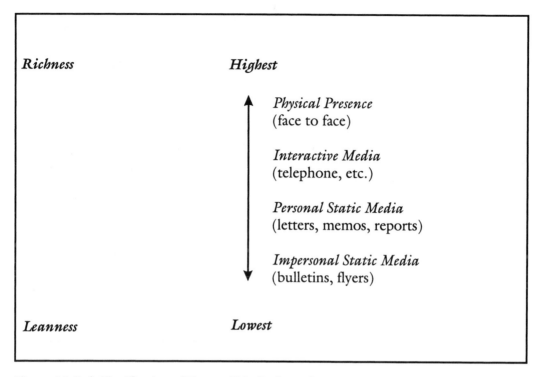

Figure 13.2. A Classification of Types of Media According to Their Communication Richness

According to Lengel and Daft, the most important thing for managers to remember in terms of matching media richness to communication needs is to use richer media for nonroutine messages and to use leaner media for routine, simple messages.[20] Complex, highly important messages should be communicated by information-rich media to be sure that the issues are clearly understood, but it is likely a waste of time to use information-rich media to convey routine messages. For instance, a supervisor would never want to tell an individual that he or she was being disciplined through a memo, but such a memo would be perfectly appropriate to use to tell a subordinate the dates of a trip out of town.

Communication Flows

Within an organization, communication flows in three directions: down, up, and horizontally.

Downward Communication

Downward communication, or communication that flows from superiors to subordinates, is the most common type of communication within the organization. The five most common types of downward communication are: specific job directives or job instruction; information designed to produce understanding of the task and the relationship to other organizational tasks, or job rationale; information about organizational procedures and practices; feedback to the subordinate about performance; and information of an ideological character to inculcate a sense of mission, or indoctrination of goals.[21]

Although employees expect to receive communication from managers, problems are often associated with downward communication in an organization. The first is that organizations rely too heavily on written or mechanical methods, such as manuals, booklets, memoranda, and newsletters, to diffuse downward communication, even when personal contact and face-to-face communication might be more effective. Second, many organizations suffer from message overload. Because of the ease of sending messages via email and by photocopied documents, some employees are overburdened with memos, bulletins, letters, announcements, and policy statements. Many employees who are inundated with too many messages respond by not reading any of the communications at all. Communication can also be hampered by poor timing. Managers should consider the timing of any communication to be sure it is advantageous for both management and employees. Finally, there is always the problem of filtering of information. Because downward communication usually goes through several layers in an organization, messages may be changed, shortened, or lengthened, and some employees may not receive a message at all. For these reasons, downward communication in many organizations is relatively inefficient.[22]

Upward Communication

Upward communication consists of messages that flow from subordinates to superiors. Most of these messages ask questions, provide feedback, or make suggestions. An organization that is inhospitable to upward communication inhibits such communication, despite the fact that upward communication is essential to an organization's effectiveness. Even in organizations that pride themselves on their open-door policy, it is not uncommon to find employees who are afraid to take information to their superiors, especially when that information concerns problems or bad news. Employees are more likely to send upward messages that enhance their own status or credibility and are much less likely to send up messages that make them look bad.

> In the vast majority of companies, if workers know that what they say will be passed along to management with their names attached, they won't speak (or write) their minds. It is the rare organization that is so attuned to its people and so trusted by them that employees feel comfortable telling the whole truth. Besides, compensation for many managers today is partly based on group performance; there can be pressures on team members to be positive. Herein lies the challenge for companies: How can organizations get the kind of unfiltered and vital information critical to their operations—even, perhaps to their survival?[23]
>
> —Barbara Ettorre,
> "The Unvarnished Truth"

Davis points out that it takes a certain amount of courage for workers, especially lower-level workers, to approach their supervisors. "A manager often does not realize how great the upward communication barrier can be especially for blue-collar workers."[24] A manager has status and prestige, often talks and dresses differently from lower-status workers, and has more practice in communication skills. The worker is further impeded because he or she is usually not familiar with the work or the responsibilities of the manager. For that reason, there is often little upward communication in an organization unless the manager encourages it.[25]

Managers who want to benefit from the flow of upward communication should be sensitive to the barriers that can be placed in the way of such communications. If managers want to remove some of the barriers, they must be sympathetic listeners and make a practice of encouraging informal contacts with workers. Some methods commonly used to achieve upward communication include grievance procedures, suggestion systems, focus groups, hotlines, group meetings, opinion surveys, and informal meetings between the manager and workers. In addition, managers should remember that the same sort of filtering and misinterpreting that is found in downward communication is also prevalent in upward communication.

Horizontal Communication

Horizontal communication is the lateral or diagonal exchange of information within an organization; it typically fulfills the following purposes: task coordination, problem-solving, information sharing, and conflict resolution. In today's flatter, team-based organizations, horizontal communication is more important than it ever was in the past. This type of communication may occur within or across departments.

Several factors tend to limit horizontal communication within organizations. Information is not always shared in competitive organizations because the employee who possesses the information wants to retain a competitive advantage over others. Specialization also impedes horizontal communication. Most organizations are subdivided into specialized subunits, and members of these subunits may want to further their own subunit's goals rather than communicate with other managers on the same level in order to advance company goals. In addition, excessive specialization may make it difficult for members of one subunit to speak the language of another; even if they were willing to exchange information, they might find it difficult to bridge the horizontal communications gap. Finally, horizontal communication often does not take place because managers have not encouraged frequent horizontal communication nor have they rewarded those who engage in such practices.

Because horizontal communication does not follow the chain of command, precautions must be taken to prevent potential problems. This type of communication should rest on the understanding that these relationships will be encouraged when they are appropriate, subordinates will refrain from making commitments beyond their authority, and subordinates will keep superiors informed of important interdepartmental activities. Although horizontal communication may create some difficulties, it is essential in most organizations to respond to the needs of a complex and dynamic environment. As organizations grow more dependent on a team approach to work, the importance of lateral communication increases.

> Central to the evolution of flatter, customer-focused, dynamic organizations is the availability of information within the organization. The traditional movement of information within an organization was based on models derived from a strong hierarchical orientation and from cost constraints that made it very expensive to move information throughout the organization. The availability of information technology and information "highways" now makes it feasible to move information relatively cheaply in multiple directions throughout an organization.[26]
>
> —Jay Galbraith et al.,
> *Organizing for the Future*

Much horizontal flow of information takes place in meetings. Some employees spend a great deal of their time in meetings; often these meetings are frustrating and ineffective because they are poorly planned and conceived. Managers at all levels should try to develop the skills and understanding about how to make meetings successful.[27]

Changing Flows of Communication

There is some indication that new channels of communication, such as email, may be changing the flow of communication within the organization. As John Seely Brown explains:

> Email plays quite a different role than it did five years ago. Email has started to seriously change hierarchy. It keeps you more aware of the edge of what's happening in your company. You can sense the heartbeat of the organization when you skim the messages. It's like reading body language.[28]

Because it is more informal than a letter and less threatening than face-to-face conversation, some workers send electronic mail not only to workers on their own level but upward in the organization, to immediate supervisors and to managers even higher up in the organizational structure. Some employees are using email messages or websites to raise complaints publicly against organizations and their practices.[29] As Robert Zmud has stated, "Traditionally, an organization member's zone of influence has been limited by a number of constraints, most of which reflect task design, authority relationships, and physical, geographic, and temporal boundaries. New information technologies are relaxing many, if not most, of these constraints."[30] Just as the telephone revolutionized organizational communication, the new communication media will bring vast changes to how employees within organizations communicate with each other and the outside world. There is evidence that effective communication through computer-mediated channels may be a unique skill that needs to be developed and that "even experienced email users will not necessarily be able to communicate richly with a new partner, or about a new topic, or within a new organizational context, without first developing these unique knowledge bases."[31] More research needs to be done to discover how new communication media such as email, voice mail, and teleconferencing are affecting organizational communication.

Informal Organizational Communication

Most of what has been discussed so far concerns the formal communication channels within an organization. These are the message channels that follow the official path directed by the organizational hierarchy. But every organization also has an informal communication system. Two of the most common of these are the "grapevine" and the activity often referred to as "managing by walking around." Although informal channels are neither as predictable nor as neatly designed as those of the formal communication structure, they are remarkably efficient at moving information.

The Grapevine

Every organization has an informal communication network commonly termed the grapevine. The grapevine "moves upward, downward, and diagonally, within and without chains of command, between workers and managers, and even within and without a company."[32] Studies of the grapevine have shown that this means of communication is fairly accurate, with more than 75 percent of the messages being transmitted correctly.[33] In addition, the grapevine is usually much faster at moving information than are formal channels. However, nearly all of the information within the grapevine is undocumented and thus is open to change and interpretation as it moves through the network.

> The grapevine grows most vigorously in organizations where secrecy, poor communication by management, and autocratic leadership behaviors are found.[34]
>
> —Paul Hersey, Kenneth Blanchard, and Dewey Johnson,
> *Management of Organizational Behavior*

Although the grapevine can sometimes cause trouble, this informal communication channel is endemic in all organizations. Managers are not able to destroy the grapevine because it serves an essential human need for information. Given the existence of the grapevine, a manager's task is to make it contribute to the accomplishment of the organization's objectives. Managers can do this by using the grapevine, either personally or through trusted staff members. It can be very useful in supplementing formal channels. A manager who wants to relay information can feed the grapevine accurate information, which will be transmitted quickly throughout the organization. In addition, the manager should be aware of the messages that circulate on the grapevine. If managers are able to find out what employees are talking about via the grapevine, they may be able to intercept and correct misleading rumors that could damage morale. Thus, intelligent managers admit the existence of the grapevine and use it to their advantage.

The grapevine can be curtailed somewhat by clear, concise, timely, and complete communication through formal communication channels. Rumors often arise because workers are anxious about some situation about which they have received little or no information. Fewer rumors would circulate on the grapevine if managers would provide sufficient information about issues of interest and concern to workers.

Managing by Walking Around

Another good way for managers to supplement information gotten from formal channels of communication is for the managers to get out of their offices, walk around the organization, and spend some time with employees. This means of ensuring informal communication is usually referred to as "managing by walking around" or MBWA. Just as managers should be aware of what is being circulated on the grapevine, they should also be aware of what is going on in parts of the organization away from their offices.

Managers need to make themselves visible and to spend time getting a general feel for what is going on throughout the organization. The best managers spend a part of their time visiting employees in their work locations. Whether it is walking through the catalog department, visiting the mailroom, or talking to shelvers as they do their job, a manager finds out things about the library that he or she would never know without emerging from the office on a periodic basis. Most workers are flattered when top administrators come to their work area and speak with them. It makes them feel significant. As Robert Goffee and Gareth Jones have written, "Followers will give their hearts and souls to authority figures who say, 'You really matter,' no matter how small the followers' contributions may be."[35] The most highly regarded managers are those who are able to communicate to their employees that they are interested in them and in what they are doing. MBWA is a proven way to allow managers and workers to communicate on an informal basis, and because it is done on the employee's turf instead of in the manager's office, it provides a different dimension to organizational communication.

In summary, both formal and informal communication is critical to organizations. Managers should pay close attention to the communication within an organization in an attempt to make it as open and free from distortion as possible. Managers should always be trying to improve their communication skills. Twenty tips for good communication can be seen in Table 13.1.

Table 13.1. Twenty Ways to Communicate with Your Employees

1. Include affected employees in goal setting.

2. Give frequent and meaningful recognition for a job well done.

3. Interact with employees on an informal basis.

4. Go to employees' work areas. Meet them on their own turf.

5. Ask for workers' opinions and listen with an open mind. Try to understand their point of view.

6. Share nonconfidential information with employees, and ask for their input and response on issues.

7. Offset demoralizing actions and events by emphasizing what went well, and use the experience as a learning opportunity.

8. Listen 80 percent of the time, and talk 20 percent.

9. Ask employees what rumors they have heard, and address them.

10. Get into the "trenches" with employees. Look for opportunities to understand employees' jobs better.

11. Give information to employees after management meetings.

12. Ask employees, "Have I made our vision, mission, and goals clear and understandable?"

13. Ask employees, "What can I do to help you with your job, and what am I doing that gets in your way?"

14. Ask employees, "What is making our clients/customers the most and/or the least satisfied?"

15. Praise in public, and give feedback in private.

16. Find something to like about each staff member with whom you work.

17. Actively make a point of speaking to all employees whom you see in a day.

18. Build bridges with people with whom you are uncomfortable.

19. Set goals each month on ways to accomplish "Managing by Walking Around."

20. Occasionally have lunch with staff members. Use this as an opportunity to build trust.[36]

Adapted from a "Checklist for Managers" by Robin Reid

Conflict

One of the common results of poor communication is conflict. Conflict situations often arise from problems in communication. One person may misunderstand another. Someone may have said something that he or she really didn't mean to say. Or someone may have missed a message that was supposed to be sent. Communication or miscommunication often leads to conflict. Then once conflict exists, people cease to talk to one another, which exacerbates the conflict. Good communication skills are an important part of preventing and resolving conflicts.

Some managers will do almost anything to try to avoid conflicts within the units they manage. Some even feel that the mere existence of conflict is a reflection on their ability to manage. This is not so. Conflict is not bad in itself, and it may result in either positive or negative outcomes. Although uncontrolled conflict can be detrimental to an organization and its employees, properly managed conflict can often be helpful.

Managers who feel that they spend a great deal of time trying to resolve conflict situations are probably correct. One study showed that managers reported spending up to twenty percent of their time dealing with conflict and its impact.[37] Another study showed that forty-two percent of a manager's time is spent on reaching agreement with others after conflicts occur.[38]

> Top managers are often stymied by the difficulties of managing conflict. They know that conflict over issues is natural and even necessary. Reasonable people, making decisions under conditions of uncertainty, are likely to have honest disagreements over the best path for their company's future. Management teams whose members challenge one another's thinking develop a more complete understanding of the choices, create a richer range of options, and ultimately make the kinds of effective decisions necessary in today's competitive environments.[39]
>
> —Kathleen M Eisenhardt et al.,
> "How Management Teams Can Have a Good Fight"

Conflict is usually characterized as being interpersonal or intergroup. Interpersonal conflict, conflict between two people, is often the result of incompatible personalities or different values or points of view. Intergroup conflict, conflict between groups of employees, can be caused by a number of factors within organizations and often arises as a result of competition over scarce resources. Both interpersonal and intergroup conflicts are often heightened by poor communication.

People react to conflict situations in different ways. Research has identified five primary styles of handling conflict: avoiding, compromising, competing, accommodating, and collaborating. Avoiders try to prevent conflict; usually they suppress their feelings and withdraw from conflict situations. Compromisers try to seek a solution that satisfies both parties; they are willing to split differences down the middle. Competitors seek to dominate and impose their viewpoints. Accommodators almost always give in to opposition and acquiesce to the demands of others. Collaborators try to work to find a mutually satisfactory outcome for all parties.[40] These approaches are affected by how assertive and how cooperative individuals are. These different styles are illustrated in Figure 13.2; although the figure shows five discrete positions, it is possible for an individual's orientation on conflict to fall anywhere on the diagram.

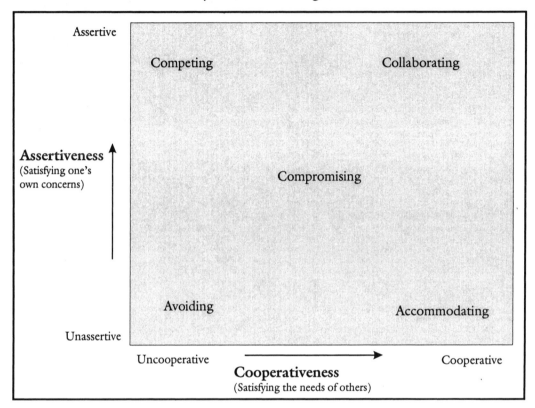

Figure 13.3. Five Styles of Handling Conflict (adapted from Thomas, "Conflict and Conflict Management")

Of the five styles, the collaborative one is generally considered best because it leads to a result that is usually described as a "win-win" outcome. This type of outcome occurs when all parties perceive that they have emerged from the conflict in a better position than before. For instance, if two employees were in conflict about the scheduling of weekend and evening hours, it is possible that you might end up with a win-win situation if you discovered that one really didn't mind working weekend hours, and the other really didn't mind working evenings, and thus you were able to arrange their schedules to conform with their preferences. Although win-win solutions are not possible in all cases, managers who are skilled as negotiators are often able to deal effectively with conflict by arriving at solutions that make all parties feel that they have come out ahead.

Results of Conflict

Organizational conflict can have both negative and positive effects. The more negative effects are usually thought of first. Working in an environment with a great deal of conflict can lead to stress and divert employees' attention from the work that has to be done. The morale of employees often suffers, as well as their motivation to perform well. In cases of extreme conflict, workers have been known to disparage or even sabotage the work of others. Conflict between departments can cause groups to close ranks and hamper cooperation. Unmanaged and unresolved conflict is a destructive force. It can destroy relationships, decrease productivity and quality of work, break down communication, and make people feel at odds with others in the group or organization.

On the other hand, sometimes conflict plays a useful role. Conflict can bring previously hidden problems to light so that solutions may be sought. Conflict is considered essential to innovation. If everyone thinks the same thing, changes will not occur. Innovation "takes place when different ideas, perceptions, and ways of processing and judging information collide."[41] At Microsoft, one of the most innovative U.S. corporations, the chair, Bill Gates, advocates a management style called "armed truce" because employees are encouraged to challenge everyone, including the chair. Conflict is said to be at the heart of every decision in a company "constantly at war with not only outsiders but also with itself."[42] Properly managed conflict can be energizing. When people debate their opposing ideas and positions in a calm and reasonable fashion, this type of conflict may:

♦ prevent stagnation;

♦ stimulate interest and curiosity;

♦ encourage the examination and exploration of problems;

♦ lead to the solving of problems and the making of decisions;

♦ facilitate personal growth and development;

♦ promote group identity and cohesion;

♦ help relieve tensions;

♦ provide the basis for change;

♦ encourage interpersonal communication, better understanding, and critical self-reflection;

♦ strengthen personal relationships; and

♦ promote the exploration and awareness of feelings, needs, and opinions of other people.[43]

In summary, conflict is an inevitable part of working in organizations. Whenever people are put together in an organization, they become interdependent, and thus grounds for competition and conflict arise. Long-term, chronic conflict typically has negative results, but short-term, managed conflict can be valuable. The ability to discuss topics openly is a strength in any organization. It is far healthier for individuals to be able to debate, to present opposing viewpoints, and to invite freewheeling conversation on any topic than to keep opinions bottled up inside. Conflicts that are suppressed typically reemerge.

However, there are some people who think that perhaps we have become too contentious, that we have begun to argue for the sake of argument. In our culture, people have been conditioned to compete and to achieve, and the cultures that develop within organizations tend to exaggerate this trait.[44] Tannen has termed this an "argument culture," which she describes as one that

> urges us to approach the world—and the people in it—in an adversarial frame of mind. It rests on the assumption that opposition is the best way to get anything done. The best way to discuss an idea is to set up a debate; the best way to cover news is to find spokespeople who express the most extreme, polarized views and present them as "both sides"; the best way to settle disputes is litigation that pits one party against another; the best way to begin an essay is to attack someone; the best way to show you are really thinking is to criticize.[45]

As Tannen goes on to say, often this type of opposition does not lead to truth because usually an issue is not composed of two opposing views but instead is a "crystal of many sides."[46]

Managers need to find a way to strike the right balance between too much conflict and not enough. In other words, they have to find a way to manage conflict so that the organization will reap its benefits and avoid its negative aspects.

Managing Conflict

How can conflict be managed? The first step is for managers to realize that a certain amount of conflict is inevitable within any organization. The worst thing managers at any level can do is to try to suppress conflict. It is much better to bring it out, to open the lines of communication, and to try to come to a mutually beneficial solution. Even if a win-win solution cannot be achieved, employees will be better satisfied if conflicts are recognized and solutions are sought in a supportive manner.

The second step is to try to deal with the conflict before it escalates. Conflicts typically escalate in three ways:

1. Expansion of interests. The conflict goes from a relatively simple one focused on a few issues to one with a larger number of areas of disagreements. Such escalation can be very destructive and makes the conflict far harder to resolve.

2. Involvement of self-esteem or self-image. Suddenly the conflict switches from one that is issue-oriented to one that is personal. People become defensive and try to save face.

3. Creation of a new reality. The final form of escalation occurs when the conflict itself begins to create its own reality. Participants base their choices on only the immediate conflict situation. Winning the conflict takes on a symbolic importance that transcends everything else. Individuals begin to focus wholly on their incentives to compete rather than their incentives to cooperate.[47]

Anytime a dispute escalates, it becomes more difficult to resolve it satisfactorily.

> Since stressful conversations are so common—and so painful—why don't we work harder to improve them? The reason is precisely because our feelings are so enmeshed. When we are not emotionally entangled in an issue, we know that conflict is normal, that it can be resolved—or at least managed. But when feelings get stirred up, most of us are thrown off balance. Like a quarterback who chokes in a tight play, we lose all hope of ever making it to the goal line.[48]
>
> —Holly Weeks,
> "Taking the Stress Out of Stressful Conversations"

The third step is to try to resolve a conflict in a way that allows the participants to feel positive about the outcome. The best result will be if the manager can help the parties to the conflict emerge with a win-win solution. Some useful tactics to keep in mind include:

♦ Help develop goals that supersede the short-term conflict the parties are experiencing. Employees should be reminded that there is always an explicit superordinate goal—that of resolving the conflict in the interest of the organization.

♦ Separate the people from the problem. Try not to personalize the conflict or problem.

♦ Focus on interests, not on positions. Positions are the demands that each party makes; interests underline these demands. Often, shared interests underline incompatible positions.

♦ Try to come up with options for mutual gain. Go beyond obvious solutions and look for broader solutions.

♦ Develop objective criteria. No matter how hard you try, it is likely that there will be incompatible interests. In those cases, framing disagreements on searches for fair standards is likely to be more fruitful than focusing on who will win. Deciding what is fair requires both parties to understand the criteria for judging fairness. Each side must be open and reasonable.

♦ Communication is the key to managing conflict. Good communication involves all parties being calm, reasonable, and open-minded.[49]

Conflict management is a necessary managerial skill. Inevitably managers will be called in to act as the third party in management of a great number of conflict situations. Managers get better at handling conflict with experience. Understanding conflict and its impact on others increases a manager's ability to make interventions. Managers learn from smaller conflict situations how to deal with larger ones, and they learn from their successes as well as their failures. Managers may fear conflict but should always be ready to manage the conflicts rather than having the conflict control them or the situation. Some practical tips for managing conflicts may be seen in Table 13.2.

Table 13.2. Some Practical Tips for Managing Conflicts

• Don't let conflict situations go on. Take care of conflict as soon as possible.
• Avoid power struggles where someone has to win and someone has to lose.
• Show concern for both the problem and the individuals involved.
• Beware of projecting your own beliefs and standards onto others because this often leads to misperceptions about the motivations for others' actions.
• Listen more than you talk.
• Don't be dogmatic or argumentative.
• Avoid exaggerating the problem.
• Restrain your own emotions; becoming angry or upset almost always adds to the problem.
• Realize that learning to manage conflict is an investment in a better organization.[50]
Adapted from Lucille Wilson's *People Skills for Library Managers*

Team-Building

A managerial innovation that is becoming more common in many types of organizations, including libraries, is the use of teams. More and more organizations are employing teams to do work that previously had been done by individuals. To use teams successfully, managers need to call upon all of the skills of leading that have been discussed thus far. Effective team management requires managers who are skilled at motivating, leading, and communicating. This section of the chapter focuses on teams—how to form successful teams, how to manage them, and how to communicate with them. Team-building is being discussed in the chapter on communication because of the importance of communication in that process, but the other skills are also important. In fact, the use of teams affects most aspects of management, and more information relating to teams, such as group decision making and the impact of teams on organizational structure, can be found in previous chapters.

Although some multinational organizations are employing virtual teams, that is, teams whose members are geographically dispersed and who work together using computer technology and groupware, this discussion will consider only teams working in the same physical location because that is the type of team that is most prevalent in libraries. However, many librarians who are active on committees in professional associations or who work with consortia often have to function, at least part of the time, as members of virtual teams.

Before any organization begins to think about the implementation of the team approach, its managers need to think carefully about the implications of such a change. A manager cannot just create teams and expect them to work effectively. Instead, successful teams are built and developed. Individuals act differently when they are part of a group than when they are alone, so any manager contemplating establishing teams should become familiar with the literature concerning group behavior. Some managers have found it difficult to switch from management in a traditional hierarchical organization to a team-based one because it takes different skills to manage in a team-based organization.

First, we need to define the word "team." Obviously there are many types of teams, ranging from sports teams to debating teams. Although all teams share a number of similarities, the focus in this chapter will be on work teams. A work team is a group of people who interact and coordinate their work in order to accomplish specific work goals. All teams are groups, but not all groups are teams. Teams differ from groups in many aspects. The most important of these are listed in Table 13.3.

As can be seen in Table 13.3, teams differ from groups in that there is greater unity of purpose and loyalty in a team. There is also a greater tendency in teams to hold one another (rather than a supervisor) mutually accountable for achieving the team's goals. Work teams typically are led in one of two ways. Some of them are self-managed or self-directed—that is, they provide their own leadership. Other teams have a leader who coordinates the team's activities. That position sometimes rotates among the members of the team. A team is almost always able to perform at a higher level than a group because its members are committed to a team goal that they are willing to put ahead of their own self-interest. "Teamwork is purposeful interdependency, which has the synergistic effect of accomplishing more than the sum of the parts."[52]

Table 13.3. Differences Between Teams and Groups

Differences Between Teams and Groups	
Teams	**Groups**
Share or rotate leadership roles	Have a designated leader
Share authority and responsibility	Have little sharing of authority or responsibility
Have individual and group accountability	Have individual accountability
Have members who work together to produce results	Have results that are produced by individual effort
Have collective work products	Have individual work products
Share results and rewards	Have little sharing of results and awards
Discuss, decide, and share work.	Discuss, decide, and delegate work to individuals.[51]

Characteristics of Effective Teams

No team that is expected to work well together should be put together haphazardly Instead managers have to choose team members carefully, ensuring that the mix is right for the task that has to be accomplished. Research on teams has shown that certain characteristics are associated with successful teams. The most successful teams demonstrate:

- ♦ Relevant skills. The members of a team have to have both the technical and the interpersonal skills needed to allow the team to be effective.

- ♦ Mutual trust. The participants in effective teams trust the other members of the team.

- ♦ An appropriate size. Although teams vary in number of members, the most effective team size is usually considered to be from five to twelve members. These numbers produce a team large enough to have varying points of view but still small enough to remain workable.

- ♦ Good communication. The most effective teams have learned to communicate well. They convey messages that are understood, and they have learned to incorporate feedback from other team members and from management.

- ♦ Appropriate leadership. Effective teams have leaders to help them achieve. These leaders aren't necessarily managers; they can be members of the team itself, as is common in self-managed teams. The role of the manager in a team is not so much to provide direction as to serve as a coach and a facilitator.

♦ Clear goals. The most effective teams know what their goals are and how to measure progress toward those goals. The clarity of goals helps ensure the team members' commitment to the achievement of the goals.

♦ Loyalty. Effective team members display loyalty to their group. They identify with the team and are willing to work hard to help the team accomplish its goals.[53]

Stages of Team Development

No team, no matter how carefully its members are chosen, functions at high efficiency when it is first formed. People who are asked to work together for the first time have to get to know each other and learn how to work together. There is a sequence of development that most teams go through. The best-known model of how teams evolve over time is called the five-stage model.[54] These stages—forming, storming, norming, performing, and adjourning—are illustrated in Figure 13.4.

Figure 13.4. Stages of Team Building (adapted from Tuckman and Jensen[55])

Stage 1

Forming

Stage 2

Storming

Stage 3

Norming

Stage 4

Performing

Stage 5

Adjourning

When individuals are first placed in a team, the team begins to take shape. In organizations, people are usually placed in a team because of a work assignment. The first stage, that of *forming*, occurs when the team is first organized and when the definitions of the purpose, structure, and leadership of the team begin to be decided.

The second stage, usually called *storming*, takes place in the early stages of a team's development. The new members of the team are questioning many things, including who has control of the team and what is the team's direction.

After the storming stage is finished, the *norming* stage begins. This is a relatively tranquil period. There is now a sense of the team's identity and purpose. The team has assimilated a common set of expectations, the "norms," about what is expected of each team member.

The *performing* stage exists when the team is fully functional. Team energy has gone from getting to know one another and setting the norms to accomplishing the tasks.

The last stage, *adjourning*, takes place in teams that have a limited time span, such as committees or task forces. The team has completed its task and is preparing to disband. The team turns away from task performance and directs its attention to disbanding. If the team's work has gone well, there is a feeling of accomplishment. Many in the team may feel sadness because of the breakup of the team and the loss of camaraderie.

Basic Steps in Team Building

> A group of people does not make a team. Naming a group a team does not make it one. A group saying that it is a team does not make it one either. For instance, a group of managers is not a team just because they call themselves a management team and meet together regularly. A work unit may call itself a team when it is actually more like an armed camp. Effective, high-performance teams have structure and operate under conditions that enable the team to perform effectively.[56]
>
> —Ruth Metz,
> *Coaching in the Library*

Requiring people to work together does not ensure that a team will result. A team must be developed. Lucile Wilson has delineated the basic steps that managers should follow in setting up successful work teams.

- First, focus on competencies when assigning team members. Look for self-starters and those who take pride in their work.

- Next, establish clear team goals and communicate the desired goals. Be sure to allow time for the team to invest in the goals and make them their own.

- Establish deadlines and ground rules at the first meeting. Devoting attention at the beginning of the project prevents trouble later on.

- Involve each member of the team in the project. Use individual talents. Take advantage of opportunities for personal growth of staff members.

♦ Maintain a results-oriented team structure. Monitor progress to be sure everyone is on track. Frequent feedback reduces miscommunication.

♦ Provide a collaborative climate and share power. Managers gain, not lose, power when teams share responsibility and authority.

♦ Strive for consensus. Explore all sides of an issue and get agreement from the group on solutions.

♦ Keep the group motivated. To meet team goals and fulfill library objectives, a manager needs strong skills in motivating.

♦ Build confidence. Make each team member feel important and essential.

♦ Build trust and respect. Although team members must earn trust and mutual respect from each other, a manager can set examples of these qualities.

♦ Be flexible. Both team members and leaders function better if all can adapt to needed change. If a new approach is needed, try it.

♦ Furnish external support and recognition. Provide recognition for group and individual accomplishments; recognize the team when it reaches major goals.[57]

Team Communication

A team's effectiveness to a large extent depends on communication. Obviously, the ability of team members to understand and to communicate enables them to work together collaboratively. All of the factors discussed previously related to improving communication are applicable to team communication. But in addition to inter-team communication, in any team-based organization there is communication that takes place between the managers and the members of the teams.

Managing teams requires different types of managerial skills. As just discussed, it requires team-building skills. The manager's style of communication has to change also. Organizations that are employing teams have abandoned the old "command and control" model of management, and managers have to learn how to communicate in a fashion that fits this new model. Instead of being a boss, a team leader functions more like a facilitator. The manager goes from someone who tells employees how to do things to one who facilitates the employees doing it on their own. Coaching is a term that is used often in describing the type of communication that occurs between managers and members of teams. Coaching is defined as "the purposeful and skillful effort by one individual to help another achieve specific performance goals."[58]

If a library has self-directed work teams, coaches can be useful in a number of situations. Sometimes they are needed when goals need to be redefined or clarified, when new skills have to be acquired, or when a team is struggling and appears to have gotten off track. Sometimes difficult tasks confronted by a team, such as allocation of resources, are facilitated by a coach.[59] Managers who are skillful coaches help their organization get the most out of teams.

The Future of Work Teams in Libraries

Some libraries that have switched to a team-based approach have been highly successful. For instance, the professional librarians at Dowling College are organized into a self-managed team, and they report that it has worked very well. The librarians there "work well together, trust each other, value their differences, mentor one another and respect each other, as well as enjoy working, laughing and having fun together."[60] Many other libraries have similar success stories to report about using teams. They have found that teams produce high-quality work, and they are beneficial for the employees because "teaming people up to grapple with challenging service issues, even if the process is inefficient by some standards, gives people a place at the learning table.[61]

Other libraries have either experimented with teams and abandoned them or decided not even to explore the approach. The team-based organization provides benefits, but to implement it successfully, a library has to be willing to invest considerable time and resources in the effort. For some libraries the benefits that result from the team approach are not worth the cost. The answer will be different for each library, and the correct approach may change as an organization evolves. To date, no one has been able to show conclusively that the team approach to management is better than the more traditional, hierarchical approach.

Conclusion

Many varying and often contradictory perspectives on leading have been covered in the preceding chapters. What is clear is that neither behavioral scientists nor experts from any other discipline have been able to provide managers with a specific prescription or universal theory about the most effective way to lead. Unlike early theorists in management who relied on principles to provide the one best way, most modern management theorists are convinced that there are few across-the-board concepts that apply in all instances. The situations with which managers deal are much more complex than originally realized, and different variables require managers to adopt different approaches. Instead of advocating a universal best theory, most contemporary management experts urge managers to be flexible and to adapt to the situation at hand. These experts, if asked how a manager should act, would say, "It all depends."

Managers should not become skeptical about the diversified approaches to management being offered to them. Instead, they should realize that in the case of leading, as in most other instances, "one size does not fit all." There is no quick fix or magic solution. But this does not mean that managers should not become familiar with as many of the approaches or "tools" as possible. All of these new methods are useful, but none of them is guaranteed to be effective in every situation. Instead, managers have to look at the organization and its goals and then adopt a management strategy that will match the overall needs of the organization, its employees, and its customers.

Nor should managers completely deride management fads as useless practices that will go away if only ignored. Reexamination of some recently dismissed fads seems to indicate that they have survived, developed a new life, and remained influential in managerial practices. For instance, although MBO is not being followed in its pure form in many organizations, its principles can still be found in much of our current thinking about goal setting. Even though quality circles and TQM are not as popular as they once were, current interests in continuous quality and team-based initiatives have direct links to those earlier popular fads.[62] The best parts of these fads have survived and have been recycled, albeit in a different form.

Unfortunately, for those who are looking for one "right" way to manage, that one right way does not exist. Good management is more complex than that. Contingency or situational theory, discussed briefly in chapter 2, provides managers with a way to bring all of the disparate approaches together in an approach that provides the flexibility necessary to manage modern organizations. Contingency theory recognizes that every organization is unique, existing in a unique environment with unique workers and a unique purpose. Contingency theory is used to analyze individual situations and to understand the interrelationships among the variables to help managers determine what specific managerial actions are necessary in any particular situation. What is appropriate in one situation may be inappropriate in another. According to contingency theory, effective management differs depending on the variables associated with various individual situations. The best techniques can be selected only after one is aware of the particular circumstances of each case.

Many managerial experts have advocated the contingency approach to management. For instance, the contingency leadership theory of Fred Feidler was described in the last chapter. In short, contingency management suggests there be a fit between the task, the people, the organization, and the external environment. In each organization, managers must be sure that each unit develops structures, measurement schemes, and reward practices that encourage its members to focus on the appropriate set of activities and issues.

> One of the most difficult things for most of us to understand is that organizations are dynamic. Particularly as one moves up the organizational ladder, matters become less tangible and less predictable. A primary characteristic of managing, particularly at higher levels, is the confrontation of change, ambiguity, and contradiction. Managers spend much of their time living in fields of perceived tensions. They are constantly forced to make trade-offs, and often find that there are no right answers. The higher one goes in an organization, the more exaggerated this phenomenon becomes.[63]
>
> —Robert E. Quinn,
> *Beyond Rational Management*

Managers who wish to use the contingency approach must understand the complex and interrelated causes of behavior in an organization and then use their intelligence and creative ability to invent a new solution or to judge which existing solutions might best be used.[64] Library managers using this approach might decide that different sections of the library would benefit from different styles of leading. For example, a part of a technical services department that performs highly standardized, repetitive work might benefit from a more task-oriented style of management. In the same library, a more people-oriented style of management might be appropriate for the reference department.

The contingency theory can be used in functions of management other than leading. For instance, there is no one best way for an institution to be organized. There are also no sure-fire approaches to planning, controlling, or managing human resources. Many variables, such as size, type of organization, and type of tasks being performed, play a role in the choice to be made. In the broadest sense, contingency theory applies to all of the managerial functions.

Although the contingency theory requires a fundamental shift from the traditional concept that there is one best way of doing things, it provides managers with a comprehensive model that can be used to achieve maximum effectiveness in all managerial functions. With the contingency approach, the performance of managerial functions is closely tied to analysis of the total system—the organization, its subsystems, and its environment. Contingency theory offers a flexible approach that is better suited to the complexity of management than are other approaches. "The basic deficiency with earlier approaches is that they did not recognize the variability in tasks and people which produces this complexity. The strength of the contingency approach . . . is that it begins to provide a way of thinking about this complexity, rather than ignoring it."[65] Although the contingency approach to management certainly does not provide all of the answers, it points to a new direction in which management theory and practice appear to be evolving. It provides a way of making sense of a number of disparate approaches.

In summary, this section has dealt with the function of leading, which is the most interpersonal aspect of management. The chapters have dealt primarily with how to motivate, lead, and communicate, but other related topics such as ethics and team-building have been included. The ultimate aim of leading is to allow the organization to achieve its objectives through the activities of the people employed within it. Leading means getting employees to work efficiently and to produce results that are beneficial to the organization. In short, leading is getting things done through other people for the good of the organization.

Because leading is complex and multifaceted, managers often find it one of their most challenging and important tasks. The need for managers to excel at leading becomes more pressing as organizations grow larger, as the rate of change in the environment increases, and as demands by employees for a more rewarding work life proliferate. The next section of this book discusses ways that managers coordinate a modern organization. Then some of the challenges and rewards of managing in the twenty-first century will be discussed in the last chapter of this book.

Notes

1. Nigel Nicholson, *Managing the Human Animal* (London: Texere, 2000), 205.

2. Chester I. Barnard, *The Functions of the Executive* (Cambridge, MA: Harvard University Press, 1938).

3. Henry Mintzberg, "The Manager's Job: Folklore and Fact," *Harvard Business Review* 53 (July–August 1975): 52.

4. Alex Bavels and Dermot Barrett, "An Experimental Approach to Organization Communication," *Personnel* (March 1951): 368.

5. Peter F. Drucker, *Managing the Non-Profit Organization* (New York: Harper Business, 1990), 115.

6. Gerald M. Goldhaber, *Organizational Communication*, 6th ed. (New York: McGraw-Hill, 1993), 14–15.

7. *Ibid.*

8. Joan Giesecke, *Practical Strategies for Library Managers* (Chicago: American Library Association, 2001), 77.

9. Deborah Tannen, *You Just Don't Understand: Women and Men in Conversation* (New York: William Morrow, 1990).

10. Patrick A. Hall, "Peanuts: A Note on Intercultural Communication," *Journal of Academic Librarianship* 18 (September 1992): 211–13.

11. Deborah Tannen, *Talking from 9 to 5: How Women's and Men's Conversational Styles Affect Who Gets Heard, Who Gets Credit, and What Gets Done at Work* (New York: William Morrow, 1994), 291.

12. Kathleen Huddleston, *Back on the Quality Track: How Organizations Derailed and Recovered* (New York: American Management Association, 1995), 113.

13. Marco Adria, "Making the Most of E-Mail," *Academy of Management Review* 14 (February 2000): 153.

14. Patricia S. Eyres, "Avoiding Costly E-Mail Disasters," *Journal of Property Management* 67 (January/February 2002): 74.

15. Nicholson, *Managing the Human Animal*, 221–23.

16. Jenny C. McCune, "Get the Message," *Management Review* 38 (January 1997): 10–11.

17. Eyres, "Avoiding Costly E-Mail Disasters," 75.

18. These and other examples of nonverbal communication can be found in Jack Griffin, *How to Say It at Work* (Englewood Cliffs, NJ: Prentice-Hall, 1998), 26–28.

19. Robert H. Lengel and Richard L. Daft, "The Selection of Communication Media as an Executive Skill," *Academy of Management Executive* 2 (1988): 225–32.

20. *Ibid.*

21. Daniel Katz and Robert L. Kahn, *The Social Psychology of Organizations* (New York: John Wiley & Sons, 1966), 239.

22. Goldhaber, *Organizational Communication*, 141–42.

23. Barbara Ettorre, "The Unvarnished Truth," *Management Review* 49 (June 1997): 54.

24. Keith Davis, cited in Goldhaber, *Organizational Communication*, 138–39.

25. *Ibid.*

26. Jay R. Galbraith, Edward E. Lawler III, and Associates, *Organizing for the Future: The New Logic for Managing Complex Organizations* (San Francisco: Jossey-Bass, 1993), 296–97.

27. A helpful guide to effective meetings is Barbara I. Dewey and Sheila D. Creth, *Team Power: Making Library Meetings Work* (Chicago: American Library Association, 1993).

28. Karen Southwick, "Back in Touch," *Forbes* 169 (March 25, 2002): 46.

29.   Bill Leonard, "Cyberventing," *HR Magazine* 44 (November 1999): 35–39.

30.   Robert W. Zmud, "Opportunities for Strategic Information Manipulation Through New Information Technology," in Janet Fulk and Charles Steinfield, eds., *Organizations and Communication Technology* (Newbury Park, CA: Sage Publications, 1990), 115.

31.   John R. Carlson and Robert W. Zmud, "Channel Expansion Theory and the Experiential Nature of Media Richness Perceptions," *Academy of Management Journal* 42 (April 1999): 163.

32.   Keith Davis, "Grapevine Communication Among Lower and Middle Managers," *Personnel Journal* (April 1969): 272.

33.   Keith Davis and John W. Newstrom, *Human Behavior at Work: Organizational Behavior*, 8th ed. (New York: McGraw-Hill, 1989), 371.

34.   Paul Hersey, Kenneth Blanchard, and Dewey E. Johnson, *Management of Organizational Behavior: Utilizing Human Resources*, 7th ed. (Upper Saddle River, NJ: Prentice-Hall, 1996), 355.

35.   Robert Goffee and Gareth Jones, "Followership," *Harvard Business Review* 79 (December 2001): 148.

36.   Robin Reid, "A Checklist for Managers." Available on the web at http://www.improve.org /mbwa.html.

37.   Kenneth W. Thomas and Warren H. Schmidt, "A Survey of Managerial Interests with Respect to Conflict," *Academy of Management Journal* 10 (June 1976): 315–18.

38.   C. Watson and R. Hoffman, "Managers as Negotiators," *Leadership Quarterly* 7 (1996).

39.   Kathleen M. Eisenhardt, Jean L. Kahwajy, and L. J. Bourgeois III, "How Management Teams Can Have a Good Fight," *Harvard Business Review* 75 (July/August 1997): 77.

40.   Kenneth W. Thomas, "Conflict and Conflict Management," in Marvin D. Dunnette, ed., *Handbook of Industrial and Organizational Psychology* (Skokie, IL: Rand McNally, 1976), 889–936.

41.   Dorothy Leonard and Susana Straus, "Putting Your Company's Whole Brain to Work," *Harvard Business Review* 75 (July/August 1997): 111.

42.   Herbert S. White, "Never Mind Being Innovative and Effective—Just Be Nice," *Library Journal* 120 (September 15, 1995): 47.

43.   Gregory Tillett, *Resolving Conflict: A Practical Approach* (South Melbourne, Australia: Sydney University Press, 1991), 6.

44.   Charles Conrad and Marshall Scott Poole, *Strategic Organizational Communication: Into the Twenty-First Century*, 4th ed.(New York: Harcourt Brace, 1998), 340.

45.   Deborah Tannen, *The Argument Culture: Stopping America's War of Words* (New York: Ballentine, 1999), 3–4.

46.   *Ibid.*, 10.

47.   Conrad and Poole, *Strategic Organizational Communication*, 338–40.

48.   Holly Weeks, "Taking the Stress Out of Stressful Conversations," *Harvard Business Review* 79 (July–August 2001): 114.

49.   Linda K. Stroh, Gregory B. Northcraft, and Margaret A. Neale, *Organizational Behavior: A Management Challenge*, 3d ed. (Mahwah, NJ: Lawrence Erlbaum Associates, 2002), 133–34.

50.   Lucile Wilson, *People Skills for Library Managers: A Common Sense Guide for Beginners* (Englewood, CO: Libraries Unlimited, 1996), 72–73.

51.   David I. Cleland, *Strategic Management of Teams* (New York: John Wiley & Sons, 1996), 38.

52.   Ruth F. Metz, *Coaching in the Library; A Management Strategy for Achieving Excellence* (Chicago: American Library Association, 2001), 46.

53.   J. Richard Hackman, ed., *Groups That Work (and Those That Don't)* (San Francisco: Jossey-Bass, 1990); Eric Sundstrom, Kenneth P. deMeuse, and David Futrell, "Work Teams: Applications and Effectiveness," *American Psychologist* 45 (1990): 122–24; Dean Tjosvold, *Team Organization: An Enduring Competitive Advantage* (New York: John Wiley & Sons, 1991).

54.   Bruce W. Tuckman and Mary Ann C. Jensen, "Stages of Small Group Development Revisited," *Group and Organizational Studies* 2 (1977): 419–27.

55.   *Ibid.*

56.   Metz, *Coaching in the Library*, 45.

57.   Wilson, *People Skills for Library Managers*, 50–52.

58.   Metz, *Coaching in the Library*, 7.

59.   *Ibid.*, 46–48.

60.   Francie C. Davis, "Calling the Shots: A Self-Managed Team in an Academic Library," Proceedings of the 10th National ACRL Conference, 2001, 240–49 (available online at http://www.ala.org/acrl/papers01/davis.pdf).

61.   Metz, *Coaching in the Library*, 47.

62.   Jane Whitney Gibson and Dana V. Tesone, "Management Fads: Emergence, Evolution, and Implications for Managers." *Academy of Management Executive* 15 (November 2001): 128–29.

63.   Robert E. Quinn, *Beyond Rational Management* (San Francisco: Jossey-Bass, 1988), 3.

64.   Jay W. Lorsch, "Making Behavioral Science More Useful," *Harvard Business Review* 57 (March–April 1979): 174.

65.   John J. Morse and Jay W. Lorsch, "Beyond Theory Y," *Harvard Business Review* 48 (May–June 1970): 68.

Section 6: Coordinating

Addressing quality control in library and information service requires establishing human and mechanical measures that identify weaknesses, correct those weaknesses, and then evaluate the results. Accountability and evaluation techniques, such as performance measures, output indicators, operation indicators, program impact indicators, and tools—including unit cost, cost accounting, cost benefit analysis, cost effectiveness, and budgeting— are examples of techniques and tools being employed to measure effectiveness and efficiency. One primary consideration is that of financing because no other element can be effectively developed without money. However, many things cannot and should not be measured in strictly monetary terms. These include both effective performance of services and customer satisfaction.

Coordination implies the existence of plans with identified goals and the regulation of the organization's activities toward those goals. With that in place, tools and techniques strengthen accountability and serve as guides for the library's progress toward meeting its established goals. In order to remain accountable, the library and information center is expected to evaluate its performance to ensure that the human and material resources are effectively and efficiently employed toward achieving their goals and those of the larger institution.

Both quantitative and qualitative measures are important. Goal setting takes information about past performance and introduces it into decisions about adjustments that are needed for future actions. This type of coordination is inextricably tied to the planning process because it is impossible to evaluate unless it is known what is to be evaluated. If the whole management process is viewed as a circle, the evaluation step in the decision making process brings one full-circle back to future planning, with continuous change as a given. The function of coordinating and controlling so that good decisions can be made requires accurate and timely information. This process is heavily dependent upon technology to enhance efficient information gathering. Budgeting pulls together the various pieces of the operational plan and relates it to the services plan in monetary terms. In essence, the budget is the monetary expression of the strategic plan.

Readings

Abbott, Christine. *Performance Measurement in Library and Information Services*. London: Aslib, 1994.

Adams, Roy, et al. *Decision Support Systems and Performance Assessment in Academic Libraries*. New Providence, NJ: Bowker-Saur, 1995.

Association of College and Research Libraries. *Standards for College Libraries 2000*. www.ala .orgacrl/guides/college.html.

Association of Research Libraries. *Developing Indicators for Academic Library Performance: Ratios from the ARL Statistics*. Washington, DC: Association of Research Libraries. Annual.

Baker, Sharon L., and F. Wilfrid Lancaster. *The Measurement and Evaluation of Library Services*. Arlington, VA: Information Resources Press, 1991.

Bertot, John C., et al. *Statistics and Performance Measures for Public Library Networked Services*. Chicago: American Library Association, 2000.

Bloor, Ian. *Performance Indicators and Decision Support Systems for Libraries*. (British Library Research Paper 93.) Boston Spa: British Library, 1993.

Bradburn, Frances Bryant. *Output Measures for School Library Media Programs*. New York: Neal-Schuman, 1999.

Brophy, Peter. *Management Information and Decision Support Systems in Libraries*. Brookfield, VT: Gower, 1986.

Brophy, Peter, and Peter M. Wynne. *Management Information Systems and Performance Measurement for the Electronic Library: eLib Supporting Study* (MIEL2, Final Report). Preston: University of Central Lancashire Centre for Research in Library & Information Management (CERLIM), June 1997.

Childers, Thomas A., and Nancy A. Van House. *What's Good: Describing Your Public Library's Effectiveness*. Chicago: American Library Association, 1993.

Crawford, John. *Evaluation of Library and Information Services*. London: Aslib, 1996.

Creswell, J. W. *Qualitative Inquiry and Research Design: Choosing Among Five Traditions*. Thousand Oaks, CA: Sage, 1998.

Daubert, Madeline J. *Control of Administrative and Financial Operations in Special Libraries*. Washington, DC: Special Libraries Association, 1996.

Daubert, Madeline J. *Financial Management for Small and Medium-sized Libraries*. Chicago: American Library Association, 1993.

DeCandido, GraceAnne A. *After the User Survey, What Then?* (ARL SPEC Kit 226). Washington, DC: Association of Research Libraries, 1997.

Developing Indicators for Academic Library Performance. Washington, DC: Association of Research Libraries, 1995.

Everhart, Nancy. *Evaluating the School Library Media Center: Analysis Techniques and Research Practices*. Englewood, CO: Libraries Unlimited, 1998.

Expert Systems in ARL Libraries. (ARL SPEC Kit 174). Washington, DC: Association of Research Libraries, 1991.

Framer, Lesley S. *When Your Library Budget Is Almost Zero*. Englewood, CO: Libraries Unlimited, 1993.

Hafner, Arthur W. *Descriptive Statistical Techniques for Libraries*. 2d ed. Chicago: American Library Association, 1998.

Hernon, Peter, and Ellen Altman. *Service Quality in Academic Libraries*. Norwood, NJ: Ablex, 1996.

———. *Assessing Service Quality: Satisfying the Expectations of Library Customers*. Chicago: American Library Association, 1998.

Hernon, Peter, and Robert E. Dugan. *Action Plan for Outcome Assessment in Your Library*. Chicago: American Library Association, 2002.

Hill, Malcolm. *Budgeting and Record Keeping in the Small Library*. 2d ed. Chicago: American Library Association, 1993.

Holsapple, Clyde W., and Andrew B. Whinston. *Decision Support Systems: A Knowledge Based Approach*. Cambridge, MA: Course Technologies, 1996.

ISO 11620. *Information and Documentation—Library Performance Indicators*. Geneva: International Organization for Standardization, June 1998.

Joint Funding Councils' Ad-hoc Group on Performance Indicators for Libraries. *The Effective Academic Library: A Framework for Evaluating the Performance of UK Academic Libraries*. Bristol: HEFCE Publications, March 1995.

Keys to Success: Performance Indicators for Public Libraries. London: UK Office of Arts and Libraries, 1990.

Kingma, Bruce R. *The Economics of Information: A Guide to Economic and Cost-Benefit Analysis for Information Professionals*. Englewood, CO: Libraries Unlimited, 1996.

Measuring Quality: International Guidelines for Performance Measurement in Academic Libraries. (IFLA Publication, v. 76). New Providence, NJ: Bowker-Saur, 1997.

Nas, Tefik F. *Cost-Benefit Analysis: Theory and Application*. London: Sage, 1996.

Poll, Roswintha, and Peter te Boekhorst. *Measuring Quality: International Guidelines for Performance Measurement in Academic Libraries*. London: K. G. Saur, 1996.

Prentice, Ann E. *Financial Planning for Libraries*. 2d ed. Lanham, MD: Scarecrow Press, 1996.

Robbins, Jane B., and Douglas L. Zweizig. *Keeping the Book$: Public Library Financial Practices*. Fort Atkinson, WI: Highsmith Press, 1992.

Roberts, Stephen A. *Financial and Cost Management for Libraries and Information Services*. 2d ed. New Providence, NJ: Bowker-Saur, 1998.

Rounds, Richard S. *Budgeting Practices for Librarians*. 2d ed. Chicago: American Library Association, 1994.

Smith, G. Stevenson. *Managerial Accounting for Libraries and Other Non-Profit Organizations*. 2d ed. Chicago: American Library Association, 2002.

Stephen, Peter, and Susan Hornby. *Simple Statistics for Library and Information Professionals.* 2d ed. London: Library Association, 1997.

Van House, Nancy, et al. *Measuring Academic Library Performance: A Practical Approach.* Chicago: American Library Association, 1990.

———. *Output Measures for Public Libraries: A Manual of Standardized Procedures.* 2d ed. Chicago: American Library Association, 1987.

Wallace, Danny P., and Connie Van Fleet, eds. *Library Evaluation: A Casebook and Can-Do Guide.* Englewood, CO: Libraries Unlimited, 2001.

Ward, Suzanne, et al. *Library Performance Indicators and Library Management Tools.* Luxembourg: European Commission DG-XIII-E3, 1995.

Warner, Alice Sizer. *Budgeting.* (How-To-Do-It Manual 79). New York: Neal-Schuman, 1998.

Zweizig, Douglas, et al. *The TELL IT Manual: The Complete Program for Evaluating Library Performance.* Chicago: American Library Association, 1996.

Chapter 14

Coordinating and Reporting

*People are now beginning to turn to the prospect of using
information and performance measurement and reporting
as more flexible instruments for improving the linkage
between strategy and execution. These strategic performance
measurements are the integrated set of measurements and
management processes that link strategy to execution.[1]*

—James V. McGee and Laurence Prusak,
Managing Information Strategically

Measuring and Evaluating Organizational Performance

In recent years interest in performance measurement and evaluation has become intense among information professionals, and various techniques and tools are being examined, researched, and written about in the literature The reason for such interest is easy to identify, with intense pressure on resources, greater demands on access, and the need for quality control of electronic resources being primary factors. Combined, they have led to a search for greater efficiency of operation and effectiveness in meeting users' needs. Funding authorities demand that value for money be achieved and that it be demonstrated through factual data. Users and other stakeholders are more sophisticated and demanding than ever before, and change is rampant as libraries and information centers become more flexible with self-organizing units, self-managed teams, and networked settings cultivating empowerment among employees, thereby allowing organizations to become more immediately responsive and adaptable in providing needed services. As the nature of information services organizations has changed, so has the coordinating and control aspects, with workers at all levels supporting the accountability process and actively participating in outcomes.

Coordinating is viewed by most forward-looking thinkers as a progressive element, with techniques being applied toward achieving success rather than a more traditional and negative view of stifling initiative. With this positive approach, the coordinating initiative permeates this text—from the discussion of setting goals and evaluating the organization's progress toward achieving them, to organizing libraries and information centers in order to provide value-added services to customers, to staffing and leadership and the motivational factors desirable in integrating the individual employee's talents with those of the organization. Evaluation, accountability, and cost measures, all necessary components, are intertwined. Greater accountability and attention to quality, with a balance between cost effectiveness, cost benefits, and efficiency, are the focus for libraries and information centers intent upon fulfilling their mission and achieving their goals.

A gradual shift in the orientation from a preoccupation with input measures, mostly internal in nature and somewhat limited in effectiveness, to a user orientation, with primary emphasis on output measures, results, and accountability, has tended to balance quantitative and qualitative factors in the coordinating process. Currently as much emphasis is being placed on the output factors of service and performance as was formerly placed on statistics and paper pushing. Performance indicators are being examined, not only from the perspective of librarians, but also by stakeholders, including customers and funding authorities, who often have varying attitudes about what constitutes efficient and effective information services.

> The measurement of quality will come back to the questions of who are the users, what are the inputs, what are the outputs, do we produce the outputs in a way that meets the needs of the users, and what do those outputs contribute to the productivity and accomplishment of those users.[2]
> —Sarah M. Prichard,
> "Determining Quality in Academic Libraries"

Quality control, quality audit, and quality assessment are terms common in the measurement literature today. This reorientation has removed coordination from the mundane, stationary category and placed it on a fluid, innovation-seeking plateau, with less a view of "looking over the shoulder" than one of working together to identify weaknesses that need to be corrected, correcting those weaknesses, and then evaluating the results. Evaluation techniques, such as performance measures; output indicators; operation indicators; program impact indicators; and tools, including unit cost, cost accounting, cost benefit analysis, and cost effectiveness, are examples of techniques and tools being employed to measure effectiveness and efficiency.

Initially, in any discussion of coordination, some distinction must be made between the act of coordinating and the control mechanisms used to accomplish it. The two are obviously interrelated—effective "coordinating" within an organization depends on the types of controls that are in place. Coordinating is the act and controls are the means that provide information for decision making. The former pertains to an end, whereas the latter is the means; the first is concerned with events, and the other with facts; one is analytical and operational, concerned with what was and is, whereas the other deals with expectations.[3] The management of resources requires determination of what resources the organization has at its disposal, or should make available, and how those resources can be employed to achieve the mission of the organization. It requires strong financial planning and feedback mechanisms to ensure success.

An all-encompassing definition of controls would take into account any action or process that leads to altered results. In that regard, it is a global term, not narrowly defined, and involves setting standards, establishing criteria, developing policies and budgets, conducting performance evaluations, and scheduling actions to achieve objectives, then monitoring the outcome on a periodic basis, and, finally, providing some type of feedback mechanism to ensure efficiency and effectiveness in the achievement, the latter suggesting corrective measures for adjustments or alternatives to the situation. In a library or information center context, controls relate to physical resources, information resources, and human resources, the latter of which has already been discussed in section 3. Although the primary aspect is usually a financial one, because no other element can be effectively developed without money, some things cannot and should not be measured in monetary terms. These include both effective performance of services and customer satisfaction.

Who Controls What?

The ultimate act of controlling in the library and information services setting is, to a degree, external because most information centers are accountable to higher public or private sector authorities that provide primary impetus and funding for the operations of the library. The library or information center in an academic setting is legally bound by constitutional provisions, charters, articles of incorporation, and general or special laws applicable to the educational institution as a whole and is coordinated by the chancellor and/or president and his or her boards of overseers. In special or corporate libraries, a similar controlling responsibility is exercised through one of the divisions of the organization—usually the research division, the sales division, or the manufacturing division—on behalf of the ultimate coordinating body, which is the corporate or company board of directors. Public libraries and school libraries are usually controlled by statutes carried out by the city manager, mayor, or superintendent, who acts on behalf of the ultimate coordinating body, that being the city council, school committee, or another governing authority. These external authorities are responsible through their overall institutional or societal charge and because of their funding and fiduciary mandate.

Besides those bodies directly related to the controlling function of an information services organization, numerous outside groups, some with sanctioning powers, are involved in various aspects of the operation, including standard setting; certification; and accreditation of libraries, librarians, and other information specialists. For example, the North Central Association of College and Secondary Schools, a regional agency in the United States, is a responsible accrediting body that observes and makes recommendations on libraries as a part of their overall review of higher education institutions. The American Library Association influences libraries through the establishment of standards for various types of libraries and library services and through its Committee on Accreditation, which is responsible for setting standards for library and information science education and accrediting those institutions that meet the set standards. State departments of education establish guidelines for the certification of school librarians or media specialists and establish standard formulae for the allocation of funds, and specialty-specific interest groups, such as the Medical Library Association, set certification standards and continuing education requirements for their members.

Some groups and agencies exist primarily to regulate activities of organizations and institutions and to measure, to one extent or another, their actions and outputs. Laws, including local, state, national, and international ones, regulate certain activities. For example, planning, constructing, and maintaining library buildings may be controlled through municipal ordinances and regulations, building codes, zoning, and fire regulations; and international copyright agreements or international standards promulgated by the International Standards Organization (ISO) or the World Intellectual Property Organization (WIPO) may direct the services or activities of an information center. Comprehensive legislation, for instance, state and federal funding legislation in the United States, places certain other types of control on the operation of libraries and information centers within their jurisdiction. Such regulatory agencies and their authority vary from one part of the world to another, but their influence remains the same and can be observed in Atlanta as well as Zanzibar.

Other bodies that exert some external control on libraries include unions, special interests groups, and political bodies. Through collective bargaining, unions can influence hiring, salaries, working conditions, fringe benefits, and so forth, and political bodies can influence the appointments of individuals, the allocation of monies, and even the disbursal of funds within libraries and information centers. Often pressures are placed on information services by outside bodies, in areas of hiring new staff and in issues relating to collection development, censorship and intellectual freedom, and use of library services and facilities. Use of the Internet and access to information through libraries is a heatedly debated topic today. Friends of the Library groups are an example of well-meaning supporters that may expect to have some say in the directions libraries will take, sometimes in exchange for their charitable contributions.

Requirements for Control

Controls are concerned with keeping things on track, successful progress toward meeting specified objectives, and, therefore, locating any operational weakness so that corrective action can be taken. Whereas plans determine what should be done, controls assure that it is done, acting as the tools and techniques for implementing the planning process. In order to avoid failure, controls are both desirable and, if applied consistently and fairly, necessary. At the operational level, controlling techniques relate to such things as policies, procedures, task analyses, and job audits. Control implies the existence of goals and plans and the regulation of the organization's activities toward those goals. The most effective controls prevent deviations from plans by anticipating that such deviations will occur unless immediate action is taken. However, other types of control are also necessary for feedback, and they naturally emanate from the planning process.

Controls are necessary in all types of organizations, but in a large organization they are particularly important to provide decision makers with facts in a comprehensible form when they are required. In a strictly theoretical sense, controls are guides for the organization; they indicate how effectively the organization is progressing toward meeting its established goals. The focus is accountability, the obligation of reporting to a higher authority on the exercise of responsibility and authority, and the responsibility of meeting expectations of those for whom the information service exists. As nonprofit organizations, most libraries and information centers do not have the monetary profit incentive of for-profit organizations and, therefore, establish different controls and measurements, or at least take a different approach in using them. All types of information centers must demonstrate the "value of service" or "value-added" aspect to the larger organization of which they are a part and to their constituencies. Through accountability, the library and information center is, more than ever before, expected to evaluate the institution's performance to ensure that the human and material resources are effectively and efficiently employed toward achieving its goals and those of the larger institution. In the past some libraries relied on the "public good" view of library services. This is no longer adequate in the current competitive environment.

> Assessment and evaluation are intended as means to demonstrate institutional effectiveness, foster institutional improvement, and demonstrate accountability.[4]
>
> —Ronald L. Baker,
> "Evaluating Quality and Effectiveness"

To be effective, controls must be objective and must reflect the job they are to perform. In addition, they should be established and agreed upon before they are needed to minimize conflict and to optimize efforts. At the least, the controls should point out exceptions at critical points. In addition, any control system that does not pose corrective actions after deviations occur is little more than an interesting exercise. In other words, there must be an action plan accompanying the evaluation process. After activities have been initiated, some sort of control mechanism must be established to monitor progress and correct actions, as needed, to achieve goals. Given those guidelines, individuals at all levels are responsible for steering the organization on the right course. Controls, wherever they are found and whatever they control, involve three basic steps:

1. establishing standards;

2. measuring performance against standards; and

3. correcting deviations.

Techniques for Evaluating and Reporting Activities

Developing Standards

Standards are established criteria against which subsequent performance can be compared and evaluations can be made. Most often they are developed, or at least devised, from organizational goals.[5] Standards fall into two basic classes:

1. those relating to material and performance—including quality, quantity, cost, and time—and

2. those relating to moral aspects—including the organization's value system and ethical criteria that may be used to establish some sort of code of ethics.

Standards may be physical, representing quantities of products, units of service, work hours, and similar things that can be evidenced and measured through time-and-motion studies; they may be stated in monetary terms, such as costs, revenues, or investments, which are evidenced through record keeping, cost analysis, and budget presentation; or they may be expressed in other terms that measure performance, such as performance ratings and appraisal systems. Of course, there are some other factors that are difficult to evaluate and measure, and they require a different approach to measurement. For instance, how does one measure commitment on the part of individuals to organizational goals?

General standards, such as those developed by the American Library Association's various units, are important as guides, but they cannot necessarily provide meaningful evaluation for the individual library or information center for a number of reasons:

♦ Most of the standards are descriptive in nature.

♦ Most of the standards that prescribe quantitative objectives are arbitrarily formulated.

♦ The emphasis of the standards is directed toward evaluating the input resources of the library.

♦ The standards discourage experimentation with different programs and different allocations of input resources.[6]

Some standards are nebulous and almost impossible to measure, some are simply guidelines for proceeding,[7] and others combine qualitative evaluation with quantitative formulae.[8] If a scientific control method is to be used, then the standard is most likely measurable to the extent possible. In any case, to be effective, standards should be acceptable to those whose performance is regulated by them. The process of applying performance standards should be explained and agreed upon rather than forced. It is only human nature that if standards are forced upon individuals, some resistance is likely to occur.

> The first step is to measure whatever can be easily measured. This is OK as far as it goes. The second step is to disregard that which can't be easily measured or to give it an arbitrary quantitative value. This is artificial and misleading. The third step is to presume that what can't be measured easily really isn't important. This is blindness. The fourth step is to say that what can't be easily measured really doesn't exist. This is suicide.[9]
>
> —McNamara Fallacy,
> *The Age of Paradox*

Measuring Performance

Performance measurement is embedded in the strategic planning process and is an essential feedback mechanism to support decision making in libraries and information services. Such measures are expressed in both quantitative and qualitative forms, including economic value and financial adequacy to image, value, competency, cost of quality, etc. Feedback, or measuring performance, is an important factor in the controlling process. It is primarily important as a technique for establishing the "value" of information services to the intended customers or funding authorities.

The third aspect of control, then, is the measurement of performance in relation to standards. After standards have been agreed upon, some sort of analysis must be performed to measure the activity against the standard. Techniques such as cost-benefit analysis and time-and-motion studies, are commonly employed to measure the standards of performance for operations. Of course, not everything can be quantified; judgment and flexibility are necessary. However, great care must be taken because subjective judgment may obviate actual performance. Some types of performance are more difficult to measure because they are more complex, less regulated, and require greater initiative and thus are less quantifiable. In other words, not all quantitative measures accurately reflect the quality of an activity. For example, a rare books cataloger may perform original cataloging on two items during an eight-hour period. The quality of that activity must be measured delicately, objectively, and with full understanding of all nuances involved.

Increasing attention has been paid to performance measures in libraries and information services, as is particularly evident in four recent international conferences on the topic.[10] There are a number of questions that "outline the different 'hows' of measurement and, in effect, encompass input, output, performance, and outcomes measures. The questions can be used individually or in groups. In fact, some of the 'hows' are calculated by using data derived from other 'hows.'" Simply stated, these questions focus on "how much?" "how many?" "how economical?" "how prompt?" "how valuable?" "how reliable?" "how courteous?" and "how satisfied?"[11] Therefore, measures can be conducted on aspects of extensiveness (i.e., amount of service provided), effectiveness, efficiency, costing (i.e., cost-benefit or cost-effectiveness), service quality, satisfaction, or any number of other factors. It is obvious from the large number of reports and studies that measuring performance is a continuous and continuing process, whether it is related to systems measurement or personnel performance.

One continuing issue is that researchers and practitioners have not yet adequately developed a set of representative outcome measures that convey customer expectations from which libraries can choose which ones to use (or modify) for local benchmarking, nor have they produced meaningful frameworks for interpreting qualitative outcomes of service quality.[12] It is recognized that those performance metrics must be in place, with an infrastructure to collect, filter, analyze, and disseminate them both within and outside the organization. Many groups are working on such activities. For instance, in 1999 the Association of Research Libraries began an ARL New Measures Initiative to assess how well libraries meet stakeholder needs and how they use their resources and services. The measures address the issue of impact of the library's resources and services and how this can be evaluated in terms of the difference between the user's expectations and the perception of what is delivered. The ARL "LibQUAL+" project is one example of such efforts.[13]

Quantitative and descriptive statistics are important and easier to develop and measure than qualitative ones, particularly when benchmarking is used. Such statistics are compiled by a number of organizations, again particularly by ARL, which has collected and published statistics of its member institutions annually for the past forty years. Those describe, for instance, collections, expenditures, staffing, and service activities, and in 2000 they began to include data on the size and kind of members' electronic resources.[14]

What is important in all measurement activities is to keep accurate records of what is done so that the process can be monitored on an ongoing basis. If records are not kept, if there is lack of control, if the output cannot be measured objectively, then it is difficult to assess how much actual performance deviates from the planned performance and to determine a measure of success. A number of research reports prove helpful in this activity. Perhaps the most comprehensive is that developed by the International Organization for Standardization, which specifies a set of twenty-nine indicators grouped in three areas:

1. user satisfaction;

2. public services, which include general indicators as well as specific indicators on providing documents, retrieving documents, lending documents, document delivery from external sources, inquiry and reference services, information searching, and facilities; and

3. technical services, including indicators in the area of acquiring, processing, and cataloging documents.[15]

Besides feedback, the other type of basic control is prevention, which attempts to predict what will happen by setting parameters. Goal setting in the planning process is a good example of this type of control. Goal setting takes information about past performance and introduces it into decisions about adjustments that are needed for future actions. Such a process is just as important to an ordinary control process as it is to a more complex, automated one.

Preventative control processes, as the name implies, attempt to prevent deviations from developing in the conduct of organizational behavior. Feedback control processes rely on information from actual performance and are designed to correct deviations after they have developed.[16]

—W. Jack Duncan,
Essentials of Management

Correcting Deviations

Correcting any deviations from the norm is a vital step in the process. This correction can be achieved by exercising organizational prerogative, for instance, in the case of personnel, by reassignment or clarification of duties, by additional staffing, by better selection and training of staff, or by some other method of restaffing. Corrections can also be made by adjusting goals, developing new or alternative plans, or altering ways of doing things.

A simplified example of detecting deviations in libraries, which combines elements of goal setting and feedback, is a monthly budget balance sheet that might show, for instance, that by the month of July, three-fourths of the amount budgeted for telephone calls for the year has already been expended and that, unless corrective action is taken, the organization will overrun the budgeted amount in that category well before the end of the calendar year. A decision must be made on how to keep this from happening.

Cybernetics, which has become increasingly important in the control feedback process, studies the interaction of communication and control as fundamental factors in all human activity and now is being applied to many large organizations, including libraries and information centers. Basically, cybernetics is a self-regulating method by which messages that the system sends to itself indicate deviations from the desired course. This may be expressed in a very simplified diagram that shows how the information flow makes possible the self-regulation of the system (see Figure 14.1).

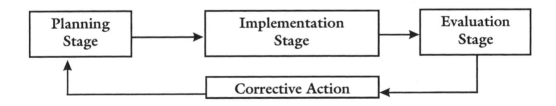

Figure 14.1. With Cybernetics, an Organization Can Provide Feedback to Itself

Communication is the most important aspect of a feedback control system because it involves transmitting and receiving messages or information—in this case, data used to make the decisions that control the system's behavior. Again, a simplified diagram illustrates the process (see Figure 14.2).

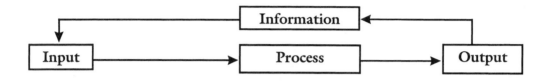

Figure 14.2. Communication Is Key to a Feedback Control System

Evaluating Efforts

The evaluation process is a complex one that identifies areas needing improvement with an aim toward taking corrective action. It is a process and should not be considered a one-time thing or even a sometime thing but rather an ongoing review of operations. This aspect of controlling is inextricably tied to the planning process because it is impossible to evaluate unless it is known what is to be evaluated. How effectively and efficiently a library or information center is meeting the goals and objectives identified in the planning process can be measured through this evaluation. If the whole process is viewed as a circle, the evaluation step in the decision-making process brings one full circle back to planning for change. There are at least three factors one must consider in evaluation:

1. The input to the service, or the application of resources necessary for library services to occur, including staff, materials, space, and equipment. They can be measured in terms of the amount of resources involved and their cost. Those are all measures of input one should consider.

2. The output should be considered in terms of the quantities of output of the services and how that can be cost factored, including price, quality, timeliness, availability, and accessibility, all contributing to the value of the services. Measures of use and nonuse of the services require examining the factors that affect use and nonuse and assessment of the importance and satisfaction with specific attributes of those services.

3. The outcomes include such elements as saving time, improving productivity, improving quality of life and work, and enhancing timeliness. It is the relationship of those measures that begins to illustrate the usefulness and value of libraries that has some bearing on justifying the budget and resources.

Evaluation requires that several questions will have been answered: Are you now able to make decisions that you wanted to be able to make as a result of your evaluation? Was the primary audience adequately identified and solicited for the results? Was the information needed actually received in the process? Where was that information sought and received, and how? Were resources adequate to get the information, analyze it, and report it? Basically, those are the same questions one will have asked before the beginning of the process. Evaluation requires careful collection and analysis of that type of data in order to make decisions.

Evaluation can come from a variety of sources. Cost-benefit analysis, budget analysis, performance evaluation, and collection evaluation are examples of techniques used in the evaluation process. Accountability in libraries has fostered the development of many prescriptive techniques to measure the efficiency of library operations and the effectiveness of library services.

> Evaluation is the process of identifying and collecting data about an organization or its specific programs, operations, and/or services. These data, viewed within a decision-making or policy-setting context, provide insights into the effectiveness, efficiency, impact, and value of a program, operation, or service.[17]
>
> —Peter Hernon and Ellen Altman,
> *Service Quality in Academic Libraries*

When one thinks of internal controls, mechanical controls come to mind first, including circulation control, automated serials, and the like. These technological controls are only examples of tools that are used to measure library operations. The computer has become an invaluable aid to decision making, particularly for larger library organizations. It has been used effectively, although in a limited number of situations, in establishing models for library operations through decision theory, game theory, graph theory, queuing theory, and simulation exercises, among other applications. Many more basic techniques and tools are employed in the control process in the library, particularly as libraries become more accountable for their operations. These include varying sophisticated tools, such as decision support systems and operations research.

Tools That Support Techniques of Coordination

> We now know that the source of wealth is something, specifically human knowledge. If we apply knowledge to tasks that we obviously know how to do, we call it productivity. If we apply knowledge to tasks that are new and different, we call it innovation. Only knowledge allows us to achieve those two goals.[18]
>
> —Justin Hibbard,
> "Knowing What We Know"

The function of coordinating and controlling so that good decisions can be made requires accurate and timely information for the control and monitoring of specific kinds of data. This process has become heavily dependent upon technology to enhance efficient information gathering. This combination of human expertise within the organization and technology to facilitate its use is what one might identify at the core of discussions about the knowledge management initiative or "knowledge networking" today. The "process of locating, organizing, transferring, and using information and expertise within the organization,"[19] made more efficient and effective by the use of technology, fits appropriately in any discussion of tools for decision making. Automated systems have the capacity to crunch enormous amounts of information relating both to input and output of information for decision making in libraries. A few of those will be discussed here.

However, caution must always be exercised in employing some of these tools because, in the hands of amateurs, the quantitative systems and tools frequently produce misleading or wrong solutions. In addition, mechanistic formulas for dealing with complex realities are not always appropriate. However, several elements can be identified in a library context that lend themselves to adequate measurement tools, and these can prove helpful in meeting goals and objectives as they coordinate and measure performance.

Cost-Benefit Analysis

A cost-benefit evaluation is conducted to determine whether the potential worth or value of a service is greater than or less than the cost of providing it; in other words, is the service justified? Developing a cost-benefit analysis process need not be an intimidating undertaking. Most people, in fact, engage in some level of intuitive cost-benefit analysis in their daily work. In its simplest form, cost-benefit analysis is little more than a formalized approach for identifying and weighing the advantages and drawbacks associated with a decision. In general, cost-benefit analysis provides a useful tool for evaluating the efficiency of a regulation. At its best, it can separate good intentions from good ideas. It is, however, only a tool, and as with any tool, it can be used effectively or misused. Cost-benefit analysis is flexible and can be adapted to focus on specific functions or aggregated on the costs and benefits of the system as a whole. Some cost-benefit activities appear to have little to do with control—financial reports, status reports, project reports—but they all require some type of monitoring, an overview of what is being done, how it is being done, and if it is being done efficiently.

One of the most difficult aspects for libraries is placing a monetary figure on the benefit of operations, unlike many other organizations that can calculate benefits for service from the financial charge of that service, which somewhat reflects the "value" of providing that service. Cost-benefit analysis is a set of procedures to measure the merit of actions in monetary terms. The process reduces uncertainty by helping to make decisions about the best of options available. It is used as a counterpart to private-sector profitability accounting. The difference is that most public actions to improve public well-being do not have well-established private markets that generate price information on which to judge their value or benefits. "Cost-benefit analysis can be defined as a systematic approach which seeks to

♦ determine whether or not a particular program or proposal is justified,

♦ rank various alternatives appropriate to a given set of objectives, and

♦ ascertain the optimal course of action to attain these objectives."[20]

It is a form of analysis which considers both direct and indirect costs in the allocation of resources. The technique is used to examine both the current budget allocation process and to ascertain the level of financial support required to establish some specified benefits of both new and existing programs. It requires a statement of the problem, accompanied by estimation of costs and benefits associated with each alternative identified in order to compare them with each other and with the benefits which are sought. The objective is to identify that one alternative that offers the greatest benefits at the lowest costs. However, it must be remembered that sometimes the cost of a service may not outweigh its direct benefit, but there may be an intangible benefit that must be considered as well.

Several factors must be identified in the process, including any external constraints that must be built into the mathematical models as parameters. The process also requires identification of input costs and output benefits. Time factor consideration requires delineation of costs involving research and development, investment, and operations. There must be recognition that there will likely be a time lag between initiation and achievement of the initial benefits. Because the topic is a detailed one, requiring extensive description, it is only mentioned here to give the reader some idea of its approach. The process has been lauded and lambasted, calling it "an infallible means of reaching the new Utopia to a waste of resources in attempting to measure the unmeasurable."[21]

The technique of cost-benefit analysis, simply stated, involves choosing from alternatives when measurement in monetary or other specific measures may not be enough or even possible. Wherever possible, however, some specific measures should be established. For instance, if the objective is the improvement of referral service at the information desk, effectiveness can be measured by the number of in-person, telephone, or online inquiries answered or unanswered as well as patrons' judgment of staff and satisfaction with the service. As the term suggests, cost-benefit analysis is used to identify not only the cost of a program but also the benefits of the various alternatives that must be considered. The emphasis of cost effectiveness is on output; each alternative is weighed in terms of effectiveness or costs against the objective that has been set. In some cases, cost models can be developed to show cost estimates for each alternative, or effectiveness models can be developed to show relationships between the alternatives and their effectiveness. Cost-benefit analysis is often confused with cost effectiveness, but there is a subtle difference.[22] Cost-benefit analysis is concerned with the cost, cost effectiveness, and value. Cost-benefit analysis asks, "Which is the best (least expensive, or efficient) way to perform an operation?" whereas cost effectiveness asks, "Because this is what the service costs, is it worth it (is it effective)?" which is a measure of quality.

The process of cost-benefits analysis has been greatly enhanced by the development of software packages.

Benchmarking

Benchmarking was first more commonly identified as a TQM tool used to measure and compare the work processes in one's organization with those in other organizations. It has since come into its own in libraries as they recognize the benefits of using it in measurement of activities. Benchmarking is information-driven and requires libraries to examine their work processes and functions and to measure their productivity against that of others. By monitoring others, they can be encouraged to enhance their own performance by adopting, or adapting, the best practices of others. Benchmarking is an excellent tool to determine how effectively, efficiently, and economically an institution rates against others in its peer group. The goal of benchmarking is to increase performance by:

♦ identifying libraries with best practices as partners;

♦ measuring and comparing a selected work process against others in the peer group; and

♦ emulating, or adapting, the identified best practices for the local library or information center situation.

Of course "best practices" are not stagnant and are always evolving; therefore, benchmarking is a continuous adjustment process. As a tool, it requires an organization to focus efforts on improving the effectiveness and efficiency of delivery of products and services. Benefits of benchmarking include the possibility of demonstrating the value of a library system and services in numerical terms; in addition, it allows comparison with libraries in the peer group. ARL's statistics are good examples of that activity, and when one examines strategic plans of ARL member libraries, they often cite those statistics. There is even a Public Libraries Benchmarking Club in the UK.[23]

In some cases a benchmarking study can be used to prevent a decrease in services, including financial and systems initiatives. The desired outcomes of benchmarking are efficiency and effectiveness—reduction of costs and improvement in customer service. Several types of benchmarking are being used in libraries: internal benchmarking used to measure similar activities performed by different units; functional benchmarking comparing an organization's practices with those identified as leaders within the same service area; generic benchmarking that compares an organization's functions or practices that cross different types of organizations; and competitive benchmarking, which compares a unit's performance of a service or process with that of a competitor.[24]

Program Evaluation and Review Techniques (PERT)

Program Evaluation and Review Techniques is a common sense tool that helps remind people of the preparation work needed before an event and helps them check if the tasks will be completed on schedule. PERT is a technique of control in the planning process that is highly applicable to library operations. PERT was developed a number of years ago by the U.S. Navy's Special Projects Office to plan the Polaris weapon system. A method of planning and scheduling work, PERT is sometimes called the Critical Path Method (CPM). It involves identifying all of the key activities in a particular project; devising the sequence of activities and arranging them in a flow diagram; and, finally, assigning duration of time for the performance of each phase of the work to be done. This technique consists of enumerating events whose completion can be measured. "Most likely" times are then calculated for the accomplishment of each event, so that one can see how long it would take for the progression of events to be completed. This model-building network approach is most effectively used for major projects that are one-time events. An example would be the opening of a new library. Activities can be plotted to allow the librarian to determine the most expeditious route—or critical path—that can be taken to carry out the event. As with other techniques discussed, in PERT one must be able to state objectives, then activities must be enumerated and estimates must be given for the time required for each of these activities. The abbreviated, two-path diagram in Figure 14.3 illustrates the concept.

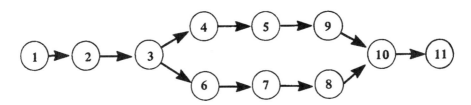

Figure 14.3. PERT Diagram Shows the Planned Schedule of a Task, in Graphic Format, of a Two-Path Approach

Figure 14.3 suggests that there are two paths to be taken—say, from the time the idea of a new library is formulated until the building is ready for occupancy (O represents events and → represents activities). Times would be assigned for each activity, say, three weeks between events 4 and 5, one week between 6 and 7. As illustrated, either path 1-2-3-4-5-9-10-11 or path 1-2-3-6-7-8-10-11 can be taken. If time is of the essence, the shorter route might be more desirable. Time is the key element in the critical path schedule. Perhaps a bit more detail, illustrating the CPM concept, can demonstrate the critical issue of time (see Figure 14.4). The time required to complete the series is the greatest sum of the combined time requirements. Of the four paths illustrated (1-2-5-8; 1-3-5-8; 1-4-6-8; and 1-2-7-8), the longest path, with work going forth on all four paths simultaneously, is 1-2-7-8. This path takes fifteen weeks to complete and is the critical path that controls the schedule, more or less, for the whole project.

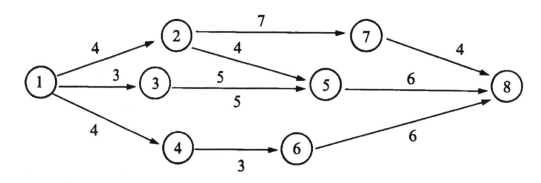

Figure 14.4. A Four-Path PERT Diagram Can Be Used to Illustrate the Critical Paths of Complex, Multipart Projects

The PERT/CPM technique allows one to analyze a project in depth before it is initiated. This not only gives the decision-maker an idea of the time frame involved but also aids in identifying potential weaknesses. The biggest disadvantage of PERT is its overemphasis on time at the expense of more detailed attention to cost. This disadvantage has led to the development of PERT/COST, which introduces the cost factor into the process. When the system to be studied is complex and when a number of events are involved, it becomes very expensive to establish a cost for each event. PERT is used mainly in industry, but some library systems have explored its value in the planning process, particularly when the process is a complex and lengthy one.

This brief discussion in no way conveys the importance or potential of mathematical or statistical controls and does not even begin to present all of their variations. Volumes have been written on each of the topics; interested readers should consult the appropriate headings in the library literature for a fuller discussion.

As was mentioned earlier, technology is having great influence on the management of library operations. The effects of electronic data processing on circulation control, acquisitions of library materials, serials control, and other functions are significant. In addition, computerized services, such as online cataloging through networks and access to bibliographic databases, enable libraries to measure more adequately service output and costs. The possibility of using mathematical or statistical control techniques, therefore, becomes greater. Expert systems have been developed to monitor performance and are being widely applied in problem-solving activities of information services.

> At different times . . . different management systems are in vogue. Some of these systems represent real innovation; more often someone 'reinvents the wheel.'[25]
>
> —Bruce H. DeWoolfson Jr.,
> "Public Sector MBO and PPBS:
> Cross Fertilization in Management Systems"

Information Systems

Over the years, several basic tools have been developed to measure the output of services, and some of them have been employed in libraries. These include a number of techniques relating to operations control, among them Management Information Systems (MIS), which was one of the first technological tools to gather internal data, summarize it, organize it for decision making, and present it as information to be used in the control process, particularly by senior decision makers. Its biggest failing was that it did not adequately take into account external intelligence.

Management information systems are viewed as ways of collecting data to improve efficiency and effectiveness. Well-ordered management information systems can be enhanced through control and evaluation techniques and tools, including Program Evaluation Review Technique (PERT), the Gantt Chart, On-line Analytical Process (OLAP), and the Critical Path Method (CPM). Typically, they involve financial information, personnel information, performance information, and user information, all related to the feedback aspect of control. Some of these tools have received recent criticism from those who believe that management information systems represent simply a process, sometimes with adequate reference to strategic planning, operations planning, or budgets, and that their objectives have no relationship to other developments. There is no doubt that to be effective, any kind of management information system must be reviewed and, if adopted, have a direct relationship to what is desired as far as information retrieval for library operations is concerned. Technology has made it easier to standardize procedures and to apply mechanical methods to measure them. Newer techniques, such as expert systems, are beginning to affect management of libraries and have taken over the impact that technology now provides.

Decision Support Systems (DSS)

> Librarians, as information managers, have been slow to recognize the distinction between information as the particular commodity in which libraries and information specialists deal, and the concept of management information as an organizational or corporate resource. A significant resource for better performance in libraries is therefore under-utilized.[26]
>
> —Rowena Cullen,
> "A Model of a Management Information
> System for Library and Information Service Managers"

The concept of management systems eventually metamorphosed from Management Information Systems (MIS) into the Decision Support Systems (DSS), which in itself is not an electronic data processing and software system but rather a process that employs data processing and other online analysis to provide required information. Such a system, combining the capacities of technology and human knowledge, can improve the quality of decision making.

It is an organized method of providing past, present, and projection information related to internal operations and external operations, the latter being related to the environmental scanning process mentioned under the topic of strategic planning. This implies "a structured organized approach with the assistance of some automated mechanism."[27] DSS supports the planning, control, and operational functions of an organization by furnishing information in the proper time frame to assist in the decision-making process.

DSS covers a variety of systems, tools, and technologies that incorporate both data and models and that are now being transposed to create a knowledge-based system as state of the art. Newer terms that focus on certain types of decisions, including Executive Support Systems, Executive Information Systems, Intelligent Information Systems, Organizational Support Systems, Controlling Information Systems, and the like, are now prominent. The concept takes advantage of the continuous development in the database management and modeling arena to offer software that supports computerized decision making. It is more interactive in that it can respond to messages and can project alternative approaches upon which decisions can be made. It can simulate situations and project outcomes. This computer-assisted analysis is an effective tool for financial planning, among other activities. It allows for testing assumptions, factoring risks, and exploring alternatives. It is particularly useful when managers are presented with problems that have more than one solution, thereby enhancing the manager's decision-making options, for instance, through time-and-motion study.

Time-and-Motion Studies

Motion studies enable a library system to record in flow chart form the present method of doing things, to analyze the method's effectiveness, and, from this analysis, to improve the method. The new method of doing things can then be timed to report the performance standard. Time studies complement motion studies in determining performance standards. A third element in this quantifying process is cost—that is, attaching a monetary figure to the activities of an individual. Both time and cost vary with the level of expertise of the individual performing the task and the institution in which the work is taking place. Many time-and-motion studies have been and are being done in libraries, particularly relating to routine tasks, such as pasting pockets in books, typing subject headings on preprinted cards for those still using card catalogs, or preparing items for the bindery.

Operations Research

Making objectives explicit, deriving suitable measures of the extent of meeting them, developing simple quantitative relations between input and output, and identifying constraints that one should strive to remove have proved considerably more valuable than the mere manipulation of complicated mathematical models.[28]

—M. Elton and Brian Vicker,
"The Scope of Operational Research
in the Library and Information Field"

Two terms that are closely related and often used interchangeably are Operations Research and Systems Analysis. Actually, the latter emerges from the former. Operations Research (OR) today is largely identified with specific techniques, such as linear programming, queuing theory analysis, dynamic programming, statistical models, Monte Carlo (randomizing) methods, gaming and game theory, and other computer simulation models. It grew out of military needs during World War II and occupies the interest of a number of different groups, particularly statisticians and mathematicians.

Operations Research is an "experimental and applied science devoted to observing, understanding and predicting the behavior of purposeful [worker-machine] systems, and operations researchers are actively engaged in applying this knowledge to practical problems."[29] This definition can be further refined to: "the use of scientific methods to study the functions of an organization so as to develop better methods of planning and controlling changes in the organization. It can be viewed as a branch of management, engineering or science. As part of the field of management, its purpose is to assist decision makers in choosing preferred future courses of action by systematically identifying and examining the alternatives which are available to the manager, and by predicting the possible outcomes for such actions."[30]

From the late 1960s up until now, applied Operations Research has come into its own in the library decision-making process. This is primarily because in recent years decision making in general has emphasized the mathematical and statistical approach rather than a judgment-based approach. The emphasis of the mathematical approach was facilitated primarily by the application of scientific methods and technological development, the major impact coming with the development of the computer, which was necessary for the manipulation of complex data. One use to which computers have been put is modeling organizations or systems. Conceptual models used for decision making are simply computer-based attempts at simulating reality. They are powerful means of testing various alternatives without changing the commitments involved in a typical decision. The primary approach of Operations Research consists of a broad view of the problem by the whole organization. This is succeeded by a team initiative, using personnel with different backgrounds from different departments, with the team addressing the economic-technical aspects of the total system. The key components to the process, then, are application of the scientific method; using a systems approach to problem-solving; and employing mathematical, probability, and statistical techniques and computer modeling. Statistical analysis is made easier with the technologies available today, software systems for modeling. However, some types of statistical analysis require a different approach to gathering data that can then be analyzed electronically.

In terms of control, the major contribution of Operations Research has been in constructing models that can be used in the decision-making process. To accomplish this, a basic knowledge of systems analysis is necessary. Again, the important first step, as in most techniques, is to identify objectives and then to look at variables that might influence the objectives. These are expressed mathematically to determine the best alternative in terms of the objectives set. The system currently in use is described. Based upon this analysis, a series of mathematical models is developed to describe the interrelationships within the organization. Data are then collected to measure the system, or if data are not available, assumptions or speculations are made. This information provides the basis for a working model for a new system. With this information in hand, the librarian is able to make decisions based on the alternatives presented. The analytical statistical technique and the techniques of probability theory are employed.

It has been pointed out that the use of Operations Research in libraries is based on the application of the scientific approach to practical problems: "It normally operates in four distinctive stages:

1. Description of the system being considered, especially by means of mathematical models and computer simulations;

2. Measurement, using objective data wherever these can be obtained;

3. Evaluation, the presentation of relevant information to the system manager (here the librarian) to aid in making decisions between different courses of action;

4. Operational control, assisting the development of ways and means of achieving the objectives aimed for over a period of time."[31]

The greatest potential of operations research lies in predicting the future by employing the mathematical models rather than in knowing the present by analyzing past experimental data.[32] Because of the technique's complexity and its use of mathematics and computers, as well as the costs of modeling, most librarians have not yet applied Operations Research to improving managerial control.

Also, there are limits to this approach. The quantitative method can be no better than the assumptions and estimates used in it. Its greatest limitation to use in libraries is that quantitative analysis is not adaptable to all situations. Some variables in libraries are very difficult to quantify, yet to achieve a proper quantitative analysis, all variables must be assigned quantitative weights either through amassed data or through estimates. Therefore, a great deal of judgment is required, first to know when to use the quantitative method, and then to know how to estimate costs of activities. In addition, quantitative analysis can become very elaborate and costly. One criticism of the technique is that it does not emphasize human factors enough because such factors are difficult to model mathematically. Also, this method demands some knowledge of mathematics and statistical concepts, and these are areas where librarians are thought to be at their weakest; we have relied heavily on nonlibrarians to provide this expertise. Finally, it should be remembered that use of quantitative tools concerns only one phase of the decision-making process. It is a kind of management information that is infrequently used to identify the problem or to develop alternatives.

One specific technique used by operations researchers is linear programming. Certain conditions much exist to make its use effective:

♦ "Goals must be stated in mathematical terms;

♦ Alternatives must be available and stated;

♦ Resources (are required which) are usually limited;

♦ Variables must be interrelated."[33]

Sometimes the cost of linear programming outweighs its benefits because it is difficult, if not impossible, to quantify the required data. "Linear programming is concerned with optimizing a decision problem by analyzing interrelationships of system components and contributions of these components to the objective function."[34]

Knowledge Management

Just as MIS was reinvented in the form of DSS, so has the concept of information resource management been assumed under the concept of knowledge management, a developing system that attempts to capture the knowledge and expertise of human capital as well as documents, repositories, routines, processes, practices, and norms within and flowing into the organization by creating a computerized system to do that. Such a systematic process of transferring knowledge within the organization is made easier by technologies, using DSS, statistical analysis software, artificial intelligence, and other developing tools. The question of systematically acquiring outside knowledge, with benchmarking being a good example for identifying best practices, is incorporated in the process. The elements of knowledge management systems include accessing, evaluating, managing, organizing, filtering, and distributing knowledge.

Reporting Results

The process of monitoring and feedback is the best way of expressing accountability in library and information services in both qualitative and quantitative terms. It provides checks and balances for the service goal. Based on evaluation as part of the reporting mechanism, decision makers decide whether or not changes are desirable, either in the system or in the strategic goals of the organization. Such reporting mechanisms are not only important to evaluate results and to correct deviations but also as marketing strategies intended for funding authorities, customers, and all staff within the organization.

Communication tools, which have been used in libraries and information centers that measure performance, include personal observation, meetings, email, statistical data, oral reports, and written print-on-paper and electronically generated reports. Other publications help facilitate the process of reporting results. When one searches the Internet, it is obvious that the web is also being used to report "to the world," not just to constituents, on activities, and on outcomes. This reporting activity is conducted in a number of ways, internally and externally. Sometimes it is on a monthly basis to review results; sometimes it is carried out internally on a daily basis by keeping a "score card" of projects and progress toward their goal accomplishment. Other times, for various audiences, reviews and reports are presented on a less frequent basis. Occasionally, such reports are required at specific intervals, for accrediting or other control purposes, by outside agencies or organizations.

Techniques such as "story boarding," where goals and objectives are compared with performance to date to identify progress, are sometimes used. Most important, data should be reported and performance explained internally, and performance information should be consolidated and reporting mechanisms consistent across the organization. Results should not only be shared internally, but also externally with customers and stakeholders through annual reports. Basically, data from the several techniques available fall into one of three primary categories:

1. Statistics (counting inputs, staff, materials, services).

2. Performance indicators (how well are we doing?).

3. Economic value (how much are we worth, in monetary terms?).

In the reporting process, it is important to recognized that there are strong relationships among resource allocation, strategic planning, and performance measurement; each builds upon the other and creates a circle of service. The budget is allocated according to primary goals and objectives that have been identified in the strategic plan, which should have identified some of the measure to be used in terms of output. Because the library is not a static organization, evaluation must be made from that perspective. As the goals and needs of society change, so the library or information center must respond. Therefore, past measures may no longer be important, and new ones may need to be found. A good example is in the area of access and ownership of materials as a criterion of quality.

Conclusion

Coordinating functions are created to facilitate the achievement of goals and objectives in libraries and information centers. Those standard-setting activities and evaluation and measurement techniques provide vital feedback information to management and staff as activities are carried out to achieve the mission. Some tools are more sophisticated and have greater application for larger organizations, whereas others can be used in all types and sizes of libraries and information centers. Both techniques and tools are important parts of the process of accountability and reporting on success.

Notes

1. James V. McGee and Laurence Prusak, *Managing Information Strategically* (New York: John Wiley & Sons, 1993), 183.

2. Sarah M. Pritchard, "Determining Quality in Academic Libraries," *Library Trends* 44, (1996): 591–92.

3. Peter F. Drucker, "Controls, Control and Management," in C. P. Bonini, R. K. Jaedicke, and H. M. Wanger, eds., *Managerial Controls: New Directions in Basic Research* (New York: McGraw-Hill, 1964), 286.

4.   Ronald L. Baker, "Evaluating Quality and Effectiveness: Regional Accreditation Principles and Practices," *Journal of Academic Librarianship* 28 (January–March 2002): 5.

5.   George Schreyogg and Horst Steinman, "Strategic Control: A New Perspective," *Academy of Management Review* 12 (January 1987): 91.

6.   Morris Hamburg et al., *Library Planning and Decision-Making Systems* (Cambridge, MA: MIT Press, 1974), 38–39.

7.   For example, "Guidelines for Two-Year College Learning Resources Programs," *College & Research Libraries News* 33 (December 1972): 305–15.

8.   For example, "Standards for College Libraries, 1985," *College & Research Libraries News* 46 (May 1985): 241–52.

9.   McNamara Fallacy, quoted in *The Age of Paradox* by Charles Handy (Boston: Harvard Business School Press, 1994), 221.

10.   *Proceedings of the Northumbria International Conference on Performance Measurement in Libraries and Information Services*, 1st 1995; 2d 1997, 3d 1999, 4th 2001 (Newcastle: University of Northumbria, Information North).

11.   Peter Hernon and Ellen Altman, *Assessing Service Quality: Satisfying the Expectations of Library Customers* (Chicago: American Library Association, 1998), 51–53.

12.   Peter Hernon, "Service Quality and Outcome Measures," *Journal of Academic Librarianship* 23 (January 1997): 1.

13.   Colleen Cook et al., "LibQUAL+: Service Quality Assessment in Research Libraries," *IFLA Journal* 27 (2000): 264–68.

14.   www.arl.org/stats/program/timeline.html.

15.   International Organization for Standardization, *ISO 11620, Information and Documentation—Library Performance Indicators* (Geneva: International Organization for Standardization, 1998).

16.   Walter Jack Duncan, *Essentials of Management*, 2d ed. (Hinsdale, IL: Dryden Press, 1978), 408.

17.   Peter Hernon and Ellen Altman, *Service Quality in Academic Libraries* (Norwood, NJ: Ablex, 1996), 15.

18.   Justin Hibbard, "Knowing What We Know," *Information Week* 20 (October 1997): 46.

19.   http://www.apqc.org/b2/b2.htm.

20.   Alan Walter Steiss, *Strategic Management and Organizational Decision Making* (Lexington, MA: Lexington Books, 1985), 117.

21.   A. R. Prest and R. Turvey, "Cost Benefit Analysis: A Survey," *The Economic Journal* 85 (March 1965): 583.

22.   F. Wilfred Lancaster, "The Evaluation of Library and Information Services," in F. W. Lancaster and C. W. Cleverdon, eds., *Evaluation and Scientific Management of Libraries and Information Centers* (Leyden, The Netherlands: Noordhoff, 1977), 4.

23.   Public Libraries Benchmarking Club, UK www.ipf.co.uk/benchmarking/libraries /default.htm.

24.   T. M. Peischel, "Benchmarking: A Process for Improvement," *Library Administration and Management* 9 (Spring 1995): 99–101.

25.   Bruce H. DeWoolfson Jr., "Public Sector MBO and PPBS: Cross Fertilization in Management Styles," *Public Administration Review* 36 (July–August 1975): 387.

26.   Rowena Cullen, "A Model of a Management Information System for Library and Information Service Managers," *International Journal of Information and Library Research* 2 (1990): 24.

27.   Michael E. D. Koenig, *Information Driven Management Concepts and Themes: A Toolkit for Librarians*, IFLA Pub. No. 86 (New Providence, NJ: Bowker-Saur, 1998), 49.

28.   M. Elton and Brian Vicker, "The Scope of Operational Research in the Library and Information Field," *ASLIB Proceedings* 25 (1973): 319.

29.   "Guidelines for the Practice of Operations Research," *Operations Research* 19 (September 1971): 1138.

30.   Ferdinand F. Leimkuhler, "Operations Research and Systems Analysis," in F. W. Lancaster and C. W. Cleverdon, eds., *Evaluation and Scientific Management of Libraries and Information Centers* (Leyden, The Netherlands: Noordhoff, 1977), 131.

31.   A. Graham Mackenzie and Michael K. Buckland, "Operations Research," in *British Librarianship and Information Science*, 1966–1970 ed. (London: Library Association, 1972), 24.

32.   Ching-chih Chen, *Applications of Operations Research Models to Libraries* (Cambridge, MA: MIT Press, 1976), 3.

33.   Richard I. Levin and Charles A. Kirkpatrick, *Quantitative Approaches to Management*, 2d ed. (New York: McGraw-Hill, 1971), 161.

34.   Sang M. Lee and L. J. Moore, *Introduction to Decision Science* (New York: Petrocelli-Charter, 1975), 90.

Chapter 15

Financial Control

As a planning document, the budget is a presentation of the library's objectives in terms of specific programs to be carried out within a specified period of time. In that regard, it can be considered a plan set forth in financial terms. As a political document, the budget, when stated and approved in terms of full funding for "visible" programs, is a statement of the importance of library services relative to other . . . services.

—Ann E. Prentice,
Public Library Finances

Budgeting

The link between planned activities and financial outcomes becomes stronger and more necessary as organizations grow and missions broaden. "Which comes first, planning or budgeting?" is a question often asked. "Neither," must be the answer because they are inextricably tied and cannot stand alone; cost predictions must be based upon a realistic picture of what is available to accomplish service objectives, both those already in existence and those being planned, which must be based upon what monies are likely to be available. Planning and budgeting must be linked in the preparation and presentation of a budget because the adoption of a planning and budgeting framework should reflect the organization's commitment to effective planning and resource allocation, quality leadership, and accountability.

One of the most important of all planning activities is to determine how resources will be allocated among the various alternatives facing the organization. Budgeting, then, is the concept that pulls together the various pieces of the operational plan and relates it to the services plan in monetary terms. It is a process that must be viewed as a whole, with equally important parts being linked together through the goals and objectives of the organization. In essence, the budget is the monetary expression of the strategic plan.

One good definition of budgetary control is that stated by the International Management Institute, which defines it as a method of rationalization whereby estimates covering different periods of time are, by the study of statistical records and analytical research of all kinds, established for everything that affects the life of a business concern and that can be expressed in figures. "A budget is not only a financial plan that sets forth cost and . . . goals . . . but also a device for control, coordination, communication, performance evaluation and motivation."[2]

Budgeting relies on predicting and justifying what will be needed by the organization to function financially in the future. Therefore, budgeting can be viewed as both a planning technique and a controlling technique. In that regard, the budget is one of the best and most important control devices to measure information services programs' performance. In the preliminary stages of developing a strategic plan for the library, each potential goal, when it is financially analyzed, is assigned a monetary figure based upon projected resources necessary to accomplish it. A preliminary budget for each of those goals is developed so that benefits can be compared with costs before finally choosing among the various potential goals.

Budgets—Planning and Evaluation Tools

In its simplest form, the budget can be stated in terms of income and expenses. The operating budget is a stated program that reflects the goals and objectives of information service and defines the manager's authority to act in that regard. It is also a political document, expressing policy decisions about priorities of programs. Budgets, when viewed as evaluation tools, are commitments or contracts with funding authorities for services and programs to be rendered, and they can facilitate the process of evaluating how successfully the goals and objectives are being addressed. Budgeting is that part of the total planning equation that assures that resources are obtained and then used effectively and efficiently in accomplishing objectives. Libraries and information centers usually budget on a yearly cycle, although it is sometimes necessary to construct operational plans that project two or three years into the future. The budget for any current cycle, or even for future ones, will inevitably be affected by past commitments, established standards of service, existing organizational structure, and current methods of operations, as well as future changes. If changes are proposed, consideration must be given to preparing the organization for change and altering the budgetary justification and allocation. The three phases of a budgeting cycle include:

1. preparation of the budget (some forms are included here, access to others is given on the website to illustrate this phase);

2. presentation to funding authorities, with full justification linking inputs (financial) with outputs (results); and

3. implementation of the actual beginning of the phase for which the budget has been allocated.

There are several different types of budgets. For libraries and information centers, the operations budget is the primary type of budget with its focus on revenue and expenses. In addition, a second type of budget, a capital budget, involved with capital investments such as a new building, is periodically necessary. The capital expense type of budget is developed to reflect expenditures over the estimated period of a project's development. Other types of budgets, which primarily relate to for-profit organizations, are not discussed here. Some components, which are typically taught in accounting courses, such as the financial budget, with subsets of cash-flow, capital expenditures, and balance sheets, are important, and a detailed discussion can be found in textbooks on financial accounting.

The Funding Process

The budgetary process is not just a controlling mechanism conducted on the inside by a stereotypical arm-banded, green-visor-shaded accountant, hovering over huge, figure-laden tomes in a dimly lit back room. Libraries and information centers are accountable for their actions, and charged with wisely expending allocated monies. External forces—political, economic, social, and technological—are constant factors that affect the budget and the process of budgeting. In other sections of this volume, factors—including values, organizational culture, commitment, and vision—are discussed, and they also affect the budgetary process. Primarily they influence priorities within the monetary allocations arena.

Funds may come to the library directly or to the parent organization, with designation for library use. Within the income categories for libraries, funds come from a variety of sources: from the larger organization's (university or college, city or town government, school district, company, foundation, or another type of business) operating budget; from local taxes; from local, state, regional, provincial, federal and/or national government support; from private foundations' or other philanthropic organizations' grants; from Friends of Libraries groups, gifts, or endowments; from fees or fines; etc. Noninstitutional funding is likely to fluctuate more widely than institutional support, and institutional support can depend on the parent organization's commitment to seeking the various types of funds that are then funneled to the library and on the projected fiscal year's budget outlook. Therefore, the budget is not a stable, sure thing.

That is why external sources such as gifts and grants are becoming more vital as direct financial support no longer adequately meets needs, and that is why fund-raising has become such an important part of every library's activities. Financial challenges are steadily compounded by the reality of inflation, reduced budgets, and the information explosion, and libraries are finding themselves forced to seek alternative routes for funding. In recent years all types of libraries and information centers have engaged in fund-raising activities, tapping nontraditional areas for budgetary support for special projects and for capital expenditures. A new political role, with extensive public relations requirements, is being forced on libraries and librarians. Many types of libraries now depend on private-sector support to expand the monies available for their budgets. Special projects and capital budgets are often supported by outside funding sources. Both ongoing annual fundraising activities and major capital campaigns are becoming integral parts of library programs. Fund-raising, through lobbying and direct solicitation, has become a way of life for enhancing budgets. Libraries have become innovative and assertive in seeking funds outside normal budgeting sources and channels.

Nevertheless, the greatest amount of budgetary support in most institutions comes from the parent body. Determination of the actual amount is usually based on expressed needs, which are justified by services offered or projected and, to a lesser extent, on standards that have been established for particular types of libraries or information centers, such as ALA standards for public, school, junior college, college, and university libraries that are often used by accrediting authorities as they consider the quality of institutions. These needs are often defined on budget forms such as those included on this volume's website.

The capital budget has less relevance in this discussion because needs are occasional rather than periodic. Capital costs are large-expense items to be planned for in projected future budgets. After capital costs are funded, yearly expenses are calculated and transferred to the operations budget as deposits and are then charged against that budget. For instance, approval and installation of a mainframe computer system would be considered a capital expense, requested separately and budgeted in the capital budget. Expenditure of funds to pay for the mainframe would be reflected, most probably, in a separate account. The two types of budgets discussed here are presented as distinct; however, a combination of budgeting systems is often used.

As a total process, the budgeting concept involves several discrete steps, from the guidelines that are issued by upper management in the larger organization or unit of which the library is a part; to the execution of the budget through the fiscal year's appropriation and expenditures; to the point when an audit is conducted to determine, in retrospect, how the allocated funds were actually spent. In between are the most important parts of the process: preparation of the budget, with justification for amounts and categories being requested, and review and approval by funding authorities. The latter step provides the best opportunity for the library to present its case, to enlighten authorities about not only what is being requested but, more importantly, why it is being requested. However, this excellent marketing opportunity is a delicate session in which a balance must be achieved between just the right amount of information and information overload. To strike that balance, librarians resort to all sorts of public relations gambits to get across their program objectives.

One great danger in budgeting is the problem of disguised needs. Librarians are often accused of asking for more than they actually need and basing current budget justifications on past budgets. Such an incremental approach is no longer valid in the fast-changing environment of today's information services. In all fairness, the approach is frequently encouraged by the budgeting technique being employed by the parent institutions where the incremental mentality can prompt automatic reductions in library budgets by those who hold the purse strings, whether they are city managers, college or company presidents, or school superintendents.

The budgeting process is a time-delayed process. A budget is usually prepared one year—or, in some cases, two or three years—in advance. In the latter instances, it is extremely difficult to project what the needs will be even with a strategic thinking mentality. Still, the budget is expected to forecast realistically expected revenues, support, and expenses for the period of time covered by the budget request. In most cases, a library must follow the budget system and budgeting cycle used by the larger system, whether that is the university, college, city government, school district, corporation, or board. Usually guidelines for the preparation of the budget come from the school committee, the state or local funding agency, the college or university administration, or the corporation's fiscal officer.

Although many libraries have a separate staff concerned primarily with budgets and the accounting process, most involve a number of employees in the budget-planning process. Some larger libraries and information centers have internal budgeting committees composed of representatives from various units of the organization. Budget requests for programs or units frequently originate from the supervisor or a team most familiar with a particular unit, program, project, or other aspect of the operation. A coordinating agent or group—either the director, his or her representative, or a committee—is responsible for pulling the various budget requests together and presenting a comprehensive budget to the funding authority. Timetables for budget preparation, presentation, and overview are essential so that wide support can be gained. Two principles guide the development and presentation of budgets: effectiveness and efficiency, involving what sources of funds will be tapped and how maximum benefit at minimum cost will be accomplished.

The budgetary aspect of control becomes even more important as costs rise. This has focused greater attention on library or information center budgets, with the determination and justification of budget allocations taking on new meaning and urgency. More and more, as there is greater financial constraint, librarians find themselves spending greater amounts of time in budgeting review, analysis, evaluation, and presentation. With rising costs, librarians are forced to prepare comprehensive reports on the library's financial status so that effective allocation, as well as accurate projections for future funding, can be made. Most often, the librarian is required to make a formal budget presentation, which is substantiated by back-up documentation, such as an index of inflation for library materials, technological impact, or trends in higher education that affect libraries. The website for this textbook includes a number of budgets and budgetary activities.

Budgeting Techniques

Adequate financial resources must be available to ensure payment of obligations arising from current operations. Materials must be purchased, wages paid, and interest charges and due dates met. The principal means of controlling the availability and costs of financial resources is budgeting.[3]

—J. H. Donnelly et al.,
Fundamentals of Management

Library budgeting techniques include traditional approaches used by many types of organizations and more innovative techniques that have only recently found their way into libraries. The former are more fixed in their approach, whereas the latter are more flexible. The shift in focus, just as in the planning process, has taken place as budgets are presented in terms of output, or performance, rather than as input—"all that money going into the library, and for what?" The most traditional types of budgeting, to be discussed below, include line-item, where expenses are divided into categories such as salaries, benefits, materials, equipment, etc.; and lump-sum allocation, based primarily on an incremental approach where percentage increases are related to the previous year's budget. An interim view of budgets is represented in such techniques as performance budgeting where performance measures are instituted to support justifying input costs as a factor of output measures. PPBS and ZBB are budgeting approaches that look at programs, objectives, and benchmark costs, respectively. Each of the approaches has advocates who promote advantages of the various approaches. A library or information center considering a switch to another process must be clear on the advantages and disadvantages before it decides to switch from one to another.

Line-Item Budgets

Probably the most common type of budget because of its simplicity, the line-item budget divides objects of expenditure into broad input classes or categories, such as salaries and wages, materials and supplies, equipment, capital expenditures, etc., with further subdivisions within those categories. It is often referred to as: 1) the historical approach because expenditure requests are based upon historical data; or 2) lump-sum approach because the attitude is one of "Here it is, do with it what you will." Critics believe this approach is no longer effective because such an incremental approach is based upon the past, maintaining the status quo, with no real review of accomplishments. Its primary disadvantage is that items within those various established categories can be designated to such a degree that it becomes difficult, if not impossible, to shift them, thus being inflexible. For example, within the broad category of materials and supplies, it may become desirable to add subscription money for new online periodicals after the budget has been set. One might wish to accomplish this by transferring money from equipment because it has been determined that the library can do without an additional personal computer, and the subscription can be justified as technology-applicable. However, budgeting authorities might frown upon this kind of transfer. If it is not completely discouraged, it is often made very difficult to accomplish because of the paperwork and red tape involved. Line-item budgeting, or incremental budgeting, tends to assume that all currently existing programs are good and necessary. That approach usually requires no evaluation of services and no projection of future accomplishments.

Table 15.1. The Line-Item Budget, with Expenditures Assigned to Broad Categories

| | | | **BUDGET REQUEST FORM I** | |
| | | | **SUMMARY** | |

Department or Program: LIBRARY

Department No.: 02876

For Fiscal Year: 2002–2003

Control Number	Expenditures	Actual Prior Year 2000–2001	Budget Current Year 2001–2002	Budget Request 2002–2003
	SALARIES			
100	Full-time emp.	730,000	784,750	809,500
101	Part-time emp.	27,050	27,860	29,200
102	Hourly wages	34,000	35,360	40,000
	STAFF BENEFITS			
103	Social Security	54,750	58,855	60,700
104	Retirement Acct.	65,700	70,625	72,850
105	Unemployment Comp.	4,675	5,025	5,200
106	Worker's Comp.	4,160	4,475	4,600
107	Life Insurance	3,505	3,765	3,900
108	Health Insurance	39,600	42,250	49,175
109	Accident Ins.	400	470	485
110	Disability Ins.	5,250	5,600	6,300
	MATERIALS			
120	Books	120,000	127,200	137,375
121	Serials	180,000	165,500	180,400
122	Binding	36,000	37,800	40,450
123	Media	86,500	92,300	97,650
124	Inst. Materials	17,000	17,850	18,750
	OTHER			
150	Utilities	39,000	40,150	42,150
151	Supplies	25,500'	26,500	27,825
152	Telephone	22,000	22,880	23,950
153	Travel	19,200	19,975	20,975
154	Postage	9,500	9,975	10,475
155	Insurance	8,000	8,450	8,900
156	Equipment	23,700	36,500	38,300
157	Vehicle cost	17,600	18,850	19,800
158	Service contracts	15,800	16,600	17,450
159	Consultants	3,700	3,850	3,850
	TOTAL	1,592,590	1,683,415	1,770,210

There are several advantages to the line-item approach. For one thing, line-item budgets are easy to prepare. Most are done by projecting current expenditures to the next year, taking cost increases into account. This type of budget is easy to understand and to justify because it can be shown that the allocated funds were spent in the areas for which they were budgeted. The funding authority can understand a request to add a new position or to increase the communication and supplies budgets by ten percent because that is the average amount that postage, telephone charges, and other supplies rose last year. The greatest disadvantage to the line-item approach is that there is almost no relationship at all between the budget request and the objectives of the organization. Using the line-item approach simply projects the past and present into the future. In recent years, there has been a sharp rise in what is categorized as "other" (that is, software, contracts, etc.) because of the increased costs of implementing technological innovations, from the purchase of computer equipment to telecommunications and online database searching charges.

A more primitive variation on the traditional line-item approach is the lump-sum approach. In this form of budgeting, a certain dollar amount is allocated to the library, and it becomes the responsibility of the library to decide how that sum is broken into categories that can be identified. These categories are usually the same ones mentioned under line-item budgeting: salaries and wages, materials and supplies, equipment, capital expenditures, and miscellaneous or overhead. This might seem more flexible than line-item budgeting, but it still does not relate the objectives to services. Libraries using this technique are forced to develop programs within the dollar figure allocated, instead of the other way around.

Formula Budgets

Formula budgeting uses predetermined standards for allocation of monetary resources. In the past this approach has been adopted by several large library systems, particularly academic libraries and state library agencies for appropriating state funds. One reason it became popular was that, after the criteria for budget requests had been established, they could be applied across the board to all units within the library system. The popularity of a formula budget is reflected in several factors:

1.   A formula budget is mechanical and easy to prepare.

2.   The formula budget process applies to all institutions in the political jurisdiction.

3.   Governing bodies have a sense of equity because each institution in the system is measured against the same criteria.

4.   Fewer budgeting and planning skills are required to prepare and administer a formula budget.

Additional advantages of formula budgets, which are accepted in a large number of U.S. statewide systems of higher education, are that they:

♦ facilitate inter-institutional comparison;

♦ facilitate comparisons from year to year;

♦ reduce paperwork in the budgeting process;

♦ eliminate extraneous details;

♦ provide a systematic, objective allocation technique; and

♦ connote mathematical infallibility.[4]

The formulae, which are usually expressed in terms of a percentage of the total institutional cost, focus on input rather than activities and are, therefore, more applicable to specific aspects of library operations, for instance, collection development. They determine what the library will get, not how the library will spend it. In that sense, formula budget allocations may be thought of as a combination lump-sum and formula approach.

Some formulae in education institutions have applied a fixed dollar figure per full-time equivalent student and faculty or have attached collection and staff figures to programs offered. This approach to formula budgeting in libraries probably got its impetus from the Clapp-Jordan formula, which developed a theoretical model for measuring the adequacy of academic library resources.[5] Although colleges and universities have tended to move away from such strict formula budgeting, Table 15.2 is a good example of how it facilitates meeting standards promulgated by outside accrediting organizations. Earlier "Standards for College Libraries" related three formulae to budget development: holdings (formula A); staff (formula B); and facilities (formula C).[6] Formula A from the 1986 Standards is given here for illustration (see latest standards: "Standards for College Libraries 2000" at www.ala.orgacrl/guides/college/html).

The best recent example of a formula approach is the Pennsylvania Model—Public Library Funding, which ties state aid to performance standards.[7] Other examples of formulae that were developed by state agencies include the Michigan system formula, the California University formula, and the Washington State formula.[8] Budget formulae vary in degree of sophistication. One disadvantage to formula budgeting is that some functions cannot be related to those formulae and must receive separate justification. Perhaps the biggest fallacy in such an approach is that it assumes a relationship between the quantity being expressed and the quality of service.

Table 15.2. "Standards for College Libraries," Formula A—Holdings. Reprinted with permission of the American Library Association, excerpt taken from "Standards for College Libraries 1986," prepared by the College Library Standards Committee, which appeared in *College & Research Libraries News* 47 (March 1986)

FORMULA A—

1.	Basic collection	85,000 vols.
2.	Allowance per FTE faculty member	100 vols.
3.	Allowance per FTE student	15 vols.
4.	Allowance per undergraduate major or minor field	350 vols.
5.	Allowance per master's field, when no higher degree is offered in the field	6,000 vols.
6.	Allowance per master's field, when a higher degree is offered in the field	3,000 vols.
7.	Allowance per 6th-year specialist degree field	6,000 vols.
8.	Allowance per doctoral field	25,000 vols.

A "volume" is defined as a physical unit of a work which has been printed or otherwise reproduced, typewritten, or handwritten, contained in one binding or portfolio, hardbound or paperbound, which has been catalogued, classified, and/or otherwise prepared for use. Microform holdings should be converted to volume-equivalents, whether by actual count or by an averaging formula which considers each reel of microfilm, or five pieces of any other microform, as one volume-equivalent.

Program Budgeting

The program budgeting process is concerned with the organization's activities, as opposed to individual items or expenditures, which is the concern of the line-item and formula-based approaches. In that regard it is similar to the Planning Programming Budgeting System (PPBS), discussed below, but is somewhat more flexible. Its approach maintains that it is possible to relate programs to the accomplishment of time/action objectives or activities that are stated in output terms in the strategic planning process. In a way, it can be said that program budgeting developed along with strategic planning because that type of planning process is based upon establishing costs of individual programs, which requires accounting as well as budgeting. A program budget emphasizes the library's activities so that monetary figures can be assigned to programs or services provided. For example, if a public library system provides bookmobile service for the community, the total cost of that service (staffing, materials, maintenance, overhead, etc.) is calculated. In this way, one can see exactly what the bookmobile service costs. Based on the total program and its objectives, one can decide whether to continue, to modify, or to delete the service. "Program budget is the most effective . . . method of explaining needs to funding bodies," but it is rarely used in libraries.[9] Focus is on consideration of all alternatives. For instance, other than simply withholding funds from the next lower ranked services in a priority list, other alternatives can be explored, including trying to reduce the cost of providing a certain level of services for those already chosen, thereby allowing the next listed priority to be funded. Another alternative might be to increase charges, say for value-added services to individuals and organizations, thereby adding to the pool of nondirect sources of funds, which might in turn support the next level on the priority list. An example of a program budget is given in Table 15.3.

Table 15.3. Program Budget Sheet

Organization: COUNTY LIBRARY	
Program: BOOKMOBILE SERVICE	
Objective: This service is offered to county residents who reside more than three miles from a public library. Specific services offered include providing basic reference collection of encyclopedias, handbooks, and dictionaries and a rotating collection of circulating materials on a variety of subjects for all levels of readers. Makes two stops per day, covers seven miles, five days per week.	
Costs:	
Personnel Service	
Librarian	$28,500
Driver	20,000
Stocker (to load, unload truck, 4 hrs. per week @ $6.00 x 52 weeks)	1,248
Benefits	9,700
SUBTOTAL	$59,448 (1)
Materials	
Books (2,000 volume collection x $36 average + $10.20 processing costs	$72,000
Periodicals (15 subscriptions @ $40 each)	600
Repairs, binding, etc.	175
SUBTOTAL	$72,775 (2)
Other	
Vehicle depreciation	$1,600
Maintenance, gasoline (30 mi. per week x 52 weeks x 26¢ per mile)	405
Insurance	600
SUBTOTAL	$2,605 (3)
TOTAL (Subtotals 1 + 2 + 3)	$134,828

Performance Budgeting

A technique similar to program budgeting is performance budgeting, which bases expenditures on the performance of activities and emphasizes efficiency of operations. Performance budgeting measures quantity rather than quality of service. This approach requires the careful accumulation of quantitative data over a period of time. Techniques of cost-benefit analysis are required to measure the performance and to establish norms. Performance budgeting has been criticized because the economic aspect overshadows the service aspect. This approach is sometimes called function budgeting because costs are presented in terms of work to be accomplished. A good example of this is processing materials—from submission of an order until the time that the volume is on the shelf and the bibliographic information is in the online or print catalog. All activities involved (verifying the author, title, and so forth; ordering, receiving, cataloging, and classifying; providing book pockets, call number, and catalog cards or electronic data; filing cards in the catalog or the information in the database; and placing the volume on the shelf) can be analyzed as to average time for the activity and average cost per item. Therefore, careful cost and work measurements are applied to each activity. Fixed costs of building maintenance, heating, lights, equipment, and other items that are variable but are directly related to the work being done must also be added to the final cost. With such detailed budgeting activity, benefits of awareness and participation may be overshadowed by the costly time and efforts involved in maintaining the process. Two techniques, PPBS and zero-based budgeting (ZBB), are spin-offs of program budgeting.

Planning Programming Budgeting System (PPBS)

Planning Programming Budgeting System (PPBS) was developed by Rand Corporation and introduced to the Department of Defense by Robert McNamara in 1961. President Lyndon Johnson directed all principal government agencies to implement it, and by 1965 it was being used by all federal government agencies. Some complex organizations all over the world have at some point used PPBS or some modification of it. These include state and local governments, college and university systems, and industry. It is basically a refinement of the program approach discussed above. Like management by objectives (MBO), which has lost its popularity in recent years, PPBS is not currently as widely promoted as it once was.

PPBS differs from traditional budgeting processes by focusing less on an existing base, with consideration of annual incremental improvements, and more on objectives and purposes with long-term alternative means for achieving them. As a result, PPBS brings together planning and budgeting by means of programming, a process that defines a procedure for distributing available resources equitably among the competing or possible programs.

The PPBS approach combines the best of both program budgeting and performance budgeting. The emphasis is on planning. Like MBO and program budgeting, it begins with the establishment of goals and objectives, but the controlling aspect of measurement, which is paramount in performance budgeting, is also part of PPBS. It emphasizes the cost of accomplishing goals (programs) set by the library instead of stressing objects, which the more traditional budgets highlight. This approach forces one to think of the budget as a tool to allocate resources rather than to control operations. The steps important in PPBS are

1. identifying the objectives of the library;

2. presenting alternative ways to achieve those objectives—with cost-benefit ratios presented for each;

3. identifying the activities that are necessary for each program; and

4. evaluating the result so that corrective actions can be taken.

In essence, PPBS is a scientific approach to budgeting that improves the decision-making process by calling for a systematic analysis of alternative ways of meeting objectives. The crux of PPBS is the selection of appropriate criteria for evaluating each alternative against relevant objectives; it combines the functions of planning (identifying objectives), translating that to a program (staff and materials), and, finally, stating those requirements in budgetary terms (financing). Headings for a PPBS summary sheet are shown in Figure 15.1.

County of:	Program Summary
Operating Budget: (Year)	
Program: (Title of program)	
Goal: (Brief operational goal)	
Description: (Brief description of program)	

Figure 15.1. Headings for a PPBS Summary Sheet

The PPBS approach allows one to enumerate programs and assign costs to those programs. The figures that are the outcome of PPBS are "extremely useful in determining future priorities and direction, in requesting funds, and in justifying the value of libraries and their services."[10] It also allows funding agencies to place programs into perspective and to evaluate the effects of cutting monies from or adding monies to the budget. As one can imagine, the required detailed examination of every aspect of the operation is not only time-consuming but cumbersome as well. It requires goals, objectives, and activities to be stated in measurable terms and then mandates the follow-up activity of measuring the results. Despite these drawbacks, some modification of the intent of this approach is being used in some libraries today.

An early modified PPBS approach can be seen in the example of the Vigo County (Indiana) Public Library summary of activities with its eight program categories (see Table 15.4).

Table 15.4. Community Use of a Public Library. Reprinted by permission of the American Library Association from "Toward PPBS in the Public Library," Edward N. Howard, *American Libraries* April 1971: 391

Community Use of the Vigo County Public Library for the Six Months' Period January to June 1969				
Input Cost	Service Category	Program Objective	Output Totals	Cost per Output
$92,866	SELF SERVICE	Provide facilities, library materials and equipment.	203,587 persons	$ .45
$77,524	LENDING SERVICE	Lend library materials for home and office use.	324,481 items	$ .24
$42,398	INDIVIDUAL SERVICE	Furnish information, reader advisory, and reference assistance.	40,301 persons	$ 1.05
$ 7,878	ALERTING SERVICE	Promote awareness of the library and use of its resources.	908 productions	$ 8.67
$ 5,202	OUTREACH SERVICE	Provide library materials for the physically or environmentally handicapped.	10 stations	$520.20
$14,288	CONTROL SERVICE	Maintain control of materials through registration of patrons and overdue reminders to borrowers.	12,173 persons	$ 1.17
$20,106	GROUP SERVICE	Provide specialized services to groups, agencies, and organizations.	459 groups	$ 43.80
$ 3,720	RESEARCH SERVICE	Perform research service for public officials, ministers, business and industry managers, labor, and other civic leaders.	150 researchers	$ 24.80

Zero-Based Budgeting (ZBB)

ZBB focuses its activities on answering two basic questions: a) are the current activities efficient and effective? and b) should current activities be eliminated or reduced to fund higher-priority new programs or to reduce the current budget?[11]

—P. A. Phyrr,
"The Zero-Base Approach to Government Budgeting"

Another technique of budgeting, which was originally used primarily in industry and government but more and more in different types of libraries and information centers, is zero-based budgeting (ZBB). International interest in this approach began to develop in the late 1960s and early 1970s. The method was popularized by U.S. President Jimmy Carter when he was governor of Georgia. However, the U.S. Department of Agriculture used a form of it as early as 1962, and it is still used by some government agencies.

The ZBB approach is not a strict procedural one but rather an approach that requires organizations to review and to evaluate each of their service programs and activities on the basis of both output measures and costs. Efficiency and effectiveness are key considerations, and both are highly evaluated as each program is justified according to its level of importance in achieving the mission of the organization. Each activity is expressed in a decision package that is reviewed and ranked in priority order in relation to all other identified decision packages. With all of the decision packages developed and gathered, using objectives as guides, they are ranked in priority order and are presented for approval or rejection, depending upon a package's position in the hierarchy and on affordability. At some level in the hierarchy of priorities is a cut-off level, and decision packages that fall below it are not funded. Because setting priorities at the organization level involves every unit within the organization, clear guidelines for ranking must be established. The process of priority formulation helps the manager to rank and, in some cases, to delete activities because of obsolescence, inefficiency, or change of policy or objectives.[12]

Ranking "decision packages," or setting priorities within each unit of the organization, forces decisions about the most important activities within that unit of the organization. The technique allocates limited resources by forcing decision makers to concentrate on identifying the most important programs and projects to be funded. Each unit of the organization conducts the same process. After each unit identifies its priorities, the priorities of all units are amalgamated into one pool, and the process is repeated in light of the decision packages' importance to the total organization. Each decision package relates to some extent to others, and this interrelationship must be considered in ranking them because related decision packages share costs of personnel and resources. For example, ready reference is dependent upon an up-to-date, fully processed reference collection, which depends upon the selection, acquisition, and processing of materials—involving staff and materials budgets in those units.

The most important initial steps in ZBB are:

1. identifying decision packages or units;

2. ranking of those packages;

3. determining the cutoff point below which packages cannot be supported; and

4. preparing operating budgets which reflect those units.

In identification of decision packages, a package should be the lowest unit for which a budget can be prepared. A unit may be described along functional lines (e.g., circulation), by smaller units in larger organizations (e.g., reserve function of circulation), or as a special program of the organization (e.g., outreach services to the under-served). However, care must be exercised so that decision units are large enough to reflect major portions of a person's time; smaller distribution would probably be meaningless because it might, for instance, eliminate only a small fraction of a full-time salary. This process of description requires the identification of goals and objectives of the package and how they relate to the mission of the organization, a statement of alternatives, the reason for the activity, consequences of not introducing the package, detailed measurement of performance, projected outcomes in the implementation process, and the costs of the activity. Of course, the size and complexity of the organization determines the number of units that can be identified and supported.

When ZBB budgets are first introduced into an organization, the process of reviewing current activities must be broken into units and placed in a hierarchy of importance. In this examination, duplication of efforts can be more easily detected. Options for reviewing those existing activities include:

♦ Should the activity be kept as it is or, perhaps, expanded?

♦ Should it be eliminated altogether or, perhaps, reduced in support?

♦ Should it be centralized or decentralized?

♦ Should it be integrated into other programs or broken down into more finite units?

Analysis in this ranking process of establishing priorities also allows for the selection of the alternatives that have the greatest potential for achieving the objectives in each of the decision packages. Therefore, the process of specifically identifying decision packages also focuses on the "best way" of doing things, either through cost savings or efficiency of service. The last processes of ZBB, just as should be the case in any budgeting process, are monitoring and evaluation. Adjustments may be essential during the budgeted time period in order to achieve the decision package objectives, and there is a need to know whether or not the goals of the various packages are being accomplished and at what level. The monitoring and evaluation process of ZBB requires establishing measures of performance and reporting. Specifically relating to costs, quantitative measures must be established to monitor output, which is expressed in financial terms.

Basically, ZBB is not concerned with what happened previously but with what is required in the future. In this approach and in its development, ZBB is very similar to PPBS; it requires careful analysis of activities that should take place in the library and requires justification for each unit of work identified. By forcing an organization to identify areas of greater and lesser importance, ZBB emphasizes planning and fosters an understanding, by all units, of the total organization. It helps maintain vitality in the organization by constantly assessing and questioning programs.[13] It forces each unit manager and the unit workers to identify priorities within their unit of the organization. Identifying priorities and stating them in terms of cost forces the unit to answer: "Is it really worth it?" and "Are there alternatives to achieving this objective?" The ZBB approach requires that justification for each program start at point "zero" and it requires that this be done each year. Of course, after a decision unit has been identified, that particular unit does not need to be reidentified each year; it needs to be further described only if changes occur, although it still must be considered in the list of priorities and costs must be recalculated.

The ZBB process should provide an indication of the real cost of various library activities, an estimate of the minimum cost level necessary to provide each service, a ranking of library functions to facilitate support, a discovery of unnecessary duplication of effort, and a framework for the establishment of criteria for continuous evaluation of performance.

It is assumed in the ZBB model that the sum of those units receiving top priority status is less than the current budgeted amount and that a cut-off will occur at some point. This attitude allows for a reduced level at which activities can be carried out to meet the essential objectives of the organization. Tables 15.5 and 15.6 illustrate, in an abbreviated way, the process involved in establishing a decision package statement and how that package might fit into the priorities of the organization. This approach requires effective communication and efficient training of personnel involved in the approach.

Text continues on page 458.

Table 15.5. Form for Decision Package Statement

DECISION PACKAGE STATEMENT	Prepared by: Ralph Lorenzo Date: 11 / 22 / 1986

Program Name: Children's Division	**Priority Rank:** 1

Department: Public Services Department Hillsdale Public Library	**Level:** 1 of 3

Statement of Purpose (Goals and Objectives—what is to be accomplished):
Provide library services to children (preschool to teen-aged years).
Work in conjunction with town's school department to offer comprehensive services to children of the town.

Description of Activity: 1) Direct summer reading program for children of the town; 2) Offer story hour and puppet shows for preschool through second grade; 3) Select children's materials for the public library collection; 4) Interpret questions of informational, educational, and recreational nature; 5) Coordinate library services for children in the community.

Benefits Desired Results: Enable children to explore, with guidance, good literature; aid in providing informational services to school children both in their school work and in their quest for knowledge, encourage children to explore areas of interest on their own.

Related Activities: School library service in the town's elementary schools.

Alternatives, Other Options (to achieve same or partial results):
1) Let schools assume full responsibility
2) Public Services (general) assume responsibility for limited services

Consequences (If activity is not approved/is eliminated):
Service to children would be seriously curtailed, thereby abrogating one of the original charges from the town to the library.

Costs/Resources Required:	Prior Period	Budgeting Period
Personnel:		
Professional (3/4)	13,200	14,900
Paraprofessional (1/2)	6,650	7,100
Hourly wages (10 per week @ $3.65)	1,898	1,898
Secretarial (1/4)	3,750	4,010
Operations:		
Supplies	800	880
Equipment	300	450
Materials	8,200	9,600
Travel	—	350
Other	150	190
TOTAL	$34,948	$39,378

Approved by: Myrna Avrey	Title: Library Director	Date: 12/3/86

Table 15.6. A Ranking System Form That Indicates the Cutoff Point for Funding

Level of Effort	Rank within System	Package Name	Current Year Commitment	Planned Addition/Deletion to Current Commitment	Projected Addition to Commitments	Cumulative Expenses
1	1	Administrative Services	$ 43,040	$ 3,300		$ 46,340
1	2	Public Services (general)	67,042	4,800		71,842
1	3	Technical Services	95,972	12,350		108,322
1	4	Children's Division	34,948	4,430		39,378
2	5	Branch Library (North)		103,500		103,500 *
2	6	Young Adult Division			$ 25,370	25,370
2	7	Bookmobile Service			29,100	29,100
2	8	Branch Library (East)			92,600	92,600
2	9	Music & Art Division			15,600	15,600
TOTAL			$241,002	$128,380	$162,670	$532,052

Organization: Town of Hilsdale
Department: Hilsdale Public Library
Prepared by: Myrna Avrey
Date: 12/19/86

FISCAL YEAR: 1987-88

*Note: Example indicates that, in addition to current unit commitments with increases, the town has agreed to fund second priority level unit which is ranked number 5 in the priorities of the library. This means that the budget for the fiscal year 1987-88 will be $369,382, an increase of $128,380. (It should be remembered that this example is given to show a priority system and not to indicate "next year" potential funding of all priorities. One can see that the extent of priorities listed in this example and the costs involved are certainly long-range. For this reason individual managers would be discouraged from preparing such "ideal" priority lists using the ZBB model because the time involved in establishing such an extensive list would be great.)

Recent Techniques for Financial Allocation

Entrepreneurial Budgeting

Entrepreneurial budgeting is a recently developed attitude toward budgeting that is being experimented with in both the public and private sectors. It differs from traditional techniques in that the ultimate controlling authority decides beforehand what the budget base will be, for example, not more that last year's budget plus five percent. Initially, this appears to be the same as an incremental budget, but in fact it is quite different. Simply stated, it allocates a pool of money to the unit or organization which is then responsible for managing it within the program priorities identified. If there are funds left over at the end of the year, they are rolled forward, thus avoiding the usual rush at the end of a fiscal year when the "use it or lose it" mentality takes over. It is reported that this "profit sharing" approach improves morale and supposedly management.[14] It decentralizes decision making with incentives to be more innovative.

Allocation Decision Accountability Performance (ADAP)

Allocation Decision Accountability Performance (ADAP) is an innovative technique that is only mentioned here because there is little experience with its use in libraries and information service agencies. A budgetary hybrid, it combines aspects of both PPBS and ZBB. It has received awards worldwide and is being adapted by a number of local government agencies. The key aspect is that three budgets must be submitted: the first requesting an increase, the second recognizing a modest decrease, and the third presenting a budget below which the organization cannot function. Administrators are asked to identify whole programs that could be eliminated if necessary. Budgeting authorities can compare the current year's budget with preceding years, and if the same programs are identified as expendable with some frequency, they become candidates for elimination. Despite this pitfall, it is an acceptable way to budget because it allows the administrator to eliminate programs that have relatively poor performance.[15]

Integrated Planning and Control System (IPCS)

Recently, there have been attempts to bring together the planning and control phases of operations into one system, called Integrated Planning and Control System (IPCS). However, this approach is more useful in for-profit institutions and is only mentioned here because it is so new. The IPCS does suggest that budgetary control cannot be thought of in isolation.

Best, Optimistic, and Pessimistic (BOP)

Rolling budgets, variable budgets, contingency budgets, and flexible budgets are all based on varying revenue projections, again applying primarily to for-profit organizations. Sometimes the set of assumptions in this approach are called best, optimistic, and pessimistic (BOP) assumptions. *Best* assumes normal operating conditions; *optimistic* assumes there will be problems, but the problems can be surmounted; and *pessimistic* assumes "if everything goes wrong."[16] By participating in such exercises, management becomes aware of the broad range of possibilities, in both possibilities and coping strategies. In these economic times, that is not a useless exercise.

Responsibility Center Budgeting

Rising costs and tightening budgets have forced greater accountability among institutions of higher education. Responsibility center budgeting is the approach of "each tub on its own bottom" and is being implemented in several large universities, having found its way into higher education through the corporate sector. It forces institutions to identify their units that are capable of self-support, including all academic units with tuition- and fee-paying students; faculty capable of bringing in contracts and grants; and other central administrative units as well as academic support units, including libraries and information centers. Direct institutional support is augmented by other sources of funding—appropriations from governments, contracts, endowments, and contributions. Again, fund-raising on the part of libraries is an important component in this mix. Basically, this approach forces decision making down into all of those units where costs are directly related to academic priorities. Heated debates revolve around how the central administration allocates funds to units. For example, "how charges for space, libraries, and other services (will) be allocated; and how the hardware and software needed to run the new information systems (will) be configured."[17] It requires that the administration recognize and support units that exist for the "public good—such as the physical plant, technology, and the library (and that they) must receive funding that is adequate, but at taxation levels that the academic units can support financially and intellectually without seriously attenuating RCM's (Responsibility Center Management) underlying incentives."[18]

Bracket Budgeting

Bracket budgeting is an analytical procedure that complements conventional budgeting techniques. It is a combination of modeling and simulation in which the computer performs an integral role. The computer must be programmed to perform various calculations, which requires considerable computer expertise and probably is much too complex to be beneficial in most library situations. It is most useful in for-profit organizations, where uncertainty can wreak havoc on the profit.

Software Applications

Information technology turns the budget into a meaningful set of instructions that optimize ... performance under changing conditions.[19]
—W. J. Burns Jr. and F. W. McFarlan,
"Information Technology Puts Power in Control Systems"

Many libraries use computers in preparing budgets. Indeed, budgetary control was one of the first functions to make use of the computer in libraries. Several financial modeling, budget, financial planning, and data manipulation software packages are applicable to library budgeting. These have been developed both commercially and in-house for specific organizations. They are available for purchase or license or, sometimes, are in the public domain. Budgeting makes use of software called an electronic spreadsheet, and spreadsheets, such as Lotus 1-2-3, SuperCalc, MultiPlan, Perfect-Calc, Context MBA, Excel, .dbf, SAS, ORacle, ClarisWorks, SQL Server, SPSS for Windows, and Framework, have been powerful decision tools in the controlling process for libraries. As the name implies, a spreadsheet is an electronic version of the columnar worksheet used for years.[20] Other computer software for planning and budgeting include Budget Express and What's Best!. There are also software packages for forecasting, including Forecast! GFX, Tomorrow, Forecast Pro, and Forecast Plus.[21] Because spreadsheets make number crunching easy, libraries can adjust or revise budgets and projections without expending great amounts in terms of personnel and time. Some libraries even use computer modeling and forecasting to prepare financial plans. However, software tools are only one part of the budgeting process—the mechanical part. Thought and imagination are also needed to prepare successfully and to defend a budget.

Accountability and Reporting

The final aspect of budgeting to be mentioned here is keeping accurate records of what has been disbursed, what has been encumbered, and what remains. Before the budget has been approved by the proper authority, a mechanism for keeping track of both expenditures and encumbrances must be in place to keep track of not only what has been spent but also to set aside funds for items ordered but not yet received so that funds will be reserved and available for their payment when they do arrive. Established account categories and numbers play a vital role in this process to identify such items as salaries, materials acquired or ordered, equipment installed, etc. Periodic statements of expenditures and an audit of the expenses at the end of the year provide important feedback to the budgetary process. An accounting process allows for efficient and effective adjustments to the process, when and where they are needed. The process has been greatly enhanced by the use of electronic spreadsheets and other software packages available for financial planning on microcomputers and other equipment. These systems have helped the auditing process, reduced the need for double bookkeeping records, and facilitated reporting by allowing projections of cost activities. Reporting is usually accomplished through monthly records prepared by the accounting office, either of which usually is a part of the library or as a part of the larger organization, such as the city government. Monthly statements can act as benchmarks to inform the library staff of how they are progressing, financially, toward the library's objectives and, at the same time, alert them to potential problem areas (i.e., overexpenditures). This monthly summary statement, or balance sheet, is typical in most organizations.

Because accounting is an independent function, many large libraries employ accountants in staff positions; their primary responsibility is to report facts as they exist or have existed. Such accountants are not normally responsible for making decisions that affect the operations of the library. However, they are most helpful in collecting relevant cost data for anticipated decisions and in making cost studies that might be keys to decision making.

> The role of the accounting system in any organization is to assist management in performing its duties and achieving the organization's goals. In this capacity accounting systems and accounting reports are not ends in themselves. Rather, they are tools to assist managers in performing their function.[22]
>
> —Jacob Birnberg,
> "Accounting Information for Operating Decisions"

Along with accounting goes the important element of reporting—reporting to the funding authority, reporting to the staff, and reporting to the public, however that might be defined. Reporting procedures can take a variety of forms: formal written reports, with detailed statistical documentation, or informal reports, such as memos, staff meetings, board meetings, or newspaper articles. In reporting, the librarian's public relations responsibility becomes most evident. Only by conscientiously selling the library and its services can the librarian hope to maintain a high level of activity and funding. The purpose is to be so convincing that support for library activities will increase or, at minimum, remain the same. Public relations for librarians is an art through which information and persuasion solicit public support for the causes that are set forth in the goals of the library. Public relations is an integral part of the goals and objectives and the budgeting procedure in a library. This is the library's primary means of gaining and holding the support necessary to develop programs. It is also a way of expanding that support through new financial initiatives.

Conclusion

Budgeting is the ultimate controlling operation because it is the monetary expression of a plan of information services in libraries and other information centers. Various types and levels of budgeting are used to plan for information services. Some are more applicable to not-for-profit organizations than others, but all are being used, in one form or another, in libraries and information centers. The process of budgeting is important because it is the way organizations remain financially accountable.

Notes

1. Ann E. Prentice, *Financial Planning for Libraries*, 2d ed.(Lanham, MD: Scarecrow Press, 1996), 1.

2. Izzettin Kennis, "Effects of Budgetary Goal Characteristics on Managerial Attitudes and Performance," *The Accounting Review* 54 (October 1979): 707.

3.   James H. Donnelly et al., *Fundamentals of Management* (Homewood, IL: Business One-Irwin, 1992), 272.

4.   Gary M. Shirk, "Allocation Formulas for Budgeting Library Materials: Science or Procedure?" *Collection Management* 6 (Fall–Winter 1984): 37–38.

5.   Verner W. Clapp and Robert J. Jordan, "Quantitative Criteria for Adequacy of Academic Library Collections," *College & Research Libraries* 26 (September 1965): 371–80.

6.   "Standards for College Libraries, 1985," *College & Research Libraries News* 46, no. 5 (May 1985): 244, 247, 249.

7.   Charles R. McClure, principal investigator, et al. www.kkkpl.gov/plfig/pamodel.html.

8.   Robert E. Burton, "Formula Budgeting: An Example," *Special Libraries* 66 (February 1975): 61–67; University of California, Office of the Vice President for Finance, "Library Workload Measures" (Berkeley: University of California, 1963, Mimeographed), 1–20; University of Washington, Office of Interinstitutional Business Studies, *Model Budget Analysis System for Program 05 Libraries* (Olympia: University of Washington, 1970, Mimeographed), 1–16.

9.   Michael E. D. Koenig and Diedre C. Stam, "Budgeting and Financial Planning for Libraries," in *Advances in Library Administration*, vol. 4 (Greenwich, CT: JAI Press, 1985), 92.

10.   Marilyn J. Sharrow, "Budgeting Experience—at the University of Toronto Library," *Canadian Library Journal* 40 (August 1983): 207.

11.   P. A. Phyrr, "The Zero-Base Approach to Government Budgeting," *Public Administration Review* 37 (January–February 1977): 1.

12.   Ching-chih Chen, *Zero Based Budgeting in Library Management* (New York: Gaylord Professional Books, 1980), 36.

13.   Ricky W. Griffin, *Management*, 3d ed. (Boston: Houghton Mifflin, 1990), 697.

14.   Dan A. Cothran, "Entrepreneurial Budgeting: An Emerging Reform?" *Budgeting and the Management of Public Spending* (Cheltenham, UK: Elgar, 1996), 446.

15.   Sarah Ann Long and Donald J. Sager, "Management for Tough Times," *American Libraries* 20 (June 1989): 546.

16.   Jay H. Loevy, "Microcomputer Applications in Budgeting," in H. W. A. Sweeney and R. Rachlin, eds., *Handbook of Budgeting*, 2d ed. (New York: John Wiley & Sons, 1987), 770.

17.   W. W. Wilms, C. Teruya, and M. Walpole, "Fiscal Reform at UCLA: The Clash of Accountability and Academic Freedom," *Change* 29 (September–October 1997): 43.

18.   D. L. Slocum and P. M. Rooney, "Responding to Resource Constraints," *Change* 29 (September–October 1997): 56.

19.   W. J. Burns Jr. and F. W. McFarlan, "Information Technology Puts Power in Control Systems," in *Revolution in Real Time* (Cambridge: Harvard Business Review Book, 1991), 206.

20.   Robert M. Donnelly, "Organizing and Administering the Budgeting Process," in H. W. A. Sweeney and R. Rachlin, eds., *Handbook of Budgeting*, 2d ed. (New York: John Wiley & Sons, 1987), 119.

21.   Jae K. Shim and Joel G. Siegel, *Financial Management for Nonprofits* (New York: McGraw-Hill, 1997), 358–62.

22.   Jacob Birnberg, "Accounting Information for Operating Decisions," in Gerlad Zaltman, ed., *Management Principles for Nonprofit Agencies and Organizations* (New York: AMACOM, 1979), 478.

Managers looking to get ahead in the 21st century will need a...(substantially) different set of tools than their counterparts in the last century. . . . With change the only constant, managers will have to be far more entrepreneurial. Anyone inclined to wait for orders or follow established procedures will simply be lost. While the Industrial Age put a premium on machines and proprietary systems, the Information Age relies on the ideas and skills that reside in workers' heads. With technology, products, markets, and customers all in flux, the corporation will need group-oriented leaders who can thrive amid uncertainty.[1]

—Diane Brady,
"Wanted: Eclectic Visionary with a Sense of Humor"

Good people in management positions are vital to the existence of library and information service organizations. Every reader of this textbook on library and information center management, with its focus upon theories and practice, should take to heart the admonishment to consider the option of becoming a manager and should begin to prepare for that eventuality. In any case, it should be recognized that whether a person is a manager or the one being managed in the organization, all are involved in the process—team building, strategic planning, motivation, quality control. To be committed to customer services requires every member of the organization's total dedication to the vision and mission of the knowledge-based organization. When that happens, society benefits.

Readings

Library Links—For Information Professionals:

> http://www.emeraldinsight.com/librarylink/management/index.htm
> http://www.managementfirst.com/index.html

Continuing Education—Librarians in the Twenty-First Century:

> http://istweb.syr.edu/21stcenlib/becoming/cont_ed.html

Yahoo's List of Library Organizations:

> http://istweb.syr.edu/21stcenlib/becoming/cont_ed.html

Chapter 16

Managers—The Next Generation

Imagine Melvil Dewey waking from a 100-year long Rip Van Winkle-like nap and suddenly being confronted with the twenty-first-century library. He and his counterpart library directors from 100 years ago would be astounded at some of the changes encountered. Where is the card catalog? What are these beige metal boxes with windows on them? Have three-dimensional books been reduced to that single dimension, a flat image on a dull screen? What about new library buildings? Has the monumentality of great libraries been reduced to a minimality of a twelve-inch dull gray screen? What about library directors? Women seem to be sitting in director's chairs. What about the library staff? Librarians seem to have been transformed into information navigators, surfing what is called the Internet with zeal and devotion. What is all this talk of metadata and Dublin Core, OCLC, and ARL LibQual+ measurements; outsourcing and customer satisfaction; self-directed teams and flattened organizations; change management and strategic planning? The transformation of the library that has taken place over the past 100 years would likely leave Mr. Dewey bothered and bewildered.

There is, of course, a bit of nostalgia associated with this scenario, a sense of regret for the passing of simpler days. Stability and continuity are no longer characteristics to be applied to the library profession, and certainly not to the manager's responsibilities. The profession is now best characterized by change, discontinuity, and opportunity. Managers are at the core of all that is happening and are responsible for making it happen efficiently and effectively. Perhaps an appropriate slogan for the manager might be "if you sense calm, it's only because you're in the eye of the typhoon." Only a few traces of bygone days seem to remain. Information service has entered a new era, and the only way libraries, under the leadership and initiative of directors, can conserve the good that has been built in the past while performing a more challenging, vital mission in the future is by innovating. The challenge is to achieve a balance between preserving the good aspects of the past while moving toward a new vision of the future.

Perhaps, then, the one stable managerial element that can be identified is that of challenge. Although the purpose of librarianship and the issues facing managers have not changed, the tasks, techniques, and technology certainly have. The nature of the work being done; the types of technologies employed; the speed with which activities are accomplished; and the way workers think, talk, and react have all been drastically altered. Managers of the early twenty-first century still face many of the same issues that confronted their predecessors: How does one motivate workers? How can a realistic budget be developed? How can the organization be both more effective and more efficient? How can library organizations capitalize upon the fact that workers are better educated, more involved in decision making, more motivated toward identifying goals and objectives, and more committed to interacting with customers than ever before?

As previously discussed in the introductory chapters of this volume, management practices and procedures have evolved over the years, drawing upon the theories developed during the last century to cope with developing trends. Management and the techniques used to practice it have changed, but the need for managers remains constant. Many of the interpersonal and organizational skills that made managers successful in the past remain important for modern managers to emulate. But in addition, managers in twenty-first-century organizations require augmented skills and talents to lead new types of organizations. Many of the readers of this textbook will be those new managers of the twenty-first-century library. The future of libraries and information services rests squarely in the hands of that new breed of managers.

Deciding to Become a Manager

Some readers may question their need for knowledge about principles and practices of management, maintaining that they never want to be managers. Nonetheless, most will be managers, if not in the first job, then later as they grow in professional expertise. Even those who never become managers will be managed—everyone is involved in the management process. Understanding the principles of management is important in analyzing why things are done as they are.

Some readers have already taken initial steps toward a management career. They have been, perhaps, intrigued by the idea of managing an organization or trying to make things work better. Others may be working in jobs where the management approach has been poor and believe that they can initiate necessary improvements. Others are intrigued by the idea of putting into practice some of the theories and techniques discussed in this text.

There is a great need for good managers in twenty-first-century libraries. Talented professionals committed to becoming managers are in great demand. The work of a manager, though often difficult, is never dull and is usually rewarding. Deciding whether to become a manager deserves thoughtful consideration by all new professionals.

Learning to be a manager in a rapidly changing era involves learning about a great many things. The cliché that management is both an art and a skill is an accurate one. The primary intention of this text is to provide some of the background "art" so that the "skill" can be developed. Of course, many management skills are developed through long practice. But it takes more than just time to become a good manager. Through concerted effort, librarians can improve their managerial skills as they acquire experience and advance in management positions.

Henry Mintzberg, in a seminal study, examined the work that managers do.[2] He actually sat in the offices of managers, followed them around, and recorded their activities. He found that managers work at demanding jobs that are characterized by their variety, fragmentation, and brevity. In other words, managers rarely have long stretches of uninterrupted time to spend on any one task. They simultaneously work at a variety of tasks, each for a short period of time. Their days are fragmented, and there are many demands on their time. The manager also performs a great deal of work at a very fast pace and is required to make ultimate decisions after due consideration. For most managers there is usually more to be done than there is time in which to do it.

> Knowledge management is a fancy term for a simple idea. You're managing data, documents, and people's efforts. Your aim should be to enhance the way people work together, share ideas, sometimes wrangle, and build on one another's ideas—and then act in concert for a common purpose.[3]
>
> —Bill Gates,
> *Business @ the Speed of Thought*

Managers are required to assume a great deal of responsibility. They are responsible for other people, their actions, and the success or failure of the enterprise. "The Buck Stops Here!" mentality continues because managers are accountable, at various levels, for the operation of a team, a unit, a division, or a whole organization. With a focus upon customers and their needs, the idea of the library as a knowledge organization whose responsibility is knowledge management becomes the most important part of the manager's daily work life. They typically have heavy workloads and often feel stress because of their managerial duties.

Under such circumstances, why would anyone want to be a manager? Although there are many challenges and difficulties associated with management, most competent managers enjoy their jobs. They like the feeling of autonomy and setting their own agenda, while at the same time feeling proud of being able to make a difference and performing well. They are challenged by the diversity of the work they do and the people—staff, customers, and other stakeholders—with whom they work. Most managers appreciate higher salaries that accompany managerial positions. Managers are monetarily recognized because they are accountable for the actions of others and for achievement of organizational objectives.

Becoming a manager is usually never accomplished in just one easy step. Although a few new graduates do begin their careers as directors of small libraries or information services units, most managers-in-training have the opportunity to learn about management through a series of positions and promotions.

In most large libraries, management is divided into three primary levels: first-line managers (often called supervisors), middle managers, and top-level managers. Many recent graduates immediately become supervisors. They are assigned responsibility for supervising a group of nonmanagement employees and direct specific services or procedures. Middle managers are in charge of departments or, perhaps, projects or teams. Top management is responsible for the entire organization. This layer of management is comprised of directors and their immediate deputies.

If a newly qualified professional begins work in a very small library, he or she may be the only professional and thus becomes the top manager automatically. In those cases, the new manager is required to work with other managers, in the larger organization of which the library is a part, to develop the expertise needed in the job. However, more frequently new graduates go to work in larger organizations, where they have a chance to learn management skills from their supervisors before they themselves become either middle- or top-level managers.

Skills Needed by Managers

Managers need different sets of skills at different levels of management. Technical skills are more important at the first-line level. To be effective there, a manager has to understand the process that is being carried out. It would be very difficult to supervise a group of copy catalogers without knowing about cataloging and classification. At the upper level, managers need to have more conceptual skills and be able to look at the "big picture" of the organization. All managers should aim at achieving a requisite set of skills:

Political Skills: Organizations are first and foremost social systems, and awareness of this is vital to survival in today's climate. Organizations are hotly and intensely political, both internally and in their relationship to forces outside the organization. Flexibility is required to maintain an equilibrium for the organization in the political arena. Risk-taking, although threatening in such a climate, is vital.

Analytical Skills: Managers as change agents must be good at analysis. Insight, of course, is useful but often insights are difficult to defend. Therefore, more is required. A lucid, rational, well-argued analysis is much more difficult to overturn.

Problem-Solving Skills: A reliable set of problem-solving skills is perhaps the single most important attribute of managers.

People Skills: Working with colleagues is at the heart of an organization. These skills come with many communication and interpersonal dimensions that must be developed and refined. A sense of humor is core to development of this skill. Seeing things through the eyes of others in the organization can facilitate cooperation and reduce conflict among disparate points of view. It helps if those who work for you know that you are concerned about their careers and take an active interest in guiding their development.

System Skills: There's much more to this than learning about computers, although most do need to learn about computer-based information systems. A system is not only a technological one but also an arrangement of resources and routines intended to produce specified results. Much of what happens in today's library occurs within the boundaries of its system.

Business Skills: This entails an understanding of money—where it comes from, where it goes, and how to get it. This also requires marketing skills because promoting libraries and information services is vital in today's information services arena.

Taken together these involve:

♦ creation of a vision and motivating a commitment to it, and thereby creating a climate conducive to strategic thinking and action;

♦ coordination of greater team-based initiatives in knowledge-based learning organization, consultation with funding authorities, within the organization and in the greater environment, developing fund-raising skills and attitudes;

♦ communication of ideas and services effectively to constituents—customers, clients, patrons, users, and potential users of information services; and

♦ consolidation of a positive attitude toward change management, with flexibility being the key to success and change being the only constant.

Most people receiving their library and information science degrees graduate with a rudimentary knowledge of most of those skills. Some they may have acquired from past job experience, others they have learned during their professional education program, still others, including analytical and people skills, they were either born with or have acquired in their life experience. But few individuals graduate knowing enough to become a top-level manager. Persons who maintain a life-long learning attitude can acquire or improve their abilities in all of these skill areas.

Acquiring Management Skills

Some graduates know that they are interested in becoming managers or in some cases are already lower-level managers. If one is interested in learning and acquiring more management skills, where can one acquire that knowledge? If one is already a manager, how can management skills be improved, and how does one keep up-to-date with all the changes in the field? One or two courses during the initial degree program certainly will not be enough.

Of course, one place to learn is on the job. Organizations themselves often function as laboratories for new managers. All managers learn from doing. Frequently, mistakes are made, and one learns from making mistakes. Managers learn from failures, and perhaps the most important lesson is that no manager is ever always right. A manager who has never made a mistake has never taken a risk, and we all know that risk management is part of a good manager's profile.

New managers also learn from other managers in the organization and from professional colleagues outside the organization, through mentoring and networking. Observation and on-the-job training are important aspects of development as a manager. One can learn from other managers who are higher in the management structure, as well as from those that are on the same level. New managers can learn a great deal from more experienced managers who have already acquired many of the skills and the characteristics that the new manager would like to emulate. They can also observe bad managers demonstrating things to avoid and ways not to do things.

Another way to acquire more knowledge about management skills is through continuing education, which is a responsibility of the individual, or staff development, which should be part of the organizational development. Many individuals, when taking management courses as part of their degree program, are exposed to the knowledge before they have an opportunity to use it. Because they are not managers at that time, they are not able to put into perspective some of the theories discussed. They really begin to need the management information when they are already out of school and in the workplace. That is why it is so important to think in terms of continuing education for managers, whether it is a commitment on their part to their professional growth or whether it is to staff development on the part of the organization. Both approaches are important because many of the "change management" discussions are focused upon preparing managers to lead organizations into an unknown future.

> The voice of the aggrieved alumnus is always loud in the land, and, no matter what the profession, the burden of complaint is the same. In the first five years after graduation, alumni say that they should have been taught more practical techniques. In the next five years, they say that they should have had more basic theory. In the tenth to the fifteenth years, they inform the faculty that they should have been taught more about administration or about their relations with their co-workers and subordinates. In the subsequent five years, they condemn the failure of their professors to put the profession in its larger historical, social and economic context.[5]
>
> —Cyril Houle,
> "The Role of Continuing Education
> in Professional Development"

Some larger libraries conduct staff development programs to augment management skills of managers within the organizations. Library and information science organizations, state, national, regional, and international, provide another important vehicle for learning management skills. These organizations routinely offer preconferences, workshops, self-learning modules, web-based courses, and institutes on specific topics. OCLC Institute classes and Association of Research Libraries web-based courses are good examples. Many library and information management departments and schools are sponsors of continuing education programs. Various library consortia often contract consultants, LIS schools, or other organizations to offer classes on specific management topics for their members. For example, regional networks—Nelinet, Solinet, Amigos—offer suites of courses on an ongoing basis. State, regional, and national library associations and state library funding agencies also sponsor continuing education programs.

These types of courses and programs are also offered by other organizations throughout the world. Examples can be identified of programs in Great Britain, Australia, and other countries, as well as programs offered by regional associations, such as CONSAL (Congress of Southeast Asia Librarians) and by UNESCO through its Principal Regional Offices in various regions of the world, and international programs by the International Federation of Library Associations and Institutions (IFLA). The British, French, and U.S governments, among others, also support management development programs for librarians in host countries internationally. Various types of courses are offered online by businesses and LIS schools so that managers can learn new techniques and skills without having to leave home. As a result of the growing interest in leadership, a number of leadership institutes have been developed to prepare managers for change and to equip them with techniques and skills to lead the next generation of information services personnel.

Continuing education is an important part of every professional's career development, particularly because graduate programs in North America, Great Britain, Australia, New Zealand, and other countries, as well as undergraduate programs in some countries, are limited by time and the amount of material that can be incorporated into the first professional degree programs. Additionally, the amount of core knowledge required in those programs has expanded tremendously in the past few years, thereby further reducing options for additional management study at the first professional degree. Although some LIS programs offer courses such as marketing, human resources management, and strategic planning, few students have time to take any management classes beyond the basic introductory one. Newly minted librarians and information managers leave degree programs with sufficient preparation for a first position, but they must have a commitment to continue to learn and develop, not only if they want to advance, but also if they are going to stay current in their present job.

Library managers sometimes decide to acquire an additional degree in the field of management or public administration, having recognized that to manage large and complex organizations requires a great deal of advanced management expertise. One important component in every manager's continuing education portfolio must be keeping up-to-date by reading both library and information management literature and the management literature in general. In addition, there is a wealth of management information available at one's fingertips through the Internet. Indeed, there is so much material available on the web that individuals are required to use their good judgment about the accuracy, timeliness, and authenticity of material found there. See the website for this volume for some pertinent sources.

As was discussed in chapter 10, career development is the responsibility of each professional. Organizations have a role to play in helping their employees grow and develop, but the ultimate responsibility to shape a career belongs to each individual. Individuals have to take responsibility for themselves rather than depending on the organization. As Peter Drucker notes, even today remarkably few Americans are prepared to select jobs for themselves. "When you ask, 'Do you know what you are good at? Do you know your limitations?' they look at you with a blank stare. Or they often respond in terms of subject knowledge, which is the wrong answer. When they prepare their résumés, they still try to list positions like steps up a ladder. It is time to give up thinking of jobs or career paths as we once did and think in terms of taking on assignments one after the other."[6]

Twenty-first-century library and information services managers need to develop their own portfolios of management skills that will permit them the flexibility to respond to a rapidly changing environment.

Opportunities for good managers are unlimited. This means that many organizations are competing for a limited number of talented managers of the twenty-first century. Those professionals, wearing the two hats of librarians and managers, have unlimited opportunities to assume new, more challenging positions. They are able to advance in their managerial positions to achieve their professional goals. They have learned to network effectively, to think strategically, and to manage skillfully. Consequently, they are given opportunities to advance through the managerial ranks and to assume top positions at leading institutions. If questioned about their career goals, it is likely that most would describe a plan, a strategy, with at least a ten-year timeline. They have identified and developed the skills necessary to succeed in the present position, while developing strategies for the next one.

Conclusion

Good people in management positions are vital to the existence of library and information service organizations. The authors hope that every reader of this textbook considers the option of becoming a manager and begins to prepare for that eventuality. In any case, it should be recognized that whether a person is a manager or the one being managed, management in successful organizations is a process that involves many individuals, from top-level managers to the team leaders. To be committed to customer services requires every employee's total dedication to the vision and mission of the knowledge-based organization.

This chapter began by imagining Melvil Dewey awakening from a long nap, and it will close with him. As a manager, Melvil Dewey had a great impact on the libraries of his day. Because of his efforts, the library profession came of age in the late nineteenth century.[7] Managers like Dewey can have a great influence on their individual organizations and on a profession as a whole.

Due to efforts of managers such as Dewey, our libraries and information agencies have had an organization and a structure that has worked well in the past. At the present time, these institutions are in the process of making a major transition from paper-based to digitally-based material. They are confronting increasing competition and new challenges. Library managers are needed to prepare libraries to meet the demands of tomorrow. To ensure their continued existence, libraries need managers who will be the Melvil Deweys of the twenty-first century. We hope that the readers of this book will be those managers.

Notes

1. Diane Brady, "Wanted: Eclectic Visionary with a Sense of Humor," *Business Week* 3696 (August 21, 2000): 143.

2. Henry Mintzberg, *The Nature of Managerial Work* (Englewood Cliffs, NJ: Prentice-Hall, 1980).

3. Bill Gates, *Business @ the Speed of Thought* (New York: Warner Books, 1999), 260.

4. Robert E. Quinn, *Beyond Rational Management* (San Francisco: Jossey-Bass, 1988), 3.

5. Cyril Houle, "The Role of Continuing Education in Professional Development," *ALA Bulletin* (March 1967): 263.

6. T. George Harris, "The Post-Capitalist Executive: An Interview with Peter F. Drucker," in Joan Margretta, ed., *Managing in the New Economy* (Boston: Harvard Business School, 1999), 163.

7. See Wayne A. Wiegand's *Irrepressible Reformer: A Biography of Melvil Dewey* (Chicago: American Library Association, 1996), for more about Dewey as a manager.

Index

About the Authors

Robert D. Stueart

Robert D. Stueart is professor and dean emeritus of Simmons College in Boston, where he was dean for 20 years. From 1994 through 1997, he served as professor of information management in the School of Advanced Technologies and as executive director of the Center for Library and Information Resources at the Asian Institute of Technology in Bangkok, Thailand, where he developed both Ph.D. and masters programs in information management. During his career, he also served on faculties of the University of Denver, the University of Wales (UK), and the University of Pittsburgh, as well as on the senior administrative staffs of libraries at both the University of Colorado and Pennsylvania State University.

Dr. Stueart has received many honors, including the Melvil Dewey medal for "creative professional achievement" and the Beta Phi Mu award for service to education "nationally and internationally." Both of those awards are presented by the American Library Association (ALA). In 1994, he was presented the Humphrey/OCLC/Forest Press International Award, given for "significant contributions to International Librarianship." He has received Outstanding Alumni Awards from all three of his degree-granting universities.

Professor Stueart has served in leadership roles in many professional organizations, including the executive board and the council of the American Library Association, and the executive board of the International Federation of Library Associations and Institutions. He has also served as president of three library associations: the Association for Library and Information Education; Beta Phi Mu, the international library science society; and the former Library Education Division of ALA.

He received both the John F. Kennedy International Scholar award, twice, and a Fulbright fellowship to Thailand, helping to develop information management, library, and information science curricula. From 1987 until its dissolution, he chaired the joint US-USSR Commission on Library Cooperation, co-sponsored by the American Council on Learned Societies and the USSR Ministry of Culture.

Dr. Stueart has consulted and lectured for the U.S. government, UNESCO, OCLC, foundations, and other governments in many countries in Asia (including China, Hong Kong, India, Indonesia, Japan, Korea, Laos, Malaysia, Myanmar, Singapore, Thailand, and Vietnam) and Europe (Belarus, England, Germany, Russia, Ukraine, and Wales). He has made professional visits to Africa, Australia, New Zealand, the Middle East, and Latin America. In addition, he has conducted many workshops, has facilitated strategic planning exercises, and has completed management evaluations in many of those countries. He is currently working with a foundation on program development in Vietnam, serving as an "expert" for UNESCO's project on developing ICT training courses for librarians in developing countries of Asia, and serving as external examiner for a major university in Malaysia. He also participated in a

UNESCO seminar and worked on the development of "A Curriculum for an Information Society: Educating and Training Information Professionals in the Asia-Pacific Region," which was published in 1998. He is a sought-after facilitator for strategic issue identification and strategic planning.

His books include a two-volume, award-winning work on collection development. He has edited or written more than a dozen monographs, including co-editing the reference work entitled *World Guide to Library Archive and Information Science Education*. He has written more than 50 refereed articles in journals and has served on the editorial boards of three major international professional journals.

Barbara B. Moran

Barbara B. Moran received an AB from Mount Holyoke College, an M.Ln. from Emory University, and a Ph.D. from the State University of New York at Buffalo. Before beginning her Ph.D. studies, she worked as a school and academic librarian. She joined the faculty at the School of Information and Library Science at the University of North Carolina at Chapel Hill in 1981 and became dean there in 1990. In January 1999, she rejoined the faculty. At the present time, she teaches primarily in the management area and has a special interest in human resources management. She has authored or co-authored four books and more than fifty articles and is currently engaged in research focusing on new organizational structures in academic libraries and on the individuals working in these new structures.